MANAGERIAL ECONOMICS

Text and Cases

MANAGERIAL ECONOMICS
Text and Cases

CHARLES J. CHRISTENSON
Thomas Henry Carroll Ford Foundation
Professor of Business Administration

RICHARD F. VANCIL
Professor of Business Administration

PAUL W. MARSHALL
Associate Professor of Business Administration

All of the Graduate School of Business Administration
Harvard University

with the assistance of

Stanley I. Buchin, D.B.A.
President, Applied Decision Systems, Inc.

Revised Edition   1973

 RICHARD D. IRWIN, INC. *Homewood, Illinois 60430*

IRWIN-DORSEY LIMITED *Georgetown, Ontario L7G 4B3*

Revised Edition

First Printing, July 1973
Second Printing. May 1974
Third Printing, June 1975
Fourth Printing, January 1976
Fifth Printing, November 1976
Sixth Printing, March 1977
Seventh Printing, August 1977

Case material of the Harvard Graduate School of
Business Administration is made possible by the
cooperation of business firms who may wish to remain
anonymous by having names, quantities, and other
identifying details disguised while basic relationships
are maintained. Cases are prepared as the basis for
class discussion rather than to illustrate either effective
or ineffective handling of administrative situations.

ISBN   0–256–00089–1
Library of Congress Catalog Card No. 73–169354
Printed in the United States of America

PREFACE

Perhaps the most obvious difference between this revised edition and the original edition of this book is an increase in the proportion of expository text material. About one quarter of the pages of the first edition were devoted to text; here the proportion is closer to half. This increase has been prompted by requests from a number of adopters of the first edition, who reported that many of their students were not sufficiently familiar with some of the terminology and techniques drawn upon in the cases to deal effectively with some of the more difficult cases. With the addition of the new text material, we believe that the book will be more suitable than before for undergraduate-level courses.

In addition, the entire book has been restructured to reflect three major categories of managerial decisions: to create product, to create demand, and to create capacity. The rationale for this division is developed in the Introduction and in Chapter 1 and so we need not go into it here, but we believe that it makes for a more orderly and logical development of the underlying concepts than in the first edition.

Finally, this edition includes six cases on federal government agencies. As the Introduction points out, managerial economics is concerned with purposive resource allocation within an enterprise that produces goods and services. There is no presumption that the enterprise is profit- or market-oriented. In recent years, there has been considerable emphasis on techniques such as cost-effectiveness analysis or systems analysis which are intended to improve the resource allocation process in not-for-profit agencies. We believe it is important to recognize this trend in a course on managerial economics.

ACKNOWLEDGMENTS

There are two of our former colleagues to whom we owe a special obligation. Neil E. Harlan, now a director of McKinsey & Co., Inc., had the original conception for this book when he was a member of the Harvard faculty and was senior author of the first edition. We greatly miss his counsel and assistance on this revision.

Stanley I. Buchin was to have succeeded Neil as the third principal author of this edition. He participated, in fact, in the early planning for the revision, wrote preliminary drafts of some of the new text, and prepared a number of the problems and cases. Stan, too, decided to become more actively involved in the improvement of managerial decision making, resigning from Harvard to become president of Applied Decision Systems, Inc. At that point Marshall joined with Christenson and Vancil to complete the revision. But we are greatly indebted to Stan for his contributions and consider it appropriate that they be recognized on the title page of this edition.

We are also obligated to others of our colleagues, present and past, who have written or supervised the writing of cases included herein. They are: Robert N. Anthony, John E. Bishop, Charles A. Bliss, David F. Hawkins, Erich A. Helfert, Malcolm P. McNair, Clarence B. Nickerson, Robert Schlaifer, Frank L. Tucker, Paul A. Vatter, Ross G. Walker, and John R. Yeager.

Professors Wiley S. Mitchell and James C. Taylor authored cases included in both editions of this book while teaching at l'Institute pour l'Etude des Methodes de Direction de l'Enterprise (IMEDE), Lausanne, Switzerland. These cases are used with their kind permission and that of the trustees of IMEDE.

We would also like to express our appreciation to Graeme M. Taylor, Vice President of Management Analysis Center, Inc., who administered the project which led to the six federal agency cases included herein and wrote several of the cases himself.

With the exception of the cases noted in the two preceding paragraphs, all cases in this book are copyrighted by the President and Fellows of Harvard College and we are grateful for their permission to reproduce them. We also wish to acknowledge our appreciation for the support provided to us by the administration of the Harvard Business School, and, most of all, for the cooperation of the many managers whose time has been so generously contributed to make these cases possible.

June 1973   CHARLES CHRISTENSON
                                         RICHARD F. VANCIL
                                         PAUL W. MARSHALL

CONTENTS

Introduction: The Economics of Managerial Decisions . . . 1

Case Prendergarth Shipping Company, 7

PART I: DECISIONS TO CREATE PRODUCT

1. Types of Costs 19

Case 1–1 Sylvania Electric Products Inc. (A), 48
1–2 White Eagle Oil Company (A), 67
1–3 The Atlantic Monthly Company (A), 88
1–4 Condon Leather Company, 102

2. Short-Run Cost Minimization 108

Case 2–1 Bob Mogielnicki, 139
2–2 Almond Apparatus Company, 143
2–3 Post Office Department (D), 146
2–4 Sherman Motor Company, 156
2–5 The Lockbourne Company, 160

3. Cost-Price-Volume Relationships 163

Case 3–1 Bill French, Accountant, 196
3–2 The Astra Company, 202
3–3 Post Office Department (B), 206
3–4 Stardust Grinder Company, 217
3–5 Nuthatch National Forest (A), 221

4. Decision Analysis: Structure and Uncertainty 227

Case 4–1 Conerly Chemical Company, 255
4–2 Warren Agency, Inc., 257
4–3 Weston Manufacturing Company, 259
4–4 Technotronics Corporation, 264
4–5 Waco Wildcat Company, 266

PART II: DECISIONS TO CREATE DEMAND

5. Probability: Measuring Uncertainty 271

6. Forecasting Demand 292
  Case 6–1 Newporter Fashions (A), 315
      6–2 Newporter Fashions (B), 317
      6–3 The Davison Press, Inc., 319
      6–4 The Walsh Company, 327
      6–5 Forest Service (A), 330

7. Analysis for Pricing Decisions 340
  Case 7–1 Sylvania Electric Products Inc. (B), 366
      7–2 General Motors Corporation, 371
      7–3 Benton Textiles, Inc., 379
      7–4 Liquid Cleanse, 386

8. Competitive Bidding 397
  Case 8–1 Mats Electronics, Inc., 409
      8–2 White Eagle Oil Company (B), 412
      8–3 Adamian Metallurgical Corporation, 420
      8–4 J. L. Jessup & Sons, 432

PART III: DECISIONS TO CREATE CAPACITY

9. Discounted Cash Flow Analysis 443
  Case 9–1 Federal Aviation Agency (A), 464
      9–2 Monitor Textile Company (A), 471
      9–3 Nuthatch National Forest (B), 476
      9–4 The Atlantic Monthly Company (B), 480
      9–5 Consolidated Mining and Manufacturing Corporation, 490

10. Simulation: Analysis of Complex Decisions 498
  Case 10–1 Weatherburn Aircraft Engine Company, 512
      10–2 Tomlinson Steel Corporation, 514
      10–3 Hurley Home Products Company, 516
      10–4 Apex Drilling Company, 518

11. Financial Structure and the Cost of Capital 521
  Case 11–1 F. F. Fierce & Company, 545
      11–2 Monitor Textile Company (B), 553
      11–3 McCarthy's Bowl Inn, 554

APPENDIXES

Appendix A. Random Number Tables 563

Appendix B. Tables for the Analysis of Capital Expenditures . . 569

INDEXES

Index of Cases 573

Subject Index 575

Introduction

THE ECONOMICS OF MANAGERIAL DECISIONS

If you are like most readers of this book, you come to it having already taken at least an introductory course in economics. "What," you may ask, "is *managerial* economics, how is it related to and how does it differ from what I have already studied?" Briefly stated, the distinction between the two disciplines is as follows:

Economics is the systematic study of	*Managerial economics* is the systematic study of
• how resources *are* allocated	• how resources *should be* allocated
• in *society as a whole*	• in a *particular productive enterprise*
• through the *interaction in markets* of many individual choices.	• through *purposive decisions* made by the managers of the enterprise.

Like most distinctions (especially briefly stated ones!), this one is not quite as clear-cut in practice as it appears in cold print, and so let us elaborate on it a bit.

First, economics per se, is, like managerial economics, concerned with the particular productive enterprise, since such enterprises make many of the choices which influence the behavior of markets. But this is only part of the concern of economics. The main focus of economics is on resource allocation at the aggregate level. For this purpose the economist can and does use an abstract model of the enterprise, much as the physicist uses the abstract concept of a particle of mass without spatial extension. Managerial economics, in contrast, is more concrete and situational, since it must cope with the messy details of real choices faced by real decision makers.

1

Second, economics per se, like managerial economics, assumes that the individual enterprise behaves purposively, that is, that it allocates the resources under its control in accordance with some goal.[1] Economics, however, places substantial emphasis on the nonpurposive, *automatic* allocation of resources through market mechanisms, while managerial economics is mainly concerned with purposive *managed* processes of allocation.

It is a remarkable fact that the automatic functioning of a market system can be a very effective allocation mechanism. Adam Smith, the first economist to set forth a detailed theory of a market economy, was so impressed by this fact that he referred to the market as governed by an "Invisible Hand." This is only a metaphor, of course, since the point is that there is no single intelligence "managing" the marketplace. Furthermore, the effectiveness of a market system depends upon its structure (how competitive it is, for instance); one of the main interests of the economist is in exploring the relationship between structure and performance.

Since resources can be allocated by either an automatic or a managed process, it is a matter of choice in any given context as to which process is adopted. This choice can be made at a number of different levels, from the level of an entire economy to that of an individual enterprise. The United States and Western Europe, for example, rely predominantly on the market system, but managed allocation takes place not only within individual private enterprises but also, and to a substantial degree, through governmental regulation of private enterprises or even through direct governmental ownership and management. Managed allocation of resources is predominant in the socialist countries of Eastern Europe, but even there market mechanisms are assigned a role (and, it seems, a growing one).

An individual enterprise exists, in a sense, primarily to manage a resource allocation process, but many of the larger firms have found it desirable to use market mechanisms internally. Each of the product divisions of General Motors, for example, is measured on its own profitability, and buying and selling of components and services takes place between divisions. Control by the central headquarters is exer-

---

[1] This assumption, while traditional, is not in fact necessary to explain the functioning of markets. Armen A. Alchian has shown that a sort of Darwinian selection in the marketplace would permit the survival of only those enterprises that *appeared* to be maximizing their profits whether or not this was their conscious purpose ("Uncertainty, Evolution, and Economic Theory," *Journal of Political Economy,* Vol. 58 [June 1950], pp. 211–21).

cised by establishing general policies rather than by prescribing decisions in detail.[2]

Most of the problems, examples, and cases in this book involve choices faced by business enterprises. The methods of analysis, however, are relevant to anyone managing the allocation of resources, whether in a business organized for profit, a governmental agency, or a private not-for-profit organization, and some of our cases do come from non-business contexts.

The Criterion Problem

The typical situation we will deal with in this book involves three main elements:

1. A set of proposed alternative uses for resources;
2. A criterion, or measure of merit, in terms of which the alternatives can be evaluated; and
3. A method for calculating a criterion value for each of the alternatives.

The first element, the set of alternatives, is clearly of critical importance. The most brilliant analysis of a poor set of alternatives can only result in a poor use of resources. But generating alternatives for consideration requires creativity and imagination more than method and rigor, and so we will not have much to say in our expository text about this step. You will, of course, have many opportunities to exercise your creativity and imagination in dealing with the case studies (and you will find in the process that a good analysis *can* be a stimulus to the imagination, although it cannot replace it).

The second element, the criterion, gives managerial economics its purposive focus. We will put as much emphasis on picking the right criterion as on picking the right alternative given the criterion. There are two reasons for this emphasis.

First, picking the right criterion is *important*. It is important because it almost amounts to picking the best alternative! Suppose, for instance, that both the set of alternatives to be considered and the criterion to be applied have already been determined. Then finding the best alternative becomes a matter of just fact-finding and arithmetic.

---

[2] Some years ago, the president of General Motors was nominated as Secretary of Defense. He aroused a furor when during his confirmation hearings before a Senate subcommittee, he stated that "What's good for General Motors is good for the United States, and vice versa." Given the parallel described above, it might have been more appropriate if he had said "Soviet Union" instead of "United States"! Joking aside, Eastern European economists have shown considerable interest in the management methods developed by American corporations.

These aren't unworthy activities, but they are relatively routine and the sort of thing that a manager can usually delegate to a subordinate.

The first point wouldn't matter much if it weren't for the second: picking the right criterion is *difficult*. How is this? In response, let us distinguish between an ultimate criterion and an immediate criterion. An ultimate criterion is one which is self-evidently valid, one about which you wouldn't think of raising the question "why." In principle, then, there should be no problem in picking the right ultimate criterion. The problem comes in using it. Chances are it achieves its self-evidential character by being so general that it's hard to see how it fits any particular concrete situation. Take, for example, Jeremy Bentham's criterion for social choice: "The greatest good for the greatest number."

An immediate criterion is one which is tailored to the concrete facts of a particular decision problem so that it is relatively easy to apply. By being so specific, however, it opens itself up to questioning and criticism. Suppose, for example, we ask you why you chose the particular school or college you are now attending. In other words, what were your immediate criteria? You might, let us say, answer:

- It's close to home;
- It has a good reputation;
- The tuition is reasonable;
- A good friend had decided to go there.

Here, first of all, we have an example of multiple criteria, which is quite common when we look at immediate rather than ultimate criteria. We might ask: Since "closeness to home" was one of your criteria, did you choose the school that was closest? No, you might reply, because that one didn't have as good a reputation. So, with multiple criteria you have the possibility of conflict and the question of how you would resolve that conflict—or, as an economist would put it, how you would "trade off" one criterion against another.

We won't push the multiple criteria issue any further at this point. Instead, we will ask you another question: Why was "reputation" important to you? (Now, you see, we are asking for the criteria for your criterion!) You might respond:

- It's an indication of educational quality;
- It will help me get a better job after graduation;
- And so forth.

But then we could ask you why you chose those reasons! In other words, the criteria you used (being immediate, not ultimate) are far from self-evident. Therefore they are subject to questioning and criticism of the sort we have been carrying out.

Now simply because we can question and *criticize* the criteria you used in choosing a college does not mean that the *choice* itself was a bad one nor, for that matter, that the *process* you followed in choosing was defective. *Any* criterion which is specific enough to be useful in making a concrete choice is going to be subject to criticism. The important thing is how well the criterion stands up to the criticism. Does it seem to be reasonably related to higher level goals? Does it handle "tradeoffs" in an appropriate way? These are questions we must consider in deciding what criteria to use in a particular situation.

Types of Resource Allocation Decisions

Fortunately, we do not have to tackle afresh the task of picking a criterion with each new resource allocation decision we face. The kinds of decisions that the managers of an enterprise must make tend to be repetitive. Once we have identified the appropriate criterion for a particular type of decision, we can use that same criterion whenever we meet the same kind of decision again.

With that fact in mind, this book is organized around three main types of resource allocation decisions:

- Decisions to create *product*;
- Decisions to create *demand*; and
- Decisions to create *capacity*.

By *product* we mean the goods and services that are the output of a productive enterprise. By *demand* we mean requirements for the enterprise's product imposed on it either by the market, if it disposes of its product by sale, or by a planning agency, if it disposes of its product in some other way. We assume that the kind and amount of product the enterprise can create in a given period of time are limited by factors such as the kind and amount of people it is employing and the plant and equipment it operates, and by *capacity* we mean these limitations.

In the first part of the book, in dealing with the decision to create product, we will take the demand for the product and the capacity of the enterprise as "givens." The problem then is whether and in what way the product should be produced.

In the second part of the book, we relax the first "given"—that the demand for the product is specified. We look at how to evaluate some of the things that an enterprise can do to influence demand. This section is most obviously relevant to profit-making enterprises, which influence demand for their goods and services through pricing, advertising, and so forth. But even not-for-profit enterprises may make such decisions. You can be sure, for example, that your college tries to anticipate the effect on demand when deciding on a change in tuition!

In the third section of the book we relax the second "given"—that the capacity of the enterprise is fixed. In economics, this is sometimes referred to as going from "short-run" to "long-run" decisions, but that terminology can be confusing. As Lord Keynes once quipped, "In the long run we're all dead." Decisions to vary capacity must be made in the here and now, just as decisions to vary production and demand, and not in some mystical "long run." The point is that, relative to other decisions, decisions to create capacity have long-lasting effects, so that in making them we must anticipate the needs of the enterprise for a long time into the future.

Putting It All Together

The classification of decisions into three types is a neat one. It helps, as we have said, in dealing with the problem of picking the right criterion. But isn't it a little *too* neat? Why should we, in analyzing a decision to produce, assume that demand and capacity are given? What if demand exceeds capacity, shouldn't we make some adjustment? These are the types of questions you may have started to ask.

And you would be quite right to do so. We are not ultimately dealing with three separate, unrelated kinds of decisions, but with the productive enterprise as an interrelated whole. In the "long run" (that phrase again!), the three variables of production, demand, and capacity should be brought into balance with each other in a way that is consistent with the overall goals of the enterprise. You should not lose sight of the problem of achieving overall balance while you're concentrating on just one of the variables.

The case at the end of this Introduction, Prendergarth Shipping Company, is intended to give you some appreciation of the interrelatedness of the three kinds of decisions before we begin focusing on them one at a time. This is a difficult and complex problem, so you shouldn't be too discouraged if you find it tough going—things will get easier later on! To help smooth the way, however, we have put some "leading questions" at the end of the case. Besides answering these questions, you might ask yourself why they are useful questions to ask. What do they reveal about the structure of this decision problem and how might this structure apply to other problems?

PRENDERGARTH SHIPPING COMPANY

Mr. William Thomas, president of Prendergarth Shipping Company, was considering what action he should take regarding the reassignment of one of the company's vessels in May 1964. In view of the market for ships at that time, it had become evident that the possibility of selling the vessel was not feasible; the ship had to be assigned where it would best serve the company's interests.

History of the Vessel

The vessel in question, the Prendergarth Warrior, had been purchased in October 1963. It was the only vessel purchased during the year ended December 31, 1963. In contrast with the remaining 27 vessels of the Prendergarth fleet, which were all about 12,500 tons burden, the Warrior was a small ship of only 4,500 tons (the burden of a freighter is the weight of freight of a standard bulk it can carry). It had been acquired to allow the Prendergarth company to compete for the tapioca trade in the port of Balik Papan in South Borneo. The Warrior was making the voyage from Singapore to Balik Papan and back at a rate of 50 round trips a year at the present time. The freight rates on this commodity were satisfactory, but the harbor channel was such that only small vessels like the Warrior could get into Balik Papan to take advantage of these revenues. The cost per dollar of revenue of operating a small vessel, fully laden, was higher than that of a larger ship, were the latter able to navigate the channel.

Operating costs for the two sizes of vessel owned by Prendergarth are given in Exhibit 1. The behavior of these and other costs is discussed in Exhibit 2.

Recent Developments

In April 1964, the port authority of Balik Papan had obtained a grant to deepen the harbor channel. The plan, which had just arrived at the Prendergarth head office, showed that ships of up to 15,000 tons would be able to use the port after the deepening operation had been completed. This work was expected to be completed in September or October of 1964. It would therefore be possible for the larger vessels of the line to serve Balik Papan. The greater carrying capacity of the larger ships should, it was thought, more than compensate for the higher total operating costs of such vessels, since the quantities of tapioca available were substantial and the demand was great. The estimated costs of having the larger vessel deviate from the normal route to put in at Balik Papan are described in Exhibit 3. The larger vessels would have to call at Balik Papan as frequently as the Warrior had called there in order to fulfill shippers' requirements. If the big ships called at Balik Papan, they would have to call twice at Singapore, once before Balik Papan and once after. This was because (1) the tapioca had to be transshipped at Singapore, (2) the large vessels were usually too full of cargo on the eastward run to get the tapioca in as well before calling at Singapore, and (3) the cargo to be moved from Singapore to Balik Papan had to be loaded.

The possibility of using both the Warrior *and* the larger vessels on this route had been considered but had been rejected because "it would slow down the big ships too much."

Alternative Use of the Warrior

The only feasible alternative use of the Warrior that Mr. Thomas was considering was on the route from Dar-es-Salaam (in East Africa) to Zanzibar. Some financial aspects of this alternative are discussed in Exhibit 4. At present, the large vessels of the line called at both of these ports, incurring port charges as detailed in Exhibit 5. The Prendergarth ships used lighters in place of docking in all the ports listed in Exhibit 5 because it was less expensive and often quicker for the amounts of cargo involved. The cargo, which consisted of dates and ground nuts from Dar-es-Salaam, and coconuts, copra, and special timbers from Zanzibar, was usually carried to the United States; the freight rates from Zanzibar and Dar-es-Salaam to the United States were virtually identical.

If the Warrior were to be used on this alternative route, it would shuttle the cargo from one of the two ports to the other, so that the large vessel need make only one call in the area on a given run, thereby saving time and portage dues. The portage dues incurred by the Warrior at the two ports would have to be considered, of course. The freight normally collected at the two ports amounted to about 3,850 tons per pair of calls.

The Problem

Mr. Thomas was anxious to decide between the two possible assignments of the Warrior within the next few days rather than wait until the problem became critical in the fall. The reason for haste was that an opportunity had arisen to move the Warrior from Singapore to Zanzibar with a cargo which would not only pay for the cost of moving the ship but would also pay for the lighterage expenses that would be needed at Balik Papan until the new harbor channel was ready. As this was a very unusual cargo, it was not thought likely that a similar opportunity would arise before the fall.

Mr. Thomas was anxious to keep all the ships as active as possible. Because the company had a very good reputation among shippers, it had been able to fill its ships at all times. This fact made the line one of very few fully booked shipping lines in the business.

The most recent income statement of the company is shown in Exhibit 6. The year ended December 31, 1963 was considered a typical year in the company's history. Maps of the areas under review are presented in Exhibit 7.

Questions

1. Assume that a vessel is already scheduled to make a round trip between Balik Papan and Singapore and that it has room for additional cargo in each direction. How much additional profit can be earned by carrying one additional ton of tapioca from Balik Papan to Singapore, dock to dock, after deducting onloading and offloading costs at each port? How much can be earned by carrying one additional ton of general merchandise from Singapore to Balik Papan?

2. Assume that Prendergarth has already decided to operate all of its present fleet and therefore to commit itself to the costs which result from that decision but that it has not decided how to allocate vessels to routes. What are the additional costs of sending the Warrior on a round trip from Singapore to Balik Papan and return? One of the large vessels?

3. Combining your answers to the first two questions, how much will each of the two vessel types earn per round trip if used on the Singapore–Balik Papan route? How much per year?

4. If the Warrior is transferred to the East Africa route, which is the preferred port of call for the large vessels: Zanzibar or Dar-es-Salaam? What costs can be saved by having the large vessels avoid the other port, and how much will these savings amount to in a year?

5. What would be the cost per year (both tonnage- and voyage-related) of using the Warrior on the East Africa shuttle run?

6. What action should Mr. Thomas take?

Exhibit 1

PRENDERGARTH SHIPPING COMPANY

ANNUAL OPERATING COSTS OF VESSELS

Item	Costs Typical for Size of Vessel	
	4,500 Tons	12,500 Tons
Payroll	$143,594	$210,877
Depreciation	222,956	363,228
Repairs	40,000	47,500
Overhead costs	8,225	16,900
Stores and provisions	32,657	39,283
Insurance	36,030	46,750
Miscellaneous	4,750	5,625
Total annual cost	$488,212	$730,163

On the average, there were 345 operating days
in a year, so the cost per operating day was......$ 1,415 $ 2,116
In addition, bunkering costs (i.e., fuel costs) were
incurred amounting to (per mile)...............$ 0.73 $ 1.27

Exhibit 2

PRENDERGARTH SHIPPING COMPANY

DISCUSSION OF COST BEHAVIOR

Cost item	Behavior of Cost
Payroll	Payroll expense is, in the short run, a fixed item. The complement of the ship is virtually fixed over a year, and in the course of one voyage it is completely fixed. No change in union rates is expected in the near future.
Depreciation	Depreciation is charged on a straight-line basis on the original cost of the vessel.
Repairs	This amount varies randomly. The figures shown are the average annual amounts expended in the industry on ships of the sizes indicated.
Overhead	This includes all expense items incurred on board the vessel and is fixed.
Stores and provisions	This varies with the payroll and is therefore virtually fixed.
Insurance	There is fixed charge of $30,000 per ship annually, plus an annual charge of $1.34 per ton.
Miscellaneous	Fixed.
Bunkerage	Fuel costs will depend on the routes being traveled, as the price of fuel varies to some extent from place to place. For calculation purposes, however, the figures shown may be taken as suitable averages.

Exhibit 3

PRENDERGARTH SHIPPING COMPANY

Calls at Balik Papan by Large Vessels   May 1964

Since the normal terminal point of the voyages of the larger vessels was Singapore on the eastward run, and since Balik Papan was further east than Singapore, it would have been necessary for the large vessels to make a round trip in order to call at Balik Papan. The feasibility of additional calls at Brunei, Djakarta, and other ports had not been investigated, but it was thought that these were not likely to be profitable.

The distance from Singapore to Balik Papan by the best navigable route was 480 sea miles, or 960 sea miles round trip. At their normal sailing speed in these waters of 16 knots, the larger vessels required about 60 hours steaming time round trip, or $2\frac{1}{2}$ steaming days, approximately. This time compares with the slightly less than $3\frac{1}{2}$ days that the Warrior required.

The carrying capacity of the larger vessels was 6,850 tons of tapioca on each voyage from Balik Papan to Singapore, as against the 3,950 tons of the Warrior. It was thought that the bookings of manufactured goods that were currently being taken from Singapore to Balik Papan by the Warrior would be the same for the larger vessels; there were no indications that any additional bookings could be obtained. The Warrior had been carrying 3,150 tons of manufactured goods on a typical voyage from Singapore to Balik Papan, at an average rate of $2.70 per ton. The difference in tonnage between the tapioca and manufactured goods was caused by the relative bulk of the two types of cargo.

The current freight rates for tapioca, amounting to $5.10 per ton for the trip from Balik Papan to Singapore, seemed likely to remain in force for some considerable time. Most of the tapioca was sent out on contracts, and there appeared to be a constant or increasing demand for the commodity. While the rate might go up in the future, it was reasonable to assume that it would not go down.

The turn-around time (the period between the ship's arrival at a port and departure from it) at Balik Papan was relatively slow. Because of the inadequacy of the cranage facilities, it would take three days to turn one of the large vessels as against $2\frac{1}{2}$ days to turn the Warrior. This difference was caused by the greater amount of cargo to be moved in the larger vessels.

Because of the extensive facilities at Singapore, all ships of the size being considered could be turned around in one day at that port, regardless of the amounts being loaded or discharged.

Exhibit 4

PRENDERGARTH SHIPPING COMPANY

Calls at Zanzibar and Dar-es-Salaam May 1964

The cargoes that were shipped from these ports were made up of the five commodities listed below. The rates shown were those for shipping one ton of the commodity from either port to the United States, and the tonnage listed was the average amount of each commodity that had been carried per voyage in all voyages in the last six months. The remaining capacity of the larger vessels was used by freight from other ports. The large vessels collectively called at each of the two ports 80 times a year.

Commodity	Port	Rate per Ton	Average Tonnage
Dates	Dar-es-Salaam	$88	500
Ground nuts	Dar-es-Salaam	84	850
Coconuts	Zanzibar	74	400
Copra	Zanzibar	66	1,600
Special timbers	Zanzibar	65	500

The turn-around time in Zanzibar had averaged two days for the larger vessels, and the use of the Warrior would not shorten this. The turnaround at Dar-es-Salaam had been two days with the larger vessels; the Warrior could be turned around in one day.

The sailing time between the two ports was very short, and this distance (72 miles) was such that only one day (two days round trip) was involved no matter which vessel is being used. The higher speed of the larger vessels had no noticeable effect over such a short trip. It was thought that an overall savings of three days per voyage would be attained by the large vessels (one port call and a day of steaming in transit) if the Warrior were used on the Zanzibar/Dar-es-Salaam run.

If the Warrior were to be used as a "shuttle," it would be necessary for scheduling purposes to have the larger ships call at the same port each time. It would be impractical to try to arrange for the large ships to call at whichever port the Warrior had most recently served because of complications in the booking of freight at other ports which would be called on subsequently.

The larger ships passed through the area with sufficient frequency to permit the Warrior to shuttle as frequently as it could.

Exhibit 5

PRENDERGARTH SHIPPING COMPANY

COST OF CALLING AT PORTS

Cost Item	Varies with—	Units	Balik Papan	Singapore	Zanzibar	Dar-es-Salaam
Portage dues	Tonnage	$/day in port/ton burden	0.14	0.20	0.13	0.31
Lighterage*	Freight moved	$/ton of freight moved	0.25	0.16	0.14	0.15
Stevedoring	Freight moved	$/ton of freight moved	0.56	0.32	0.32	0.32
Lighthouse	Fixed	$/visit	73.0	126.0	...	62.0
Cranage	Freight moved	$/ton of freight moved	†	0.14	0.13	0.13
Special assessment			‡			

* Lighterage expense is the cost of having small barges called lighters come alongside the vessel in order to facilitate loading and unloading of cargo. The Balik Papan lighterage charge is for ships anchoring in the harbor channel; having lighters come out to the channel mouth would involve a total charge of $0.97. Portage dues are required on entering a port and are independent of the above charges.

† There is no cranage charge at Balik Papan because the freight is manhandled. This considerably increases the charge for stevedoring relative to other ports.

‡ All ships exceeding 8,000 tons burden were to be assessed $2,000 for each port call (in addition to portage dues). This assessment was intended to contribute to the investment in and maintenance of the new deep channel that these ships required.

Exhibit 6

PRENDERGARTH SHIPPING COMPANY

INCOME STATEMENT FOR THE YEAR TO DECEMBER 31, 1963

Voyage revenues for the year	$49,661,000
Voyage expenses	33,480,000
Gross margin	$16,181,000
Shore support expenses	6,318,000
Administrative and other expenses	3,916,000
Net income before tax	$ 5,947,000
Income tax expense	3,088,000
Net income	$ 2,859,000

Exhibit 7

PRENDERGARTH SHIPPING COMPANY

MAPS OF AREAS RELEVANT TO THE ASSIGNMENT
OF THE PRENDERGARTH WARRIOR

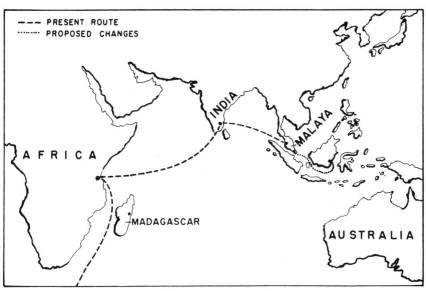

PART I

Decisions to Create Product

Chapter 1

TYPES OF COST

The word "cost" is a ubiquitous one in our language. In business usage, we speak of the cost of inventories or of equipment used for production, the cost of goods sold, the cost of operating the machining department, or the cost of making a certain part in-plant rather than purchasing it outside. Government officials talk of cost-benefit or cost-effectiveness analysis.

The possibilities for confusion are compounded because of the fact that the word "cost" is used in different ways by accountants and economists. Both these professions would agree with the most general definition of cost: a measure, usually in monetary terms, of the resources consumed in achieving a given objective. The word by itself is empty of meaning until we have specified the purpose for which the resources were consumed.

The difference between the accountant's and the economist's concept of cost comes in the different principles they use to value the resources consumed. Accountants generally use the concept of *acquisition cost,* by which they mean the amount of cash or other financial resource which was originally paid out by the enterprise when it acquired the resource in question. Accountants are basically historians, reporting on the results of past events.

Economists, on the other hand, measure resources in terms of their *opportunity cost.* By this they mean the return the resources would bring if they had instead been devoted to the best alternative opportunity. Economists have traditionally been interested in the optimal allocation of resources, which involves the decision-making function. No decision made today can affect what has already happened. Hence the costs economists consider relevant are *future* costs rather than the historical costs considered by accountants.

Opportunity cost may be either greater or less than acquisition cost. Suppose, for example, that a firm is considering the production of an item which would require the use of material on hand for which $100 was originally paid; the acquisition cost, then, is $100. If the material could currently be sold on the market for $125, however, its opportunity cost must be $125, because the use of the material requires the firm to forego the opportunity of receiving $125. If, on the other hand, the material currently has no market value or alternative use, its opportunity cost is zero.

The businessman lives with both these concepts of cost. For decision-making purposes, the economist's concept of opportunity cost is the relevant one; a rational decision must involve the comparison of alternative courses of action. We shall see that all the business decisions studied in this course require the analysis and measurement of opportunity costs. The accountant's role as a "scorekeeper" for outside investors is also important to the businessman. Moreover, accounting records are often a primary source of information for decision-making purposes. For these reasons, it is important for the student to understand both the differences and the similarities in the two approaches, an understanding we hope will be fostered through grappling with the two concepts in the cases in this book.

CLASSIFICATION OF COSTS

In order to sharpen our discussion of costs relevant for business decisions, we will first indicate three possible ways in which costs can be classified—by product identification, by variability, and by objective.

By Product Identification

One way to classify costs, which is quite familiar to accountants is by the degree to which the resources which have been consumed in generating revenue can be identified with specific units of product. Under this scheme, total costs are divided into two classifications, *prime costs* and *overhead costs.*

Prime costs represent those which are supposedly identifiable with specific units of end product. These costs include *direct material* and *direct labor,* both of which are dependent directly upon the products in such a way that it is possible to say that specific units of resource *input* were consumed in producing specific units of product *output.*

Overhead costs represent general support activities which are not directly identifiable with specific units of product. Overhead, in turn, is commonly further classified into three subclasses: factory overhead, selling expense, and general and administrative expense.

The distinction between prime costs and overhead costs is to some extent a matter of convenience. Some overhead costs could no doubt be directly identifiable with specific units of product given sufficient effort on the part of the accountant. The inclusion of such costs within the classification of overhead generally results from a determination that ·greater precision would require more effort than it is worth.

By Variability

This second basis of classification is quite similar to the first. It also divides costs into two categories, this time depending upon whether or not the total amount of cost incurred in a period of time varies with the quantity of product produced during that period.

Direct costs often called variable costs, are those costs whose total *does* vary. Direct costs generally include prime costs, as defined above, and also *direct overhead,* that portion of overhead costs which varies with the quantity of production.

The other category of cost is called *period cost.* These costs are so named because they are assumed to be constant relative to the quantity of production and hence can be expressed as so much "per period." Period costs are also often called *fixed costs.*

It is often assumed in practice that direct costs vary in direct proportion to production, which implies that the *average* direct cost per unit of production is the same regardless of the level of production. (In economic terms, marginal variable cost equals average variable cost at all levels of production.) This assumption, while not necessarily true under all circumstances, often turns out to be a satisfactory empirical approximation. When it is true, direct cost is a linear function of the quantity of production, as illustrated in Figure 1–1.

Figure 1–1

COST VARIABILITY WITH VOLUME

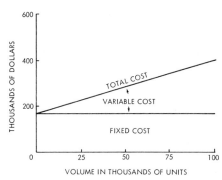

By Objectives

Cost represents resource consumption, and a business would normally try to avoid consumption of any of its resources unless some valid purpose were accomplished thereby. Hence, it is useful to classify costs according to the result which the business expects when it permits the resources to be consumed. Three major classes of objectives can be distinguished: creation of product, creation of capacity, and creation of demand.

Costs resulting in *creation of product* occur when the resource consumption results in a storable product for sale. These costs include what we have previously defined as prime costs and direct factory overhead. The costs are, therefore, quite similar to direct costs, except that they exclude direct costs (i.e., costs which vary with production) which do not *result* in production. Allowing for the difference in valuation principles between acquisition costs and opportunity costs, product-creating costs are also quite similar in concept to the economist's variable costs. Costs incurred in the production of services, as distinguished from goods, would not generally fall in this category since services are not storable, but would instead come in the category "creation of capacity," to be discussed below.

Costs associated with *creation of capacity* represent resource consumptions which result in capacity to produce goods or services in the future. Capacity can be in the form of bricks and mortar or of hardware, but it can also be in the form of an organization and the people required to carry on a business of a certain size. If, for example, a business has a salaried work force which will be paid regardless of whether there is a demand for its product, the cost of this salaried work force is a capacity-creating cost rather than as a product-creating cost; the cost does not necessarily result in creation of product.

Capacity-creating costs vary in terms of the degree of permanence associated with the capacity. Buildings and equipment purchased by the business represent relatively long-term capacity and the highest order of permanence. Fixed assets leased by the business on intermediate-term or long-term leases and employees paid on a salaried basis with a reasonably permanent commitment fall into an intermediate category of semipermanent capacity. It is also possible for the business to adjust its capacity over the very short run through such devices as overtime, and the premium pay for this purpose would constitute a temporary capacity-creating cost. The judgment as to what effort to use in creating capacity will depend upon the degree of permanence anticipated in the underlying demand situation.

Capacity is, of course, itself a resource, and its consumption therefore results in a cost. Commonly, consumption of capacity is a function of elapsed time rather than of physical production (and hence falls in the category of period, or fixed, cost), in contrast to product-creating costs which are a function of physical production. It is in connection with capacity-creating costs that the distinction between the accountant's acquisition cost principle of valuation and the economist's opportunity cost principle is likely to become more pronounced. Because it is difficult in the very short run to make major adjustments in capacity, the amount of capacity available in any period may be considerably out of balance with that required. If, for example, the amount of capacity available is considerably in excess of that required, then the *opportunity* cost of this nonrequired capacity will be zero, regardless of its *acquisition* cost. In contrast, if the firm is faced with a strong demand situation, it may find that it does not have enough capacity to meet its requirements. In this case the available capacity may have an *opportunity* cost which exceeds its *acquisition* cost because of the very profitable alternative uses which the business has available.

Since the elementary economic theory of price determination does not ordinarily consider methods of stimulating demand other than price changes, product-creating costs and capacity-creating costs correspond closely with the economist's concepts of variable costs and fixed cost, respectively.

Costs associated with *creation of demand* occur when the resource consumption results in a demand for the firm's product. Demand-creating costs *may* be direct costs, such as sales commissions paid on a percentage or per unit basis, but more likely these costs are period costs. Firms often budget some of these costs on the basis of anticipated sales revenues; it is quite common, for example, to base advertising expenditures on a forecast of sales. It is important to note, however, that the advertising budget is based on a *forecast* rather than on actual sales; hence advertising expenditures are not in fact a direct cost, at least in the short run.

Classifying costs by objectives is analytically useful because business managers are naturally inclined to think of their problems in these terms. A businessman is not usually worried much about hairsplitting distinctions between various theoretical classifications of costs: "I've got a production problem," he will say, or a "pricing problem" or a "capacity problem." In many situations, cost analysis can be helpful in resolving these problems, and for this reason we have adopted the objectives classification as the basic structure for the remainder of this book. The balance of this chapter plus the next two are devoted to product-creating costs; subsequent chapters then deal with demand-creating and capacity-creating costs.

ESTIMATING PRODUCT COSTS

The accounting records of an enterprise are a primary source of data about product costs. Utilizing accounting data for decision-making purposes, however, is not as straightforward as it might first appear. The manager who asks his accountant, "What's the unit cost of product X?" must be very careful how he uses a simple answer such as, "Two dollars and sixty-seven cents." More likely, the accountant will reply, "Why do you want to know?" because the accountant is well aware of two important limitations on his data:

1. Accounting figures are historical. The $2.67 may have been the "cost" of product X last month, but the manager's current decision can't change last month's results. The manager really wants to know what the cost of product X will be next month.
2. Product cost, as determined by the accountant, is a general-purpose figure. The manager, however, has a specific decision to make and, more than likely, will need a special-purpose product cost figure for his analysis.

Despite these limitations, accounting records are too valuable as a source of information to be ignored. The manager who understands *how* the accountant determines his general-purpose product cost figure is in a good position to modify that figure in order to arrive at an estimate of future product costs that are relevant for the decision he has to make. Therefore, the starting point for estimating product costs is an understanding of the way that accountants traditionally determine product costs. The following discussion describes these typical accounting procedures at several levels of sophistication and illustrates the application of these procedures in a hypothetical company called Essex Corporation.

Actual Costs

Even the simplest accounting records for a manufacturing company are usually structured in such a way to yield a historical measure of actual product costs. Table 1–1 represents an operating statement for the Essex Corporation which fulfills this purpose. The company manufactures only one product, and during 1972 it sold 972,418 units for a total revenue of $3,782,789. The total costs charged against this revenue amounted to $3,385,681, and the accountant has divided these costs into two broad categories: costs of goods sold, and selling and administrative expenses. With this classification, the "actual" cost of the units sold during the year was $2.68 each. As may be noted, however, even this cost figure is an average; some of the units sold during 1972 had been manufactured in 1971 at an actual cost of $2.76 each, the balance of the units sold during 1972 were produced during that year at a manufacturing cost of $2.67 each.

The accounting system from which the statement in Table 1–1 was prepared is an extremely simple one but is typical of the systems still used by thousands of small businesses in this country today. All that is required to arrive at a product cost figure is to add together all of the

Table 1–1

ESSEX CORPORATION

OPERATING STATEMENT FOR 1972

	Number of Units	Amount per Unit	Total	Amount
Net sales..............................	972,418	$3.89		$3,782,789
Cost of goods sold:				
Beginning factory inventories...............	177,412	$2.76	$ 489,621	
Manufacturing costs:				
Materials used in production..............			$ 703,642	
Factory payroll........................			1,046,915	
Fringe benefits.........................			128,868	
Fuel and electricity.....................			115,406	
Factory supplies........................			102,574	
Repairs and maintenance.................			198,412	
Depreciation...........................			230,705	
General factory expense.................			110,956	
Property taxes and insurance..............			25,770	
Total manufacturing costs..............	998,684	$2.67	$2,663,248	
Subtotal.........................	1,176,096		$3,152,869	
Less: Ending inventories..................	203,678	$2.67	543,820	
Cost of goods sold.......................	972,418	$2.68	$2,609,049	2,609,049
Gross profit on sales......................	972,418	$1.21		$1,173,740
Selling and administrative expenses:				
Office payroll...........................			$ 118,162	
Sales salaries and commissions.............			201,386	
Fringe benefits.........................			55,962	
Advertising and sales expense..............			217,624	
Audit and legal.........................			21,933	
Interest expense........................			88,233	
Travel and telephone....................			27,022	
Bad debts..............................			3,589	
Office supplies and postage................			16,019	
Miscellaneous..........................			26,702	
Total expenses......................	972,418	0.80	$ 776,632	776,632
Net profit before income taxes...............	972,418	$0.41		$ 397,108

manufacturing costs that have been incurred and divide that total by the number of units produced. The Essex Corporation did spend $2,663,248 in its factory during the year, it did produce 998,684 units, and therefore these units cost $2.67 each. This cost figure is quite useful for some purposes, such as valuing the ending inventory of 203,678 units in order to determine the company's profit for the year. The cost figure may also be useful as a crude sort of evaluation of pricing policies and manufacturing efficiency, but as soon as the manager begins to think about the kinds of actions he might take to improve profitability, a more careful analysis of product costs is required.

Product-Creating Costs

One way to begin an analysis of manufacturing costs is to classify them by the objectives for which resources have been consumed, as suggested earlier. Table 1–2 illustrates how this might be done for Essex

Table 1–2

ESSEX CORPORATION

ANALYSIS OF MANUFACTURING COSTS FOR 1972

Cost Item	Total Cost	Product-Creating Costs	Capacity-Creating Costs
Materials used in production	$ 703,642	$ 703,642	...
Factory payroll	1,046,915	816,219	$230,696
Fringe benefits (12.3%)	128,868	100,395	28,473
Fuel and electricity	115,406	41,312	74,094
Factory supplies	102,574	58,967	43,607
Repairs and maintenance	198,412	83,543	114,869
Depreciation	230,705	...	230,705
General factory expense	110,956	21,471	89,485
Property taxes and insurance	25,770	...	25,770
Total	$2,663,248	$1,825,549	$837,699

Units produced: 998,684. Product costs per unit: $\dfrac{\$1,825,549}{998,684} = \$1.83$

Corporation for 1972. None of the manufacturing costs fall into the "demand-creating" category; manufacturing costs are incurred either to create products or to maintain the capacity to do so. As may be noted, several of the cost elements are split between these two classifications, as explained below.

Factory Payroll. This item—the largest single manufacturing cost —includes all the people employed in the factory: production workers, foremen, supervisors, materials handlers, and even janitors and watchmen. While all of these people were necessary in order for the factory to operate, there is a significant distinction to be drawn between the purposes of their activities. Some of the employees, such as the plant superintendent and the watchman, are the human resources required to have any sort of productive capability at all; we don't need two watchmen no matter how many units of product we turn out, but we can't even stay in business without having one watchman. Other employees—those involved directly in production such as machine tool operators or assemblers—are usually identifiable with the products they create. In between these two extremes is another group of employees that are somewhat harder to classify, perhaps best typified by the young men with hand trucks who move materials between departments, as well as other types of "indirect" labor. A minimum number of such people are probably required at any level of operations and, just like the watchman, might therefore be regarded as part of the costs of maintaining productive capacity. Additional people may be needed as the volume of production increases, and even though they are not directly identifiable with specific units of product, their wages are a product-creating cost.

Fringe Benefits. Once the payroll costs have been split between the two classifications, fringe benefits for social security taxes, pension contributions, and the like, may easily be split along these same lines.

Other Manufacturing Costs. Each of the remaining cost items would also have to be analyzed using the same line of reasoning applied to factory payroll. Heat and light for the plant are capacity-creating costs, but some part of the electricity bill is also used to drive productive equipment and is directly identifiable with units of production. Factory supplies in the Essex Corporation's accounting system include packing materials, and these product-related costs should be differentiated from those supplies needed to keep the factory running at any level of production. And, as Table 1–2 shows, even in this simple accounting system, some cost elements are pure: materials used in production are strictly product-creating costs; while depreciation, property taxes, and insurance represent the cost of maintaining productive capability.

The net effect of classifying costs by objective, at least in this example, is the recognition that some substantial fraction of total manufacturing costs are capacity-related rather than product-related. For the Essex Corporation in 1972, product-creating costs amounted to $1.83 per unit; the balance of the manufacturing costs were really incurred to maintain the general productive capability of the company. Classifying manufacturing costs in this way is a useful start in the analysis of product costs. This classification scheme is not, however, the one commonly used by accountants. If Essex Corporation's accounting system were a little more elaborate than that represented in Table 1–1, it would probably draw a distinction between prime costs and overhead costs.

Conventional Cost Classifications. The analysis of each cost element necessary to prepare the cost classification, such as that shown in

Table 1–3

ESSEX CORPORATION

CONVENTIONAL BREAKDOWN OF DIRECT COSTS
AND MANUFACTURING OVERHEAD

Direct materials:		
Production	$703,642	
Packing supplies	58,967	
Total		$ 762,609
Direct labor:		
Payroll	$714,219	
Fringe benefits—direct	87,849	
Total		802,068
Total "prime costs"		$1,564,677
Factory overhead:		
Supervision and indirect labor	$332,696	
Fringe benefits—overhead labor	41,019	
Fuel and electricity	115,406	
Factory supplies	43,607	
Repairs and maintenance	198,412	
Depreciation	230,705	
General factory expense	110,956	
Property taxes and insurance	25,770	
Total overhead		1,098,571
Total manufacturing costs		$2,663,248

Table 1–2, is quite time consuming; and as will be seen in the next chapter, the classification of some cost items may shift from one category to another from time to time. While cost classification by objectives is an extremely useful way for the manager to think about his costs and the way that he can influence them by the decisions that he makes, it is almost impossible to reflect such a classification scheme in the accounting records of the company. Instead, the accountant typically uses the classification of manufacturing costs as illustrated in Table 1–3, thereby producing a crude approximation of the cost classifications used in Table 1–2. The accountant's "prime" costs for direct materials and

direct labor used in production are fairly easy to identify separately in the accounting records. All other manufacturing costs, which include both product-creating and capacity-creating costs, are called factory overhead. The most common procedure is to deal with these overhead costs as a group, as shown in Table 1–3, although some sophisticated accounting systems differentiate between variable overhead costs and fixed overhead costs.

A line-by-line comparison of Tables 1–2 and 1–3 illustrates some of the dangers inherent in using the data found in conventional accounting systems: factory overhead costs are *not* simply the fixed costs related to the maintenance of productive capability. For example, factory overhead in many accounting systems includes indirect labor ($102,000 in the Essex example) that could be reduced as output decreases or vice versa. Nevertheless, the accountant's classification as shown in Table 1–3 is much more useful than no classification at all (see Table 1–1). The typical accounting classification has the further advantage of facilitating *consistent* cost collection from one year to the next, thus providing a time series of cost data which may then be analyzed systematically. This analysis will be discussed in Chapter 6. Because of the advantages of this consistency, the accountant's classification system is probably as useful as any that could be devised for general-purpose use. The analysis of such data and its adaptation to the needs of a specific problem will continue to be the task of the manager who seeks to use accounting data.

The other major drawback of accounting information, its historical nature, is a problem which can be mitigated by the further sophistication of a company's accounting system. The techniques and procedures that are commonly used for this purpose are described below.

Standard Prime Costs

The only thing that is certain about historical product costs is that—like the stock market—they will fluctuate. The manager who is responsible for making decisions when the need arises is also responsible for determining *when* the need has arisen for making a decision. For this purpose, he monitors actual product costs on a continuous basis, trying to understand why costs have changed and whether or not the change is a signal that some action is needed on his part. This monitoring process, sometimes called management control, is a critical task for the manager; and because of its importance, a variety of accounting techniques have been developed to assist him in fulfilling it. Two of the more important of these techniques, standard prime costs and overhead budgets, are valuable not only for control purposes but they also provide the manager with cost information which can be very useful in his analysis of decision problems.

In order to evaluate the implications of a fluctuation in actual manufacturing costs, the manager must have some concept of what the costs *should* have been; actual cost performance has been either favorable or unfavorable against this criterion. Even in simple accounting systems,

Table 1–4

ESSEX CORPORATION

STANDARD PRIME COSTS PER UNIT

	Type of Material	Quantity per Unit	Cost of Material	Cost per Unit
Direct materials:				
Production:	A	0.68 lb.	$0.51/lb.	$0.35
	B	8 pieces	0.041/piece	0.33
Packing supplies:	C	0.16 lb.	0.18/lb.	0.03
	D	1 piece	0.03/piece	0.03
Total materials...				$0.74

	Department	Hours per Unit	Cost per Hour*	
Direct labor:				
Production:	1	0.06	$2.40	$0.14
	2	0.08	2.57	0.21
	3	0.08	2.26	0.18
	4	0.07	2.28	0.16
Shipping...................5	5	0.06	2.14	0.13
Total labor				$0.82
Total prime costs...				$1.56

* Including payroll fringe benefit costs of 12.3%

such as that shown for the Essex Corporation in Table 1–1, an evaluation of cost performance is possible simply by comparing 1972's costs to those incurred in 1971; the prior year's costs are used as a "standard" against which the current year is measured. Such an evaluation is facilitated, however, by the preparation of a formal standard cost such as that illustrated in Table 1–4.

Table 1–4 illustrates the calculation of standard prime costs for the product manufactured by the Essex Corporation. As is usually true, the production process is well defined; management knows that a finished unit will contain four different types of materials and will pass through five different departments in the factory. Nevertheless, each line on Table 1–4 requires two separate estimates in order to determine the standard cost of one unit. Management must estimate the standard *quantity* of each type of input (material or labor) needed to produce a finished product and the standard *price* that the company will have to pay for each unit of input. These two standards are then multiplied together to yield the standard cost per unit.

The degree of management's uncertainty about each of these estimates may vary considerably. Material quantities, for example, usually include an allowance for "normal" spoilage or waste during production. The product in Table 1–4 requires 0.68 pounds of material A, even though a unit of finished product contains only 0.57 pounds of that material; the remainder is wasted as the raw material is processed. The actual amount of waste for any particular unit of finished product may be more or less than 0.11 pounds, depending upon the efficiency of the production machinery and the man operating it at the particular time that a unit is produced. On the other hand, material B is a finished part purchased from an outside supplier; there is little uncertainty that a completed unit of product will contain eight such parts.

Labor quantities also reflect expected normal performance and thus include an even greater variety of standard allowances. In Department 1, for example, the standard hours per unit is 0.06. This standard implies that a man working in that department would produce 16.67 units per hour (1 hour/0.06 per unit). In fact, when the man is actually working he can produce 20 units per hour; one unit can be produced in 0.05 hours. The standard quantity, however, reflects the fact that the man does not produce units constantly at the rate of 20 per hour; he is permitted to take a rest period in the morning and afternoon and a washup period at the end of his shift. In addition, management knows that the machine may be shut down sporadically for minor maintenance and that some of the units produced on the equipment will be defective. The standard labor quantity per unit reflects all of these factors. The standard says, in effect, that the worker will be paid for 8 hours and is expected to produce 133 good pieces of product during that period.

Standard prices for materials and labor are also subject to estimating errors. Material prices, particularly for some commodities, may change frequently. At the other extreme, management may enter into long-term supply contracts for some materials, thus eliminating the uncertainty about future prices. Labor costs may also be a contractual matter with a labor union, but even then there may be different rates paid to individuals in the same department, depending upon their seniority and the definition of their job. Standard prices for both materials and labor reflect management's best estimates of the average expected cost of acquiring these inputs during the coming period.

Standard prime costs determined in this manner may be extremely useful for many types of management decisions. The relevant product-creating costs for a unit of finished product should not be based on theoretical maximum efficiency which cannot be maintained over a period of more than a few hours. The relevant labor input in Department 1 is 0.06 hours per unit, not 0.05. Standard prime costs which reflect normal efficiency are, therefore, an important source of product cost information for management.

Overhead Budgets

Expense budgets for overhead costs are another valuable source of information for estimating future product-creating costs. As with standard prime costs, overhead budgets have been developed by management primarily as a tool for management control; the budget represents a "standard" level of expense against which the actual level of expense may be compared and evaluated. If the budget has been prepared carefully, however, it may yield valuable information about the way that certain costs will vary as the volume of products created changes. Factory overhead budgets, in particular, are sometimes prepared in such a way as to recognize explicitly the fact that some overhead costs will increase as production volume increases. Such a budget, commonly called a "variable budget," is illustrated in Table 1–5 for the Essex Corporation. Each element of expense in Table 1–5 has its own peculiar character-

Table 1–5

ESSEX CORPORATION
VARIABLE BUDGET FOR FACTORY OVERHEAD

Overhead Item	Budgeted Expense for Specified Units of Annual Production				
	800,000	900,000	1,000,000	1,100,000	1,200,000
Supervision and indirect labor	$ 310,000	$ 325,000	$ 340,000	$ 355,000	$ 370,000
Fringe benefits	38,000	40,000	42,000	44,000	46,000
Fuel and electricity	102,000	106,000	110,000	114,000	118,000
Factory supplies	41,000	43,000	45,000	47,000	49,000
Repairs and maintenance	200,000	205,000	210,000	218,000	228,000
Depreciation	230,000	230,000	230,000	230,000	230,000
General factory expense	106,000	108,000	110,000	112,000	115,000
Taxes and insurance	26,000	26,000	26,000	26,000	26,000
Total	$1,053,000	$1,083,000	$1,113,000	$1,146,000	$1,182,000
Factory overhead per unit	$1.32	$1.20	$1.11	$1.04	$0.99
Incremental overhead budget	...	$30,000	$30,000	$33,000	$36,000
Incremental overhead per unit	...	$0.30	$0.30	$0.33	$0.36

istics in terms of cost variability. An item such as indirect labor for materials handling will increase as production increases but it is not strictly variable for each unit of production. That is, if production expands enough, an additional materials handler will be hired, thus providing enough additional capacity to handle the higher volume of materials. If production increases from 900,000 units to 1 million units, management recognizes that three additional materials handlers will be required. Thus, the cost of materials handlers might be viewed as fixed between a production range of 900,000 to 933,000 units, and then jumps to a new level of fixed cost that is $5,000 higher for the next increment of 33,000 units; the cost is variable with production, but in a "stepwise" fashion.

Other items in the overhead budget, such as electricity and supplies, may include some costs that are strictly variable with production. The implication from reading those items in Table 1–5 is that electricity costs about 4 cents per unit of production and supplies cost about 2 cents per unit. Repairs and maintenance, in this example at least, appear to vary according to a different rule. As volume increases to 1,200,000 units per year, the rate of increase in this cost item increases, perhaps because the equipment is being used more intensively and must be repaired on an emergency basis rather than according to a schedule of preventive maintenance. Finally, some elements of factory overhead, such as depreciation, taxes, and insurance, may be truly fixed expenses which do not vary as production quantities change.

Despite these differences in the variability of individual items of overhead, the most common practice today is to treat these costs as a group, using a technique such as a variable budget to specify the normal level of such costs at various rates of production. In terms of the total of these costs, Table 1–5 shows that they tend to increase about 3% for each 10% increase in production. As noted earlier in Table 7–2, the variable portion of these costs are really product-creating costs, but the difficulty of differentiating actual cost data between product and capacity costs is a strong argument for ignoring this distinction in a company's accounting records.

A variable budget such as that shown in Table 1–5 has at least three important uses, and while only one of these relates directly to our purpose of analyzing cost data for decision making, the other two purposes need to be understood.

1. *Cost Control.* The cost actually incurred for any given item of expense can be quickly evaluated against a well-prepared variable budget. If the factory

produced 80,000 units in a particular month, the variable budget tells us that the expense for factory supplies during that month should be about $3,700. (The annual production rate is 960,000 units; annual expense at that rate would be a little more than $44,000; one twelfth of $44,000 is about $3,700.) If the actual expenditure for factory supplies differs significantly from $3,700, management will want to investigate the reason for the variation.

2. *Inventory Valuation.* A value must be assigned to the units in inventory at the end of any accounting period, as was done in Table 1–1, in order to determine the cost of goods sold during the period and the resulting profit for the period. For this purpose, most accounting systems prorate the total amount of factory overhead over the entire number of units produced in the year. Thus, if 900,000 units were produced and total factory overhead amounted to $1,083,000, factory overhead of $1.20 would be assigned to each unit produced. This amount would be added to the prime cost per unit ($1.56 in this example) to arrive at a value per unit of $2.76, as was shown in Table 1–1 for the inventory on January 1, 1972. This $2.76, while commonly referred to as the "cost" per unit, has limited usefulness for many kinds of management decisions.

3. *Decision Making.* Frequently, a management decision may be influenced by the *variable* cost of incremental units of product. While variable costs are very hard to estimate, data from a variable budget, such as that in Table 1–5, may help to provide a good approximation. If management is considering some sort of marketing activity which would increase production by 4,000 units per month, the relevant cost per unit is not $2.76. A better approximation of variable costs might be the $1.56 of prime costs plus 30 cents per unit of variable overhead, as shown on the last two lines of Table 1–5. Even this figure of $1.86 per unit is, at best, only an approximation; specific items of overhead expense will not vary directly with the increase in production. (An increase of units per year will require about $1\frac{1}{2}$ additional materials handlers, but the factory will have to hire two handlers—unless there's a little slack at the current level of production in which case only one additional man might be needed.) On the other hand, there is probably little point in being overly precise in trying to estimate variable overhead expenses for a specific decision. Management makes decisions all the time which will influence the level of production, and a variable cost figure of 30 cents per unit may, in fact, be more useful for a group of such decisions than a different cost figure for each decision which might be computed on the level of production at each specific decision point.

The accounting records of a company can be a valuable source of information in preparing estimates of product costs for decision-making purposes. But the accounting system is designed to serve other purposes as well. The manager, therefore, must understand how the accounting system operates so that he can then modify the accounting data to make it more useful for his specific purpose. If the company uses a relatively sophisticated system with standard prime costs and variable overhead budgets, the necessary modifications may not be too difficult. Even very simple accounting systems, however, usually provide a stream of historical cost data prepared on a consistent basis. Careful analysis of historical data is, therefore, another way to gain valuable insights about product-creating costs. Such analyses also are desirable even when a standard cost system is being used by the company. It is to this topic that we now turn our attention.

ANALYZING PRODUCT COSTS

In situations in which management needs an estimate of variable product costs for decision-making purposes, the essence of the analytical task is understanding *which* costs will vary as a result of the decision and *why* those costs vary. Based on this knowledge, the analyst can then estimate *how much* each element will vary as a result of a specific decision. One procedure for gaining such an understanding, obviously is a frontal attack on the problem; the analyst can attempt to think through the implications of the decision in terms of its effect on each element of cost. The other basic approach to the problem, admittedly more pedestrian, is to examine how costs have changed in the past. The primary advantage of the latter approach is its comprehensiveness; if the analyst understands which costs have varied in the past and why, he is less likely to overlook the possibility that those costs will vary as a result of future actions. As a practical matter, of course, a combination of both approaches is needed because the current decision may have some unusual effects on cost behavior. But a thorough understanding of historical cost behavior is a good grounding for more creative thinking that may be required to quantify the cost effects of alternative courses of future action.

In this section we shall demonstrate some of the more common techniques of cost analysis. To insure comprehensiveness, we will start with a broad analysis of all the factors that may cause a change in total profitability. Our main concern in this chapter, however, is with product-creating costs; and we will focus our attention, in turn, on prime costs and factory overhead expenses.

Analysis of Profit Changes

Continuing with the Essex Corporation as an example, we note in Table 1–1 that the company's profit for 1972 was $397,108. Taken by itself, that figure is difficult to evaluate. Instead, management is interested in either or both of the following two questions:

1. Why is this year's profit more or less than last year's?
2. Why is this year's profit greater or less than we expected it would be?

Table 1–6

ESSEX CORPORATION

PROFIT PLAN FOR 1972

Sales—900,000 units at $3.95 . . . .$3,555,000

	Per Unit	Total for 900,000 Units
Cost of goods sold:		
Materials	$0.74	$ 666,000
Labor	0.82	738,000
Factory overhead	1.20	1,083,000
Total	$2.76	2,487,000

Gross profit on sales $1,068,000
Selling and administration expenses 752,000
Net profit before taxes . . . .$ 316,000

In fact, there is little difference between these two questions. In many companies, particularly small and relatively stable ones, management uses the prior year's operating results as an implicit statement of their expectations for the current year. In companies that have more formal procedures for budgeting and profit planning, a statement of the expected profit for the coming year is prepared at the beginning of the year; and in preparing such a statement, management deals with the question of *why* they expect this year's profit to be different than the profit of the prior year. In either situation, some explicit statement of management's expectations (even if only the prior year's results) is needed in order to do a comparative analysis of profit changes. For the Essex Corporation, a statement of these expectations is presented in Table 1–6.

A comparison of the 1972 profit plan against 1972 actual results, as shown in Table 1–7, now permits us to deal with a much more specific question: Why was the 1972 profit $81,108 higher than expected?

Table 1–7

ESSEX CORPORATION

COMPUTATION OF 1972 PROFIT VARIANCE

	1972 Budget	1972 Actual	Effect on Profit Increase or (Decrease)
Sales	$3,555,000	$3,782,789	$ 227,789
Cost of goods sold	2,487,000	2,609,049	(122,049)
Gross profit on sales	$1,068,000	$1,173,740	$ 105,740
Selling and administrative expenses . . .	752,000	776,632	(24,632)
Net profit before taxes	$ 316,000	$ 397,108	$ 81,108

A simple statement of the increases or decreases in the revenue and expense items, as shown in the last column of Table 1–7, doesn't really reveal very much. A more analytical treatment of the profit variance is displayed in Table 1–8.

Table 1–8, which is really just the beginning of a more detailed analysis, identifies four major causes of the 1972 profit increase. This analysis focuses primarily on the change in gross margin, identifying

Table 1–8

ESSEX CORPORATION

CAUSES OF 1972 PROFIT INCREASE

	Profit Increase or (Decrease)
Increase in sales volume:	
Expected gross profit per unit: $3.95 − 2.76 = $1.19	
Actual sales volume at expected gross margin:	
972,418 units @ $1.19...................................$1,157,177	
Expected gross margin on 900,000 units (Table 1–6).............. 1,068,000	
Profit increase due to higher volume.......................	$ 89,177
Reduction in selling price:	
Expected revenue at $3.95 per unit on 972,418 units..............$3,841,051	
Actual sales revenue (Table 1–7)............................ 3,782,789	
Profit decrease due to lower price.........................	(58,262)
Reduction in manufacturing costs:	
Expected manufacturing costs of $2.76 per unit on 972,418 units....$2,683,874	
Actual manufacturing costs (Table 1–7)....................... 2,609,049	
Profit increase due to lower manufacturing costs..............	74,825
Subtotal: Change in gross profit...............................	$105,740
Increase in selling and administrative expenses:	
Actual expenses (Table 1–7)................................$ 776,632	
Expected expenses (Table 1–6)............................... 752,000	
Profit decrease due to higher expenses......................	(24,632)
Net increase in profit before taxes...........................	$ 81,108

three primary causes of the change: the number of units sold, the selling price per unit, and the manufacturing costs per unit. Using the expected gross margin per unit of $1.19 as a basic statement of management's profit expectation, changes in gross profit due to these three factors may be quantified as described in Table 1–8.

It should be recognized immediately that the three primary causes of the increase in gross profit are closely interrelated. For example, the implication in Table 1–8 that profits could have been higher by an additional $58,262, if only management had not lowered the selling

price, is probably false; the slight reduction in selling price may have
been a major reason why the volume sold increased by 72,418 units.
Similarly, although perhaps a little more subtle, the reduction in manufacturing costs per unit is almost totally due to the fact that the volume
of production increased because of higher sales. As Table 1–7 shows,
1972 actual manufacturing costs were $122,049 higher than the
budget. Table 1–8 recasts this fact to recognize that manufacturing costs
are expected to increase when volume increases, but that in 1972 the
increase in manufacturing costs was less than proportionate to the increase in sales volume. Management, of course, would have expected a
less-than-proportionate increase, so the $74,825 shown on Table 1–8
requires further analysis.

At this point in our analysis, however, we have made some progress.
Each of the four major causes of profit change for 1972 needs to be
analyzed in more detail, but we have made a start at a comprehensive
profit analysis. We will spend the rest of this chapter in a detailed
analysis of the $74,825 of reduction in manufacturing costs and defer
our detailed analysis of the other three items to subsequent chapters.
The focus of our analysis is thus narrowed to such questions as *which*
manufacturing costs changed in 1972? Why did those costs change?
And how did the change in those costs measure up against our expectations?

Analysis of Prime Cost Variances

If the Essex Corporation were maintaining a formal standard cost
accounting system, the system would be of great help in analyzing
the changes in manufacturing costs during 1972. Table 1–9 displays
the operating statement for 1972 that would be produced by a standard
cost system and, as may be noted, the system is designed to break the
total "variance" that we are interested in into its major cost components.
In the absence of a formal cost accounting system, our first step in trying to understand the $74,825 variance would be to prepare a more de-
tailed statement of management's expectations about manufacturing
costs. In fact, a standard cost system is nothing more than a formal
statement of such expectations, and we have seen earlier (Tables 1–4
and 1–5) how such statements might be prepared. The analysis of actual results against these expectations may proceed regardless of whether
or not the expectations have been incorporated into the company's regular accounting system. Table 1–10 is a somewhat more detailed breakdown of the way in which the variance for each cost element is deter-

Table 1–9

ESSEX CORPORATION

OPERATING STATEMENT FOR 1972 USING A STANDARD COST SYSTEM

Net sales—972,418 units at $3.89.................	$3,782,789
Cost of goods sold:	
Standard cost—972,418 units at $2.76............	$2,683,874

	(Favorable) or *Unfavorable*	
Manufacturing variances:		
Materials...............................	$ 23,583	
Labor..................................	(16,853)	
Factory overhead.........................	(99,850)	
Inventory adjustment.....................	18,295	(74,825)
Total cost of goods sold..................		$2,609,049
Gross profit on sales...........................		$1,173,740
Selling and administrative expenses (Table 1–1)......		776,632
Net profit before taxes.........................		$ 397,108

mined. A standard cost system determines these variances using accounting procedures, but an analyst can also calculate them directly from a statement of expectations such as that shown in Tables 1–4 and 1–5.

The analysis in Table 1–10 thus permits us to further narrow the focus of our inquiry. We now know, for example, that our direct labor costs were $16,853 less than we expected; the question now is *why* this occurred. More precisely, for decision-making purposes we need some estimate of what future product-creating costs will be, and we know that

Table 1–10

ESSEX CORPORATION

CALCULATION OF MANUFACTURING COST VARIANCES

	Material	*Labor*	*Overhead*	*Total*
Standard (expected) costs:				
Prime costs/unit (Table 1–4)............	$0.74	$0.82		$1.56
Overhead costs/unit at a volume of 900,000				
units (Table 1–5).....................			$1.20	1.20
Total costs/unit...................	$0.74	$0.82	$1.20	$2.76
Total cost to manufacture				
998,684 units....................	$739,026	$818,921	$1,198,421	$2,756,368
Actual costs:				
To manufacture 998,684 units (Table 1–3)	762,609	802,068	1,098,571	2,663,248
Manufacturing variances:				
Favorable (unfavorable)...............	$(23,583)	$ 16,853	$ 99,850	$ 93,120

labor will be a major element in that cost figure. Should we be estimating that future labor costs will be 82 cents per unit or should that figure be adjusted to reflect our actual cost experience during 1972?

One way to answer that question is to do an even more detailed analysis of the actual labor costs during 1972. We know from Table 1–4 that there are four direct labor departments and that for each department we have specified our expectations about the quantity of labor required for processing one unit and the cost of a labor hour in that department. Table 1–11 uses those expectations for Department 1 as a

Table 1–11

ESSEX CORPORATION

ANALYSIS OF DIRECT LABOR VARIANCE
(Department 1)

Standard labor cost:
  0.06 hours per unit @ $2.40/hour = $0.144/unit
Actual production volume during the year: 998,684 units
Standard labor value of production: $0.144 × 998,684 = $143,811
Actual labor cost: 62,318 hours @ $2.42/hour =   150,810
        Labor variance—unfavorable.............................$ 6,999
Labor "rate" variance: $2.42 − $2.40 = $0.02/hour
                         62,318 hours × 0.02 =   1,246
Balance—labor "efficiency" variance—unfavorable.................$ 5,753

Proof: Standard number of hours required to produce
         998,684 units:
              0.06 × 998,684 =   59,921
         Actual labor hours spent.......................62,318
              Inefficient labor hours.................... 2,397
         2,397 hours at standard cost per hour of $2.40 = $ 5,753

basis for analyzing the actual results in that department. In order to do such an analysis, three pieces of information are required: the number of units actually produced by the department, the number of labor hours actually spent, and the cost per labor hour for the total payroll cost for the department. The analysis shows that Department 1 had an unfavorable labor variance of $6,999, despite the fact that the labor variance for the factory as a whole was favorable. A similar analysis of the other four labor departments would show that the net effect of the labor variances in the five departments would be favorable to the extent of $16,853.

Table 1–11 also permits us to isolate the difference between actual results and our expectations. We had expected that units processed in

Department 1 would require 0.06 labor hours at a cost of $2.40 per hour. With the data in Table 1–11 we can now state that the actual results were 0.0625 hours per unit at a cost of $2.42 per hour. The total labor variance for the department may thus be broken down into two components: a "rate" variance caused by the fact that the labor rate was $2.42 rather than $2.40, and an "efficiency" variance caused by the fact that the labor hours spent did not produce quite as many units as we had expected.

As a more general statement, any element of prime costs may be analyzed in this fashion. Both the *quantity* of labor or material required per unit and the *cost* per unit of input are estimates which are subject to error. Actual results may be stated in terms of actual quantities used and actual costs, and thus quantify the extent of the estimating errors.

An analysis such as that shown in Table 1–11 may be useful to management in evaluating the performance of Department 1 during 1972, but it also has value for the analyst who is preparing the estimate of future product-creating costs. At the beginning of 1972, our best estimate of direct labor costs per unit in Department 1 was $0.144 per unit. We now know that actual costs were $0.151 per unit. Which figure should be used as an estimate of labor costs in Department 1 in 1973? The answer to this question turns on the answers to two other questions: (1) Is the increase in the labor rate to $2.42 per hour expected to continue in 1973? and (2) will the efficiency of labor in the department improve during 1973? If management believes that the actual results during 1972 were due to known temporary factors, it might continue to use the cost of $0.144 as its expected labor cost for the department. On the other hand, if there has been an increase in labor rates, for example, to $2.45 per hour (resulting in an average cost during 1972 of $2.42), management would want to adopt the new rate in arriving at its expected cost for the coming year. The analysis such as that shown in Table 1–11 helps to identify the specific elements of estimated future costs which may need to be updated to be useful for decision making.

Analysis of Overhead Variances

The largest single item of manufacturing variance shown in Table 1–9 was a $99,850 favorable variance for factory overhead. Analyzing this variance also requires an explicit statement of management's expectations, such as that shown earlier on Table 1–5. Such data, in conjunction with information about the actual number of units produced and the actual expenditures for factory overhead, may be used to prepare an analysis such as that shown in Table 1–12 which breaks the factory overhead variance into two components. In this example, the bigger component by far is what is usually called the "volume" variance, the variance that results from the fact that actual volume was different from the volume of production that was expected at the beginning of the year.

Table 1–12

ESSEX CORPORATION

ANALYSIS OF FACTORY OVERHEAD VARIANCE

		(Favorable) or Unfavorable
Volume variance:		
Absorption rate at standard volume of		
900,000 units =	$1.20/unit	
Adjusted rate based on actual volume........	1.11/unit	
Adjustment in absorption rate...........	0.09	
Applied to 998,684 units @ $0.09........		$(89,882)
Spending variance:		
Overhead budget at a volume of 1,000,000		
units/year is $1.11; 998,684 units produced @ $1.11 =	$1,108,539	
Actually spent...........................	1,098,571	
Spending variance—(favorable).........		(9,968)
Total factory overhead variance.......		$(99,850)

Volume Variance

A volume variance, such as that calculated in Table 1–12, is normally calculated only when a company is using a formal standard cost system; it results from the accounting procedures that are used to record factory overhead costs as a part of the total standard cost of units produced. The volume variance should be ignored by the analyst who is trying to adjust historical cost data to yield an estimate of future, *variable* product-creating costs. Nevertheless, the analyst should understand what a volume variance is and how it is calculated in order to be able to focus his attention on that part of the overhead variance which may be relevant for his estimates.

At the beginning of 1972, management estimated that 900,000 units would be produced during the year and, as shown in Table 1–5, the factory overhead would amount to $1,083,000. Actual results for the year were that the factory produced nearly a million units and the actual overhead expense amounted to $1,098,571. Table 1–5 also shows us that these results were not far out of line from management's expectations; if management had predicted a production volume of a million units, it would have expected factory overhead to amount to $1,113,000. The volume variance shows up in the accounting system because, based on its original estimate of the production volume, factory overhead of $1.20 per unit was included in the standard manufacturing costs. If the original volume estimate had been one million units, only $1.11 per unit of factory overhead would have been applied. Thus, the volume variance arises due to the fact that the original estimate of production volume was erroneous. On each unit produced during the year, the accountant has applied 9 cents per unit of overhead in excess of the amount that would have been applied based on the actual production volume. We see in Table 1–9 that the standard cost per unit produced in 1972 was $2.76. In fact, as we now know, we should have been using a standard cost of only $2.67 per unit, 9 cents lower because of the difference in factory overhead as shown in Table 1–12. Thus, the volume variance is nothing more than a retroactive adjustment of the standard cost. We have already seen, however, that neither the $1.20 per unit of factory overhead nor the $1.11 per unit is useful as a measure of the variable product-creating costs; an accounting adjustment of these irrelevant numbers, therefore, may be ignored by the cost analyst. If a standard cost system is being used, however, the analyst needs to isolate the volume variance component in order to turn his attention to the other component, sometimes called the "spending" variance.

Spending Variance. In Table 1–5, management has stated its expectations about factory overhead expenses at various levels of production. The cost analyst can use these estimates as one source of information about the variable component of overhead costs, but in so doing it is prudent to validate the accuracy of management's cost expectations. As the lower part of Table 1–12 shows, these expectations were reasonably accurate for 1972; at a volume of 998,684 units, the expected expense would have been approximately $1,108,539.[1] In fact, actual expenses were $9,968 less than this. A more detailed analysis of

---

[1] A more precise calculation would be possible here, recognizing that the variable component of overhead is only 30 cents per unit. The expected expenditures would then be $1,083,000 for the first 900,000 units plus 30 cents per unit for the additional 98,684 units. An offsetting adjustment in the calculation of the volume variance would be required if the sum of the two variances were still to total $99,850.

each of the eight elements of factory overhead cost would identify which specific items caused this spending variance. The final step in the analysis, analogous to that described earlier for prime costs, would be to determine why these variances occurred, whether or not the factors causing the variances are temporary or permanent, and whether the expectation of future overhead costs should be modified.

Inventory Adjustment. The final item listed under manufacturing variances in Table 1–9 deserves a brief comment. An unfavorable inventory adjustment of $18,295 has been recorded, thus reducing profits for the year by that amount. As with the volume variance, this variance arises from the fact that the Essex Corporation is using a standard cost system. Table 1–13 calculates the amount of the inventory adjustment,

Table 1–13

ESSEX CORPORATION

CALCULATION OF INVENTORY ADJUSTMENT
BASED ON NEW STANDARD COST

	Units	Amount
Beginning inventory	177,412	$489,621
Added to inventory at standard cost of $2.76/unit	26,266	72,494
Total inventory	203,678	$562,115
Value at new standard of $2.67		543,820
Inventory adjustment		$ 18,295

reflecting the fact that for the coming year, Essex has adopted a new standard cost of $2.67 per unit. Management believes that the increased volume of sales experienced in 1972 is likely to continue in the coming year and, therefore, has adopted one million units as its "standard volume" for 1973. Thus, only $1.11 of factory overhead will be charged to each unit produced, resulting in a total standard cost of $2.67 per unit. At the end of 1972, however, the company has 203,678 units in its finished good inventory. Because a lower volume estimate was used during 1972, these units are valued at $2.76 each, and the valuation must now be reduced to $2.67. Such an adjustment would not be necessary if management thought that the increase in units sold during 1972 were only temporary and that volume would return to the 900,000 unit level in 1973; a temporary good year such as 1972 would thus show a higher profit by $18,295.

Summary

Careful estimates of variable product-creating costs are useful for many types of management decisions. The accounting records of the company frequently provide a useful starting point for the analyst preparing such estimates. Accounting records are historical, while management is interested in the future. Thus it is *expected* future costs that are relevant for management's decisions. Nevertheless, the accounting records are useful for two reasons:

1. The accounting system is comprehensive; it records all costs that have been incurred in the past. Preparing estimates of future costs based on accounting records does help to insure that no elements of cost are overlooked.
2. Accounting records provide data which may be analyzed against management's previous cost expectations, whether or not those expectations have been formalized through use of a standard cost system. Such an analysis not only provides some sort of quality check on management's ability to make cost estimates but it also makes use of previous estimates (rather than starting from scratch each time) and pinpoints those estimates which may need modification.

In order to capitalize on the potential value of accounting records, the cost analyst must understand how the accounting system works so that he may modify the accounting data as necessary to deal with the specific decisions under consideration. The problems and cases which follow provide an opportunity for the student to develop his skill in making such modifications.

PROBLEMS

Problem 1–1. Assume that instead of the profit plan shown in Table 1–6, the management of Essex Corporation had made the following estimates of the year's results:

a) During the year, 972,418 units would be manufactured.
b) Sales volume would equal production; the 972,418 units sold would yield a revenue of $3,782,789.
c) Manufacturing cost estimates would be the same as those shown in Tables 1–4 and 1–5.
d) Selling and administrative expenses would amount to $775,174.

Using these new estimates, complete the assignment below in the sequence listed:

1. Calculate the new unit cost figure for factory overhead that should be used in place of the $1.20 figure shown in Table 1–6. (Round off your calculation to the nearest penny.)

2. Prepare a profit plan for 1972 in the format shown in Table 1–6.
3. Compute the profit variance for 1967 against your profit plan, similar to the calculation in Table 1–7.
4. Analyze the variance in cost of goods sold, using such procedures as shown in Tables 1–8 through 1–13 as may be appropriate. (Hint: The total manufacturing variance should be a favorable $16,480.) Based on your analysis, you should be able to answer the following questions:

   a) Why is there no change in the prime cost variances from the amounts shown in Table 1–10?

   b) What is the significance, if any, of the change in the factory overhead volume variance?

   c) Why is the amount of the inventory adjustment different from that calculated in Table 1–13?

Problem 1–2. The machining department of the Wellington Corporation produced two metal parts that were subsequently incorporated into the company's finished products. In January 1973, the plant superintendent was reviewing the cost performance of the department for the preceding year. A summary of the historical data relating to productivity, labor cost, and material cost is shown below:

		1972
Number of good parts produced:		
Part No. 683		4,451,328
Part No. 845		975,744
Total		5,427,072
Pounds of steel rod used		1,770,739 lbs.
Cost of steel rod used		$460,392
Number of labor hours		34,500 hrs.
Labor cost		$103,500

The machining department operated two types of automatic screw machines: the Acme model 106 machines were used to produce part No. 683, while the Detroit model X7 machines were used for part No. 845. The Acme machines were faster and more efficient in that they could produce 60 pieces per hour and one operator could serve four machines. The department had 48 Acme machines, and during 1972 these machines had been operated at full capacity (40 hours per week for 50 weeks) because of a strong demand for the product which used this part. During the year, therefore, 12 men had always been assigned to the Acme machines; and in order to achieve maximum output, the foreman had always assigned his most highly skilled operators to this equipment. The Detroit machines had a theoretical capacity of 40 units per hour of part No. 845, and a skilled operator could serve only three of these machines. While there were 24 Detroit machines in the department, full utilization had not been necessary during 1972. The department's normal total work force was 17 men, but this number varied from day to day depending on the production of part No. 845 required. Some workers might be temporarily assigned to or from another department to handle these fluctuating requirements. Wellington's contract with the labor union specified that all men assigned to the machining department were to receive the same wage ($3 per hour); for this reason, the payroll accounting department kept track of all temporary transfers, and the machining department was charged only for the time spent by men actually assigned to the department.

A study of the labor efficiency in the machining department conducted in the fall of 1971 indicated that the machines normally operated about 90% of the time. Half of the 10% downtime was due to regularly scheduled rest periods for the machine operators, the other 5% was the time required by a worker of average skill to make adjustments to the machine settings.

Both parts produced by the department were made from the same type of tempered steel rod. Wellington's major domestic supplier had announced a list price for this rod, f.o.b. Wellington's plant, of 28 cents per pound in late 1971. During 1972, however, Wellington's purchasing agent had found that imported rod of equal quality could be purchased on similar terms for 24 cents per pound. By the end of 1972, all of Wellington's rod were being supplied by the foreign producer.

Part No. 683 was smaller than part No. 845; a finished piece of the smaller part weighed 0.20 pounds, while a finished unit of the larger part weighed 0.40 pounds. Because some material was wasted in the machining process, 0.45 pounds of rod were required to produce one piece of part No. 845, while 0.24 pounds were needed for one piece of No. 683. In addition, some of the finished pieces were scrapped because the machine settings tended to become out of adjustment. The company's historical experience had been that part No. 683, the more complex part, incurred a 20% scrappage rate while No. 845 had only a 10% scrappage rate. According to the foreman in the department, however, the actual scrappage on part No. 683 during 1972 had been lower than normal—only 16%—because the more skilled workers on the Acme machines were better able to keep the machines in adjustment. The proceeds (10 cents per pound) received from the sale of both metal shavings and scrapped parts were regarded by Wellington's management as "other income," and were not credited to the materials cost account of the machining department.

Assignment

1. Prepare a statement of estimated or standard prime costs for each part, as of the beginning of 1972. Analyze the actual results for that year in terms of these standards, and compute quantity and price variances in as detailed a manner as is possible with the information available.

2. Wellintgon's management was considering an opportunity to enter into a one-year supply contract with a major mail-order house for the product which used part No. 845. The contract would require at least 15,000 units of the part each month. As part of the analysis in deciding what price to offer on this contract, management has asked you to prepare an estimate of prime costs for the coming year which you think would be relevant for this bid.

SYLVANIA ELECTRIC PRODUCTS
INC. (A)

In November, 1954, Mr. H. D. Lloyd, plant accountant at the Danvers fluorescent lamp plant of Sylvania Electric Products Inc. and his staff were working on the annual revisions of standard type cost sheets, to go into effect January 1, 1955.

Sylvania Electric Products Inc. was one of the country's principal producers of incandescent lamps, fluorescent lamps and fixtures, photoflash lamps, radio receiving tubes, television picture tubes, television and radio sets, specialized electronic devices, and related parts and materials. The company assumed its present corporate form in 1931 as a result of a merger of three concerns engaged in the manufacture of incandescent lamps and radio receiving tubes.

The oldest of these three predecessor manufacturing companies was founded in the year 1901, and the second of these companies was founded in 1906. Both companies were established to produce incandescent lamps. In addition, both companies had entered into the business of manufacturing radio tubes in the 1920's.[1]

Sylvania was, in 1938, one of the first companies to introduce fluorescent lamps commercially. Between 1938 and 1954, the company's vigorous promotional efforts rapidly placed it in the second position in the domestic fluorescent market. The company's market position was maintained largely as a result of its research activities, which had contributed a number of new developments to the field while helping to lower the cost of manufacture. The company's entire output of fluorescent lamps in 1954 was produced in a modern plant at Danvers, Massachusetts.

---

[1] Subsequent to the date of this case, in 1959, Sylvania Electric Products Inc. was merged with General Telephone and Electronics Corporation, of which it is now an operating subsidiary.

MANUFACTURE OF FLUORESCENT LAMPS[2]

A fluorescent lamp[3] consists of three basic subassemblies: a coated bulb, two mounts, and two bases. These three subassemblies plus small quantities of solder, mercury, and argon gas make up the physical components of a lamp. In the process of manufacture, the subassemblies passed through from six to eight cost centers.[4] The flow of these materials through cost centers is depicted in Exhibit 1.

A coated bulb is a piece of glass tubing with its ends slightly turned in and coated on its inner surface with a fluorescent powder. This powder becomes activated when subjected to ultraviolet radiation and emits visible light. The coated bulbs were prepared in the coating and baking centers on the first floor of the plant. About 25 different sizes of bulbs were used in the production of fluorescent lamps, although in 1954 one size accounted for approximately 50% of production. Individual lamps might also differ from one another in the type of fluorescent coating used.

In the coating center, bulbs were unpacked and sent through a washing tunnel where all traces of dirt were removed, especially from the inner surface. The washed and dried bulbs then moved into an air-conditioned room where the fluorescent powder coating was applied by flushing a lacquer suspension of the fluorescent powder down from the top of the bulb. A certain amount of this suspension adhered to the glass wall of the bulb as the lacquer dried. The drying operation was performed in a long tunnel immediately after the coating operation.

Before the coated bulb could be used in a finished lamp, the lacquer had to be burned out by baking the bulb at a high temperature. This operation was accomplished in large conveyor-type ovens on the first floor. Following the baking, bulbs were inspected and loaded onto buggies for transfer to the assembly floor.

The second basic subassembly was the mount. In essence, the mount was the electrical contact, one being needed at each end of the lamp. The mount consisted of a flare, an exhaust tube, two lead wires, and a tungsten coil coated with an electron-emitting material. The flare was a bell-

---

[2] This section is adapted almost verbatim from an article written by Bruce Goldsmith, supervisor of plant engineering of the Danvers plant, which appeared in the *Sylvan Corps,* a company publication.

[3] The terminology used in the industry differs somewhat from popular usage. The word "bulb" refers only to the glass envelope, or tube, which encloses the lamp. The complete assembly is called a "lamp."

[4] For the time being, the term "cost center" may be taken as synonymous with "production department."

shaped piece of glass. It was produced from glass tubing in the flare center on a fully automatic machine.

In the automount center, the exhaust tube, the two lead wires, and the tungsten coil were assembled with the flare into a completed mount. The mount assembly was performed on an automatic machine, which automatically fed the required parts from hoppers into the machine.

The base of the fluorescent lamp, one of which was used on each end, is a dish-shaped metal or plastic cap into which is mounted two metal pins to be used as the electrical contact with the lamp socket. These were prepared in the base preparation center. This subassembly was filled with a green-colored cement which hardened very slowly under room conditions, but which could be "set" by the application of moderate heat.

The three basic subassemblies were then supplied to the finishing center, where the assembly into a finished lamp was accomplished. A typical assembly unit consisted of a sealing machine, an exhaust machine, and a basing machine. There were a number of these units on the assembly floor, each doing essentially the same job on different sizes of lamps. In terms both of area and of number of employees, the finishing center was easily the largest department in the plant.

The sealing machine securely attached a mount to each end of a coated bulb. This was done by melting the lip of the bulb and the rim of the flare together until they melted into a single piece of glass without cracks or air holes which might permit the lamp to leak.

The sealed lamp was then conveyed to a rotary exhaust machine. The exhaust machine extracted the air from inside the bulb through the small exhaust tube in one of the mounts, substituted for the air a very small quantity of mercury and argon gas, and then broke off the exhaust tube and sealed the opening. The application of heat to the coating on the tungsten coil during the exhaust process activated the coating.

A cement-filled base was then placed on each end of the lamp and baked into place on a second rotary machine. After the lamp had been based, it was physically complete. All that remained was a process of aging, which consisted of actual operation under controlled conditions to stabilize the electrical properties of the lamp. This was done automatically on a tall conveyor-like machine located at the end of the finishing unit.

At the same time as the lamps were being aged, automatic test equipment tested each lamp for all important electrical characteristics and rejected all unsatisfactory lamps. The completed lamps were then packed into shipping cartons and sent to the warehouse on a conveyor belt.

A few types of lamps passed through two cost centers which have not been described in this case. These two centers, the stem and hand-mount centers, were relatively small. They performed operations similar to that performed in the automount center.

DETERMINATION OF STANDARD TYPE COSTS

In 1949, Sylvania adopted what is called a "standard cost system." This system was in most important respects similar to the standard cost systems found in many industrial companies. A "standard type cost" was determined annually for each type of lamp. These standard costs had three major purposes. First, they simplified the determination of certain accounting entries. Second, they were used to evaluate performance, since differences, or variances, could be developed between actual and standard cost. Third, the standard costs were used as a basis of pricing products for sale.

As an illustration of the methods used by Sylvania, this case will discuss the determination of the standard costs for a single type of fluorescent lamp, the 40 T-12 White lamp.[5] The same procedures would be followed in the case of any type manufactured in the Danvers plant, a total of about 800 types. In many cases, only minor variations distinguished one type from another. For example, the 40 T-12 Daylight lamp would differ from the 40 T-12 White only in the composition of the interior fluorescent coating.

The standard costs of each individual type of lamp were summarized on a standard type cost sheet, which was brought up to date annually by the plant cost department. The standard type cost sheet for the 40 T-12 White lamp is shown in Exhibit 2. The standard costs in effect during calendar year 1954 are given in the columns headed "January 1, 1954." The sheet also indicates some of the components of cost for calendar year 1955.

Sylvania's accounting manual defined standard costs as "the costs we would expect to incur at the level of production accepted as standard." By "expected costs," the company meant to imply costs which would be reasonably attainable. While the standards were used in cost control, they were *not* intended to be interpreted as "bogeys" or long-run goals. Consequently, past experience and reasonably expectable cost changes were the most important considerations in setting standard type costs.

---

[5] The code designation signifies a 40-watt lamp using a tubular (T) bulb whose largest diameter is $\frac{12}{8}$ inches, i.e., $1\frac{1}{2}$ inches. Similar designations were used for each type of lamp. Each type was also assigned a numerical code, in this case No. 4001.

Direct material and direct labor were classified as "prime costs." Other costs were called "burden costs," or occasionally "overhead expense." These two major types of costs required substantially different treatment in the preparation of the standard type cost sheet and will therefore be discussed separately.

A. *Prime Costs*

1. *Material Costs.* The material cost items on the standard type cost sheet included only those materials which could be *directly* associated with a particular type. Manufacturing supplies which could not be associated with a type, such as fuel gas, were classified as burden costs. The material components of standard type cost were based on specifications prepared for each type of lamp and furnished to the cost department by the plant engineering department. The specifications gave the specification number and description of each component of a particular type of lamp. For each class of material, the theoretical quantity required for a thousand lamps was indicated.[6]

The theoretical quantity was the physical quantity of the material contained in the specified number of *finished* lamps, as determined by engineering analysis. For example, the theoretical quantity for bulbs would be 1,000, since 1,000 completed lamps would of course contain 1,000 bulbs. To produce these 1,000 lamps, however, would actually require more than 1,000 bulbs, since there would be some loss, or "shrinkage," in production. The term "theoretical" was used by Sylvania to indicate that the quantity was that which would be required if there were *no* shrinkage.

The cost department posted the theoretical quantities to a standard material cost sheet similar to Exhibit 3. The materials were subdivided on this sheet into the major categories listed on the standard type cost sheet.[7] The quantities were then extended to a theoretical cost per thousand, using a standard purchase price for the material. This standard purchase price was generally based on the most recent invoice price for the material, but it might be adjusted for prospective price changes after consultation with the purchasing department.

---

[6] Standard type cost sheets were based on lots of 1,000 lamps rather than on a single lamp because of the relatively low unit cost of a lamp. Lamps were not necessarily produced in lots of 1,000.

[7] Most of these categories should be recognizable from the description of the manufacturing process earlier in this case. Sylcote is a wax coating used in certain types of lamps; none was required for the 40 T-12 White lamp.

In the case of bulbs, Exhibit 3 might be interpreted as follows: A lot of 1,000 completed 40 T-12 White lamps would contain 1,000 bulbs with the specification number 40 T12AG4C. The standard purchase price of these bulbs, based on recent invoice prices, was $52.95 per thousand. Hence, the theoretical cost per thousand for bulbs for this type of lamp was $52.95.

When all of the materials had been priced and extended, the theoretical costs were posted to the standard type cost sheet. In order to determine standard costs, it was next necessary to determine the *efficiency* of usage of each item. "Efficiency" was defined as output divided by input; that is, the ratio of the quantity of each material which would *complete* production in finished lamps to the quantity which was *originally placed* in production. In the case of bulbs, for example, the efficiency of 89% indicated that for every 89 completed lamps it was necessary to start 100 bulbs into production. Thus, it was expected that eleven bulbs out of each 100 started into production would be broken or spoiled *at some point* in the production process. Part of the shrinkage would occur in the coating department, part in the baking department, and part in the finishing department; the total shrinkage in the three departments which handled bulbs was 11%.

Actual efficiency was tabulated for a two-year period for each major class of material. These figures, particularly those for the most recent six months, were then discussed by Mr. Lloyd with the engineering department and with the foremen concerned, who might suggest reasons for making changes, such as improved mechanical techniques. After agreement was reached, the efficiency percentage was posted to the standard type cost sheet. The standard cost per thousand for the particular material was then determined by dividing the theoretical cost by the efficiency (expressed as a decimal).

After this process had been repeated for each component material, all of the items were totaled. An allowance for freight on materials purchased was added in to complete the determination of standard material costs for the type. This allowance was based on the average transportation charges per lamp during the current year, adjusted for the relative weights of the various types.

It is important to distinguish between *standard purchase prices* and *standard material costs*. The former referred to the price paid for raw materials, and was usually expressed in terms of the physical quantity which was used as an ordering unit in purchasing the material. Standard material cost, however, referred to the material cost involved in bringing a lamp to the completed stage and was expressed in terms of 1,000 completed lamps.

2. *Direct Labor Costs.* Direct labor included only "that labor expended directly in processing particular products, between the time the materials enter the production department and the products enter finished stock, and which can be measured through time study and allocated specifically to such products."[8] The company collected labor expenses in three other major categories: indirect labor, expense labor, and premium labor. These categories were considered burden costs and will be discussed subsequently.

As the definition indicates, all direct labor operations had been time-studied. The time studies were prepared by divisional industrial engineers operating out of the division headquarters in Salem in order to insure uniformity in the application of time-study principles from one plant to another. The standards were set at the level which it was expected an average worker would achieve under normal operating conditions; they were expressed initially in terms of production per hour and were later converted into hours per thousand lamps. Allowance was made in setting the standards for such elements as fatigue, but no allowance was made for the actual efficiency of the workers in a cost center if it was expected to differ from that of average workers. Hence, this standard was a "theoretical" standard of much the same type as the material theoretical. The standards were discussed with the foremen concerned, whose approval was required before the standards could be used.

The cost department posted the theoretical standards for each job to a direct labor standard sheet such as that shown in Exhibit 4 for the coating cost center. One of these sheets was prepared for each cost center through which the type of lamp passed. The rate applicable to each job was also posted. (All direct labor employees were paid on an hourly basis.) The rate used was the top rate paid on the job, presumably the rate which would be earned by an experienced normal worker.

Before the operation could be priced, it was necessary to determine whether there were any "bottleneck" operations. If there were, each operation whose speed was controlled by the bottleneck was adjusted to reflect this condition. Such adjustments have already been made in Exhibit 4.

Next, each operation was extended by the rate on the job. This ex-

---

[8] From the company's *Accounting Manual*.

tension gave the theoretical cost per thousand of the particular operation. For example, for the operation "unpack bulbs," this extension consisted of multiplying $1.51 by 0.324 hours. The theoretical costs were summed for each cost center, and the sum posted to the standard type cost sheet.

Like the theoreticals on material, those on direct labor had to be adjusted for anticipated efficiency. The direct labor efficiencies were affected, of course, by the level of operating proficiency in the departments where that level differed from the performance expected of an average worker. To some extent, the fact that a less efficient worker would probably not receive the top rate on the job compensated for this factor. Since all employees were on hourly rates rather than piece rates, compensation was generally not directly proportional to productivity (although pay rates were based in part on proficiency) and some adjustment had to be made. In addition, the degree of machine utilization compared with the normal conditions assumed in setting the theoretical standards would affect efficiency.

These intradepartmental conditions were estimated chiefly from the average experience of the three- to six-month period just preceding the preparation of the standard type cost sheet, unless there appeared to be good reasons for change. A change might be warranted, for example, if unusual mechanical difficulties had been experienced in the three-month period which were now believed to be under control. These factors were also discussed with the foremen concerned.

Labor efficiency was affected not only by the intradepartmental factors just mentioned but also by the shrinkage expected to occur in the materials worked on as they passed through subsequent operations. This situation was analogous to the materials efficiency. Not all bulbs started into the coating center, for example, would end up in finished lamps; about 11 out of every 100 would be lost through shrinkage. Since the standard type cost sheets were supposed to give the cost of completed lamps, the production in each cost center had to be related to the number of completed lamps which could be produced from it.

For example, labor efficiency in the coating department during 1954 was budgeted at 53%. This percentage was arrived at by first estimating the operating proficiency of the workers in the department; in 1954 this estimate was 60%. Next the 60% efficiency was adjusted for shrinkage in the coating department. Only 97% of the bulbs started into coating were completed. The labor expended in coating these bulbs, as well as the bulb itself, was lost, reducing the coating department labor efficiency to 58%. Finally, shrinkage of coated bulbs in the baking center was estimated to be 4%, and shrinkage of coated and baked bulbs in the finishing center was estimated to be 5%. Allowing for these losses reduced the final coating department labor efficiency to 53% (i.e., 58% times 96% times 95%).[9]

A figure for labor efficiency was obtained combining all three of the elements mentioned above, and this was posted to the standard type cost sheet. Standard cost per thousand for each cost center was then obtained by dividing efficiency into theoretical, just as was done for materials.

B. *Standard Burden Costs*

All factory costs other than prime costs were classified as burden costs. Since burden costs were associated with the operation of the plant generally and not with the production of any particular type, it was necessary to determine some reasonable basis of distribution to types. Furthermore, these costs included many items, such as property taxes, depreciation, supervisory salaries, and so forth, which were partially fixed; that is, they did not vary in proportion to the volume of production. As a result, total burden cost would have a different percentage relationship to the value of production at different levels of production.

In the company's definition of standard cost quoted earlier in this case, it was stated that these costs were the costs expected to be incurred at the "level of production accepted as standard." This definition further said that "the standard level of production will be the production *budgeted for the year* and, for plant operation, will be expressed in terms of *direct labor hours* required to produce the units budgeted for the period" [emphasis supplied]. It was the burden costs at the budgeted level of production, therefore, which were distributed to individual types. The determination of burden standards was thus tied in with the company's over-all budget procedure.

1. *The Budget Process.* In September of each year, the corporate sales research department in New York made a forecast of fluorescent sales for the entire industry during the next calendar year. This forecast was used by the top executives of the company in budgeting company sales for the year.

The sales budget was converted into a production budget by type of lamp. For this purpose, only the major type classifications were used; minor variations having little effect on costs were ignored. The forecast

---

[9] The bulb efficiency of 89% was the result of the material shrinkage in the three departments involved, i.e., $100\% \times 97\% \times 96\% \times 95\% = 88.5\%$ (rounded to 89%).

usually listed about 50 major type groups of lamps and their budgeted annual production. This information was supplied to the cost department at the Danvers plant.

At the plant, the monthly standard level of production was determined by dividing annual production by $11\frac{1}{2}$ (thereby allowing for a two-week vacation shutdown in July). For 1954, this monthly level was 2,950,000 lamps. This level referred, of course, to the particular mix of lamps assumed in the annual production budget. The company did not consider unit production a satisfactory measure of plant activity. It would be acceptable, for example, for costs to go up even if unit production stayed at 2,950,000 lamps, if the mix changed so that a greater proportion of expensive lamps was being produced. For this reason, the lighting division used *standard direct labor dollars* as the basic measure of plant activity.

To obtain the standard level of direct labor dollars, the direct labor component of the standard level of production was priced, using the labor standards prepared for the standard type cost sheet. The corresponding level of direct labor hours was also determined. An average direct labor rate per hour was determined for each cost center by dividing the total hours into the total dollars (see Exhibit 5).

The foreman or other person responsible for each category of burden expense was asked by Mr. Lloyd to make an estimate of the expense in his category at the standard level of production. Estimates for indirect labor and expense labor were the responsibility of departmental foremen. Other items, such as engineering expense, factory supplies, and so forth, were variously assigned. These estimates were compared by the cost department with historical costs and discussed with the persons making them. The estimates agreed upon were then summarized by expense class and posted to a schedule of burden expense (see Exhibit 6), where they appeared on the top half of the sheet in the column "Allowable Monthly Costs—Standard."[10]

2. *Burden Distribution to Cost Centers.* Burden expenses at the *standard level* were then distributed to cost centers. Four methods of distribution were used:

a) *Analysis.* If possible, Mr. Lloyd tried to determine which cost center was actually responsible for incurring each item of expense. For example, the mechanical maintenance foreman might report that 40% of his department's time was spent working in the finishing center, so

---

[10] The columns headed "Budget Formula" will be explained at a later point in this case.

that 40% of his budget would be allocated to finishing. Indirect labor was allocated entirely on the basis of analysis, since all workers classed as indirect labor were assigned to specific cost centers. It was possible to allocate about 70% of all burden expense on the basis of analysis.

b) Floor Space. Occupancy expenses—depreciation on buildings, heat, property taxes, and plant maintenance, etc.—were distributed in proportion to floor space in each center. About 6% of all burden costs were assigned to cost centers on this basis.

c) Direct Labor Dollars. Payroll taxes, employee benefits, and other expenses which tended to vary in proportion to payroll were distributed on the basis of the standard direct labor dollars for each center. This basis accounted for about 12% of all burden costs.

d) Direct Labor Hours. Expenses which tended to vary with the number of employees rather than with their pay—such as plant supervision—were distributed on the basis of the standard direct labor hours for each cost center. Departmental supervision, of course, was allocated by analysis. Distribution by direct labor hours also accounted for about 12% of burden.

These distributions were made on work sheets but were summarized in the lower half of Exhibit 6 (standard burden costs).

3. *Distribution of Burden to Types.* When the distribution to cost centers was completed, the total burden expense for each cost center at the standard level of production was divided by the standard direct labor dollars for the same level. For the coating center, this consisted of dividing $23,345 by $7,650. The quotient, 305%, was posted to Exhibit 6 in the column entitled "Overhead Per Cent of Direct Labor at Standard Production." This calculation was repeated for each cost center.

This last figure was the basis for the distribution of burden to individual types. The percentage rate computed for each cost center was posted to each of the individual type cost sheets of types passing through that center, in the column headed "Rate." This rate was then multiplied by the standard direct labor dollars for that type in that center, giving a standard burden cost per thousand for that center. Referring again to Exhibit 2, the standard burden cost for the coating center was determined by multiplying the standard burden rate, 305%, by the standard direct labor cost for the center, $3.11. The result, $9.49, was entered on the standard type cost sheet.

When this process had been repeated for all centers, the total burden cost for the type was summed. Adding together the three components of cost, the cost clerk preparing the sheet obtained the total manufacturing cost (TMC) of the type. This clerk also calculated and posted the percentage of total manufacturing cost to the list price of the lamp. List price, which was given at the top of the sheet, was the basis for setting the selling price of the lamp. Sales were made at list price less a trade discount which varied with the volume and class of the customer. The calculation of "per cent to list" completed the preparation of the standard type cost sheet.

C. *Variable Budgets*

Since burden expenses were partly fixed and partly variable, the cost department was interested in determining the extent to which these expenses might be expected to vary with the volume of production. For this reason, the person making the budget estimate for each category of expense was also asked to make an estimate of the amount of change which would occur in this category if production increased or decreased by 35%; these estimates are also given in Exhibit 6. The cost department calculated the direct labor cost of a 35% change in output and summarized this calculation on Exhibit 5; these figures were exactly 35% of direct labor costs at standard production since direct labor costs, being used as the measure of volume, would necessarily vary proportionately with volume.

The cost department then determined the rate of change of each burden item relative to direct labor dollars. In the case of manufacturing expense, for example, this was obtained by dividing $28,860 (the estimated change in manufacturing expense at a change of 35% from the standard level, as shown on Exhibit 6) by $41,125 (the change in total direct labor at a change of 35% from the standard level). The quotient, 70.170%, was the percentage of standard direct labor dollars which comprised the variable cost component of the budget formula for manufacturing expense, indicating that for every change of one dollar in direct labor, manufacturing expense could be expected to change by slightly more than 70 cents.

The fixed portion of the variable budget formula was found by extrapolation. Using the same example, the factor of 70.170% would be multiplied by the standard level of labor dollars (Exhibit 5, $117,500), giving $82,450. This amount, which represented the variable portion at the standard level, was subtracted from the standard level budget for manufacturing expense. The difference of $66,200 was considered to be the fixed portion. This procedure may give the impression that Sylvania assumed that variable unit costs were constant at all levels of volume.

Such was not the case. The variable budget formula was regarded as being applicable only within the range of from 65% to 135% of the standard volume. The calculation of fixed costs was done only as a means of arriving at the formula, and the figure for fixed cost was not considered as being the cost that would be incurred at zero production.

REVISION OF STANDARDS FOR 40 T-12 WHITE LAMP

As of November, 1954, most of the work involved in the annual revision of standard type cost sheets had already been completed. Mr. Lloyd was working on the partially completed sheet for the 40 T-12 White lamp (Exhibit 2). Theoretical costs for material and labor, based on revised specifications, purchase prices, and wage rates, had been posted to the sheet. Most of the changes in theoretical costs from the 1954 revision were due to price or wage rate changes.

Based upon discussions with the foreman, Mr. Lloyd had tentatively decided upon efficiencies for most categories of material and labor. These efficiencies had been posted to the standard type cost sheet, and the corresponding standard costs had been calculated.

The new theoretical cost for direct labor in the automount center was the result of a change in machine design which had been developed by the mechanical design department. The new operation was scheduled to go into effect shortly after the first of the year.

From past experience, Mr. Lloyd expected that the labor efficiency of the automount center would initially average about 75% on this type, compared with 86% in 1954. This change would be due principally to higher shrinkage resulting from mechanical problems involved in breaking in the new equipment. As the "bugs" were ironed out of the process, however, the shrinkage would be reduced. Mr. Lloyd thought that the operation would reach 85% efficiency by the middle of the year and stabilize at that level.

Mr. Lloyd was also aware that since the increased shrinkage would occur on the last operation on the mount, he would have to adjust the tentative efficiency on the preceding direct labor operations in the flare center. If it were not for the new process in the automount center, the efficiency in the flare center was expected to be the same as in 1954. In addition, he knew that the increased shrinkage would affect the efficiency on all the materials required to produce a mount. Except for the effect of the new operation, Mr. Lloyd expected no changes in these material and labor efficiencies from the 1954 level.

When Mr. Lloyd completed the standards for prime costs for the 40 T-12 White lamp, he next had to complete his determination of the standard level of production for the plant. The direct labor dollars for all other types had already been computed (see Exhibit 7), and it was therefore necessary only to add the standard direct labor dollars for the 40 T-12 White lamp. The monthly production of this type was budgeted at 200,000 units.

Mr. Lloyd also had to determine the appropriate burden loading rates to be used. For this purpose, he had summarized all burden costs as distributed to cost centers (see Exhibit 8).

Included as burden costs in Exhibit 8 were the expenses of the mechanical maintenance department. The foreman of the mechanical maintenance department had estimated his monthly expense at the standard level to be $15,000. Of this total, $3,000 had been allocated to the automount center, since the mechanical maintenance foreman estimated that 20% of his department's time would be spent working for that department. He commented that about $1,250 of this expense would be in connection with the new operation on the 40 T-12 White lamp, although that type would amount to only about 10% of the production passing through the automount center in terms of direct labor dollars.

Question

Complete the calculations of standard total manufacturing cost for the 40 T-12 White lamp. (Slide rule accuracy is sufficient.)

Exhibit 1

SYLVANIA ELECTRIC PRODUCTS INC. (A)

MANUFACTURE OF FLUORESCENT LAMPS

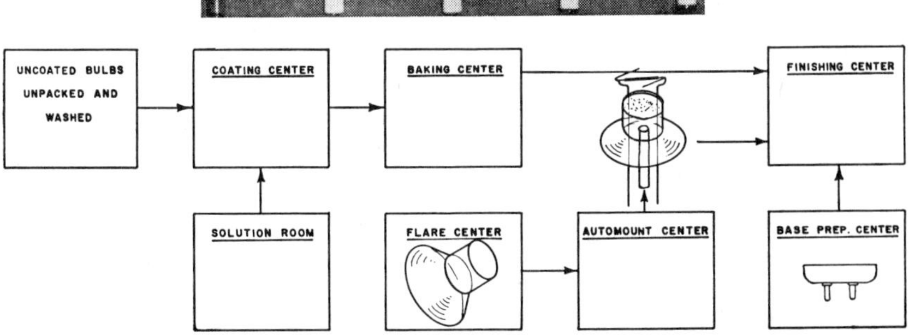

Exhibit 2

SYLVANIA ELECTRIC PRODUCTS INC. (A)

STANDARD TYPE COST   Type 40 T-12 White

Product **Fluorescent Lamps**

Plant **Danvers**   Code No. 4001   List/M $ 1,100.00

Date	JAN 1- 1954			JAN 1- 1955					

MATERIAL COST

Acct. No.	DESCRIPTION	Theoretical Cost/M	Standard % Eff.	Standard Cost/M	Theoretical Cost/M	Standard % Eff.	Standard Cost/M	Theoretical Cost/M	Standard % Eff.	Standard Cost/M
01	Bulbs	52 95	89	59 47	52 95	89	59 47			
03	Bases	15 80	92	17 17	15 35	92	16 68			
04	Basing Material	1 61	88	1 83	1 61	90	1 79			
05	Glass Tubing	3 29	77	4 27	3 29					
07	Lead Wires	2 96	88	3 36	2 96					
10	Coils	.11 27	89	12 66	11 15					
13	Powder	22 11	83	26 64	22 11	85	26 01			
95	Miscellaneous	1 00	85	1 18	1 00	85	1 18			
96	Packing	18 33	99.5	18 42	18 50	99.5	18 59			
32	Solvents	2 01	-	2 01	2 01	-	2 01			
114	Sylcote									
	Sub-Total	131 33		147 01	130 93					
	Transportation			6 25			6 50			
	Total Material			153 26						

DIRECT LABOR COST

COST CENTER	Theoretical Cost/M	Standard % Eff.	Standard Cost/M	Theoretical Cost/M	% Eff.	Cost/M	Theoretical Cost/M	% Eff.	Cost/M
Coating	1 65	53	3 11	1 70	58	2 93			
Baking	1 61	66	2 44	1 66	75	2 21			
Flare	62	77	81	64					
Stem									
Hand Mount									
Automount	3 84	86	4 47	3 46					
Base Preparation	71	83	86	73	85	86			
Finishing	28 42	85	33 44	29 27	86	34 03			
Total Direct Labor	36 85		45 13	37 46					

BURDEN COST

COST CENTER	Rate	Cost/M	Rate	Cost/M	Rate	Cost/M
Coating	305%	9 49				
Baking	348	8 49				
Flare	250	2 02				
Stem						
Hand Mount						
Automount	187	8 36				
Base Preparation	146	1 26				
Finishing	285	95 28				
Special Burden						
Total Burden	277%	124 90				
Standard T. M. C.		323 90				
% Cost/List		29.4%				
Posted By		✓				

Exhibit 3

SYLVANIA ELECTRIC PRODUCTS INC. (A)

STANDARD MATERIAL COST

PRODUCT Fluorescent Lamps   DATE **JAN 1- 1954**

TYPE #4001   40 T-12 White

	DESCRIPTION	QTY/M	UNIT COST	THEO. COST/M	UNIT COST	THEO. COST/M	UNIT COST	THEO. COST/M
01	Bulb - 40 T12A040	1,000	52.95	52.95				
03	Base - T12 Med. Bipin	2,000	7.90	15.80				
04	Basing Material							
	Cement	10.2#	.127	1.29				
	Alcohol	.85 pt	.13	.11				
	Solder	.35#	.60	.21				
				1.61				
05	Glass Tubing							
	Flare Tubing #469	16.0#	.14	2.24				
	Exhaust Tubing #177	5.5#	.19	1.05				
				3.29				
07	Lead Wires - 2018	4,000	.74	2.96				
10	Coils - 40 wt.	2,000	5.635	11.27				
13	Powder	10.05	2.20	22.11				
95	Miscellaneous		.10	1.00				
96	Packing							
	Wrappers - T1248	1,000	8.25	8.25				
	Cases - T1248	41.7	210.50	8.78				
	Pads - T12	83.3	15.60	1.30				
				18.33				
52	Solvents		.20	2.01				

Exhibit 4

SYLVANIA ELECTRIC PRODUCTS INC. (A)

DIRECT LABOR STANDARDS

Date: January 1, 1954   Type #4001
Ref. 40 T-12

Coating	Job		Theoretical Standard		
	Class	Rate	Production per Hour	Hours per Thousand	Cost per Thousand
Unpack bulbs	G-5	$1.51	3,075	0.324	$0.489
Load tray	G-5	1.51	3,075	0.324	0.489
Deliver to coater	G-7	1.66	19,250	0.052	0.086
Mill and mix powder	G-7	1.66	50,000	0.020	0.033
Mix cathode coating	G-7	1.66	40,000	0.025	0.041
Mix cathode coating (female)	G-3	1.49	166,000	0.006	0.008
Coat bulbs	G-3	1.49	2,940	0.340	0.507
Total					$1.653

Exhibit 5

SYLVANIA ELECTRIC PRODUCTS INC. (A)

LIGHTING DIVISION—FLUORESCENT PLANT

STANDARD DIRECT LABOR COSTS

Product Fluorescent	Unit Production at Standard Level 2,950,000	Effective Date: January 1, 1954 Revision No.: 6 Schedule: A		
			Direct Labor	
Cost Centers	Average Hourly Rate	Standard Hours	Standard Dollars	Change at 35% Increase from Standard Level
Coating.......................	$1.52	5,033	$ 7,650	$ 2,675
Baking........................	1.52	3,549	5,395	1,890
Flare..........................	1.76	923	1,625	570
Stem..........................	1.41	762	1,075	375
Handmount....................	1.41	2,681	3,780	1,325
Automount....................	1.44	5,979	8,610	3,015
Base preparation...............	1.44	2,021	2,910	1,020
Finishing.....................	1.44	60,038	86,455	30,255
Total fluorescent............	$1.45	80,986	$117,500	$41,125

Exhibit 6

SYLVANIA ELECTRIC PRODUCTS INC. (A)

LIGHTING DIVISION—FLUORESCENT PLANT
SCHEDULE OF BURDEN EXPENSE

Effective Date: January 1, 1954
Revision No.: 6
Schedule: B

Product: Fluorescent

Unit Production at Standard Level: 2,950,000

		Allowable Monthly Costs — Change at 35% Increase or Decrease from Standard Level	O.H. % of D.L. at Standard Production	Budget Formula	
	Standard			Fixed	% Std. D.L. $
Class of expense:					
Indirect labor	$ 12,880	$ 2,800	11	$ 4,880	6.809
Expense labor	22,800	3,590	19	12,540	8.732
Overtime and premium labor	7,600	3,780	6	(3,200)	9.191
Manufacturing expense	148,650	28,860	127	66,200	70.170
Mechanical design expense	41,200	......	35	41,200	......
Division manufacturing prorate	17,000	......	14	17,000	......
Division engineering prorate	32,500	......	28	32,500	......
Danvers engineering expense	25,980	1,575	22	21,480	3.830
Warehousing	8,320	1,420	7	4,260	3.455
Total fluorescent	$316,930	$42,025	269	$196,860	102.187
Cost centers:					
Coating	$ 23,345	$ 3,920	305	$ 12,150	146.340
Baking	18,785	3,060	348	10,045	162.002
Flare	4,070	600	250	2,360	105.231
Stem	1,220	150	113	790	40.000
Handmount	2,830	455	75	1,525	34.524
Automount	16,100	2,530	187	8,875	83.914
Base preparation	4,260	610	146	2,515	59.966
Finishing	246,320	30,700	285	158,600	101.471
Total fluorescent	$316,930	$42,025	269	$196,860	102.187

Exhibit 7

SYLVANIA ELECTRIC PRODUCTS INC. (A)

WORK SHEET FOR COMPUTATION OF PLANT ACTIVITY

| | Monthly Standard Level of Direct Labor Dollars | | |
	40 T-12 White	All Other Types	Total
Coating	$ 586	$ 7,546	$ 8,132
Baking	442	5,296	5,738
Flare	....	1,566	....
Stem	0	1,135	1,135
Handmount	0	3,992	3,992
Automount	....	8,260	....
Base preparation	172	2,918	3,090
Finishing	6,806	86,378	93,184
	$	$117,091	$ ....

Exhibit 8

SYLVANIA ELECTRIC PRODUCTS INC. (A)

BURDEN DISTRIBUTION TO COST CENTERS

	Allocated Burden
Coating	$ 23,595
Baking	18,600
Flare	3,950
Stem	1,200
Handmount	2,860
Automount	16,585
Base preparation	4,320
Finishing	258,640
	$329,750

WHITE EAGLE OIL COMPANY (A)

The rotary drilling committee of White Eagle Oil Company met bi-weekly to review the operations of the contract drilling department and analyze the results of contracts (wells) completed since the last meeting. These meetings were conducted by Mr. Lee Daniel, vice-president in charge of drilling, and were regularly attended by Mr. Carl Young and Mr. S. J. Brown of the contract drilling department; Mr. Robert W. Haigh, controller; and Mr. R. G. Gambrell, assistant controller. Frequently, Mr. Walter H. Helmerich, III, executive vice-president, would attend a portion or all of the meetings. An organization chart of White Eagle Oil Company appears in Exhibit 1.

History of White Eagle Oil Company

In 1920, Mr. Walter H. Helmerich and a partner organized a small contract drilling company. The company was incorporated as Helmerich & Payne, Inc., in the year 1926. Several years later, the partner elected to sell his interest in the company to Mr. Helmerich.

As an adjunct to its drilling business, Helmerich & Payne, Inc., and its predecessor company took an interest in many oil and gas exploration and producing deals. As a result, the company operated successfully through the years as an oil and gas producer and drilling contractor. In 1944 the company's name was changed to White Eagle Oil Company and a new subsidiary, Helmerich & Payne, Inc., was organized to conduct contract drilling operations. In 1952, there was a public offering of White Eagle Oil Company stock.

In 1957 the Helmerich family still owned a 43% interest in White Eagle. The remaining shares were publicly held, and the stock was quoted daily in "over-the-counter" listings. Contract drilling by the Helmerich & Payne subsidiary continued to account for more than 50% of the total revenue of White Eagle, but as the over-all size of the company increased, other activities became increasingly more important.

Consolidated financial statements for White Eagle Oil Company for the fiscal year ended September 30, 1956, are presented in Exhibits 2 and 3.

The Meeting of March 8, 1957

In March, 1957, the rotary drilling committee was engaged in the process of trying to improve management control over drilling operations. Several new cost and analytical reports had been designed and put into use in the closing months of 1956 (Exhibits 4 through 12, discussed individually below). The meeting on March 8 started off with an examination of the most recent H & P daily progress report (Exhibit 4) for March 4, 1957. This report summarized, by area, the activities of each of the company's 21 domestic drilling rigs. As may be noted from the report, three rigs in the Kansas-Oklahoma area and three in the West Texas–New Mexico area were "stacked" (dismantled and not operating), and had been inactive for periods varying from 9 to 277 days. The remaining rigs were under contract to the various "operators" (companies engaged in oil exploration activities) listed.

The columnar data in Exhibit 4 may be defined briefly as follows. "Spud in" was the date on which drilling of the well was started. "Depth" was the cumulative total footage drilled as of midnight on March 4, 1957. "Degree" was a measure of the angle of deviation of the hole from the perpendicular. Contracts typically specified the maximum number of degrees of deviation permissible.

"Hours-daywork" indicated the number of hours on March 4 for which the operator would be billed for use of the rig at the daywork rate. Some contracts, such as those for rig Nos. 33 and 8, were strictly daywork jobs under which the operator, in effect, hired the rig and its crew at a specified amount for each day employed on the job. Under the more usual drilling contract, H & P agreed to drill the well to a specified depth at an agreed price of so much per foot drilled. Under such a "footage" contract, a daywork rate was also agreed upon and H & P was paid at this rate for all delays during the drilling that were requested by the operator. For example, rig No. 36 was on daywork (and not drilling) for 12 hours on March 4 while the operator ran a "core" test to inspect the geological structure that had been drilled through in order to evaluate the possibilities of having passed through an oil bearing stratum. "Hours-delay" indicated the number of nondrilling hours on March 4 which were not chargeable against the operator as daywork (repairs to equipment, etc.).

The "Remarks" column contained several pieces of information. For a footage contract this column showed the estimated total depth (TD) to be drilled at the agreed price per foot, the estimated number of drilling days required, and parenthetically the cumulative number of day-work days. These data were useful for comparing actual drilling progress with the estimated time required. For example, the remarks column for rig No. 44 indicated that the well was flowing at 80 barrels per hour at a TD of 11,988 feet. Although estimated footage was 12,200, no further drilling would be done since the well was producing at a slightly shallower depth. Sixty-three days had elapsed since the well was spudded, but $4\frac{1}{2}$ days had been spent on daywork. Therefore $58\frac{1}{2}$ days had been spent drilling, compared to an estimated time of 63 days required for drilling the full 12,200 feet. Other comments in the remarks column explained the type of geological formation being drilled through (lime, chert, etc.), or other unusual features of a particular rig's operation.

After examining the daily progress report and raising any questions about particular rigs, the committee turned to an examination of the final results of any contracts completed since the last meeting. Rig No. 41 had completed a contract on February 23, 1957, and the final actual cost data were examined and over-all performance of the job evaluated. Mr. Daniel also pointed out that rig No. 44 would complete its contract within a few days and final figures on it would be available for the next meeting of the committee.

The Meeting on March 22, 1957

The meeting of the rotary drilling committee on March 22 opened with an examination of the most recent daily progress report, and then turned to an analysis of the final results of the Harris Well No. 1 completed by rig No. 44 on March 12. Mr. Young distributed copies of Exhibits 5 through 8, and Mr. Gambrell distributed Exhibits 9 through 12.

Exhibit 5 is a copy of the bid sheet that had been prepared at the time H & P had submitted a bid on the job to Sinclair. Costs per foot of $8.34 had been estimated, and the company's bid of $8.65 per foot had been accepted. A description of the methods used to determine the bid is presented in the Appendix.

Exhibit 6 is a copy of the drilling procedure prepared by the H & P home office for use by the "tool pusher" (supervisor located at the drilling site). As may be noted, the diameter of the hole to be drilled varied depending upon the depth. For the first 350 feet a $13\frac{3}{8}$-inch hole was drilled. After drilling the proper depth for each diameter, the hole was "cased" with pipe provided by the operator. Casing of the 7-inch hole (5,000 feet to TD) would not be done unless the well was productive. The drilling bits and lubricating mud to be used were carefully programmed. The operator typically specified the type of mud he would provide for each drilling zone, and H & P then determined the best type of bits to use and the number required. The type of mud used had an important effect on the drilling operations, since a heavy (thick) mud could increase the friction against which the drill pipe rotated, thus reducing the drilling penetration rate. Lubricating mud was frequently a carefully compounded chemical solution, and the cost of mud for a well could run as high as the cost of the contract drilling.

Exhibit 7 is an analysis of actual time spent by the rig during the $75\frac{1}{3}$ days it was on the drilling location. For example, $283\frac{3}{4}$ hours were spent running "trips" (pulling up the string of drill pipe to replace the bit and letting the string of pipe back down into the hole), 37 hours were spent conditioning the hole and installing casing, 140 hours were spent waiting on cement (WOC) used to fix the casing pipe in the hole, and $1\frac{1}{4}$ hours were lost when the drill pipe got stuck in the hole and had to be jarred loose. The number of bits actually used, in addition to one $17\frac{1}{4}$-inch bit, was also shown on Exhibit 7.

On the left side of Exhibit 8, several key sets of data are plotted graphically: the type of formation, size of bits used and the depth at which each change was made, deviation, and weight on the bit. The upper lines on the big graph in Exhibit 8 show rotating hours (read on the right axis) plotted against elapsed time. The lower line of the three represents 75% rotating hours; the upper line, 50%. The middle line is the actual number of rotating hours, an indicated 59.2% for the complete job (per Exhibit 7). H & P considered performance within the 50%–75% range to be satisfactory. The lower three lines on the big graph plot depth against elapsed time, and permit a comparison between actual performance, estimated performance, and the fastest drilling time for a comparable well in that oil field. Time spent on daywork was not plotted for any data in Exhibit 8.

Exhibit 9 gives a breakdown of total variable costs for rig No. 44 on Harris Well No. 1. The account numbers refer to White Eagle's chart of accounts. Account 111, for example, reflects the payroll cost of time spent by the drilling crew while they were waiting on location (WOL) when the rig was being moved in from its prior site. Maintenance expense accounts are two or three digit numbers beginning with a three, and where individual items exceed $300 they are annotated at the bottom of the report.

In Exhibits 10 and 11, the total actual rig costs are divided between footage and daywork costs. Mr. Gambrell explained that daywork costs were charged at the estimated or factor daily rate for all cost elements except variable costs which were specifically identified with the daywork. Drill pipe depreciation was charged to daywork for only 4.1 days out of $9\frac{1}{2}$ days of daywork. Daywork costs as shown in Exhibit 11 were then subtracted from total direct rig costs (Exhibit 9), and the balance entered on Exhibit 10 as footage costs.[1] Using this distribution, Mr. Gambrell was able to prepare Exhibit 12 as a summary statement of drilling profit and loss, indicating that daywork had done slightly less than break even and the footage work had produced a profit of $2,922.95.

The Committee's Analysis of Harris No. 1

After examining all the reports on Harris Well No. 1, Mr. Daniel said, "I'm pretty proud of our performance on this job. We estimated our footage cost at $8.34, and it actually ran $8.41—a variance of less than 1%. This indicates to me that both the estimating done in the home office and cost control in the field are being properly handled."

Mr. Brown said, "I'm out in the field a great deal, and from the casual conversation I pick up I think we're one of the few drillers that are able to cover full costs and earn a $2\frac{1}{2}\%$ profit. I think this is a good performance in times like these."

"Even our maintenance factor made money for us on this job," Mr. Gambrell pointed out, "although the overabsorbed maintenance probably only indicates that this rig was in pretty good shape when it started on the contract."

Mr. Haigh, however, shook his head. "We have a wealth of data here concerning this contract," he said, "and it seems to me we ought to be able to pin down pretty closely the reasons for our profit variance. As

---

[1] Reconciliation of Exhibits 10 and 11 with Exhibit 9 may be illustrated as follows:

Total direct out-of-pocket costs:		
Contract footage (Exhibit 10)		$87,542.97
Daywork (Exhibit 11)		8,052.29
Total		$95,595.26
Less: Home and field office overhead:		
Contract footage (Exhibit 10)	$8,312.50	
Daywork (Exhibit 11)	1,187.50	
Overabsorbed maintenance (Exhibit 12)	2,793.65	12,293.65
Total direct rig costs (Exhibit 9)		$83,301.61

I figure it, on our footage bid we expected to make a profit of $3,841, yet we only made $2,923. Not only is this a net reduction in profit of nearly 25%, but also I suspect that this 'loss' is really a net figure reflecting several cost fluctuations that might be significant if examined individually. I think it would be worthwhile to pursue our analysis of this data further. Let me work on this problem, and I will try to come up with something for our next meeting."

Questions

1. Compute the cash contribution to overhead and profit resulting from the Harris No. 1 contract. Of what use to management is this figure, if any?

2. Analyze the variance between actual and estimated profit on Harris Well No. 1. If possible, design a one-page analytical report form that might be useful for highlighting significant causes of variance on drilling contracts.

APPENDIX

DESCRIPTION OF METHODS USED TO DETERMINE BID ON HARRIS WELL NO. 1
(References Are to Exhibit 5 of the Case)

Labor and supervision were estimated for the 16-man crew (three five-man shifts and the "tool pusher"), allowing for maximum overtime payments on a seven-days-per-week schedule. For the Harris Well No. 1, this cost was estimated at $351 per day, including payroll taxes, insurance, and fringe benefits. Supplies and maintenance were estimated based on historical "factors" determined by taking an average of actual costs per day on prior jobs. These factors were reviewed quarterly by the accounting department to keep them in line with the company's most recent cost experience.

Contrary to rig operating costs which were estimated on a daily basis and multiplied to get a total, variable costs were estimated in total and divided by the number of days to yield a daily cost. Estimates for bits and transportation were detailed at the bottom of the bid form. For the Harris Well No. 1, it was estimated that the cost of having a subcontractor prepare the location and erect the rig would be $3,000. The 86 bits and five reamers estimated as required for the job would cost $23,625. Fuel cost, which varied depending on the type of fuel most economically available, was estimated at $3,060. The cost of drilling two water wells (subcontracted) was estimated at $700. Miscellaneous costs included an estimate of the cost of having a specialist subcontractor install "casing pipe" (steel pipe placed down in the hole to prevent cave-ins), another subcontractor to dig the "rat hole" and "mouse hole" (shallow holes in the ground near the rig used to hold the drilling table mechanism at times when it was removed to give access to the main hole during testing and changing bits), insurance on the rig, and an allowance for contingencies.

Home and field office overhead was estimated on a factor basis similar to supplies and maintenance. These costs included a share of executive salaries and other administrative expenses of White Eagle's home office as well as the costs of field offices maintained by H & P in each of the three areas where it operated. The cost-per-day factor computed to cover these costs was predicted on a 70% rig utilization, and the factor was reviewed semiannually to make sure it reflected current operations.

The factor for rig depreciation was not based on historical actual costs but was, as Mr. Gambrell described it, "a competitive factor, designed to reflect the estimated average depreciation costs of our competitor's equipment." The estimated life of a drilling rig was ten years, and White Eagle had conducted a study which showed that the cost of a given type of rig had risen 6% per year (compounded annually) since 1947. The average cost of a rig in the field was thus determined by taking the current cost of a new rig and discounting it back for five years at 6%. The resulting "average competitor's cost" was then depreciated over nine years with an estimated 10% salvage value. This procedure was done for each of the three classes of rigs operated by H & P. Rigs were classified by depth capabilities: Kansas-Oklahoma area rigs were efficient between 5,500–8,500 feet, North Dakota–Montana rigs between 6,500–10,000 feet, and West Texas–New Mexico rigs between 10,000–15,000 feet. "Competitive depreciation" for a rig similar to H & P rig No. 44 was estimated at $140 per day (70% utilization) in 1957. Depreciation factors were revised annually to allow for the 6% increase in replacement costs each year.

Drill pipe (D.P.) depreciation was also figured on a complex "factor" basis. Drill pipe is $3\frac{1}{2}$–5 inch diameter steel pipe, typically in 30-foot sections, which is joined together to make the "drill string" to which the cutting bit is attached. Lubricating "mud," used to cool the bit and carry away the cuttings, was forced down through the drill pipe and out through holes (jets) in the bit. The mud then flowed around the outside of the drill pipe up the hole to the surface where it was filtered and recirculated. Since the drill pipe rotates in the hole during actual drilling, the life of the pipe depends to a great extent on the abrasiveness of the cuttings carried in the mud from the formations being drilled through. The depth of the well being drilled was also a factor since a deep hole exposed more pipe to the abrasive action of the cuttings from the well. H & P figured drill pipe costs in terms of average cost per day for each of its three geographical areas, considering average well depths and typical geological formations in each area. For its deep rigs like No. 44, H & P estimated drill pipe depreciation at $75.39 per day. This factor was adjusted each time the price of steel was increased.

In addition to submitting a footage bid, H & P also submitted (at the operator's request) a daywork bid at various depths. The daywork bid also varied depending on whether or not H & P was required to use its drill pipe while so employed. Thus, the minimum daywork bid on Harris Well No. 1, without drill pipe, was determined as follows:

Rig operating costs	$562
Fuel	45
Home and field office overhead	125
Rig depreciation	140
Allowance for contingencies and profit	28
Total	$900

The daywork bid was scaled higher at greater depths to allow for the greater strain on equipment when laboring under heavier loads. The "standby" bid was applicable in those situations when the drilling crew was inactive and waiting for further instructions from the operator, and therefore included no allowance for supplies, maintenance, fuel, or rig depreciation.

Exhibit 1

WHITE EAGLE OIL COMPANY (A)

PARTIAL ORGANIZATION CHART AS OF MARCH, 1957

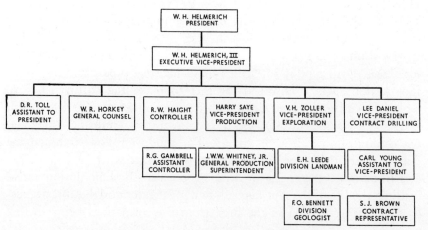

Exhibit 2

WHITE EAGLE OIL COMPANY (A)

CONSOLIDATED STATEMENT OF FINANCIAL POSITION AS OF
SEPTEMBER 30, 1955, AND 1956

	September 30	
	1955	*1956*
Current assets:		
Cash	$ 471,001	$ 1,583,727
Accounts, notes receivable, etc.	1,615,097	1,748,597
Inventories (drilling wells, warehouse stocks, etc.)	2,124,518	2,179,083
Total current assets	$ 4,210,616	$ 5,511,407
Current liabilities:		
Notes payable	$ 759,788	$ 1,168,044
Accounts payable	957,723	749,521
Accrued taxes, interest, etc.	88,733	141,026
Total current liabilities	$ 1,806,244	$ 2,058,591
Working capital	$ 2,404,372	$ 3,452,816
Other receivables	$ 325,828	$ 144,818
Investments	$ 5,577	$ 551,000
Properties, plant, and equipment:		
Producing properties and equipment (pledged)	$13,958,250	$15,447,292
Drilling tools, pipeline construction equipment, gasoline plant, etc.	7,573,143	8,483,449
Land and buildings	759,253	755,750
Undeveloped leases and royalties	1,469,995	1,520,641
	$23,760,641	$26,207,132
Less: Accumulated depletion and depreciation	11,607,048	13,085,462
Net properties, plant, and equipment	$12,153,593	$13,121,670
Deferred charges	$ 304,428	$ 182,187
Total assets less current liabilities	$15,193,798	$17,452,491
Deductions:		
4% first-mortgage promissory notes (payable monthly from oil and gas sales)	$ 7,173,141	$ 8,649,582
Deferred items	149,061	213,671
Total deductions	$ 7,322,202	$ 8,863,253
Net assets	$ 7,871,596	$ 8,589,238
Stockholders' equity:		
Capital stock issued	$ 136,304	$ 149,882
Reinvested earnings employed in business	7,760,167	8,439,356
	$ 7,896,471	$ 8,589,238
Less: Treasury stock 2,500 shares (cost)	24,875	....
Total stockholders' equity	$ 7,871,596	$ 8,589,238

Exhibit 3

WHITE EAGLE OIL COMPANY (A)

CONSOLIDATED INCOME STATEMENTS

FISCAL YEARS ENDED SEPTEMBER 30, 1955, AND 1956

	Year Ended September 30	
	1955	1956
Income:		
Drilling tool revenue (contract wells)........................	$ 5,515,595	$ 6,971,507
Oil and gas sales..	3,528,289	3,903,182
Pipeline construction revenue.............................	4,076,241	1,066,333
Miscellaneous...	244,452	305,397
Total...	$13,364,577	$12,246,419
Operating expenses:		
Drilling tool expense......................................	$ 4,397,226	$ 5,537,773
Production and pipeline expense............................	934,279	990,634
Pipeline construction expense..............................	3,767,588	914,628
General and administrative expense.........................	728,908	860,177
Lease rentals and expirations..............................	252,599	161,601
Geological and geophysical expense.........................	113,895	224,836
Miscellaneous...	38,074	14,098
Total...	$10,232,569	$ 8,703,747
Net income from operations.................................	$ 3,132,008	$ 3,542,672
Other income:		
(Interest, discounts, profit on sale of assets, etc.).............	226,458	261,765
	$ 3,358,466	$ 3,804,437
Less: Interest expense......................................	354,521	445,021
Net income before depletion, depreciation, dry holes, and abandonments...	$ 3,003,945	$ 3,359,416
Less:		
Depletion...	$ 669,735	$ 684,003
Depreciation..	1,555,486	1,558,548
Dry holes and abandonments..............................	512,320	375,160
Total...	$ 2,737,541	$ 2,617,711
Net income before income taxes.............................	$ 266,404	$ 741,705
Provision for federal and state income taxes...................	8,870	None
Net income for year.......................................	$ 257,534	$ 741,705

Exhibit 4

WHITE EAGLE OIL COMPANY (A)

HELMERICH & PAYNE, INC.

DAILY PROGRESS REPORT — ROTARY   DATE: March 4, 1957

COMPANY AND STATE		RIG NO.	WELL NAME	SPUD IN	DAYS DOWN	DEPTH	FOOTAGE DRILLED TODAY	DEG.	HOURS DW-DELAY	DAYS FROM SPUD	REMARKS
Shell	0	36	Barby Unit B-#1	2/1		7,025	83		12	31	7600 - 25 days (7 days DW) Core
United Prod	0	26	Nina Mayo No. 4	2/8		6,225	191		2	24	7100 - 26 days (2 days DW) CBS
Shell	0	24	Boyd No. 1	2/22		3,404	31	12	3/4	9	11600 - 60 days (1/2 day DW) Log
Shell	0	7	Lonker "B" Unit #1	3/2		630	475			2	6300 - 22 days 12-1/4 Hole
	0	40			277						
	0	35			246						
	0	38			26						
Champlin	T	46	Myrtle M. Nausbaum #1		7		RUR				7600 - 29 days
WEST TEXAS											
Magnolia	T	9	Reynolds-Parks No. 7	11/2		13,225			24	122	13500 - 95 days (15 days DW) Swab @ 12,230'
Sinclair	T	25	University 212 No. 4	12/15		12,505			24	79	12800 - 72 days (3-1/2 days DW) Drlg cement
Sinclair	T	32	A. R. Brownfield No. 1	12/17		11,065	85	1-3/4		77	13250 - 93 days (11-1/2 days DW) LI - SH 80 Bbls p/Hr.
Sinclair	NM	44	Harris No. 1	12/31		11,988			24	63	12200 - 63 days (4-1/2 days DW) DST - Flow
Gulf	T	42	O. W. Pool No. 1-D	1/15		10,732	118	2		48	11900 - 57 days LI - SH
Tex Pacific	T	37	W. W. McClure No. 5	2/3		6,760	160	3-1/4		29	12000 - 100 days LI-Sand-Chert
	T	39			85						
	NM	43			52						
	T	41			9						
WILLISTON BASIN											
Murphy	M	29	McIntosh No. 1	12/30		9,377	69	1-1/2		63	9200 - 35 days (11-1/2 days DW) LI CBS
Shell	M	15	State 44x-16	2/7		7,560	194			25	11000 - 60 days (5 days DW) LI
Amerada	M	33	R. W. Ruesegger No. 1	2/13		6,965	154		24	19	Daywork LI
Amerada	ND	8	ND "F" No. 6	2/20		7,272	142		24	12	Daywork LI
			TOTAL		702						

Exhibit 5

WHITE EAGLE OIL COMPANY (A)

HELMERICH & PAYNE, INC. CONTRACT FOOTAGE BID

```
                                                          Date  12-19-56
                                                          Depth 12,200'
OPERATOR   Sinclair Oil & Gas          WELL      Harris No. 1
ADDRESS                                ATTENTION OF
STATE   New Mexico    COUNTY   Lea     LOCATION Section 18-12S-38E  1980 FNL 660 FEL
BID WITH RIG   44   LOCATION    East Lovington
RIG UP   3  TEAR DOWN  2   DRLG.   63   OTHER                        TOTAL DAYS  68
REMARKS
```

	Total	Av Per Day Days	Av Per Ft Ft			
DIRECT OUT-OF-POCKET COSTS						
RIG OPERATING COSTS						
Labor & Supervision	23,868.00	351.00				
Supplies	2,788.00	41.00				
Maintenance	11,560.00	170.00				
Sub-Total	38,216.00	562.00				
VARIABLE COSTS						
Bits	23,625.00	347.43		**Footage Bid**		8.65
Transportation	5,500.00	80.88				
Location ___Dk___	3,000.00	44.11		5%	8.75	
Fuel & Lines	3,060.00	45.00				
Water & Lines	700.00	10.29		10%		
Fishing etc. ___Da___						
Other _____				15%		
_____	4,400.00	64.70				
Sub-Total	40,285.00	592.41				

FIXED OUT-OF-POCKET COSTS				W/DP	WO/DP
Home Office Overhead					
Field Office Overhead			0 - 10,000	950	900
~~Interest & Insurance~~			10 - 11,000	1000	950
			11 - 12,200	1050	1000
Sub-Total	8,500.00	125.00	Standby $750.00		

```
TOT DIR OUT-OF-POCKET COSTS  87,001.00   1,279.41

RECOVERY-OF-EQUIP COSTS
Rig Depreciation              9,520.00    140.00
D P Depr. _____Da___        5,168.00     76.00

TOT RECOVERY-OF-EQUIP COSTS  14,688.00    216.00

GRAND TOTAL COSTS           101,689.00   1,495.41    8.34

PROFIT   _____

EARNINGS
```

Casing	Depth	No. Bits	Size	Price	Total	Transportation	
13-3/4	350	1	17 1/4	200	200	Move, Skid:	
9 5/8	5000	10	12 1/4	300	3000	30/40 Miles	4,000
7	12200	70	8 3/4	200	14000	Rig Up	900
		5	8 3/4	1135	5675	Tear Down	600
		Rms. 5	8 3/4	150	750	Incidental	
		Total			23625	Total	5,500

Exhibit 6

WHITE EAGLE OIL COMPANY (A)

RIG NO. __44__

DRILLING PROCEDURE: WELL NAME___Henry A. Harris #1___

LOCATION   1980' from the North line and 660' from the East Line of Section 18,
T-12-S, R-38-E, Lea County, N.M.
OPERATOR   Sinclair Oil & Gas Company

       Mr. C. C. Salter, Dist. Prod. Supt., Hobbs, N.M.

       Phone EX 3-4150 or EX 3-4159

CASING AND HOLE PROGRAM

    13-3/8" casing cemented at approximately 350'

     9-5/8" casing cemented at approximately 5000'

    7"   casing cemented at approximately 12,200' or on top or through the Devonian.

FORMATIONS EXPECTED

DEPTH	DESCRIPTION
0 - 250	Sand and Caliche
250 - 2000	Red Beds
2000 - 2115	Anhydrite
2115 - 3450	Salt and Anhydrite
3450 - 5000	Anhydrite, Dolomite and Lime
5000 - 8500	Dolomite, Anhydrite and Shale
8500 - 9700	Shale and Lime
9700 - 10500	Lime and Shale
10500 - 10800	Shale and Lime
10800 - 11900	Lime, Sand and Chert
11900 - T.D.	Dolomite and Lime

DEVIATION: The contract deviation is as follows: 2° from surface to 1000'; 3° from 1000-3000'; 4° from 3000-4500'; and 5° from 4500 - T.D. The deviation is not a critical factor in drilling this well, and the deviation should be under three degrees most all the well. It is recommended, therefore, that a stabilizer be run only when

Exhibit 6 (Continued)

REMARKS

deviation rises above 2° which is expected at approximately 8000'. Constant weight on the bit when using a stabilizer will give the maximum benefit from stabilization. The stabilizer should be used at 60' except with a reamer, then it should be placed at 30' above the reamer.

BITS: Use jet bits with 5/8" jets to 5000' with a circulation rate of 800 GPM. When using 8" liners, 800 GPM can be maintained with 50 SPM and when using 7" liners, 800 GPM can be obtained with 60 SPM.

From 5000-9500' jet bits can be used to get maximum hole from our bits. Jet bits with 9/16" jets should be used with a circulation rate of 450 GPM. Below 9500' conventional bits should be used with a circulation rate of 350-400 GPM.

From the bits used in this area, chert bits can possibly be used to good advantage from 11350-11800. Three chert bits should be sufficient to drill this section.

HOLE CONDITIONS: From studying the wells drilled in the area, there seems to be no serious hole problems except crooked hole and this is not of a serious nature.

MUD: Salt saturated water will be used in drilling the intermediate hole. If possible, use the reserve pit as a settling tank. Clear water will be used below the intermediate casing to approximately 5000'. A gel-chemical mud will be used below 9500' to T.D.

REPORTS; Please show that all measurements of casing records, formations encountered, daily drilling reports and log of the well, including depth used in the payment of footage bill, are taken from surface or ground level:

Also make sure that the distance from the Kelly Drive Bushing to Ground Level is recorded on the tour sheets.

12-18-56

JEP

Exhibit 7

WHITE EAGLE OIL COMPANY (A)

HELMERICH & PAYNE, INC.   ANALYSIS OF RIG TIME

WELL NAME __Henry A. Harris No. 1__   OWNER __Sinclair Oil & Gas Company__

STATE __New Mexico__   COUNTY __Lea__   LOCATION __Section 18-12S-38E__   DEPTH __11,988'__

RIG NO. __44__   TOOL PUSHER __Ray Marsh__   RIG UP __12-27-56__   TEAR DOWN __3-12-57__

	FOOTAGE		DAYWORK		TOTAL	
	HOURS	%	HOURS	%	HOURS	%
RIG UP	80	5.9			80	4.4
TEAR DOWN	40	2.4			40	2.2
DRILLING BIT ON BOTTOM:	936 1/2	59.2			936 1/2	51.8
FOOTAGE_____						
DAYWORK_____						
TRIPS	283 3/4	17.8			283 3/4	15.7
RUN CSG. — INCLUDING COND. HOLE	37	2.3			37	2.0
WOC	140	8.8			140	7.7
STRAIGHT HOLE TEST	19 3/4	1.1			19 3/4	1.0
MIX MUD	8 3/4	.5			8 3/4	.5
LOST CIRCULATION						
RIG REPAIRS	9 3/4	.6			9 3/4	.5
RIG SERVICE	14	.9			14	.9
REAMING:	8 1/2	.4			8 1/2	.5
FOOTAGE_____						
DAYWORK_____						
FISHING — INCLUDING TRIPS						
STUCK PIPE	1 1/4	.1			1 1/4	.1
DAYWORK — OTHER			228 3/4	100.	228 3/4	12.7
FOOTAGE DELAY TIME						
TOTAL	1579 1/4	100.	228 3/4	100.	1808	100

DRLG. W/10,000 LBS. OR
LESS ON BIT: _____

CORING FOOTAGE _____

TOTAL TIME   HOURS 1808
LESS: DAYWORK   228 3/4
    FISHING
    STUCK PIPE   1 1/4
    L. C.
    REPAIRS   9 3/4
    OTHER   239 3/4
        1568 1/4

	WEIGHT ON BIT	DEGREES OFF	No. D. C.
1,000'	46,000	1 1/4	12
2,000'	46,000	3/4	12
3,000'	46,000	1 1/2	12
4,000'	50,000	1 1/2	15
5,000'	60,000	3/4	25
6,000'	60,000	3/4	25
7,000'	60,000	1	25
8,000'	60,000	1 3/4	25
9,000'	60,000	1	25
10,000'	60,000	1 1/2	25
11,000'	60,000	1 3/4	25
12,000'			
13,000'			
14,000'			

CASING PROGRAM:

13-3/8" Spiral Weld Csg. @ 300' w/400 sxs.
9-5/8" @ 4496' w/2600 sxs.

BIT SUMMARY: 7" @ TD
  6 - 12 1/4
  64 - 8 3/4

SPUDDED: 12-31-56
RIG RELEASED: 3-11-57

MAX. DEGREES OF: 1 3/4 @ 11,755'

DAYS W/DP   FTG. 53.
            DW   4.1

Exhibit 8

WHITE EAGLE OIL COMPANY (A)

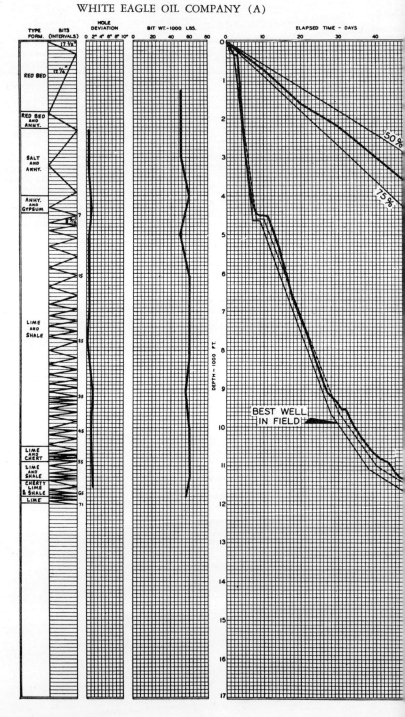

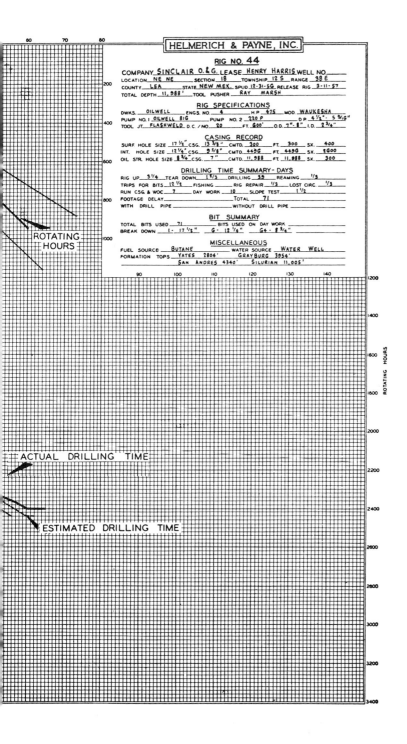

Exhibit 9

WHITE EAGLE OIL COMPANY (A)

HELMERICH & PAYNE, INC.   DIRECT RIG COSTS

Tool Pusher __Ray Marsh__   Rig __44__ Well __Harris #1__

Location __Lea Co., New Mexico__   Operator __Sinclair Oil & Gas Co.__

Operating Days __76__   Date __12-27-56 to 3-12-57__

Acc't.	Item	Total Cost For Period		Average Cost Per Day (Period)		Remarks
111	Labor; W.O.L., Move	595.19		7.83		
112	Labor, Rig Up	1,155.50		15.20		
113	Labor, Drilling	22,695.74		298.63		
114	Labor, Tear Down	292.41		3.85		
12	Supervision	3,534.37		46.50		
	Sub Total-Labor		28,273.21			372.01
21	Rig Supplies	929.58		12.23		
22	Hand Tools	234.41		3.08		
23	Valves & Fittings	91.87		1.21		
24	Oil & Grease	2,182.23		28.72		
	Sub Total-Supplies		3,438.09			45.24
311	Drawworks	169.93		2.24		
1. 312	Compound & Chain	963.13		12.67		
321	Mud Pump, Fluid End	778.81		10.25		
322	Mud Pump, Power End	50.49		.66		
323	Mud System	380.51		5.01		
324	Other Pumps	66.38		.87		
2. 331	Drilling Engines	3,794.30		49.92		
334	Other Engines	461.98		6.08		
34	Overhead String	344.81		4.54		
343	Wire Line					
3. 35	Other Equipment	1,546.11		20.35		
363	Maintenance Trucking					
364	Welding	212.20		2.79		
38	Drill Pipe	114.00		1.50		
4. 391	Drill Collars	1,214.78		15.98		
392	Subs	28.92		.38		
	Sub Total-Maintenance		10,126.35			133.24
	Total Rig Operating Costs		41,837.65			550.49
41	Bits & Reamers	20,716.64				
421	Trucking In	4,919.98				
422	Other Transportation	1,385.82				
423	Rig Up	642.00				
424	Tear Down	45.00				
51	Location	2,543.76				
52	Fuel & Lines	8,928.43				
53	Water & Lines	595.66				
	Csg. Crews	1,246.85				
	Rat & Mouse Hole	102.00				
	Misc.	337.82				
	Total-Variable Costs		41,463.96			545.58
	Grand Total		83,301.61			1,096.07

1. Compound Chain - Sextuple   759.63
2. Rework 4-Heads & Valve jobs   3,052.84
3. Convert 4YC Air Comp. to 5YC   685.84
4. Hardband 10-7" D.C.   500.00
    Stub 1-6-1/2 D.C.   371.20

Exhibit 10

WHITE EAGLE OIL COMPANY (A)

HELMERICH & PAYNE, INC. CONTRACT FOOTAGE COST

HP

OPERATOR ___Sinclair Oil & Gas Co.___ WELL __Harris #1__

STATE __New Mexico__ COUNTY __Lea__   LOCATION __Section 18-12S-38E__

RIG NO. __44__ TOOL PUSHER __Ray Marsh__ RIG UP __12-27-56__ TEAR DOWN __3-12-57__

	TOTAL	AV. PER DAY 66.5 DAYS	AV. PER FT. 11988 FT.
DIRECT OUT-OF-POCKET COSTS			
RIG OPERATING COSTS			
Labor & Supervision	24,938.71	375.02	2.08
Supplies	3,048.59	45.84	.25
Maintenance	11,305.00	170.00	.95
SUB-TOTAL: RIG OPERATING COSTS	39,292.30	590.86	3.28
VARIABLE COSTS			
Bits	20,716.64	311.53	1.73
Transportation	6,597.00	99.20	.55
Location __541.50__ Derrick __2002.26__	2,543.76	38.25	.21
Fuel & Lines	7,835.02	117.82	.65
Water & Lines	595.66	8.96	.05
Fishing, etc. _____ Days _____			
Other __Csg. Crews__	1,246.85	18.75	.10
__Misc & Spec. Ins.__	403.24	6.06	.04
SUB-TOTAL: VARIABLE COSTS	39,938.17	600.57	3.33
FIXED OUT-OF-POCKET COSTS			
Home Office Overhead			
Field Office Overhead			
Interest & Insurance			
SUB-TOTAL: FIXED OUT-OF-POCKET COSTS	8,312.50	125.00	.69
TOTAL DIRECT OUT-OF-POCKET COSTS	87,542.97	1,316.43	7.30
RECOVERY-OF-EQUIPMENT COSTS			
Rig Depreciation	9,310.00	140.00	.78
Drill Pipe Depreciation __52__ Days __75.39__	3,920.28	58.95	.33
TOTAL RECOVERY-OF-EQUIPMENT COSTS	13,230.28	198.95	1.11
GRAND TOTAL COSTS	100,773.25	1,515.38	8.41
PROFIT _____	2,922.95	43.96	.24
EARNINGS	103,696.20	1,559.34	8.65
11,988' @ 8.65 per foot.			

CASING	DEPTH	NO. BITS	SIZE	PRICE	TOTAL	TRANSPORTATION	
13 3/8	300	1	17 1/2	Retips	87.50	Move, Skid:	
9 5/8	4496	6	12 1/4		2,117.07	__40__ Miles	4,524.18
7	T.D.	61	8 3/4		13,100.16	Rig Up	642.00
		3	8 3/4-R-1		3,279.09	Tear Down	45.00
T.D.	11988	Rms. 15	8 3/4- Chert		2,132.82	Incidental	1,385.82
		TOTAL			20,716.64	TOTAL	6,597.00

Exhibit 11

WHITE EAGLE OIL COMPANY (A)

HELMERICH & PAYNE, INC.   DAYWORK COST

HP

OPERATOR __Sinclair Oil & Gas Co.__   WELL __Harris #1__

STATE __New Mexico__ COUNTY __Lea__   LOCATION __Section 18-12S-38E__

RIG NO. __44__ TOOL PUSHER __Ray Marsh__   RIG UP __12-27-56__ TEAR DOWN __3-12-57__

	TOTAL	AV. PER DAY 9.5 DAYS
DIRECT OUT-OF-POCKET COSTS		
RIG OPERATING COSTS		
Labor & Supervision	3,334.50	351.00
Supplies	389.50	41.00
Maintenance	1,615.00	170.00
SUB-TOTAL: RIG OPERATING COSTS	5,339.00	562.00
VARIABLE COSTS		
Bits		
Transportation	395.80	41.66
Location _____ Derrick _____		
Fuel & Lines	1,093.41	115.10
Water & Lines		
Fishing, etc. _____ Days _____		
Other __Spec. Ins.__	36.58	3.85
SUB-TOTAL: VARIABLE COSTS	1,525.79	160.61
FIXED OUT-OF-POCKET COSTS		
Home Office Overhead		
Field Office Overhead		
Interest & Insurance		
SUB-TOTAL: FIXED OUT-OF-POCKET COSTS	1,187.50	125.00
TOTAL DIRECT OUT-OF-POCKET COSTS	8,052.29	847.61
RECOVERY-OF-EQUIPMENT COSTS		
Rig Depreciation	1,330.00	140.00
Drill Pipe Depreciation __4.1__ Days __75.39__	309.10	32.54
TOTAL RECOVERY-OF-EQUIPMENT COSTS	1,639.10	172.54
GRAND TOTAL COSTS	9,691.39	1,020.15
PROFIT _____	(156.51)	(16.48)
EARNINGS	9,534.88	1,003.67

CASING	DEPTH		W/DP	WO/DP
____	____	0 - 10,000	950.00	900.00
____	____	10 - 11,000	1,000.00	950.00
____	____	11 - 12,000	1,050.00	1,000.00
____	____			

Exhibit 12

WHITE EAGLE OIL COMPANY (A)

HELMERICH & PAYNE, INC.

STATEMENT OF DRILLING PROFIT AND LOSS

OPERATOR___Sinclair Oil & Gas Co.___   WELL NAME___Harris #1___

STATE__New Mexico__COUNTY___Lea___   LOCATION___Section 18-12S-38E___

RIG NO.__44_TOOL PUSHER__Ray Marsh___   RIG UP¹²⁻²⁷⁻⁵⁶TEAR DOWN___3-12-57___

	Contract	Daywork	Total
EARNINGS	103,696.20	9,534.88	113,231.08
COST	100,773.25	9,691.39	110,464.64
PROFIT	2,922.95	(156.51)	2,766.44
%PROFIT	2.9%	(1.6%)	2.5%
OPERATING DAYS	66.5	9.5	76
AVERAGE EARNINGS PER DAY	1,559.34	1,003.67	1,489.88
AVERAGE COST PER DAY	1,515.38	1,020.15	1,453.48
AVERAGE PROFIT PER DAY	43.96	(16.48)	36.40
TOTAL DEPTH	11988		

Actual Maintenance	$ 10,126.35
Maintenance Factor	12,920.00
Overabsorbed Main-tenance	$ 2,793.65

THE ATLANTIC MONTHLY COMPANY (A)

Late in January 1964, Donald B. Snyder, since 1933 the publisher of *The Atlantic Monthly* magazine, was preparing a report for the company's board of directors. For many years it had been Mr. Snyder's practice to submit a comprehensive report for discussion at the January board meeting; the report served as the primary basis on which the board reviewed the performance of the magazine during the preceding calendar year. Mr. Snyder thought his 1964 report was particularly important because (1) he was planning to retire later that year and he wanted to make a careful assessment of the recent progress of the magazine and its current situation at the time that he turned his job over to his successor, and (2) the 1963 operating results provided the first real opportunity to review the effect of the price increase that he had made in 1962. Mr. Snyder was convinced that the price increase had been a wise decision, but he thought that it would be useful for the board to review the results of that action.

History of the Atlantic

The Atlantic Monthly, a magazine published in Boston, Massachusetts, was founded in 1857 by the following group of distinguished New England literary and political leaders:

James Russell Lowell	Henry Wadsworth Longfellow
Ralph Waldo Emerson	Oliver Wendell Holmes
Francis H. Underwood	James Elliott Cabot
John Lothrop Motley	Moses Dresser Phillips

The original prospectus of the magazine stated that its aim was "to concentrate the efforts of the best writers upon literature and politics, under the light of the highest morals." In 1957, this editorial policy was reaffirmed by the editor, Edward A. Weeks, in his introduction to the 100th Anniversary Issue:

> The aims of the magazine were clearly defined in the first issue. It was to be primarily an American undertaking. "The publishers wish to say," so runs the prospectus, "that while native writers will receive the most solid encouragement, and will be mainly relied on to fill the pages of the *Atlantic,* they will not hesitate to draw from the foreign sources at their command, as occasion may require, relying rather on the competency of an author to treat a particular subject, than on any other claim whatever." In this way they hoped to make their periodical "welcome wherever the English tongue is spoken or read." We have from the first relied upon "the competency" of our authors; we have not tried to water down what they wrote but have given them the latitude to express conflicting and at times highly controversial opinions, for we still believe, as did our founders, that the free competition of ideas has made this country what it is.
>
> "In Politics," so runs our charter, "the *Atlantic* will be the organ of no party or clique, but will honestly endeavor to be the exponent of what its conductors believe to be the American idea. . . . It will not rank itself with any sect of anties, but with that body of men which is in favor of Freedom, National Progress, and Honor, whether public or private." To the founders the Union was sacred, and ever since the Reconstruction we have held to the pledge that the magazine would be nonpartisan. At the time of national elections, as tempers have risen, we have had to resist the pressure of well-meaning friends who would have us become a Republican or a Democratic organ. Our refusal to do so has sometimes cost us readers and advertising, but we believe that it has increased our sense of responsibility and our value.[1]

From the very beginning, the *Atlantic* was a critical success, enjoying an increasing reputation for publishing excellent literary essays and critiques, high-quality fiction and poetry, and provocative political and topical articles. Financially, however, the *Atlantic*'s success as a self-supporting commercial venture was somewhat less consistent. For the first 51 years of its existence, the *Atlantic* was published as an auxiliary activity by a variety of book publishing companies; the publishing rights changed hands seven times during these years. In 1908, the magazine became an independent enterprise when Ellery Sedgwick formed The Atlantic Monthly Company and purchased the magazine from Houghton Mifflin Company. During the first 15 years under Mr. Sedgwick's direction, the circulation of the *Atlantic* increased from less than 40,000 copies per issue to more than 125,000 copies.

The depression years of the 1930s affected the *Atlantic* as it did many other businesses; circulation dropped from 126,000 in 1930 to 101,000 in 1935. In 1938, Mr. Sedgwick sold his stock in the company

---

[1] *The Atlantic Monthly,* Vol. 200 (November, 1957), pp. 37–38.

to Richard E. Danielson; and under the new owner, Mr. Weeks, who had joined the organization in 1924 as associate editor, continued as editor, and Mr. Snyder as publisher, positions still held by these two men in 1964.

The *Atlantic*'s progress during the years 1950 to 1963 is documented in Exhibits 1, 2, and 3. Exhibit 1 presents comparative statistical data for the *Atlantic* and its most direct competitor, *Harper's Magazine.* Total average paid circulation of the *Atlantic* increased from 102,000 in 1940 to 170,000 in 1950 and 269,000 in 1963. The volume of advertising carried by the magazine also increased substantially during this period. Exhibit 2 presents income statements for The Atlantic Monthly Company for the five years 1959 to 1963.

Excerpts from the balance sheet of The Atlantic Monthly Company are presented in Exhibit 3. The major liability shown on Exhibit 3 was for unearned magazine subscriptions. Subscriptions were sold at a variety of prices; the regular prices were 12 issues for $8.50, 24 issues for $16, and 36 issues for $23. In addition, trial subscriptions were sold on special offers, such as 8 issues for $2.84 or 12 issues for $4.50. The subscription price was collected or billed at the time the subscription was entered, but recognition of the revenue from the subscription was spread pro rata over the number of issues to be delivered. The subscription liability account thus represented the revenue to be recognized in the future based upon (1) the number of copies to be delivered in the future and (2) the revenue per copy on those copies. As a practical matter, the calculation of the liability was made at the end of each fiscal year. The new "revenue per copy" rate was a weighted average of (1) the unit revenue of the beginning "inventory" of the subscription liability account plus (2) the unit revenue for new subscriptions sold during the year. The subscription revenue recognized during the year was equal to the number of copies sold times the revenue per copy. In effect, therefore, the averaging procedure used in accounting for subscription revenue smoothed out the impact of changes in subscription prices and changes in the mix (trials versus long renewals) of subscriptions sold.

In a similar manner, the expenses incurred in selling subscriptions were deferred at the time the subscription was sold and charged against income as the subscription was delivered. These deferred circulation costs amounted to $391,313 on April 30, 1963. For purposes of computing federal income taxes, however, magazine publishers had been permitted, since 1957, to deduct circulation promotion expenses in the year in which the expenses were incurred, and the *Atlantic* followed this procedure in computing its tax liability. As a result, the *Atlantic*'s balance sheet also contained a figure for deferred federal income tax. This liability account arose because the company's accountants had provided for estimated income tax expense based on the profit as reported to stockholders each year; the actual income tax liability had been less than this estimate because taxable profits were reduced by the full write-off of circulation promotion costs. The difference between taxable profits and profits reported to stockholders during the years 1957–63 amounted to about $150,000, the amount by which deferred circulation costs had increased during the period. When the tax law was changed in 1957, deferred circulation costs amounted to about $240,000. These costs were written off for tax purposes, and the resulting tax refund of approximately $120,000 was credited directly to Retained Earnings because "it was the opinion of the management that the level of annual expenditures for subscription procurement achieved by 1957 constituted a plateau from which the company could not conceivably retreat."[2]

The Price Increase in 1962

According to Mr. Snyder, the *Atlantic* had raised its newsstand and subscription prices in 1962 because, as he said,

Our profit margin became too thin. Profits, which were satisfactory in 1959 and 1960, dropped significantly in 1961 and continued to drop in 1962. The reasons for the decline were complex; a combination of increases in our production costs and some decline in the editorial appeal of our product. Then, in January 1962, the House of Representatives passed a bill drastically raising postal rates on second-class and third-class mailings. We didn't wait for the bill to be acted on by the Senate; we raised our prices effective with the March 1962 issue. Fortunately, the Senate scaled down the postal rate increases, but we needed the higher price anyway.

Exhibit 4, 5, and 6 present detailed statistical data for The Atlantic Monthly Company for the years 1959 to 1963. Mr. Snyder's comments about these data and some of the developments reflected by these data are quoted below:

Number of Pages. We didn't feel that we could raise our prices unless we simultaneously offered a bigger and better magazine. The result was our *Atlantic* "Extra," a regular monthly supplement which explores an important topic in some depth. In the old days, our "saddle" (the main block of editorial material, which contained no advertising) was usually 44 pages per issue, with the

---

[2] The 1960 Annual Report of The Atlantic Monthly Company.

exception of three "Supplement" issues that might contain an 88-page saddle. Now our policy is to have 12- or 16-page "Extras" in nine issues and 32- or 48-page "Supplements" in the other three, in addition to our 44 pages of regular text. The net effect has been to increase the quantity of saddle text annually by about 100 pages or so.

During the last few years we have also seen a steady increase in the number of pages of editorial material printed as regular features by our "departments." Our readership surveys show that our *Atlantic* "Reports" on political developments around the world are important to a large percentage of our subscribers, and we've also increased the space devoted to "Accent on Living" and "Pleasures and Places." The department text is interspersed through the advertising sections that precede and follow the saddle, and to some extent at least, the increase in department text was necessary in order to space out the increased number of advertising pages we've been running. But department text is not "filler" in any sense of the word; it must make our total editorial package more attractive or we won't print it. In other words, more advertising gives us an opportunity to run more pages of department text, and we try to use the opportunity to make the *Atlantic* an even better magazine.

Paper and Printing Costs. Contrary to the practices of most magazines, we keep a careful breakdown of our costs as between text pages and advertising pages. We find that advertising pages are considerably more expensive to manufacture because the use of color requires a heavier paper as well as higher printing costs. In general, the costs for paper and printing have been creeping up for several years, although the trend took a breather in 1963. We began using a slightly lighter, and therefore less expensive, paper stock in the fall of 1961 in an attempt to hold our costs down. And, of course, the increase in printing costs has been mitigated to some extent as we have been able to spread our fixed costs for plates and setup over an increasing number of copies printed.

Mailing and Distribution Costs. In a similar fashion, we separate the costs of distribution as between text pages and advertising pages. For copies mailed to subscribers this breakdown reflects the differences in postal rates: editorial material may be mailed anywhere in the country for $2\frac{1}{2}$ cents per pound; advertising material is figured on a postal zone basis and ranges from 5 cents per pound for a Boston address to 14 cents per pound for the West Coast. The shipping costs on newsstand copies are a straight charge based on weight without regard to the type of material, so we merely prorate those costs between editorial and advertising.

Editorial Costs. Although editorial costs are only a fraction of our costs for manufacturing and distribution, they are our most important product cost. The *Atlantic* is an editor's magazine, by which I mean that it is editorial judgment which really determines the success of the magazine. Without attractive material we would have neither readers nor the advertisers that pursue them. Over the years, I've worked closely with Ted Weeks, continually trying to assess the effectiveness of our editorial policies in attracting and holding readers. The job is a lot tougher than just trying to figure out what the readers want; a good editor is always a step or two ahead of his audience, giving them what they want before they even know they want it.

I'm not really concerned that our editorial costs have risen steadily over the last several years. The important thing is that, month after month, we're publishing an increasingly better magazine.

Advertising Revenue. Perhaps the most dramatic change in our business in the last few years is the growing recognition by advertisers of the efficiency with which a small magazine such as the *Atlantic* reaches an important and influential group of readers. We really don't compete with television and the mass magazines for the advertiser's dollar; rather, we compete with other media for our reader's leisure time. It's because we've won that battle that the advertisers are turning to our pages as a way of communicating with our selective, thoughtful subscribers.

Here's a summary of our advertising rates during the last several years:

	Rate Card				
	No. 32	*No. 31*	*No. 30*	*No. 29*	*No. 28*
Effective date	Sept. 1963	July 1960	Jan. 1959	May 1958	Jan. 1954
Guaranteed paid circulation	262,500	255,000	240,000	215,000	200,000
Cost of one insertion:					
Black-and-white page	$ 2,275	$ 2,100	$ 1,950	$ 1,750	$ 1,500
Four-color page	3,525	3,250	2,925	2,650	2,200
Cost per thousand circulation for black-and-white page	$8.67	$8.24	$8.13	$8.14	$7.50

Actually, our rates involve a complex series of discounts based on the size and frequency of the insertion, and we have a special rate card for book publishers. On card No. 31, for example, the one-time rate for a black-and-white page was $2,100 for a general advertiser but only $1,400 for a book publisher. These rates dropped to $1,890 and $1,260 if the advertiser made 12 insertions in any 12-month period. From these gross rates, the advertising agency deducts a 15% commission, and the revenue shown in our books is the 85% that they remit to us. The increase in revenue in the last few years is primarily due to (1) selling more pages of advertising and (2) realizing more revenue per page as a result of more color ads and selling a higher percentage of our space at the general rate rather than the book publishers' rate. We raised our guarantee again, effective in September 1963, to 262,500. Based on that increase and the fact that advertisers are increasingly aware of the selectivity of our audience, our new rate card shows an average page-rate increase of about 8%.

Advertising Promotion Expenses. We discovered an interesting thing in a major readership survey done back in the early 1950s: very few people read both *Harper's* and the *Atlantic* in any one month. Both magazines are edited for essentially the same audience, and there's a lot of switching back and forth by these readers, but very little direct overlap at any one point of time. The upshot of this fact was that we got together with *Harper's* to form the Harper-Atlantic Sales Company to sell advertising in both magazines. Up to that time we'd each had our own sales force, with all the duplication of effort that that involved. Now we each own 50% of the sales company, and it's run on essentially a break-even basis.

This new sales approach has worked out exceedingly well. It's both more efficient in terms of calling on advertisers, as well as giving us a bigger package to sell. We find that an increasing number of advertisers are running the same insertion in both magazines the same month, and we offer a special 10% discount on the combined package. In terms of costs, we've really benefited from the economies of scale during the last few years. Each magazine pays a commission to the sales company based on the net revenue produced. The commission rates are on a declining scale based on the volume of net revenue billed by each magazine. Currently, the rates begin at 40% and drop to a low of 17% on billings in excess of $1 million per year. We crossed that magic line for the first time in 1963.

Newsstand Circulation. Our newsstand distribution is handled by Curtis Circulation Company, the same firm that distributes *Saturday Evening Post, Look, The New Yorker,* and many other magazines. Newsstand sales are important to the *Atlantic;* they're an important segment of our total circulation, and the net revenue from newsstand sales is substantially higher than the net revenue from subscriptions.

Our volume on the newsstand has held up well in the face of the price increase, in part because we've increased the number of copies we're distributing. We used to distribute about 80,000 copies of each issue, but the average was over 92,000 in fiscal 1963 and is currently running higher than that. These extra copies have increased our exposure in terms of the number of newsstands where we're offered. Of course, when you put two copies on a marginal newsstand and only sell one, the efficiency of your total newsstand distribution drops. But single copy sales are a good way to broaden our readership base. For the same reason, most of our newsstand promotion costs, typically small ads in newspapers and other media, are aimed at college towns where we think our natural market is concentrated.

Subscription Circulation. The trickiest part of this business, without a doubt, is subscription circulation. There's nothing quite as comforting to a publisher as a nice solid core of dedicated subscribers—and the *Atlantic* has it. A high percentage of our regular subscribers renew year after year. These renewals, which are mostly at our regular rates, yield over $7 of revenue for 12 copies, and it only costs us about $1 for mailing and so forth to sell the renewal. Clearly, this is the most profitable source of circulation we have.

The problem is that since about 30% of our regular subscribers don't renew each year, we have to go out and sell new subscriptions in sizable quantities. To make the job easier, we offer trial subscriptions at half price, although we worry about making our regular subscribers unhappy when we ask them to pay full price. In 1963 we decided to start going to the considerable expense of "unduplicating" our trail offer mailing lists, just to make sure that a current subscriber wasn't tempted to throw away our renewal notice and enter a new trial at half the price. So, the way it works out, we feel lucky if the revenue from a new trial subscription is enough to cover the costs of selling the trial. The thing that makes it worthwhile is that many trial subscribers are converted to regular subscribers when it comes time to renew.

In addition to subscription promotion costs, we have a considerable expense in "fulfilling" a subscription, a term used in the trade to refer to the cost of keeping the mailing list of subscribers up to date, processing changes of address, and so forth. Taking everything together, subscription circulation involves a lot of costs in order to build, maintain, and serve that core of subscribers we want. The profitability of this type of circulation really depends on the renewal experience we enjoy both on our trial subscribers and on our regulars. And the renewal rates, of course, are a reflection of how well our readers like our editorial product.

Questions

1. Using data in the case for fiscal years ended April 30, try to isolate the reasons for the profit increase between 1962 and 1963. Specifically, try to deal with the following items:

  a) The *net* effect on profit of selling more advertising.
  b) The *net* effect on profit of increasing the price of the magazine.
  c) The *net* effect on profit of reducing the total paid circulation from 277,824 to 271,471.

Note: Unit costs, ratios, and percentages are presented in Exhibits 4 to 6. Not all these calculations are necessarily relevant, nor are these necessarily the only relevant calculations.

2. Think about how you might go about designing a model of a magazine publishing company. Ideally, such a model, when supplied with the input data for any particular year, would yield an approximation of the profit or loss for that year. What problems do you see in working out such a model? What would be the value, if any, to the management of The Atlantic Monthly Company of having such a model?

Exhibit 1

THE ATLANTIC MONTHLY COMPANY

COMPARATIVE STATISTICS FOR *The Atlantic Monthly* AND
Harper's Magazine, SELECTED YEARS, 1950 TO 1963

	1963	1962	1961	1960	1955	1950
Average monthly paid circulation (calendar year):						
Subscriptions:						
Atlantic.............	219,186	223,791	227,165	220,729	165,800	138,000
Harper's.............	220,540	234,076	212,471	186,905	151,800	126,000
Newsstand:						
Atlantic.............	49,413	50,196	54,764	44,505	42,500	31,500
Harper's.............	49,388	52,427	52,426	52,086	36,900	35,300
Total:						
Atlantic.........	268,599	273,987	281,929	265,234	208,300	169,500
Harper's.........	269,928	286,503	264,897	238,991	188,700	161,300
Regular prices on December 31:						
One-year subscription:						
Atlantic.............	$8.50	$8.50	$7.50	$7.50	$6.00	$6.00
Harper's.............	7.00	7.00	6.00	6.00	6.00	5.00
Single copy:						
Atlantic.............	0.75	0.75	0.60	0.60	0.50	0.50
Harper's.............	0.60	0.60	0.60	0.60	0.50	0.50
Advertising volume (calendar year):						
Pages:						
Atlantic.............	620	491	481	535	341	239
Harper's.............	569	468	460	509	314	326
Gross revenue:						
Atlantic.............	$1,562,798	$1,206,867	$1,135,432	$1,181,815	$481,804	$237,759
Harper's.............	1,448,168	1,165,542	1,012,613	1,046,262	369,808	350,207

Sources: Audit Bureau of Circulation, Standard Rate and Data Service, and Publishers Information Bureau.

Exhibit 2

THE ATLANTIC MONTHLY COMPANY
COMPARATIVE STATEMENTS OF OPERATIONS, 1959–63

	Twelve Months Ended April 30				
	1963	*1962*	*1961*	*1960*	*1959*
Operating revenues:					
Subscriptions earned............	$1,080,349	$1,058,565	$1,036,243	$1,026,410	$1,004,694
Newsstand sales................	249,716	240,350	194,564	202,659	204,024
Advertising sales..............	1,024,067	856,387	932,404	745,356	587,735
Total....................	$2,354,132	$2,155,302	$2,163,211	$1,974,425	$1,796,453
Operating expenses:					
Paper and paper handling.......	$ 367,501	$ 362,804	$ 358,997	$ 307,406	$ 282,685
Printing......................	348,887	331,360	302,121	257,486	225,837
Mailing......................	158,497	151,035	138,435	120,077	102,222
Subscription promotion.........	437,754	408,154	405,149	351,155	326,516
Subscription fulfillment........	117,580	117,615	113,046	112,704	113,292
Manuscripts...................	136,662	131,226	106,825	102,376	101,595
Other editorial costs...........	169,985	157,963	168,414	146,608	137,147
Newsstand promotion..........	29,211	31,941	35,086	29,081	21,863
Advertising promotion..........	367,632	329,927	341,767	306,847	243,650
General and administration.....	128,906	136,895	122,036	116,263	115,577
Total....................	$2,262,615	$2,158,920	$2,091,876	$1,850,003	$1,670,384
Operating profit before taxes......	$ 91,517	$ (3,618)	$ 71,335	$ 124,422	$ 126,069

Exhibit 3

THE ATLANTIC MONTHLY COMPANY

EXCERPTS FROM THE BALANCE SHEET OF APRIL 30, 1963

ASSETS

Current assets:

Cash and investments*............................		$ 251,416
Accounts receivable:		
Advertisers...................................$108,715		
Subscribers.................................... 51,020		
Other... 10,832		
Reserve for uncollected accounts................. (3,000)		167,567
Inventories:		
Paper.......................................$102,513		
Manuscripts.................................. 39,647		
Other... 13,991		156,151
Advances to authors.............................		18,186
Prepaid expenses................................		21,981
Total current assets...........................		$ 615,301
Fixed assets:		
Office equipment and leasehold improvements (net)		60,839
Sundry assets.....................................		32,754
Intangible assets:		
Deferred circulation costs.........................		391,313
Total assets..............................		$1,100,207

LIABILITIES AND CAPITAL

Current liabilities:		
Accounts payable...............................		$ 110,624
Accrued federal income tax........................		87,000
Other accruals..................................		39,939
Total current liabilities.......................		$ 237,563
Deferred credits to future operations:		
Unearned magazine subscriptions..................$784,916		
Deferred federal income tax...................... 77,727		862,643
Capital stock and retained earnings*.................		1
Total liabilities and capital................		$1,100,207

* Certain asset and liability accounts not pertaining to magazine operations have been eliminated, and the balances of the Cash and Investments and Capital Stock and Retained Earnings accounts have been modified in order to avoid the disclosure of confidential information.

TABLE 4. THE ATLANTIC MONTHLY COMPANY

MANUFACTURING AND DISTRIBUTION COSTS, 1959–63

Line	Items	Lines Used in Computations	1963	1962	1961	1960	1959
					Twelve Months Ended April 30		
1	Number of pages printed during year:						
2	Saddle text		834	782	729	685	740
3	Department text		336	330	306	300	262
4	Paid advertising		584	498	567	507	429
5	Other advertising		32	31	24	46	31
6	Total		1,786	1,641	1,626	1,538	1,462
7							
8	Number of copies printed per issue	23 + 29	327,905	329,653	323,483	313,675	310,705
9							
10	Paper cost for the 12 months:						
11	Text pages		$230,026	$233,580	$216,634	$189,100	$187,235
12	Cost per M pages	11 ÷ [(2 + 3) × 8]	0.600	0.637	0.647	0.612	0.601
13	Advertising pages		137,475	129,224	142,363	118,306	95,450
14	Cost per M pages	13 ÷ [(4 + 5) × 8]	0.681	0.741	0.745	0.682	0.668
15							
16	Printing cost for the 12 months:						
17	Text pages		$180,276	$174,469	$152,699	$138,953	$135,639
18	Cost per M impressions	17 ÷ [(2 + 3) × 8]	0.470	0.476	0.456	0.450	0.436
19	Advertising pages		168,611	156,891	149,422	118,533	90,198
20	Cost per M impressions	19 ÷ [(4 + 5) × 8]	0.835	0.900	0.782	0.683	0.631
21							
22	Mailing subscriber copies:						
23	No. of copies mailed (12 mo. av.)		235,707	244,414	244,588	233,929	229,385
24	Cost of mailing text pages		$ 57,656	$ 57,110	$ 47,892	$ 43,248	$ 38,318
25	Cost per subscription year	24 ÷ 23	0.245	0.234	0.196	0.185	0.167
26	Cost per M text pages	25 ÷ (2 + 3)	0.209	0.210	0.189	0.188	0.167
27							
28	Newsstand distribution costs:						
29	No. of copies distributed (12 mo. av.)		92,198	85,239	78,895	79,746	81,320
30	Cost of shipping pages		$ 25,990	$ 23,123	$ 19,296	$ 18,239	$ 16,171
31	Cost per 12 copies	30 ÷ 29	0.282	0.271	0.245	0.229	0.199
32	Cost per M text pages	31 ÷ (2 + 3)	0.241	0.244	0.237	0.232	0.199
33							
34	Advertising distribution costs:						
35	Cost of mailing & shipping ad. pages		$ 74,851	$ 70,802	$ 71,247	$ 58,590	$ 47,733
36	Cost per M pages	35 ÷ [(4 + 5) × 8]	0.371	0.406	0.373	0.338	0.334

Exhibit 5

THE ATLANTIC MONTHLY COMPANY

EDITORIAL AND ADVERTISING STATISTICS, 1959–63

Line	Item	Lines Used in Computations	Twelve Months Ended April 30				
			1963	1962	1961	1960	1959
1	Number of pages printed during year:						
2	Saddle text.........		834	782	729	685	740
3	Department text......		336	330	306	300	262
4	Paid advertising........		584	498	567	507	429
5	Other advertising.......		32	31	24	46	31
6	Total........		1,786	1,641	1,626	1,538	1,462
7							
8	Editorial costs for 12 months:						
9	Cost of manuscripts..........		$136,662	$131,226	$106,825	$102,376	$101,595
10	Cost/page of saddle text....	9 ÷ 2	164	168	147	149	137
11	Cost/page of total text......	9 ÷ (2 + 3)	117	118	103	104	101
12	Salaries and overhead costs...		169,985	157,693	168,414	146,608	137,147
13	Total editorial costs......	9 + 12	306,647	288,919	275,239	248,984	238,742
14	Cost/page of text......	13 ÷ (2 + 3)	262	260	266	253	238
15							
16	Advertising revenue and expense:						
17	Total advertising revenue......		$1,024,067	$856,387	$932,404	$745,356	$587,735
18	Average revenue/page......	17 ÷ 4	1,754	1,720	1,644	1,470	1,370
19	Average paid circulation/issue...		271,471	277,824	271,924	265,420	261,002
20	Average revenue/page/M paid...	18 ÷ 19	$ 6.46	$ 6.19	$ 6.05	$ 5.54	$ 5.25
21	Commissions to *Harper's-Atlantic*.		320,054	284,841	296,528	274,740	227,182
22	Cost/page of advertising sold...	21 ÷ 4	548	572	523	542	530
23	% of advertising revenue.......	21 ÷ 17	31.3%	33.3%	31.8%	36.9%	38.7%
24	Other promotion costs:						
25	Cash discounts (2%)........		$ 19,668	$ 16,579	$ 18,749	$ 14,106	$ 11,269
26	Salaries and overhead......		27,910	28,507	26,490	18,001	5,199
27	Total promotion costs......	21 + 25 + 26	367,632	329,927	341,767	306,847	243,650
28	Cost/page of advertising sold...	27 ÷ 4	630	663	603	605	568
29	% of advertising revenue......	27 ÷ 17	35.9%	38.5%	36.7%	41.2%	41.5%

CIRCULATION STATISTICS, 1959–63

Line	Item	Lines Used in Computations	Twelve Months Ended April 30				
			1963	1962	1961	1960	1959
1	Newsstand circulation:						
2	Cover price at year-end		$ 0.75	$ 0.75	$ 0.60*	$ 0.60*	$ 0.60*
3	Distribution/issue (12 mo. av.)		92,198	85,239	78,895	79,746	81,320
4	Sales/issue		52,230	52,893	46,557	45,438	47,390
5	Net revenue during year†		$ 249,716	$ 240,350	$ 194,564	$ 202,659	$ 204,024
6	Average revenue/12 copies sold	5 ÷ 4	$ 4.78	$ 4.54	$ 4.18	$ 4.46	$ 4.31
7							
8	Subscription circulation:						
9	One year regular rate at year-end		$ 8.50	$ 8.50	$ 7.50	$ 7.50	$ 7.50
10	Paid circulation/issue (12 mo. av.)		219,241	224,931	225,367	219,982	213,612
11	Sub. revenue recognized during year		$1,080,349	$1,058,565	$1,036,243	$1,026,410	$1,004,694
12	Average revenue/subscription year	11 ÷ 10	$ 4.93	$ 4.71	$ 4.60	$ 4.67	$ 4.70
13							
14	Combined circulation:						
15	Total circulation revenue	5 + 11	$1,330,065	$1,298,915	$1,230,807	$1,229,069	$1,208,718
16	Paid circulation/issue (12 mo. av.)	4 + 10	271,471	277,824	271,924	265,420	261,002
17	Average revenue/12 copies sold	15 ÷ 16	$ 4.90	$ 4.68	$ 4.53	$ 4.63	$ 4.63
18							
19	Subscription promotion costs:						
20	Promotion costs written off		$ 437,754	$ 408,154	$ 405,149	$ 351,155	$ 326,516
21	Costs/subscription year (paid)	20 ÷ 10	2.00	1.81	1.80	1.60	1.53
22							
23	Subscription fulfillment costs:						
24	Total fulfillment costs		$ 117,580	$ 117,615	$ 113,046	$ 112,704	$ 113,292
25	Costs/subscription year (paid)	24 ÷ 10	0.54	0.52	0.50	0.51	0.53
26							
27	Newsstand promotion activities:						
28	Total promotion costs		$ 29,211	$ 31,941	$ 35,086	$ 29,081	$ 21,863
29	Promotion costs/12 copies sold	28 ÷ 4	0.56	0.60	0.75	0.64	0.46
30							
31	Net circulation revenue:						
32	Newsstand net revenue	5 − 28	$ 220,505	$ 208,409	$ 159,478	$ 173,578	$ 182,161
33	Net/12 copies sold	32 ÷ 4	4.22	3.94	3.43	3.82	3.84
34	Subscription net revenue	11 − (24 + 20)	525,015	532,796	518,048	562,551	564,886
35	Net/subscription year (paid)	34 ÷ 10	2.39	2.38	2.30	2.56	2.64

* One issue during the year carried a cover price of $1.

† Taken from the accounting records. This figure does not reflect the lag in giving credit for returns of unsold copies.

CONDON LEATHER COMPANY

In the fall of 1938, executives of the Condon Leather Company reexamined the basis of allocating costs to its two products, counters and innersoles. Some of the executives believed that the method then being used resulted in inaccurate cost figures which led to unsound pricing and purchase policy. Other executives contended that the current method yielded figures which were reasonably accurate, and that the difficulties in which the company then found itself were the result of misinterpretation of the figures, rather than the figures themselves.

Counters were the leather forms fitted on the inside of the heel of a shoe, and their manufacture was a specialty in which the company had acquired the reputation of doing unusually good work. Counters were the main product of the company. Because of its ability to produce a superior product, it had been able to secure a slight differential in price, even in a highly competitive market. There were two distinct types of counters, the flat and the molded, and within these two types there existed a large variety of styles, grades, and patterns. The flat type was shaped and fitted during the manufacture of a shoe and in general was used only in higher grades of shoes because additional labor was involved in fabricating the shoe. Molded counters were molded in the shape of a heel. They varied in quality, depending both upon material and workmanship, and were used in a wide range of shoes.

Innersoles required no forming; they were made simply by cutting out leather in various sizes and putting these pieces through an inexpensive finishing operation. They were manufactured by a large number of companies, and this fact had an important bearing on the question of cost allocation. There were approximately 12 grades of innersoles; the grade depended on the quality of the leather used and the nature of the finishing operation.

Raw Material

A hide varies in texture considerably in its different parts (see Exhibit 1). Hides also differ in quality within a given lot, in spite of

102

grading. The lack of uniformity of raw material leads to a variety of grades for the finished products and restricts the manufacture of some products to certain parts. Thus, only the belly centers were used by the company in manufacturing its leading product, counters. The leather here was of proper quality, satisfactory in thickness and neither too tough nor too flexible. Usually, the company purchased entire bellies which included, in addition to the belly center, the flank, shanks, and shins. These sections could not be cut into counters and were therefore either cut into innersoles or were resold without processing, depending upon market conditions. Under certain conditions, other parts of the hide, such as the butt, shoulder, or neck, were purchased and cut into innersoles.

Belly centers were rarely purchased separately. Tanners typically separated the entire belly from the bend and shoulder, but did not cut it into parts. It was possible to purchase centers from leather dealers, but the cost was ordinarily higher than the net cost of belly centers obtained from entire bellies, taking into account the amount that could be realized by reselling the other parts. Even the belly center could not be completely used for the manufacturer of counters; some parts of it had to be cut into innersoles.

One or more of the following courses of action could be followed at any one time, depending on the price of leather, the price of the various parts of the hide (centers, shanks, etc.), which did not necessarily vary in proportion to the price of leather, and the price of counters and innersoles:

a) Purchase entire bellies; cut the centers into counters and innersoles, and the remainder into innersoles.

b) Purchase entire bellies; cut the centers into counters and innersoles, and sell the shanks, flanks, and shins without processing.

c) Purchase belly centers alone, and cut them into counters and innersoles.

d) Purchase other parts of the hide and cut them into innersoles.

e) In connection with any of the above, hold either the counters or the innersoles, or both, in inventory in anticipation of a higher market price. Usually, however, counters were made only after orders for them had been received, and innersoles would thus be the only product held in inventory.

In connection with all of these alternatives, matters of utilization of plant capacity, customer relations, and working capital position were important considerations.

Allocation of Belly Cost to Sections

When parts of the hide, such as the shoulder or neck, were purchased for the purpose of making innersoles, it was a simple matter to allocate cost to the product, since the material "cost" of a lot of inner-soles was simply the cost of the leather used less the amount received from the sales of scraps. But when complete bellies were purchased, it was difficult to decide how much of the cost should be allocated to centers from which the counters were cut, and how much should be allocated to the other sections, which could either be sold without processing or cut into innersoles.

In costing, the company used a procedure which was in a sense a by-product approach but which overcame certain of the disadvantages inherent in the pure by-product method. Raw material costs were as-signed to all sections of the belly except the centers; these costs were set at an arbitrary amount (e.g., 1 cent per pound) less than the current market price of the section. The total of these costs was then subtracted from the total cost of the lot, and the remainder of the cost of the lot was allocated to counters. To illustrate this method, assume that a lot of 500 pounds of bellies was bought for 13 cents per pound, a total cost of $65. The lot was cut into hind shanks, fore shanks, flanks, and centers as shown below. The assumed quantities cut, market prices, per pound allowances, and values allocated to the sections were as follows:

Section	Pounds	Market	Allowance	Net Value
Hind shanks	150	$0.12	$0.010	$16.50
Fore shanks	110	0.09	0.005	9.35
Flanks	60	0.08	0.005	4.50
	320			$30.35

Total cost of lot....................................$65.00
Values assigned to parts as above...................... 30.35
Assumed cost of centers ($34.65 divided by 180 [pounds of centers cut] results in cost of $0.1925 per pound for centers)..$34.65

The cost of labor in cutting and the standard departmental burden charge based on labor cost were charged entirely to the centers.

This arbitrary allowance resulted in a "standard" profit for the sections sold (assuming them to be sold before a change in leather prices) or a standard reduction in the cost of the raw material if the section was to be used in the manufacture of innersoles. Profits made in this manner were considered operating income, not a reduction in the cost of manufacturing counters.

Allocating Costs to Products

It was a relatively simple matter to determine the cost of innersoles made from shanks, shins, and flanks, once the "cost" of the raw material had been determined by the method described above. Costs were collected for each production lot, and consisted of direct material, direct labor, and a standard burden charge (a certain amount per pair) less the value of scrap material. The unit cost was determined by dividing the total cost of the lot by the number of good pairs produced. No attempt was made to assign different costs to the different sizes and grades of innersoles which made up any single lot.

When both counters and innersoles were cut from the same lot of material, as was the case with belly centers, the costs of the lot had to be allocated to the two products on an arbitrary basis. It was the practice to divide the material costs on the basis of the relative weight of the completed products. Labor costs were divided on a per-pair basis, on the assumption that it took as much time and skill to cut the innersoles as it did the counters; all cutters were paid on an hourly basis. Overhead costs were allocated by means of the standard per-pair charge.

Situation in 1938

It was the practice of the company not to cut counters until an order had been received at a price high enough to cover material costs, costs of conversion, and a reasonable profit. Throughout 1936 and 1937, the company had been able to adhere to this policy and still get a reasonable volume of business. But the production of counters was always accompanied by the production of a certain number of innersoles cut from the same belly centers, and it had become increasingly difficult to sell these innersoles at a price above their computed cost. Every effort was made to cut the maximum number of counters from the belly centers, but certain parts of the belly center were not of a suitable quality for counters and had to be cut into innersoles to get any good out of them. Consequently, for nearly two years, an increasing number of innersoles was carried in inventory. By the fall of 1938, the inventory investment was so large that it threatened to impair the working capital of the company It was evident that action would have to be taken.

The treasurer placed the blame on the cost accounting system. He asserted that the company had actually been selling counters at a loss in that it had allocated too much of the cost to innersoles and not enough to counters. Since belly centers were cut primarily to obtain counters, he advocated costing by the "pure" by-product method. Under this method counters would be charged with all costs less whatever could be obtained by selling innersoles, sections, and scrap at the current market price. The sales manager stated that this proposal would result in a price for counters which was much higher than that for which they could be sold under current market conditions. To this objection the treasurer countered that the emergency situation could be met by eliminating part or all of the overhead charge from the cost computations, reducing cost to approximately market price.

The factory manager opposed any change in the cost accounting system. He argued that the disposition of the innersole inventory was a matter of business, not of cost accounting. In his opinion the cost accounting system should yield consistently accurate costs for their purpose, and the current price situation should be met by the intelligent consideration of all factors, of which past cost was only one, rather than by seeking for an answer in juggling the figures.

Questions

1. What position would you have taken toward the disposition of the innersole inventories?

2. Try to frame general "costing" policies to govern the future buying, manufacturing, and selling decisions of the company.

Exhibit 1

CONDON LEATHER COMPANY
PARTS OF SIDE OF SOLE LEATHER

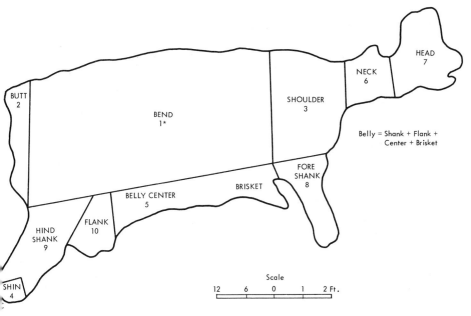

* Figures indicate relative texture; No. 1 equals highest quality, No. 2 next, etc.

Chapter 2
SHORT-RUN COST MINIMIZATION

Product-creating costs are frequently used to evaluate the financial implications of alternative courses of action. As we have seen in the previous chapter, historical data about product costs may be an important source of information in preparing a conditional estimate of future product costs. But a conditional analysis, which recognizes explicitly that management's decisions can influence the future, must use a somewhat different definition of "cost" than the one used by the accountant in accumulating historical data. This broader concept which economists call "opportunity cost" will be discussed in this chapter in terms of one simple class of problems. Opportunity cost, as defined briefly in Chapter 1, is the value of a particular resource measured in terms of the return it could earn if it were used in the best possible way.

The unique aspect of the concept of opportunity cost is the idea that the cost of any resource is determined by its "value in use"; if the resource cannot be used productively by someone, its opportunity cost is zero no matter how much was paid to acquire it. Most resources, however, can be used in some way, and because such resources are scarce, a resource usually has a value in use. The value of a resource in its *best* use is called its opportunity cost because if the resource is used in some other way, its owner foregoes the opportunity of receiving the highest possible return that he could have received and, in effect, incurs a penalty by misusing the resource. The concept is not very difficult to apply in the case of individual types of resources, but its application becomes complex in business situations which commonly involve a combination of resources.

Types of Resources

The basic resource of business is money, or perhaps more precisely, the power that money has in our society to command the primary resources, the labor provided by men and the materials provided by nature. Money by itself is powerless, however, without a manager or entrepreneur to decide how to put it to work. Even then, capital does not become productive until it is exchanged for more tangible resources than imagination: labor, raw materials, and combinations of labor and materials in the form of products manufactured by other business. In the "raw" state, as money, the wise utilization of resources is difficult; it becomes even more difficult once the money resource has been exchanged for a wide variety of heterogeneous resources, each with a specialized productive capability.

An operating business possesses a variety of resources in addition to money: a building which is adaptable to a greater or lesser variety of uses, equipment which can be used to produce a range of products with varying degrees of efficiency, and employees whose productive skills may embrace a broad spectrum. At first glance, the problem of allocating physical resources might not seem vastly different from that of allocating money. All of these resources have been purchased with money, and their values can be measured in monetary terms. Why, then, did Henry J. Kaiser, a man with adequate capital resources and a reputation as an efficient shipbuilder during World War II, fail in his attempt to establish a new line of passenger cars in the late 1940s? It is not an easy task to convert raw capital into an efficient combination of productive resources. And the converse is also true: It is very difficult to measure the value of an existing set of productive resources in monetary terms.

In the "long run," money is the basic business resource. But business decisions are made in the short run, and money, the best available common denominator for all resources, is an imperfect yardstick. At the core of the broad problem of resource allocation, therefore, is the problem of measurement. Actually, the measurement problem can usefully be broken into two parts for purposes of analysis: (1) what types of resources will be required in order to carry out each course of action being considered? and (2) what is the value (or cost) of the combination of resources required for each alternative? We shall discuss some of the aspects of these questions in the remainder of this chapter.

Classification of Problems

As a practical matter, businessmen rarely refer to their problems as problems in resource allocation. Rather, they say, "I've got a make-or-buy problem," or a "capital expenditure problem," or a "pricing problem," and so forth. This "specific problem" orientation is not necessarily due to a failure to recognize the resource allocation characteristic of the problem—it is simply an attempt to find a practical way to begin the analysis that will eventually lead to a decision.

Dividing business decisions into problem categories has two advantages:

1. From his prior experience with similar problems in the past, the businessman may have observed the kinds of resources that typically are involved in the evaluation of alternatives, and may be familiar with some of the most common problems in measuring the cost of the resources required. Categorizing the problem facilitates making maximum use of this experience.

2. Some types of problems may be best resolved using analytical techniques that have been developed specifically for that class of problems. Identifying the type of problem thus serves to identify the techniques which may aid in the solution.

There is a danger, too, in the classification of business problems: the danger of a closed mind that can only follow familiar decision patterns used in the past rather than searching imaginatively for new and better ways to grapple with the problems of today and tomorrow.

The three main parts of this book are organized by problem classification in order to secure the advantages listed above. The remainder of this chapter will deal with the simplest class of decisions, a class sometimes referred to as "cost minimization" problems because it is concerned with decisions in which the objective is to determine the least costly method of accomplishing a given end.

Formulating the Problem

In order to illustrate some of the most common problems of cost analysis, let us examine the decision process in a simple example. The Webber Company manufactures industrial equipment in a small plant with 50 employees. A recent increase in orders has taxed the one-shift capacity of the plant, and management can see that the company will fail to meet its delivery schedules unless some action is taken. What should be done?

The first step in analyzing this problem, and the most important step by far, is to determine the alternative courses of action that might solve the problem. The list is longer than one might first suppose. There are three main types of actions which might be taken: restricting the quantity sold to the present capacity of the plant; increasing the plant capacity on a permanent or semipermanent basis; or increasing capacity on a temporary basis. Under each of these broad headings, further actions can be identified, as the list below demonstrates.

1. Restricting the quantity sold by—
   a) Refusing to accept orders in excess of present plant capacity.
   b) Accepting all orders and apologizing to customers when deliveries are late.
   c) Raising prices enough to reduce volume of orders down to present plant capacity.
2. Increasing plant capacity by—
   a) Building an addition to the present plant.
   b) Operating the present plant on two shifts.
3. Providing temporary capacity by—
   a) Using overtime.
   b) Buying some components from another manufacturer rather than making them.

This initial stage of formulating the problem is vital to wise decision making. It is a waste of time to do a careful analysis of three alternatives and to select the best of the three if a fourth course of action which is far better is completely overlooked. Analysis is no substitute for imagination. A few extra minutes devoted exclusively to the preparation of an exhaustive list of alternatives will nearly always be time well spent.

So that the exhaustive list does not become exhausting, the next (and sometimes simultaneous) step in problem formulation is to select those alternatives that merit further investigation. Several alternatives on Webber Company's list may be eliminated in this screening process. Items 1 (*a*) and 1 (*c*) would have the effect of reducing the demands placed on the factory. If the company had long-run growth in sales volume as one of its objectives, these two actions might be rejected as incompatible with the goal. Even if the company's only goal were "maximization of long-run profits" (as we will usually assume, in the absence of a specific statement of goals), alternative 1 (*a*) is not acceptable if the additional product could be produced profitably. The profit effect of raising prices is more difficult to assess. In the next chapter we will discuss how to evaluate alternatives involving price changes; for the moment let us simply assume that we are interested in determining the best course of action at the present price in order to compare it with the results obtainable at a higher price.

Alternative 1 (*b*) might appear attractive as a method of accepting the available orders without incurring additional production costs. Evaluation of this alternative should, however, recognize that it involves the consumption of an intangible business resource, customer "goodwill." Depending upon competition and normal trade practices in Webber's industry, it may be that stretching out of delivery schedules is the best solution to the problem. In most industries, however, this practice might be a costly one, and we will eliminate it from further consideration here.

The remaining four alternatives are ways to provide increased production in order to meet the increased demand. It is difficult to reject any of these solutions based only on a cursory analysis. It may be useful, however, to realize that there are major differences in type and magnitude of the resources required for each course of action. Expanding the plant or adding a second shift will cause significant changes in Webber's fixed costs as well as in its productive capacity. A plant addition is permanent and involves a special set of considerations to be discussed in Part III. Even a second shift is a semipermanent action that involves hiring new supervisors as well as laborers, and may require a heavy expenditure of the vital *management* resource. Neither of these two actions would be wise unless Webber's management believed that the increase in demand was a relatively permanent one.

As a temporary solution to their problem, therefore, Webber's management might decide to narrow their analysis to a choice between alternatives 3(a) and 3(b), the use of overtime in the plant or the purchase of some components from outside vendors. The selection of either of these solutions can easily be changed in the future, and a few months from now management may be in a better position to assess the permanence of the current spurt in demand.

The final stage in formulating the problem is now at hand. How shall we evaluate the alternatives that we have decided to examine? What is the criterion on which we shall make our decision? A careful restatement of the problem at this point may help us to see the best way to point our subsequent analysis. It is little help at this point to say that we have a problem in resource allocation. It may be of more use to define the problem as "fulfilling our production requirements while minimizing the consumption of our resources." The businessman would say simply, "Which parts, if any, would it be cheaper to buy outside?"

In situations such as this where the decision has no revenue implications (we have already decided to accept all orders and deliver them on time), the best course of action is the one that costs the least. Realizing that we are equating "cost" with "resource consumption," therefore, we may say that our decision rule will be to choose the "least cost" alternative, and we may then turn our attention to measuring the cost of pursuing each course of action.

RELEVANT COSTS

Before we can begin a detailed analysis, we will need a more precise statement of the alternatives. For this purpose, we will assume that the anticipated capacity problem will arise only in the machining department of the Webber Company. Normally this department does the machining of all the component parts in the Webber product. Most of the parts are produced in small lots and require specialized skills not possessed by many outside vendors. Two parts, however, are produced in rather large quantities, and the machining operations on them are routine. Clearly these parts are the best candidates for outside purchase. If they were purchased outside, the machining department would have no trouble making all the remaining components on schedule.

Having identified the alternatives, we must next determine the resources required to execute them. According to engineering estimates, the production of one unit of part A requires raw materials costing $3 and a half hour of the time of a machine operator, while the production of one unit of part B requires $8 of raw materials and one hour of operator time. The purchasing agent, after checking with several vendors, informs us that the Smithy Corporation, a reliable source, will deliver part A for $4.50 each and part B for $11.50 each.

The next step is to determine the cost of the resources required. Earlier we referred to the different cost concepts used by accountants and economists and we argued that the economist's notion of opportunity cost is more appropriate for decision making than the accountant's notion of acquisition cost. Accounting records provide a useful source of cost data, however, and so we will begin by presenting the costs of the alternatives to the Webber Company as its accountants might prepare them; then we will indicate how these accounting costs must be analyzed and modified to reflect opportunity costs.

Accounting Costs

After being supplied with the list of resources required as given above, the accounting department of the Webber Company provides the following schedule of manufacturing costs:

	Cost per Unit	
	Part A	Part B
Prime cost:		
Raw materials	$3.00	$ 8.00
Direct labor @ $2/hour	1.00	2.00
Total prime costs	$4.00	$10.00
Factory overhead @ 100% of labor	1.00	2.00
Normal manufacturing cost	$5.00	$12.00
Overtime premium @ 50% of labor	0.50	1.00
Overtime manufacturing cost	$5.50	$13.00

The accounting department explains its calculations as follows. The purchase of raw materials is, of course, a direct out-of-pocket cost. The machine operators are paid $2 per hour, and this rate is applied to the time requirements to arrive at the direct labor cost. Production of the parts would also require the use of certain common resources of the company: plant, equipment, supervision, and the like. The acquisition costs of these resources allocated to the machining department are given in Table 2–1. Because total allocated overhead costs are equal to total direct labor costs, a charge of 100% of direct labor is made to cover these overhead costs. Finally, if work were done on overtime, an additional cost of 50% of direct labor would be incurred for overtime premium pay.

If we look at accounting costs, therefore, both parts are apparently cheaper to buy from Smithy than to produce in our own plant—even ignoring the premium paid for overtime work! But we must take a closer look at the behavior of manufacturing costs. Analysis of the over-

Table 2–1

WEBBER COMPANY

MONTHLY BUDGET FOR MACHINING DEPARTMENT

Direct labor (2,000 hours @ $2)	$4,000
Overhead:	
Indirect labor—materials handling	$ 300
Department foreman	400
Payroll taxes, vacation and holiday pay, pension contributions, and other fringe benefits	900
Heat, light, and power	250
Shop supplies	150
Depreciation of machinery	800
Repairs and maintenance—machinery	600
Allocated share of plantwide costs (superintendent, building depreciation and maintenance, property taxes and insurance, watchman, etc.)	600
Total overhead	$4,000

head costs listed in Table 2–1, for example, might reveal the following facts about the behavior of overhead costs under two circumstances: (*a*) at present volume if one man is laid off and parts are purchased outside and (*b*) at the anticipated increased volume if overtime is used.

1. *Indirect Labor.* One man is employed as a materials handler in the department. If a machinist were laid off there would be no saving in the wages paid to this man; he would just be a little less busy. If the department worked overtime, however, the materials handling function would have to be performed by someone, either the machinist himself (thereby lowering his productive efficiency) or by the materials handler also working overtime.

2. *Department Foreman.* This cost probably would not vary with either a small decrease or small increase in production. The machining work to be performed on overtime might not require the presence of a supervisor; if it did, the overtime paid to the supervisor would be relevant.

3. *Payroll Taxes, etc.* These costs amount to nearly 20% of Webber's expenses for labor and supervision. If a man were laid off, the entire 20% might be saved. There would be some increase in these costs on overtime, but the workers would not get more holidays or longer vacations. The variable portion, using overtime, might be 10% of the labor cost.

4. *Heat, Light, Power, and Shop Supplies.* These costs are difficult to analyze. There might be an insignificant saving in power if one machine were shut down. On overtime, additional power and light would be required.

5. *Depreciation.* This cost is not a cash expenditure but a pro rata portion of the original cost of the equipment. This cost, caused simply by the passage of time, will not be changed by management's decision to either lay off a man or use overtime.

6. *Repairs and Maintenance.* This expense is made up of two components: routine, preventive maintenance and the repair of breakdowns. The former is the larger expense, and might be reduced somewhat if one machine were shut down completely. The latter probably bears some relationship to the volume of work put through the equipment and would vary for either a decrease or increase in production.

7. *Allocated Plant Costs.* These overhead costs occur at the next higher level in the company, and would not change as a result of a minor change in production volume in the department.

We may now recapitulate the results of our analysis. Direct labor seems to be a useful measure of volume in this department because each man operates one machine and costs that vary in relation to machine utilization will also vary with labor costs. In Table 2–2, therefore, we have computed the direct overhead cost for each of the two circumstances mentioned above (laying off one man or using overtime).

How variable are overhead costs? The preceding analysis illustrates how difficult it is to answer that question in a practical way. It seems

Table 2–2

WEBBER COMPANY

OVERHEAD COST ANALYSIS

| Overhead Item | —Monthly Budget Cost— | | Variable Cost as a Percent of —Direct Labor Cost Change If— | |
	Amount	Percent of Direct Labor	One Man Laid Off	Overtime Used
Indirect labor—materials handler.......$	300	7.5	...	7.5
Department foreman...................	400	10.0	...	...
Payroll taxes, etc.....................	900	22.5*	19.1	10.8
Heat, light, and power...............	250	6.2	1.0	2.0
Shop supplies.......................	150	3.8	...	...
Depreciation of machinery.............	800	20.0	...	...
Repairs and maintenance.............	600	15.0	12.0	5.0
Allocated plant costs.................	600	15.0	...	...
Total........................$	4,000	100.0	32.1	25.3

* Stated as a percentage of total departmental payroll, this cost is $\frac{900}{4,700} = 19.1\%$. On overtime, it is estimated here that direct payroll taxes would be 10% of wage costs but would also apply to the materials handler (10% of 7.5%).

safe to say that overhead is not completely variable, as might be inferred from the accountant's allocation mechanism. Saving $1 in labor cost will not save $1 in overhead in the machining department. But any further general statement about overhead variability is useless. For decision-making purposes, the most useful answer is one based on an analysis of the specific cost items in the specific situation in which a specific decision is to be made. Fortunately, it is possible to gain skill in this kind of analysis, with a concomitant reduction in the analytical time required. This is a skill worth developing, because reliance on rules of thumb or general cost variability classifications is a poor, and sometimes dangerous, substitute for such skill.

Opportunity Costs

The accountant measures the cost of resources consumed in terms of the outlay originally made to acquire them. The economist, in contrast, measures their cost in relation to alternative opportunities for their employment. Let us see how these two concepts differ in the Webber Company example.

On some costs, the accountant and the economist would agree. This would probably be true, for example, of the cost of buying the parts from the Smithy Corporation or the cost of the raw materials if the parts are manufactured. In these cases, the foregone opportunity is to refrain from buying the parts or the raw material so that the opportunity cost and the acquisition cost would be identical.

It might seem, in fact, that opportunity cost is identical with the accounting concept of direct cost. While there is a close relationship between opportunity cost and direct cost and while they are often identical, there are important differences which must be borne in mind.

We can illustrate this point using the direct labor cost in the company example. The company employs 11 machinists in the machining department; approximately 2,000 hours of production labor are available each month. Before the company's anticipated sales volume increase, these men spent about 1,550 hours per month on machining the special, low-volume parts and used the balance of their time, as available, to turn out parts A and B. Forgetting for the moment about the increase in volume, how would you decide whether or not to have parts A and B made by Smithy? Are the labor costs true opportunity costs? The answer depends on what action Webber's management would take if the parts were purchased outside. A total of 450 labor hours could be saved. Would $2\frac{1}{2}$ machinists be laid off? Such action might mean reducing the range of skills now available in an 11-man force, and might cause morale problems for the man working a short week. If, in fact, only one man would be laid off, then we should not say that the entire labor cost used in producing the parts is an opportunity cost of the parts. The relevant cost in this situation is the *total* amount of money that will be spent for labor under each course of action. If labor costs $2 per hour, the cost would be $4,000 if both parts are manufactured inside and about $3,660 if one man is laid off and some parts were purchased. Although Webber's accountant would say that $900 is spent each month on machining labor for parts A and B, the *opportunity cost* of that labor is only $340. The other $560 is perhaps best conceived of as a "capacity-creating" cost; it is spent primarily to maintain a balanced labor force with the necessary variety of skills—skills that may be a vital resource in Webber's overall success.

On the other hand, now that the demand for Webber's product is expected to increase, what is the relevant labor cost in deciding whether to use overtime to meet the requirements? With a 10% increase in demand, 1,705 hours per month are needed for low-volume parts and 495 hours of machining are needed for parts A and B. Hiring a twelfth man might provide most of the 200 extra hours needed, but there is no room in the plant for another machine. If overtime is used, the additional labor will cost $3 per hour, or $600. This cost is relevant to the decision because its expenditure depends upon the course of action management selects.

Even in the relatively simple case of direct labor, therefore, opportunity cost is not necessarily identical with direct cost. In the example just considered, opportunity cost was less than direct cost, but the reverse could also be true, as we will demonstrate shortly. While the acquisition cost of fixed resources (i.e., the fixed overhead) is neither a direct cost nor an opportunity cost, there may be an opportunity cost associated with employing these facilities in one use rather than in an alternative. This opportunity cost is relevant in making decisions regarding the use of the fixed resources, although it is not an acquisition cost.

Opportunity cost, then, depends upon the context of a particular decision whereas direct cost does not. The two concepts are similar enough to create both an advantage and a danger: an advantage in that direct cost can often be used to estimate opportunity cost; a danger in that this process can be carried farther than appropriate.

COMPARISON OF ALTERNATIVES

After the problem has been formulated and the relevant costs determined, the next step in the analysis of a decision problem is to recapitulate the results of our analysis to determine which alternative is least costly. If the problem has been formulated properly and the cost analysis done systematically, this ranking task is a simple one. Illustrative calculations for the Webber Company's make-or-buy decisions are shown in Tables 2–3, and 2–4.

Table 2–3 is an evaluation of the alternatives that faced Webber under its "normal" demand conditions, that is, before the anticipated increase in demand. As a result of our analysis, the most promising alternatives have now been more sharply defined. Only one man would be laid off if any parts were purchased outside, eliminating 170 labor hours per month. If this were done, Webber would then have to buy outside either 340 units of A or 170 units of B. In terms of total costs, the best alternative is to continue to manufacture all our requirements inside. The only difficult cost calculation is the overhead cost. If all parts were made inside, the labor and overhead budgets would be unchanged at $4,000 each per month. If one man were laid off, labor cost would decline by $340 and the overhead budget would fall by 32.1% of that amount (Table 2–2).

An alternative analysis in Table 2–3 arrives at the same conclusion

Table 2–3

WEBBER COMPANY

MAKE-OR-BUY ANALYSIS

CONDITION NO. 1: NORMAL DEMAND

	Make 500 Units of A and 200 of B	—Lay Off One Machinist and— Buy 340 Units of A	Buy 170 Units of B
Raw material costs:			
Part A	$ 1,500	$ 480	$ 1,500
Part B	1,600	1,600	240
Purchased parts	...	1,530	1,955
Direct labor	4,000	3,660	3,660
Overhead costs	4,000	3,891	3,891
Total cost	$11,100	$11,161	$11,246

ALTERNATIVE ANALYSIS

	Opportunity Cost of —Manufacturing— Part A	Part B
Raw material costs	$ 3.00	$ 8.00
Direct labor—one man	1.00	2.00
Overhead at 32.1% of labor	0.32	0.64
Total opportunity cost	$ 4.32	$ 10.64
Purchase price	4.50	11.50
Saving due to manufacturing	$ 0.18	$ 0.86
Number of units produced in 170 hours	340	170
Total savings	$61.00	$146.00

in terms of opportunity costs. According to the cost accountant's statement on page 114, the "normal" cost of one unit of part A was $5. We have seen that this figure is not useful for decision-making purposes; we are interested in the opportunity cost of manufacturing part A. To measure opportunity cost, we must answer the question, "What costs (resources) will be saved if the parts are purchased outside?" For part A, we will save $3 of raw material for each unit, the labor cost of one man divided by the units he could produce, and approximately 32% in overhead costs related to labor. What costs (resources) will be required to achieve those savings? Part A must be purchased at a price of $4.50 each. The savings are less than the additional cost, indicating that outside purchase is not the cheapest course of action. It is no coincidence that the total saving due to manufacturing is equal to the difference in the total costs of the alternatives as computed in the upper part of Table 2–3.

Table 2–4 is a similar set of calculations after a 10% increase in demand. The overhead cost increase of $138 was computed in two

Table 2–4

WEBBER COMPANY

MAKE-OR-BUY ANALYSIS

CONDITION NO. 2: INCREASED DEMAND

	Use 200 Hours of Overtime; Make 550 Units of A and 200 Units of B	—Use No Overtime and— Buy 400 Units of A	Buy 200 Units of B
Raw material costs:			
Part A...........................	$ 1,650	$ 450	$ 1,650
Part B...........................	1,760	1,760	160
Purchased parts.................	.....	1,800	2,300
Direct labor—straight time........	4,400	4,000	4,000
Overhead costs..................	4,000	4,000	4,000
Overtime premium................	200	.....	.....
Overhead costs applied to premium pay...	138	.....	.....
Total cost..................	$12,148	$12,010	$12,110

ALTERNATIVE ANALYSIS

	Opportunity Cost of —Manufacturing— Part A	Part B
Raw material costs..........................	$ 3.00	$ 8.00
Direct labor—200 hours......................	1.00	2.00
Overhead at 25.3% of labor..................	0.25	0.51
Overtime premium...........................	0.50	1.00
Overhead at 18.3% of premium...............	0.09	0.18
Total opportunity cost...................	$ 4.84	$11.69
Purchase price.............................	4.50	11.50
Saving due to purchase......................	$ 0.34	$ 0.19
Number of units produced in 200 hours........	400	200
Total savings from purchase............	$138.00	$38.00

stages as follows: Variable overhead was estimated at 25.3% of labor in Table 2–2, and this percentage was applied to the $400 straight time cost of the added labor. In addition, indirect labor and payroll taxes (18.3% of labor) would vary as a function of labor cost (not time), so that percentage was applied to the $200 of overtime premium pay. The best alternative is to buy 400 units per month of part A rather than to use overtime.

We have said that most decision problems are basically problems in resource allocation. Cost analysis is used to solve these problems because money is the best common denominator for resources, and because money is the basic "scarce resource" which the business would like to utilize in an optimal fashion. In the Webber Company's overtime decision it is useful to conceive of the problem somewhat differently. The company has 2,000 hours of machining capacity available, and our analysis in Table 2–3 has shown that this capacity should not be reduced. As demand increases, Webber's real question is, "How should the 2,000 hours be allocated among the available jobs?" The special, low-volume parts are of first priority and require 1,705 of the available hours. The remaining 295 hours should be used in such a way as to maximize their value to Webber.

In Table 2–5 we have computed the contribution per labor hour

Table 2–5

WEBBER COMPANY

CALCULATION OF CONTRIBUTION PER LABOR HOUR

Hours available:

Total...		.2,000
Required for low-volume, special parts...............		.1,705
Available for parts A or B.........................		295

	Part A	Part B
Purchase price per unit...............................	$ 4.50	$11.50
Raw material cost per unit..........................	3.00	8.00
Materials savings per unit...........................	$ 1.50	$ 3.50
Number of units produced per labor hour..............	2	1
Contribution per labor hour.........................	$ 3.00	$ 3.50
Cost of adding additional labor hours:		
Labor per hour.........................$2.00		
Overhead at 25.3%..................... 0.51		
Overtime premium per hour............. 1.00		
Overhead at 18.3% of premium......... 0.18		
Total cost...........................$3.69	3.69	3.69
Excess cost per hour of making rather than buying......$ 0.69	$ 0.19	
Total excess cost for 200 hours... .... $138.00	$38.00	

that would be earned by using the available hours to manufacture part A or part B. Labor and its related overhead costs are ignored in this calculation since these costs will not change as a result of our decision. They are part of the fixed resources we desire to allocate optimally. We will spend a total of $4,000 for labor and $4,000 for overhead; our decision is to determine *how* to use this capacity. Additional cash resources are required only for materials. For every unit of part A manufactured we will pay only $3 for materials rather than $4.50 for the completed part, a saving of $1.50 per unit or $3 per labor hour. Manufacturing part B is even more attractive because we will save $3.50 per labor hour. In order to get maximum value from our scarce resource (capacity), we should manufacture all of our requirements of part B before we use any of the capacity to manufacture part A.

Next, we must decide whether it would be worthwhile to buy additional capacity by using overtime. The cost of adding capacity is $3.69 per hour (Table 2–5). Since this cost exceeds the contribution earned by the labor hours, the use of overtime is not warranted. The last calculation on Table 2–5 is proof that this method of analysis is consistent with the two methods shown in Table 2–4.

The Importance of Judgment

A final step in the decision process remains: we must test and temper our quantitative analysis against the subjective standard of "sound judgment." Analysis is a powerful tool, but not a perfect one. It is almost impossible to measure quantitatively all the ramifications of a business decision, or the measurement may be so crude that we may not have complete confidence that we will obtain the predicted results. It is usually wise, therefore, to devote a little time after the analysis is completed to viewing the problem in a broader perspective to attempt to discover any factors that have been overlooked.

Should the Webber Company use overtime? The quantitative analysis says no; such an action would cost $138 more than the best course of action of purchasing 400 units of part A each month from Smithy Corporation. Although we have had to make several estimates of the effect of overtime on our overhead costs, we might justifiably feel that our cost estimates are quite accurate. Have we failed to measure any important resource? Perhaps so. What would be the effect of overtime on the morale of the workers in the machining department? They might complain about it, but a 10% increase in their work hours would mean a 15% increase in their income. The use of overtime might create an atmosphere of purposeful activity in the department, the beehive-type "hum" that is conducive to a higher level of production efficiency. If we buy from Smithy, we pay them $1,800; if we use overtime, we pay $1,200 for raw materials but most of the remaining $738 goes into the pockets of our employees. Webber's final decision is far from a sterile one based solely on cost analysis; it will depend importantly on management's evaluation of the possible intangible benefits of overtime balanced against the additional cost of about $138 per month.

Optimal location of scarce resources is a primary task of the businessman. The Webber Company example is a simple illustration of what is involved in this task. We now turn to the discussion of a more formalized technique that can be used for accomplishing this goal under certain conditions.

PROGRAMMING OF INTERDEPENDENT ACTIVITIES

In this section we will present a systematic procedure for analyzing certain types of resource allocation problems. This procedure, called *mathematical programming,* has been developed in recent years through the combined efforts of mathematicians and economists. While a considerable amount of erudite mathematics has been employed in developing linear programming procedures and proving that they work (in the sense of leading to an optimal use of the resources), the basic steps involved are relatively elementary and can be understood intuitively on economic grounds alone. The discussion in this section will emphasize the economic rationale of linear programming rather than its mathematical aspects.

In the ensuing discussion, we will refer to resource uses as *activities* and to resource limitations as *constraints.* The problem is to determine the *level* at which each activity is to be carried on. An activity might consist, for example, of the production of a certain commodity; the level of the activity, then, would be the number of units produced. A list of the levels at which each activity is to be carried on is called a *program.* Because of the constraints, the levels at which the activities can be carried on are interdependent; for example, if the constraints consist of limited capacities of production equipment, then if more of one product is produced it might be necessary to produce less of another. For this reason, the term *programming of interdependent activities* is sometimes used to describe the resource allocation problem.

The description above is quite general. The following examples are typical of business decision problems that have been analyzed through the use of mathematical programming:

A Product Mix Problem. A company produces a variety of products each of which utilizes, in varying degrees, the various pieces of production equipment in the company's plant. The production of each product is an activity, and the levels of the activities are mutually dependent on the capacities of the equipment.

A Blending Problem. In oil refining, inputs of crude oil and a number of additives are used to produce as outputs a variety of petroleum products. The use of a particular input to produce a particular output is an activity. The quantity of each input used in the production of a given output will depend not only on the availabilities of the inputs but also on the technical specifications of the outputs.

A Shipping Problem. A product produced in several plants is distributed through a number of geographically dispersed warehouses. Each possible shipping route is an activity, and the quantities which can be shipped over each route are governed by the requirements of meeting each warehouse's demand while not exceeding any plant's capacity.

Linear and Nonlinear Programming

Mathematical programming methods have achieved their greatest success in the subclass of programming problems known as *linear programming*. In economic terms, this subclass of problems has the following characteristics:

1. The cost and/or revenues of each activity are *proportioned* to the level of the activity (resource use); that is, marginal cost and/or marginal revenue are constant.
2. For each constraint (resource limitation), the *rates of substitution* between activities are *constant*.

The meaning of these assumptions will be made more explicit later when we consider linear programming methods in more detail.

If the assumptions given above are not even approximately true, then the problem is one of *nonlinear programming*. Practical methods of solving nonlinear problems have been discovered only for some special cases. Considerable research is being done in this area by mathematicians and economists, and we may expect that an increasing proportion of programming problems will become susceptible to formal solution. In this introduction, however, we will emphasize linear programming methods.

In large-scale programming problems, the volume of calculation required makes the use of high-speed computing devices desirable if not absolutely essential. Smaller problems can, however, be solved with nothing more than pencil and paper and perhaps a pocket calculator.

THE TRANSPORTATION METHOD

Perhaps the simplest linear programming problems are those handled by the *transportation method*. This method is so called because it was first used to solve problems of the following sort: A commodity is available at six sources in predetermined quantities and is required at eight destinations, likewise in predetermined quantities; these quantities constitute the constraints. Since each source can ship to any destination, there are a total of 6 × 8 = 48 routes; these routes constitute the activities. The cost of shipping one unit of the commodity over each of the routes is given. Determine the minimum cost shipping program which satisfies the availabilities and the requirements.

While the transportation method was initially applied to transportation problems, it has subsequently developed that other classes of problems may be formulated within the same framework. A variant of the transportation method, for example, called the assignment method, is used to assign personnel to jobs according to their capabilities.

To illustrate the transportation method, however, we will use a classical shipping example. The essential details of the example are summarized in Table 2–6. There are three sources—labeled I, II, and

Table 2–6

STATEMENT OF TRANSPORTATION EXAMPLE

Sources	A	B	C	D	Total Available
	(Shipping Costs per Unit)				
I	10	15	8	20	7
II	3	2	7	15	5
III	8	11	12	18	3
Total required	4	2	3	6	15

III—of a commodity which is to be supplied to four destinations—labeled A, B, C, D. The quantities available at each source and required at each destination are given in the right and bottom margins of the table respectively, while the unit shipping costs (in dollars) over each of the 12 routes are given in the body of the table.[1]

Solution of the Problem

Initial Program. Solution of a linear programming problem, whether a transportation problem or not, is an iterative procedure starting from an arbitrarily selected initial program. There is just one restriction which must be observed in selecting an initial program in a transportation problem: the number of routes used must not be greater than $(m + n - 1)$, where m is the number of sources and n is the

[1] In this problem, the quantities available and the quantities required add to the same grand total. If this were not the case, equality could be achieved by introducing into the problem either a fictitious source (to ship the excess requirements) or a fictitious destination (to receive the excess availabilities). The cost of shipping to or from such a point is zero.

number of destinations.[2] An initial program satisfying this requirement can always be found by applying the so-called "northwest corner rule," to wit: starting with the route I-A in the "northwest corner" of Table 2–6, set the level of this route at either the requirments of A or the availability of I, whichever is smaller. Proceed across the table in a general northwest-to-southeast direction, exhausting the availabilities of one row before moving down to the next and exhausting the requirements of one column before moving on to the next.

The initial program obtained from Table 2–6 by application of the "northwest corner" rule is shown in Table 2–7a; the shipments over

Table 2–7a

INITIAL PROGRAM FOR TRANSPORTATION EXAMPLE

	A	B	C	D
I	10　　4　　　10	15　　2　　　15	8　　1　　　8	20　　0　　　16
II	3　　0　　　9	2　　0　　　14	7　　2　　　7	15　　3　　　15
III	8　　0　　　12	11　　0　　　17	12　　0　　　10	18　　3　　　18

each route are given in the center of the cell representing that route. The cost of this program can be determined to be $191 by multiplying the cost per unit on each route by the number of units shipped over that route.

Other information useful at the next stage of the analysis is also given in Table 2–7a. The upper left corner of each cell reproduces the cost data of Table 2–6; derivation of the data in the lower right corner of each cell will be illustrated shortly.

Pricing of Alternative Combinations. The initial program illustrated in Table 2–7a uses six routes (= 3 + 4 — 1) at a positive level and six at a zero level. The six routes used at a positive level will be

[2] Difficulty also arises if the number of routes used is *less* than $(m + n - 1)$; the problem is then said to be *degenerate*. Degeneracy can be handled, by a method to be discussed later in this introduction.

called *included routes,* and those at a zero level will be called *excluded routes.*

The *alternative combination* to an excluded route is defined as the combination of changes that would be required on included routes if one unit were shipped over the excluded route. (Changes would be required because of the constraints.) Let us take the excluded route I-D as an example. If one unit were to be shipped over this route, it would be necessary, because of the restrictions on availabilities and requirements, to:

1. Decrease shipments over I-C by one unit.
2. Increase shipments over II-C by one unit.
3. Decrease shipments over II-D by one unit.

If one unit were shipped over route I-D, there would be a net saving on the alternative combination of $16, calculated as follows:

> Decreased costs:
>   Route I-C.............................$ 8
>   Route II-D.................................. 15
> $23
>
> Less increased costs:
>   Route II-C............................. 7
> $16

Thus, $16 may be considered as the cost of shipping one unit over the alternative combination to route I-D rather than over route I-D itself. It is instructive to think of this $16 as the *opportunity cost of leaving route I-D unused,* since this cost could be saved on the alternative combination if route I-D were used. This cost is entered in the lower right corner of cell I-D in Table 2–7*a*. Since the cost of not using route I-D ($16 per unit) is less than the cost of using the route ($20 per unit), the route is better left unused; each unit shipped over the route would raise total costs by $4.

The costs of the alternative combinations to other excluded routes may be calculated in the same way and are shown in Table 2–7*a* in the lower right corners of the cells. The alternative combination in terms of included routes to any included route is, of course, that route itself. To represent the cost of this alternative combination, therefore, we simply transfer the cost given in the upper left corner of any cell representing an included route to its lower left corner.

Inspection of the values in the lower right cell corners in Table 2–7*a* will reveal the following fact: between any two rows, there is a constant difference in the values from column to column, and likewise between any two columns there is a constant difference from row to row. The values in column B, for example, are always 5 more than those in column A. The constant row-to-row or column-to-column differences have an important economic interpretation to which we will return later.[3]

Improving the Program. If the cost of using an excluded route is less than the cost of using its alternative combination, then total costs will be reduced by substituting the excluded route for its alternative combination. In Table 2–7*a,* four excluded routes satisfy this standard: II-A, II-B, III-A, and III-B.

The method of solution of a linear programming problem requires, however, that only one excluded route at a time be introduced into the program. If a choice must be made, the rule customarily followed is to select the route where the unit advantage from substitution is the greatest. In Table 2–7*a,* this would be route II-B, since its cost is only $2 per unit while the cost of its alternative combination is $14 per unit; a saving of $12 per unit can therefore be realized on every unit substituted.

Since $12 will be saved for every unit moved over route II-B, it is desirable to use the route to the maximum extent feasible. Because of the constraints, the controlling factor here will be the quantities shipped over routes included in the equivalent combination which will be reduced as a result of the substitution; the substitution can be made only until one or more of these quantities has been reduced to 0. Only two units are being shipped over routes I-B and II-C, both of which are in the alternative combination to II-B. Hence only two units can be transferred to II-B from its alternative combination.

The revised program obtained by transferring two units to route II-B from its alternative combination is shown in Table 2–7*b.* The cost of this program is $167, as can be verified either by direct calculation or by subtracting $2 \times \$12 = \$24$ from the cost of the program represented by Table 2–7*a.*

Degeneracy. Table 2–7*b* illustrates a difficulty that may arise in the solution of a transportation problem. In going from Table 2–7*a* to Table 2–7*b,* both routes I-B and II-C were eliminated from the program, while only route II-B was added. As a result, the revised program

---

[3] They also form the basis for a short-cut method of deriving the costs of alternative combinations, as described in the appendix to this chapter.

involves only five included routes. A program which includes fewer than $(m + n - 1)$ routes (six in this case) is said to be *degenerate*.

The reason why a degenerate program presents difficulties is that it is no longer possible to find alternative combinations for each excluded route. The student may verify in Table 2–7b that excluded route III-B has an alternative combination in terms of included routes, but that none of the other excluded routes do. Thus we cannot perform the test to determine whether an excluded route should be substituted for its alternative combination.

Table 2–7b

FIRST REVISED PROGRAM FOR TRANSPORTATION
EXAMPLE

	A	B	C	D

I	10
	4
	    10
		15
		0
		    9
			8
			3
			    8
				20
				0
				    22

II	3
	0*
	    3
		2
		2
		    2
			7
			0
			    1
				15
				3
				    15

III	8
	0
	    6
		11
		0
		    5
			12
			0
			    4
				18
				3
				    18

Fortunately, the difficulties created by degeneracy can be overcome by a remarkably simple trick: we simply *assume* that one of the excluded routes is included. In Table 2–7b, for example, we have assumed that route II-A is included and have indicated this fact by starring it; any excluded route could have been selected. When this has been done, we have the required $(m + n - 1)$ included routes and are able to carry through the procedures as before.[4]

Final Program. A further improvement is possible in the program represented by Table 2–7b, since route I-D has a unit cost of \$20 while its alternative combination has a unit cost of \$22. Decreasing its al-

---

[4] Suppose route II-C had been starred in Table 2–7b rather than route II-A. Following through on the procedure of substituting an excluded route for its alternative combination when the route is less costly, it would be found that no such change in Table 2–7b would be feasible. In such a case, another route (such as II-A) should be starred and the procedure attempted again.

ternative combination involves decreasing routes I-A and II-D while increasing route II-A, which has been assumed to be an included route. Route I-D can be substituted for its alternative combination to the extent of the three units being shipped over route II-D. The resulting program is given in Table 2–7c.

The cost of this program is $161, which may be obtained by direct calculation or by subtracting $3 \times \$2 = \$6$ from the cost of the preceding program. When the costs of the alternative combinations to all excluded routes have been calculated, it is found that no further improvement is possible; in no case is the cost of using an excluded route less

Table 2–7c

FINAL PROGRAM FOR TRANSPORTATION EXAMPLE

	A	B	C	D
I	10 1 10	15 0 9	8 3 8	20 3 20
II	3 3 3	2 2 2	7 0 1	15 0 13
III	8 0 8	11 0 7	12 0 6	18 3 18

than the cost of using its alternative combination. Hence Table 2–7c represents an optimal program.

In one case, however, the cost of an excluded route (III-A) and of its alternative combination are equal. This implies that route III-A could be substituted for its alternative combination with no change in total cost. The resulting program, exhibited in Table 2–7d, also costs $161.

In the final program, it will be noted, the two most costly routes (I-D and III-D) are both utilized. This is a result which might very easily have been overlooked by a traffic manager operating without the benefit of formal methods.[5]

---

[5] Although once we know the result we can rationalize it: if we had supplied destination D from its cheapest source, II, that source would not have been able to ship over routes II-A and II-B, the cheapest routes. Overall optimization, therefore, requires use of the costliest routes.

Table 2–7d

ALTERNATE OPTIMAL PROGRAM FOR
TRANSPORTATION EXAMPLE

	A	B	C	D
I	10 0 10	15 0 9	8 3 8	20 4 20
II	3 3 3	2 2 2	7 0 1	15 0 13
III	8 1 8	11 0 7	12 0 6	18 2 18

Interpretation of the Row and Column Differences

It was noted earlier that the costs in the lower right cell corners of the table representing any program always differ by a constant amount from row to row and from column to column. In the optimal program for our example (Table 2–7c or 2–7d), the second row is uniformly $7 less than the first, and the third row is uniformly $2 less than the first. Similarly, the last column is always $10 more than the first.

In the optimal program, these row and column differences have an important economic interpretation: they represent the *relative locational advantages* of the sources and destinations. A unit of the commodity is worth $2 more at source III than at source I, for example, because since source III is closer on the average to the destination, it is able to supply them at a lower shipping cost (compare routes I-D and III-D which are both used in the optimal program). Similarly, it costs $10 more to have a unit delivered at destination D than at destination A (compare routes III-A and III-D).

These values, which appear as by-products in the determination of the optimal shipping program, thus have managerial significance of their own. From them we can determine, for example, that if the market at destination D is to be as desirable as that at destination A, the price must be $10 per unit higher. If we could expand capacity by one unit at some source, we should prefer to do so at source II, since this would enable us to reduce shipping costs by $7, by shipping one less unit from source I and one more unit from sources II. The student may wish to verify this conclusion as an exercise.

THE GENERAL LINEAR PROGAMMING METHOD

As we have seen in the transportation method, an important step in the solution of a linear programming problem is the determination for each excluded activity in a given program of its alternative combination in terms of included activities. This step is necessary in order to test whether the excluded activity should be substituted for its alternative combination.

In the transportation method, the determination of alternative combinations and their costs is a relatively simple matter. This is due to the fact that the substitution rate between activities (routes) is always equal to plus or minus one. Thus, an increase in one unit shipped over an excluded route always results in either a decrease or an increase of exactly one unit shipped over each route in its alternative combination. The whole problem can be handled, therefore, with no more arithmetic than addition and subtraction.

When the substitution rate between activities is not equal to plus or minus one, the transportation method cannot be applied and the determination of alternative combinations becomes more difficult. In this section, we will discuss a general method which will solve any linear programming problem, even when substitution rates are not equal to plus or minus one. The details of this method of solution (called the "simplex method") may be found in the references cited at the end of this introduction, but we will indicate in a general way how and why it works.

To illustrate the general method, we will use the following example: A chemical company manufactures two compounds, A and B. Compound A passes through three processes in the course of manufacture, while compound B requires the use of only two of these. In the production of one barrel of each compound, the following percentages of the daily capacities of each process are required:

	Compound A	Compound B
	(% of Daily Capacity per Barrel)	
Process 1	$\frac{1}{3}$	$\frac{1}{2}$
Process 2	$\frac{2}{3}$	$\frac{1}{3}$
Process 3	1	0

Compound A is sold to yield a contribution, after variable costs of manufacture, of \$4 per barrel, while compound B yields \$5 per barrel. It is desired to find the product mix which maximizes contribution.

Graphical Solution of the Example

When there are only two activities (in this case production of compound A and compound B respectively) with a direct effect on cost or profit, a linear programming problem can be solved graphically. The approach is illustrated in Figure 2–1. The quantity of compound A pro-

Figure 2–1

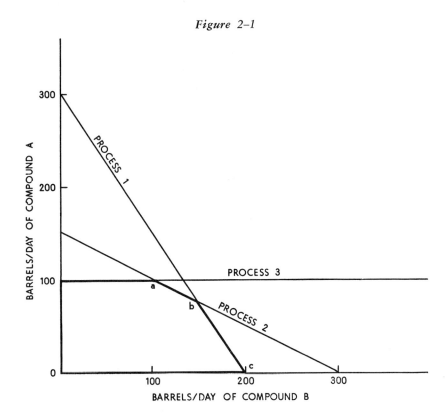

duced is indicated by the distance above the horizontal axis, while the quantity of compound B produced is indicated by the distance to the right of the vertical axis. The capacity limits of the three processes (i.e., the constraints) are indicated by straight lines drawn on the graph. The capacity of process 1, for instance, is adequate for either 300 barrels/day of compound A or 200 barrels/day of compound B or, in general, for any combination of A and B represented by a point southwest of the line connecting 300 on the vertical axis with 200 on the horizontal axis. Any combination of A and B can be produced, therefore, which can be represented by a point falling within or on the boundary of the polygon bounded by heavy linear segments.

It is not difficult to guess that the optimal production mix will lie somewhere along the northeast boundary of the polygon, from the point *a* to the point *c*. If a mix not on this boundary is selected, it is always possible to increase production of at least one compound without decreasing production of the other; and since both products are profitable, such a move should be made.

The precise optimum can be found by moving along the boundary in the following way. Start, say, at point *a*. Will it pay to move toward point *b?* Along this segment of the boundary, the substitution rate between compounds A and B is 1 to 2; for each reduction of one barrel in output of A, two barrels of B can be added. Considering contribution, the loss of one barrel of A loses $4, but the two barrels of B return $10, for a net gain of $6 per barrel of A. The substitution should be made, therefore, and to the maximum extent feasible (i.e., to point *b*).

At point *b,* the substitution rate changes to 3 to 2. For each barrel of A given up, therefore, only two thirds of a barrel of B can be substituted. The tradeoff is unprofitable in terms of contribution: $4 per barrel of A given up permits an increase of only $\frac{2}{3} \times \$5 = \$3.33$ in contribution from B. Thus, point *b* represents the optimal production mix. At this point, production consists of 75 barrels per day of compound A and 150 barrels per day of compound B.[6] Processes 1 and 2 are used to capacity, but 25% of process 3 capacity is unused. Total contribution is $1,050 per day.

The graphical method of solution just illustrated is, of course, applicable to only the very simplest programming problems. For larger problems, a numerical method must be employed. This method proceeds to a solution in much the same manner as the transportation method: An initial program is first selected. Possible improvements in the program are tested by comparing the cost or profit of each excluded activity with the cost or profit of its alternative combination in terms of included activities. Substitutions are made until no further improvement is possible.

---

[6] These results can be calculated by solving simultaneously the two equations representing process 1 and process 2 capacity, viz.:

$$y = 300 - (\tfrac{3}{5})x$$
$$y = 150 - (\tfrac{1}{2})x$$

where *y* represents compound A production and *x* represents compound B production.

Summary

Two methods of solving linear programming problems have been presented in this section. While the two methods differ in their computational details, because of differences in the structure of the problems to which they are applied, they have a number of features in common. These common features will be reviewed in this summary.

In a linear programming problem, it is desired to set the levels of a number of *activities,* or resource uses, in such a way as to maximize profits or minimize costs. The feasible activity levels are governed by certain *constraints,* or resource limitations.

An iterative technique is employed to solve a linear programming problem. The general outline of this technique is as follows:

1. An initial program (i.e., determination of the level of each of the activities) is selected arbitrarily. In this program, some of the activities will be set at a zero level; these are called *excluded activities.* The others, which will be set at a positive level, are called *included activities.*
2. For each excluded activity, a test is performed to determine whether total profit will be increased or total cost decreased if the activity is included. If the activity is included it will be necessary, because of the constraints, to change the levels of some of the included activities. The first step in testing each excluded activity, therefore, is to determine its *alternative combination,* that is, those included activities which must be eliminated if the level of the excluded activity is raised by one unit. The alternative combination is then priced. Comparing the return or cost of the alternative combination with that of the excluded activity, it is thus possible to determine whether it is advantageous to substitute the excluded activity for its alternative combination.
3. If there is an excluded activity which should be included according to the above test, it is substituted in the program for its alternative combination to the extent permitted by the conditions of the problem. (If there is more than one such excluded activity, only one is selected for inclusion.) Thus a new program can be found which is at least as good and possibly better than the first.
4. Steps 2 and 3 are then repeated on the new program. This process continues until step 2 reveals that no further improvement is possible. At this point the optimal program has been achieved.

The methods discussed in this section are applicable only to *linear* programming problems. As stated on page 124, this means that marginal costs and/or marginal revenues of each activity must be constant and that for each constraint, the rates of substitution between activities are constant. Methods are also available for solving some problems where these assumptions are not satisfied, but others remain unsolved.

APPENDIX

This appendix discusses briefly some practical computational methods used in solving a transportation problem. Further details may be found in the references cited above which also present clerical procedures for handling the general linear programming method.

In the transportation method, the most tedious step is the determination of the costs of shipping over alternative combinations to excluded routes (see Table 2–7a on page 126, these costs are included in the lower right corners of the cells). These costs can be calculated by a short-cut procedure described below. Table 2–7a will be used as an illustration, but the procedure can be used at any step in the analysis.

1. First enter in the lower right corner of the table the costs of shipping over *included* routes, as specified in the cost table (Table 2–6). At this point, Table 2–7a would appear as given below. (It is suggested that the student follow the steps as given by entering the required numbers in this table.)

	A	B	C	D	Row Values
I	10 4 10	15 2 15	8 1 8	20 0	
II	3 0	2 0	7 2 7	15 3 15	
III	8 0	11 0	12 0	18 3 18	
Column Values					

2. Select an arbitrary value for any one row and enter it in the column headed "row values." We will, for example, select a value of zero for row I.

3. For every *included route* in the row to which a value was assigned, determine a value for its column in such a way that (row value) + (column value) = (cost of included route). With a value of zero assigned to row I, for example, the value of column C must be 8.

4. Now use the column values just assigned to find new row values in the same way; that is, for every included route in a column with a value assigned, determine a value for its row in such a way that (column value) + (row value) = (cost of included route). With a value of 8 assigned to column C, for example, the value of row II must be −1.

5. Continue alternating between steps 3 and 4 until a value has been assigned to each row and column.

6. Now, for each excluded route, obtain the cost to be entered in the lower right corner of its cell by adding together the appropriate row value and column value.

If the student has carried out these steps on the table given above, he should now compare that table with Table 2–7*a* in the text. The bodies of the two tables will be seen to be identical.

PROBLEMS

Problem 2–1. The Kramer Company manufactured a line of power and hand tools for home workshops which were marketed under its own brand name. In addition, the company produced parts and accessories for power tools which were marketed by a large retail chain under its name. The Kramer Company had to meet the quality standards and delivery schedules required by the chain.

During 1955, sales of parts and accessories to the chain had exceeded $400,000. The president of the Kramer Company felt that these sales to the chain contributed significantly to overhead and profit while stabilizing employment. In the past, during periods of high activity, the Kramer Company had purchased parts from smaller firms for use in its own product line as well as to complete orders for the chain.

In March 1956, the treasurer, production manager, and purchasing agent met to decide whether to produce or purchase from an outside supplier 82,000 reduction gears which were part of an order from the retail chain.

The Kramer Company cost accounting system recorded actual material costs. Product costing of direct labor was at a uniform average rate per hour. The treasurer recognized that this use of a uniform average rate per hour resulted in some error in costing individual parts. He believed, however, that the average direct labor rate was accurate enough for practical purposes since actual labor rates did not vary widely and in most instances parts passed through similar machining operations.

Both fixed and variable overhead were charged to products at a uniform rate per direct labor hour. See Table 2–8 for the overhead accounts grouped as fixed or variable costs.

Table 2–8

OVERHEAD ACCOUNTS GROUPED AS FIXED OR VARIABLE COSTS

Fixed Overhead	*Variable Overhead*
Administrative expenses	Foremanship (above basic budget)
Selling expense	Indirect labor
Taxes	Supplies
Insurance	Engineering
Factory superintendence	Cost accounting department labor
Foremanship (basic budget)	Heat, light, and power
Repairs and depreciation (building)	Social security taxes
Equipment depreciation	Workman's compensation taxes

At the time of the meeting, the plantwide average costs per direct labor hour, exclusive of material, were:

Direct labor...............................$1.65
Variable overhead.......................... 1.94
Fixed overhead............................ 1.45
Total per hour......................$5.04

The production manager stated that the Kramer Company could make the gears in a continuous production run (i.e., involving only one setup) at 480 per hour. Furthermore, by deferring production of other parts intended for inventory accumulation, machine time could be made available for producing the reduction gears. The material for the gears would cost $1,220.

The purchasing agent observed that a smaller company would sell the gears to the Kramer Company at a price of $0.0234 per gear. Past experience indicated that this firm was reliable. He remarked that at other meetings on production versus purchase of parts the treatment of fixed factory overhead in the cost comparison had been discussed. However, he wanted to know what should be done when evaluating a purchase price which obviously included the administrative, marketing, and profit elements the outside supplier included in his price.

Assignment

1. Should the Kramer Company produce or buy the reduction gears? Support your conclusions with cost comparison figures.
2. Comment on the question of the purchasing agent relative to the administrative, marketing, and profit elements included in a supplier's price.
3. With respect to the present make-or-buy decision, comment on the deficiencies, if any, in the use of the overhead costs.

Problem 2–2. The Henderson Corporation, Inc. operated three factories producing the same product for national distribution through four warehouses. The table below states the freight rates from each plant to each warehouse, the capacity of each plant, and the requirements of each warehouse.

	—Freight Rates per Unit to Each Warehouse—			Warehouse
	Factory I	*Factory II*	*Factory III*	*Requirements*
Warehouse:				
A......................$1.05		$0.90	$2.00	35
B...................... 2.30		1.40	1.40	10
C...................... 1.80		1.00	1.20	35
D...................... 1.00		1.75	1.10	25
Factory capacity (units)..... 5		60	40	105

Assignment

Using the transportation method described in this chapter, find the optimal shipping schedule from the plants to the warehouses. What would the total freight cost be using this schedule?

BOB MOGIELNICKI

On receiving his M.B.A. degree in June 1957, Bob Mogielnicki went to work for the Brandywine Corporation, a medium-sized manufacturer of electrical controls and electronic devices. Although his undergraduate degree was in mechanical engineering, summer jobs and a brief stint as an engineer before entering military service had convinced Bob that he was not interested in an engineering career. Accordingly, after completing his three-year tour in the Air Force, he entered business school in the fall of 1955.

What particularly attracted Bob to the job offer from Brandywine was the fact that it presented an opportunity to assume line responsibilities after a brief training period. The position in question was that of supervisor of the parts fabrication shop at the company's San Jose plant.

In the fall of 1957, then, Bob Mogielnicki assumed his new duties. At that time, the staff of the parts fabrication shop consisted of 10 machine operators and two clerks in addition to the supervisor. The shop was producing five parts which were used by other departments of the San Jose plant in the assembly of final products. A statement of costs incurred by the parts fabrication shop during the first week of Bob's supervision is attached as Exhibit 1.

When he took over the parts fabrication shop, Bob was told by the plant manager, Mr. Wallis, that it was his responsibility to see that the five parts being produced by the shop were acquired at the lowest possible cost to the company. For this reason, he had the authority to buy all or any of these parts from outside sources if he found this to be more advantageous to the company.

In order to carry out his responsibility for "make-or-buy" decisions, Bob felt he needed more cost information than was supplied by the weekly cost statement (such as Exhibit 1). He discussed his needs with the plant accountant, Mr. Dreyfus, and together they agreed on a format for a second weekly report, which would show the actual cost of producing 100 of each of the parts during the week in question. The first such report, corresponding to the cost statement of Exhibit 1, is attached as Exhibit 2. The figures in Exhibit 2 were obtained as follows:

1. *Direct labor/hundred.* Each machine operator kept a time sheet indicating the time (in hours and tenths of an hour) he spent on each part. These times were accumulated for each part and costed at the direct labor rate of $3.50/hour. The total cost for each part was then divided by the amount of production.
2. *Direct materials/hundred.* When materials were drawn from the storeroom, an issue slip was prepared indicating the amount drawn and the part on which the materials were to be used. The amounts were totaled for each part and the totals divided by the amount of production.
3. *Overhead/hundred.* The total of all overhead costs charged to the department was divided by the number of direct labor hours to produce a cost per hour. This figure was multiplied by the number of direct labor hours charged to each part and the product was then divided by the amount of production.

After receiving the information in Exhibit 2 from Mr. Dreyfus, Bob Mogielnicki solicited bids on each of the five parts from several small shops in the San Jose area. The lowest bid received on each part was as follows:

Part No.	Lowest Bid
101	$65.00
102	90.00
103	37.50
104	60.00
105	34.50

Clearly, then, it was more advantageous to the company to continue making each part in its own shop.

. . . .

In the spring of 1958, demand for Brandywine's products fell sharply because of a business recession. This decline was naturally reflected in the work load in the parts fabrication shop. Because of the reduced work load, Bob Mogielnicki had laid off one machine operator and had transferred another to performing maintenance of equipment which had been deferred during the period of higher production.

When Bob received his product cost report for the week of April 14, 1958, shown in Exhibit 3, he discovered that costs were up on all five parts, and that part 103, in particular, now cost more to make than the bid of $37.50 per hundred he had received in the fall. Bob called up the owner of the shop who had made that bid and asked him for an updated bid. The owner responded with a bid of $36 per hundred, saying that his business was off and so he was willing to shave his earlier price a bit if it would help to keep his shop busy. Bob promptly accepted the reduced offer and asked the purchasing agent of the San Jose plant to issue a purchase order to the outside source for 4,000 units (about a two-week supply at the current usage rate). Bob estimated that his decision would save Brandywine about $140.

The cost reports for the week of April 28, 1958 (see Exhibit 4) showed a further rise. Once again Bob checked with the sources of earlier bids, this time on parts 102 and 105, and learned that in both cases the bidders were sticking by their earlier quotes.

Question

1. What should Bob Mogielnicki do with regard to parts 102 and 105?

Exhibit 1

BOB MOGIELNICKI

Cost Statement for Week of September 16, 1957

Prime cost:

Labor	$1,397.56
Materials	3,116.80
Total prime cost	$4,514.36
Departmental overhead:	
Departmental supervision and services	$1,002.16
Depreciation	1,200.00
Total departmental overhead	$2,202.16
General overhead	$1,500.00
Total costs	$8,216.52

Exhibit 2

BOB MOGIELNICKI

Product Cost Report for Week of September 16, 1957

	Cost per 100 Units of Part No.				
Cost element:	*101*	*102*	*103*	*104*	*105*
Labor	$ 8.48	$13.30	$ 5.25	$ 7.33	$ 4.31
Material	18.40	24.00	14.80	17.20	13.60
Total prime cost	$26.88	$37.30	$20.05	$24.53	$17.91
Overhead	22.42	35.15	13.88	19.38	11.39
Total cost	$49.30	$72.45	$33.93	$43.91	$29.30
Production (100 units)	33	40	32	42	26

Exhibit 3

BOB MOGIELNICKI

PRODUCT COST REPORT FOR WEEK OF APRIL 14, 1958

	Cost per 100 Units of Part No.				
Cost element:	101	102	103	104	105
Labor........................	$ 9.02	$14.00	$ 5.60	$ 7.82	$ 4.33
Material.....................	18.43	24.01	14.78	17.20	13.59
Total prime cost.............	$27.45	$38.01	$20.38	$25.02	$17.92
Overhead.....................	30.92	48.00	19.20	26.80	14.86
Total cost.................	$58.37	$86.01	$39.58	$51.82	$32.78
Production (100 units)...........	26	32	20	30	21

Exhibit 4

BOB MOGIELNICKI

PRODUCT COST REPORT FOR WEEK OF APRIL 28, 1958

	Cost per 100 Units of Part No.				
Cost element:	101	102	103	104	105
Labor........................	$ 8.68	$13.33	...	$ 7.50	$ 4.50
Material.....................	18.43	24.00	...	17.20	13.55
Total prime cost.............	$27.11	$37.33	...	$24.70	$18.05
Overhead.....................	37.60	58.00	...	32.14	18.00
Total cost.................	$64.71	$95.33	...	$56.84	$36.05
Production (100 units)...........	25	30	...	28	20

ALMOND APPARATUS COMPANY

In the late summer of 1957, Bob Jones, manager of the Almond Apparatus Company, was faced with the inevitable shutdown of a key part of one of his processing operations because of the need for major overhaul and alteration. Sales of Product X, the chief product of this process, had been very good and quite uniform throughout the year; indeed they were so good that it had been impossible to build up any inventory against the inevitable shutdown. (The process was run 24 hours a day.) Bob Jones believed, however, that most if not all his customers could get along all right for the 30-day period that he estimated the process would be down for repairs, for he had been warning them for some months now that the interruption to their supply was going to be absolutely necessary. He suspected, although he was not sure, that they had anticipated the shutdown and were keeping their own stocks somewhat on the high side. On the other hand, he realized his chief competitor would make the most of any opportunity to take customers away from him.

The Almond Apparatus Company enjoyed an excellent reputation for its products which were of a uniformly high quality and a little better, most people thought, than the products of its chief competitor, and much better than the four or five other brands in the market. One reason why Bob Jones was anxious to get the shutdown over with was that it was increasingly possible, he feared, that something might suddenly go wrong and some poor-quality product would slip by his inspectors. Moreover, he contemplated that in the overhaul process some minor improvements might be introduced that would raise still higher the quality of the output.

The total demand for Product X, the chief product of the process to be shut down, had been growing steadily but slowly. Profits on this part of the business (80% Product X) had been $5,300 in a typical 30-day period in the summer of 1957 (see Exhibit 1). As yet total demand

143

would not warrant an entirely new extra facility that could be built and in operation before the shutdown. However, Bob Jones thought that by some changes in layout and an improvement at one critical point, an increase of 10% in capacity could be had when the process started up again. There would be no difficulty, he was sure, in selling this extra output.

The engineer's estimates of the cost of the 30-day overhaul and alteration operation were as follows:

Personnel:

One engineer............$36 per 8-hour day...........$1,080		
One foreman............ 24 per 8-hour day.......... 720		
Two welders............ 18 per 8-hour day.......... 1,080		
Two pipefitters.......... 17 per 8-hour day.......... 1,020		
One riveter............. 18 per 8-hour day 540		
Six laborers............. 12 per 8-hour day.......... 2,160		
Total labor.....................................	$ 6,600	
Materials and supplies, etc............................	3,100	
Overhead at 100% of labor...........................	6,600	
Total..	$16,300	

The overhead charge of 100% of labor was the standard charge that the company used in all its cost work and represented its best estimate of the average cost relationship between labor and overhead.

In view of the great advantage of minimizing the interruptions to the company's operation, Bob Jones was considering the possibility of having the alteration work done on an around-the-clock basis. If the work were done with three crews, there would be no overtime work but there would be an additional 10% compensation for the one night shift. In addition he believed that they would not realize the same performance on the night shift as in the day. There might be, he estimated, as much as 20% difference between the work accomplished on the night shift and that accomplished on the day shift. The second day shift would be subject to the same influences, he believed, but not to the same degree—the loss in efficiency would not exceed 10%. Also, because the same crew would not be doing all the work, Bob Jones estimated that the over-all time required would be increased by about 10%, even granting full efficiency of the extra shifts. The other extra expenses of night operations, including light and other services, were expected to amount to no more than $50 a day.

As far as Bob Jones could see there were problems both ways. If the work were to take the scheduled 30 days, he knew he would be under pressure from his customers before the time was out, especially from

one important but irascible gentleman who had some custom processing put through every once in a while as a special order. On the other
hand, he realized that extra shifts meant extra costs and extra troubles.
He thought he could get the extra labor without too much trouble but it
would be a nuisance, and he was not sure how much the speedup would
be worth, other than in possible goodwill. He really was not worried
very much about the loss of goodwill, for he was convinced his customers understood his problem and appreciated the high quality of his merchandise. If any customers chose to drop out, he thought that there were
one or two good ones that had been waiting to get on the list.

Questions

1. What would it cost Bob Jones, net, to speed up the overhaul work? Make
as precise an estimate as you can, using the figures in the case, and assuming no
shift in customer loyalties if the work is not accelerated.

2. What would you decide if you were Bob Jones?

Exhibit 1

ALMOND APPARATUS COMPANY

ESTIMATED SALES AND PROFITS, PRODUCT X AND ALLIED PRODUCTS

THIRTY-DAY PERIOD, SUMMER, 1957

Sales...		$35,000
Cost:		
Direct labor................................	$ 6,000	
Material....................................	12,200	
Fixed overhead..............................	6,000	24,200
Gross margin.................................		$10,800
Allocated administrative expense....................		2,000
Selling expense*................................		3,500
Estimated profit...............................		$ 5,300

* Commission on sales, 10%.

POST OFFICE DEPARTMENT (D)[1]
Presort Discount for First-Class Mail

In July 1966, staff analysts in the Bureau of Finance and Administration of the Post Office Department were entering the final stages of an analysis concerning the desirability of presort discounts to large users of first-class mail. Reduced rates were already offered to second- and third-class bulk mailers and had proven mutually advantageous to both mailers and the Post Office Department.

Bulk Discounts on Second- and Third-Class Mail

In the summer of 1965 the Post Office Department revised its bulk rate sorting requirements for second- and third-class mail. Previously, second- and third-class mail qualified for a bulk discount if it was presorted into city, state, and mixed-state bundles by the mailer. The Post Office had established the following conditions governing bulk rate sorting of third-class mail:

1. To qualify for a discount on second- or third-class mail a minimum of 200 pieces or 50 pounds had to be mailed at one time.
2. The mail was to be sorted into the most detailed bundles of 10 or more pieces possible. If 10 or more pieces were addressed to the same city, a city bundle could be created. Mail addressed to cities receiving less than 10 pieces was bundled by state or by mixed states if 10 or more pieces were not available for one state.
3. Bundles were to be placed in sacks according to a similar minimum limitation. In preparing sacks the mailer followed essentially the same procedure as for preparing bundles, only the minimum was defined as one third of a sack.

---

[1] This case is intended for class discussion only, and certain names and facts may have been changed which, while avoiding the disclosure of confidential information, do not materially lessen the value of the case for educational purposes. This case is not intended to represent either effective or ineffective handling of an administrative situation, nor does it purport to be a statement of policy by the agency involved.

146

A discount of $1\frac{1}{8}$ cents off the normal 4-cent third-class rate was given to mailers for abiding by these sorting requirements. The discount and sorting requirements for second-class mail were essentially the same as for third-class mail.

The revised bulk rate sorting requirements for second- and third-class mail were issued in 1965, but not effective until January 1, 1967. The new requirements were designed to encourage second- and third-class mailers to presort their mail by ZIP code rather than by city, state, and mixed states. The sizes of the second- and third-class discounts were not changed, nor was the minimum size of one mailing (200 pieces or 50 pounds). Exhibit 1 presents a pictorial explanation of the new bulk rate sorting requirements. Excerpts from the Department's explanation of the new procedures are quoted below:

> All mail entered at second-class or third-class bulk rates after January 1, 1967, must be sorted. (Mail sorted to carrier routes, however, need not show the ZIP code on individual pieces.) In third-class, 10 or more pieces bearing the same five digits must be tied out to five-digit bundles; remaining city mail (10 or more pieces) must be made up to city bundles; 10 or more pieces for the same Sectional Center (i.e., having the same first three digits in the ZIP code) must be made up to Sectional Center bundles and state and mixed-state bundles and sacks are made up as at present. The same requirements apply to second-class mail except that six or more pieces to the same area must be bundled together.
>
> If there are sufficient five-digit bundles to the same destination to make one-third sack or more, they should be placed in a sack labelled to the five-digit address. Remaining five-digit bundles for a city, along with city bundles, should be placed into a city sack, if one makes up. Remaining city and five-digit bundles, if any, should go into a Sectional Center sack, along with any three-digit bundles which have been prepared for that Sectional Center.
>
> When such mail for a Sectional Center is less than one-third sack, it should be combined with state working bundles in a state sack.

Bulk rates for presorting mail were economical for both the Post Office and the mailer. The mailer, of course, benefited from the reduced rates, while the Post Office saved money in the handling and sorting of the mail. In addition, the mailer could mechanize the sorting of mail by proper geographical arrangement of his mailing lists. Thus, by a one-time arrangement of his mailing lists, the mailer could eliminate the necessity of hand sorting each time a mailing was made. This natural leverage which the mailer had over the organization of his mail made it economically desirable for the Post Office to encourage the mailer to take responsibility for his own sorting.

Proposed First-Class Discount

Even though presort discounts were common for bulk mailings of second- and third-class mail, no discount had ever been offered for presorting first-class mail. As a result of the attention given to presort procedures during the summer of 1965, serious interest developed concerning the potential for a first-class mail presort discount. One of the first formal expressions of this interest was contained in a memorandum from the Bureau of Finance and Administration to the Deputy Postmaster General, dated September 28, 1965. Excerpts from that memo were as follows:

> The basic reason for offering a pre-sort discount (for first-class mail) is to increase the volume of pre-sorting by mailers. The economic value to the Post Office Department is measured by the *difference* between cost savings from pre-sort and reduced revenue resulting from a mailer discount. If the Department were to offer a discount there is little question that pre-sorting would increase. However, the discount would also apply to mail now being pre-sorted "free," without a discount. For this mail, providing a discount would result in a net loss to the Post Office Department.
>
> The economic return from a pre-sort discount approach depends on the cost savings per piece in relation to the discount per piece and, also, on the level of "free" pre-sorting we would obtain without a discount.
>
> As an illustration, if mailer pre-sort results in savings of 5 cents per piece and we offer a discount of 3 cents per piece, the level of mailer pre-sort with the discount would have to increase 150% over the present "free" level simply to break even.
>
> In the light of these arguments it would seem advisable to withhold any decision on a pre-sort discount until a market analysis can be performed to determine the present level of mailer pre-sort and the estimated increase which might be expected from a pre-sort discount.

Much of the information necessary to make an intelligent decision regarding a presort discount for first-class mail could only be obtained through an extensive market survey. This information included the size of the demand for presort bulk rates, the degree of voluntary presort, and the quality of the presort which the Department could expect to receive. In order to obtain this information the Bureau of Finance and Administration began constructing a questionnaire to be sent to a sample of large first-class mailers.

Sorting Procedures

While this questionnaire was being prepared, the Bureau also began gathering statistics regarding the Department's cost for sorting first-class mail. There was a possible total of six sorts in processing first-class mail. Performing these six sorting operations was the primary responsibility of the mail handler and window service clerks. Mail-handler and window service costs, and other Department expenses allocated to first-class mail in fiscal year 1965, are shown in Exhibit 2. Exhibit 2 also contains volume statistics for first-class mail in fiscal year 1965.

The six sorting operations performed in processing first-class mail were primary outgoing, secondary outgoing, interim sorting, sectional center sorting, incoming primary, and incoming secondary. These sorting operations were described as follows:

> Primary outgoing—First sorting operation after receipt in Post Office. Separated into 49 categories, including local, high-volume destinations, and general groupings.
> Secondary outgoing—Further separation of the general groupings created in primary.
> Interim sorting—Separation en route, often of mail destined for small cities in low mail-volume areas.
> Sectional Center—Detailed sorting to specific offices within Sectional Center Region.
> Incoming primary—Separation of post office destination into postal districts.
> Incoming secondary—Further explosion of districts into carrier routes.

Not all first-class mail had to be processed through all six of these operations. Local mail (mail with a common Post Office of origin and destination), which accounted for an estimated 30% of first-class volume, required a maximum of only three sorts. Local mail received one separation at the outgoing primary and was sent directly to the office's incoming primary. Incoming primary distributed local mail to postal districts, and the incoming secondary further exploded the districts into carrier routes. Mail collection boxes were usually separated between local and out-of-town mail. Thus, it was estimated that 60% of local mail bypassed the primary outgoing sort and went directly to incoming primary. All local mail had to pass through the incoming primary sort, but an estimated 20% of the total local volume could be routed directly from the incoming primary to the addressee, thereby avoiding the incoming secondary sort.

First-class mail with out-of-town destinations could require all six sorting operations. If it was not presorted, all of the out-of-town mail had to pass through the primary outgoing distribution. An estimated 30% of total out-of-town mail was sorted directly to its post office destination in this primary distribution. The remainder was processed through secondary outgoing distribution, where another 30% of the total out-of-town mail was identified by post office destination. After secondary outgoing distribution, 40% of the total out-of-town was identified only by state or region of the country. Thus, the interim sort was required on this mail and was performed as it was being transported toward its general destination. Interim (en route) sorting identified an additional 20% of the total out-of-town mail by post office destination, leaving a final 20% of the total to be sorted at the Sectional Center and finally identified by destination. All out-of-town mail was subjected to the incoming primary distribution upon arrival at the destination post office. However, as with local mail, an estimated 20% of the total out-of-town mail could be routed directly to the addressee and thereby avoid the final incoming secondary sort. This pattern for unsorted mail is diagrammed in Exhibit 3.

With this understanding of the sorting process the Bureau next estimated the number of sortings eliminated by various degrees of presorting. It was observed that local mail bundles presorted to the five-digit ZIP code (postal district) would not require outgoing primary or incoming primary sorting; such mail would require only one sort in the incoming secondary, where the mail is distributed to carrier routes. Local mail bundles presorted to the city (separated from out-of-town) would not require primary outgoing sorting but would be transferred directly to the incoming primary sort for that city.

Presorting of out-of-town mail promised even larger savings. The following table indicates the sorts that would be eliminated and the first sort that would be required for each type of presorted mail. Subsequent sorts, after the first one, were expected to follow the pattern shown in Exhibit 3. For example, out-of-town mail presorted by states would all go through the incoming primary sort, but 60% of it could be sorted directly to its post office destination. The other 40% would go through an interim sort, and half of that would also go through the Sectional Center.

Bundles Presorted by	Sorting Completely Eliminated	Initial Sort Required
Five-digit ZIP code	Primary outgoing Secondary outgoing Interim sorting Sectional Center sorting Incoming primary	Incoming secondary
City	Primary outgoing Secondary outgoing Interim sorting Sectional Center sorting	Incoming primary
Sectional Center facility	Primary outgoing Secondary outgoing Interim sorting	Sectional Center
State	Primary outgoing	Secondary outgoing

The Market Survey

In January 1966, a questionnaire for surveying the first-class mail market was completed. This questionnaire was distributed to 8,000 businesses in industry classifications known to have significant volumes of first-class mail. By July 1966, the questionnaire responses had been summarized and analyzed, providing initial information about the demand for first-class mail presort discounts. Exhibit 4 contains some of the more important information obtained in the survey. This information concerned the relationship between the requirement for the minimum size of the mailing and three important determinants of the desirability of a first-class mail presort discount. These determinants were:

1. Share of first-class mail qualifying for presort discount broken down between local and out-of-town mail.
2. The size of the voluntary presort of first-class mail (mail already presorted without a discount) broken down between local and out-of-town mail.
3. The quality of the presort of first-class mail for the local mail market and out-of-town mail market. Quality was used to designate the expected distribution of mail among the five categories (five-digit ZIP code, city, Sectional Center facility, state, mixed states).

In examining each of these relationships it was assumed that the regulations governing bundling and sacking of first-class mail would be the same as the new third-class mail regulations. These regulations established a general limitation of 10 pieces to a bundle and a third of a sack to a sack in sorting the mail.

Structuring the Final Analysis

By the end of July 1966, the Bureau of Finance and Administration had gathered most of the material which they believed was relevant to the first-class presort discount question. At that point the staff was considering how to combine the available information into a special study of the presort discount question. They were concerned with presenting information on the following topics in the final presort discount special study:

1. For various minimum size of mailing requirements, what is the relationship between the per piece discount given the mailer and the volume of presorted mail needed to break even?
2. For various minimum size of mailing requirements, what volume of presorted mail would be required to break even if the presort discount is

set at the minimum level which would still be significant to the mailer?

3. Would the Post Office be likely to receive the break-even volume calculated in (2) above?

The staff was also concerned about the possibility of changes in the cost of sorting mail in the future. Although the historical sorting cost per piece was easily estimated, there was a strong possibility that this cost might be reduced in the future. This reduction in cost was expected to result from increased automation of the sorting operations. The Postmaster General described these expectations in the 1965 Post Office Annual Report as follows:

If there is one central feature of the Department's service improvement effort it is the development and implementation of the ZIP Code Program. It is the core of our program, and we think it will provide us in the next few years with a veritable mail-handling revolution in this country. We cannot emphasize too strongly its importance, in the long run, to the handling of mail. . . .

The Department's optical scanning research program continued to occupy top priority.

We awarded a contract for six of the improved high-speed optical readers, mentioned in last year's report, to be installed in two of our largest, highly mechanized post offices. Each optical reader letter-sorting machine system will be capable of reading and sorting mail with printed or typed ZIP-coded addresses at a rate of 36,000 per hour.

Because of the uncertainty concerning the impact of automation upon sorting costs, the staff also wanted to measure the relationship between the expected cost (and therefore, savings) per sort and the break-even point as computed in (2) above.

In general, the staff felt that they could recommend a presort discount only if (1) the volume of presorted mail was almost certain to exceed the break-even point, (2) the discount could be applied as a single rate rather than creating a different discount for different types of mailers, and (3) the discount could be expected to continue for at least a five-year period.

Questions

1. Using data in the case about the number of sorts required for the historical distribution pattern of first-class mail and the cost and volume data in Exhibit 2, calculate the "average cost per sort" in 1965. Could this figure be used in calculating the relationship between the per piece discount and break-even volume, as suggested near the end of the case? What implicit assumptions about this average "cost per sort" would have to hold true in order to use the figure for this purpose?

2. Asssuming that a discount of $\frac{1}{2}$ cent per piece were allowed for presorted

first-class mail in quantities of 200 or more pieces, what is the volume of presorted mail needed to break even?

3. Compute the break-even volume required for one other combination of presort discount and minimum quantity, that is, for a discount of $\frac{1}{4}$ cent per piece on quantities of 5,000 or more. You may select any of the four quantity ranges in Exhibit 4, and any discount (in $\frac{1}{4}$ cent increments) from $\frac{1}{4}$ cent to $1\frac{1}{4}$ cents per piece.

4. Which alternative presort policies seem worthy of further exploration? Based on your analysis thus far, which discount structure, if any, would you recommend? What additional fact finding and analysis, if any, seems desirable before a decision can be made?

Exhibit 1

POST OFFICE DEPARTMENT (D)

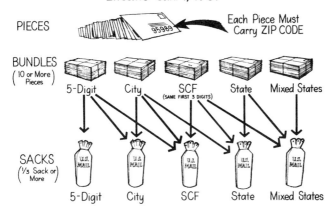

BULK RATE SORTING REQUIREMENTS
Effective Jan. 1, 1967

Exhibit 2

POST OFFICE DEPARTMENT (D)

SUMMARY OF APPORTIONED COSTS, FISCAL YEAR 1965

	Total Post Office (000's)	First-Class Mail (000's)
Income and associated expense (operating revenue).........	$ 4,483,390	$ 2,192,790
Postal operation expenses:		
Administration of post office operations..................	$ 510,733	$ 206,198
Mail handling and window service......................	1,766,627	813,930
Collection and delivery...............................	1,542,540	587,281
Local transportation.................................	91,195	29,516
Operation and care of buildings........................	267,273	56,376
Postal supply services................................	23,076	5,832
Other expense..	40,848	16,204
Mail handling in transit..............................	132,476	75,518
Total operating expense	$ 4,374,768	$ 1,790,855
Transportation of mails	$ 613,240	$ 68,479
General overhead	97,053	32,243
Nonfund expense	90,675	26,050
Redistribution of expense	. . .	47,539
Total nonoperating	$ 800,968	$ 174,311
Total expense (net income [deficit]) before public service losses and costs..........................	$ 5,175,736	$ 1,965,166
	$ (692,346)	$ 227,624
Pieces of mail (000's).................................	71,873,166	38,067,778

Exhibit 3

POST OFFICE DEPARTMENT (D)

PERCENTAGES OF FIRST-CLASS MAIL FLOWING THROUGH EACH SORTING OPERATION

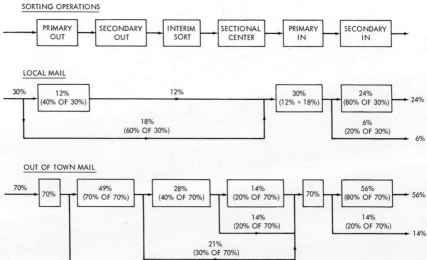

Exhibit 4

POST OFFICE DEPARTMENT (D)

PRESORT DISCOUNT QUESTIONNAIRE, SUMMARY OF RESPONSES

1. Share of first-class mail qualifying for discount under various minimum quantity restrictions:

Minimum Size of Mailing to Qualify for Presort Discount	*Share of Local Mail Market*	*Share of Out-of-Town Mail Market*
200	57%	20%
500	42	15
1,000	33	12
5,000	22	10

2. Size of voluntary presort under various minimum quantity restrictions:

Minimum Size of Mailing to Qualify for Presort Discount	*Share of Local Mail Market*	*Share of Out-of-Town Mail Market*
200	16%	8%
500	14	6
1,000	12	5
5,000	10	4

3. Quality of the presort under various minimum quantity restrictions:

Percent of Mail Presorted by—	*Minimum Size of Qualifying Mailing (Local Mail)*			
	200	*500*	*1,000*	*5,000*
Five-digit ZIP code	65%	70%	80%	95%
City	35	30	20	5
SCF	...	...	...	...
State	...	...	...	...
Mixed states	...	...	...	...
Total	100%	100%	100%	100%

Percent of Mail Presorted by—	*Minimum Size of Qualifying Mailing (Out-of-Town Mail)*			
	200	*500*	*1,000*	*5,000*
Five-digit ZIP code	15%	15%	10%	10%
City	20	25	30	35
SCF	20	25	30	35
State	30	25	20	15
Mixed states	15	10	10	5
Total	100%	100%	100%	100%

SHERMAN MOTOR COMPANY[1]

The Sherman Motor Company manufactured two specialized models of trucks in a single plant. Manufacturing operations were grouped into four departments: metal stamping, engine assembly, model 101 assembly, and model 102 assembly. Monthly production capacity in each department was limited as follows, assuming that each department devoted full time to the model in question:

Department	*Monthly Capacity* Model 101	Model 102
Metal stamping	2,500	3,500
Engine assembly	3,333	1,667
Model 101 assembly	2,250	...
Model 102 assembly	...	1,500

That is, the capacity of the metal stamping department was sufficient to produce stampings for either 2,500 model 101 trucks or 3,500 model 102 trucks per month if it devoted full time to either model. It could also produce stampings for both models with a corresponding reduction in the potential output of each. Since each model 102 truck required five-sevenths as much of the capacity of the department as one model 101 truck, for every seven model 102 trucks produced it would be necessary to subtract five from the capacity remaining for model 101. If, for example, 1,400 model 102 trucks were produced, there would be sufficient stamping capacity available for $2,500 - (\frac{5}{7})(1,400) = 1,500$ model 101 trucks. Thus, the capacity restrictions in the four departments could be represented by the straight lines shown in Exhibit 1. Any production combination within the area bounded by the heavy portion of the lines was feasible from a capacity standpoint.

The prices to dealers of the two models, F.O.B. the Sherman plant, were $2,100 for model 101 and $2,000 for model 102. Sherman

---

[1] Adapted from an example used by Robert Dorfman in "Mathematical or 'Linear' Programming: A Nonmathematical Approach," *American Economic Review*, December, 1953.

followed the price leadership of one of the larger manufacturers in the industry.

As a result of a sellers' market in 1953, Sherman was able to sell as many trucks as it could produce. The production schedules it had followed during the first six months of the year resulted in a monthly output of 333 model 101 trucks and 1,500 model 102 trucks. At this level of production, both the model 102 assembly and the engine assembly departments were operating at capacity, but the metal stamping department was operating at only 56.2% of capacity and the model 101 assembly department was at only 14.8%. Standard costs at this level of production are given in Exhibit 2, and further details on overhead costs are given in Exhibit 3.

At a monthly planning session of the company's executives in July, 1953, dissatisfaction was expressed with the company's profit performance as reported in the six-month income statement just prepared (see Exhibit 4). The sales manager pointed out that it was impossible to sell the model 101 truck to yield a profit and suggested that it be dropped from the line in order to improve over-all profitability.

The controller objected to this suggestion. "The real trouble, Dick, is that we are trying to absorb the entire fixed overhead of the model 101 assembly department with only a small number of units production. Actually these units are making a contribution to overhead, even though it's not adequate to cover fixed costs, and we'd be worse off without them. In fact, it seems to me quite possible that we'd be better off by *increasing* production of model 101 trucks, cutting back if necessary on model 102 production."

The production manager pointed out that there was another way in which output of model 101 trucks could be stepped up, which would not require a cutback in model 102 production. This would be through purchase of engines from an outside supplier, thus relieving the present capacity problem in the engine assembly department. If this course of action were followed, Sherman would probably furnish the supplier with the necessary materials but would reimburse him for his labor and overhead.

At this point the president entered the discussion. He asked the controller, the sales manager, and the production manager to get together to consider the two questions raised by their comments and to report their recommendations to him the next day. The two questions were: (1) Assuming no change in present capacity and demand, what would be the most profitable product mix? (2) What was the maximum labor and overhead charge Sherman could afford to pay for engines if it purchased them from an outside supplier?

Question

What would be your reply to the questions raised by the president?

Exhibit 1

SHERMAN MOTOR COMPANY

DIAGRAM SHOWING PRODUCTION POSSIBILITIES

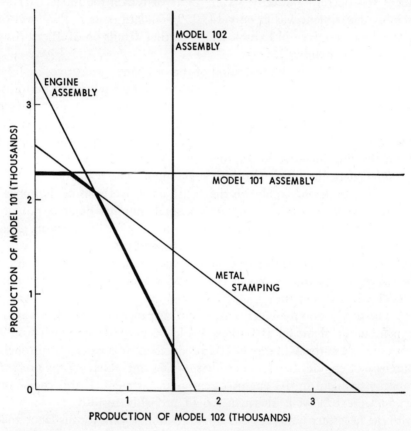

Exhibit 2

SHERMAN MOTOR COMPANY

STANDARD COSTS OF TWO TRUCK MODELS

	Model 101		Model 102	
Direct materials...................		$1,200		$1,000
Direct labor:				
Metal stamping.................$ 40			$ 30	
Engine assembly................. 60			120	
Final assembly.................. 100	200		75	225
Overhead:*				
Metal stamping................$216			$169	
Engine assembly................ 130			251	
Final assembly.................. 445	791		175	595
Total.......................		$2,191		$1,820

*See Exhibit 3.

Exhibit 3

SHERMAN MOTOR COMPANY

OVERHEAD BUDGET FOR 1953

Department	Total Overhead per Month*	Fixed Overhead per Month†	Variable Overhead per Unit	
			Model 101	Model 102
Metal stamping..................$ 325,000		$135,000	$120	$100
Engine assembly................ 420,000		85,000	105	200
Model 101 assembly.............. 148,000		90,000	175	...
Model 102 assembly.............. 262,000		75,000	...	125
	$1,155,000	$385,000	$400	$425

* Based on planned 1953 production rate of 333 model 101 trucks and 1,500 model 102 trucks per month.
† Fixed overhead was distributed to models in proportion to degree of capacity utilization.

Exhibit 4

SHERMAN MOTOR COMPANY

INCOME STATEMENT FOR SIX MONTHS ENDING
JUNE 30, 1953

(Dollar figures in thousands)

Net sales.......................................	$21,950
Cost of goods sold.............................	20,683
Gross margin...................................	$ 1,267
Selling, administrative, and general expense.........	1,051
Net income before taxes.........................	$ 216
Taxes on income................................	115
Net income after taxes...........................	$ 101

THE LOCKBOURNE COMPANY

The Lockbourne Company was one of the country's leading manufacturers and distributors of a line of packaged goods which it sold nationally under the trade name of Burn-Loc Products. The company operated three factories from which it shipped to regional warehouses or directly to large outlets.

In 1957, demand for Burn-Loc Products was 3,200,000 "equivalent" cases, distributed as follows according to the five sales regions:

Sales Region	Demand (Hundred Thousand Cases)
Atlanta	5
Los Angeles	4
Dallas	4
Chicago	11
New York	8
	32

One-shift production capacity in each of the three plants was as follows:

Plant	Production Capacity (Hundred Thousand Cases)
Home City	12
Branch No. 1	7
Branch No. 2	15
	34

Estimated freight costs per case from each of the factories to each distribution center are given in Exhibit 1. While not all shipments were routed through regional warehouses, on the average the freight cost on direct shipments to outlets was quite close to the cost which would have been incurred if the shipment had been routed through the servicing warehouse.

Lockbourne followed a philosophy of decentralized management. Top executives favored this approach for a number of reasons. First, by enriching the experience of subordinate managers, it provided better training for ultimate top-management responsibility. Second, it insured that, insofar as possible, operating decisions were made by those persons most familiar with the detailed circumstances which would determine the success or failure of the decisions. Under the decentralized approach, subordinate managers were held responsible for the profitability of operations under their control.

Consistent with the policy of decentralization, each of the five regional warehouses was under the direct supervision of a regional sales manager. The warehouses were not assigned to a particular plant for servicing, since demand shifts made a certain amount of flexibility necessary. Rather, the regional sales manager or a delegated subordinate decided upon which plant to place an order. The price paid by the warehouse was $6.25 per case F.O.B. the plant. This price was set to recover costs plus a reasonable return on investment for the manufacturing division.[1] Since the regional warehouse was required to absorb the freight costs, it was expected that the regional sales managers would place their orders so as to minimize their own freight costs and hence those of the company as a whole.

Over a period of time, this procedure had led to increasing amounts of organizational friction, and in early 1958 some officials of Lockbourne were beginning to question whether the procedure was even achieving the objective of minimizing freight costs. Because Branch No. 2 was not the closest plant to any of the regional warehouses, it was never deliberately selected as a source by a regional sales manager. Rather, the managers would initially order from the Home City or Branch No. 1, whichever was closer. Since these plants had inadequate capacity to meet all sales demands, it was then necessary for the plant managers to reject some orders. No consistent procedure was followed in determining which orders would be accepted, but it was largely a matter of "first-come-first-served." The regional managers whose orders were rejected were then usually forced to take them to Branch No. 2, typically at a considerable increase in freight cost. This aspect of the situation resulted in much grumbling by the regional managers.

Moreover, since the orders placed with Branch No. 2 were not placed there in a conscious effort to minimize freight costs, there appeared to be a strong possibility that the resulting over-all shipping program was not optimal. For this reason, some executives felt that the practice of leaving shipping decisions to the decentralized judgments of

_____
[1] Variable costs of manufacture were quite similar in the three plants.

regional managers should be discontinued. They proposed instead that all orders be routed through a central office which could then determine an optimal shipping program from an over-all company point of view. The actual quantities shipped over each possible route in 1957 are given in Exhibit 2; total shipping costs that year were about $2,275,000.

Other executives were concerned about the effect such a proposal would have on the general effectiveness of decentralized management. They also observed that one result of the proposal would be to saddle the regional sales managers with freight costs over which they could exercise no control.

Question

Evaluate the proposal to establish centralized control over shipping programs. Does this case demonstrate an inherent contradiction between decentralized decision making and over-all optimization?

Exhibit 1

THE LOCKBOURNE COMPANY

SCHEDULE OF FREIGHT RATES

(Dollars per case)

Factory	Atlanta	Los Angeles	Dallas	Chicago	New York
Home City	$0.95	$1.05	$0.80	$0.15	$1.00
Branch No. 1	0.35	1.80	1.40	0.80	0.30
Branch No. 2	0.90	1.80	1.60	0.70	0.85

Regional Warehouse

Exhibit 2

THE LOCKBOURNE COMPANY

SHIPPING PROGRAM IN 1957

(Hundred thousand cases)

Factory	Atlanta	Los Angeles	Dallas	Chicago	New York	Total
Home City	0	1	2	9	0	12
Branch No. 1	3	0	0	2	2	7
Branch No. 2	2	3	2	0	6	13
Total	5	4	4	11	8	32

Regional Warehouse

Chapter 3

COST-PRICE-VOLUME
RELATIONSHIPS

The prices charged by a business enterprise for the goods and services it sells affect its profit in three different ways. There is first, of course, the direct effect which results from the fact that price is "revenue per unit," since the total revenue is price times quantity sold. Second, the quantity the enterprise is able to sell depends itself upon the price charged; economists express this price-quantity relationship in the form of a *demand function* or *demand schedule.* Finally, as we have seen in the preceding two chapters, the quantity sold will be an important determinant of cost. Thus, three major variables—price, volume, and cost—which together determine total profit are all affected by pricing decisions.

In this chapter, we shall examine the interrelationships among these three variables, focusing our attention particularly on the ways that price and volume affect *product-creating* costs. In terms of the broad framework for this book, price is viewed as the major *demand-creating* cost; the difficult art of price determination is thus the major topic of Part II. The objective of this chapter, therefore, is to explore some of the cost implications of pricing decisions so that we will be better able to evaluate the profit consequences of alternative pricing policies in subsequent chapters.

The Concept of Contribution

The most fundamental concept used to analyze the interrelationships of costs, price, and volume is the concept of *contribution to overhead and profit.* Consider, as a simple example, the following income statement for the Clinton Company in 1972:

163

```
Net sales.....................................$500,000
Cost of goods sold...........................  300,000
Gross manufacturing profit.....................$200,000
Selling, general, and administrative expenses.......  100,000
Net profit before taxes.........................$100,000
```

The Clinton Company manufactures only one product, and in 1972, it sold 100,000 units at a price of $5 each. For a single-product company such as this, the historical price and volume factors in the profitability equation may be relatively easy to establish. The cost factors, however, may require further analysis. The fact that the "cost of goods sold" was $3 per unit is not pertinent to our analysis because it reflects the combined effect of the total manufacturing costs for the year and the volume produced and sold. Some of these costs were incurred in order to create and maintain the company's production capacity; at different volume levels, the total cost per unit would reflect the spreading of these relatively fixed costs over a greater or lesser number of units. Let us assume that an analysis of the $300,000 of manufacturing costs reveals that $175,000 was spent for product-creating costs such as direct labor and materials, and $125,000 was for supervision, property taxes, insurance, and other capacity-creating costs. A similar analysis of selling, general, and administrative expenses discloses that sales commissions of 10% of the selling price is the only item of demand-creating cost that is variable directly with the quantity sold. Thus, average variable costs at the 1972 volume were $2.25 per unit ($1.75 manufacturing cost and $0.50 sales commissions).

The difference between price and average variable cost is called *contribution per unit.* The average contribution earned on each unit sold by the Clinton Company in 1972, for example, was $5.00 — $2.25 = $2.75. The word "contribution" is intended to suggest that the price on each unit sold, after first being applied to cover its variable product-creating and demand-creating costs, is able to "contribute" to a pool of funds out of which the company's fixed, or capacity-creating, costs will be met. Any residual in this pool of funds after payment of fixed costs then becomes the company's profit.

The concept of contribution may be illustrated by recasting the Clinton Company's income statement in the following instructive way:

```
Contribution to fixed overhead and profit:
    Selling price per unit............................$5.00
    Average variable cost per unit....................  2.25
       Contribution per unit..........................$2.75
          Total contribution on 100,000 units...........    $275,000
    Less: Fixed overhead..............................     175,000
    Net profit........................................     $100,000
```

This simple concept of contribution to overhead and profit is a crude but powerful analytical tool. Suppose, for example, that the management of the Clinton Company wished to explore the effect of reducing the price on their product from $5 to $4.50, an action which they expected might increase the sales volume to 125,000 units. A rough calculation of the effect of this change takes less than a minute:

```
Contribution at a price of $4.50:
  Selling price per unit..........................$4.50
  Variable costs per unit:
    Manufacturing..............................$1.75
    Sales commission—10%.....................  0.45    2.20
  Contribution per unit.........................          $2.30
       Total contribution on 125,000 units..........              $287,500
```

Comparing this calculation to the preceding one, we see that the contribution to overhead and profit is $12,500 higher than it was at the $5 price; the price reduction would be a profitable one if 125,000 units could be sold. The value of the contribution concept lies in its efficiency as a calculating procedure; it is neither more nor less accurate than

Table 3–1

CLINTON COMPANY

EVALUATING THE EFFECT OF A PRICE DECREASE

	100,000 Units at $5 Price	125,000 Units at $4.50 Price
Net sales..	$500,000	$562,500
Cost of goods sold:		
Variable costs @ $1.75...............................	$175,000	$218,750
Fixed factory overhead..............................	125,000	125,000
Total cost of sales................................	$300,000	$343,750
Gross manufacturing profit..........................	$200,000	$218,000
Selling, general, and administrative expenses:		
Sales commissions @ 10%............................	$ 50,000	$ 56,250
Fixed other overhead...............................	50,000	50,000
Total selling, general and administrative expenses.....	$100,000	$106,250
Net profit before taxes.............................	$100,000	$112,500

the estimates of cost variability on which it rests. But it is more efficient, as illustrated by the longer, more traditional calculation shown in Table 3–1 which is based on the same cost estimates and, inevitably, arrives at the same conclusion.

Break-even Point Analysis

One very common way of demonstrating the interrelationships of the three variables, price, cost, and volume, is through the use of a *profitgraph* or *break-even chart.* An example of such a chart, using the Clinton Company's data for 1972, is shown in Figure 3–1. One line, representing total revenue, rises at the rate of $5 per unit. Another line, representing total cost, rises at the rate of $2.25 per unit, starting from the point representing the fixed costs of $175,000 per year.

The term "break-even chart" refers to the fact that the chart can

Figure 3–1

CLINTON COMPANY

PROFITGRAPH

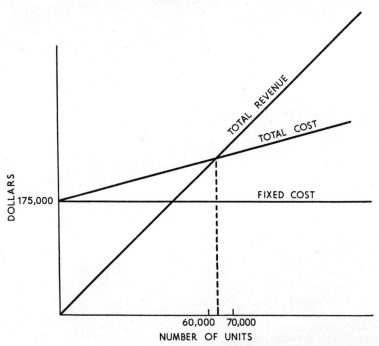

be used to determine the *break-even point* for the company, that is, the volume at which profit would be zero. This point is represented on the horizontal axis immediately below the intersection of the total revenue and total cost lines since at this point total revenue and total cost are equal. The break-even volume can also be determined by dividing the fixed overhead by the contribution per unit, for example, $175,000 divided by $2.75 per unit equals 63,637 units.

The profitgraph can also be used to explore the effects of alternative decisions on the company's total profits, which are represented by the vertical distance between the total revenue and total cost lines. For example, to evaluate the change in price to $4.50 per unit, the slope of both the total revenue and total cost lines would be redrawn, respectively, at $4.50 and $2.20 per unit. The break-even point would then be 76,087 units. Can you explain why the break-even point rises, even though the price reduction appears profitable?

The profitgraph as it is customarily drawn is a severely over-simplified picture of reality, and this fact must be kept in mind when interpreting any conclusions derived from it. For one thing, the total costs graphed are generally taken from accounting records and hence include only accounting costs. As we have seen in Chapter 1, there are often costs relevant for decision making which do not appear in the accounts. The opportunity costs of using fixed facilities when they are in scarce supply is an example.

As a corollary to the point just made, the costs graphed in Figure 3–1 are not only accounting costs but historical costs. The cost-volume relationship may be changing over time, and hence the profitgraph derived from historical records may be misleading for making decisions about the future.

Then, even if we consider only accounting costs, the assumption implicit in Figure 3–1 that average variable cost is the same at all volumes is subject to question. As we argued in Chapter 1, variable costs have a tendency to change in discrete units (as, for example, when another worker is added to the payroll). Moreover, the efficiency of operations may depend upon volume. At relatively high volumes, for example, less efficient facilities may have to be brought into service and less skilled workers employed.

But probably the most serious weakness of the profitgraph is that it ignores the interrelationship between price and volume: total revenue is assumed to increase in direct proportion to volume. This assumption, for most businesses, is literally unrealistic. Except for the effect of environmental factors, it is most unlikely that the Clinton Company could sell 125,000 units of its product at a price of $5. Management, of course, can influence the number of units that will be sold by changing the price, but as we have just seen, such a change means that we must now draw a new profitgraph to reflect the change in revenue and costs per unit.

In spite of these several limitations concerning unrealistic assumptions, once the break-even chart is understood it can be interrogated to produce a good deal of useful information. For example, although Figure 3–1 does not picture a true price-quantity relationship or demand curve, in the absence of any information about this curve we might be interested in knowing what quantity would have to be sold in order to break even. Looking at Figure 3–1, we can determine that given the cost and price assumptions embodied therein, the break-even volume would be 63,637. This represents the break-even volume only for the particular price graphed, $5. If we were interested in learning

Figure 3–2

CLINTON COMPANY

BREAK-EVEN VOLUME AS FUNCTION OF PRICE

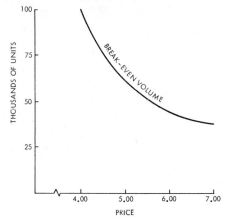

the effect of a price change on the break-even volume, we could obtain this information by constructing additional profitgraphs utilizing different assumptions about the price. Each one of these profitgraphs would give us the break-even point corresponding to that particular price. By doing this a number of times, we could develop another graph, such as the one shown in Figure 3–2, which gives break-even point as a function of price. This information, presented to the pricing decision maker, would enable him to evaluate any particular price alternative against his intuitive judgment as to the probable demand at that price.

Rather than a break-even price, the decision maker may be interested in a price which would bring in a specified amount of profit. Information about this price could be obtained just as readily as the break-even price. If a certain number of dollars of profit are desired, these dollars can simply be added to the total cost function on the break-even chart, raising it uniformly by an amount representing the profit goal. We are thus able to determine a new "break-even" volume, where the break-even now includes not only actual costs but also the desired level of profit.

The technique of break-even analysis is a useful extension of the contribution concept. In order to determine the contribution per unit, we must divide all costs into variable and fixed categories; break-even analysis then links these two types of costs together again in order to find the total volume necessary for total contribution to equal total fixed costs. Despite the simplicity of this concept, its practical application is often difficult because of the intricate interrelationships between the three profit variables of cost, price, and volume. A single analysis involving the manipulations of the three variables simultaneously may make it difficult to grasp the significance of the relationship between any two of the variables. An easier approach, illustrated in Figure 3–1, is to hold one of the variables constant (the cost function in that case) in order to observe how the other two interact. We shall use this approach in the balance of this chapter, dealing in turn with each of the three pairs of two-variable combinations.

PRICE-VOLUME RELATIONSHIPS

Let us return now to the Essex Corporation, the illustrative company used for our discussion in Chapter 1, and turn our attention to an analysis of that company's cost-price-volume relationships. In Chapter 1 we attempted to explain why the actual 1972 profit was different from the profit plan for that year, and we found (Table 1–8) that several aspects of the profit variance were attributable to the price-volume relationship. We did not fully explore the impact of the price-volume change in that chapter, but now, armed with the concept of contribution to overhead and profit and the technique of break-even analysis, we can return to that task.

Referring back to Tables 1–1 and 1–6, we may characterize our problem in the following way: At the beginning of 1972, the profit plan for Essex was to sell 900,000 units at a price of $3.95. During the year, management lowered the price so that the average for the year was $3.89 per unit and 972,418 units were sold. What effect did this price-volume change have on the company's profit for the year?

The first step in dealing with this question is to complete our analysis of all the costs incurred by the company, dividing the costs into those that vary with the quantity sold and those that are fixed. We have already done this analysis for the manufacturing costs (Tables 1–4 and 1–5) by examining the distinction between product-creating costs and capacity-creating costs in Table 1–3. We must now do a similar analysis of the other major group of costs: selling and administrative expenses.

Demand-Creating Costs

A useful starting point in an analysis of selling and administrative expenses is to examine the objectives for which each element of cost has been incurred. While the accounting records, as illustrated in Table 1–1, separate these costs into 10 accounts, that breakdown is a functional one showing what the money was spent for rather than why it was spent. Slicing these same costs a different way leads to the analysis shown in Table 3–2.

While it is conceptually useful to distinguish between demand-creating costs and capacity-creating costs, the application of this distinction in a practical situation is sometimes difficult. The value of attempting to make such distinctions is that it provides the basis for a more careful examination of those demand-creating costs which tend to vary with the volume of sales. Some selling and administrative expenses are clearly capacity-creating costs; they must be incurred if the company is to do business at all. In this sense, the expense for auditing and legal services is directly analogous to the expense for property taxes and insurance that is commonly classified as a part of manufacturing overhead. Somewhat more subtle, the salary of the sales manager is also a capacity-creating cost analogous to the salary of the production

Table 3–2

ESSEX CORPORATION

ANALYSIS OF SELLING AND ADMINISTRATIVE EXPENSES FOR 1972

Expense Item	Total Cost	Demand-Creating Costs	Capacity-Creating Costs
Office payroll	$118,162	$ 15,401	$102,761
Sales salaries and commissions	201,386	201,386	. . .
Fringe benefits (17.5%)	55,962	37,979	17,983
Advertising and sales expenses	217,624	217,624	. . .
Audit and legal	21,933	. . .	21,933
Interest expense	88,233	. . .	88,233
Travel and telephone	27,022	18,581	8,441
Bad debts	3,589	3,589	. . .
Office supplies and postage	16,019	4,794	11,225
Miscellaneous	26,702	8,814	17,888
Total	$776,632	$508,168	$268,464

superintendent; although both men have functional responsibilities related to the creation of demand or the creation of product, their roles are so fundamental to the very existence of the company that they are probably best viewed as part of the basic capacity of the company.

Nevertheless, the group of costs identified as demand-creating costs in Table 3–2 is not "pure" in the sense of being strictly variable with sales volume. It is true that all eight expense categories do vary with sales to some extent, but the variability, as with some elements of manufacture overhead, is less than strictly proportional. In total, for the year 1972, these costs amounted to 13.4% of sales revenue, but this does not mean that this cost would change by 13 cents for every change of $1 in sales revenue. Advertising expense is a good example of this phenomenon. Management of the Essex Company has found, over the years, that a certain critical mass of advertising exposure is necessary in their industry before the desired result can be achieved. Beyond that point there is a marginal value from additional advertising such that, although the company does increase its advertising budget as the sales volume grows, only a small part of the advertising budget is variable in this way. The same thing is true of other expenses that might be called "sales support activities," such as salesmen's travel, telephone expenses, and bad debts. There are also some expenses incurred in the home office for clerical work in preparing invoices and handling sales inquiries which tend to vary with the volume of sales.

An examination of each of the elements of demand-creating costs will lead finally to an estimate of the portion of those costs that are variable with sales volume. Some companies, in fact, prepare a variable budget for these expenses analogous to the manufacturing overhead budget shown in Table 1–5. We will take a somewhat less precise approach in this chapter, and will estimate that the variable portion of these costs is equal to 8% of sales revenue; roughly 4% for sales commissions and 4% for sales support activities. Note that the variable percentage is stated in terms of sales revenue rather than as a cost per unit sold, reflecting the fact that these costs tend to be incurred or controlled in relationship to sales dollars rather than in relationship to units.

Break-even Point

With this estimate of the variable portion of demand-creating costs, combined with our analysis in Chapter 1 of variable product-creating costs, we may now compute the break-even point for the Essex Corporation as shown in Table 3–3. Basing our calculation on the profit

Table 3–3

ESSEX CORPORATION

CALCULATION OF BREAK-EVEN POINT BASED ON 1972 PROFIT PLAN

Selling price per unit...	$3.95
Variable costs per unit:	
Prime manufacturing costs (Table 1–4)............................$1.56	
Variable factory overhead (Table 1–5)............................ 0.30	
Variable selling expenses:	
Sales commissions..............................4% of sales	
Sales support costs..............................4% of sales	
Total.......................................8% of $3.95 0.32	
Total variable costs..	2.18
Contribution per unit to fixed overhead and profit....................	$1.77

	Factory Overhead	Selling and Administrative Expenses	Total Overhead
Fixed costs:			
Variable cost per unit (above).............	$0.30	$0.32	$0.62
Total budget for 1972 (Table 1–6)..........$1,083,000		$752,000	$1,835,000
Total variable for 900,000 units............	270,000	288,000	558,000
Fixed overhead..........................$	813,000	$464,000	$1,277,000

$$\text{Break-even point: } \frac{\text{Fixed costs}}{\text{Contribution per unit}} = \frac{\$1,277,000}{\$1.77} = 721,469 \text{ units}$$

plan for 1972, we find that the contribution per unit to fixed overhead and profit is $1.77. Dividing this figure into the total fixed overhead of $1,277,000 yields a break-even point of 721,469 units. While the break-even point, thus determined, is a precise figure, it is really nothing more than a concise encapsulation of a myriad of estimates and assumptions built into the calculations in Table 3–3. In particular, it should be noted that the calculation is based on a planned sales volume of 900,000 units to be sold at a price of $3.95 each.

Using these estimates, we may now recalculate the 1972 profit plan very simply, as shown below:

	Per Unit	Total for 900,000 Units
Sales....................................$3.95		$3,555,000
Variable costs.............................. 2.18		1,962,000
Contribution to fixed costs and profit...........$1.77		$1,593,000
Fixed costs.................................		1,277,000
Profit before taxes..........................		$ 316,000

Proof that this calculation is consistent with the break-even point in Table 3–3 is perfectly straightforward: If 900,000 units are sold, the volume will exceed the break-even point by 178,531 units. Each of these units will yield a contribution of $1.77, and because all fixed overhead has been covered by the contribution on the first 721,469 units, the entire contribution of the excess units comes through as profit. The profit on the excess units amounts to $316,000.

While the above calculation is accurate, a more useful way of arriving at the same contribution per unit is shown below:

```
Selling price............................100%
Variable selling expenses...................  8
Net sales revenue..........................  92%
Net revenue at a price of $3.95.............        $3.63
Variable product costs......................         1.86
Contribution per unit.......................        $1.77
```

It is true that the total variable costs per unit for this product amount to $2.18, but this figure holds true only at a price of $3.95. We are interested in looking at the price-volume relationship, and thus we need to recognize explicitly that some costs vary directly with the selling price, while others vary with the quantity of units sold, as illustrated in the above calculation.

Effect of a Price Change

Let us now return to the question stated earlier concerning the effect of a price change on Essex's profitability. We know that the company sold 72,418 units more than originally planned, but that the price was dropped to $3.89. About the only thing that we can be sure of is that the volume change was not *solely* attributable to the price change; a great many other factors are at work in a competitive situation. An 8% increase in volume as a result of a $1\frac{1}{2}$% price cut is not very likely in most markets; some portion of the volume increase is probably attributable to either a general growth in the market as a whole and/or ineffective action by Essex's competitors. Nevertheless, let us act as though the volume increase were due simply to the price drop, and determine what effect that action had on profits. Using the new price-volume relationship, we may prepare a revised profit plan for Essex as shown below:

```
92% of $3.89 per unit........................$3.58
Less: Variable production costs................ 1.86
   Contribution per unit.....................$1.72
Total contribution on 972,418 units.............    $1,672,559
Fixed costs.................................     1,277,000
   Revised profit..........................    $ 395,559
```

This calculation indicates that the company's profit would increase by $79,559, the difference between the revised profit shown above and the $316,000 profit in the original plan. Actually, this profit increase is the result of two simultaneous changes: (1) a loss in revenue on the units that could have been sold at the original price of $3.95, offset by (2) the additional contribution to profit on the incremental units that are sold at a lower price. The following calculation displays these two effects:

Revenue loss (net) of $0.05/unit on 900,000 units.................$(45,000)
Additional contribution of $1.72/unit on 72,418 incremental units.... 124,559
Net gain from price-volume change............................$ 79,559

Note that the price reduction of 6 cents per unit results in a net revenue loss of only 5 cents per unit because of the offsetting effect of variable selling expenses. Even more important, the calculation immediately above is an extremely useful way of evaluating price changes in general, and we will return to it in more detail in our discussion of pricing decisions in Chapter 7.

The calculations above are sufficient to permit us to complete our analysis of the profit variance for the Essex Corporation in 1972. We saw in Table 1–7 that the total profit variance for the year was $81,108, and our calculation of the effect of the price change above indicates that nearly all of that variance was due to the price change. The easiest way to complete our analysis is to first recast the original profit plan as though the company had intended all along to lower the price and achieve the higher sales volume. Such a calculation, shown in Table 3–4, yields approximately the same results shown above except for a small difference due to rounding in our earlier rough calculations.

Using this adjusted profit plan we may now prepare Table 3–5 in a format similar to that shown earlier for Table 1–7, thus focusing our analysis on the small profit variance of $1,466 which was due to causes other than the price-volume change. Analyzing this variance, which is quite similar to the problem assigned as Problem 1–1, will not be discussed in detail here. A summary of such an analysis, however, is presented in Table 3–6 and shows that in addition to the effect of the price-volume change measured earlier, there were two other causes for the profit variance in 1972: (1) actual expenditures in all cost categories varied slightly from the standard or budgeted amounts and (2) the higher volume of production created a favorable over-

Table 3–4

ESSEX CORPORATION

EFFECT OF PRICE-VOLUME CHANGE ON 1972 PROFIT PLAN

	Original Profit Plan		Revised Profit Plan		Increase (Decrease) in Profit
	per Unit	Total	per Unit	Total	
Number of units manufactured and sold...................		900,000		972,418	
Sales revenue...................	$3.95	$3,555,000	$3.89	$3,782,789	$227,789
Variable manufacturing costs:					
Material.....................	$0.74	$ 666,000	$0.74	$ 719,589	$(53,589)
Labor........................	0.82	738,000	0.82	797,383	(59,383)
Factory overhead...............	0.30	270,000	0.30	291,725	(21,725)
Total.....................	$1.86	$1,674,000	$1.86	$1,808,697	
Fixed factory overhead............		813,000		813,000	
Total cost of sales..........		$2,487,000		$2,621,697	
Gross profit on sales..............		$1,068,000		$1,161,092	
Variable selling costs (8%)........	$0.32	$ 288,000	$0.31	$ 301,450	(13,450)
Fixed selling and administrative expenses....................		464,000		464,000	
Total selling and administrative expenses..............		$ 752,000		$ 765,450	
Profit before taxes................		$ 316,000		$ 395,642	$ 79,642

head volume variance which was offset to some extent by an inventory adjustment. Table 3–6 represents a substantial improvement over the earlier analysis shown in Table 1–8 because the interrelated cost-price-volume effects of the price change have been pulled together in a single figure.

In this section we have examined the effect of a price-volume change, basing our analysis on the asumption that the underlying cost functions would not change as a result of a pricing action. We have

Table 3–5

ESSEX CORPORATION

COMPUTATION OF 1972 PROFIT VARIANCE FROM ADJUSTED PROFIT PLAN

	1972 Adjusted Profit Plan	1972 Actual Results	Effect on Profit Increase or (Decrease)
Sales.....................................	$3,782,789	$3,782,789	...
Cost of goods sold...........................	2,621,697	2,609,049	$12,648
Gross profit on sales........................	$1,161,092	$1,173,740	$12,648
Selling and administrative expenses.............	765,450	776,632	(11,182)
Net profit before taxes......................	$ 395,642	$ 397,108	$ 1,466

Table 3–6

ESSEX CORPORATION

RECAST STATEMENT OF CAUSES OF 1972 PROFIT INCREASE

Original 1972 profit plan..................................	$316,000
Effect of price-volume change:	
Sold 72,418 additional units but lowered the price from $3.95	
to $3.89 (Table 3–4)..................................	$ 79,642

<table>
<tr><td></td><td align="center">Favorable or
(Unfavorable)</td><td></td></tr>
<tr><td>Spending variances:</td><td></td><td></td></tr>
<tr><td> Materials variance from standard..........................</td><td align="right">$(23,583)</td><td></td></tr>
<tr><td> Labor variance from standard.............................</td><td align="right">16,853</td><td></td></tr>
<tr><td> Factory overhead variance from budget....................</td><td align="right">9,968</td><td></td></tr>
<tr><td> Selling and administrative variance</td><td></td><td></td></tr>
<tr><td>   from budget..</td><td align="right">(11,182)</td><td></td></tr>
<tr><td>   Total spending variances...........................</td><td></td><td align="right">(7,944)</td></tr>
<tr><td>Overhead volume variance and inventory adjustment...........</td><td></td><td align="right">9,410</td></tr>
<tr><td>   Total profit variance for 1972.....................</td><td></td><td align="right">$ 81,108</td></tr>
<tr><td>Actual 1972 profit before taxes.............................</td><td></td><td align="right">$397,108</td></tr>
</table>

not assumed that costs would not change; clearly they would change as a result of changes in volume, as demonstrated in Table 3–4. Rather, we have assumed that fixed costs would remain constant, and that the *rates* of cost variability would continue to hold even at different volume levels. These assumptions are convenient ones because they permit us to get a better picture of the price-volume relationship. Using these assumptions, we could prepare a graph similar to Figure 3–2 for the Essex Company and compute the effect that the price cut would have on the company's break-even point. We turn our attention now to the relationship between another pair of cost-price-volume variables and will proceed in our analysis in a similar fashion.

COST-VOLUME RELATIONSHIPS

By far the most important idea that is useful in the examination of the cost-volume relationship is the idea that has been a central theme of this chapter and the two preceding ones: Costs should be segregated into two categories, those that are relatively variable with the quantity of units produced and/or sold, and those that are relatively fixed. We have devoted considerable space to analyzing the Essex Corporation's costs in this fashion, and our analysis thus far may be summarized very compactly in the following profit equation:

Profit = No. of units sold × (92% of selling price − $1.86) − $1,277,000.

With this background, we are now in a position to explore two additional aspects of the cost-volume relationship. Each of these focus on a class of decisions which management is frequently called upon to make:

1. Should the cost structure be changed by raising the level of fixed costs in order to reduce the variable costs per unit, or vice versa? The most common example of this type of decision is the acquisition of a piece of laborsaving equipment, but the same kind of analysis is also appropriate for demand-creating costs such as the establishment of branch offices with salaried salesmen to replace a sales force that is paid strictly on commissions.

2. Should the quality of the product be changed, either through a change in the variable costs per unit or through a change in fixed costs which influence quality, in order to influence the attractiveness of our product to the customer? A change in the "design cost" of a product need not necessarily be reflected by a change in selling price; the selling price may be held constant, and the effect of the change in design cost would then be reflected in the quality of units sold.

These two classes of decisions, both important aspects of the cost-volume relationship, are discussed in turn below.

Fixed Costs versus Variable Costs

Let us illustrate this sort of problem by taking a simple example from the Essex Corporation. The company's current procedure for moving materials around in the plant is to employ relatively unskilled workers with hand trucks. The company is considering acquiring a fleet of motorized lift trucks for use within the plant. A careful study of how these trucks might be used indicates that one truck, with a driver, could accomplish as much as three men with hand trucks; the saving in labor costs might be substantial. The investment required, on the other hand, is also substantial, and the question is: Should the trucks be acquired?

The most critical task in resolving this question is a careful analysis of the effect that decision would have on both variable costs per unit and fixed costs for the company. We will not go through such an analysis here, because the student will have plenty of opportunity to do so in the problems and cases which follow. Also, in this example, involving a capital investment, the problem is even more complex because the fixed cost increase occurs mainly in the form of the purchase price of the trucks. As will be seen later in Part III of this book, one way of handling capital investments in a situation such as this is to calculate the "equivalent annual cost" represented by the investment; this figure may then be used as an approximation of the increase in annual fixed costs which would result from a decision to buy the trucks. We will assume here that all the necessary analysis has been done, and that the conclusions are that acquiring the trucks would result in a savings in variable costs per unit of 10 cents, while fixed costs would increase by $65,000 per year. Using these numbers, the evaluation of the decision is now relatively straightforward.

As a first step, let us calculate a "Project Break-even Point" for the decision to acquire the lift trucks:

Project Break-even Point

$$\frac{\$65,000 \text{ increase in fixed costs}}{\$0.10/\text{unit savings in variable costs}} = 650,000 \text{ units}$$

Against this break-even point of 650,000 units, we need to only look at the planned production volume of 900,000 units to see that the project looks fairly attractive. If the lift trucks are acquired, and if 900,000 units are produced, total savings will be $90,000, thus resulting in an increase in profit before taxes of $25,000.

There is another aspect of most such projects, however, which management would normally want to consider before making the decision. This action, in effect, trades a variable cost per unit for a fixed annual cost thereby reducing, to some extent at least, the company's flexibility and responsiveness to changes in volume. What effect would this action have on the company's total break-even point? The calculation is shown below:

Revised Company Break-even Point

$$\frac{\text{Total fixed costs}}{\text{Contribution/unit}} = \frac{\$1,277,000 + \$65,000}{\$1.77 + \$0.10} = \frac{\$1,342,000}{\$1.87} = 717.647 \text{ units}$$

Note that in the calculation shown above, the 10 cents saving in variable cost per unit is added to the contribution calculated earlier at a $3.95 price. In our earlier calculation of the break-even point we found that it was 721,469 units. The lift truck project thus reduces the company's break-even point slightly. Since the company is already operating at a volume level substantially above its break-even point, and since this project does not raise the break-even point, management would probably decide that the project was a desirable one.

A little thought about the calculation just above should make it obvious that such a calculation is unnecessary in order to arrive at the conclusions we did. The reason why the company's total break-even point declined slightly was because the break-even point for the project itself was less than the company's original break-even point. In effect, the new break-even point of 717,647 units is a weighted average of the original break-even point of 721,469 and the project break-even point of 650,000. Thus, calculating the project break-even point is all that is required in order to determine whether or not the project will raise or lower the total break-even point for the company.

Extending this line of reasoning, we may now say that all such decisions that involve a tradeoff of fixed and variable costs will fall into one of the following three categories:

1. The project break-even point is less than the total break-even point. Such a project is almost unquestionably desirable because it not only "pays for itself" but does so at less risk than the risk already inherent in the company's cost structure.

2. The project break-even point is above the expected sales volume. If the cost savings on the lift truck project were only 5 cents per unit, the project break-even point would be 1,300,000 units, and this is far beyond the quantity that the company expects to sell. Accepting this project, therefore, would lower the profits of the company and increase the company's total break-even point at the same time.

3. The project break-even point is higher than the company's total break-even point but less than the expected sales volume. Suppose the lift truck project was expected to save 10 cents per unit but the increase in fixed costs would amount to $80,000. We can see immediately that the project break-even point of 800,000 units would result in a slight increase in the company's total break-even point, but if the planned sales volume of 900,000 units is achieved, profit before taxes will increase by $10,000. The project is, therefore, desirable in terms of profits, but these profits are earned at a somewhat greater risk than that inherent in the company's existing cost structure.

Projects in the third category, of course, are the most difficult to evaluate. At the superficial level they involve a tradeoff of fixed for variable costs, but more fundamentally they represent the tradeoff of risk for profit. Decisions concerning this latter tradeoff are the essence of management, and no simple calculations such as we have illustrated above can be said to "solve" such problems. Nevertheless, distilling such a decision down to its essential feature does put the decision maker in a better position to exercise his judgment as to the best course of action.

Design Costs versus Product Demand

A great many consumer products, ranging all the way from auto-mobiles to candy bars, pose vexatious problems for management in the manipulation of cost-price-volume relationships. For many such products, price is not the primary form of competition between manufacturers; traditional prices have become established, and all manufacturers tend to charge the same price. If one manufacturer raises or lowers his price, all the others are likely to follow suit. Instead, one of the major forms of competition is in the unique design features by which manufacturers attempt to differentiate their products from those of their competitors. For example, so-called "popular-priced" cigarettes all sell at the same price even though they differ in terms of length, the quality of the tobacco used, and the complexity of the filter (if any) attached to the end.

In markets such as these, the cost-volume relationship is of paramount importance. Our previous analyses have indicated how costs will change *if* volume changes, but we are now concerned with a much more complex problem: How will volume change if we intentionally change our costs? In reality, this is just another form of the pricing problem, and dealing with it involves forecasting demand under uncertainty, a topic which is dealt with in Part II of this book. Side-stepping that problem, then, until the next chapter, we may nevertheless explore this aspect of the cost-volume relationship in a manner analogous to that used earlier for the price-volume relationship.

Using the Essex Corporation as our example again, let us suppose that the company has developed a new feature for its product which it thinks will be attractive to consumers. The feature, which involves a new purchased part and a slight additional amount of assembly labor, will increase variable costs by 14 cents per unit. As one alternative, management wishes to explore the desirability of introducing this feature without increasing the selling price of the product. No change in fixed factory overhead or demand-creating costs is anticipated, although the company's advertising program would be recast to highlight the desirability of the new feature. Management believes that the new feature is sufficiently attractive so that 100,000 additional units of the product could be sold at the $3.95 price. What effect would this course of action have on the company's profitability?

If we base our calculations on the company's original profit plan of 900,000 units at a price of $3.95 each, the revised profit reflecting the assumption stated above is as follows:

```
92% of $3.95 per unit..........................$3.63
Less: Variable production costs.................  2.00
     Contribution per unit.....................$1.63
        Total contribution on 1,000,000 units......    $1,630,000
Fixed costs...................................     1,277,000
Revised profit...............................     $  353,000
```

As a result of the increase in volume, profits would be $37,000 higher than the $316,000 original profit plan. Another way to calculate that same result is as follows:

```
Contribution loss of $0.14/unit on 900,000 units.................$(126,000)
Additional contribution of $1.63/unit on 100,000 incremental units..   163,000
Net gain from cost-volume change...........................$  37,000
```

It is interesting to note that the profitability of this volume increase is influenced not only by the increase in variable production costs per unit but also by the base volume against which the increase is calculated. Suppose, for example, that Essex had expected to sell 1 million units at a price of $3.95 without the new product feature, and that the feature would raise the total sales volume to 1,100,000 units. The profit effect would be as follows:

```
Contribution loss of $0.14/unit on 1,000,000 units...............$(140,000)
Additional contribution of $1.72/unit on 100,000 incremental units..   163,000
Net gain from cost-volume change...........................$  23,000
```

The difference between this calculation and the preceding one is the base volume. In effect, the company is giving away 14 cents per unit on 100,000 more units than before, and this reduces the profitability of the cost-volume change by $14,000.

Another way to evaluate the desirability of introducing the new feature without a price increase is to observe the effect it will have on the company's total break-even point:

Break-even Point with a New Product Feature

$$\frac{\text{Total fixed costs}}{\text{Revised contribution/unit}} = \frac{\$1,277,000}{\$1.63/\text{unit}} = 783,436 \text{ units}$$

We know, of course, that such an action will raise the break-even point because we are increasing our variable costs without increasing the selling price, thereby reducing the contribution per unit. This has the effect of increasing the break-even point more than 60,000 units. Note that *this* calculation is not dependent upon the base volume used in the profit plan; it requires only an estimate of total fixed costs and the revised contribution per unit.

Calculation of a revised break-even point may not help management very much in appraising the desirability of the proposed cost-volume change. Essex is already operating substantially above its break-even point. The real question is: Will the cost-volume change increase the company's profitability? To help deal with this question, it may be more useful to provide management with a calculation showing the volume required in order to earn the same profit that would have been earned if the new feature were not introduced at all:

Volume Required for Constant Profit with New Feature

$$\frac{\text{Total contribution without feature}}{\text{Revised contribution/unit}} = \frac{\$1,593,000}{\$1.63/\text{unit}} = 977,301$$

Here, the $316,000 profit under the original profit plan has been added to the total fixed costs in order to calculate the volume required to earn the same $316,000 profit. Management is now in a better position to evaluate the desirability of introducing the new feature in this way. It may be quite difficult for management to come up with an estimate of the increase in demand that would result from the feature, but they may be able to appraise the likelihood of achieving a volume increase of 77,301 units above the original planned volume of 900,000 units. It should be noted, however, that the calculation immediately above *is* dependent upon an explicit profit estimate or profit goal. If such a profit goal is stated, it is then possible to prepare a chart such as that shown in Figure 3–3. This chart depicts graphically the relationship between sales volume and variable costs, in terms of both the volume required to cover fixed costs and the volume required to earn a stated profit. It should be noted that other, parallel lines could easily be entered on this chart representing other profit goals. If a few such additional lines were drawn on the chart, management could then use it in two ways: (1) using the line for the current profit goal, management could read off the sales volume necessary to maintain that level of profitability; and (2) if management had some estimate of what the total demand might be with the new feature, it could then find a profit line which went through the intersection of that volume at the stated variable costs per unit—that profit line would then represent the profit that would be earned if the assumed volume were achieved. A series of such lines on a chart such as Figure 3–3 are called *isoprofit* lines; each line represents the combination of two variables which would be necessary in order to achieve the stated profit.

A graph such as Figure 3–3 might also be prepared to reflect the relationship between fixed costs and sales volume, in order to deal with those circumstances where the action being considered has an impact

Figure 3–3

ESSEX CORPORATION

BREAK-EVEN VOLUME AS A FUNCTION OF VARIABLE COSTS

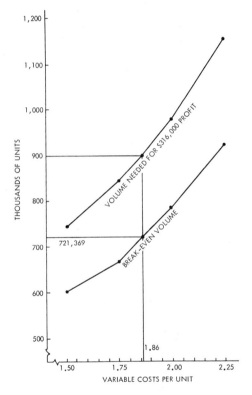

on fixed costs rather than variable costs. And, conceptually, a three-dimensional chart might be visualized which had variable costs per unit on one axis, total fixed costs on another, and sales volume on the third.

This section has discussed two classes of management decisions for which an analysis of cost-volume relationships may be useful. We turn our attention now to the third pair of variables in the cost-price-volume formula.

COST-PRICE RELATIONSHIPS

Another common problem which businessmen frequently face is that of dealing with increasing costs and the explicit relationship between costs and prices. Even in a highly industrialized economy where productivity is increasing, the decrease in unit costs from higher productivity is sometimes more than offset by cost increases due to inflation. This "cost-price squeeze," as it is sometimes called, is the main topic of this section. Before turning to that topic, however, we shall deal briefly with another type of decision involving manipulation of the cost-price relationship: exploitation of a new product feature. In the preceding section we dealt briefly with the cost-volume aspect of this problem, but we can now consider a broader range of alternatives.

Exploiting a New Feature

If, as was assumed earlier, the Essex Corporation has developed a new product feature which costs 14 cents per unit if incorporated in the present product, one way to capitalize on this development is to hold the price constant and reap the benefits of increased volume. The risk of such a course of action, as we have seen, is that contribution per unit sold is decreased and the break-even point of the firm rises. Unless the necessary incremental volume is sold, profits of the company will actually be less. A common way of avoiding this danger, therefore, is to manipulate the other variable in the cost-price-volume relationship: increase the price of the product to offset the increased costs of the new feature.

Such a price increase can be accomplished in either of two ways. One approach would be to incorporate the feature into the existing product and raise the price for all units sold. Applying that approach requires either an explicit assumption about the volume that will be sold at the new price with the new feature, or an implicit assumption that even at a higher price the new feature is attractive enough that the same volume will be sold as would have been sold at the old price without the feature. Testing this latter assumption first yields the following calculation:

PRICE INCREASE TO COVER INCREASE IN VARIABLE COSTS

Present contribution per unit................$1.77
Variable product costs with new feature....... 2.00
Net revenue per unit required................$3.77

New selling price: $\dfrac{\$3.77}{0.92} = \$4.10$

The 14-cent increase in variable costs results in a price increase of 15 cents because variable selling expenses amounting to 8% of sales revenue will also increase slightly. Much more important, however, is the validity of the implicit assumption in the above calculation. While it may be highly likely that some customers will find the new feature attractive and will be willing to pay 15 cents more for the product, it is far less certain that all 900,000 customers will be willing to do so. If the demand for the new product is at all price-sensitive, raising the price even with a new feature could actually result in a decrease in the total volume sold. The uncertainty, of course, runs in the other direction, too. The new feature may be sufficiently attractive that even at a slightly higher price, more than 900,000 units will be sold. The point is that changing the existing product and changing its price will probably result in a change in volume, and the direction of this change may be very hard to predict.

The other approach to pricing for a new product feature avoids these complications. The existing product is continued at its current price, and a deluxe model which offers the new feature is introduced at a somewhat higher price. This approach offers many advantages to both the manufacturer and the consumer. The manufacturer's risk is minimized because the consumers who were happy with the old standard product may continue to use it; no customers will be forced to switch to the standard product offered by our competitors. Further, the deluxe model may be priced higher than might otherwise be the case, reflecting the value that it has in the eyes of those consumers who are really attracted by it. In the example used here, the deluxe model might be priced at $4.25 or even higher, both to create a significant price difference between the two products, and to recover those additional costs that will result from offering two products rather than one. Finally, Essex may find that sales of the standard product increase as a result of the improved reputation of the company's products; some customers may buy Essex's standard product even though they do not wish to pay the price for the deluxe model because they have more confidence in the company which is a leader in product innovation. The customer, too, is better served by this approach. He now has two products to choose from at two different prices and can decide which one he prefers.

Selecting the strategy for exploiting a new product feature is further complicated by the continuing evolution of most products. If there is a typical pattern, it seems to be that the initial introduction of a new feature is reflected in the price charged, frequently through the creation of a deluxe model. This phase is sometimes called "skimming the cream" off the market, and involves cost-price manipulation. If the new product is successful, however, the feature may ultimately be incorporated into the standard product with little or no price increase because of the larger volume of the improved product that can be sold. In this second stage, the cost-volume relationship becomes the more important, but that relationship may then be analyzed with greater knowledge, and less risk, because of the success of the first stage.

The Cost-Price Squeeze

What happens when the costs that a manufacturer incurs for wages and materials go up? In some industries, continuing improvements in the efficiency of the production process tend to offset these cost increases so that a manufacturer can continue to earn a reasonable profit without increasing the price that he charges for his product. Some industries offer products which continue to gain increased consumer acceptance, and these volume increases may be sufficient to yield the necessary profit without a price increase. But many times, even though these two factors may serve to mitigate the effect of cost increases, the manufacturer may be forced to increase his prices if he is to maintain the growth and profitability of his business.

In a highly competitive economy, similar products produced by different manufacturers tend to be sold at approximately the same price. Without some distinguishing product feature, one manufacturer can raise his price only against the expectation that the volume that he sells will decline. But if all manufacturers are faced with an increase in their costs, there may be a general increase in the price charged by all manufacturers, with very little effect on the market share held by each manufacturer. Total sales of the industry may decline if the product is subject to substitution by other products for which the price has not increased, but even this effect may be minimized if there is a general upward pressure on all prices due to inflation.

Price increases of this sort, as may be readily observed, do not occur in a nice orderly manner across all segments of an economy simultaneously. On the other hand, we frequently see an almost-simultaneous increase in prices for a particular group of products by all manufacturers, usually as a result of "price leadership" by one producer who raises his prices and is promptly followed by many of his competitors.

Such price increases are a good example of the way that the cost-price relationship operates, and we will illustrate it using the Essex Corporation again as our example.

In order to make the example as realistic as possible, we must first recognize that cost increases may occur in both the fixed and variable components of product costs. Increases in variable costs are fairly easy to deal with. In the example used just above, and assuming for the moment no increase in fixed costs, a 14 cents per unit in variable costs for Essex would indicate that a 15 cents per unit price increase might be appropriate. The word "appropriate" is used here in a quite specific sense; it assumes (1) that Essex is in an industry that had a relatively stable competitive situation before the cost increase occurred; (2) that all manufacturers in the industry are faced with the same increase in costs; and (3) that a price increase reflecting the cost increase will, therefore, be followed by all manufacturers with no change in their relative competitive situation. If Essex wishes to be the price leader for its industry, its management might accept these assumptions and raise the price by 15 cents per unit in the expectation that other manufacturers would follow.

In fact, of course, the effects of inflationary cost increases are even more complex. Fixed costs will probably be increasing too. And at the same time, an aggressive management will be seeking ways to improve productive efficiency so that even though some price increase might be almost inevitable, it may be minimized in order to keep the industry's products as competitive as possible in the larger array of choices open to consumers. As we saw in the earlier section on cost-volume relationships, many productivity gains are the results of investments in labor-saving equipment which have the effect of reducing variable costs by more than enough to justify the resulting increase in the fixed costs. The net effect of all these forces is a change in the cost structure of the firm. Inflation drives up both fixed and variable costs, while the drive for efficiency tends to substitute fixed cost increases for variable costs decreases. In order to examine this complex set of changes, let us simplify it a little and assume that the variable costs per unit for Essex are not expected to change because improved productivity will offset the increased labor and material costs. Fixed costs, on the other hand, are expected to increase by $100,000 reflecting both the effect of inflation and the additional costs incurred to improve productivity. A cost-based price increase in this situation is somewhat more complex to calculate, as illustrated below:

PRICE INCREASE TO COVER INCREASE IN FIXED COSTS

Present fixed costs.............................	$1,277,000
Fixed cost increase...........................	100,000
New fixed costs...........................	$1,377,000
Present profit before taxes......................	316,000
Total contribution required..............	$1,693,000

Contribution required per unit, if

$$900{,}000 \text{ units are sold:} \quad \frac{\$1{,}693{,}000}{900{,}000} = \$1.88$$

Variable costs per unit.................	1.86
Net revenue per unit required..........	$3.74

$$\text{New selling price:} \quad \frac{\$3.74}{0.92} = \$4.07$$

The two important assumptions embodied in this calculation are that (1) the company's profit target will be held constant at \$316,000 and (2) other manufacturers will follow Essex's price increase, with the result that Essex will still be able to sell 900,000 units. Under these assumptions, a price increase to \$4.07 per unit is justified. The same conclusion could have been reached more directly by recognizing that what Essex is trying to do is to spread the \$100,000 increase in fixed

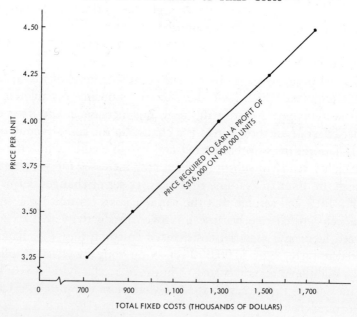

Figure 3–4

ESSEX CORPORATION

PRICE AS A FUNCTION OF FIXED COSTS

costs across its 900,000 units of volume, a cost increase of 11 cents per unit. Variable selling expenses will also increase as a result of the price increase, so that the total price increase necessary is 12 cents per unit.

Figure 3–4 is a graph showing the relationship between product price and total fixed costs, under the two assumptions stated in the preceding paragraph. Either of these assumptions could be changed, of course, and a new line drawn on that chart reflect the new assumptions.

Another effect of an increase in fixed costs, even though offset by a price increase, is a change in the break-even point for the company. If the Essex Corporation raised its price to $4.07 per unit, its break-even point would increase slightly, as shown below:

Effect of Higher Fixed Costs on the Break-even Point

$$\frac{\text{Total fixed costs}}{\text{Contribution/unit}} = \frac{\$1,377,000}{\$1.88} = 732,447 \text{ units}$$

Thus, management might feel that even though the price increase is adequate to yield the same profit as before, the business is now somewhat riskier than it was because of the change in its cost structure. One way to offset the undesirable effect of a higher break-even point would be to calculate the price increase necessary to result in the same break-even point as had previously existed. Such a calculation is shown below:

PRICE INCREASE REQUIRED TO HOLD BREAK-EVEN POINT CONSTANT

Present break-even point............................. 721,469 units
New total fixed costs............................... $1,377,000

Contribution required per unit: $\dfrac{\$1,377,000}{721,469} = \$1.91$

Variable costs per unit........................ 1.86
Net revenue per unit required................. $3.77

New selling price: $\dfrac{\$3.77}{0.92} = \$4.10$

In effect, the calculation above spreads the $100,000 increase in fixed costs across the break-even volume of 721,469 units, a cost increase of about 14 cents per unit which, when adjusted for variable selling expenses, results in a 15 cents price increase. A price of $4.10 per unit would, therefore, leave the company's break-even point unchanged. On the other hand, if such a price increase were followed by the other manufacturers, and if Essex continued to sell 900,000 units at the new price, the company's profit would be higher, which the following calculation illustrates:

EXPECTED PROFIT IF 900,000 UNITS ARE SOLD AT A
PRICE OF $4.10

Contribution on 900,000 units at $1.91....$1,719,000
Total fixed costs...................... 1,377,000
Profit before taxes....................$ 342,000

These calculations concerning the effect on the company's break-even point only serve to illustrate some of the complexities of pricing for a cost increase. The real question that a price leader must grapple with is the extent to which his price increase will be matched by his competitors in the face of a complex environment where other products may be substituted for those of his industry. And this problem is even more complex if we turn our attention explicitly to the further problem of profit margins and the way that they are affected by cost increases.

Maintaining Profit Margins

If price increases are necessary as a result of inflationary cost increases, there is another "cost" element which must be recognized: the "cost" or profit due to the owners of the business who have supplied the capital and taken the risks to start and maintain the enterprise. Management is well aware that stockholders, just like employees, need wage (profit) increases to offset the effects of inflation. One way to accomplish this is to insure that any cost-based price increase is adequate to maintain the profit margins of the company, rather than to simply maintain the total dollars of profit that the company had expected to earn before the cost increase occurred. The profit margin for the Essex Corporation is stated below:

COSTS AND PROFIT AS A PERCENT OF SELLING PRICE

	Amount per Unit	Percent of Selling Price
Selling price......................................	$3.95	100
Variable selling expenses.........................	0.32	8
Net revenue......................................	$3.63	92
Variable product costs...........................	1.86	47
Contribution per unit............................	$1.77	45
Fixed costs $\dfrac{\$1,277,000}{900,000}$	1.42	36
Profit before taxes..............................	$0.35	9

If Essex wishes to maintain a 9% margin of profit before taxes, a somewhat more complex pricing formula is required to arrive at the new price necessary to reflect a $100,000 increase in fixed costs. The implicit assumption in the formula shown below is that maintaining the margin of profit at 9% will provide adequate protection for the owners of the Essex Corporation against the impact of a general inflation of costs and prices in the economy.

Price Formula for Specified Profit Margin

Price/unit =

$$\left(\frac{\text{Total fixed costs}}{\text{Estimated volume}} + \text{Variable costs/unit} \right) \div \frac{\text{Net revenue percentage}}{100\%}$$

where net revenue percentage = 100% — (Percent variable selling expenses + Percent profit margin desired)

For Essex

$$\text{Price} = \left(\frac{\$1,377,000}{900,000} + \$1.86 \right) \div \frac{100\% - (8\% + 9\%)}{100\%}$$

$$= (\$1.53 + \$1.86) \div 0.83$$

$$= \frac{\$3.39}{0.83} = \$4.08$$

As with our earlier calculations, there is a quicker way to arrive at the conclusion that the necessary price is $4.08 per unit. In effect, the formula above treats the 9% profit margin as though it were a variable expense related to sales. Net revenue is thus only 83% of the selling price. A $100,000 increase in fixed costs spread over 900,000 units amounts to an 11 cents per unit increase, but this amount must be divided by 0.83 to arrive at the 13 cents price increase necessary to maintain the company's profit margin. It should also be noted that as with our earlier calculations, a volume assumption must be specified in order to permit us to deal solely with the cost-price relationship.

While it is true that a price of $4.08 per unit would have the effect of maintaining a 9% profit margin for Essex, even this calculation is somewhat oversimplified. If the primary contribution of the owners of the business is in the form of capital, then the real obligation on the part of management is to maintain the profit margin that would continue to yield the owners a reasonable return on their capital. More sophisticated pricing techniques based on this return on investment approach are, therefore, probably more appropriate. These techniques will be discussed in Chapter 7. The analysis shown above, however, is adequate to draw the tentative conclusion that if Essex were faced with a $100,000 increase in fixed costs, a price increase to about $4.10 per unit might achieve wide following by other companies in the industry. Such an increase is adequate to cover the increase in costs, avoid any increase in the break-even point for the company, and maintain or slightly improve the profit margins of the company.

SUMMARY

This chapter has explored the interrelationships between costs, prices, and volume, attempting to illustrate the interaction of these three variables in the profit equation. Management's simultaneous manipulation of these three variables is a wonderfully complex task; the very complexity of it is one of the primary reasons why the job of a businessman is so challenging. In this chapter, however, we have simplified the task considerably by looking at three pairs of these variables, holding one constant in order that we might observe the interrelationship between the other two. This oversimplification does not reflect the way the world works, but it is a useful starting point in gaining an understanding of some of the complexities of business before we then attempt to manipulate all three variables at once.

Cost-price-volume relationships are complex because each of these variables are subject to change for a variety of reasons. Costs, the element in the equation over which management has the most control, change because of technological advances which may permit increases in productivity, inflationary factors which drive up the costs of acquiring resources, and the sheer quality of management itself which may permit an improvement in the efficiency with which the work force goes about its tasks. Prices change as a result of changes in the consumer tastes and preferences, product innovations, and the actions of competitors in both the particular industry and in the market as a whole. And volume, which ought to be totally dependent on the two preceding sets of causes, is always erratic and unpredictable due in part to the actions of competitors, but also in some part to the company's own effectiveness in its sales and promotion activities.

All these complexities, in the face of all the uncertainties in the marketplace, do not wipe out the need for and the value of careful quantitative analysis. Many of the calculations illustrated in this chapter require two or three crude but crucial assumptions in order to carry a given calculation through to its conclusion. Even crude calculations, however, are frequently better than none at all. The simple concept of contribution to overhead is a very powerful analytical device, crystalizing in a single figure both price and variable costs. The other primary analytical tool we have employed is the concept of a break-even point, which makes it possible to relate total fixed costs to contribution per unit. Neither of these concepts can be employed in a definitive way, in the sense of dictating the decisions that management must make. But when they are used with full appreciation of the assumptions required, they can have great value for management in improving the decision maker's understanding of the implications of his decisions.

PROBLEMS

Problem 3–1. In preparing its profit plan for 1968, the management of the Cotter Co., Inc. realized that its sales were subject to monthly seasonal variations, but expected that for the year as a whole the profit before taxes would total $240,000, as shown below:

	1968 Budget Amount	Percent of Sales
Sales	$2,400,000	100
Standard cost of goods sold:		
Prime costs	$ 960,000	40
Factory overhead	840,000	35
Total standard cost	$1,800,000	75
Gross profit	$ 600,000	25
Selling and general overhead	360,000	15
Profit before taxes	$ 240,000	10

Management defined "prime costs" as those costs for labor and materials which were strictly variable with the quantity of production in the factory. The overhead in the factory included both fixed and variable costs; management's estimate was that within a sales volume range of plus or minus $1,000,000 per year, variable factory overhead would be equal to 25% of prime costs. Thus the total factory overhead budgeted for 1968 consisted of $240,000 of variable costs (25% of $960,000) and $600,000 of fixed costs. All of the selling and general overhead was fixed, except for commissions on sales equal to 5% of the selling price.

Mr. Cotter, the president of the company, approved the budget, stating that "A profit of $20,000 a month isn't bad for a little company in this business." During January, however, sales suffered the normal seasonal dips, and production in the factory was also cut back to keep inventories in line. The result, which came as some surprise to the president, was that January showed a loss of $7,000.

OPERATING STATEMENT, JANUARY 1968

Sales...	$140,000
Standard cost of goods sold......................	105,000
Standard gross profit............................	$ 35,000

Favorable or
(Unfavorable)

Manufacturing variances:		
Prime cost variance............................	$(3,500)	
Factory overhead:		
Spending variance............................	1,000	
Volume variance.............................	(12,500)	(15,000)
Actual gross profit..............................		$ 20,000
Selling and general overhead......................		27,000
Loss before taxes................................		$ (7,000)

Assignment

Explain, as best you can with the data available, why the January profit was $27,000 less than the average monthly profit expected by the president.

Problem 3–2. In January 1968, Mr. George Kenney, marketing manager of Willman Electronics Company, was preparing a market forecast for the company for the next two years as his part in the companywide budgeting process. As was his usual custom, he was trying to develop separate estimates of total unit sales and average price per unit, as this had proven a most accurate combination in the past.

The Willman Electronics Company was a small manufacturer of silicon diodes and other semiconductor devices. The company had been formed in 1955 by three engineers from a major Eastern electronics firm. Willman's products were used in miniature electronic circuits, primarily in missiles and computers. The silicon semiconductor market had seen a considerable depression in industrywide prices during the late 1950s and early 1960s due to a disproportionate growth in industry capacity compared with sales. In more recent years, the industrywide prices had once again stabilized, and in fact, Mr. Kenney now believed some increases were likely in 1968 and 1969.

It had been the policy of the Willman Electronics Company to concentrate its efforts on the higher priced semiconductors, offering considerable engineering assistance to its customers as well as a high-quality product. This policy had consistently yielded profits since 1962 and was likely to be continued in the future. During 1967, the average unit price of the Willman Electronics Company was $1, about $0.20 above the industrywide average of $0.80 per unit. Willman's sales amounted to 10 million units in 1967.

Mr. Kenney expected the industry average sales price to rise to $0.90 during 1968 and $1 during 1969. He believed Willman could maintain its 10 million unit sales level by raising its prices by $0.10 in 1968 and another $0.10 in 1969, keeping up with the anticipated industry price increases.

Mr. Kenney wondered, though, as to the desirability of trying to continue the $0.20 price differential. He felt that a decrease in the differential by $0.10 would help the Willman Electronics Company increase its business by one million units per year. He did not think that Willman's pricing practices would influence the industrywide average price appreciably, since Willman had so small a share of the total market.

Mr. James Stiefel, the company treasurer, was given all of the above information by Mr. Kenney. Mr. Stiefel had an assistant draw up a statement of projected company costs. This statement was as follows:

UNIT PRODUCTION PER YEAR

	—————Unit Production per Year—————		
	10,000,000	11,000,000	12,000,000
Materials costs.........$3,000,000		$3,300,000	$3,600,000
Labor costs........... 1,500,000		1,600,000	1,700,000
Overhead costs......... 3,500,000		3,700,000	3,900,000
Total...........$8,000,000		$8,600,000	$9,200,000

In addition, the company's general, administrative, and selling expenses were projected as follows: $1,000,000 + 10% of sales value.

The Willman Electronics Company produced primarily to customer order.

Assignment

1. Prepare a profit budget for the Willman Electronics Company for 1968 and 1969 if the $0.20 price differential is maintained.

2. Should the Willman Electronics Company maintain this price differential?

3. How would you change your price recommendation and budget if the industrywide price level remains constant at $0.80 in 1968 and 1969?

BILL FRENCH, ACCOUNTANT

Bill French picked up the phone and called his boss, Wes Davidson, controller of Duo-Products Corporation. "Say, Wes, I'm all set for the meeting this afternoon. I've put together a set of break-even statements that should really make the boys sit up and take notice—and I think they'll be able to understand them, too." After a brief conversation about other matters, the call was concluded and French turned to his charts for one last check-out before the meeting.

French had been hired six months earlier as a staff accountant. He was directly responsible to Davidson and, up to the time of this case, had been doing routine types of analysis work. French was an alumnus of a liberal arts undergraduate school and graduate business school, and was considered by his associates to be quite capable and unusually conscientious. It was this latter characteristic that had apparently caused him to "rub some of the working guys the wrong way," as one of his co-workers put it. French was well aware of his capabilities and took advantage of every opportunity that arose to try to educate those around him. Wes Davidson's invitation for French to attend an informal manager's meeting had come as some surprise to others in the accounting group. However, when French requested permission to make a presentation of some break-even data, Davidson acquiesced. The Duo-Products Corporation had not been making use of this type of analysis in its review or planning programs.

Basically, what French had done was to determine the level of operation at which the company must operate in order to break even. As he phrased it, "The company must be able to at least sell a sufficient volume of goods that it will cover all of the variable costs of producing and selling the goods; further, it will not make a profit unless it covers the fixed, or nonvariable, costs as well. The level of operation at which total costs (that is, variable plus nonvariable) are just covered is the break-even volume. This should be the lower limit in all of our planning."

196

The accounting records had provided the following information which French used in constructing his chart:

> Plant capacity—2,000,000 units
> Past year's level of operations—1,500,000 units
> Average unit selling price—$1.20
> Total fixed costs—$520,000
> Average variable unit cost—$0.75

From this information, he observed that each unit contributed $0.45 to fixed overhead after covering the variable costs. Given total fixed costs of $520,000, he calculated that 1,155,556 units must be sold in order to break even. He verified this conclusion by calculating the dollar sales volume that was required to break even. Since the variable costs per unit were 62.5% of the selling price, French reasoned that 37.5% of every sales dollar was left available to cover fixed costs. Thus, fixed costs of $520,000 require sales of $1,386,667 in order to break even.

When he constructed a break-even chart to present the information graphically, his conclusions were further verified. The chart also made it clear that the firm was operating at a fair margin over the break-even requirements, and that the profits accruing (at the rate of 37.5% of every sales dollar over break-even) increased rapidly as volume increased (see Exhibit 1).

Shortly after lunch, French and Davidson left for the meeting. Several representatives of the manufacturing departments were present, as well as the general sales manager, two assistant sales managers, the purchasing officer, and two men from the product engineering office. Davidson introduced French to the few men that he had not already met and then the meeting got under way. French's presentation was the last item on Davidson's agenda, and in due time the controller introduced French, explaining his interest in cost control and analysis.

French had prepared enough copies of his chart and supporting calculations so that they could be distributed to everyone at the meeting. He described carefully what he had done and explained how the chart pointed to a profitable year, dependent on meeting the volume of sales activity that had been maintained in the past. It soon became apparent that some of the participants had known in advance what French planned to discuss; they had come prepared to challenge him and soon had taken control of the meeting. The following exchange ensued:

COOPER (*production control*): You know, Bill, I'm really concerned that you haven't allowed for our planned changes in volume next year. It seems to to me that you should have allowed for the sales department's guess that we'll boost sales by 20%, unitwise. We'll be pushing 90% of what we call capacity then. It sure seems that this would make quite a difference in your figuring.

FRENCH: That might be true, but as you can see, all you have to do is read the cost and profit relationship right off the chart for the new volume. Let's see —at a million point eight units we'd . . . .

WILLIAMS (*manufacturing*):   Wait a minute, now!!! If you're going to talk in terms of 90% of capacity, and it looks like that's what it will be, you damn well better note that we'll be shelling out some more for the plant. We've already got okays on investment money that will boost your fixed costs by ten thousand dollars a month, easy. And that may not be all. We may call it 90% of plant capacity, but there are a lot of places where we're just full up and we can't pull things up any tighter.

COOPER: See, Bill? Fred Williams is right, but I'm not finished on this bit about volume changes. According to the information that I've got here—and it came from your office—I'm not sure that your break-even chart can really be used even if there were to be no changes next year. Looks to me like you've got average figures that don't allow for the fact that we're dealing with three basic products. Your report here (see Exhibit 2) on costs, according to product lines, for last year makes it pretty clear that the "average" is way out of line. How would the break-even point look if we took this on an individual product basis?

FRENCH: Well, I'm not sure. Seems to me that there is only one break-even point for the firm. Whether we take it product by product or in total, we've got to hit that point. I'll be glad to check for you if you want, but . . . .

BRADSHAW (*assistant sales manager*):   Guess I may as well get in on this one, Bill. If you're going to do anything with individual products, you ought to know that we're looking for a big swing in our product mix. Might even start before we get into the new season. The "A" line is really losing out, and I imagine that we'll be lucky to hold two-thirds of the volume there next year. Wouldn't you buy that Arnie? [Agreement from the general sales manager.] That's not too bad, though, because we expect that we should pick up the 200,000 that we lose, and about a quarter million units more, over in "C" production. We don't see anything that shows much of a change in "B." That's been solid for years and shouldn't change much now.

WINETKI (*general sales manager*):   Bradshaw's called it about as we figure it, but there's something else here too. We've talked about our pricing on "C" enough, and now I'm really going to push our side of it. Ray's estimate of maybe half a million—four hundred fifty thousand I guess it was—up on "C" for next year is on the basis of doubling the price with no change in cost. We've been priced so low on this item that it's been a crime—we've got to raise, but good, for two reasons. First, for our reputation; the price is out of line classwise and is completely inconsistent with our quality reputation. Second, if we don't raise the price, we'll be swamped and we can't handle it. You heard what Williams said about capacity. The way the whole "C" field is exploding, we'll have to answer to another half million units in unsatisfied orders if we don't jack that price up. We can't afford to expand that much for this product.

At this point, Hugh Fraser, administrative assistant to the president, walked up toward the front of the room from where he had been standing near the rear door. The discussion broke for a minute, and he took advantage of the lull to interject a few comments:

FRASER: This has certainly been enlightening. Looks like you fellows are pretty well up on this whole operation. As long as you're going to try to get all of the things together that you ought to pin down for next year, let's see what I can add to help you.

Number One: Let's remember that everything that shows in the profit area here on Bill's chart is divided just about evenly between the government and us. Now, for last year we can read a profit of about $150,000. Well, that's right. But we were left with half of that, and then paid out dividends of $50,000 to the stockholders. Since we've got an anniversary year coming up, we'd like to put out a special dividend about 50 per cent extra. We ought to hold $25,000 in for the business, too. This means that we'd like to hit $100,000 *after* the costs of being governed.

Number Two: From where I sit, it looks like we're going to have to talk with the union again, and this time it's liable to cost us. All the indications are —and this isn't public—that we may have to meet demands that will boost our production costs—what do you call them here, Bill—variable costs—by 10 per cent across the board. This may kill the bonus-dividend plans, but we've got to hold the line on past profits. This means that we can give that much to the union only if we can make it in added revenues. I guess you'd say that that raises your break-even point, Bill—and for that one I'd consider the company's profit to be a fixed cost.

Number Three: Maybe this is the time to think about switching our product emphasis. Arnie Winetki may know better than I which of the products is more profitable. You check me out on this Arnie—and it might be a good idea for you and Bill French to get together on this one, too. These figures that I have (Exhibit 2) make it look like the percentage contribution on line "A" is the lowest of the bunch. If we're losing volume there as rapidly as you sales folks say, and if we're as hard pressed for space as Fred Williams has indicated, maybe we'd be better off grabbing some of that big demand for "C" by shifting some of the facilities over there from "A."

That's all I've got to say. Looks to me like you've all got plenty to think about.

DAVIDSON: Thanks, Hugh. I sort of figured that we'd get wound up here as soon as Bill brought out his charts. This is an approach that we've barely touched, but, as you can see, you've all got ideas that have got to be made to fit here somewhere. I'll tell you what let's do. Bill, suppose you rework your chart and try to bring into it some of the points that were made here today. I'll see if I can summarize what everyone seems to be looking for.

First of all, I have the idea buzzing around in the back of my mind that your presentation is based on a rather important series of assumptions. Most of the questions that were raised were really about those assumptions; it might help us all if you try to set the assumptions down in black and white so that we can see just how they influence the analysis.

Then, I think that Cooper would like to see the unit sales increase taken up, and he'd also like to see whether there's any difference if you base the calculations on an analysis of individual product lines. Also, as Bradshaw suggested, since the product mix is bound to change, why not see how things look if the shift materializes as sales has forecast.

Arnie Winetki would like to see the influence of a price increase in the "C" line; Fred Williams looks toward an increase in fixed manufacturing costs of ten thousand a month; and Hugh Fraser has suggested that we should consider taxes, dividends, expected union demands, and the question of product emphasis.

I think that ties it all together. Let's hold off on our next meeting, fellows, until Bill has time to work this all into shape.

With that, the participants broke off into small groups and the meeting disbanded. French and Wes Davidson headed back to their offices, and French, in a tone of concern asked Davidson, "Why didn't you warn me about the hornet's nest I was walking into?"

"Bill, you didn't ask!"

Questions

1. What are the assumptions implicit in Bill French's determination of his company's break-even point?
2. On the basis of French's revised information, what does next year look like:
    a) What is the break-even point?
    b) What level of operations must be achieved to pay the extra dividend, ignoring union demands?
    c) What level of operations must be achieved to meet the union demands, ignoring bonus dividends?
    d) What level of operations must be achieved to meet both dividend and expected union requirements?
3. Can the break-even analysis help the company decide whether to alter the existing product emphasis? What can the company afford to invest for additional "C" capacity?
4. Is this type of analysis of any value? For what can it be used?

Exhibit 1

BILL FRENCH, ACCOUNTANT

DUO-PRODUCTS CORPORATION

BREAK-EVEN CHART—TOTAL BUSINESS

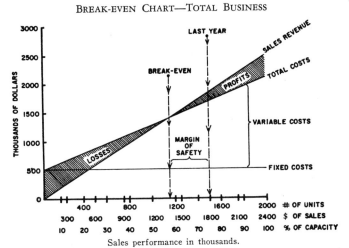

Sales performance in thousands.

Break-even volume = 1,156,000 units, or $1,387,000.

Exhibit 2

BILL FRENCH, ACCOUNTANT

DUO-PRODUCTS CORPORATION

PRODUCT CLASS COST ANALYSIS

(Normal year)

	Aggregate	"A"	"B"	"C"
Sales at full capacity (units)	2,000,000			
Actual sales volume (units)	1,500,000	600,000	400,000	500,000
Unit sales price	$1.20	$1.67	$1.50	$0.40
Total sales revenue	$1,800,000	$1,000,000	$600,000	$200,000
Variable cost per unit	$0.75	$1.25	$0.625	$0.25
Total variable cost	$1,125,000	$ 750,000	$250,000	$125,000
Fixed costs	$ 520,000	$ 170,000	$275,000	$ 75,000
Net profit	$ 155,000	$ 80,000	$ 75,000	—0—
Ratios:				
Variable cost to sales	0.63	0.75	0.42	0.63
Variable income to sales	0.37	0.25	0.58	0.37
Utilization of capacity	75.0%	30.0%	20.0%	25.0%

Breakeven volume

		170K	275K	75K
		.42	.875	.15

THE ASTRA COMPANY[1]

In October, 1959, the board of directors of the Astra Company, a large Brussels manufacturer specializing in candy, ice cream, and fruit bread, received a proposal from Eltsen, Ltd., a foreign confection manufacturer, whereby Astra would sell the basic piece in Eltsen's line of candies in Belgium under the Astra brand name. The product in question was a high-quality, medium-priced chocolate-coated candy packaged in an attractive wrapper.

It was the first time Astra had considered handling through their own selling organization a product which they did not manufacture themselves. Actually, Astra, with their existing facilities, could have produced a chocolate candy similar to the one proposed by Eltsen. However, at that time the company was operating at capacity and neither a change in the product mix nor an increase in production facilities was contemplated.

The directors were inclined to be favorable towards the proposal, feeling that a chocolate candy would improve the competitive position of their candy line. Before making a decision, the board asked Mr. Bourque, the controller, to determine if a profit could be realized on the sale of the product under consideration.

In order to provide the directors with the required information, Mr. Bourque asked the marketing manager, Mr. Faickney, to include the new product in the sales forecast for the following year. This involved an appraisal of the market situation to determine the price at which each product could be sold and the volume which could be attained at that price.

When the marketing department had obtained the figure for total sales, they established the advertising allowance which, according to company policy, was set at 7% of total sales. Forty per cent of this al-

[1] Copyright 1960, by l'Institute pour l'Etude des Methodes de Direction de l'Enterprise (IMEDE), Lausanne, Switzerland. Reprinted by permission.

lowance was earmarked for general advertising, while the balance was assigned to specific products according to estimates of the effect of added advertising on sales.

The budgets for general and administrative and for selling expenses were established by the central accounting department on the basis of past experience and budgeted sales volume. To determine the budget for general and administrative expenses, the assumption was made that these expenses would vary with volume in a straight-line relationship.

The following procedure was used to estimate this relationship: From the records, figures were obtained for the sales volume in francs[2] and for general and administrative expenses over the past two years. Expenses at the lower volume were subtracted from those at the higher volume. The difference in expenses was divided by the difference in volumes to give the variable expense per unit of volume. Either of the volume figures was then multiplied by this amount, and the product representing total variable expense subtracted from total expenses at that volume. The remainder was therefore the nonvariable expense.

By multiplying the estimated variable expense per sales franc by the expected sales volume for the following year and adding the fixed allowance, it was then possible to compute the budget for general and administrative expenses. This was distributed among the various products in proportion to sales francs.

Selling expenses were divided into six categories:

a) *Commissions.* These were set at a percentage of the wholesale price which varied among products, depending on the amount of advertising devoted to each. Using figures for expected franc sales, it was possible to determine the amount of commissions to be paid on each product.

b) *Free Samples and Fairs.* A fixed allowance per year was distributed to each product in proportion to sales francs.

c) *Returns, Deliveries, Sales Salaries, and Other Selling Expenses.* The budget for each of these items was established following the procedure described for general and administrative expenses. Returns were allowed, and deliveries made at company expense only on certain products. Therefore expense allowances for these two items were distributed on a sales-franc basis only among the products involved. Sales salaries and other selling expenses were distributed among all products also as a percentage of franc sales.

Mr. Bourque summarized the cost estimates for all product lines in Exhibit 1. On the evidence of the figures in Exhibit 1, he concluded that the new product would show a loss since the gross margin which had

---

[2] The Belgian franc (B. Fr.) was worth approximately $0.02 in U.S. money.

to absorb the general and administrative, advertising, and selling expenses was only 30% of the wholesale price established by the marketing department.

Before forwarding this information to the board of directors, Mr. Bourque again contacted Mr. Faickney asking if it would be feasible to raise the wholesale price. Mr. Faickney in return took issue with the procedure followed by the central accounting office in allocating the indirect expenses to the new product. He argued that Eltsen had already included its own share of these expenses plus profit in the selling price quoted to Astra. Mr. Faickney suggested therefore that the controller calculate the cost that Astra would incur should the product be manufactured with the company's own facilities. The difference between this cost and the acquisition price should, he said, be deducted from the indirect expenses allocated to the chocolate candy and uniformly reallocated to all products on a sales-franc basis.

Mr. Bourque estimated that Astra could manufacture a chocolate candy similar to the one it planned to acquire at 85% of the acquisition price, but felt that by charging expenses at a reduced rate, the company would incur the risk of judging incorrectly whether or not the new product would be profitable, since the company's administrative and selling organizations would perform identical operations for the new product and for those which were being manufactured.

The objection raised by Mr. Faickney, however, made Mr. Bourque question if his calculations of net profit by product line was a valid criterion for judging the desirability of a product.

Question

1. Should Astra accept the offer from Eltsen, Ltd?

Exhibit 1

THE ASTRA COMPANY

ALLOCATION OF BUDGETED GENERAL AND ADMINISTRATIVE, ADVERTISING, AND SELLING EXPENSES TO PRODUCT LINES

(All amounts in hundreds of Belgian francs)

Product Lines	Forecasted Sales Volume in Belgian Francs	General and Administrative Expense Budget		Advertising Budget		Selling Expense Budget												Total
						Commissions		Returns		Transportation		Free Samples and Fairs		Sales Salaries		Other Selling Expenses		
		Direct	In-direct	Direct	In-direct	Direct	In-direct	Direct	In-direct	Direct	In-direct	Direct	In-direct	Direct	In-direct	Direct	In-direct	
Fruit bread	516,000	.....	30,960	25,800	14,448	41,280	.....	8,447	.....	7,161	.....	.....	17,412	.....	15,480	.....	10,370	171,308
Ice cream	258,000	.....	15,480	6,300	7,224	24,400	.....	4,223	.....	3,580	.....	.....	8,706	.....	7,740	.....	5,160	82,813
Candy	64,500	.....	3,870	2,547	1,806	9,030	.....	955	.....	809	.....	.....	2,176	.....	1,935	.....	1,290	24,418
Chocolate candy	21,500	.....	1,290	1,473	602	2,150	.....	.....	.....	.....	.....	.....	726	.....	645	.....	430	7,316
Total	860,000	.....	51,600	36,120	24,080	76,860	.....	13,625	.....	11,550	.....	.....	29,020	.....	25,800	.....	17,200	285,855

Note: The following percentages of each of the expenses were considered to be variable:

General and administrative = 10%
Advertising budget = 100
Commissions = 100
Returns = 85
Transportation = 80
Free samples and fairs = 0
Sales salaries = 10
Other selling expenses = 15

POST OFFICE DEPARTMENT (B)[1]
Money Order Analysis

In February 1965, staff members in the Bureau of Finance and Administration in the Post Office Department were preparing to review the economic aspects of the Department's money order service. Evaluation of the Post Office's "Special Services" was an almost continuous task for the economics staff. These services included money order, special delivery, registry, insurance, certified mail, cash on delivery, and postal savings. Special Services were not directly related to the Post Office's primary mail responsibility but were congressionally required activities for the Department.

The Postal Policy Act of 1958 affected Special Services in two ways. First, Congress authorized the Postmaster General to establish rates for Special Services, a responsibility previously reserved by Congress. Second, losses incurred for Special Services were categorized by Congress as Public Service Losses. By this action Congress indicated that Post Office Special Services were provided in the public interest and that losses incurred in providing these services would be automatically sanctioned by Congress.

Postal rates were officially exempt from the President's policy regarding user charges, which was expressed in BOB Circular A-25 as follows:

> Where a service (or privilege) provides special benefits to an identifiable recipient above and beyond those which accrue to the public at large, a charge should be imposed to relieve the full cost to the federal government of rendering that service.

Special Service fees were not considered to be postal rates. Rather, because these services had a clearly identifiable recipient and because the

---

[1] This case is intended for class discussion only, and certain names and facts may have been changed which, while avoiding the disclosure of confidential information, do not materially lessen the value of the case for educational purposes. This case is not intended to represent either effective or ineffective handling of an administrative situation, nor does it purport to be a statement of policy by the agency involved.

Postmaster General was given the authority to establish the Special Service fee, some postal officials believed these services were subject to the user charge policy. Reassertion of this policy by the President in February 1965 led the Postmaster General to request a complete review of the nonpostal services provided by the Department. Money orders was one such service which was carefully scrutinized by Post Office officials.

Background

Money orders were sold in all of the Department's 45,000 outlets. In addition, applications for money orders were provided to rural customers directly by the carriers. Cash received from money order sales was forwarded by the selling post office to the Treasury Department. The buyer entered the name of the payee on the money order and forwarded it to the payee. The money order could be redeemed at any post office, bank, or at most retail merchants. The form was processed, like a check, through the Federal Reserve System and eventually honored by the Treasury Department.

At larger post offices, money orders were sold at special money order windows. Any office which issued over 350 orders per day was felt to require a special window. Officials estimated that the 321 Class A, B, and C offices had special money order windows, while the remaining 33,719 offices issued the money orders at general-purpose windows. The clerical expense allocated to money orders at the A, B, and C class offices totaled $12.5 million in fiscal year 1964 out of a total of $1,095.9 million.

The revenue from the Postal Money Order Service had never equaled the full cost of providing the service. Exhibits 1 and 2 show the revenue and expenses allocated to the service under the Post Office's Cost Ascertainment System. This system was based on time studies taken during one week per quarter at a selected sample of approximately 500 post office branches. This survey was used as the basis of distributing the direct expense for collection and delivery, and mail handling and window service to the various services provided by the Post Office Department. If the survey recorded idle time, the expense for this idle time was spread in proportion to the productive labor cost for each post office service.

In small post offices the cost of administration of post office operations was also distributed on the basis of a time study survey. Also, postal supply expenses which could be identified directly with a particular service were charged to that service. All other expense classifications contained in the Cost Ascertainment report were allocated to the services on the basis of the relationship between the direct costs, as determined above, and the total direct costs for the department.

Since the end of the Korean War the allocation of expenses to the money order service in most expense categories had steadily declined. In spite of this reduced allocation to money orders, none of these expense categories declined in total (for the entire Post Office). In fact the allocations to all other Post Office services increased during this period, with the exception of postal savings.

The primary cause of the reduction in allocated money order expenses was the decrease in money order transactions after the early 1950s. Exhibit 3 presents historical statistics for domestic money order transactions and the total value of money order sales.

As a reaction to the changes in allocated costs and transaction values, three money order rate changes had been made since the end of World War II. A summary of these rate changes, from the creation of money orders in 1864 to the rate change in 1961, is presented as Exhibit 4.

Competition

Postal money orders had two traditional sources of competition. The first was the commercial money order firms, the largest of which was the American Express Company. In 1960 it was estimated that American Express money orders were available at 25,000 locations, although the value of the company's money order transactions was less than $100 million. Commercial money order rates were generally equal to or higher than the postal money order rates. Commercial money orders often were sold in stores offering extended, late evening hours for the purchase of money orders.

The following excerpt from the American Express Company annual report to stockholders for 1959 gave an indication of their competitive viewpoint:

> To strengthen our position in a competitive market, the Money Order Sales Department had at the end of 1959 a record number of money order subagency sales outlets, which include thousands of retail stores, such as supermarkets, drug and department stores around the country, as well as Western Union, Railway Express Agency and our own American Express offices.
> Sales programming for the year 1959 included countrywide solicitations, a colorful promotion portfolio, subagency incentive contests, sales brochures, and

mailing pieces. An attractive film promoting money orders as an important service at supermarket courtesy centers was prepared and will be shown widely during 1960 to trade associations and other meetings.

Another source of money order competition was the banking industry. This competition took the form of increasing public acceptance of regular and special checking accounts, as well as bank money orders.

A 1960 survey of 18 important banking firms, throughout the nation, revealed that these banks generally charged less than the Post Office for large money orders. Among the 18 banks surveyed, 13 offered money orders under a single fee arrangement, while five had graduated fees. In every instance, bank money order fees for money orders over $10 were less than Post Office fees. And in all but two instances, bank fees for money orders from $5 to $10 were equal to or less than postal money order fees.

Both the commercial and bank institutions offering money order service benefited from the "float" created by the service. The amount of this float was estimated at between six and eight days of sales in 1960. This time period represented the delay between the receipt of cash and the payout of the cash for the money order.

The high-value money order customer represented a larger share of the Post Office's money order revenue than of the money order transactions. In 1959 the Post Office's distribution of transactions and revenue was as follows:

Value of Money Order	Share of Total Revenue (1959)	Share of Total Transaction (1959)
$ 0.01–$ 5	19%	29%
5.01– 10	21	24
10.01– 50	50	39
50.01– 100	10	8

In spite of the decline in postal money order volume after the Korean War, both commercial and banking money order suppliers believed that the total market for money orders had expanded. This expansion was attributed to the increase in population and greater dependence by the public upon charge accounts and other credit facilities.

The Meeting in February 1965

As a result of the Postmaster General's request, three staff members of the Bureau of Finance and Administration held an informal meeting in mid-February 1965 to discuss the approach they should use in their analysis. Excerpts from this discussion are quoted below:

CARL JACOBSON: There is no good reason why the Post Office should continue to provide money order service for the public. They're a losing proposition. They lost $12 million in 1964. The money order market is filled with competitors. American Express, Travelers Express, and every bank in the country provide money order service. I just don't understand why the Post Office should continue to conduct a Special Service at a loss when the same service is provided by commercial competition.

HOWARD WHITMORE: The Post Office provides a very real service in rural areas. We carry money right to the door of rural customers, where commercial firms can't afford to provide the service.

Also, money orders are important for our c.o.d. service. After the cash for a collect parcel is collected by our carriers, it is returned to the mailer by the money order process. These c.o.d. remittances represent 10% of our money order volume.

PAUL BERMAN: What about this so-called loss on money orders? Certainly a loss under Cost Ascertainment's full cost allocation of expenses does not mean that the Post Office is suffering an out-of-pocket loss. As a matter of fact I've found that money orders make a substantial contribution to the Department's overhead. To do this I went through the Cost Ascertainment expense categories in detail (Exhibit 2) and separated the expense into a fixed and incremental component. After reviewing these expenses, I'm sure that money orders make a substantial contribution to the Department's overhead.

HOWARD WHITMORE: I think your approach is reasonable. If I understand what you've done, you're saying, "What costs would we still incur if the Post Office went out of the money order business?" When looked at in this manner, practically all of the costs are fixed because a great many men who handle money orders 25% or 50% of their time would not be eliminated if money orders were discontinued.

CARL JACOBSON: I just cannot agree with this line of reasoning. If you take this viewpoint it is impossible to make decisions regarding any of the Department's services. For instance, assume that a man at a general-purpose window spends 40% of his time on money orders, 30% on c.o.d.'s, 15% on printed stamped envelopes, and 15% on postal savings. All of these activities are revenue-deficient activities. If we look at these activities individually, it appears that there is no direct labor cost for conducting the activity. The man will be there in any event. However, if we look at all of the activities together, the entire cost of the man becomes variable.

The point is that elimination or substantial curtailment of several revenue-deficient services promises far more in cost saving possibilities than the sum of the estimated cost savings if each, in isolation from the rest, were considered for termination.

HOWARD WHITMORE: Does this mean that there actually was a loss on money orders in 1964?

CARL JACOBSON: No. Items of expense, such as overhead, operation, and care of buildings, etc., are certainly fixed as Paul indicated. But I feel strongly that the expense for mail handling and window service must be viewed as primarily direct expense.

PAUL BERMAN: No matter how you view these expenses, I think you must agree that our pricing policy should be designed to maximize revenue. This is a different consideration than the question of whether we should be in or out of the business.

The money order fee increases in 1957 and 1961 decreased money order revenue dramatically. This not only is costing the Post Office money but is slowly pricing us out of the money order business. I doubt if Congress would appreciate our taking over the function of determining what services the Department will provide by gradually going out of the money order business. Also, haven't they indicated that they feel money order service is in the public interest by covering it under Public Service Losses?

HOWARD WHITMORE: There have been a number of questions raised here. Let's see if we can't make a better start on the problem by first doing some preliminary analysis. There are several interrelated questions to which we ought to be able to get some approximate quantitative answers, and based on that we can then see how to proceed for a more detailed and precise analysis.

The questions that I think we ought to address ourselves to are:

1. What impact did the rate increases in 1957 and 1961 have on money order volume?
2. What was the net effect of these two rate increases in terms of the overall financial performance of the Department?
3. What might we expect to happen if we changed rates again? We could have a 5-cent across-the-board increase, or we might even cut rates if the higher volume would justify it.
4. Finally, would a single-fee rate structure, similar to that used by banks, improve the financial performance of money orders?

Exhibit 1

POST OFFICE DEPARTMENT (B)

POSTAL MONEY ORDERS—HISTORICAL INCOME AND APPORTIONED EXPENSES, 1955–64

	1964	1963	1962	1961	1960	1959	1958	1957	1956	1955
Income and associated expense:										
Operating revenue	$ 60,744	$ 62,142	$ 64,251	$ 62,606	$64,613	$ 67,089	$71,018	$ 63,880	$ 65,405	$ 65,649
Unclaimed money orders	1,411	1,738	1,531	1,558	16,576					
Total income	$ 62,155	$ 63,880	$ 65,782	$ 64,164	$81,189	$ 67,089	$71,018	$ 63,880	$ 65,405	$ 65,649
Postal operation expenses:										
Administration of Post Office operations	$ 18,772	$ 19,659	$ 20,552	$ 23,309	$23,016	$ 23,536	$23,612	$ 23,199	$ 25,866	$ 26,022
Mail handling and window service	39,834	40,688	40,744	41,804	40,419	40,560	39,719	40,601	48,886	51,969
Collection and delivery	1,601	1,719	1,896	1,958	2,036	1,941	2,291	2,520	2,495	2,475
Local transportation	4	6	8	11	7	4	2	2	3	3
Operation and care of buildings	3,432	3,364	3,357	3,317	3,296	3,043	3,124	4,416	3,261	3,284
Postal supply services	1,209	1,413	1,497	1,734	1,749	1,975	547	718	900	767
Other expense	627	918	549	538	568	555	927	1,386	1,614	2,670
Total postal operations	$ 65,479	$ 67,767	$ 68,603	$ 72,671	$71,091	$ 71,614	$70,222	$ 72,842	$ 83,025	$ 87,190
Transportation of mails	$ 75	$ 83	$ 86	$ 81	$ 82	$ 39	$ 46	$ 44	$ 41	$ 32
General overhead	2,610	3,160	4,464	4,595	7,416	3,541	4,493	2,520	2,636	4,480
Nonfund expense	1,033	1,142	(104)	(291)						
Redistribution of expense	3,891	3,536	3,889	3,983	4,119	3,607	4,244	4,189	4,717	
Total nonoperating	$ 7,609	$ 7,921	$ 8,335	$ 8,368	$11,617	$ 7,187	$ 8,783	$ 6,753	$ 7,394	$ 4,512
Total expense	$ 73,088	$ 75,688	$ 76,938	$ 81,039	$82,708	$ 78,801	$79,005	$ 79,595	$ 90,419	$ 91,702
Net (deficit)	$(10,933)	$(11,808)	$(11,156)	$(16,875)	$(1,519)	$(11,712)	$(7,987)	$(15,715)	$(25,014)	$(26,053)

Source: U.S. Post Office, Cost Ascertainment Report 1955-64.

Exhibit 2

POST OFFICE DEPARTMENT (B)

POSTAL MONEY ORDERS—APPORTIONMENT OF POST OFFICE EXPENSES
(000's)

	Fiscal Year 1964		Fiscal Year 1955	
	Total Expense	Money Order Allocations	Total Expense	Money Order Allocations
Postmasters:				
First-class offices:				
Class A	$ 425	$ 3	$ 37,289	$ 891
Class B	764	6	35,188	1,793
Class C	3,110	23	9,960	519
Class D	3,279	41	14,803	829
Class E	6,979	113	14,639	1,025
Class F	11,061	312	18,282	3,122
Class G	16,956	1,136	...	...
Total first-class offices	$ 42,576	$ 1,634	$130,161	$ 8,180
Second-class offices	55,799	3,366	36,587	7,377
Third-class offices	81,020	6,936	50,375	6,227
Fourth-class offices	26,876	1,815	31,710	4,238
Postmaster's grand total	$ 206,271	$13,751	$248,833	$26,022
Supervisors:				
First-class offices:				
Class A	$ 80,336	$ 535	...	...
Class B	38,312	402	...	...
Class C	50,335	639	...	...
Class D	21,696	291	...	...
Class E	26,117	444	...	...
Class F	20,142	451	...	...
Class G	15,963	1,630	...	...
Total first-class offices	$ 252,903	$ 4,392		
Second-class offices	9,819	629	...	...
Other facilities	9,497	...	...	...
Supervisors' grand total	$ 272,219	$ 5,021		
Administration expense total	$ 478,490	$18,772	$248,833	$26,022
Mail handling and window service:				
First-class offices:				
Class A	$ 635,213	$ 6,075	$369,671	$ 8,012
Class B	226,587	3,079	186,761	7,450
Class C	234,116	3,315	37,177	1,680
Class D	91,839	2,605	52,585	4,527
Class E	100,626	3,961	40,160	5,457
Class F	73,630	4,338	40,898	6,822
Class G	60,289	4,876	...	...
Total first-class offices	$1,422,300	$28,249	$727,252	$33,948
Second-class offices	94,507	6,302	69,535	12,647
Third-class offices	446	3,007	29,150	3,602
Miscellaneous offices	53,551	...	...	...
Contract station service	10,505	2,276	7,340	1,772
Total clerical expense	$1,616,303	$39,834	$833,277	$51,969

Exhibit 2 *continued*

	Fiscal Year 1964		Fiscal Year 1955	
	Total Expense	Money Order Allocations	Total Expense	Money Order Allocations
Collection and delivery rural carriers:				
First-class offices..............$	85,748	$ 210	. . .	. . .
Second-class offices............	81,757	394	. . .	. . .
Third-class offices..............	74,289	919	. . .	. . .
Fourth-class offices............	9,732	78	. . .	. . .
Total rural carriers' expense..................$	251,526	$ 1,601	$194,945	$ 2,475
Operation and care of building:				
Custodial service, salaried and personnel costs...............$	118,422	$ 1,540	$ 59,538	$ 1,387
Communication services.........	6,165	88	2,710	95
Building occupancy—rents......	85,721	1,098	32,113	769
Rental—fourth-class offices.....	3,427	231	4,176	558
Building occupancy—fuel and utility services..............	30,296	438	11,070	269
Custodial supplies.............	2,879	37	8,591	206
Total expense.............$	246,910	$ 3,432	$118,198	$ 3,284
Postal supply services:				
Stamps and accountable paper...$	17,758	$ 891	$ 14,560	$ 767
Facilities field personnel.......	6,900	57	3,164	. . .
Money order processing by Federal Reserve Board........	450	261	. . .	. . .
Total postal supply........$	25,108	$ 1,209	$ 17,724	$ 767
General overhead expense:				
Administration and regional operations costs.............$	78,060	. . .	$ 21,013	. . .
Processing money orders (U.S. Treasury)....................	600	. . .	516	. . .
Operations costs...............	. . .	. . .	11,765	. . .
Transportation costs............	4	. . .	1,505	. . .
Facilities costs.................	886	. . .	3,399	. . .
Plant and equipment costs.......	. . .	. . .	. . .	. . .
Research development costs.....	10,512	. . .	. . .	. . .
Total general overhead.....$	90,062	$ 2,610	$ 38,198	$ 4,480
Nonfund expense:				
Depreciation...................$	51,825	$ 465	. . .	. . .
Freight and expendable equipment........................	5,858	168	. . .	. . .
Supply items...................	737	. . .	. . .	. . .
Maintenance building services....	20,876	271	. . .	. . .
Unemployment compensation....	8,100	129	. . .	. . .
Total nonfund.............$	87,396	$ 1,033		
Redistribution of expense:				
Post Office penalty.............	. . .	$ 498	. . .	. . .
Post Office registry.............	. . .	3,393	. . .	. . .
Total redistribution........		$ 3,891		

* FY 1965 includes both postmaster and supervisors under Postmaster Account.

Exhibit 3

POST OFFICE DEPARTMENT (B)

MONEY ORDER SERVICE—HISTORICAL STATISTICAL INFORMATION

Fiscal Year	Domestic Transactions (Thousands)	Average Domestic Fee (Cents)	Domestic Value of Sales (Millions)	Average Domestic Value (Dollars)
1964	235,414	25.6	4,719	20.0
1963	242,871	25.4	4,709	19.4
1962	251,842	25.3	4,787	19.0
1961	264,267	23.5	4,958	18.8
1960	273,633	23.4	5,031	18.4
1959	286,647	23.2	5,158	18.0
1958	311,025	22.6	5,442	17.5
1957	334,882	18.9	5,880	17.6
1956	346,505	...	5,926	17.1
1955	349,273	18.6	5,865	16.8
1954	359,685	18.6	6,049	16.8
1953	368,762	18.3	6,032	16.4
1952	375,215	18.1	5,946	15.8
1951	321,797	18.4	5,236	16.3
1950	302,848	17.7	4,641	15.3
1949	312,725	14.7	4,874	15.6
1948	296,817	11.3	4,589	15.4
1947	282,702	10.9	4,222	14.9
1946	270,787	11.5	4,766	17.6
1945	282,421	14.0	4,827	17.1
1944	306,257	12.8	4,584	15.0
1943	346,441	10.5	4,445	12.8
1942	316,066	9.9	3,112	9.8
1941	274,869	9.5	2,367	8.6
1940	255,502	9.4	2,103	8.2
1939	250,794	9.3	2,058	8.2
1938	248,529	9.4	2,158	8.7
1937	246,481	9.4	2,117	8.6
1936	228,633	9.3	1,927	8.4
1935	213,351	9.3	1,829	8.6
1934	198,656	9.3	1,785	9.0
1933	171,480	9.4	1,655	9.7
1932	179,385	8.4	1,549	8.6
1931	190,877	8.3	1,578	8.3
1930	203,307	8.4	1,735	8.5
1929	200,336	8.4	1,681	8.4
1928	197,337	8.4	1,650	8.4
1927	195,207	8.4	1,667	8.5
1926	194,375	8.4	1,611	8.3

Exhibit 4

POST OFFICE DEPARTMENT (B)

MONEY ORDER SERVICE—DOMESTIC POSTAL RATE HISTORY

(Cents)

Value	Nov. 1, 1864	July 1, 1866	Sept. 1, 1868	July 15, 1872	July 1, 1875	July 2, 1883	July 26, 1886	July 1, 1894	Apr. 15, 1925	July 20, 1932	Mar. 26, 1944	Nov. 1, 1944	Jan. 1, 1949	July 1, 1957	July 1, 1961
$ 0 to $ 2.50	.10	10	10	5	10	8	5	3	5	6	10	6	10	15	20
2.51 to 5.00	.10	10	10	5	10	8	5	5	7	8	14	8	10	15	20
5.01 to 10.00	.10	10	10	5	10	8	8	8	10	11	19	11	15	20	20
10.01 to 15.00	.15	10	10	10	10	10	10	10	12	13	22	13	25	30	30
15.01 to 20.00	.15	10	10	10	15	15	15	10	12	13	22	13	25	30	30
20.01 to 30.00	.20	25	15	15	15	15	15	12	15	15	25	15	25	30	30
30.01 to 40.00		25	20	20	20	20	20	15	15	15	25	15	25	30	30
40.01 to 50.00		25	25	25	25	25	25	18	18	18	30	18	25	30	30
50.01 to 60.00						30	30	20	18	18	30	18	35	30	35
60.01 to 70.00						35	35	25	20	20	34	20	35	30	35
70.01 to 75.00						40	40	25	20	20	34	20	35	30	35
75.01 to 80.00						40	40	30	20	20	34	20	35	30	35
80.01 to 100.00						45	45	30	22	22	37	22	35	30	35

[1] The 66⅔% increase prescribed in 1944 was to apply until 6 months after the termination of hostilities of World War II; however, the Act was repealed and on Nov. 11, 1944, the previous rates were restored.

[2] Original act prescribed that money orders be not issued for amounts less than $1. Restriction removed in 1866.

STARDUST GRINDER COMPANY[1]

In May, 1968, Mr. Sorrel, the general manager of the English plant of the Stardust Grinder Company was considering what he should do at a meeting he was to attend that afternoon with his sales manager, accountant, and development engineer. The meeting was to discuss the introduction by Adolph Müller & Company, a German competitor, of a plastic ring to take the place of a steel ring presently used in certain machines sold by the company. The new ring, which had been put on the market only a few weeks previously, not only had a much longer life than the Stardust steel ring but also had a much lower cost. Mr. Sorrel's problem stemmed from the fact that his company had a large quantity of the steel rings on hand and had a substantial inventory of special steel for their manufacture which, after a thorough survey, he had found could not be sold even for scrap. The total value of these inventories was in excess of £6,000.[2]

For over 60 years the Stardust Grinder Company had manufactured industrial machines which it sold in a number of countries. The particular machine involved in Mr. Sorrel's decision was made only at the English plant situated in Manchester which employed over 6,000 persons. The different models were priced between £250 and £400 and were sold by a separate sales organization. Parts which in total accounted for a substantial part of the company's business were sold separately sometimes, as in the case of the steel rings, for use on similar machines manufactured by competitors. The company's head office was in Switzerland. In general, the separate plants were allowed considerable leeway in administering their own affairs. However, the executives in Switzerland

---

[1] Copyright 1959, by l'Institute pour l'Etude des Methodes de Direction de l'Enterprise (IMEDE), Lausanne, Switzerland. Reprinted by permission.

[2] The English pound (£) was worth approximately $2.80 in U.S. money.

could be approached easily for advice either by correspondence and tele-phone or during their visits to the individual plants.

Throughout its history the company followed the practice of provid-ing the best quality it could at reasonable prices. As a result it had established a good reputation everywhere. In some countries competition hardly existed. In others, despite strong efforts by competitors, it had succeeded in keeping large shares of the available markets. In recent years, however, particularly since the Korean war, the competition had become much stronger. Japanese manufacturers had had more than a little success in entering the field with low-priced spare parts. Other companies had appeared with lower-quality and lower-priced machines. There was little doubt that in the future, competition would become more intense. Technological developments would come faster and have a much greater impact on competitive activities.

The sales manager, Mr. Matthews, had learned of the new plastic ring shortly after its appearance and had immediately asked when the Stardust company would be able to supply it, particularly for sale to customers in Germany where Adolph Müller & Company was providing probably the strongest competition faced by the Stardust company. Mr. Lanergan, the development engineer, estimated that the plastic rings could be produced by September. The company already had a plastics division which was not operating at full capacity. The additional tools and equipment necessary could be obtained for about £200. At this point Mr. Lanergan had raised the question about the investment in steel ring inventories which would not be used up by September. Mr. Matthews said that if the new ring could be produced at a substantially lower cost than the steel ones, the inventory problem was irrelevant. It should be sold for whatever could be obtained, or even thrown away if it could not be sold. However, the size of the inventory, which he esti-mated might be equal to more than a year's supply, caused Mr. Sorrel to question this suggestion. He recalled that the size of the inventory was the result of having to order the highly specialized steel in large amounts in order to find a mill willing to handle the order.

The discussion then became very heated. Mr. Matthews insisted that the company could not hope to retain its position unless it provided its customers with the best quality of parts available. He furthermore em-phasized that as Adolph Müller & Company were said to be selling the plastic ring at about the same price as the Stardust steel ring, and as the cost of the former would be much less than the latter, the company was refusing profits as well. Finally it was decided that the company should prepare to manufacture the new ring as soon as possible but that they would only be sold in those markets where they were offered by competitors until the inventories of the old model and the steel were exhausted. No one expected that the new rings would be produced by any company other than Adolph Müller for some time. This meant that not more than 10% of the company's markets would be affected.

Shortly after this, Mr. Schmid of the parent company in Switzerland visited Manchester. During a review of company problems, the plastic ring case was discussed. Mr. Schmid agreed that the company should proceed with plans for its production and try to find some other use for the steel. He then said, "If this does not seem possible, I would, of course, expect you to use this material and produce the steel rings." But he added that as the additional revenue of the plastic ring might well offset the cost of carrying the inventory of the steel parts plus the cost of the raw material involved, it could be economically feasible to introduce the new ring much sooner than would be expected. He suggested that this possibility be explored without delay.

Within a few days after Mr. Schmid's visit, both Mr. Lanergan and Mr. Matthews came in to see Mr. Sorrel. The former came because he felt that the plastic ring would completely destroy demand for the steel ring as tests had indicated that it had at least four times the wearing properties. However, because he understood that the price of the competitive ring was very high (perhaps even higher than the Stardust steel ring), he felt that the decision to sell the plastic ring only in the market areas where difficulties existed was a good one. "In this way we would probably be able to continue supplying the steel ring at least until stocks of processed parts were used up."

Mr. Matthews, the sales manager, was still strongly, even violently, against selling any steel rings after the new ones became available. The company had always prided itself on giving its customers the best available. If steel rings were sold in some areas, while plastic rings were being sold elsewhere, customers in the former would eventually find out. The result would affect the sale of machines, the selling price of which was many times that of the rings. He produced figures to show that if the selling price of both rings remained at £43. per hundred, the additional profit from the plastic rings, which would cost £8.7. per hundred as contrasted with £38.45 per hundred for the steel, would more than cover the "so-called" investment in the steel inventory within less than a year at present volume levels. Mr. Sorrel refused to change his decision of the previous meeting but agreed to have another discussion within a week.

In anticipation of the meeting and also having in mind Mr. Schmid's suggestion, Mr. Sorrel obtained the following estimates from the cost department on the cost of plastic and steel rings:

	Cost per 100 Rings	
	Plastic Rings	Steel Rings
Material...	£ .44	£11.57
Direct labor.....................................	2.04	7.26
Overhead:*		
Departmental.................................	4.59	14.33
Administrative................................	1.63	5.29
Total (per 100 rings).........................	£8.70	£38.45

*Overhead was allocated on the basis of direct labor.

Although no attempt had ever been made to separate variable and fixed overheads, it was estimated that the variable costs included in the above summary would be within 25 to 50% of the departmental amounts.

Mr. Sorrel also learned that the inventory of special steel of 17,200 pounds had cost £2,700 and was equal to a 70 weeks' supply if sales continued at about 340 rings per week. At this rate the supply of finished rings would be about 7,800 by the time in September when the plastic rings could first be produced. It then occurred to him that during the next two or three months the plant would not be operating at capacity. As the company had a policy of employing its excess labor during slack periods at about 70% of regular wages on maintenance and repair projects rather than laying the men off, he wondered if it would be a good idea to convert the steel inventory into rings during this period and so save on the labor cost.

Questions

1. What alternatives are available to Mr. Sorrel?
2. Which alternative should he choose? Why?

NUTHATCH NATIONAL FOREST (A)[1]

In January 1966, Mr. Lionel Ursus, the supervisor of Nuthatch National Forest, was considering offering for sale federal timber from some 2,000 acres of choice old-growth stands. This particular area consisted of mixed conifers, mainly ponderosa pine (60%) and true fir (40%). The estimated amount involved was 50 million board feet of timber.

Nuthatch National Forest occupied about 1.4 million acres of rolling timberland in Nemorensis County, a remote section of one of the mountain states. The local economy was primarily dependent on the forest products industry, although for some time county and state officials had been attempting to devise means to exploit the undoubted recreational potential of their beautiful region. A constant concern was the steady loss of young people to the nearest large town, Inverness, located near an interstate highway 300 miles away.

Three sawmills were located in Blairgowrie, 10 miles from the proposed timber sale area along Forest Highway 357. The Cameron mill, with a capacity of 75 million board feet per year, was a division of a nationwide corporation which owned several hundred thousand acres of timberland adjacent to Nuthatch. The MacLeod and Affleck mills were each capable of handling six million board feet per year: neither owned any land. The 100 families dependent on the MacLeod and Affleck mills were all descendants of the original Scottish settlers of Nemorensis County.

Mr. Ursus had two alternative proposals before him.

---

[1] This case is intended for class discussion only, and certain names and facts may have been changed which, while avoiding the disclosure of confidential information, do not materially lessen the value of the case for educational purposes. This case is not intended to represent either effective or ineffective handling of an administrative situation, nor does it purport to be a statement of policy by the agency involved.

222   *MANAGERIAL ECONOMICS: TEXT AND CASES*

Sale Alternative 1

The Cameron mill had indicated that they would bid $43/Mbf (thousand board feet) for the ponderosa pine and $2/Mbf for the true fir. They would build all roads involved (roads A, B, C, and D in Exhibit 1) to Forest Service standards for single-lane unpaved roads and would remove all timber during the first logging season (1967) after the roads were completed. If the Forest Service should decide that the main access road, road A, should be double-lane and paved, and that they should therefore supplement Cameron's road-building outlays to the extent of the necessary difference in construction costs, then Cameron's bid would be $57.36/Mbf for ponderosa pine and $9/Mbf for the true fir. Cameron would pay the Forest Service for the timber in seven monthly installments beginning April 1, 1967.

Sale Alternative 2

The MacLeod and Affleck mills had submitted a joint proposal. Like Cameron, they too intended to build roads A, B, C, and D and commence logging operations by April 1, 1967. They intended to remove the timber according to the following schedule: 12,000 Mbf in 1967, 1968, and 1969, with the balance of 14,000 Mbf being removed by November 1, 1970. (The logging season in Nuthatch National Forest consisted of the seven months from April through October.)

Their bid was $45.33/Mbf for the ponderosa pine and $2/Mbf for the true fir. If road A were paved, their bids would be $59.91/Mbf for the ponderosa pine and $9.25/Mbf for the true fir. They proposed to pay for the timber in 28 equal installments, a payment to be made on the first of each month of logging operations.

The cost to the Forest Service of administering the Cameron proposal was estimated at $20,000, whereas the second proposal would cost an estimated $30,000. (Most of these costs would be incurred in the year the sale was offered for bid.)

The main access road (road A) would be 8 miles long; spur roads B, C, and D would be 2.5 miles, 2 miles, and 3 miles, respectively. Road construction costs were estimated at $15,000 per mile for single-lane unpaved roads and $165,000 per mile for two-lane paved roads. All roads could be built within 12 months. Maintenance costs were estimated at $300 per mile per year for double-lane paved roads, $1,200 per mile per year for single-lane unpaved roads during logging, and $200 per mile per year for single-lane unpaved roads when not used for logging.

Unpaved roads would be adequate for logging purposes only. However, should Mr. Ursus decide to open up this section of Nuthatch for recreational purposes, the 8-mile main access road would certainly have to be double-lane and paved. Since "prudent operator" standards in Forest Service timber management regulations necessitated only that timber purchasers be required to build roads to meet logging needs, the Forest Service would have to supplement the timber operator's road-building outlays. Maintenance of the roads would be the responsibility of the timber operator until logging operations ceased: thereafter, the Forest Service would have to assume the maintenance costs for whichever roads it decided to keep open.

Calculation of Stumpage Price

"Stumpage price," the proceeds per thousand board feet of timber (Mbf) anticipated by the Forest Service from the sale, would be calculated in the following manner.

The timber in the section of Nuthatch under consideration had been appraised as likely to yield sawn lumber with an average value (selling price) of $140/Mbf for the ponderosa pine and $90/Mbf for the true fir. From these figures, the mill's milling costs would be deducted (estimated at $15/Mbf). A profit margin of 10% of the appraised selling price would also be allowed. Deduction of profit and milling costs from appraised selling price would give the estimated value of the logs as they arrived at the mill.

From this, transportation and logging costs would have to be deducted. Logging costs (consisting of costs of felling, limbing, bucking, and skidding) were estimated at $14/Mbf. Road construction costs would be calculated per Mbf by dividing the timber operator's road-building costs (exclusive of any Forest Service supplement) by the amount of timber for which he had contracted. (In the case of the second alternative method of sale, should the MacLeod and Affleck mills be awarded the contract, these operators would pool their road-building resources and prorate their share of construction costs according to their share of the timber.) Road maintenance costs would be calculated and deducted in the same manner. Actual hauling costs from the stands to the mill were estimated at $4/Mbf per mile over unpaved roads and $2/Mbf per mile over paved roads. (For the purpose of calculation, it may be assumed that one third of all timber involved would travel over each of the three spur roads, and that the timber was evenly distributed along each spur road.)

As a final item, $2/Mbf would have to be deducted for deposit in funds under the "K-V Act"[2] to provide minimum regeneration of the area logged.

The balance would be the minimum stumpage price that Mr. Ursus would accept from bidders, with the proviso that should the stumpage price calculated as above prove to be less than $20/Mbf for ponderosa pine or $2/Mbf for true fir, these latter prices would be the minimum acceptable. (The Forest Service required such minimum prices for each species and grade.) Of the stumpage price received by the Forest Service, 25% would have to be turned over to Nemorensis County.

Proposed Recreation Area

In considering the possibility of opening up this section of the forest to recreational use, Mr. Ursus had on his desk a preliminary report outlining the recreational possibilities and planned facilities for the area.

The area contained four lakes and 50 miles of excellent fishing streams, four sites for campgrounds, each with space for 200 family units, and two possible picnic areas with space for 100 family units each.

Campground construction costs were estimated at $1,000 per unit; picnic areas would cost $300 per unit to prepare.

In addition, a commercial developer proposed to build a lodge, parking lot, restaurant, and boat-launching ramp at a cost of $750,000. He estimated his gross revenue per season would amount to $1 million, on which he expected to make 15% before federal and state taxes. Federal taxes would probably come to 30% of his before-tax margin, and state taxes would be 2%. County property taxes would amount to an additional $3,000 per year. His expected margin of 15% before taxes had been calculated with the understanding that he would pay 3% of his gross to the Forest Service for use of the area and 1% to the county.

Forest Service estimates of use of the proposed area ranged from 750 to 2,000 family automobiles per day during the tourist season, with an average of three persons per automobile. (The tourist season was expected to last from June 1st until Labor Day.) Ten percent of the people visiting the area were expected to spend most of their time fishing; 10% would be exclusively interested in camping and hiking.

---

[2] Knutson-Vandenberg Act, June 9, 1930.

The remainder would probably want to picnic or bathe in the lakes, besides using the other facilities from time to time.

It would cost the state $30,000 per year to keep the streams stocked with fish. A state fishing license cost $4 per year. Deer hunting would probably prove popular in season: up to 1,000 hunters were expected to pay the state $8 each for a license. Past experience in similar areas indicated that approximately 50 deer might be killed per season, thus relieving the state of a control program expense for that area amounting to $6,000 annually. A game warden would have to be hired, however, to patrol the area during the season: his salary and housing would cost the state an estimated $9,000 per year. The Wildlife Department at the state capital estimated that a deer carcass might be worth $200 commercially.

The area under consideration contained grazing land which could support up to 500 cattle for the four-month grazing season. The Forest Service would receive $1 per head per month for use of this land, of which 25% would have to be turned over to the county.

Lightning fires were a constant problem in Nuthatch National Forest. In the area under consideration, suppression costs had averaged $30,000 per year, with an annual loss of timber whose stumpage value was estimated approximately at $25,000. The road system contemplated would lower suppression costs by 50% and would reduce timber losses from fire to negligible amounts. However, if the roads were open to recreationists, experience had shown that additional fire prevention measures would need to be taken, costing an estimated $2,000 per month during the tourist season.

If the area was opened to recreation, the Forest Service would have to recruit additional staff to supervise the various facilities. It was estimated that two year-round men would be needed at a cost of $10,000 per man, including housing. During the tourist season, six college students from the state university in Inverness could be hired at $700 per month each, including transportation and housing.

Mr. Ursus felt that he was faced with three interrelated decisions:

1. Which bid should he accept?
2. Should he have road A paved?
3. Should he authorize the proposed plans for development of the recreational facilities?

He was aware that building the recreational facilities could not commence until logging operations ceased. The developer and Forest

Service officials felt that the area would be ready for the public 17 months after work began on the various facilities. Mr. Ursus had received a note from the regional forester pointing out that recreational facilities in the nearest national park, some 60 miles away in a neighboring state, were already overcrowded. He also had on his desk a letter from the Nemorensis County authorities advising him that the MacLeod and Affleck mills were running dangerously low on work in process. This letter also reminded Mr. Ursus that the county was hoping to use a portion of future timber receipts in a cooperative venture with the state university to retrain local high school dropouts.

Question

1. What action should Mr. Ursus take on the three interrelated decisions listed above?

Exhibit 1

NUTHATCH NATIONAL FOREST (A)

SCHEMATIC OF PROPOSED ROAD SYSTEM FOR TIMBER SALE AREA

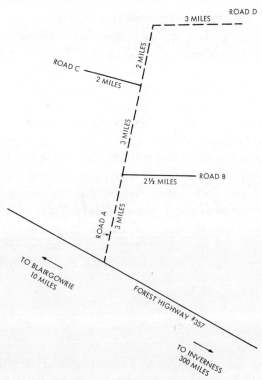

Chapter 4

DECISION ANALYSIS: STRUCTURE AND UNCERTAINTY

The decisions you can make today can only influence the future. This is an obvious fact, yet it is often ignored in practice. There have been many cases where a decision has been made to continue some project mainly because of the large amount of resources already spent on the project. We have discussed this phenomenon previously and have concluded that the only relevant costs and revenues are those that can be influenced by some decision available to the decision maker. Clearly such costs and revenues must occur sometime in the future. In this relevant-cost type of problem, the important question is which set of future outcomes are the best to have happen. These problems can be very complicated to analyze because the number of possible choices may be very large and the objectives that the decision maker wishes to satisfy may be ill-defined and conflicting. However, one major simplifying assumption has always been present in our analyses: The future was completely within the decision maker's control, that is, there was no uncertainty about what would happen *once* the decision had been made. This is obviously an unrealistic assumption for most problems, and we are now ready to discuss problems where the future is not known for sure.

Conceptually it is not difficult to say what must be done to analyze a problem when the future is not known with certainty. We must forecast the future and then analyze the alternatives available relative to this forecast. A typical approach to forecasting is to select one future outcome and assume that it will happen for sure. This selection process may be elaborate and consume a great amount of time; but regardless of the details of the process, the end result is a selection of *"The* future outcome." The next step in the analysis is to select the course of action that will best satisfy some goal if the future turns out to be as predicted. This is called a conditional analysis, because it selects the best course of action conditional on some future outcome occurring. The basic weakness of making a decision based on a conditional analysis is that there may be no agreement on what the future outcome will be. In fact, it may be possible to envision many possible outcomes in the future, and then your decision should be based on an analysis that takes into account all the reasonable possibilities.

When there is no agreement about the future, a conditional analysis can be made for all possible outcomes. A decision can be made if you find some course of action that is best in all future situations. As an example, suppose you want to decide if you should introduce a new product that will require an increase in your production capacity. There are many possible future sales volumes for this product. If, however, for all these sales volumes the total contribution from the product will more than cover the costs of increasing capacity, then you would make the decision to introduce the product. This decision could be made with confidence even when you did not know what the "true" sales volume would be.

Unfortunately, quite often this conditional analysis will indicate that for some future outcomes one action is best, and for another outcome some other action is best. It is this situation that presents the real challenge to the decision maker and that will be the subject of this chapter. How can a decision maker select among various courses of action today when he does not know for certain what will happen tomorrow, but he does know that for some possible outcomes one action is best and for some other outcomes another action would be preferred?

AN EXAMPLE OF A DECISION UNDER UNCERTAINTY

For the purpose of focusing our discussion it will be useful to have a simple decision problem for consideration. Consider Mr. Fred Owens' problem of deciding whether or not to introduce a new novelty toy into the Owens Novelty Company product line. Mr. Owens already offers many other novelties and therefore does not believe this is a major strategic decision, but he does want to be systematic and careful in his analysis, since his success ultimately depends on decisions of this type. Because of the short life of most novelties he is willing to consider only one year into the future.

Mr. Owens has determined that this particular novelty can be made by one of two manufacturing processes, one using a standard machine, the other a highly automated machine. In either case he has decided to lease the manufacturing equipment. The standard machine rents for $1,000 for the year and will result in directly variable costs of $1 per item produced. The automated equipment can be leased for $5,000 per year and will result in directly variable costs of $0.50 per item produced. He knows that this novelty is similar to some already on the market and that the existing price for this type of toy is $1.50 net to the manufacturer. Since he does not wish to try and change the price structure of this market, he has decided that if he introduces this product it will be at the $1.50 price.

The forecast of possible sales has occupied most of Mr. Owens' recent thinking on this problem. He knows that there are many possible sales volumes; however, he has decided to concentrate on only three typical situations. He thinks that there is a possibility that the novelty will be a failure and he will sell only about 1,000 items. If it goes fairly well he could sell 5,000 items. If it really takes off he might sell 12,000 items. In summary, Mr. Owens is willing to assume that sales will either be 1,000, 5,000, or 12,000 units.

THE BASIC STRUCTURE OF THE PROBLEM

In its simplest form any decision problem has only two components. First, there are choices that can be made by the decision maker; we shall call these *acts*. Second, there are occurrences that are not controlled by the decision maker but instead happen to him; these we shall call *events*. An event can be the act of a competitor or the act of a large number of consumers, or an act of nature; the common characteristic is that it is beyond the *complete* control of the decision maker. It is obvious that we need only forecast the outcomes of events, because acts, even if they will be taken in the future, are completely within the decision maker's control.

How to Select Acts

There is very little that can be said about how to select the acts of a decision problem. This depends upon the creativity and imagination of the decision maker. No analytical technique will generate the alternatives to be considered; this can only be accomplished by careful evaluation of the situation by someone familiar with the basic problem. Many excellent acts are ignored because they were not considered until after the decision had been made. One general point can be made, however, concerning what is often not thought of as an act.

To take no action should always be evaluated as an alternative. Doing nothing has consequences in the future; and doing nothing is under the control of the decision maker—therefore, to do nothing is an act.

In Mr. Owens' problem the acts are: (1) do nothing, that is, do not introduce the novelty; (2) introduce the novelty and use the standard machine; and (3) introduce the novelty and use the automated machine.

The Selection of Events

The selection of what events to consider in a decision problem is also a matter of judgment. It is possible to include everything that is beyond your control. For example, Mr. Owens might consider whether or not his competition will react to the introduction, and if so how soon. He might worry about government policy on taxation and whether this will increase or decrease the disposable income available to buy toys and so on. All of these factors may influence the forecast of the future sales. If they do, he must think about them, but it would be useful to have a simpler framework for actual analysis. This can be achieved if he will follow some simple rules in selecting events.

First, for a specific analysis the decision maker should recognize only those events that will result in different consequences for the actions being considered. For example, if Mr. Owens is able to finance this project without borrowing, then he can ignore all the possible future interest rates. Whatever the rate is in the future, it will influence all of his acts in the same way and thus for the purpose of this decision it can be ignored.

The second rule is to define the event in such a way that its consequences can be measured by the decision maker in an unambiguous way. This can be done if he thinks of an event as an occurrence at some point in time and then thinks of the possible outcomes of the event at that time. In this example, Mr. Owens really only has to think of the event: "demand for the novelty in the next year." There are many factors influencing this event, but at some point in the future the combined influence of all these factors can be measured by counting the number of orders received. This "event" can have many *outcomes,* all of which must be measurable.[1] In this case, outcomes of demand

---

[1] In some texts this "event" is called a random variable or an unknown quantity. We will use the word event to mean an occurrence at some future point in time, the results of which can be measured after the fact. The various results that can be measured will be called *outcomes.*

can be 1,000, 5,000 or 12,000 items. In thinking about the possible outcomes of an event, two rules should be observed:

1. The outcomes should be *mutually exclusive*. This means that the consequences of each outcome can be measured in an unambiguous way. It would not be useful for Owens to talk about the outcome, "demand equals more than 1,000 units," because he could not clearly measure the consequences of his various actions against this outcome.

2. The outcomes should be *collectively exhaustive*. This means that all of the possible outcomes should be determined. This rule is to ensure that all factors that can happen are being considered.

In summary, Mr. Owens can define as the only relevant event— "demand for the novelty next year." The outcomes of this event are: 1,000 units, 5,000 units, or 12,000 units.

The Payoff Table

A useful way to display the possible acts and events and their consequences is in a payoff table. Table 4–1 is a completed payoff table

Table 4–1

PAYOFF TABLE FOR OWENS' PROBLEM
(Dollars of profit before tax)

Outcomes	Acts		
	I *Do Not Introduce*	*II* *Introduce with Standard Machine*	*III* *Introduce with Automated Machine*
1,000	$0	$−500	$−4,000
5,000	$0	$1,500	$ 0
12,000	$0	$5,000	$ 7,000

for Mr. Owens' problem. There is one column for each possible act, and there is one row for each possible outcome of each relevant event. Each intersection of row and column represents a unique point in the future, and for this point we can perform a conditional analysis to determine the consequence. Mr. Owens has decided that he can measure the consequence of any future position in terms of net profit before tax. As an example, one column will be for act III, introduce with the automated process; and one row will be for the outcome, demand = 5,000 units. The calculation of profit before tax for this combination of act and event is shown in Table 4–2.

Table 4–2

PROFIT BEFORE TAX WITH DEMAND OF 5,000 UNITS USING
AUTOMATED PROCESS

Revenue................................5,000 × $1.50 =		$7,500
Variable cost..........................5,000 × 0.50 =	$2,500	
Lease cost..............................	5,000	
Total cost.....................		7,500
Profit before taxes...................		$ 0

Every cell in Table 4–1 can be completed in this manner. You assume the outcome is known for sure and measure the consequence for each action conditional on this assumption.

From the payoff table we can see that if demand were to equal 1,000 items, the best act would be not to introduce with a net profit of $0. If demand were to equal 5,000 items, the best choice would be to introduce using the standard machine with a net profit of $1,500. And finally, if demand were to equal 12,000 items, the best act would be to introduce with the automatic machine for a profit of $7,000. Mr. Owens can choose any column he would like since the choice of acts is completely under his control. Unfortunately, the choice of the row is outside his control. He would like some guidance for making his choice of acts now that takes into account this lack of control over events in the future.

Some Possible Decision Guides

There are many possible guides Mr. Owens can use in deciding which act to select. One frequent approach is to select the act that is best if the "most likely" outcome were to occur. Mr. Owens has indicated that his sales may be any of three possible levels, but suppose he believes that the most likely of the three is 12,000 units. In this case he would decide to introduce the novelty and to use the automated manufacturing process, since this act provides the best profit for his "most likely" outcome. If Mr. Owens uses this decision guide in all of his decisions, he will select the act with the best consequence for the actual outcome more often than he would using any other decision guide. Unfortunately, selecting the act with the best consequence for the actual outcome as often as possible does not assure long-run economic success. First of all, "as often as possible" may be very infrequent. If there are many outcomes, the "most likely" may not happen very often. Secondly, this guide does not consider how bad the decision might be if the "most likely" outcome does not happen. It may be possible to select some act that is about as good as the best act when the "most likely" outcome happens and that is much better when some other outcome occurs. As an example of this, Mr. Owens could introduce the novelty by using the standard machine and obtain $5,000 profit if the "most likely" outcome occurs, but if one of the lower sales levels results, he is better off than he would be if he used the automated machine.

Another decision guide is to select the action that has the "best worst case."[2] Looking at the payoff table for his problem, Mr. Owens can see that the worst that could happen if he did not introduce the novelty would be zero profits. If he introduces the novelty with standard machinery, the worst he could do is to lose $500. If he introduces the novelty by using the automated machinery, he could lose $4,000. Using the decision guide of selecting the act with the "best worst case" would result in a decision not to introduce the novelty. The obvious drawback of this decision guide is its pessimism. All surprises in the future using this decision guide will be pleasant. On the other hand, there may not be many surprises because more often than not the resulting decision is to take no action.

Both decision guides have a common characteristic. They focus on only one possible situation and ignore all other outcomes for the purpose of making the decision. In another respect, however, they are quite dissimilar. One of them focuses on the likelihood of the various outcomes and tries to choose an act that will be best for the most likely occurrence. This guide ignores the magnitude of the consequences of other actions. The other decision guide looks only at the consequences and tries to avoid the really bad results. This guide ignores how likely it is that the worst case will in fact happen and looks only at the most negative consequence for each act.

What we would like is a guide for ranking the various acts that gives consideration to all of the possible outcomes. In making a choice we would like to consider the consequences of each outcome for each of the possible actions, and also give weight to the likelihood of each of those consequences occurring. In summary, such a ranking scheme

---

[2] This decision guide applies what is called the "maximin" criterion, since the objective is to select an act that maximizes the minimum gain. A variation of this process more often used is the "minimax" criterion. In this case the payoff table consequences are measured in opportunity costs and the goal is to select an act that minimizes the maximum opportunity cost.

would try to balance the consequence and likelihood of all outcomes for every act.

Probability

We have proposed that any ranking of the acts open to the decision maker should take into account both the consequences that could result from the various outcomes of relevant events, and the likelihood that these various outcomes will in fact occur. The consequences can usually be described in some economic unit, like dollars of profit or opportunity cost. This measurement for each act and each outcome is then displayed in the payoff table. We have not discussed how to describe the likelihood of the various outcomes except in qualitative terms such as "the most likely." It is clear from these examples that any description will be a relative one. We would like to make this relative description more precise and will, therefore, use a quantitative measurement. A quantitative measure of the relative likelihood of a particular outcome will be called the *probability* of its occurrence. Various rules have been developed for assigning probabilities, and they are much like the rules of grammar. These rules cannot be proven to be correct, but their use makes it much easier to communicate your meaning.

Before describing the rules associated with the language of probability, it is useful to make some observations. First, for our purposes there is no meaning to the term "true probability" or "correct probability." We have adopted the language of probability to describe an attitude about the relative likelihood of various occurrences in the future. Thus a probability is a personal statement about the future. Two reasonable people can view a similar set of facts and assign different probabilities to future outcomes of events. If this were not true there would never be any wagers on horse races. This does not mean that probabilities can be arbitrarily assigned or that they are unimportant. In fact we shall show in the next chapters that much hard thinking should be associated with the assigning of probabilities. This leads us to a second observation, which is that the decision maker should not allow his judgment to be replaced by techniques when he assigns probabilities. There are many aids, some simple others quite complex, to assist the decision maker in assessing probabilities. These techniques may be appropriate in many cases, but the decision maker must realize that in the final analysis the probability assessment is *his personal judgment* about future outcomes. This judgment can be guided, and improved, with techniques, but it cannot be replaced.

There are three rules for assigning probabilities to the outcomes of an event:

1. Outcomes that in the opinion of the decision maker cannot occur are assigned a probability of zero.
2. The sum of the probabilities for all possible outcomes should be 1.0.
3. The probability of at least one of a set of mutually exclusive outcomes occurring is the sum of their individual probabilities of occurrence.

The first rule results because a probability is a quantitative measure of the likelihood of an outcome occurring *relative* to all the other possible outcomes. Once the collectively exhaustive list of outcomes for an event has been determined, the decision maker may believe that one outcome has no chance of occurring. The only number that can be used to quantify this feeling is zero. As an example the collectively exhaustive list of all possible outcomes for event "toss of a coin" are: (1) heads, (2) tails, and (3) the edge. Most of us would assign a probability of zero to the last outcome. In practice, any outcome with zero probability is no longer considered in the analysis. For this reason you should be careful in making this assignment since it is equivalent to saying that you no longer wish to consider this outcome in making your decision.

The second rule results from the eventual use of the probabilities. The probabilities must add to some amount. This amount is not important since we are using probabilities as a relative measure. Thus for convenience, this amount was chosen to be 1.0. We will discuss this aspect of the probabilities in more detail in the next section.

The third rule results from the way we defined the possible outcomes of an event. We said that the outcomes should be mutually exclusive. This meant that only one of them could occur. For the purpose of preparing an initial list of outcomes, this concept is useful. However, occasionally two or more outcomes will result in the same *consequence,* and for the purpose of calculation it is useful to combine these outcomes into one new outcome. The problem then is what probability should be assigned to this new outcome.

As an example suppose you have what you believe is a "fair" die (one half a set of dice). The possible outcomes of the next roll of this die are a 1, 2, 3, 4, 5, or 6. You believe that these outcomes are equally likely to occur, and thus the second rule requires you to assign the probability $\frac{1}{6}$ to each outcome. Now suppose you have a friend who is willing to play a game of chance. He will give you $1 if the number rolled is even, and you will give him $1 if the number rolled is odd.

You can now define the possible outcomes of the next roll in a different way. Only two outcomes are important to your decision: (1) the number is even and (2) the number is odd. The consequence of the first is a gain of $1, and of the second a loss of $1.

What probability should you assign to each of these newly defined outcomes? The third rule would require the probability of the winning $1 to be the sum of three mutually exclusive outcomes, namely, the probability for rolling a 2 plus the probability for rolling a 4 plus the probability for rolling a 6. Thus the probability of winning $1 is $\frac{1}{6} + \frac{1}{6} + \frac{1}{6} = \frac{1}{2}$. The probability of losing $1 can be found in the same manner, only now the mutually exclusive outcomes are 1, 3, and 5. Another way to obtain the probability for losing $1 is to remember that the only possible outcomes under the new definition are to win $1

Table 4–3

PROBABILITY OF OUTCOMES FOR THE EVENT:
DEMAND NEXT YEAR

Outcome	Probability
1,000	0.3
5,000	0.5
12,000	0.2
	1.0

or lose $1. Thus the sum of their probabilities must be 1.0 according to the second rule. Therefore, the probability of losing $1 is 1.0 minus the probability of winning $1 or $1 - 0.5 = 0.5$.

Now we can return to Mr. Owens and ask him to assign probabilities to the various outcomes of the event: demand for novelty next year. We are asking him to think hard about the various factors that influence demand and to summarize his judgment in a quantitative way by assigning probabilities.

Mr. Owens is willing to do this, and the results of his efforts are shown in Table 4–3. From this table we can see that he has not changed his mind about considering only three outcomes, since he assigned zero probability to all the other possibilities. He has also observed the second rule and made the sum of all outcomes equal 1.0. We can see he now thinks that the most likely outcome will be 5,000 units and that 1,000 is more likely than 12,000. In some sense we can view this set of probabilities as Mr. Owens' "vote of confidence" in the future, almost as if we gave him 100 votes and asked him to place them on the various outcomes in a way that would correspond to his feeling about their relative likelihood of occurrence. Regardless of how he arrived at this assessment, he has stated that it reflects his best judgment of what will happen.

Choosing the Act

So far we have proposed that Mr. Owens should think of the decision problem as a choice among various acts, all of which result in different consequences depending on the outcomes of some future event. We have suggested that in order to rank these acts he should give consideration to both the magnitude of the consequences and to the relative likelihood of the various outcomes actually occurring. We will now introduce a criterion that will allow Mr. Owens to rank his actions according to our suggestions. This criterion will be called the *certainty equivalent* for an act.

In order to assign this certainty equivalent, Mr. Owens must look at each act as though it were one of only two alternatives. The other alternative will be to accept an amount of profit for certain from someone who will then have the rights to the act. Mr. Owens should think about that minimum amount of profit that he would accept from someone else rather than take the act under consideration. In order to do this seriously he must think about the various consequences of the action and their likelihood of occurrence. He can think about each action separately and will be able to assign a certainty equivalent to each one. He should then pick that act that has the highest certainty equivalent. This act will be the one that Mr. Owens thinks has the highest value, giving weight to both the consequences of the outcomes and their probability of occurrence.

Table 4–4 is the payoff table for Mr. Owens' problem, expanded to include the probabilities assigned to each outcome. What he must do is think about each action, consider the consequences and their probabilities, and determine the minimum certain amount he would accept for this option if it were the only one available.

Consider the act not to introduce the novelty. It is clear that the minimum profit Mr. Owens should take for this act is zero. If this were the only available action, any positive profit would be better than taking that act. However, it would be better to take the act than to take a negative profit for certain. We can then say that Mr. Owens *should* assign a certainty equivalent of zero to act I.

Unfortunately, we cannot tell Mr. Owens what exact value he

should assign as a certainty equivalent to the other two acts. As an example, take the second act. The worst Mr. Owens could do is to lose $500. We can therefore conclude that he would be silly to select as a certainty equivalent anything less than —$500. He likewise can never hope to make more than $5,000 by choosing this act, so he would be unreasonable to select more than $5,000 as a certainty equivalent. We have now established a range for the certainty equivalent. In order to narrow this range we would begin an iterative process of questioning Mr. Owens. Would he rather take $4,000 for sure or select act II? He might answer that he would take the $4,000 because there is only

Table 4–4

EXPANDED PAYOFF TABLE FOR MR. OWENS' PROBLEM
(Dollars of profit before tax)

Outcomes	I Do Not Introduce	II Introduce with Standard Machine	III Introduce with Automated Machine	Probability of Outcome
		Acts		
1,000	$0	$–500	$–4,000	0.3
5,000	$0	$1,500	$ 0	0.5
12,000	$0	$5,000	$ 7,000	0.2

20% chance of doing better by taking the act, and even then he would only get $5,000. We would then ask him if he would rather take $1,000 for certain in place of act II. He might say no because he has a 70% chance of doing better, and if he does worse he would only lose $500. If he answered this way we could continue to narrow the range. It should be clear that there is some amount of profit for certain that Mr. Owens thinks is equivalent to taking act II. If we offered him more he would take the certain profit. If we offered him less he would take the act.

This amount of profit is *his* certainty equivalent for this act. If Mr. Owens can think about his acts this way he will end up with a measure of value for each act, the certainty equivalent. If he believed his judgment in this process he would then choose the action with the largest certainty equivalent.

These certainty equivalents may vary from person to person because of individual attitudes. This is consistent with our belief that the decision maker should exercise *his* judgment in making the decision and not some arbitrary guideline established by some advisor or consultant. However, in many decision problems a good argument can be made for using a particular value for the certainty equivalent. This value is called the *expected value* of the act.

Expected Value as a Certainty Equivalent

When we had Mr. Owens answer our questions about his certainty equivalent for act II, he was giving consideration to two factors: the consequences and their likelihood. In fact, this is why we introduced the concept of certainty equivalent—to get one value to repre-

Table 4–5

CALCULATION OF EXPECTED VALUE FOR ACT II
(Introduce using standard machine)

Outcome for Event Demand Next Year	Consequence C	Probability P	Consequence Times Probability C×P
1,000	−500	0.3	−150
5,000	1,500	0.5	750
12,000	5,000	0.2	1,000

$$\text{Expected value} = \frac{-150 + 750 + 1,000}{0.3 + 0.5 + 0.2} = 1,600*$$

* The expected value is found by taking a weighted average of the consequences using the probabilities as weights. This means each consequence is multiplied by its probability and these products are summed. This amount is then divided by the sum of the weights. Since the sum of probabilities for all possible outcomes must be 1.0 if the second rule of probabilities is observed, the last step of division can be ignored.

sent these two factors. A much more mechanical method for combining these factors is to take a weighted average of the consequences using the probabilities as the weights. This weighted average is called the *expected value* of the act. Table 4–5 shows a calculation of the expected value for act II.

This number $1,600, the expected value, can now be used as the certainty equivalent for act II if Mr. Owens is willing to make an assumption. This assumption is that he is willing "to play the averages." The reason for this becomes clear when we think about what the expected value represents. Suppose that instead of act II, Mr. Owens could choose to play a game of chance. This game has a fair roulette wheel with 100 marks. Being fair means that on any spin there is a 1/100 chance that the pointer on the wheel will come to rest on a given mark. Now suppose that 30 of the marks have a −$500 on them, 50 marks have +$1,500 on them, and 20 marks have +$5,000 on them. The game of chance is simple; Mr. Owens will spin the wheel and receive or pay the amount on the mark where the wheel comes to rest. On any spin the chance of winning $5,000 is 0.2, the chance of winning $1,500 is 0.5, and the chance of losing $500 is 0.3. If this is truly a fair wheel and Mr. Owens spins it many times, the average winning for a spin will be $1,600, the expected value.

This abstraction of the decision problem demonstrates the origin of the expected value as a criterion for choosing between actions. Each act can be replaced by a hypothetical roulette wheel, and the average payoff for that wheel, its expected value, can be calculated. If each act is represented by a fair roulette wheel then the decision maker should want to spin the wheel with the highest expected value.

Mr. Owens might be willing to play the averages until he remembers that he is only going to make this decision one time. He will not be able to have many spins of the wheel. Why should he use the expected value as a criterion for making this choice? We can argue that although this decision will be made only one time, there are many other decisions like this one for Mr. Owens to make. He will make each decision only one time, but he can still feel comfortable using the expected value as a criterion if he makes many similar decisions.

A final worry he may have is that even if he uses the expected value as a criterion of choice, he may choose an act that has a high average payoff but also has some very disastrous consequences for some outcomes. If one of these outcomes occurs he will no longer be able to continue in business and make decisions.

As an example, suppose he could take an act that resulted in a 50–50 gamble at making $100,000,000 or losing $50,000,000. The expected value is $25,000,000, but Mr. Owens must declare bankruptcy if he loses the $50,000,000. In this situation he would probably not want to use the expected value as his certainty equivalent. He must then judgmentally assess his certainty equivalent for this act by determining the minimum amount of cash that is equivalent to taking the act.

We can now be more specific in stating when we would use the expected value as a certainty equivalent. The decision maker should be willing to assign the expected value of an act as his certainty equivalent if—

1. He believes that there are many similar decision problems of this type that he will consider in the future.
2. None of the consequences of the acts under consideration are so disastrously bad that if that consequence were to occur, it will be impossible for the decision maker to continue in business in his *usual manner.*

This last condition is really an escape clause. What it essentially states is that when the decision maker does not feel comfortable about "playing the averages" he should not use the expected value as his certainty equivalent. Instead he should go through the process of thinking about each act and assessing a certainty equivalent for that act. We should emphasize that the decision to use the expected value as a certainty equivalent should be *explicitly* made by the decision maker and not assumed to be the "best" or "appropriate" way to proceed.

WHAT SHOULD MR. OWENS DO?

Mr. Owens has looked at his problem and concluded that he is willing to play the averages. This decision was based on his belief that he would have many similar decisions to make in his business and that he could afford to lose the $4,000 associated with act III and still be in business as usual. This last decision in no way should be influenced by the probability of losing the $4,000. When deciding on whether or not to play the averages, Mr. Owens should only consider his ability to withstand the $4,000 loss. If these are his beliefs, then we would recommend that he rank the acts according to their expected values. Table 4–6 is a payoff table with expected values for each action.

Table 4–6

PAYOFF TABLE FOR MR. OWENS' PROBLEM
(Dollars of profit before tax)

| | | Acts | | |
Outcome	I Do Not Introduce	II Introduce with Standard Machine	III Introduce with Automated Machine	Probability of Outcome
1,000	$0	$ −500	$−4,000	0.3
5,000	$0	$+1,500	$ 0	0.5
12,000	$0	$+5,000	$ 7,000	0.2
Expected value	$0	$ 1,600	$ 200	

From Table 4–6 Mr. Owens can see that act II, introduce with standard machinery, has an expected value of $1,600 and this is higher than the expected value of any other act, including act I, do nothing. Therefore, he should introduce the novelty and lease the standard machine. This is the action most consistent with his judgment.

THE VALUE OF INFORMATION

In many decision problems it is possible to obtain more information which might help in making a better analysis of the decision. For example, it is possible to conduct a test market for a product before introducing it on a large scale. Once the results of the test market are analyzed the probabilities for various sales outcomes may be revised and the certainty equivalents for the various acts would then change. In this example, and in most other cases, the information can only be obtained at some cost. For this reason it would be useful to have an estimate of how much this information was worth before spending any money to obtain it.

It is necessary to understand how additional information could have value before attempting to assign a quantitive measure to this value. In most decision problems an act can be selected without obtaining new information, and the value of information should always be measured relative to what would have been done without the information. Information can have economic value only if there is some possible outcome of the information request that will cause the decision maker to take a different act than he would take with no information. In other words, if all possible answers to a question will not change your mind about taking a certain act, then asking the question has no value. However, if the decision maker thinks it is possible that some answer to his information request will change his action, then he must attempt to measure its worth. This information can only change his action because the value of some new act is higher given the information than is the value of the previously chosen act, and this difference in value should be attributed to the information.

The value of the information will also depend on how accurate the information is. It is difficult to determine accuracy in most cases, and often for this reason an assumption is made that the information is perfect.[4] A value can be calculated for this perfect information, and

---

[4] Perfect information means that the information generating process accurately evaluates what is in the world. Specifically, when a perfect information source reports that some outcome will occur, we should be willing to assign a probability of 1.0 to that outcome.

this value then becomes the maximum amount that should be spent to obtain information. In fact, less than this amount should be spent because most real information gathering processes are less than perfect.

In order to calculate the value of information, it is helpful to measure the consequences of the decision problem in opportunity costs. The opportunity cost for an act and some specific outcome of an event is a relative measure. Specifically, the opportunity cost for an act and a given outcome is the difference between the value of that combination and the value of the "best" act that could have been taken for the given outcome. As an example, we will determine Mr. Owens' opportunity cost for not introducing the novelty if demand next year is 5,000 units. The value of this consequence is shown in Table 4–6 as $0 profit before taxes. Table 4–6 also shows that Mr. Owens' "best" act for this 5,000 unit outcome is to introduce the novelty with standard equipment, and this consequence has a value of $1,500. The opportunity cost of not introducing and having a demand of 5,000 units is the difference between these values: $1,500 — 0 = $1,500.

The opportunity cost is the penalty that a decision maker must pay because he must act before he knows for certain what will happen. Consider Mr. Owens' possible choice of using standard equipment. How large a penalty will he suffer if he takes this act and demand is 12,000 units? Table 4–6 shows the value of this consequence as $5,000 profit before tax. However, if Mr. Owens had known that demand was going to be 12,000 units, he would have chosen the automated machinery and had a profit before taxes of $7,000. Therefore, we can say he has "paid" a penalty of $2,000 to choose this act whenever the outcome of the event is 12,000 units. This penalty, or opportunity cost, can never be less than zero, because the "best" act for each outcome has an opportunity cost of zero.

Table 4–7 shows the payoff table for Mr. Owens' problem with the consequence of each act and outcome measured as an opportunity cost. The probability for each outcome is the same since nothing has been done to change his thinking about the world; we have only measured the consequences with a different yardstick. The last row of Table 4–7 shows the expected opportunity cost for each act. Assuming that Mr. Owens is still willing to play the averages, these are also his certainty equivalent for each act. The certainty equivalent cost for an act would be the maximum amount he would pay to have someone else take this act. His decision rule in this case should be to pick the act with the smallest certainty equivalent cost.

Table 4–7

PAYOFF TABLE FOR MR. OWENS' PROBLEMS
(Consequences in opportunity cost)

Outcome	Acts			Probability of Outcome
	I Do Not Introduce	II Introduce with Standard Machine	III Introduce with Automated Machine	
1,000	$ 0	$ 500	$4,000	0.3
5,000	$1,500	$ 0	$1,500	0.5
12,000	$7,000	$2,000	$ 0	0.2
Expected opportunity cost	$2,150	$ 550	$1,950	

The act with the lowest certainty equivalent is act II, introduce with standard equipment, and the expected opportunity cost of this act is $550. This $550 also can be viewed as a measure of the value of information to Mr. Owens in this problem. Look at how this $550 was obtained. First, the act, introduce with standard equipment, is the best that can be taken without information. Second, the opportunity cost for each outcome is a measure of how much could be saved if a perfect information process indicated that this particular outcome were going to occur. For example, if Mr. Owens got information telling him that demand was going to be 1,000 units, he would not introduce the novelty and cancel his order for the standard machine. This would save him $500. This $500 is the value of that particular piece of information; it is also the opportunity cost. Finally, the probability of obtaining each answer from a *perfect* information source is the same as the probability that Mr. Owens would assign to the outcome's occurring. For example, if Mr. Owens believes there is a 0.2 chance that demand will be 12,000 units and that his information source is perfect, then he must believe there is a 0.2 chance that source will say "demand is 12,000." For these reasons, the $550 is the weighted average of the value of each specific answer from a perfect source. The probability of receiving each answer is used as the weight in calculating the weighted average. This is called the *expected value of perfect information* and is an indication of the maximum amount a decision maker should be willing to spend on obtaining additional information.

THE DECISION DIAGRAM: ANOTHER APPROACH
TO STRUCTURING THE PROBLEM

Earlier we used a payoff table as a way to display the consequences of various acts and events in a decision problem. This was a useful tool to organize our thinking about a simple problem like Mr. Owens'. For problems with a large number of choices and outcomes these tables become cumbersome and confusing. Therefore, we will introduce a technique, called decision diagramming, which is more applicable to complex problems. A decision diagram is particularly useful in the analysis of sequential decision problems where the decision maker can take various actions after he learns the outcome of some event.

Decision diagrams are constructed from two types of forks: event forks and act forks. From their names it should be clear that every act fork is associated with an act and every event fork with an event. These forks are analogous to the rows and columns of the payoff table. For clarity we will represent act forks with a square and event forks with a circle. From each square one branch is drawn for each possible choice of action, and from each circle one branch is drawn for each possible outcome to the event. Figure 4–1 is a decision diagram for Mr. Owens' basic problem.

Figure 4–1

MR. OWENS' BASIC PROBLEM

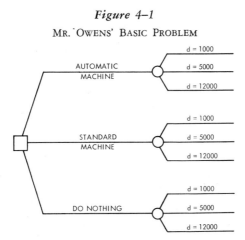

The decision diagram follows a time sequence from left to right. The first step in time is the decision on type of machine, after which demand occurs at the various levels. The diagram ends at a cutoff date in the future beyond which the decision maker does not wish to structure the problem. In Mr. Owens' case, this is one year. For every sequence of choices and outcomes there is an end point on the diagram. This end point corresponds to the intersection of a row and column in the payoff table. The consequence of each act and event is placed at the end point.

For every event fork one additional step is needed to complete the diagram. The decision maker's probabilities are placed on each branch, representing his best judgment about the relative likelihood of the various outcomes occurring. Figure 4–2 represents a decision diagram

Figure 4–2

MR. OWENS' COMPLETE DECISION DIAGRAM

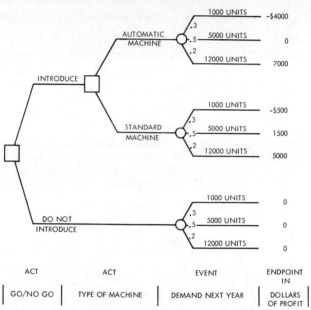

| ACT | ACT | EVENT | ENDPOINT IN |
| GO/NO GO | TYPE OF MACHINE | DEMAND NEXT YEAR | DOLLARS OF PROFIT |

for Owens' problem with the end points and probabilities included. In addition we have broken the act fork into two parts. This is to demonstrate the fact that acts can be represented sequentially or jointly as long as there are no intervening events. In fact, in this case it would be possible to put the decision about type of machine first and then follow it with an act fork for whether or not to introduce the machine, since no event of interest occurs between these two acts.

Once the problem has been structured with a decision diagram, the process of making the decision begins. In order to decide which branch he prefers at each act fork, the decision maker must decide on the worth of being at the end of each branch. This usually means that he must decide what a complete event fork is worth. We have discussed the certainty equivalent in connection with the payoff table, and the concept also applies here, despite the different type of display. Therefore, each event fork is replaced by a certainty equivalent. In this manner, a certainty equivalent will be assigned to every branch on an act fork. The decision maker would then choose the branch with the highest certainty equivalent. If Mr. Owens were still willing to play the averages and use the expected value as his certainty equivalent, we could reduce his problem to the one shown in Figure 4–3.

Figure 4–3

MR. OWENS' PROBLEM
WITH CERTAINTY EQUIVALENTS
REPLACING EVENT FORKS
(Assuming he will use expected values
for his certainty equivalent)

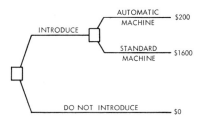

Mr. Owens controls the choice of branches at the act forks, and therefore he would go ahead with the standard machine because it has the highest certainty equivalent of $1,600.

In summary, a decision can be obtained from a decision diagram by going to the far right-hand side and working backwards, with each event fork being replaced by a certainty equivalent. At each act fork the branch with the highest certainty is selected. This certainty equivalent is then used to replace the entire act fork. This process is continued from right to left until the best choice is determined at the initial act fork. This process is called backward induction and is used to reduce complex decision diagrams so that the best initial act is selected.

A MORE COMPLEX PROBLEM

The decision diagram is most useful when the decision problem has sequential choices of acts. Mr. Owens' basic problem is not such a case.

In order to show the value of diagramming, we will consider the following extension of the basic problem. Mr. Owens has a friend, Mr. Fischer, who is in the market survey business. Mr. Fischer has offered to do an exhaustive survey on the novelty Mr. Owens is considering introducing and he absolutely guarantees that he can predict what market there will be for this toy. He plans to visit several toy wholesalers to discuss the characteristics of this product, and on the basis of this and other general economic indications he will be able to determine what will happen. Mr. Owens has been trying to decide what this service would be worth and whether he should make an offer to Fischer. In order to analyze the problem he has constructed the decision diagram shown in Figure 4–4.

Figure 4–4

DECISION DIAGRAM FOR MR. OWENS' EXPANDED PROBLEM
(End points in dollars of profit before taxes)

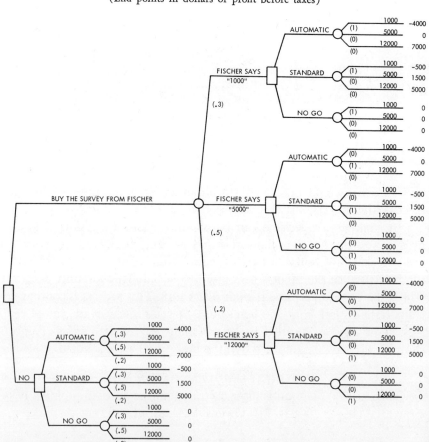

Several features of this diagram should be noted. The initial act has two forks representing the basic alternatives of whether or not to buy the survey. If the survey is not purchased, the decision problem is exactly like the problem we have already diagrammed, and thus the portion of the diagram following the "no survey" fork is exactly like the basic problem diagram shown in Figure 4–2.

The major advantage of buying the survey is the ability to delay the decision on machine types until the results of the survey are known. Therefore, immediately following the act fork "buy survey" there is an event fork representing the results of the survey. There must be one branch for each possible outcome to the survey. The probabilities assigned to this event fork depend on two things: the decision maker's feelings about the real world and his feelings about how good the survey is at revealing the real world. For the sake of simplicity, let us assume that Mr. Fischer is a perfect forecaster. This means that when Mr. Fischer finally predicts an outcome, Mr. Owens will assign a 1.0 probability to this outcome actually occurring. If this assumption is true, we can assign probabilities to the first event fork according to Table 4–8.

Table 4–8

PROBABILITIES OF OUTCOME TO EVENT:
RESULTS OF FISCHER'S SURVEY

	Probabilities
Fischer says "1,000"	0.3
Fischer says "5,000"	0.5
Fischer says "12,000"	0.2

As you can see these are the same probabilities that Mr. Owens initially assigned to the outcome of the event called, demand next year. If Mr. Owens believes that Fischer is perfect, then he will assign these same probabilities to the survey outcomes. Mr. Fischer has not promised that he will change the world, only that he will accurately reflect what is there. Since Mr. Owens' judgment about what would happen was reflected in his original assessment of the probabilities, he should not alter them because a survey is being taken. This concept is often hard to appreciate, so we will discuss an example.

Assume that there is a roulette wheel hidden from your view. You have previously inspected the wheel and you believe it is fair. This means you believe that one half the time the metal ball will end up in a black spot and the other one half of the time you believe that it will end up in a red spot. This wheel will be spun and stopped, and then you will place your bet on what color came up. Remember that you cannot see the wheel when it stops so you would want to assign a probability of one half to the outcome red. Now suppose you have a friend who can see the wheel and tell you where the ball stopped before you must place your bet. How often will this friend tell you the outcome is red? If he is honest and not color blind he will say red one half of the time. Thus you would assign a probability of one half to the outcome: "My friend says the outcome is red." This analogy is like Owens' problem. He can hire Fischer to tell him something about the world, but Owens already has a feeling about his "roulette wheel," and he will want to include this feeling in his decision making.

Returning to Figure 4–4, after each of the three outcomes of the survey result event fork there is an act fork which represents the three basic alternatives available for manufacturing. Each of these nine act forks is followed by an event fork representing the event, demand next year. You can see that we have assigned zero probabilities to the outcomes not mentioned by Fischer in each part of the diagram. This is the result of our assumption about Fischer's forecasting ability. We could have eliminated all outcomes that have zero probability from the diagram, but for illustration they were included. After each branch on this final event fork is the value of the consequence of that particular path through the diagram. No cost has been charged for the information because we are attempting to determine the value of such a survey. If the cost were fixed and known, we could include it here. As an exercise you may want to construct a payoff table for this problem. It must have one cell for each of the 36 possible consequences.

To analyze this diagram, we would start at the far right. We will assume that Mr. Owens is still willing to play the averages and will, therefore, use the expected value of each event fork as its certainty equivalent. The expected value for the event forks on the survey portion of the tree are easy to calculate because all probabilities are either zero or one. If Fischer says "1,000," the act with the highest certainty equivalent is no-go with a value of $0. If Fischer says "5,000," the best act is the standard machine with a value of $7,000. Figure 4–5 is a reduced diagram representing the conditional decisions mentioned above. The action planned, given each of Fischer's responses, is shown in parentheses and the certainty equivalent is shown at the end of each branch representing an outcome.

If we continue to reduce the diagram by replacing each event fork

Figure 4–5

REDUCED DECISION DIAGRAM
FOR EXPANDED PROBLEM

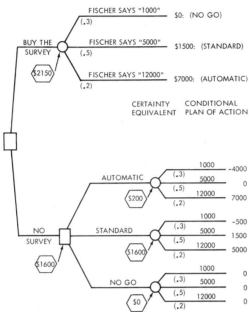

with its certainty equivalent (in this case its expected value), we will produce the circled numbers at the base of the event forks in Figure 4–5. Mr. Owens should use the standard machine if he does not buy the information because this act has the highest certainty equivalent of the three choices. Thus, as we concluded before, the certainty equivalent for the entire "no information" strategy is $1,600. The certainty equivalent for the "buy survey" strategy is shown as $2,150. Mr. Owens can conclude that the difference between these two certainty equivalents is a measure of the value he would assign to having the information. This value is $550. This should not be surprising since we have assumed that Mr. Fischer's survey is perfect and this amount matches the earlier calculation for the expected value of perfect information made using opportunity costs.

SUMMARY

We have proposed the following process for analyzing decisions when the future is not known with certainty:

1. Determine the possible actions that can be taken.
2. Determine the events in the future that can result in different consequences for the various actions.
3. Determine all the possible outcomes of these future events.
4. Assign some value to the consequence of each act and each outcome. We have used two measures for this value, profit and opportunity cost; other measurements for value may be more appropriate for other problems.

For simple problems these first four steps can be accomplished systematically by constructing a payoff table. For problems with many acts and events or with sequential decision options, a decision diagram will be more efficient. After these steps are completed the decision maker must:

5. Assess his probability for each outcome of each event.
6. Determine his certainty equivalent for each action in the problem. This can be done in one of two ways:
   a) If he is not willing to play the averages, he must think about each act in isolation and determine what *minimum* amount of profit he would accept or what maximum amount of cost he would pay as an alternative to taking this act. This amount is his certainty equivalent.
   b) If he is willing to play the averages he can assign the expected value to each act as his certainty equivalent. The expected value of an act is the weighted average of the consequences for the outcomes of the following event using the probability of each outcome's occurrence as the weights.
7. Select the act with the best certainty equivalent.

If the problem has sequential decision options, then steps 6 and 7 must be iterated starting at the far right of the decision diagram until the certainty equivalents for all the alternatives on the initial act fork have been determined.

8. In addition the decision maker may find it useful to calculate the expected value of perfect information (EVPI) to determine the maximum amount that he should spend to collect more information. The EVPI can be calculated by obtaining the expected opportunity cost of the best act. Another approach for calculating the EVPI is to assume you have as an alternative access to a source of perfect information. The EVPI is the difference between the certainty equivalent of the real problem and the certainty equivalent of the problem with the source of perfect information as an alternative.

PROBLEMS

Problem 4–1. Joel Williams, president and founder of the J. P. Williams Novelty Company, received a proposal from his research and development group for a new seasonal novelty, with the suggestion that it be added to the company's novelty line for the upcoming season. Mr. Williams thought enough of the proposed novelty that he was at least willing to explore the suggestion. Consequently, he gave the design to his production people with the question, "Do we have the capability to produce this novelty? If we do, what kind of cost will be involved?"

A few days later he received a report from the production department indicating that the company could make the proposed novelty and, in fact, could produce identically the same item by either of two production processes. The direct process would involve producing the article on a fairly standard machine. The report indicated that although the company did not now have such a machine, one could be leased for the season at a lease cost of $1,000. The production report indicated that were the direct process used, the variable cost would be expected to be very close to $1 per unit.

The alternative process was a more highly automated one. It, of course, required a more complex piece of equipment, which investigation indicated could be made available at a lease cost of $5,000 for the season. The report demonstrated that if this process were used, there would be considerable savings in labor and even some reduction in scrap relative to the direct process. The production report concluded from this that the variable cost using this process would drop to approximately 50 cents per unit.

In considering whether he should add the new item to his line, Mr. Williams recalled two long-standing policies of his firm, and he decided that he would not be willing to change them in this situation. The first policy recognized that there was a standard price for this type of novelty in the market and asserted that the Williams line would neither charge a premium price nor did it wish to run the risk of a price war by charging a lower than customary price. If this proposed novelty were to be added to the line, it would thus be priced at the traditional company price of $1.50 per unit.

The company's production policy took account of its relationship with its distributor. The agreement with the J. P. Williams distributor stated that he would purchase an original production run of 1,000 units for any novelty to determine its marketability. After this initial run, the distributor ordered only in lots of 4,000 units since its handling and storage costs were such that a smaller lot size was unattractive. The length of the season was such that it would be impossible to make more than three production runs. This policy meant that the company had no inventory problem. It also meant that sales in the season would be exactly 1,000, or exactly 5,000, or exactly 9,000 units.

Mr. Williams next called his sales manager and discussed the proposal. They considered the new novelty and how appealing it would be to the type of people who made up the novelty market. They looked at forecasts for the strength of the economy in the upcoming season and what they felt this meant for the novelty market. They thought about what they believed their competitor's lines would be and how this would affect their ability to sell the novelty under consideration. After considering all those factors they believed had an effect on the sales of the new novelty, Mr. Williams made the following statement: "I think the likelihood that we will only sell the 1,000 units is about one half. That is, I think it is about as likely that we would sell exactly 1,000 units as that I would win in an honest lottery in which I had half of the tickets." In a similar vein he stated that in his judgment, the probability of selling exactly 5,000 units was one third, and, in his opinion, the chance that there would be sales of 9,000 units was, therefore, one sixth.

The proposed novelty was one of many in the company's line. If sales turned out to be 9,000 units, the sales revenue would represent less than 1% of the firm's annual revenue.

Assignment

What should Mr. Williams do?

Problem 4–2. At one of the company's regular meetings, Mr. Walter Barry, who handled the Williams company account at Duffy and Davis Advertising Agency, learned from Mr. Williams about the new novelty and the plans for it. He said, "You know, Joel, there is still quite a bit of time before your season starts. There is even a lot of time before you have to place your order for the leased machine. Why don't we hold off for a little while and take another look? You know, our agency has at its disposal a consumer panel that has been fantastic in predicting consumer attitudes to just such novelties as you have here. We could make up some models of this novelty to show the panel. The way they operate, each member will give your novelty a one-, two-, or three-bell rating. We will coordinate the results and write you a report. If they think it's a dud, watch out, but if they get excited, you better think about the more automated machine and its variable cost advantages, for then, you could pretty well count on having a winner.

"We're counting on your having a strong line, and, to help, we'll make this service available, from making the models through to the final report, for only $600."

"I'm afraid that your price for service is a bit on the high side, Walt," replied Mr. Williams. "I could get the same information for less by simply leasing the $1,000 machine and giving things a try. The maximum I could lose without your help and still get the real information is less than your $600."

Mr. Barry was a bit troubled by Williams' reply. After scrawling on a pad of paper for a few minutes, he looked up and said, "Okay, Joel, I see your point. The numbers I was just pushing indicate that I can just cover my costs by doing the job for $350. In view of our long relationship, I'd be willing to do this job for you at cost."

Assignment

Should Mr. Williams buy Mr. Barry's information?

CONERLY CHEMICAL COMPANY

Conerly Chemical Company produced as a by-product a special volatile gas, which if not used within a week after aging, decomposed. Once decomposed it was valueless. The gas required aging for exactly one week before use.

The plant manager and the sales manager strongly disagreed (1) as to the price per tank at which the gas should be sold, and (2) as to the number of tanks of gas that should be bottled and held in inventory each week.

In 1959 the tanks were priced at $200 per tank. Analysis of several years past data revealed that the relative frequency distribution of demand in number of tanks was as follows:

Demand at $200 per Tank	Relative Frequency
0	0.05
1	0.25
2	0.40
3	0.15
4	0.15
	1.00

Production costs were such that the variable cost per tank was lowered by $10 *if* more than two tanks were bottled. The variable cost for bottling of only one tank was $100. Thus variable costs of production were:

Number of Tanks Bottled	Total Variable Cost
1	$100
2	200
3	270
4	360

There was also a fixed setup charge of $100 for the bottling operation. The sales manager maintained that the price was too high. He estimated that if the price per tank were reduced to $180, the odds that two tanks per week would be sold were four to six. He also was willing to bet that it was inconceivable that no tanks would be sold at $180. And he judged that the odds that one, three, or four tanks would be sold were six to four, each of these three levels of demand having similar odds. "If we lower the price," he reasoned, "the average number of tanks sold over the future will increase, according to my estimates, enough to increase profits."

SALES MANAGER'S ODDS

Demand at
$180 per Tank   *Odds*

Demand	Odds
0	....
1	1 to 4
2	4 to 6
3	1 to 4
4	1 to 4

On the other hand, the plant manager felt that the price should be held at $200 per tank. "In view of the short life of the gas and the uncertainty of demand," he reasoned, "we have to cover our risk by keeping the price up. Even though some cost savings can be had by producing more than two tanks a week, I'm not sure that these could be profitably sold."

Questions

1. Calculate the expected profit of the best decision if the price is maintained at $200. Assume that the probability distribution assigned to future demand is numerically equal to the relative frequency distribution of past demand for a price of $200 per tank. Show that the best amount to stock is two tanks per week, and its expected profit = + $30. Show that the best amount to stock under the price of $180 is 3.

2. Assume that you are the company president. You must resolve the pricing and stocking issues. If you were to decide what to do for *next week only* on the basis of historical information and the sales manager's assessment of demand: What price would you adopt? Why?

3. Assume that for a cost per week of $90 Conerly can obtain perfect information about demand one week in advance by contacting customers each day; that is, know exactly what demand will be one week in advance.

    a) Would you be willing to pay $90 for perfect information? Why?

    b) Assume that you were willing to pay $90 for perfect information. Which price level would you choose?

4. Assume a forecast, whether perfect or not, cost $150. Would a *long-run* assessment of this problem introduce any new considerations? (*Long-run* in contradistinction to *one week*—that is, the decision will have to be re-evaluated week after week.)

WARREN AGENCY, INC.

Mr. Thaddeus Warren operated a real estate agency which specialized in finding buyers for commercial properties. Warren was approached one day by a prospective client who had three properties which he wished to sell. The client indicated the prices he wished to receive for these properties as follows:

Property	Price
A	$ 25,000
B	50,000
C	100,000

Warren would receive a commission of 4% on any of the properties he was able to sell.

The client laid down the following conditions: "Warren, you have to sell A first. If you can't sell it within a month, the entire deal is off—no commission and no chance to sell B or C. If you sell A within a month, then I'll give you the commission on A and the option of (a) stopping at this point; or (b) selling either B or C next under the same conditions (i.e., sell within a month or no commission on the second property and no chance to sell the third property). If you succeed in selling the first two properties, you will also have the option of selling the third."

After the client had left, Warren proceeded to analyze the proposal which had been made to him to determine whether or not to accept it. He figured his selling costs and his chances of selling each property at the prices set by the client to be:

Property	Selling Costs	Warren's Assessment of Probability of Sale
A	$800	0.7
B	200	0.6
C	400	0.5

He believed that sale of a particular property would not make it any more or less likely that the two remaining properties could be sold.

Selling costs would have to be incurred whether or not a particular property was sold but could be avoided by deciding not to attempt to sell the property.

Since property A would have to be sold before any further action could be taken, Warren prepared the following table in an attempt to determine whether or not to accept property A:

		Act	
Outcome	Probability	Accept A	Refuse A
A sold............................	0.7	$ 200	$0
A not sold.........................	0.3	−800	0
Expected value....................	1.0	$−100	$0

Thus, accepting A would be unprofitable looked at by itself. Warren was not very happy with this conclusion, however, because he reasoned that success in selling A would entitle him to offer either B or C, and it looked as if either of these properties would result in an expected profit. He felt that somehow or other the value of this opportunity should be taken into consideration.

Questions

1. *a*) Develop a design diagram for Warren's problem.
   b) The diagram will terminate in one of three ways:
      (*i*) With a successful sale of all three properties;
      (*ii*) With an unsuccessful sale of any one of the properties; or
      (*iii*) With Mr. Warren's decision not to continue.
   For each of the 11 end points of the diagram, determine Mr. Warren's *cumulative* profit *conditional* on his reaching that point in the diagram. (For example, if he succeeds in selling all three properties his conditional profit will be $5,600.)
   c) Assume that Warren has succeeded in selling A and B. Should he accept C? What is his expected cumulative profit from so doing?
   d) Same as (*c*), except assume Warren has sold A and C and is considering B.
   e) Assume that Warren has succeeded in selling A. Should he accept B, accept C, or stop? What is his expected cumulative profit from so doing?
   f) Should Warren accept the client's proposition?
2. Analyze Mr. Warren's problem using a payoff table. Hint: There are eight outcomes to consider, corresponding to all the possible combinations of success or failure in attempting to sell the three properties.

WESTON MANUFACTURING COMPANY

On December 14, 1965, at 3 P.M., the quarterly meeting of Weston's board of directors was held at the company's offices. All four directors were present. From the chair, Scott Howell began the meeting by informing the directors of the background of negotiations with the Sheridan Electric Products Corporation. Sheridan was a national manufacturer of heavy-duty industrial electrical appliances, and the company's headquarters were in Dayton, Ohio, less than 100 miles from Weston.

"In 1958 Sheridan asked us to determine whether a flat-bed car with 330-ton capacity and a bed height of 26 inches could be built. The car was needed to move one of a series of new transformers from the construction area to the testing shop, a distance of $2\frac{1}{2}$ miles on the company's track. The low bed height was required because of vertical clearance constraints in the area of the construction shop. John Sanders did some figuring and wrote them that such a car could be built for about $20,000.

"It seemed to us that Sheridan was on the verge of placing the order but then decided instead to rent a car from the Baltimore and Ohio Railroad each time one of the large transformers needed to be moved. No reason was given for this decision, but I do know that we were the only people Sheridan had contacted with a view to having a car built for them. Over the next five years, Don Archer occasionally stopped by the Sheridan plant and found their interest in the purchase of the flat-bed car to vary from time to time.

"Last year Sheridan indicated interest in resuming serious talks. Bert Stokes drew up some plans according to the gauge, capacity, height, and other specifications received from Fred Shillkof, Sheridan's chief engineer. Shillkof approved the plans, and as usual, we took this as an assurance that the track was a normal, level, industrial installation, permitting the proposed simple nonoscillating design for the car. In spite of a general increase in costs in the interim, John was able to submit the original bid of $20,000. The production costs were actually $15,000. The order was placed, and the car was shipped March 23, on schedule.

"Unfortunately, Sheridan's track foundation was not adequate, and the car derailed on a banked portion of the track. Sheridan would not accept the car and returned it, at a cost of $550 to us. Bert then undertook an engineering restudy and concluded that the cost of rebuilding the car with oscillating trucks would be about $16,000. A further review of costs developed no useful shortcuts. On July 18 a revised total price of $36,000 was offered to Sheridan.

"As you know, I was more or less out of action for most of the fall due to a prolonged serious illness in the immediate family. Shortly after I returned, early in November, having received no reply to our July proposal, I sent a wire requesting that Bert and I meet with Sheridan's chief engineer, the purchasing agent, and the general manager.

"I have asked Bert to report to the board on that meeting. He will be along in a few minutes. In the meantime, has anybody any questions?"

"Yes, Scott, there is one point I'd like to clear up," said O'Brien. "Did anyone from Weston see the Sheridan track?"

"Bert and I inspected the track when we visited in November," replied Howell. "It was totally unsuited for a nonoscillating car. It turned out that Sheridan's people thought the car would flex, but any engineer could see that that would be impossible for a car with 330 tons capacity."

There was a knock at the door and Albert Stokes entered. No introductions were necessary; so Howell asked Stokes to proceed immediately with the report of their joint visit to Dayton.

"On November 22, Scott Howell and I met at Dayton, Ohio, with Sheridan's purchasing agent, Mr. Robert Casey, and Mr. James Woodruff, their general manager. Mr. Woodruff informed us that according to a report from his traffic department dated November 8, there had been four instances since March when the Weston car could have been used if it had been operating satisfactorily. In each case it was necessary to pay the B&O Railroad $300 demurrage charges. However, they foresaw that a car of 330 tons capacity could be used about 12 times a year—equivalent to $3,600 demurrage charges.

"Woodruff expressed the feeling that on the basis of a car life of 20 years, $36,000 was a greater investment than the company would consider. They felt that a suitable car should cost about $25,000. This figure was based on savings that would accrue to them if they did not have to pay the demurrage charges.

"We left the meeting with the understanding that we would review the design to see if costs could be reduced below the quotation of July 18. Scott had also suggested that they consider whether this car would not serve additional uses for Sheridan in moving and storing the new large transformers. We said we would keep in touch, although Woodruff and Casey indicated that there was 'no great rush.' "

"Bert, why wasn't Fred Shillkof at this meeting?" asked Hall.

"I don't know, Max," Stokes replied. "Neither Woodruff nor Casey gave any reason for his absence. He hasn't been fired and he wasn't off sick. I know because we walked past his office on our way from the meeting; the door was open, and he was working at his desk."

"One more question, Bert," said O'Brien. "If we rebuild the car with oscillating trucks according to the revised design, what are the chances that it will again derail?"

"Very small, even though that track of theirs is not so hot. I'd say not more than 1 chance in 100."

There being no further questions forthcoming, Stokes collected his papers together and left the room.

"Well, gentlemen," said Howell, "where do we go from here?"

The ensuing silence was broken by Sanders: "We quoted them a figure of $36,000 based on the present estimate of the costs of modification and the production cost of the original car. Now though, with an indication that a suitable car at $25,000 might be acceptable to them, we could reconsider. But I would like to remind you that it would have been impossible to have built an oscillating car originally for $25,000. Maybe we should split the difference and make a bid of $30,000. However, I would say that we would have less than an even chance of getting the order at $30,000, say around 2 in 5, whereas at $25,000 the odds would be about 9 to 1 in our favor. By the same token, at $36,000 we'd be lucky to have 1 chance in 10."

"What about trying to sell the car to someone else if Sheridan turns us down?" asked Hall.

Don Archer shook his head: "Not very good—as is we might have a 1-in-20 chance of selling the car. If we can find a customer we might get between $10,000 and $20,000, and my best estimate is about $15,000. The market is pretty small; so I don't think our selling costs would run over $200.

"If we rebuild the car with an oscillating truck, there are more firms who might be interested and the chances are about 1 in 5 of finding a customer. We should get between $15,000 and $25,000, with an average of about $20,000, but in this market, the selling costs would be around $500.

"Those are very reasonable prices, but that would be about the most we could expect in either case."

All agreed that the possibilities of bargaining further with Sheridan were nil. Sanders summarized the situation: "As I see it, we have two choices: make a firm bid proposal for a rebuilt car or absorb the loss ourselves. As scrap, the car might be worth about $3,000 to us. If we rebuild the car with oscillating trucks and it still doesn't work, its scrap value might go up to around $4,000."

"I think that just about says it, John," said Howell. "I certainly don't want to absorb any loss in view of our recent poor profit picture, but would do so in preference to a legal battle. Our lawyers have assured me that we could force Sheridan to pay a substantial cancellation charge on the grounds that the track was substandard. Another and perhaps stronger reason for demanding a cancellation charge would be the claim that Shillkof could have warned us when he saw and approved the plans. Legally we are on sure ground, but this is our first contract with Sheridan, and possible future business from such a large company could substantially help us to halt, even reverse, our present sales decline. Besides, getting your name involved with a wrangle in court never does you any good in this business, no matter how right you are in the eyes of the law. For the same reason we have to give Sheridan the right of first refusal on a working car. Only if they turn down our bid can we consider selling it elsewhere. Anyway, the next move seems to be ours, and should be made soon. However, you have only today been brought up to date and shown the details of the alternatives open to us. I would like you to give some intensive thought to this matter, and for us to reach a decision when we meet again in a month's time. Now, John, let's have that general report of yours."

Sanders opened his briefcase and took from it four copies of his general report. He passed one copy to each of the other three directors so that they could refer easily to the quantitative data contained in the report. Having cleaned his spectacles and taken a drink of water, John Sanders, reading from his own copy, went to the next report on the agenda.

Question

What action should the board of directors take?

TECHNOTRONICS CORPORATION

Technotronics Corporation of Waltham, Massachusetts, was organized in 1954 to exploit the technical talent of Dr. Robert F. Rutledge, who, until becoming president of Technotronics, had been professor of electrical engineering at a nearby university. As was typical of many of the small companies in the electronics industry, Technotronics derived the major part of its revenues from subcontracts placed with it by larger companies who held prime contracts to produce military electronics systems.

One such subcontract held by Technotronics in 1960 called for the production of a component which was later incorporated into a complete system by the Babson Aircraft Company, the prime contractor on the job. The subcontract provided for a fixed price for each unit delivered to Babson. Experience with this component had indicated that with the manufacturing process then being used, about 30% of the components produced were faulty. The flaw was not detectable by the inspection procedures then being used. When Babson subjected the completed system to its final test, however, the flaw in the component would result in failure. Babson would then be forced to disassemble the system, correct the flaw in the component, and finally reassemble the system. Under the terms of the subcontract, Babson was permitted to charge the cost of these operations, amounting to $65 per defective unit, back against Technotronics.

By adding another operation to its own manufacturing process, Technotronics could insure that none of the components would be faulty. This additional operation would add $15 to the manufacturing cost per unit, however, and since only 30% of the units actually required this operation, it was not clear that the additional cost would be justified. Dr. Rutledge had discussed the problem with the purchasing agent of Babson and had learned that Babson would not be particularly concerned if the defective rate stayed at the 30% level, since it was being ade-

264

quately reimbursed for its extra costs. Hence it seemed to Dr. Rutledge that the decision should depend upon which course of action would be least costly to Technotronics.

As an alternative to performing the additional operation on each component, it would be possible to subject each component to a test and to decide whether or not to perform the additional operation on the basis of the results of this test. Testing would add $5 to the manufacturing cost. Unfortunately, the test being considered was not capable of making a perfect discrimination between good and defective components. The test resulted in one of two possible outcomes—positive or negative—and the conditional probabilities of these outcomes for both good and defective components is given in the table below:

CONDITIONAL PROBABILITY OF TEST RESULTS

	State of Component	
Result	*Good*	*Defective*
Positive	0.75	0.20
Negative	0.25	0.80
	1.00	1.00

Thus while good components were more likely to give a positive test result than defective ones, 20% of all defectives would also give that result, so that it was not possible to say that a positive test result was a definite indication that the component was good.

Questions

1. Prepare a loss table reflecting the two possible terminal acts (i.e., those not involving testing) open to Technotronics. Which is the better act? What is the expected value of perfect information?

2. Should Technotronics use the test described in the case?

WACO WILDCAT COMPANY

In September, 1958, Mr. Arthur Bennett, exploration vice-president of Waco Wildcat Company, was trying to decide what action to take regarding the company's lease No. 4783. The lease, which gave the company exclusive rights to explore for oil and gas on 40 acres of west Texas land owned by Mr. W. T. Hatcher, had been purchased by Waco in July, 1954, for a bonus payment of $5,000. Annual rentals, payable in advance each year until drilling operations began, of $400 had been paid—a total of $2,000. The lease provided that in the event that oil or gas were found, Mr. Hatcher was to receive one-eighth of the gross production from the well, with the other seven-eighths to go to Waco. All costs of drilling and completing any well and bringing the oil or gas to the surface were to be paid by Waco.

The lease contained an automatic cancellation provision if drilling was not started within five years from the date of the lease. During the four years since the lease had been signed, Waco had not been in a position to begin drilling on the property because the company had all its funds employed in investment opportunities which it considered more attractive. The company was a medium-sized oil producer with sales in 1957 of approximately $20,000,000 and profits after taxes of about $3,000,000. In a normal year the company invested between five and six million dollars in oil exploration ventures.

Mr. Bennett knew that he must reach a decision on lease No. 4783 within a month or so if he wished to consider the alternative of "selling" (assigning Waco's rights to another party) the lease to another oil company. He believed that because the oil field in which the lease was located had proved out so well during the last four years, Waco should be able to sell the lease for approximately $15,000. In order to give the purchaser time to act on the lease, Mr. Bennett thought that it should be put on the market by the first of November, 1958.

Mr. Bennett was more interested in the possibility of having Waco drill for oil on the site of lease No. 4783. The lease was located in the Sandusky oil field, an area of roughly 35 square miles containing an unknown number of large oil and natural gas pools. The productiveness of any particular well was determined by the subsurface geological formations underneath the well. The topography in the Sandusky field was relatively uniform, but the subsurface formations varied; therefore, the results of any particular exploratory well were difficult to predict. Since exploration of the field began, 70 wildcat wells had been completed by the 23 operators active in the field. Referring to data collected by an oil industry trade association, Mr. Bennett was able to determine that 21 of these were dry holes (nonproductive), 28 were gas wells, 14 were combination oil and gas wells, and seven were oil wells. In addition, 18 wildcat dry holes had been drilled on the fringes of the field during the process of determining what the apparent boundaries of the productive zone were. Within the productive zone thus defined, the location of productive wildcats followed no particular pattern. Therefore, Mr. Bennett had no specific guide as to whether a well drilled on lease No. 4783 would be productive, but he did know that the land was clearly situated within the productive zone of the field.

From the trade association data, Mr. Bennett was also able to determine the average amount of oil and gas reserves that were recoverable from a productive well in the Sandusky field. He computed the net profit that Waco could expect each year over the ten-year life of a typical well, and found that the total, discounted to its present value, was approximately $150,000 for a gas well, $200,000 for a combination well, and $300,000 for an oil well. These amounts were the discounted total profits from the well, after deducting royalty payments and operating expenses but before deducting the estimated $100,000 cost of drilling the well.

Several of the major oil companies had been active in the exploration of the Sandusky field and had employed an exploration technique with which Waco had had no experience. These companies conducted a "seismic test" to determine in advance of drilling the type of subsurface formations that were beneath the proposed drilling site. The seismic test required a highly trained crew to bury and detonate an explosive charge, and expensive equipment to record the shock waves produced by the explosion. The resulting seismograph was then interpreted by a geologist who could predict the subsurface formations with great accuracy. In the Sandusky field, three main types of formations were commonly found. Of the 30 seismic tests that had been "shot," type A formation was indicated 12 times; type B, 15 times; and type C, 3 times.

In each case in which the tested site had then been drilled, the formation predicted by the seismic test had been actually encountered. Only four of the "A" formations had been drilled, as this was generally thought to be an unproductive type of formation. Of these four, three were dry and the fourth was a gas producing well. The B type formation was known to be a formation likely to contain gas pools. Of the 15 wells drilled on tested "B" sites, nine were gas producers and the other six were combination oil and gas wells. The "C" formation almost always yielded an oil well, and on the three "C" sites located by seismic tests, an oil well had been brought in.

Reviewing this information, Mr. Bennett was uncertain as to what action to take. Upon inquiry, however, he found that the cost of a seismic test on lease No. 4783 would be $30,000, and he suspected that the cost of the test would be impossible to justify in economic terms. He also knew that having a seismic test made would, if it yielded negative results, kill the market for the lease since no competitor would want to speculate on it if Waco had tested it and then decided not to drill on it.

Question

What course of action should Mr. Bennett take? It is suggested that you ignore the effect of income taxes in your analysis of this case.

PART II

Decisions to Create Demand

Chapter 5

PROBABILITY: MEASURING
UNCERTAINTY

In the introduction to this book we said that Part II would consider decisions to create demand. This is one of the three types of resource allocation decisions around which this book is organized. The other two are the decision to create product and the decision to create capacity. The classical demand-creating decision is the pricing decision. Some features of this problem were discussed in Chapter 3 under the topic of price-volume relationships. All of this discussion assumed that the other important parts of the problem were known with certainty. In Chapter 4 we introduced a framework for analysis when the future is not known with certainty. Therefore in Part II we would like to combine the idea of pricing decisions with analysis that specifically considers uncertainty.

In order to do this we must forecast the future demand for each possible price consideration. Techniques for making such forecasts are presented in Chapter 5 and Chapter 6. Chapter 7 addresses the pricing decision for a company selling into a mass market. Chapter 8 considers the special pricing problem of submitting a competitive bid.

Defining a Forecast

In Chapter 4 we presented a framework for analysis of decision problems. One part of that framework was the assessment of probabilities for the outcomes of future events. An event was defined as some future occurrence over which the decision maker did not have complete control. Such an assessment is what we will call a forecast. This definition of a forecast is different from some others you may have known, in that this type of forecast does not try to isolate exactly what will happen. A forecast that results in the selection of *one* outcome to represent the future is called a *point forecast*. Instead, our idea of a forecast is a description of a range of possible happenings and a statement about the relative likelihood that the various outcomes within that range will in fact occur. This type of forecast is called a *probabilistic forecast.*

Before we can discuss techniques for making these probabilistic forecasts, it will be necessary to define some terminology and present some basic concepts about probability. In Chapter 6 we will present some approaches to assessing probabilistic forecasts under varying circumstances. You should keep clearly in mind, however, that the main purpose of forecasting is to assist in making decisions that have consequences in an uncertain future. Therefore, remember that the ideas presented in this chapter and the next should be viewed as a part of the general framework for analyzing decision problems presented in Chapter 4.

PROBABILITY DISTRIBUTIONS

When Mr. Owens assigned probabilities to the various levels of demand for his new product he was assessing a probability distribution for the outcomes of the event—demand next year. The word distribution can be confusing; it is easier to understand if you recall that when you assign probabilities you are distributing a set of weights across the various outcomes of an event. There are two types of probability distribution that we will find useful, the *mass distribution* and the *cumulative distribution*. Mr. Owens' assessment was a mass probability distribution.

To distinguish between these two types of distribution, it is necessary to remember how we defined an event and its outcome. An event takes place at some point in time and has outcomes that can be measured after the occurrence of the event. In a way an event is the general description of a point in time, while an outcome is one of many specific measurements that can be made at that point in time. An example of an event is the demand for a product next week. There may be six outcomes for this event: no demand, one unit, two units, three units, four units, and more than four units. Another example of an event is the condition of a part after manufacturing. The outcomes of this event may be that the part is good or that the part is defective. The set of outcomes for an event must be mutually exclusive and collectively exhaustive. This means that the definition of each particular outcome is unique and that the set of all outcomes takes into account everything that can happen at the point in time for which the event is specified. In the first example given above the outcomes are zero, one, two, three, four, and more than four. This last outcome is acceptable because it has no overlap with the other outcomes; therefore, the outcomes are mutually exclusive, and the entire set of outcomes is collectively exhaustive. It is not required by the definition of outcomes that their description be quantitative. In fact the second example above has outcomes entitled "good" and "defective."

The Mass Distribution

A mass probability distribution assigns a probability to the possibility that when the event has taken place the result will be *exactly equal to an*

Table 5–1

MASS PROBABILITY DISTRIBUTION FOR THE EVENT:
SALES TOMORROW

Outcome Number of Units Sold N	Probability That Sales = Outcome $P(\tilde{S} = N)$
0	0.05
1	0.10
2	0.20
3	0.15
4	0.15
5	0.10
6	0.10
7	0.05
8	0.04
9	0.04
10	0.02
Sum	1.0

outcome. This distribution assigns a probability to each outcome, and the sum of these probabilities for all outcomes is 1.0. For example, suppose a retailer wishes to assess the probability for tomorrow's sales for one of his products. He knows that it is impossible to sell more than 10 units because that is all he will have in stock. He also knows from experience that he may not sell any units of this product. After much thought and analysis, he assigns the probabilities in Table 5–1. This is a mass probability distribution for the outcomes of the event, sales tomorrow, because it assigns to each outcome a probability that sales will exactly equal that outcome. The sum of these probabilities is 1.0.

The headings in Table 5–1 are also shown in symbolic form. The general name for the outcomes is "number of units sold," and the symbol for this is N. N can be any of the integers from 0 to 10. The name of the event is "sales tomorrow" and its symbol is $\tilde{S}$. The tilde over the symbol will mean that it represents an event and will have a probability distribution associated with it. The symbol for the mass probability distribution is $P(\tilde{S} = N)$ and is read: The probability that the event, $\tilde{S}$, will have an outcome exactly equal to the value N. The probability for any specific outcome can also be written symbolically. For example the probability that sales tomorrow will exactly equal 5 units is 0.10. This is written as

$$P(\tilde{S} = 5) = 0.10.$$

The mass probability distribution for our example can be drawn on a graph like the one shown in Figure 5–1. The vertical axis repre-

Figure 5–1

MASS PROBABILITY FOR RETAILER'S EVENT: SALES TOMORROW

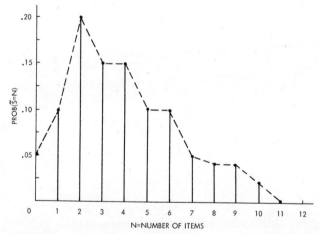

sents the probability, and the horizontal axis represents the list of outcomes.

The mass probability distribution has a positive value only for the possible outcomes of the event and has zero value for any numbers other than these outcomes. Therefore, the graph of the mass distribution in our example is actually a row of vertical lines at the integers. For graphical presentation a smooth curve is often drawn across the tops of these vertical lines like the one shown in Figure 5–1. This representation should not cause any problems as long as you remember that the only meaningful values on the smooth curve are those directly above the possible outcomes of the event.

The Cumulative Distribution

A cumulative probability distribution assigns a probability to the possibility that when the event has taken place the result will be *equal to or less than an outcome*. This distribution assigns a probability to each outcome, the sum of these probabilities has no meaning. Taking the example of the retailer we can construct the cumulative probability distribution shown in Table 5–2.

Table 5–2

CUMULATIVE PROBABILITY DISTRIBUTION FOR THE EVENT:
SALES TOMORROW

Outcome	Mass Distribution	Cumulative Distribution
Number of Units Sold	Probability That Sales Equal Outcome	Probability That Sales Equal to or Less Than Outcome
N	$P(\tilde{S} = N)$	$P(\tilde{S} \leq N)$
0	0.05	0.05
1	0.10	0.15
2	0.20	0.35
3	0.15	0.50
4	0.15	0.65
5	0.10	0.75
6	0.10	0.85
7	0.05	0.90
8	0.04	0.94
9	0.04	0.98
10	0.02	1.00
Sum	1.0	

The first two columns of this table are identical to Table 5–1; the third column, however, represents the cumulative distribution. The symbol for the cumulative probability distribution is $P(\tilde{S} \leq N)$ and is read the probability that event $\tilde{S}$ will have an outcome equal to or less than the value N.

The value of the cumulative distribution for a specific outcome can be obtained by adding the values of the mass distribution for all outcomes equal to or less than that specific outcome. As an example the value of the cumulative distribution for the outcome five units, written $P(\tilde{S} \leq 5)$, is 0.75. This can be obtained by adding the value of the mass distribution for all outcomes of five or less. This calculation is shown in Table 5–3.

Table 5–3

CALCULATION OF CUMULATIVE PROBABILITY
FOR OUTCOME FIVE UNITS

Outcome N	Mass Distribution $P(\tilde{S} = N)$
0	0.05
1	0.10
2	0.20
3	0.15
4	0.15
5	0.10
	$P(\tilde{S} \leq 5) = \overline{0.75}$

Using this approach, you can calculate the cumulative distribution whenever you have the mass distribution for an event. In a similar way it is possible to calculate the mass distribution if you know the cumulative distribution. The probabilities assigned by the cumulative distribution to two adjacent outcomes can be subtracted to obtain the probability that the mass distribution would assign to the larger of the two outcomes. For example, the calculation in Table 5–4 shows how to calculate the probability that sales tomorrow will exactly equal eight units.

Table 5–4

CALCULATION OF MASS
PROBABILITY FOR OUT-
COME OF EIGHT UNITS

$$P(\tilde{S} \leq 8) = 0.94$$
$$P(\tilde{S} \leq 7) = 0.90$$
$$\overline{0.04} = P(\tilde{S} = 8)$$

The cumulative distribution can be drawn on a graph with the vertical axis for probability and the horizontal axis for outcomes. Such a graph for the retailer's distribution is shown in Figure 5–2.

This cumulative distribution has a nonzero value for every number on the graph to the right of zero. As an example the probability that sales will be less than or equal to 3.62 units is 0.50. It is obvious that sales cannot be equal to 3.62 units but they can be less than 3.62 units and therefore the graph of the cumulative distribution has a positive value over the 3.62 value on the horizontal axis.

As in the case of the mass distribution, a smooth curve can be drawn to provide better graphical representation; such a curve is shown

Figure 5-2

CUMULATIVE PROBABILITY DISTRIBUTION FOR RETAILER'S EVENT:
SALES TOMORROW

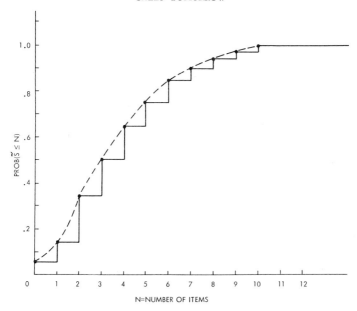

N=NUMBER OF ITEMS

with dotted lines in Figure 5–2. This smooth curve is only an approximation to the real curve, shown in solid lines. For events with hundreds or thousands of outcomes, the smooth curve will be almost exactly the same as the real cumulative curve.

APPROXIMATING A PROBABILITY DISTRIBUTION

In many cases the event for which a forecast is being made will have many possible outcomes. Think about Mr. Owens, the novelty manufacturer described in Chapter 4. The event, sales next year, could have many possible outcomes; however, he was willing to think about only a few typical outcomes for that event. This simplification was necessary so that Mr. Owens could determine the certainty equivalent or calculate the expected value for the various actions. If the payoff table had contained one row for every possible outcome, it would have been immense and for practical purposes unusable. Even a decision tree would have so many branches that calculation of expected values would become impractical. For these reasons, Mr. Owens thought about only a few typical outcomes and assessed a mass probability distribution for them. This simplification results in an approximation to the "true probability distribution"; and if the typical outcomes are selected carefully, this approximation can be used in calculations of expected values.

In analyzing realistic decision problems, the question of which few outcomes should be chosen as representative of the many possible outcomes is difficult to answer. We propose that for situations where the event has many outcomes you assess the cumulative probability distribution and then use it to guide your selection of representative outcomes. The assessment of the cumulative probability distribution will be discussed later in Chapter 6. Now we want to discuss how to select representative outcomes once you have a cumulative distribution.

Figure 5–3 is a cumulative graph for the outcomes of some event.

Figure 5–3
METHOD FOR APPROXIMATING CUMULATIVE PROBABILITY DISTRIBUTION

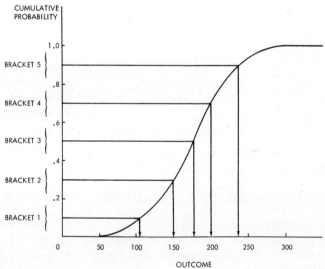

This distribution can be approximated with five outcomes. To select these five you should mark off the vertical axis in five equal brackets as shown in Figure 5–3. Starting at the midpoint of each of the brackets draw a line parallel to the horizontal axis until it intersects the cumulative graph. At these points of intersection, come directly down to the horizontal axis. The values thus selected on the horizontal axis will be the representative outcomes. In Figure 5–3 these values are

108, 153, 179, 203, and 242. Each of these outcomes is a representative for the entire bracket; therefore, you would assign the probability encompassed by each bracket to its representative outcome. This would result in the mass distribution shown in Table 5–5.

You should remember that this is only an approximation to the actual mass distribution and is used only to facilitate calculations in a decision analysis. If you wish to make a better approximation, the number of brackets selected on the vertical axis can be increased. There is no reason why the brackets need to be the same width. In fact, in some cases it is advantageous to make the sizes of the brackets different. There are other ways to approximate this distribution. Just remember

Table 5–5

MASS DISTRIBUTION APPROXIMATION FOR ACTUAL
CUMULATIVE DISTRIBUTION

Outcome N	*Mass Distribution* $P(X = N)$
108	0.2
153	0.2
179	0.2
203	0.2
242	0.2

that the goal of whatever method used should be to achieve a good approximation without requiring excessive calculations in the decision analysis.

In summary, we suggest the following approach for approximating a mass probability distribution when you have already assessed the cumulative distribution:

1. Divide the vertical axis of the cumulative graph into brackets. In most cases five brackets of equal size will be sufficient.
2. Start at the midpoint of each bracket and read over to the cumulative curve and down to the horizontal axis. The value selected is the representative outcome for that bracket.
3. Assign the probability of the entire bracket to its representative outcome. This will result in a mass probability distribution for a few outcomes which approximates the actual mass probability distribution for the many outcomes.

MEASURES OF A PROBABILITY DISTRIBUTION

We have seen that there are two basic ways to describe the probabilities for the outcomes of an event, either as a mass distribution or as a cumulative distribution. Each of these distributions can be presented in a table or by a graph. These presentations are effective although clumsy descriptions. Other measures have been developed for describing the probability distribution more concisely. In this section we shall define some of these measures. Quite often these measures will be chosen as point forecasts for the event in question.

The most common measure is the *mean* of the probability distribution, also called the "average" of the distribution. The mean of a probability distribution is calculated by taking the mass probability for each outcome and multiplying it by the value of that outcome and then summing all these products. Table 5–6 shows this calculation for

Table 5–6

CALCULATION OF THE MEAN OF THE RETAILER'S DISTRIBUTION

Mass Distribution $P(\tilde{S} = N)$	Outcome N	Product $P(\tilde{S} = N) \times N$
0.05	0	0.00
0.10	1	0.10
0.20	2	0.40
0.15	3	0.45
0.15	4	0.60
0.10	5	0.50
0.10	6	0.60
0.05	7	0.35
0.04	8	0.32
0.04	9	0.36
0.02	10	0.20
		3.88 = Mean

the retailer's probability distribution we have been using for an example.

The mean of a probability distribution is the weighted average of the outcomes using the mass probability distribution to do the weighting. In Chapter 4, this same process was used to obtain the expected value of an event fork on the decision diagram. For this reason we will also use the term—the expected value of the distribution—to describe the mean of the distribution. It is impossible to read the mean of a distribution directly from the graphs of either the cumulative or mass distribution; it must be calculated as described.

Another common measure used to describe a distribution is the *mode*. The mode of a probability distribution is the value of the most likely outcome or, in other words, the outcome to which the mass distribution assigns the largest probability. In the retailer's distribution, for example, the mode is the outcome two units, because this outcome has a probability of 0.20, which is larger than the probability for any other outcome. If two or more outcomes have an equal probability that is the largest probability in the mass distribution, then all of these outcomes are called modes.

The mode can be easily read from the graph of the mass distribution because it is the highest point on the curve. It is more difficult to read the mode from the cumulative distribution because the mode is the outcome over which the cumulative curve is rising most rapidly.

A third measure of a probability distribution is the *median.* There is a 0.50 chance that the final result of the event will exceed the median; and, likewise, there is a 0.50 chance the final result will be equal to or less than the median. In general terms the median is the midpoint of the cumulative distribution. The median can be read easily from the cumulative graph. Start at the 0.50 point on the vertical axis and move over parallel to the horizontal axis until you hit the graph. Then come straight down from the graph to the horizontal axis and that point is the median. Figure 5–4 shows such a procedure for the retailer's example. The median for this distribution is three units.

The median is really only one of many measures for the distribution that can be read directly from the cumulative graph. These measures are called *fractiles.* For example, the 0.25 fractile is the outcome for which there is 0.25 probability that the final result of the event

Figure 5–4

CUMULATIVE DISTRIBUTION FOR RETAILER'S EVENT: SALES TOMORROW

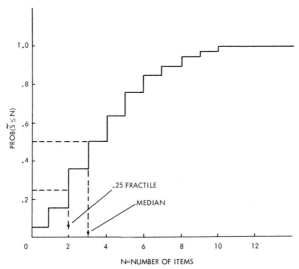

will be equal to or less than that outcome.[1] The 0.25 fractile is found by starting at 0.25 on the vertical axis of the cumulative graph and reading over to the graph and then down to the horizontal axis. The 0.25 fractile is also shown in Figure 5–3 and has a value of two units.

If you understand the definition of median and fractile, you should see that the median is merely a special name for the 0.50 fractile. All fractiles of the probability distribution can be read directly from the cumulative graph. Try to read the 0.75, 0.01, and 0.99 fractiles from Figure 5–4. You should get 5 units, 0 units, and 10 units, respectively, as the values.

There are other measures for a probability distribution, but we will not need them in our work. In summary, we have presented three measures or shorthand descriptions for a probability distribution:

1. The mean, which must be calculated using the mass distribution.
2. The mode, which can be read directly from the mass distribution.
3. The fractiles, which can be read directly from the cumulative curve. One frequently used fractile is the 0.50, and it is called the median.

OBTAINING ONE PROBABILITY DISTRIBUTION FROM ANOTHER

We have been using as an example the forecast a retailer might make for an event entitled "sales tomorrow." The upper limit on the outcome to this event has been 10 items because that was the size of his current inventory. In many situations, the level of stock in inventory is within the control of the decision maker; that is, it is an act. You can imagine that the retailer has another product that he sells for which he can place an order and receive delivery by the end of the day. If he wants to forecast the sales for this product tomorrow he has a problem, because the sales tomorrow may depend on the amount of stock he orders today. In fact, he may want to assign a different probability distribution to the event, sales tomorrow, for every possible purchase action he can take today. In addition, it is necessary to make these forecasts of sales if he wants to determine what level of stock he should order.

In situations like this where the probability distribution of an event changes for different acts, it is easy to become confused when making the assessments. One way to avoid this confusion is to define a new event that has a direct relationship to the event for which the forecast is needed, but whose probability distribution will not be influenced by

---

[1] The fractile of a probability distribution is the same as the percentile ranking used by some nationwide testing services. If you rank in the 25th percentile this means 25% of the people taking the test had a score less than or equal to your score.

the actions being considered. Then the decision maker is able to assess only one probability distribution for this new event, and to use the relationship between this event and the other events to calculate the many different probability distributions needed in the analysis.

As an example of this process, think about the following problem for the retailer. He must place an order today for delivery of a perishable item to his store tomorrow morning. If the item is unsold by the end of tomorrow, he must throw it out. He pays $0.20 for each item and can sell it for $0.50. He has never had more than five people ask for this item in any one business day and feels there is no chance that more than five of these items can be sold tomorrow. His decision problem is how many to order. Figure 5–5 is one possible decision diagram for this problem. The consequence of each act and event is measured in dollars of contribution. This contribution is $0.50 revenue for each item sold less $0.20 cost for each item ordered. Thus if he orders three items and sells two, his contribution is $2 \times \$0.50 - 3 \times \$0.20 = \$0.40$.

Before the retailer can determine his certainty equivalent for each act, he must assess probability distributions for sales tomorrow. This forecast will vary depending on how many items he orders today.

Figure 5–5

A POSSIBLE DECISION DIAGRAM

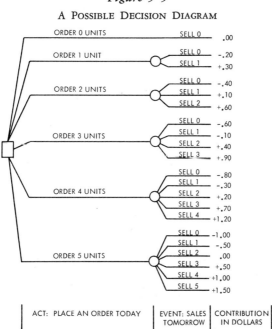

| ACT: PLACE AN ORDER TODAY | EVENT: SALES TOMORROW | CONTRIBUTION IN DOLLARS |

To make these forecasts, the retailer can define a new event called "demand tomorrow." We will use the symbol $\tilde{d}$ for this event. Since the demand for the product does not depend on the size of his order, he will only have to make one forecast. He also knows that sales and demand have a direct relationship given a level of inventory. Specifically, if the demand is less than the inventory, his sales will equal the demand. If demand is greater than inventory, his sales will only equal the inventory.

Suppose after careful thought the retailer assesses the probability distribution for the event, demand tomorrow, shown in Table 5–7.

Table 5–7
PROBABILITY DISTRIBUTION FOR EVENT: DEMAND TOMORROW

Outcome N	Mass Distribution $P(\tilde{d} = N)$
0	0.20
1	0.30
2	0.20
3	0.15
4	0.10
5	0.05 Mean = 1.80

What would he want to assess as the probability distribution for sales tomorrow if he orders three units today? Using the relationship between sales, inventory, and demand he can calculate the sales outcome for every demand outcome. If he did this he would obtain the probability distribution shown in Table 5–8.

Table 5–8
SALES OUTCOME FOR DEMAND OUTCOME IF THREE ITEMS ARE ORDERED

Demand Outcome N	Sales Outcome M	Mass Distribution $P(\tilde{S} = M)$
0	0	0.20
1	1	0.30
2	2	0.20
3	3	0.15
4	3	0.10
5	3	0.05

Since the last three sales outcomes are all for three items, the retailer can add the separate probabilities of these outcomes to obtain the total probability of selling three items. He can now forget demand and record the probability distribution for sales tomorrow if he orders three items today. This distribution is shown in Table 5–9.

Table 5–9

PROBABILITY DISTRIBUTION FOR EVENT,
SALES TOMORROW, IF THREE UNITS
ORDERED TODAY

Sales Outcome M	*Mass Probability Distribution* $P(\tilde{S} = M)$
0	0.20
1	0.30
2	0.20
3	0.30

A similar process could be followed to determine the probability
distribution for sales tomorrow at each possible inventory level. Such
a set of calculations would result in the probabilities shown on the decision diagram in Figure 5–6. Figure 5–6 also shows the expected
value for each act. As a review, you can see that for the act, order three

Figure 5–6

THE DECISION DIAGRAM REDUCED

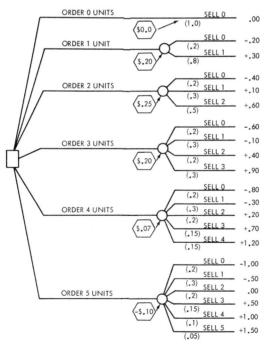

| ACT: PLACE AN ORDER TODAY | EVENT: SALES TOMORROW | CONTRIBUTION IN DOLLARS |

items, the expected value is: $0.2(-0.60) + 0.3(-0.10) + 0.2(0.40) + 0.3(0.90) = +0.20$. You can also check and see that the act with the highest expected value is order two items.

THE RISK PROFILE: A PROBABILITY DISTRIBUTION FOR THE FINAL OUTCOMES

Now that we have shown how one probability distribution can be used to calculate another distribution, we can calculate a special distribution called the *risk profile*. There is one risk profile for each act that the decision maker can select. The risk profile is the probability distribution for the event whose outcomes can be measured in the same units that the decision maker will use to measure his certainty equivalent. For example, the retailer measured his certainty equivalent in dollars of contribution. Therefore, a risk profile for each act would result from a calculation of the probability distribution for the event, contribution tomorrow. We will use the symbol $\tilde{C}$ to represent this event.

The probability distribution for the event, contribution tomorrow, can be calculated for any specific act using the procedure described in the previous section.

Consider the previous example and the act order four items. First, it is necessary to assess the distribution for some event that does not change with the various acts. Demand tomorrow in such an event, and its probability distribution is shown in Table 5–7. Next, it is necessary to determine some relationship between demand and contribution. The cost of ordering four items is $0.80, and the revenue for any demand less than or equal to four units is $0.50 times the number of items demanded. For a demand greater than four units the revenue must be $4 \times \$0.50 = \$2$. This relationship can be summarized with the following formulas:

If demand $\leq$ 4 items, contribution = (demand) $\times$ ($0.50) − $0.80
If demand $>$ 4 items, contribution = $2.00 − $0.80 = $1.20

This relationship has been used to calculate the contribution figures shown in the third column of Table 5–10. The contributions for the last two demand outcomes are identical, $1.20; therefore, their probabilities can be added together. This results in the risk profile shown in Table 5–11. Since the risk profile is a probability distribution, it can be expressed in both the cumulative and mass form, both of which are shown in Table 5–11.

Table 5-10

CALCULATIONS FOR OBTAINING CONTRIBUTION
TOMORROW IF FOUR ITEMS ARE ORDERED TODAY

Demand Outcome N	Mass Probability Distribution $P(\tilde{d} = N)$	Contribution for Demand Outcome K
0.	0.20	$-0.80
1.	0.30	-0.30
2.	0.20	0.20
3.	0.15	0.70
4.	0.10	1.20
5.	0.05	1.20

Table 5-11

RISK PROFILE FOR ACT: ORDER FOUR ITEMS

Contribution Outcome K	Mass Probability Distribution $P(\tilde{C} = K)$	Cumulative Probability Distribution $P(\tilde{C} \leq K)$
-0.80.	0.20	0.20
-0.30.	0.30	0.50
0.20.	0.20	0.70
0.70.	0.15	0.85
1.20.	0.15	1.00

Mean = $0.075

The risk profile is a special probability distribution because it contains all the information needed by the decision maker to assess his certainty equivalent. It has the outcomes measured in the final unit of value for the decision maker and the likelihood for each of these outcomes. The mean of this risk profile is the expected value for the act; and, therefore, if the decision maker is willing to play the averages, the mean should be his certainty equivalent for the act. If he is unwilling to play the averages, the risk profile describes the likelihood of his possible losses and gains. In general terms, this probability distribution represents a profile of his exposure to risk, and this idea is the origin of the name risk profile.

One problem associated with the risk profile should be mentioned. Often a decision maker decides that he is willing to play the averages. Therefore, he would like to choose the act with the highest expected value, which is the act whose risk profile has the highest mean. There is a strong temptation to skip calculating the entire risk profile and to calculate instead the mean of the risk profile directly. This approach

MANAGERIAL ECONOMICS: TEXT AND CASES

can work in special situations; however, in many situations it will not work.

Look at the example we have been using. The mean of the risk profile in Table 5–11 is $0.075 of contribution. This mean was obtained by calculating all the outcomes in dollars of contribution and their probabilities and then taking the expected value, assuming the act, order four items, was chosen. It would be easier to take the expected value of the probability distribution for the event demand tomorrow and use the relationship between demand and contribution to calculate the expected value of the contribution directly. The expected value of the probability distribution for demand tomorrow, shown in Table 5–7, is 1.8 items. For a demand of four items or less and an order of four units, the relationship for contribution is

$$\tilde{C} = \$0.50\,\tilde{d} - 4(0.20)\,.$$

Using this relationship and the expected demand of 1.8 items gives a contribution of 1.8 ($0.50) — $0.80 = $0.10. This calculation overstates the expected contribution calculated before by $0.025. This difference results because the expected demand calculation gives some weight to the possibility of a demand of five units, while the risk profile for the act, order four items, is based on an assumption that a maximum of four items can be sold. The correct expected value can always be obtained by first calculating the entire risk profile.

In summary, we have shown how to use one probability distribution to calculate another. This process is useful in real decision problems where the assessment of the probability distribution for some event is dependent on the choices available. Such a calculation can be made to obtain a special probability distribution called the risk profile. The risk profile contains all the information needed to assess the certainty equivalent for an act; and if the decision maker is willing to play the averages, the mean of the risk profile should be his certainty equivalent for that act.

PROBLEMS

Problem 5–1. Mr. A. V. Spanner is a weather reporter for a local radio station. He has an early morning program, and one feature of this broadcast is a prediction of the daily high temperature. Mr. Spanner has been trying to think how he can make this temperature forecast more useful to his listeners. He is willing to assess a cumulative probability distribution for the event, today's high temperature. The table below is his forecast for a typical day:

Outcome T	Cumulative Probability Distribution for the Event, $\bar{T}$, Today's Highest Temperature $P(\bar{T} \leq T)$
69°	0.00
70°	0.02
71°	0.07
72°	0.23
73°	0.40
74°	0.60
75°	0.75
76°	0.85
77°	0.94
78°	1.00

Assignment

1. What is the mass probability distribution for the event today's high temperature?
2. What is the mean or expected value of this distribution?
3. What is the mode of this distribution?
4. Plot the graph of the cumulative and mass probability distributions.
5. For this distribution, what is the median? the 0.25 fractile? the 0.07 fractile? and the 0.85 fractile?
6. What should Mr. Spanner predict as the high temperature for this day?

Problem 5–2. Mr. R. D. Halverson, an automotive parts manufacturer, knows that a particularly complex subassembly can be made on regular time for $37 of labor. On overtime, the labor cost for this subassembly is $56. The materials needed for this subassembly cost $110, and the finished subassembly can be sold for $375. It is possible to make two subassemblies on regular time and two additional subassemblies by scheduling all available overtime. Mr. Halverson does not have to decide on the production schedule until the orders are received. However, he has made a forecast of the orders to be received by the time he must decide on overtime. This forecast is shown below:

Number Ordered N	Probability of That Number Being Ordered $P(\tilde{d} = N)$
0	0.05
1	0.10
2	0.30
3	0.35
4	0.15
5	0.05

Assignment

1. What is the expected number of orders to be received?
2. What is the probability distribution Mr. Halverson should assign to the event, subassemblies to be sold?

3. What is the expected number of sales?
4. What is the probability distribution that Mr. Halverson should assign to the event, contribution from subassemblies, next week?
5. What is the expected contribution?

✓ **Problem 5–3.** Mr. C. C. Frolik, a newspaper dealer, can stock a particular magazine for 25 cents a copy. This magazine can be sold for 50 cents. If he stocks the magazine and does not sell it in the month before the next issue is published, he can return it and receive 15 cents. Mr. Frolik is willing to assign the following probability distribution to the event, demand next month.

Number Demanded N	Probability of That Number $P(\bar{d} = N)$
0	0.10
1	0.20
2	0.25
3	0.15
4	0.10
5	0.10
6	0.05
7	0.05

1. What is the expected demand for this magazine?
2. What probability distribution should Mr. Frolik assign to the event, sales next month, for this magazine if he orders three copies?
3. What are the expected sales if he orders three copies?
4. What is the risk profile of the act, order three copies?
5. What is the expected value of the act, order three copies?
6. How many copies should Mr. Frolik order?

✓ **Problem 5–4.** Figure 5–7 is the forecast for demand in the next month for product X assessed by Mr. H. Jones. Mr. Jones plans to produce product X only once during the month. Product X costs $3 per unit to manufacture. Each item not sold this month can be reconditioned and sold in the next month. The reconditioning cost is 50 cents per item reconditioned. He currently has an inventory of 20 reconditioned units of product X. The revenue from product X when sold is $4 per unit. Mr. Jones considers storage, carrying, and set up costs for product X to be negligible. Mr. Jones has been considering producing 220 units, while his sales manager is recommending production of 265 units.

Assignment

1. What is the expected demand for product X in the next month?
2. What is the most likely demand figure?
3. What is the median of the demand distribution?
4. What is the risk profile for the act, produce 220 units?
   What is the expected value of this act?
5. What is the risk profile for the act, produce 265 units?
   What is the expected value of this act?

6. If these are the only two acts Mr. Jones wishes to consider, which one should he choose?
7. What is the best act of the two if Mr. Jones wishes to minimize opportunity cost?
8. Outline a procedure for finding the best act for Mr. Jones.

Figure 5–7

DEMAND FORECAST FOR PRODUCT X

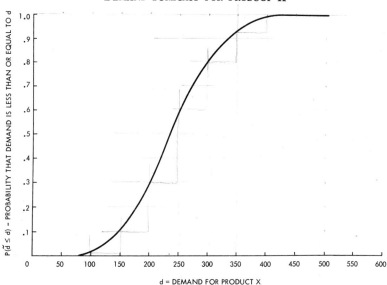

P($\tilde{d} \leq d$) – PROBABILITY THAT DEMAND IS LESS THAN OR EQUAL TO d

d = DEMAND FOR PRODUCT X

Chapter 6

FORECASTING DEMAND

This chapter is designed to help you forecast the outcomes of a future event. An event of much interest to most businessmen is demand for some product at some time in the future. Although our examples will concentrate on demand forecasting, there is no reason why the techniques cannot be used to make probabilistic forecasts for other events.

A probabilistic forecast is for a range of possible outcomes, instead of representing a single outcome, and you should express your belief about the relative likelihoods of various outcomes within this range actually occurring. Such a forecast can be obtained by assessing a probability distribution over the various outcomes for the event. This forecast will then be used within the framework for analysis presented in Chapter 4. In Chapter 5 we described two ways to represent a probability distribution. These are mass distribution and cumulative distribution. One representation can always be used to calculate the other; thus, the problem of forecasting can be stated as assessing either the mass or cumulative probability distribution over the outcomes of the event being considered.

Previously, we defined the fractile as a measure for a probability distribution. There are many fractiles for each distribution, and one special fractile is called the median. The final result of the event has a 50% chance of being below the median outcome. In general terms, the Xth fractile can be defined in the following way: There is an X% chance the final result of the event will not exceed the Xth fractile. The concept of a fractile is the basis of the approach we will suggest for assessing the probability distribution for an event. We will ask the decision maker to think about some specific fractiles for his event. Once he has made these assessments, we can construct a graph of the entire cumulative probability distribution. Following this approach, he only has to think about a few well-defined outcomes, like the median, instead of trying to conceptualize the entire distribution. His judgment can be focused on a specific part of the distribution, allowing him to express more accurately his knowledge about the event. Once again, however, we remind you that any probability distribution or forecast is an expression of judgment. Any procedure that accurately reflects the assessor's judgment is *correct.*

It is easier to discuss assessment if we think about several situations. The first situation occurs when no relevant data are available to assist in making the assessment. A second situation exists when there are relevant historical data available from previous events similar to the one under consideration. A third situation is when relevant data are available about a previous event dissimilar from, but related to, the event under consideration.

ASSESSING A PROBABILITY DISTRIBUTION FOR THE OUTCOMES OF AN EVENT WHEN NO DATA ARE AVAILABLE

Quite often a decision problem will include an event fork and the decision maker will feel that no relevant data are available to guide his judgment in assessing the probabilities for the various outcomes. This lack of data may be because no effort has been made to collect data or because none is available to be collected. In the first case it may be worthwhile to make a judgmental assessment and prepare an initial decision analysis to see if the value of information is large enough to make the collection of any data that may be available worthwhile.

If the event has only a few known outcomes, for example, if a test can only be good or bad, then the best approach is to think about the relative likelihood of each of the outcomes occurring and assess the mass probability distribution. You should assign relative weights to each possible outcome, and if these weights add to one, you have the desired mass probability distribution. If they do not, you can add all the weights and divide each individual weight by the total to get the mass distribution.

When the number of outcomes is small, you can think about each outcome individually and judgmentally assess the mass distribution. This may not seem easy, and it isn't. However, when the number of outcomes exceeds 5 or 10, this approach becomes hopeless. Try to imagine assessing the probability of a demand for exactly 118 units when you believe that demand could be anywhere from 0 to 1,000 units. For most practical situations, the outcomes for an event are numerous and it is more realistic to think about the cumulative probability distribution. It should be easier to think about demand being less than 118 units in the above example than being exactly equal to 118. Not only is it easier to think about the cumulative distribution, it is also possible to obtain a satisfactory cumulative distribution by thinking about only a few points on the distribution as opposed to thinking about them all. Once you have assessed several points on the cumulative probability distribution, you can plot them and then connect the points with a smooth graph. In most cases five points are sufficient for plotting a cumulative distribution: the median, the 0.25 and the 0.75 fractiles, and two extreme fractiles.

Figure 6–1

A WHEEL WITH ONE HALF THE AREA SHADED

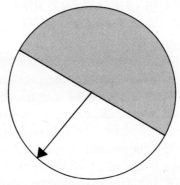

The median is by definition the outcome of the event that has a probability of one half of being exceeded. This should be the first point assessed. In order to think about the median, picture a wheel with a spinner as shown in Figure 6–1. You believe the spinner is just as likely to stop at any one point on the wheel's circumference as any other, and you have examined the wheel and believe one half of the area is shaded. The spinner on this wheel will be spun and you will receive a prize if the spinner stops in the shaded region. You will receive nothing if it falls outside the shaded area. Now think about the event for which you are assessing the probability distribution. Assume you would get the same prize if the event has an outcome equal to or less than X. Which of these two gambles do you prefer—the one based on the spin of the wheel or the one based on the outcome of the event?

If you prefer the wheel, then think of an outcome larger than X. If you prefer the event, think of an outcome smaller than X. By going through this iteration, you should finally find some outcome to the event so that you don't care whether you take the wheel or the event as a gamble for receiving the prize. In other words, there is some outcome that makes you indifferent between a 0.50 chance of receiving a prize with the wheel gamble, and a gamble where you receive the same prize if the final result of the event is less than or equal to that particular outcome. This outcome that makes you indifferent is your median for the probability distribution for the event under consideration.

The hypothetical wheel we described represents a concept called an *equivalent gamble*. The idea is to think of a situation where you clearly understand the chances of winning, like a fair roulette wheel or a fair coin, and to use this device to structure a gamble with a prize of your own choosing. The next step is to structure another gamble with the same prize, but the winning of the prize depends on some outcome of the event for which a distribution is being assessed. By changing the value of the outcome, it should be possible to find one for which you don't care which gamble you would play for the prize. At this point, in your judgment, the gambles are the same. If this is true, we can then assign the probability of the equivalent gamble to the value of outcome where you expressed indifference. Figure 6–2 shows two event forks representing two gambles.

Figure 6–2

TWO EVENT FORKS BETWEEN WHICH YOU MUST BE
INDIFFERENT FOR SOME OUTCOME, Z

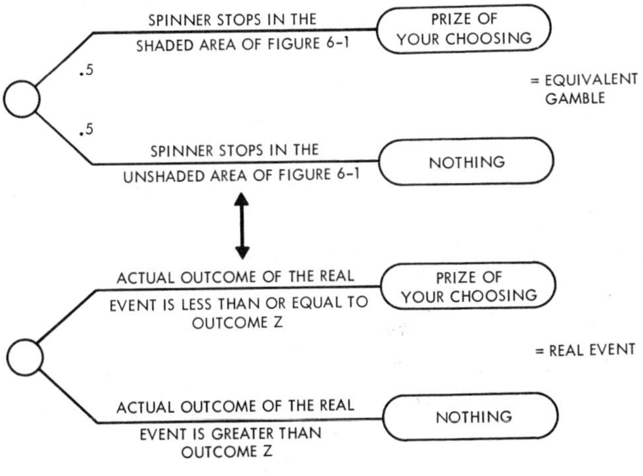

The equivalent gamble provides a prize if the spinner in Figure 6–1 stops in the shaded area and provides nothing if the spinner stops in the unshaded area. Since you believe the wheel is fair and has one half the area shaded, you should assign 0.5 to the top branch and 0.5 to the bottom branch of the equivalent gamble. The second gamble has the same prizes and no probabilities. However, there should be some value for the outcomes of the event, call it Z, that makes you indifferent between the two gambles. This value Z is the median for your distribution.

The next step in obtaining the forecast is to assess the extreme fractiles. Most people believe that it is not difficult to think about the extreme values of the probability distribution. However, in some experiments the results have indicated that this belief may be unfounded. Part of the difficulty is in defining what is meant by an extreme value. One approach is to ask for the value of the 0.01 and 0.99 fractiles. By definition, the outcome of the event should be outside these two values only twice in 100 occurrences. This is not an easy situation to conceptualize. In experiments, most people do not distinguish between the 0.99 and the 0.999 fractile or the "highest possible" outcome. Also most people tend to *underestimate* the extreme points of the distribution. For this reason we recommended that you think about the highest possible outcome and the lowest possible outcome for the extreme points of the cumulative distribution.

With the median and extreme points assessed, you should think about some fractiles between these values. A common practice is to think about the 0.75 and 0.25 fractiles. To do this we suggest again the use of an equivalent gamble. For the 0.25 fractile, think about the wheel shown in Figure 6–3 with 25% of its area shaded.

Think about a prize you would receive if the spinner stopped in the shaded area. Now think of some outcome of the event, call it Y. Imagine you will receive the prize if the final result is less than or equal to Y. The value for Y that makes you indifferent to which gamble you play is the 0.25 fractile of your distribution. A similar process can be used for the 0.75 fractile, only the wheel should have a 75% shaded area.

Other fractiles can be assessed using an equivalent gamble approach. Additional effort may improve the quality of the assessment, but it may only serve to confuse the assessor. If you stop after assessing the five points you can do some checking on yourself. You should believe that it is just as likely that the outcome of the event will be between the 0.75 and 0.25 fractiles as it is that the outcome will be below the 0.25 or above the 0.75. If this is not true you may wish to move the five points to make them more consistent with your best judgment.

Now plot your five points on a cumulative graph. The lower extreme point should be below 0.01 but above 0.00 on the vertical axis; the upper point between 0.99 and 1.00. Now connect the points with a smooth line. This process may indicate a curve you do not believe represents your best judgment. It may have an "irregular" shape in some sense that you believe is not representative of your feelings. Do not feel

Figure 6–3

A WHEEL WITH 25% OF THE AREA SHADED

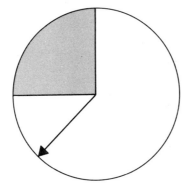

that the five original points cannot be moved. Adjust the points until you believe the *entire curve* is more to your liking. Be careful in this process. You are not seeking some artistic prize where symmetry is rewarded. If you really believe the lower and upper half of the distribution are symmetrical, then plot it that way, but *only* if you believe that a symmetrical distribution is representative of the event under consideration.

This entire process usually leaves one feeling uncertain. Remember that is where you started. The uneasiness may be caused by the fact that you *don't really know* the outcome of the event, not because you are trying to quantify your feelings about this uncertainty.

You may find that this approach is not workable for you and that you feel more comfortable assessing the distribution in some other manner. This is quite appropriate. The only point to keep in mind is that your assessment should reflect your judgment about the possible outcomes of the event, not your likes and dislikes for the outcomes or your fears and wishes.

Summary for Forecasting with No Data

In summary, when you must assess the probability distribution for an event with no relevant data, there are two approaches: one for an event with few outcomes and the other for an event with many outcomes. In the first case, you should attempt to assess the mass distribution of the event. The approach is to think about the relative likelihood of each of the few outcomes occurring. Once a set of relative weights is assigned, you should add them and divide them by their sum. This will assure that the resulting probabilities add to one.

In the second case, with many possible outcomes to the event, you should attempt to assess the cumulative probability distribution of the event. The approach is outlined below:

1. Assess the median.
2. Assess the extreme points.
3. Assess the 0.75 fractile.
4. Assess the 0.25 fractile.
5. Check to see if you believe that a value in the range between the 0.75 and 0.25 fractile is as likely to occur as a value outside the range.
6. Plot the assessed points on a cumulative graph.
7. Smooth a curve through the points.
8. Adjust the shape of curve to reflect your overall judgment.

ASSESSING A PROBABILITY DISTRIBUTION FOR THE OUTCOMES OF AN EVENT USING HISTORICAL DATA FOR AN INDISTINGUISHABLE EVENT

In the last section we presented an approach for assessing probability distributions when no relevant data were available. This is a difficult process and leaves most people with the desire to collect some data to help guide their judgment. You should keep clearly in mind, however, that even with data you are expressing a *judgment* when you make an assessment. The choices of what data to collect, how much to collect, which data should be discarded after being collected, and how to use the data not discarded are all judgmental. Too often a feeling of security is associated with data because the decision maker believes he can rely on past experience to forecast the future. This may not be true. The responsibility for deciding when data are a "good" guide to the future and when they are not should be taken as seriously as the responsibility for making a completely subjective assessment.

To approach the use of data systematically, it is useful to define an *indistinguishable event*. An indistinguishable event is one for which the decision maker has no reason to believe that the outcomes of the event are any more or less likely to occur for a given trial than they would be on any other trial. For example, the event may be the toss of a coin. The outcomes are "heads" or "tails." Now if the decision maker believes that on the fifth toss the outcome "heads" is just as likely as it is on the 29th toss, or any other toss, then this event is indistinguishable from occurrence to occurrence. Note that it is not necessary that the coin be fair (i.e., the probability of heads be 0.5), only that each toss has the same probability of coming up heads. If the event is indistinguishable from occurrence to occurrence, then the outcome of previous occurrences can be used to forecast the outcome of the next occurrence.

In most cases it is possible to find some distinguishable characteristic for various occurrences of the same event. For example, an event of interest at a newsstand may be the number of newspapers to be sold tomorrow. The various outcomes for this event are numbers of papers. The decision maker might feel differently about this event depending on the day of the week, because he knows, for example, that Sunday papers sell better (or worse) than weekday papers. In this case you would say the event is distinguishable from one day to the next.

In assessing the probability distribution for an event, one major decision required is whether you have data on events which are indistinguishable from the one under consideration. In a strict sense, this is never true, but in many cases the distinguishing characteristics are small enough so the decision maker is willing to treat the data as indistinguishable. In the newsstand example, the forecaster may exclude historical data on Saturday and Sunday sales when forecasting the number of papers he will sell on Monday. However, he may be willing to use historical sales data from previous Mondays, Tuesdays, Wednesdays, Thursdays, and Fridays because he is willing to assume all weekdays are indistinguishable when it comes to newspaper sales.

A classic example of a case where you would have data on indistinguishable events is the gambling table. Suppose you are shown a fair die and are asked to play a game where the payoffs depend on the outcome of the next roll of this die. What should you assess as the probability of each outcome?

You must decide first if you believe this is really a fair die. You can hold it and observe that it is a perfect cube and has no abnormal distribution of weight, etc. On the basis of this observation, you are willing to conclude that it is a fair die. What would your probability distribution be for this die if you had to decide? A great number of people would assess a mass distribution that assigns one-sixth probability to each of the six possible outcomes. This assessment is usually based on previous experience with fair dice that the assessor has observed. In fact, the amount of historical data is usually so large that the assessor is willing to assign the historical relative frequencies of the outcomes as the probabilities of these outcomes on the next roll.

Maybe you are not quite sure that this die is fair, so you ask for a chance to roll the die a few times. You are now really checking to see that this die is in fact indistinguishable from the others in your back-

Table 6–1
RESULTS OF 10 ROLLS

Face	Number of Times Showing in 10 Rolls
1	3
2	2
3	1
4	0
5	2
6	2
	10

ground. Suppose the results of your first 10 rolls are as shown in Table 6–1. There is not much data here; however, you are now required to assess your probability distribution. What would it be?

Many people would still say one sixth for each of the six faces. Their main reason would be that a fair die could give these results on 10 rolls and they would be unwilling to discard all the historical data they have collected on other fair dice. However, if you were convinced that this die was unfair and therefore your historical data useless, then you might assess the mass distribution shown in Table 6–2.

The process followed to obtain this assessment was to assign the historical relative frequency of each outcome as the probability of that outcome on the next roll. Note that only the data from indistinguishable events (the 10 rolls of this die) were used to calculate the relative frequencies.

Table 6–2

MASS DISTRIBUTION FOR THE EVENT NEXT
ROLL OF DIE IF THE ONLY RELEVANT DATA
ARE FROM THE 10 ROLLS

Outcome	Probability
1	0.3
2	0.2
3	0.1
4	0
5	0.2
6	0.2

If there were major uncertainty in your mind about the "fairness" of this die, you would roll it a large number of times. Suppose that in 10,000 rolls the data in Table 6–3 were obtained.

Table 6–3

RESULTS OF 10,000 ROLLS

Face	Number of Times Showing in 10,000 Rolls
1	2,980
2	2,020
3	1,010
4	3
5	2,497
6	1,490
	10,000

Now it is clear that the die is "unfair." Using the historical data on the indistinguishable event, roll of this unfair die, you should feel comfortable with the mass probability distribution for outcomes of the next roll shown in Table 6–4.

Table 6–4

MASS DISTRIBUTION FOR THE EVENT NEXT
ROLL OF DIE USING DATA FROM
10,000 ROLLS

Outcome	Probability
1	0.30
2	0.20
3	0.10
4	0
5	0.25
6	0.15

In this example the major decision has been how much data resulted from a process that was indistinguishable from the event currently under consideration. In the cases when there was a large amount of data on an indistinguishable event, the long-run relative frequency for each outcome was assigned as its probability. This was true before rolling the die, or after 10,000 rolls. In both situations, there was some comfort in assigning relative frequencies because of the large amount of data considered to be relevant. Even after 10 rolls if you were still willing to assume the die was fair, you could invoke all your experience with dice to support the assigning of one-sixth probability to each face. The uncomfortable situation was when you believed the die was "unfair" and only had 10 historical data points. This most uncomfortable situation unfortunately is also the most typical in the real world.

Making an Assessment Using a Small Amount of Data

Suppose you have been keeping track of daily sales in your new business, which has been serving customers faithfully for 10 days. Your historical sales records are shown in Table 6–5.

Table 6–5

SALES RECORDS

Number of Items	Number of Days That Amount Was Sold	Number of Items	Number of Days That Amount Was Sold
12	1	22	0
13	0	23	1
14	0	24	0
15	0	25	0
16	1	26	1
17	2	27	0
18	0	28	0
19	1	29	0
20	2	30	0
21	0	31	1

You are preparing to forecast the number of items that can be sold on the 11th day. Your first decision is whether you believe the first 10 days are indistinguishable from the 11th. Let us assume you are willing to believe this. If you don't, you should ignore the data and assess the probability distribution for the next day's sales judgmentally.

If you used the data and followed the approach of assigning relative frequencies as probabilities, you would assess the mass probability distribution shown in Table 6–6.

Table 6–6

MASS PROBABILITY DISTRIBUTION FOR
EVENT SALES ON 11TH DAY

Outcome* N	Probability That Sales = Outcome $P(\tilde{S} = N)$
12	0.1
16	0.1
17	0.2
19	0.1
20	0.2
23	0.1
26	0.1
31	0.1

* Zero probability to all other sales levels.

It seems odd that you would assign a 0.2 chance to sales being 17 and a 0.1 chance to sales being 19, but *no* chance to sales being 18. In fact, you probably believe that 18 units could be sold tomorrow. If this distribution were based on 10,000 days' sales records, and 18 items had never been sold, then a probability of zero for 18 might be believable. However, with 10 days of data such a conclusion is doubtful.

A more useful approach is to calculate the cumulative relative frequencies of the historical data as shown in Table 6–7. The cumula-

Table 6–7

HISTORICAL CUMULATIVE RELATIVE FREQUENCY OF SALES

N = Items Sold	Percent of Days N or Fewer Items Were Sold	N = Items Sold	Percent of Days N or Fewer Items Were Sold
12	0.1	22	0.7
13	0.1	23	0.8
14	0.1	24	0.8
15	0.1	25	0.8
16	0.2	26	0.9
17	0.4	27	0.9
18	0.4	28	0.9
19	0.5	29	0.9
20	0.7	30	0.9
21	0.7	31	1.0

tive relative frequencies can then be plotted on a graph. Such a graph for the data in Table 6–7 is shown as the stairsteps in Figure 6–4.

Figure 6–4

FORECAST FOR NUMBER OF ITEMS TO BE SOLD ON 11TH DAY

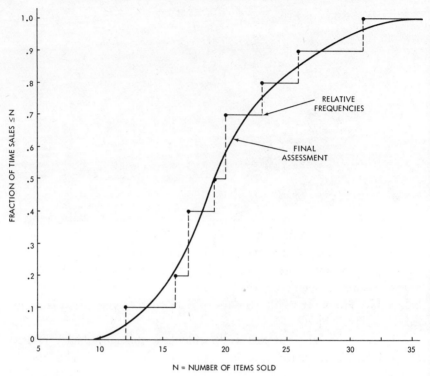

N = NUMBER OF ITEMS SOLD

Now using the stairsteps shown in Figure 6–4, you can draw a smooth curve for the cumulative probability distribution. This smooth curve should not be drawn without careful thought, since the stairsteps are only a guide based on limited data. The curve should reflect your judgment about tomorrow's sales, and this judgment can be aided, but not replaced, by the historical data.

You would probably want the curve to extend below 12 and above 31 items. There is no reason to believe that in the first 10 days you have seen the highest or lowest possible sales that may result on day 11. How far beyond these points you should extend the curve is judgmental. It might be useful for you to think about the highest and lowest sales you think are possible and plot them as the 0.001 and 0.999 fractiles before you draw the smooth curve. Note that the stairsteps are steepest between 15 and 20 items. This means that more historical occurrences were in this range. In fact 60% of the historical data is between 15 and 20. This gives you some idea about where you might want to put the mode of your assessed distribution (remember the mode has the steepest slope on the smooth cumulative curve). After thinking about the shape of the curve, draw it in over the steps. One possibility for the smooth curve is shown in Figure 6–4. At this point it may be useful to erase the stairsteps and begin to think about the overall shape and position of the curve. Once the curve satisfies your judgment, you can change the vertical axis scale from cumulative relative frequency to cumulative probability.

Summary on Forecasting Using Data on Indistinguishable Events

In summary, two approaches have been suggested for situations where you have data from indistinguishable events. The two approaches are classified for situations with much data and situations with little data.

1. With much data for indistinguishable events, you can assign the long-run relative frequency of each outcome as the probability of that outcome on the next occurrence of the event.
2. With little data for indistinguishable events, you can—
   a) Plot the cumulative relative frequency of the data.
   b) Think about the general shape and position of a cumulative probability for the event.
   c) Smooth a curve through the stairsteps of the plot keeping in mind your ideas about shape and position.
   d) Use the *smooth* curve as your cumulative probability distribution for the event.

ASSESSING A PROBABILITY DISTRIBUTION FOR THE OUTCOMES OF AN EVENT USING HISTORIC DATA FROM A DISTINGUISHABLE EVENT

In the last section we presented an approach for assessing a probability distribution for the next occurrence of an event when data were available for indistinguishable occurrences of the event. Unfortunately, in most cases the available data are not for indistinguishable events. This section will present two approaches for using data that are from events that can be distinguished by some characteristic.

For example, suppose on a Monday you are trying to forecast tomorrow's demand for a recently introduced item in a wholesaler's line of goods. The wholesaler has been offering this item to grocery stores in a large metropolitan area for the past three weeks and has collected the order data shown in Table 6–8.

Table 6–8

ACTUAL NUMBER OF ITEMS ORDERED

	Week 1	Week 2	Week 3	Average Daily Orders
Monday	133	126	146	135.0
Tuesday	110	131	130	123.7
Wednesday	126	82	79	95.7
Thursday	84	119	73	92.0
Friday	88	102	95	95.0
Saturday	52	55	61	56.0

Looking at the daily averages for the three weeks it is clear that there is a definite daily trend. Orders are higher in the early part of the week and fall sharply on Saturday. The wholesaler feels that this fact is consistent with the behavior of his grocery store customers on other items. In fact, he has kept track of dollar sales to the grocery stores for each day of the week and has developed the average daily orders shown in Table 6–9.

Table 6–9

	Average Daily Order	Adjustment Factor
Monday	$682,349	1.4
Tuesday	584,392	1.2
Wednesday	487,207	1.0
Thursday	438,962	0.9
Friday	439,005	0.9
Saturday	292,477	0.6
All days	487,399	1.0

You now have a choice in making the forecast for Tuesday's orders for the item. It is clear that Tuesday is distinguishable from the other days. Thus one choice is to discard all data on the other days and use only the three previous Tuesdays as a guide to your forecast. The second choice is to try to adjust the other days to make them indistinguishable from Tuesday and then use all 18 adjusted pieces of data to guide your judgment. If you make the first choice, you would plot the three data points as a cumulative relative frequency graph and draw a smooth curve through them which would be your probability assessment.

The second approach is more attractive if there is some reasonable basis for making the adjustment to the other days. It can be argued that the only reason for the daily pattern in ordering might be the policy of grocery stores to let their stock run down by the weekend.

This ordering pattern is reflected in the average daily dollar orders collected in Table 6–9.

If this line of argument is acceptable to the wholesaler, then you can proceed in the following way. First, define the event you believe is indistinguishable; in this example, the basic daily demand for this item. Second, define a relationship between this event and the data available. In this example, *Basic demand = Actual demand ÷ Adjustment factor*. Finally, adjust the available data to make it indistinguishable. Adjusted data are shown in Table 6–10.

Table 6–10

BASIC DEMAND FOR ITEM
(adjusted for ordering policy)

	Week 1	Week 2	Week 3
Monday	95	90	104
Tuesday	92	109	108
Wednesday	126	82	79
Thursday	93	132	81
Friday	98	113	105
Saturday	86	91	101

The data in Table 6–10 were obtained by taking the actual demand shown in Table 6–8 and dividing by the adjustment factors for each day shown in Table 6–9. This procedure is possible because we believe that the basic demand on Mondays is increased by a factor of 40% strictly by the ordering policy of the grocers and that the basic demand on Fridays is decreased by 10% because of this ordering practice.

Once the influence of the ordering policy is factored out, the data are treated as indistinguishable. Table 6–11 shows the cumulative

Table 6–11

D	Fraction of the Time Sales Were Less Than D	D	Fraction of the Time Sales Were Less Than D
79	0.056	98	0.555
81	0.111	101	0.611
82	0.167	104	0.667
86	0.222	105	0.722
90	0.278	108	0.778
91	0.333	109	0.833
92	0.389	113	0.889
93	0.444	129	0.944
95	0.500	132	1.000

relative frequencies of the basic demand. Figure 6–5 shows a plot of
these cumulative relative frequencies. A smooth curve has been drawn
through these stairsteps to represent what might be a final assessment
of the probability distribution for the event, tomorrow's basic demand.
However, since tomorrow is Tuesday, this forecast of basic demand
must be readjusted to take into account the ordering policy. This re-

Figure 6–5

PLOT OF CUMULATIVE RELATIVE FREQUENCIES OF BASIC DEMAND AND
CUMULATIVE PROBABILITY DISTRIBUTION FOR SALES ON TUESDAY

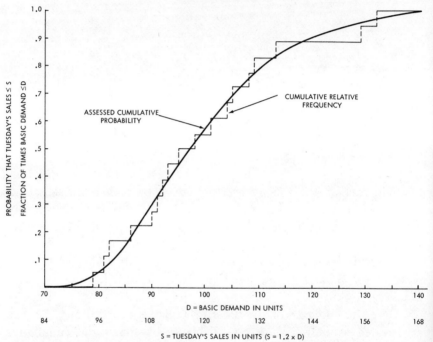

adjustment is accomplished by multiplying the basic demand on the
horizontal axis by 1.20, which is Tuesday's adjustment factor from
Table 6–9.

In this example it is possible to take into account all the factors
we believe make the data distinguishable, that is, the ordering policy
of customers. In other cases there may be so many factors that distinguish the basic data that all the needed adjustments cannot be
made. For example, if the wholesaler had run promotional deals in
the first week and advertised heavily in the third week, it would have

been necessary to adjust the data of the first and third weeks for these differences. However, there might not exist adjustment factors that you would be willing to use for advertising and promotion. If this were true, then the first and third weeks' data should not be used to forecast orders on days when different promotional or advertising policies are in effect.

THE USE OF FORECASTING MODELS

Many situations change so rapidly or are influenced by so many different factors that it is virtually impossible to adjust for all of the distinguishable characteristics in the data. In these cases it may be

Table 6–12

Year	Quarter	Forecasted Demand	Actual Demand	Absolute Error Actual − Forecast	Relative Error Actual ÷ Forecast
1970	1	100	94	−6	0.94
1970	2	450	459	9	1.02
1970	3	860	920	60	1.07
1970	4	1,300	1,196	−104	0.92
1971	1	110	122	12	1.11
1971	2	430	421	−9	0.98
1971	3	890	854	−36	0.96
1971	4	1,240	1,426	186	1.15
1972	1	190	?	?	?

possible to use a forecasting model. Such a model may be an elaborate mathematical abstraction or the judgment of an experienced employee. The basic assumption in using a forecasting model is that the model will account for all major distinguishable characteristics and be subject only to errors not attributable to any one particular factor. Whether this assumption is valid in any given case is a major judgment to be made by the decision maker.

Consider the first eight quarters of data for a product shown in Table 6–12. The last entry of 190 units is the forecast for the first quarter of 1972 made by the same model that had made the previous eight forecasts.

It is clear that there is a seasonal trend to actual sales data. The general level of the economy was changing during the period of history considered. In addition, it would be fair to assume that the marketing policy of the company selling the product and its competitors' policies may have changed during the period. All these factors make the actual sales for any quarter distinguishable from any other quarter. Our assumption is that these major factors were considered in the forecasting model and resulted in the changing forecast from quarter to quarter. In addition, we assume that the new forecast has been made by the same model after considering all major factors for the next quarter. The problem is how to use this model's point forecast.

First, look at the fifth column, the absolute error in the data. This error is obtained by subtracting the forecasted sales from the actual sales. It should be clear that the error is quite distinguishable from quarter to quarter. When the actual sales are low (quarters 1 and 2), the error is small. When the actual sales are high (quarters 3 and 4), the error is large. This is a fairly common occurrence with forecasting models (humans or otherwise) and indicates a tendency to make relative errors rather than absolute errors.

Because the size of the absolute error changes with the actual sales level, it is more useful to look at the relative error. A measure of this relative error is shown in the sixth column. This column is the actual sales divided by the forecasted sales or the "A/F ratio." The A/F ratio in this example does not have any recognizable pattern relating it to the actual sales levels; for example, it is not always greater than 1.0 for low or high actual values. If there is no distinguishable characteristic to the A/F ratio from period to period, then it becomes the undistinguishable event to be forecast.

Table 6–13

CUMULATIVE RELATIVE FREQUENCY OF
RELATIVE ERROR FOR FORECASTING MODEL

X	Fraction of Time $A/F \leq X$
0.92	0.125
0.94	0.250
0.96	0.375
0.98	0.500
1.02	0.625
1.07	0.750
1.11	0.875
1.15	1.000

Table 6–13 shows the cumulative relative frequency of the A/F ratio and Figure 6–6 shows a plot of these data.

After thinking about the shape and position of the error curve, you might draw in a smooth curve like the one shown in Figure 6–6.

This would be your probability assessment of the relative error that the forecasting model will make in its next forecast. What you are interested in, however, is a sales forecast for next quarter. This can be obtained by taking the model's point forecast of 190 for the next quarter and multiplying it by the probability distribution you have just assessed for the error of the model. This is accomplished by taking

Figure 6–6

PLOT OF CUMULATIVE RELATIVE FREQUENCIES OF RELATIVE ERROR AND
CUMULATIVE PROBABILITY DISTRIBUTION FOR SALES IN
FIRST QUARTER OF 1972

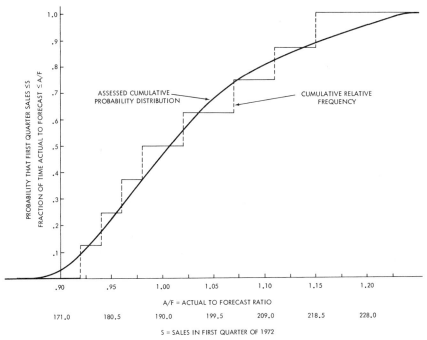

190 times the A/F's on the horizontal axis in Figure 6–6. The result of this multiplication is your probability distribution for next quarter's sales.

Summary on Forecasting Data on Distinguishable Events

In summary, there are two forecasting approaches that use historical data on distinguishable events.

1. When there is some way to adjust the data to remove the influence of the distinguishing characteristics:

    a) Determine the relationship between the distinguishing factors and the data.
    b) Adjust the data using this relationship.
    c) Forecast using the data that are indistinguishable.
    d) Readjust the forecast for the particular event under consideration, using the relationship developed in step (a).

2. When some forecasting model exists that you believe takes account of the distinguishing characteristics:

    a) Obtain the next point forecast from the model for the event of interest, and the historical data on the model's previous forecasts and the actual outcomes of the event when the model was used to forecast.
    b) Determine if the model has an indistinguishable error pattern (either absolute or relative errors).
    c) Use the indistinguishable data on historical error to forecast the probability distribution for the error in the next forecast.
    d) Adjust the point forecast by adding the probability distribution of the historic absolute error or by multiplying by the probability distribution of the historic relative error you have assessed. The result will be a probabilistic forecast for the event of interest.

PROBLEMS

Problem 6–1. Assess a probabilistic forecast for each of the five events listed below using only what knowledge you now have about them. You should not do research or collect data in preparing these forecasts, even though it clearly would make you a better forecaster. This exercise is intended to give you an opportunity to practice converting your knowledge into a cumulative probability distribution. You may want to follow the eight-step procedure in the summary for forecasting with no data.

    Event 1.   The percentage of your classmates who are registered Democrats.
    Event 2.   The percentage of your coffeedrinking classmates who drink their coffee black.
    Event 3.   The total number of runs scored in last year's World Series.
    Event 4.   The number of shares to be sold on the New York Stock Exchange tomorrow.
    Event 5.   The population of Cairo, Egypt, in 1966 in thousands (e.g., 1 million = 1,000).

Problem 6–2. National Rubber Products Company is a large manufacturer of rubber and plastic goods. The company's commercial sales division manufactures a self-inflating rubber raft. This raft is sold to distributors for $31, and each includes one carbon dioxide cylinder used for inflation.

    Several years ago the company had conducted a study of warranty claims against the raft. The major finding of this study was that the largest claim category was for malfunctioning carbon dioxide cylinders. The study recommended that no raft be shipped from the plant containing a carbon dioxide cylinder more than six months old. At that time the company decided to schedule production runs for the self-inflating raft every six months. This policy was implemented, and at the end of six months when new rafts were being manufactured, the carbon dioxide cylinders were replaced on any rafts remaining from the previous production run. The commercial division had considered buying the carbon dioxide cylinder when rafts were shipped to the distributors but found they could not get an attractive price unless they purchased in large volume. Based on this investigation, the procurement policy was established to buy carbon dioxide cylinders only for the planned production units and all rafts left in inventory. For orders of 1,000 to 5,000 units, National was paying an average of $4 per cylinder.

The rubber rafts were stored by the company in 2,500 square feet of an old warehouse that it had owned for over 50 years. This warehouse was used mainly for storage of other commercial products. The warehouse at present was only 50% occupied with no foreseeable change in occupancy. Overhead costs for the upkeep of this building were being allocated at $0.10 per square foot per month by the division accounting department. A packaged rubber raft occupied four square feet and rafts could be stacked five high.

The cost of capital tied up in the rubber raft inventory had been ignored by the company in its previous production and inventory planning.

If National received orders for self-inflatable rafts after the inventory had been depleted but before the new production run was scheduled, a standard raft could be modified to make the self-inflatable raft. What was required was to insert a special inflating mechanism by hand in a standard raft and provide a carbon dioxide cylinder. For such low volumes the cost of the cylinder was $8 per unit. In order to avoid loss of goodwill, the company supplied this modified raft at the same price as the regular self-inflating raft, $31. Because the standard raft was a high volume seller for National, there had never been a case where it had been out of stock when needed for modification into the self-inflating raft.

The variable manufacturing costs of a self-inflating raft produced in a regularly scheduled production run were $10. The variable costs for a standard raft plus the materials and labor to perform the hand modifications were $15. Neither of these costs included the price of the carbon dioxide cylinder. The setup costs for a regular production run of the self-inflating raft were $2,500.

The marketing personnel for the self-inflating raft had no reason to believe that the rate of demand would be significantly different in the next six months then it has been in the past three years. The units sold in the last six semi-annual periods were: 2,231; 2,753; 1,970; 2,256; 2,878; and 1,436.

Assignment

1. Assume that the company wishes to continue to ignore the cost of capital tied up in inventory and that they plan to produce self-inflating rafts every six months for at least the next year. There are currently no self-inflating rafts in inventory; how many should they manufacture?

2. Assume that the company plans to go out of the self-inflating raft business at the end of six months and any raft in inventory at that time will be given away to employees. How many rafts should they manufacture?

Problem 6–3. In January 1965, Mr. John Thurber, factory manager of The Lyon Company, was preparing an estimate of the factory payroll for 1965.

The Lyon Company was a small manufacturer of machine and wood screws. While the company itself was over 50 years old, in very recent years it had experienced a large increase in sales due to the introduction of several new kinds of screws used by the aircraft industry. As a result of this sales increase, the company had encountered a cash shortage which had led to the introduction of budgeting in 1960 to forecast cash needs.

Mr. Thurber had available to him the following information to estimate the 1965 payroll needs:

	Forecasted Production (Gross)	Actual Production (Gross)	Ratio of Actual to Forecasted Production	Actual Payroll	Payroll Cost per Gross of Production	
1960	120,000	125,000	1.041	$154,000	$1.23	1.28
1961	130,000	120,000	0.923	167,000	1.39	1.28
1962	150,000	160,000	1.067	192,000	1.20	1.28
1963	170,000	180,000	1.059	225,000	1.25	1.32
1964	200,000	190,000	0.950	247,000	1.30	1.24

Based on the sales manager's sales forecast and the current inventory levels, Mr. Thurber estimated that production in 1965 would be 250,000 gross. He had also been responsible for the production forecasts for 1960–64.

Mr. Thurber was unsure about the best amount to budget for factory payroll in 1965.

Assignment

1. What is your probabilistic forecast for actual production level in 1965?
2. What is the expected actual production level for 1965? What payroll costs would you expect at this production level?
3. What amount do you think Mr. Thurber should budget for payroll costs during 1965? What are the penalties for overestimating the payroll cost level? For underestimating it?

NEWPORTER FASHIONS (A)

In January 1967, Mr. Colin Barnhart, the inventory manager of Newporter Fashions, was placing orders for tweed fabrics for the company's line of men's winter sports jackets. These jackets would be produced for customer order throughout the late spring and summer of 1967.

Newporter Fashions was a medium-sized producer of men's clothing located in New England. Its 1966 sales had been $100 million, on which after-tax profits of $8 million had been realized.

Purchasing woolen cloth in early 1967 was a particularly difficult task because of the high military demands being placed on Newporter's suppliers. In fact, Mr. Barnhart was told he had to decide exactly how much he wanted of each fabric type by the end of January. There would be no opportunity for subsequent reorders in time for that selling season. However, he was promised that whatever was ordered would be delivered by the end of February, in time for that season's production.

While many of the materials being ordered were staple items with an anticipated continuing demand beyond the 1967 selling season, there were several "high fashion" new fabrics which were causing him great concern. One of these was fabric style No. 10524, a maroon worsted tweed for sports jackets. He was very unsure about what customer response would be to this item.

He wanted to avoid ordering too much, as each unused yard meant excessive inventory costs to the company. On the other hand, ordering too little meant lost profits and possible customer ill will. He felt that somehow these had to be balanced against each other.

He knew that the fabric would cost $5 per running yard (of 60-inch wide material) and that it would require about three running yards of fabric per jacket. He was unsure, however, as to what the inventory costs would be or what profit could be anticipated from the sale of each jacket. As a result, he requested Mr. Robert Scarborough, the company's chief accountant, provide him with this information. He learned the following from Mr. Scarborough: (1) any unused fabric could probably be sold after six months to a company specializing in "seconds" for $3 per running yard; (2) in addition, during the six-month period there would be an inventory carrying charge of $0.50 per running yard on fabric No. 10524; and (3) each jacket made from fabric No. 10524 would add $20 to the company's before-tax profits if the fabric cost were excluded.

When Mr. Barnhart asked Mr. John Traylor, the company's sales manager, how many jackets made up of fabric No. 10524 he thought would be sold, Mr. Traylor replied that he thought that about 2,500 jackets would be sold. When asked about how sure he was about this, Mr. Traylor said that the number would almost certainly be between 1,500 and 3,000. He then added that he felt it was as likely to be below 2,500 as it was to be 2,500 or above and that the odds were 1 in 4 it would be less than 2,250 or 2,750 or more.

Mr. Barnhart knew he was restricted to purchasing fabric in bolts of 1,000 running yards.

Question

How many bolts of fabric No. 10524 should Mr. Barnhart order?

NEWPORTER FASHIONS (B)

Mr. Colin Barnhart, the inventory manager of Newporter Fashions,[1] felt unsure how to handle the purchase of even the staple woolen fabrics during January 1967. He knew that the suppliers had indicated they could promise delivery during the spring only on orders placed before the end of January. High military demands were absorbing the remainder of the suppliers' capacities.

He felt sure that any inventory left over at the end of the season could be used the following year. He preferred to keep his inventories down, however, and leave as much supplier capacity available for the military as possible. On the other hand, he did not want Newporter to have customers whose demands could not be met later in the season.

Typical of the staple items was a grey flannel cloth (item No. 32922) used primarily in suits. This cost the company $4 per running yard (60-inch width). A typical suit required five running yards of fabric.

Cost data from Mr. Scarborough, the company's chief accountant, revealed the following: (1) the inventory carrying charge for the year on fabric No. 32922 would be $0.80 per running yard; and (2) each suit made from fabric No. 32922 would add $30 to the company's net profits before taxes if the fabric cost were excluded.

Mr. Barnhart then checked his inventory records and discovered the following:

1. Current balance on hand: 13 bolts (1,000 running yards each).
2. Withdrawals from inventory over the past five years:

$$
\begin{array}{ll}
1962 & \text{104 bolts} \\
1963 & \text{ 98 bolts} \\
1964 & \text{100 bolts} \\
1965 & \text{ 96 bolts} \\
1966 & \text{102 bolts} \\
\end{array}
$$

---

[1] See Newporter Fashions (A) for a description of the company.

3. There had been no instances during the five-year period where there had been an out-of-stock situation.

Question

How many bolts of fabric No. 32922 should Mr. Barnhart order for 1967?

THE DAVISON PRESS, INC.

In early June 1961, the general manager of the Davison Press, Mr. Frank Davison, called in his sales manager, Mr. Leroy Jervis, to discuss a production order soon to be sent to the firm's printing department for the next year's winter specialty line of diaries and calendars. It was Davison's policy to process in one lot an entire season's supply of each item of the line, since the selling season was so brief that it was impossible to foresee running out of any item before it was too late to produce a second batch without jeopardizing the company's ability to meet other commitments. Each spring, the sales manager prepared sales forecasts for all the items of the following winter's specialty line, taking into account the quantity of the same and similar merchandise sold in previous years by Davison and its competitors, the number and the volume of business of the retailers expected to be carrying the Davison line in December, and the general economic outlook. Mr. Davison's ordinary practice had been to go over Mr. Jervis' estimates with him, make revisions by agreement, and then produce a quantity equal to the forecast sales of each item.

Background

The Davison Press had been founded in 1921 in Cleveland as a small printing job shop, selling mainly to local small businesses. Letterheads, cards, price lists, and catalogs were produced to meet orders solicited by salesmen who visited nearby firms. During the next several years, Davison did an increasing trade in special-purpose forms designed in collaboration with large manufacturers to meet their special control and record-keeping needs. Acquisition of modern, high-speed machinery in the late twenties made possible the speedy and inexpensive handling of a large volume of relatively small individual orders. Setup costs (which ordinarily account for more than half the production cost of such orders) were tightly controlled. Ambitious advertising brought in customers throughout the Midwest and revenue increased to several hundred thousand dollars per year, although competitive conditions held profit margins very low.

After barely surviving the Depression under the burden of debts contracted in the purchase of the new equipment, Davison in the middle thirties sought a line of business that would tie its fortunes less tightly to the ups and downs of the business cycle, and this led to the firm's entry into the retail stationery field. Sample books were compiled and taken by salesmen to variety, drug, and department stores within a few hundred miles of Cleveland. Customers could order personalized letter paper and envelopes, making their own choice of design and paper stock and buying as few as 60 sheets. This division of the business became increasingly profitable just before and during World War II. It involved little selling cost or effort on the part of Davison, demanding only the accurate and efficient handling of orders.

After the war, attention was given to the marked seasonal character of the business. At that time, only a trickle of orders came in during the four summer months, and most of those orders were small ones. It was under these circumstances that the winter specialty line was marketed for the first time in 1951 by direct selling to the outlets that had been handling the sale of stationery. The line, originally consisting of two diaries and two appointment books, was a quick success. By 1960, sales of the line had grown to nearly $250,000 per year and were yielding a net profit of about $70,000.

Sales of the company's other lines, however, had also grown very rapidly during the decade of the 1950s. Distribution area and sales volume expanded in each succeeding year, and by 1960 Davison was marketing its goods throughout the eastern half of the country. Total sales of the firm that year were over $3,100,000, yielding a net profit of about $410,000, and the seasonal pattern in sales had virtually disappeared. In fact, overtime operation of most of the company's facilities had been necessary through a great part of 1960. Although a move to larger quarters was planned, it seemed clear that overtime operation would be called for continuously until early 1962; it was estimated that about 20% of all direct labor hours worked during the remainder of 1961 would be performed on overtime. Mr. Davison did not believe that he would have actually to refuse any orders or that the effort to obtain them should be slackened, but he did believe that it was important to estimate sales closely enough to avoid any serious overruns, since the loss arising from the printing of one diary or appointment book too many would be far greater than the profit which would be forfeited if one too few were printed to satisfy demand.

Jervis' Record and Recommendation

In the summer of 1958 the whole winter specialty line had been redesigned and Mr. Jervis had been hired as sales manager, with responsibility for all lines except the custom-designed business forms. During the past three years, the items in the winter specialty line had been as follows: No. 1 was a large (8 × 11), handsomely laid out diary, with simulated leather cover, selling at retail for about $7.50; No. 2 was a smaller (5 × 8) diary and daily appointment book, of somewhat less sumptuous appearance, retailing at around $3; No. 3 was a weekly memorandum book, with spaces for notations relating to each hour (9 through 4) and each day of the week, which sold for $1.75; and Nos. 4 and 5 were pocket diaries, one bound in leatheroid and the other in paper, selling for $1 and $0.65, respectively. Mr. Davison felt that uniformity and continuity were better buying incentives than novelty, and the 1962 line was to differ from its predecessors only to the extent necessary to accord with the change in the calendar. In general, Mr. Davison was quite satisfied with the rate of growth of winter specialty sales; the greatest potential for future growth, he felt, was in other directions, but winter specialty production would keep the expanded facilities fully employed, and on high margin goods at that.

As regards sales forecasts, Mr. Davison felt that Mr. Jervis' record in predicting sales of the winter specialty line (Exhibit 1) was amazingly good, much better than that of his predecessor and much better than Jervis' own record in predicting sales of stationery. But even though he was impressed with the small percentage error in Jervis' predictions, Mr. Davison had noticed that the predictions were frequently on the high side, where errors were more expensive; and he wondered whether the sales forecast should not be revised downward in determining the number of units to be ordered into production. His reasoning was that "producing a lot too few is no worse than producing a few too many."

Mr. Jervis disagreed strongly with this view. He pointed out that when a store or consumer wanted to buy an item and could not do so, bad will was likely to be created that would endure and make future selling more difficult. In the first place, he said, someone who bought a diary this year was far more likely to buy one next year than someone who did not; hence, failure to make a sale should be considered to entail a far greater loss than the forfeited profit on one diary. Furthermore, a store owner who was disappointed or annoyed by the situation might stop pushing the line or might even refuse to handle it at all. Therefore, Jervis concluded, it was actually *worse* rather than better to produce too little rather than too much. Because of the marked dissimilarity of the prices and uses of the various items in the line, it was unlikely that a person wishing to buy one of them would be willing to take another instead; he would buy a competitor's product or none at all.

Mr. Davison acknowledged that Jervis had made out a good case for a generous production order, but he argued that at least as good a case could be made out on the other side. For instance, many of those who bought diaries and appointment books used them only during the earliest months of the year and then neglected them, and such people could not be considered as likely sales prospects in the following year. It might even be claimed that if such a person had *wanted* to buy an item in 1962, he would buy one in 1963 only if he had *not* actually bought one in 1962; in these cases, no money except possibly a small amount of interest would be lost as a result of the undersupply. In addition, regular users of Davison products would almost surely buy their new books soon after these appeared on the market, from the first shipment their retailers received from Davison; and even when Davison did run out of stock, this never prevented filling the retailers' *initial* orders, virtually all of which were received before November 15.

As to the matter of goodwill, Davison said that the primary objective of the Press was not to increase the respect or affection it received from customers; this was a pleasant incident, not to be confused with practical, dollar-and-cents considerations. If goodwill implied potential for future profits, it should be considered; but if it referred to a state of mind not closely connected with willingness to buy, it should be ignored. In this instance, his judgment was that Jervis' case was overstated. Davison had enjoyed good relations with most of its present outlets over a period of some years, and most of them handled the lucrative stationery sales the year round. They would regard an inability to fill orders at the tag end of the season as entirely understandable and forgivable. After all, they were themselves conservative in their stocking policy, preferring as a rule to run out and have to reorder rather than have to scrap surplus or sell it at a loss. For a retailer to hide the diaries behind the counter next year would be stupidly self-destructive; the retailer had more to lose by this than Davison. The retailer's profits from the Davison line were sufficient, even if lower than they might be, to dissuade him from trying to switch to a competitor, and in any case there was no reason to think that either of Davison's chief competitors in the field of diaries and appointment books was superior to Davison as regards out-of-stocks. On balance, Mr. Davison felt that while the total loss resulting from insufficient stock was perhaps a little greater than the foregone immediate profit, the difference was almost certainly negligible. He was satisfied to treat it as zero; and if this proved wrong, to learn from the experience. This seemed better than to assume the contrary and never be able to check the validity of the assumption. Damage done would not be permanent, especially on the retailer level, where it could be excused if necessary as a single year's abberration rather than the result of any change of policy. And since overtime was being incurred this year but would probably not be needed next year, the present seemed an unusually good time to try the experiment of producing below Jervis' sales forecast.

Jervis did not contest further the matter of "goodwill" losses, but he reacted quite strongly to Davison's mention of costs. "It's no wonder these diaries look expensive when the boys down in accounting are finished with us; we're charged for everything from the watchman's salary to the paint on the back fence. It's ridiculous; they could be printed in gold ink for the costs that they've got on the books. When are we going to get a fair deal on this? And another thing, why is our work charged at the overtime rate just because the company was making business forms before it got into the diary business? Davison Press makes a much higher profit margin per press hour on diaries than it does on forms and catalogs; if we had to choose between making diaries and making forms, we would certainly choose diaries. It's the *forms* that should be charged the overtime rate. The only real expense in producing more diaries is material and labor; but instead of recognizing this, accounting is even charging diaries with depreciation on the presses that are going to be sold for scrap when we move next year. And anyway, even if the costs *were* figured right, I don't understand this business of producing some number other than the number we expect to sell. Just because one kind of mistake is cheaper than another, why commit one of the cheaper mistakes on purpose?"

What Are the Costs?

Before trying to make up his own mind about Jervis' last question, Mr. Davison decided to clear up the cost question, and with this in view he asked Mr. Herman Lewis, his chief accountant and assistant treasurer, to prepare a detailed cost breakdown for each item of the winter specialty line, showing how much it would cost per unit to produce a lot of the size recommended by Jervis for each item. The next day, Mr. Lewis came to Mr. Davison's office with the information requested of him (Exhibit 2). Mr. Davison raised the questions brought up by Mr. Jervis the previous day, with particular emphasis on the matter of overtime charges and undue overhead allocations, and Mr. Lewis vigorously defended his department's methods and results.

In the first place, he said, every penny of expense incurred by Davison had to be attributed or allocated to some product. "The reason why there is a back fence to be painted and a janitor to be paid is that we are making and selling printed pieces of paper of one kind or another. These costs wouldn't exist if we weren't here doing printing, and they are just as much a part of the total cost of the work we do as electricity and labor are. They appear on our income statement, and unless the prices we set and the revenue we receive takes account of them, we will be operating in the red and going broke. Nobody is smart enough to know what part of some of these overhead charges should be viewed as being due to production of business forms, which to stationery, and so forth, and I don't pretend that we can calculate the precise cost of each piece of paper that we sell. But the total amounts we allocate come from an overhead budget that has been very carefully prepared, and the formulas we use in allocating these amounts are consistent, reasonable, and fair. The manufacturing overhead we incur in the plant is divided among our products in proportion to direct-labor hours because the reason we have a plant is so that direct labor can be performed. Executive salaries and general office expenses are charged in proportion to what it costs us to make the products, the same as we would do if we bought the products outside, except, of course, that any expense that we can trace directly to a particular line, like the salaries of the stationery salesmen, is charged to that line. As to depreciation of buildings and equipment, it appears on our income statement as a cost and it *is* a cost, just the same as the ink we use up is a cost, whether we buy it in the same period we use it or not. Our method of cost accounting is entirely modern and accepted. Naturally, we'd all like to see the costs as low as possible; I don't blame Jervis for that. But he should see the effects beyond his own department. If we report a lower cost for one of his babies, we'll have to pile it onto someone else's, and he'll complain the same way that Jervis does now. I can't see that there's a suggestion here for a better *system* than the present one—just one fellow trying to get an advantage over someone else."

Mr. Lewis felt less certain about the proper handling of the overtime charges. Historically, of course, the winter specialty line had been taken on mainly to keep the presses running during the slack season; business forms were the bread-and-butter line. Hence, on those few occasions prior to 1961 when overtime had been necessary during the summer, its cost had been charged to winter specialties. It was true that diary sheets and appointment-book pages were produced steadily throughout the working day (during both regular and overtime hours), whereas business-form orders, which often could be run off in only a couple of hours of press time, might be printed at any time, regular or not. The plant usually ran with a reduced work force after the regular closing time; in particular, the setup men almost never worked overtime. It would be possible to calculate costs on the basis of actual press-hour charges (orders run wholly or partly after 5:30 being charged at time and a half); or the costs could be averaged out and the average rate charged to all lines alike whether run on overtime or not. Basically, Mr. Lewis felt that this was a policy question that should be settled by Mr. Davison rather than by himself.

Exhibit 1

THE DAVISON PRESS, INC.
WINTER SPECIALTY SALES AND FORECASTS
(Hundreds of units)

	No. 1	No. 2	No. 3	No. 4	No. 5
1959 estimate	82	199	388	174	585
Actual to 11/15	68	134	218	130	413
Actual total	82*	189	301	174*	584
1960 estimate	128	316	564	261	915
Actual to 11/15	88	236	370	162	673
Actual total	123	316*	552	225	915*
1961 estimate	136	320	589	273	972
Actual to 11/15	92	294	369	191	627
Actual total	134	320*	539	273*	892
1962 estimate	176	435	770	360	1,175

* Sales limited by stockout.

Exhibit 2

THE DAVISON PRESS, INC.
ESTIMATED COSTS FOR 1962 WINTER SPECIALTY PRODUCTION
(Dollars per 100)

Row	Account	No. 1	No. 2	No. 3	No. 4	No. 5
1	Setup labor	4.38	1.34	0.69	0.31	0.31
2	Pressroom labor	5.03	1.97	1.01	0.79	0.79
3	Total direct labor	9.41	3.31	1.70	1.10	1.10
4	Supervisory labor	3.51	1.23	0.63	0.41	0.41
5	Overtime premium	6.46	2.27	1.16	0.76	0.76
6	Payroll taxes, etc.	2.33	0.82	0.42	0.27	0.27
7	Setup materials and plates	12.14	4.08	2.13	0.82	0.82
8	Pressroom materials and stock	25.33	13.40	4.35	2.11	2.11
9	Power	0.78	0.64	0.61	0.42	0.42
10	Press maintenance	0.47	0.19	0.11	0.09	0.09
11	Press depreciation	2.46	0.98	0.51	0.40	0.40
12	Other plant overhead	27.67	9.73	5.00	3.23	3.23
13	Binding, fixed charge	3.41	1.15	0.65	1.11	0.08
14	Binding, per 100 units bound	81.17	29.94	20.25	12.63	3.23
15	Total manufactured cost	175.14	67.74	37.52	23.25	12.92
16	Winter specialty S and A	40.81	15.78	8.74	5.44	3.01
17	General overhead	128.20	49.59	27.46	17.09	9.46
18	Total cost	344.15	133.11	73.72	45.78	25.39
19	Price to dealers	485.00	187.50	105.00	65.00	37.50

NOTES

Row	
1, 7	Total cost divided by estimated units produced.
4	37.3% of row 3.
5	50.0% of rows 3 and 4.
6	12.0% of rows 3, 4, and 5.
11	Straight-line depreciation allocated to products by press hours.
12	294% of row 3; includes insurance and property taxes.
13, 14	Binding done by outside contractor who charges a fixed amount for each style plus an amount proportional to number of units produced.
16	23.3% of row 15.
17	73.2% of row 15.

THE WALSH COMPANY

In the early spring of 1965, the board of directors of the Walsh Company was considering the possible acquisition of the Damon Company, a medium-sized manufacturer of grinding wheels. Mr. Robert Dunn, the assistant to the president of the Walsh Company, was assigned the task of preparing a five-year forecast of sales and profits for the Damon Company for the years 1965–69. This would provide a basis for the acquisition analysis.

Mr. Dunn began his research with Damon's annual reports, in which he located summary information about sales, costs, and profits for 1960–64 (Exhibit 1).

He also learned that a grinding wheel was a combination of abrasive grain, a bonding material, and air space, and that grinding action depended on the bonding material to bring the abrasive grain into contact with the surface to be ground and to release the grain under appropriate pressure to avoid scratching the surface. The air space seemed to assist the releasing of the abrasive grain. There were two major classes of bonding materials—resinoid and vitrified. Both were used for cutting and fine finishing by the metalworking and construction industries. The resinoid bonded wheels tended to be more flexible and involved more in cutting, the vitrified wheels harder and used more for fine finishing. The resinoid bond was a low-temperature bond, the vitrified a high-temperature bond.

Mr. Dunn next visited the headquarters of the Damon Company. In his discussions with the Damon controller, Mr. George Campbell, he acquired information about the 1960–64 product line sales and costs (Exhibit 2).

He then talked with the Damon sales manager, Mr. Harry Moore, about what the future sales prospects appeared to be. Mr. Moore gave him a set of sales forecasts for the next five years (Exhibit 3). Mr. Moore added that the forecasts for the total market size and the market share had been done by his market research manager, those for the product line sales done directly by his district sales managers. He thought they coincided (at least, approximately), though.

Questions

1. How should Mr. Dunn prepare his sales forecasts? His cost forecasts?
2. How much profit do you think the Damon Company will make in 1965? In 1969?
3. If you thought that the total 1969 market size were going to be $150 million, how would you adjust your forecasts?

Exhibit 1

THE WALSH COMPANY

SUMMARY OF SALES, COSTS, AND PROFITS FROM 1960–64

	1960	1961	1962	1963	1964
Sales...............	$12,447,648	$12,153,328	$10,518,978	$14,101,628	$14,351,256
Cost of goods sold...	8,164,659	8,044,386	7,118,269	9,046,083	9,274,197
Gross profit.........	$ 4,282,989	$ 4,108,942	$ 3,400,709	$ 5,055,545	$ 5,077,059
General, administrative, selling expense............	3,446,212	3,461,078	3,347,467	3,741,676	3,779,916
Net profit before taxes............	$ 836,777	$ 647,864	$ 53,242	$ 1,313,869	$ 1,297,143
Taxes..............	435,076	336,889	27,685	683,204	673,134
Net profit after taxes............	$ 401,701	$ 310,975	$ 25,557	$ 630,665	$ 624,009

Exhibit 2

THE WALSH COMPANY

PRODUCT LINE SALES, COSTS, AND PROFIT STATISTICS FROM 1960–64

	1960	1961	1962	1963	1964
Total market size ($000,000).............	112.1	109.5	94.2	127.8	128.8
Market share (%):					
Resinoid..........................	6.30	6.55	6.65	6.90	6.95
Vitrified..........................	4.80	4.55	4.50	4.10	4.15
Total........................	11.10	11.10	11.15	11.00	11.10
Sales ($000,000):					
Resinoid..........................	7.0	7.2	6.3	8.9	9.0
Vitrified..........................	5.4	5.0	4.2	5.2	5.4
Total........................	12.4	12.2	10.5	14.1	14.4
Cost of goods sold ($000,000):					
Resinoid..........................	4.3	4.4	4.0	5.3	5.5
Vitrified..........................	3.9	3.6	3.1	3.7	3.8
Total........................	8.2	8.0	7.1	9.0	9.3
Gross profit ($000,000):					
Resinoid..........................	2.7	2.8	2.3	3.6	3.5
Vitrified..........................	1.5	1.4	1.1	1.5	1.6
Total........................	4.2	4.2	3.4	5.1	5.1
Gross profit (%):					
Resinoid..........................	38.5	38.9	36.5	40.5	38.9
Vitrified..........................	27.8	28.0	26.2	28.9	29.5
Total........................	33.9	34.4	35.7	36.2	35.4

Exhibit 3

THE WALSH COMPANY

SALES FORECASTS FOR 1965–69

	1965	1966	1967	1968	1969
Total market size ($000,000).............	120.0	140.0	160.0	180.0	180.0
Market share (%):					
Resinoid..........................	7.10	7.25	7.40	7.55	7.70
Vitrified..........................	4.00	3.85	3.70	3.55	3.40
Total........................	11.10	11.10	11.10	11.10	11.10
Sales ($000,000):					
Resinoid..........................	8.5	10.4	12.2	14.4	14.6
Vitrified..........................	4.8	5.0	5.4	5.6	5.4
Total........................	13.3	15.4	17.6	20.0	20.0

FOREST SERVICE (A)[1]

The McSweeney-McNary Forest Research Act of May 22, 1928, as amended, gave the Secretary of Agriculture authority to cooperate with appropriate officials of each state and, either through them or directly with private and other agencies, to make a comprehensive survey of:

1. Present and prospective requirements for timber and other forest products.
2. Timber supplies, including a determination of present and potential productivity of forest lands.

As part of its continuing responsibility under this Act, the Forest Service of the Department of Agriculture undertook a comprehensive review of the outlook for timber supply and demand through the year 2000. This review was published in February 1965, as *Timber Trends in the United States* (Forest Resource Report No. 17). This report was prepared by a team under the direction of H. R. Josephson, director of Forest Economics and Marketing Research in the Forest Service.

The principal conclusion of the study was that projected demand for all types of timber would rise from 11.8 billion cubic feet of roundwood in 1962 to 21.3 billion cubic feet by 2000. This would necessitate in 2000 a total "cut" from domestic growing stock of 21.6 billion cubic feet of timber (see Exhibit 1).

Against the projected demand of 21.6 billion cubic feet in 2000, projected supply was only 18 billion cubic feet (see Exhibit 2). *Timber Trends* argued that "if all commercial forest land in each region were managed as well as the better managed properties, the resulting 'realizable growth' would in time reach an estimated 27.5 billion cubic feet."

---

[1] The case is intended for class discussion only, and certain names and facts may have been changed which, while avoiding the disclosure of confidential information, do not materially lessen the value of the case for educational purposes. This case is not intended to represent either effective or ineffective handling of an administrative situation, nor does it purport to be a statement of policy by the agency involved.

Methodology of Demand Projections

The sources and methodology used in forecasting demand for timber through the year 2000 were relatively straightforward. Basic assumptions regarding the general level of economic activity which were used in the projections were clearly stated in the study.

First, it was assumed that the population would rise from 187 million in 1962 to 325 million by 2000, representing a compound annual growth rate of 1.5%. (This was compared with the average rate of 1.4% from 1910 to 1930, 0.9% from 1930 to 1935, and 1.7% from 1945 to 1960.) The figure of 325 million chosen approximated the median of a series of projections published by the U.S. Bureau of Census in 1964.

Second, it was assumed that the gross national product would increase from $546 billion in 1962 to $1,920 billion in 2000 (at 1961 prices), representing an average annual rate of increase of 3.4%. (This was compared with 3.9% between 1940 and 1960 and 3.2% between 1920 and 1960.) This projection was in turn based on assumptions such as: (1) employed labor force would increase from 70.7 million in 1962 to 126.4 million in 2000; (2) average workweek would decrease from 39 hours in 1960 to 30.5 hours in 2000; (3) product per man-hour would increase from $3.66 in 1960 to $9.56 in 2000; (4) average unemployment rate would remain at about 4%; and (5) peace would be maintained, but with a high degree of military preparedness.

Third, as a corollary to the projection of GNP, it was assumed that per capita disposable personal income would rise from $2,030 in 1962 to $4,120 in 2000. (This represented the assumption that disposable personal income would remain at the same level of 70% of GNP which it had approximately maintained over the past several decades.)

Fourth, it was assumed that the future price of timber in relation to other commodities would remain constant—that future price trends for timber products between 1962 and 2000 would "not differ significantly from price trends for competing materials, and that future price-induced substitution between competing materials and timber products consequently will be limited. Implicit in this price assumption are the further assumptions (*a*) that adequate timber supplies will be available throughout the projection period to supply the projected demands for timber products and (*b*) that technological progress in the forest industries will keep pace with that in industries producing competing materials."

Demand for timber in each of its various forms and end product uses was then projected on the basis of the overall economic and demographic assumptions stated above. Each category was examined separately and a judgment made as to the most appropriate procedure to use for that category. In the case of lumber used in residential construction, for example, the basic assumptions were first translated into forecasts of such intermediate variables as household formation and new construction. Exhibit 3 lists the categories for which projects were made and the intermediate variables used in making the projections.

Demand for Pulpwood Products

The methodology used in projecting demand for pulpwood will now be discussed in greater detail. In brief, the approach was as follows:

1. Projections were first developed for the major grades of paper and board.
2. These estimates were then converted into required amounts of wood pulp, to which were added estimates for wood pulp used in the manufacture of nonpaper products.
3. The final step was to convert these total wood pulp requirements into volumes of pulpwood.

Projections by Grade

For each grade of paper and board, historical data on annual consumption were compared with a number of different economic indicators over various periods of time. Regression analysis was applied to the data in an attempt to find the best explanatory variable, the best base period, and the equation of the curve which would best fit the data over the base period. This equation was then used in making the projections.

For example, in the case of sanitary and tissue paper, it was found that for the base period 1947–61, the equation giving the best fit was $Y = -270.5254 + 89.3336 \log_{10}X$, where Y = per capita consumption of sanitary and tissue paper in pounds, and X = per capita disposable income in dollars.

As noted earlier, per capita disposable income in 2000 was estimated at \$4,120. By substitution in the above equation, the per capita consumption of sanitary and tissue paper projected for 2000 was 53 pounds.

For each grade of paper and board, the equation finally adopted was of the form $Y = a + b \log_{10}X$, although the units of X and Y and, of course, the specific values of a and b varied from grade to grade. The values of the coefficients and the units of X are given below. (Except where otherwise noted, the units of Y are per capita consumption in pounds.)

Grade	a	b	X
Newsprint	−186.9908	77.1619	Per capita GNP
Groundwood paper	6.3556	1.1678	Per capita dpi†
Book paper	−266.2077	92.9362	Per capita dpi†
Fine paper	−145.1432	49.7961	Per capita dpi†
Coarse and industrial paper	−209.1012	75.6454	Per capita GNP
Sanitary and tissue paper	−270.5254	89.3336	Per capita dpi†
Construction paper	−2032.9031	1081.8239	Residential construction starts
Container board	−792.7026	268.6300	Per capita dpi†
Bending board	−440.5959	149.1586	Per capita dpi†
Building board	−213.8058	71.0823	Per capita dpi†
Other board*	−8769.2200	4178.7565	Total GNP (billions)

* Note: For "other board," Y was taken to be total consumption in thousands of tons.
† dpi = Disposable personal income.

Per capita figures were converted to totals by multiplying by the estimated population of 325 million in 2000. Similar calculations were performed for the years 1970, 1980, 1990; a summary of results is shown in Exhibit 4.

Of the totals projected in Exhibit 4, some would be imported. Trends in domestic consumption, net imports, and domestic production were examined. It was concluded that because of the limited supplies of pulping materials in many countries and the relatively advanced technology of pulp and paper production in Canada and the United States, both the United States and Canada would continue to export increasing tonnages of paper and board products as well as wood pulp. Some further increases in U.S. imports from Canada, particularly newsprint, were also considered likely. Accordingly, the projections in Exhibit 5 were made.

Amount of Wood Pulp Required

Wood pulp had been displacing other fibrous materials in the manufacture of paper and board. Between 1950 and 1962, for example, the use of wood pulp per ton of paper and board produced in the United States increased from 0.68 to 0.76 ton, while the use of waste paper per ton of paper and board declined from 0.33 ton to 0.24 ton. Other fibrous materials (such as straw, bagasse, and rags) dropped from 0.06 ton to about 0.03 ton per ton of paper and board.

Trends in the use of wood pulp versus competing materials were studied for each of the 11 major grades considered. Graphical analysis was performed, besides discussion with technologists in the industry regarding their judgment as to future developments. Accordingly, it was projected that the use of wood pulp per ton of paper and board produced would continue to increase, reaching 0.83 ton in 2000. Applying this factor to the projections for domestic production of paper and board resulted in the projections of domestic consumption of wood pulp for the manufacture of paper and board. To these projections were added projections, as shown in Exhibit 6, of consumption of dissolving wood pulp for use in products such as rayon. Finally, projected net imports were subtracted from projected consumption to give demand for domestic production.

Amount of Pulpwood Required

The final step was to convert the projections for wood pulp (85.7 million tons to be produced domestically in 2000) into the volumes of pulpwood required. Here it was assumed that the average conversion ratio by 2000 would be 1.482 cords of wood per ton. This projection was based on a detailed study by type of pulp to technological trends in the industry. Applying this factor to the projected domestic production in 2000 resulted in an estimated demand for pulpwood of 127 million cords (see Exhibit 7).

Once more imports had to be considered. It was assumed, again on the basis of detailed studies, that net pulpwood imports would level off at 1.5 million cords per year from 1970 through 2000.

Much of the demand for pulpwood could be met through the use of by-products from sawmills, veneer mills, and other wood-using plants; this source had provided about 20% of all pulpwood consumed at U.S. mills in 1962. This situation was expected to continue.

Subtracting net imports and plant by-products from the estimated demand for pulpwood resulted in a projection, to be met out of domestic production, of 105.5 million cords (see Exhibit 7).

One cord is equivalent to 77.44 cubic feet. Thus, 105.5 million cords is equivalent to 8.17 billion cubic feet. However, not all round-wood came from domestic, commercial growing stock. In 1962, a significant percentage came from dead and down timber, cull trees, noncommercial forest land, and other such sources. Some saw logs would also be imported.

After making adjustments for these sources, the requirements for timber to be cut from domestic commercial growing stock for pulpwood products in 2000 was projected at 7.39 billion cubic feet, which is the figure appearing in Exhibit 1.

Questions

1. Develop a flow chart illustrating the projected flow of materials in 2000 from the cutting of trees through the final production of the 10 grades of paper and board. The chart should show the quantities of materials and their sources at each stage in the process.

2. Using the same procedures employed in *Timber Trends,* test the sensitivity of the pulpwood projections to a change in GNP by calculating a new projection based on a per capita GNP which is 20% higher than that used in *Timber Trends.* (Assume that per capita disposable personal income goes up in proportion.)

3. Review your entire calculation in (2) above and try to identify the estimates and assumptions to which the demand projections are most sensitive; i.e., the factors for which a small change in the climate would make a proportionately larger change in the total projection.

Exhibit 1

FOREST SERVICE (A)

Timber Cut from Growing Stock, by Products, 1952–2000
(Billion cubic feet)

			Projections			
Product	1952	1962	1970	1980	1990	2000
Sawlogs...............	5.801	4.936	5.150	5.580	6.140	6.870
Veneer logs...........	0.392	0.725	1.110	1.350	1.640	1.980
Pulpwood.............	1.655	2.353	2.940	4.200	5.520	7.390
Miscellaneous.........	0.579	0.380	0.370	0.370	0.370	0.370
Fuel wood............	0.966	0.517	0.450	0.370	0.310	0.250
Total timber products........	9.393	8.911	10.020	11.870	13.980	16.860
Logging residues........	1.364	1.237	2.290	1.490	1.680	1.960
Total timber cut..	10.757	10.148	11.310	13.360	15.660	18.820
Adjusted* total timber cut..........	10.757	10.148	11.500	13.700	16.900	21.600

* Adjusted for expected reduction in the size of trees available for cutting in the future.

Exhibit 2

FOREST SERVICE (A)

Timber Demand, Growth, Supply, and Inventories
in the United States, 1952–2000
(Billion cubic feet of growing stock)

			Projections			
	1952	1962	1970	1980	1990	2000
Demand....................	10.8	10.1	11.5	13.7	16.9	21.6
Growth...................	14.3	16.3	17.4	18.2	17.2	17.2
Supply*..................	N.A.	17.2	18.2	18.8	17.8	18.0
Inventory.................	595.8	627.9	671.9	725.7	757.9	738.3

* Supply is defined as the sum of growth in the East, allowable cut on public lands in the West, and prospective cut on private lands in the West.

Exhibit 3

FOREST SERVICE (A)

FORMS AND CATEGORIES FOR WHICH DEMAND WAS PROJECTED

Category of Timber Use	Subcategories	Forms of Timber Involved	Measures of Demand Employed
Construction	(a) Residential	Lumber, plywood, and other panel products	(1) Estimates of future requirements for new dwellings (2) Prospective replacements of dwellings (3) Trends in size and characteristics of new dwellings (4) Trends in use of wood products in each type of dwelling
	(b) New nonresidential construction (excluding farms and railroads)	Lumber, plywood, and other panel products	(1) Trends in dollar values of expenditures on industrial buildings, commercial buildings, hotels, motels, other private buildings, public buildings, utilities, sewer, water, highways, military facilities, public service, all other.
	(c) Upkeep and improvements	Lumber, plywood, and other panel products	(1) Trends in dollar values of expenditures for repairs, alterations, and additions of residential structures (2) Trends in dollar values of expenditures for repair of nonresidential structures
	(d) Farm structures	Lumber, plywood, posts, poles, and other products	(1) Projections of farm GNP (2) Farm construction expenditures (new and repairs)
	(e) Railroad construction and maintenance	Lumber (crossties), plywood	(1) Crossties consumed (2) Railroad mileage (3) Construction and repair of railroad cars
	(f) Mine construction and maintenance	Lumber, mine ties, round and split timbers	(1) Projection of past trends in consumption of lumber and timbers
Manufacturing	…	Lumber, plywood, veneers	(1) Trends of consumption of timber by product groups a) Household furniture b) Commercial and institutional furniture c) Consumer goods d) Commercial equipment e) Industrial machinery f) Miscellaneous (2) Sales trends in these product groups
Shipping	…	Lumber, plywood, veneers	(1) Trends of lumber consumed in boxes, crates, pallets, and dunnage
Paper and board	Various grades and types	Pulpwood	(1) Trends in consumption of paper and board—10 grades considered separately (2) Trends in consumption of wood fiber versus waste paper and other sources for production of paper and board

Exhibit 4

FOREST SERVICE (A)

PAPER AND BOARD CONSUMPTION BY GRADE, 1920–2000
(Million tons)

Year	Total Paper and Board	Paper								Board				
		Total Paper	News-print	Ground wood Paper	Book Paper*	Fine Paper	Coarse and Industrial Paper	Sanitary and Tissue Paper	Construction Paper	Total Board	Container Board	Bending Board	Building Board	Other Board
1920	7.8	5.5	2.2	0.2	0.9	0.4	1.2	0.2	0.4	2.3	...	...	...	...
1930	12.3	8.4	3.5	0.2	1.4	0.7	1.8	0.4	0.5	3.9	1.9	1.0	0.1	0.9
1940	16.8	10.6	3.7	0.6	1.6	0.7	2.6	0.7	0.7	6.2	3.3	1.4	0.2	1.3
1950	29.1	16.8	5.9	0.7	2.6	1.2	3.7	1.4	1.4	12.3	5.8	3.1	1.2	2.1
1960	39.2	22.0	7.3	0.9	3.8	1.8	4.7	2.2	1.4	17.2	8.2	4.6	1.9	2.5
1962	42.3	23.2	7.5	0.9	4.0	2.0	5.0	2.4	1.4	19.1	9.5	4.8	2.1	2.8
Projections														
1970	52.7	28.3	9.0	1.0	5.0	2.4	6.0	3.2	1.6	24.4	12.0	6.7	2.7	3.1
1980	69.3	36.4	11.2	1.2	6.6	3.3	7.7	4.7	1.7	32.9	16.5	9.0	3.7	3.6
1990	90.0	46.3	13.9	1.3	8.8	4.3	9.8	6.4	1.8	43.7	22.1	12.2	5.2	4.2
2000	115.5	58.5	17.1	1.5	11.4	5.7	12.4	8.6	1.9	57.0	29.2	16.1	6.8	4.9

* Includes coated printing and converting paper.

Note: Figures in columns may not add to totals because of rounding.

Sources: 1920–40, American Paper and Pulp Association, *The Statistics of Paper*, 1960, reporting statistics published by the U.S. Department of Commerce, and Report of the Committee on Interstate and Foreign Commerce, *Pulp, Paper and Board Supply-Demand*, August 21, 1963 (88th Cong., 1st sess., Union Calendar No. 292, House Report 693). 1950–62, U.S. Department of Commerce, Bureau of the Census, Current Industrial Reports, *Pulp, Paper and Board*, Annual, and Business and Defense Services Administration, *Pulp, Paper and Board*, Quarterly. Projections, U.S. Department of Agriculture, Forest Service.

Exhibit 5

FOREST SERVICE (A)

CONSUMPTION, NET IMPORTS, AND DOMESTIC PRODUCTION
OF PAPER AND BOARD, 1920–2000
(Million tons)

Year	Consumption	Net Imports	Domestic Production
1920	7.8	0.6	7.2
1930	12.3	2.1	10.2
1940	16.8	2.3	14.5
1950	29.1	4.7	24.4
1960	39.2	4.8	34.4
1962	42.4	4.8	37.6
Projections			
1970	52.7	5.2	47.5
1980	69.3	5.6	63.7
1990	90.0	5.9	84.1
2000	115.5	7.2	108.3

Sources: 1920–50, American Paper and Pulp Association, *The Statistics of Paper*, 1960, reporting statistics published by the U.S. Department of Commerce. 1960-62, U.S. Department of Commerce, Bureau of the Census, Current Industrial Reports, *Pulp, Paper and Board*, Annual, and Business and Defense Services Administration, *Pulp, Paper and Board*, Quarterly. Projections, U.S. Department of Agriculture, Forest Service.

Exhibit 6

FOREST SERVICE (A)

CALCULATION OF REQUIREMENTS FOR DOMESTIC PRODUCTION OF WOOD PULP
TO BE CONSUMED IN THE MANUFACTURE OF PAPER AND BOARD
1940–2000
(Million tons)

	Paper and Board, Domestic Production	Wood Pulp per Ton of Paper and Board	Wood Pulp Used in Paper and Board Production	Dissolving Wood Pulp	Total Wood Pulp Consumed	Net Imports	Domestic Production of Wood Pulp
1940	14.5	0.68	9.8	0.3	9.7	0.7	9.0
1950	24.4	0.68	16.5	0.7	17.1	2.3	14.8
1960	34.4	0.75	25.7	1.1	26.6	1.2	25.3
1962	37.6	0.76	28.6	1.1	29.5	1.6	27.9
Projections							
1970	47.5	0.78	37.0	1.2	38.2	1.9	36.3
1980	63.7	0.80	51.0	1.4	52.4	2.3	50.1
1990	84.1	0.82	68.1	1.7	69.7	3.6	66.2
2000	108.3	0.83	88.8	2.0	90.8	5.1	85.7

Note: Figures in columns may not add to totals because of changes in inventories and rounding.

Exhibit 7

FOREST SERVICE (A)

CONSUMPTION OF PULPWOOD IN U.S. MILLS, 1940–2000
(Million cords)

Year	Total Consumption	Net Imports	Domestic Production	Plant By-products	Domestic Roundwood
1940....................	13.7	1.4	12.4	0.3	12.1
1950....................	23.6	1.4	20.7	1.3	19.4
1960....................	40.5	1.2	40.0	7.4	32.6
1962....................	44.1	1.3	42.8	9.0	33.8
		Projections			
1970....................	58.0	1.5	56.5	14.5	42.0
1980....................	78.5	1.5	77.0	17.0	50.0
1990....................	99.5	1.5	98.0	19.0	79.0
2000....................	127.0	1.5	125.5	20.0	105.5

Note: Figures in columns may not add to totals because of changes in inventories and rounding.

Chapter 7

ANALYSIS FOR PRICING DECISIONS

In Chapter 3 we discussed the relationships between product prices and two important factors (costs and volume) in the profit equation, and in chapter 6 we examined techniques for analyzing and summarizing historical data in order to prepare better forecasts of future demand. While these are both important topics in themselves, they are, in another sense, merely prefatory to the topic to which we now turn: the decisions and policies for the determination of product prices and the related group of demand-creating costs. In this chapter, we will draw upon the analytical techniques we have already learned, using them to help us grapple with the additional set of realistic complexities that businessmen face when they price their products in a competitive market.

The management of demand-creating costs, including price itself, is complex if only because the range of alternative actions is so broad. In the cases considered in the previous chapters, the choice could usually be narrowed down to a small number of alternatives, often only two: make or buy, choice of production process, and so forth. In pricing decisions, in contrast, the number of possible alternatives is enormous. This is true not only of the basic price at which the product is sold to the ultimate consumer but also of such other dimensions of price as trade discounts to wholesalers and retailers, discounts for quantity purchases, differentials due to type or location of customer, and so on. The complexity of the pricing problem increases manyfold in multiproduct companies. The considerations already mentioned are duplicated for each product, and there is the further necessity of insuring that a proper interrelationship exists among the various prices.

Given the complexity of pricing decisions and the frequent unavailability of much of the information required for a "textbook" solution, pricing will probably always remain an art rather than a science. To avoid spending most of their time on pricing decisions, businessmen often adopt "price policies" or rules of thumb to guide the setting of specific prices over a period of time. The establishment of price policies permits much of the detailed decision making to be delegated to subordinate levels of the business, thus conserving the time of top executives for other important responsibilities. To the extent that a policy is adhered to in the face of conditions which were not anticipated when it was established, it may not lead to the "best" price. Nevertheless, when the costs of a more sophisticated approach are considered, who is to say that use of the policy is not optimal at a broader level?

Science can, however, serve the ends of art. An understanding of the economic principles of price determination may not lead to an all-purpose pricing formula, but it can help in the establishment of a wise price policy and in the translation of such policies into effective prices on specific transactions. In this chapter and the next, therefore, we will explore some of these principles.

DEMAND

Factors Affecting Demand

Many factors influence the quantity of its product a business can sell. Some of these are environmental factors, beyond the direct control of the business' managers. Others, however, can be manipulated by the business in an effort to control its volume of sales. Each of these two classes of factors will be considered in turn below.

Environmental Factors. Among the external forces affecting the level of demand are general economic conditions, consumer tastes, and the nature of competition. These forces are, at best, subject to only very indirect influence by a particular business.

When consumers have high incomes, they are usually prepared to buy more of most things than when their incomes are low. Although there may be some products (potatoes are a possible example) whose consumption will decrease as incomes rise, even here there is a relationship between income and demand. Demand for consumer goods in turn creates a demand for the raw materials used in manufacturing them. Finally, if businesses are prosperous, they are in a better position to acquire new capital goods, thereby creating a demand for plant and equipment.

Not only consumer income but also consumer tastes affect the demand for specific products. The influence of tastes is vividly illustrated in the recent history of the automobile industry. In the decade following World War II, the long, low, and powerful car was fashionable among consumers, and automobile manufacturers strove to increase their market shares by building more of these attributes into their products. Beginning in the late 1950s, however, there was a trend in consumer preference toward the compact economy car, resulting in a sharp decline in sales for most medium-priced brands. It is interesting to note that this trend took place in the face of rising consumer incomes and was, in fact, most pronounced among higher income professional people.

While consumer tastes have been listed here as an environmental factor, they are not entirely outside the control of business management. Often advertising is intended to change consumer tastes in a manner favorable to the advertiser's product. There is great dispute about the morality and effectiveness of such advertising. One camp decries the efforts of so-called "hidden persuaders" to manipulate people's "true" wants. Another group minimizes the power of a business to influence basic wants, arguing that the best that can be done is to learn more about these wants so that the business can tailor its products to satisfy them.

Economic conditions and consumer tastes determine the size of the market for a product. The share of this market which a particular seller can obtain usually depends also upon the nature of the competition it faces. Economists distinguish several types of competition or market structure. At one extreme, there is the market situation characterized by only a single seller, which is called *monopoly*. A monopolist, of course, need not be concerned with the actions of his competitors because he has none. At the other extreme is the market with many sellers, each so small that his actions have an imperceptible effect on the demand faced by his competitors. In this type of market, characterized as *perfect competition,* price is determined by the impersonal pressures of supply and demand. While the individual seller is concerned with the actions of his competitors in the aggregate, there is nothing he can do about them.

In between these two extremes falls the broad spectrum of *monopolistic competition.* The seller in a market characterized by monopolistic competition has neither the complete freedom from competitive pressures of the monopolist nor the complete subjection to them of the seller in a perfectly competitive market. His partial insulation from competitive pressures may be the result of such factors as geographical location or product differentiation, giving the seller a submarket in which he can play something of the role of a monopolist. At the same time, the existence of close substitutes for his product limits his monopoly power.

The two extremes of monopoly and perfect competition are rarely found in practice. There are usually substitutes for most products, particularly if we look at the function the product serves rather than at its physical form. The local electric utility, for example, may have a legal monopoly of electric power transmission, but it competes with gas for cooking and heating, with private generating equipment for industrial power supply, and—if under unregulated conditions, it adopted predatory practices—even with kerosene lamps for household illumination! On the other hand, because of product differentiation and locational advantages, "textbook" examples of perfect competition are also uncommon. Most of our subsequent comments in this chapter will, therefore, be concerned with the firm in a situation of monopolistic competition.

In conclusion it should be observed that even though the individual firm may have only a modest influence on the environmental factors we have discussed, knowledge of them is obviously useful in making many business decisions. It is for this reason that businesses spend much money for economic forecasts, studies of consumer attitudes and intentions, and analyses of the behavior of competitors.

Controllable Factors. Of the variables at the disposal of management in its attempts to influence sales, price is the one most studied by economists and the one we will emphasize in this chapter. As a practical matter, however, there are many situations in which other types of demand-creating costs are of greater competitive importance. These elements of a company's total marketing strategy include expenditures for advertising and other methods of promotion, choice of channels of distribution, and size and method of compensation of the sales force. These aspects of marketing management present important analytical problems and will be discussed later in this chapter.

Demand Schedules

Economists express the relationship between price and quantity demanded in the form of a *demand schedule*. We will review here some of the relevant facts about demand schedules.

The demand schedule for a product is simply a point forecast of the quantity that would be demanded at various prices. This schedule can be in tabular form, such as Table 7–1, or in graphical form, such as Figure 7–1, both examples reflecting the demand situation assumed to face the Clinton Company in 1972.[1]

Elasticity of Demand. The phrase "elasticity of demand" refers to the price-sensitivity of the market for a particular product. The demand for a product is said to be "elastic" if customers would be willing to spend more dollars buying it at a lower price than would have been spent at a higher price. From the seller's point of view, elasticity is a measure of the effect of price on the total revenue (price times quantity) of the firm. Lowering the selling price on an item would have the effect of reducing total revenue, unless the consumer demand was so

Table 7–1

CLINTON COMPANY

DEMAND SCHEDULE—1972

Price per Unit	Quantity Demanded	Total Revenue	—Percentage Change in—		Elasticity Index
			Price	Quantity	
$5.00	100,000	$500,000			
4.75	120,000	570,000	5.0%	20.0%	4.0
4.50	135,000	607,500	5.3	12.5	2.6
4.25	142,500	605,625	5.6	5.6	1.0
4.00	145,000	580,000	5.9	1.8	0.3

price-sensitive that the increase in the quantity sold would more than make up for the price cut and result in a net increase in total revenue. When the total revenue from a product could be increased by lowering the price, the demand for the product is defined as elastic at that price; when a price cut would result in a decrease in total revenue, demand is said to be inelastic.

Using the demand schedule for the Clinton Company given in Table 7–1 we see that at a price of $5, the demand for this product is elastic because a reduction in price would result in an increase in total revenue. At a price of $4.25, the demand is inelastic because total revenue would decrease if the price were lowered. The important thing to note here is that the elasticity of demand may change over a range of prices; at a relatively high price like $5 the demand may be elastic,

[1] Columns of Table 7–1 other than the first two will be explained in due course. In Figure 7–1, quantity demanded is indicated on the vertical axis and price on the horizontal axis. This reverses the traditional economics textbook representation, but since we wish to consider quantity as the dependent variable the treatment used in Figure 7–1 is more appropriate.

Figure 7–1

CLINTON COMPANY
DEMAND CURVE

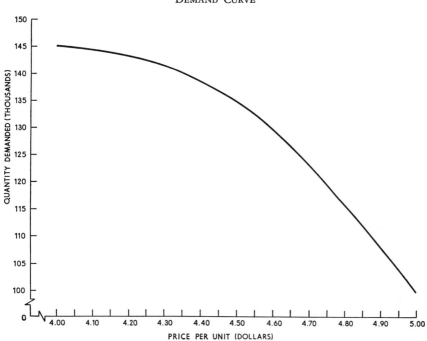

but at lower prices demand becomes inelastic. This general pattern—elasticity decreasing with price—may be described as typical for many products, since at low prices great increases in volume are necessary in order to recoup the revenue lost from lowering the unit price on the large volume base that could have been sold at a slightly higher price.

To describe the elasticity concept more precisely, economists have defined the *coefficient of elasticity* or *elasticity index*. This index is the negative of the ratio of the percentage change in quantity demanded to the percentage change in price. In terms of the data in the table above, lowering the price by 5% (from $5 to $4.75) produces an increase in demand of 20% for an elasticity coefficient of 4.0. Using this index as a yardstick, we may say that demand is elastic if the coefficient of elasticity is greater than 1.0, that is, if the percentage increase in demand exceeds the percentage decrease in price. When demand is inelastic, the index will be less than 1.0. Demand is said to be *unitary* when the coefficient is exactly 1.0. These definitions are completely consistent with our earlier definitions stated in terms of the effect on total revenue; as may be observed above, total revenue increases when the price is dropped from $4.75 to $4.50 and the index is 2.6, and total revenue decreases when the price goes from $4.25 to $4 and the index is 0.3.

The method of calculating the coefficient of elasticity just described is somewhat imprecise. In the calculations above we computed the percentage changes in price and volume on the base of the volume sold at the higher price. Since we really wish to measure elasticity within a price interval, a better calculation would be to compute the percentage changes based on the midpoints within the price interval, as shown in Table 7–2.

Table 7–2

CLINTON COMPANY

CALCULATION OF AVERAGE ELASTICITY WITHIN PRICE INTERVALS

Price per Unit	Quantity Demanded	Midpoints within Price Interval	Midpoints within Demand Interval	Percentage Change in Price	Percentage Change in Quantity	Elasticity Index
$5.00	100,000					
4.75	120,000	$4.875	110,000	5.13%	18.18%	3.54
4.50	135,000	4.625	127,500	5.41	11.76	2.17
4.25	142,500	4.375	138,750	5.71	5.41	0.95
4.00	145,000	4.125	143,750	6.06	1.74	0.29

From Table 7–2 we can see, for example, that between prices of $4.50 and $4.75 per unit, this product has an average coefficient of elasticity of 2.17.

It should be obvious that the Clinton Company would never wish to lower its price to such an extent that its total revenue would actually decrease. From the tables above it is easy to see that a price of $4.25 does not produce as much revenue as a price of $4.50, and that the *average* elasticity within that interval is 0.95. Does this mean that $4.50 is the price that yields maximum revenue? The answer is no, if some intermediate price can be used. Let us assume that Table 7–3 gives a more detailed demand schedule.

This schedule permits us to break the average elasticity index of 0.95 into an index for five smaller price intervals. The elasticity between $4.50 and $4.45 is 1.31 and between $4.30 and $4.25 it is 0.54. The price that yields maximum revenue now appears to lie in the interval between $4.40 to $4.35.

Shifts in Demand. While earlier in this section we listed a number of factors, environmental and controllable, which might exert an influence on quantity demanded, the demand schedule depicted in Figure 7–1 illustrates the effect of only one factor: price. In determining a demand schedule, it is assumed that *all factors other than price are held constant.* That is, the demand curve in Figure 7–1 reflects the influence of price on quantity demanded on the assumption that general economic conditions, consumer tastes, competitive factors, and nonprice elements of marketing strategy are not changed.

Changes in nonprice determinants of demand can be represented graphically by a "shift" in the demand curve. It is reasonable to sup-

Table 7–3

CLINTON COMPANY

FINDING UNITARY ELASTICITY BY INTERPOLATION

Price per Unit	Quantity Demanded	Total Revenue	—Midpoints within— Price Interval	Demand Interval	—Percentage Change in— Price	Quantity	Elasticity Index
$4.65	127,200	591,480					
4.60	130,100	598,460	$4.625	128,650	1.08%	2.25%	2.08
4.55	132,700	603,785	4.575	131,400	1.09	1.98	1.82
4.50	135,000	607,500	4.525	133,850	1.10	1.72	1.56
4.45	137,000	609,650	4.475	136,000	1.12	1.47	1.31
4.40	138,800	610,720	4.425	137,900	1.13	1.31	1.16
4.35	140,300	610,305	4.375	139,550	1.14	1.07	0.94
4.30	141,600	608,880	4.325	140,950	1.16	0.92	0.79
4.25	142,500	605,625	4.275	142,050	1.17	0.63	0.54

pose, for example, that a deterioration in general economic conditions would result in a leftward shift in the demand curve illustrated in Figure 7–2; that is, at any given price, a lesser quantity would be demanded. In contrast, a successful advertising campaign might result in a shift to the right.

Revenue

For decision-making purposes, our primary interest in demand is because of its effect on total revenue. The total revenue corresponding to the demand schedule faced by the Clinton Company in 1972 is tabulated in Tables 7–1, 7–2, and 7–3, and graphed in Figure 7–2. The total revenue curve in Figure 7–2, which rises to a maximum and

Figure 7–2

CLINTON COMPANY

TOTAL REVENUE

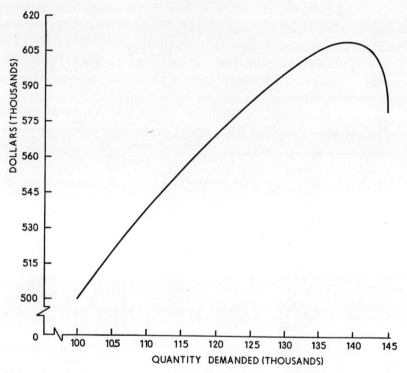

QUANTITY DEMANDED (THOUSANDS)

then declines, should be compared with that in the break-even chart discussed in Chapter 3 (Figure 3–1), in which the less realistic assumption that price and volume are independent was made.

Marginal Revenue. How much will total revenue change if the price is lowered just enough so that the quantity demanded increases by one unit? The change in total revenue will not generally be the same as the price charged for the incremental unit since, because of the price-quantity relationship expressed by the demand schedule, an across-the-board reduction in price may be necessary to secure the increase in volume. The change in total revenue will, therefore, be the net result of the two opposing influences:

1. An *increase* in total revenue resulting from applying the new price to the increase in total volume.

2. A *decrease* in total revenue resulting from applying the price decrease necessary to secure the additional volume to the preexisting volume.

These two effects can be illustrated by using the data of Table 7–3. If price is decreased from $4.55 to $4.50, quantity demanded is increased from 132,700 units to 135,000 units, a change of 2,300 units. Total revenue is thus increased by $3,715, as follows:

```
1. Increase due to volume: $4.50 × 2,300 units.............$10,350
2. Decrease due to price: $0.05 × 132,700 units..............  6,635
   Net change in total revenue...........................$ 3,715
```

The change in total revenue resulting from a change of one unit in quantity demanded, assuming no shifts in the demand schedule, is called *marginal revenue.* Marginal revenue within a price interval may

Table 7–4

CLINTON COMPANY
CALCULATION OF MARGINAL REVENUE

Price per Unit	Quantity Demanded	Total Revenue	Change within Interval Quantity	Change within Interval Total Revenue	Marginal Revenue (Average within Interval)
$5.00	100,000	$500,000			
4.75	120,000	570,000	20,000	$70,000	$3.50
4.70	123,900	582,330	3,900	12,330	3.16
4.65	127,200	591,480	3,300	9,150	2.77
4.60	130,100	598,460	2,900	6,980	2.41
4.55	132,700	603,785	2,600	5,325	2.05
4.50	135,000	607,500	2,300	3,715	1.62
4.45	137,000	609,650	2,000	2,150	1.08
4.40	138,800	610,720	1,800	1,070	0.59
4.35	140,300	610,305	1,500	(415)	(0.28)
4.25	142,500	605,625	2,200	(4,680)	(2.13)
4.00	145,000	580,000	2,500	(25,625)	(10.25)

be approximated by dividing the change in total revenue within the interval by the change in quantity demanded. Marginal revenue in the interval from $4.55 to $4.50, for example, is approximately $3,715 divided by 2,300, or $1.62 per unit. Marginal revenue within other intervals are given in Table 7–4.

Relationship of Marginal Revenue to Price and Elasticity. From Table 7–4 we can observe that (1) marginal revenue is less than price² and (2) marginal revenue is positive when demand is elastic and negative when demand is inelastic.³

Measurement of Demand

In our simple example we assumed that the Clinton Company knew exactly how many units would be sold in 1972 at each price, other things being equal. Once the demand curve is known, the remainder of the analysis was straightforward. One of the main reasons why analysis of demand of the type illustrated above is rarely used in practice is simply because companies are unable to estimate the shape of their demand curves. The raw data from which a demand curve might be drawn are sales statistics for the recent past, but the businessman can look at these data and observe many volume fluctuations that are obviously not related to price (and if price has not changed, very possibly none that are related to price). Product style changes, advertising, shelf placement, the general economic situation, and aggressive salesmanship are only a partial list of things that may cause shifts in the demand curve and make it difficult to isolate the effect of price changes. Because of these many uncertainties, in practice it is not possible to know the exact number of units that will be demanded at a given price. Therefore, it would be more appropriate to make a probablistic forecast of demand for each price level using the techniques presented in Chapter 6. Using such a forecast would require a more complicated discussion; therefore, to present the theory of pricing we will continue to talk about a demand curve with only one demand level for every price. You should think of this demand curve as a point forecast of demand at each price level. This point forecast will be a measure of the entire probabilistic forecast of demand at that price level.

DETERMINATION OF PRICE

Building, now, on our discussion of cost-price-volume relationships in Chapter 3, let us see how an explicit demand curve such as that

---

² This will be true unless quantity demanded *increases* with price, that is, unless elasticity of demand is negative.

³ The relationship between marginal revenue, price, and elasticity can be expressed by the following formula:

$$\text{Marginal revenue} = \text{Price} \times \left(1 - \frac{1}{\text{Elasticity}} \right)$$

The quantity in parentheses combines the "price" and "volume" effects on total revenue referred to earlier. If demand is elastic (elasticity greater than 1) this quantity, and hence marginal revenue, is positive. At unitary elasticity this quantity is zero, and at inelastic demands it is negative.

displayed above may be incorporated into our analysis. How can we use our point forecast of demand at various prices to arrive at the most profitable price?

Pricing for Profit Maximization

In order to find the most profitable price we must look at the difference between total revenue and total cost for each price. These calculations for the Clinton Company, assuming direct costs of $2.25 per unit and fixed, or period, costs of $175,000 per year are shown in Table 7–5.

Table 7–5

CLINTON COMPANY
CALCULATION OF TOTAL PROFIT

Price per Unit	Quantity Demanded	Total Revenue	Direct Costs @ $2.25/ Unit	Total Costs	Total Profit
$5.00	100,000	$500,000	$225,000	$400,000	$100,000
4.75	120,000	570,000	270,000	445,000	125,000
4.70	123,900	582,330	278,775	453,775	128,555
4.65	127,200	591,480	286,200	461,200	130,280
4.60	130,100	598,460	292,725	467,725	130,735
4.55	132,700	603,785	298,575	473,575	130,210
4.50	135,000	607,500	303,750	478,750	128,750
4.45	137,000	609,650	308,250	483,250	126,400
4.40	138,800	610,720	312,300	487,300	123,005
4.35	140,300	610,305	315,675	490,675	119,630
4.25	142,500	605,625	320,625	495,625	110,000
4.00	145,000	580,000	326,250	501,250	78,750

Although a price of $4.40 will yield the most total revenue, we see from the table that a price of $4.60 will yield the greatest total profit. A graphic representation, in Figure 7–3, illustrates what is happening to total costs and revenues as volume changes.

The lower part of Figure 7–3 reproduces the demand curve from Figure 7–1. (Rotating the book 90 degrees counterclockwise may make it clear that price, the independent variable, determines demand. Demand then becomes an intervening variable that determines total revenue and total cost.) Total profit in the top part of the graph is represented by the vertical distance between the total revenue and total cost curves.

Marginal Analysis. Another, and more instructive, way to find the price which yields maximum profit involves the concept of *marginal analysis.* It is relatively easy to see why a price of $4.60 is more profit-

Figure 7–3

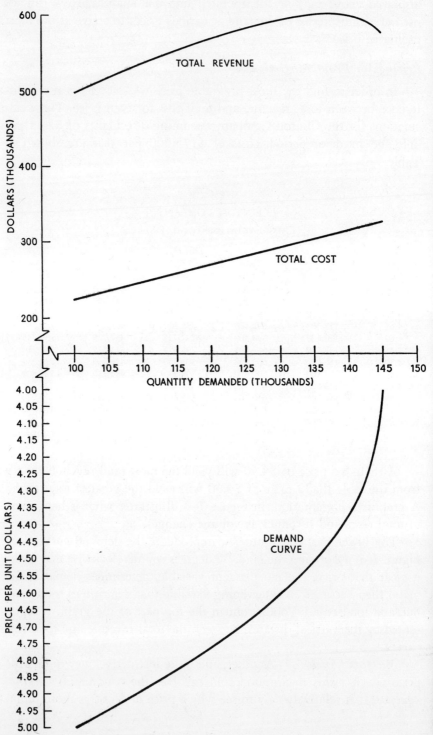

CLINTON COMPANY

Dependence of Profit and Quantity on Price

able than a price of $4.40 even though we know that total revenue is greater at the lower price: The incremental revenue that is received by lowering the price below $4.60 is inadequate to cover the incremental direct costs of producing the additional product that is demanded at the lower price. In terms of Figure 7–3, the total revenue curve rises more rapidly than the total cost curve as the price falls to $4.60 per unit; below that price the total cost increases faster than total revenue.

We have previously introduced the concept of marginal revenue, defined as the change in total revenue resulting from a change of one unit in quantity. A related concept is that of *marginal cost:* the change in total cost resulting from a change of one unit in quantity. In the Clinton Company example, since we have assumed constant direct costs of $2.25 per unit, marginal cost is also $2.25 per unit. We will return later to consider the reasonableness of this assumption of constant marginal cost.

When marginal revenue exceeds marginal cost, as it does for prices above $4.60, total profit will be increased by selling additional units. When marginal revenue is less than marginal cost, however, each additional unit sold decreases total profit. It will only be profitable, therefore, to increase volume to the point at which marginal revenue equals marginal cost. This is the so-called *marginal* condition for profit maximization.[4] Applying the technique to the Clinton Company, we see in Table 7–4 that the marginal revenue from a price reduction to $4.60 is $2.41, while a further reduction to $4.55 yields only $2.05 per unit of marginal revenue. Since $2.05 is less than the marginal cost per unit of $2.25, the price reduction to $4.55 is not profitable; the most profitable price is $4.60 per unit.

Relevant Costs for Price Determination

In our example, we have identified the marginal costs with the direct costs of $2.25 per unit derived from the Clinton Company's accounting records. This is a tempting identification to make, but except in very limited circumstances it would be an erroneous one. In most pricing problems, the relevant marginal costs are probably greater than accounting direct costs. There are some circumstances, however, in

---

[4] The condition "marginal revenue equals marginal cost" is also true when profit is minimized. To insure maximum profit it is also necessary to require, as we have been assuming, that marginal cost is increasing more rapidly than marginal revenue; at minimum profit the reverse would be true.

which marginal cost in the economist's sense might be less than direct cost in the accountant's sense.

Because accounting records often provide one of the most convenient sources of cost data for pricing, it is important to wise decision making that the differences in concept between the accountant and the economist be understood. Some of these differences have been considered already in Chapter 1, but we will review them here in the context of pricing decisions.

Average Direct Cost versus Incremental Cost. To calculate the $2.25 per unit used in the Clinton Company example, we divided total direct costs at the 1972 volume (including sales commissions) by that volume. Thus the figure represents the *average* direct cost of the product. While this may be the *average* cost (at the 1972 volume), what would be more relevant in the present context is the *incremental* cost, that is, the amount by which total cost would change if volume increased by one unit. Except by coincidence, the two concepts would lead to the same cost estimates if and only if incremental costs were the same for all units.

Actually, as we observed in Chapter 1, it is unlikely that incremental costs would be the same for all units. The incremental cost of the very first units may be quite high as a result of the necessity to hire a minimum staff and provide certain facilities. Once the minimum staff and facilities are provided, incremental cost will be less than average cost and may, in fact, be nearly constant over a considerable range of output. With increasing output, however, incremental cost may begin to rise. To produce the higher output, it may be necessary to press less efficient facilities into service, hire inexperienced workers, and cope with the difficulties created by a crowded plant. When plant capacity is reached, additional output may require the payment of overtime or night shift premiums or of subcontract costs. Eventually, as incremental costs rise, they may become greater than average costs.

Thus we see that even if we restrict our attention to accounting costs, it would be erroneous to equate average costs and incremental costs.

Opportunity Costs of Fixed Facilities. Not all the costs relevant to a pricing decision may even be included in accounting records. The opportunity costs of using fixed facilities constitute the most important exception.

These opportunity costs must *not* be confused with the accountant's allocations of the fixed costs of the same facilities. By definition, the fixed costs will not vary with the price, no matter how allocated, and hence are not relevant to the decision. To illustrate, suppose that the Clinton Company's fixed costs during 1972 included $25,000 of depreciation expense. The company's accounts might allocate this expense to the products sold during the year at the rate of $0.25 per unit. But since the total depreciation expense of $25,000 does not depend upon the quantity produced, the unit depreciation charge is not a true "variable" cost.

Suppose, on the other hand, that the Clinton Company makes two products in the same plant, and that capacity is limited so that if more of the product we are considering (which we will call product A) is made, less of the second product (product B) can be produced. In this case, any contribution to fixed costs which would have been earned by the units of product B displaced by units of product A constitute an opportunity cost of product A. This cost is clearly relevant to a decision regarding price for product A, since the Clinton Company would not want to increase the production of product A at the expense of product B unless product A earned at least as much contribution to fixed costs per unit of capacity employed as did product B.

Change of Production Technique. If a radical price cut is being considered, production methods for a greatly increased volume may be considerably changed and it may be exceptionally difficult to estimate costs. Henry Ford's conception of the assembly line as a production technique to permit the exploitation of the elastic demand for automobiles (that existed at that time) is a good example of a situation in which marginal cost was both important and difficult to estimate.

OTHER DEMAND-CREATING COSTS

While a price reduction may result in an increase in the quantity of goods that will be sold, such an action is profitable only if the "cost" of the price cut is more than offset by the profit on the sale of incremental units. In this sense, price is only one of a variety of demand-creating "costs" which may be manipulated by the businessman. To illustrate this concept of cost, let us look again at the Clinton Company's pricing analysis discussed above.

In Table 7–4, we see that management would expect to sell 127,-200 units at a price of $4.65 and that an additional 2,900 units could be sold if the price were reduced to $4.60. The "cost" of such a price reduction is measured by the loss in revenue on the units that could be sold at the higher price: $0.05 on 127,200 units = $6,360. Against this cost we can calculate the profit on the additional units; the contribution per unit is \$2.35 (\$4.60 — 2.25), a total of \$6,815 on 2,900 units. The price reduction earns a profit of \$455 because the added contribution exceeds the cost of the price cut, and this same profit increase may be observed in Table 7–5 as the difference between the total profit at the two prices. This way of looking at a price change, however, casts the decision in a somewhat different light and makes it easier to compare this method of stimulating demand to some of the other alternatives open to the businessman.

Price, particularly in highly competitive industries, is the most violent form of competitive attack. If the gasoline station on one corner of an intersection lowers its price 2 cents per gallon—and puts up a big sign to proclaim the fact—the operator of the station across the street may feel he has little choice but to lower his price as well. When all the stations in town follow suit, given a relatively inelastic demand for the product, the net effect may be simply that all stations earn a lower profit. For any one seller, the potential profits that would result from increasing his volume are great enough to make some sort of effort worthwhile, but more subtle forms of demand-stimulation may be more effective than a price cut because they are harder for a competitor to counteract. Thus, the major oil companies offer various forms of games and prizes through their outlets, while the price wars of a decade earlier are almost unknown. At the same time, retail food chains, which had been through an analogous cycle of promotion with trading stamps, saw some members of the industry giving up stamps and beginning to promote on the basis of lower prices. Clearly, in a great many situations, price reductions and direct promotional expenses are simply alternative types of demand-creating costs.

Viewed in this way, the analysis of demand-creating costs (other than price changes) is not much different, nor any easier, than the analysis for the determination of an optimum price discussed above. Although the way in which demand-creating costs are incurred may differ, the crux of any decision still turns on the estimate of the effect that such costs will have on the quantity demanded. To illustrate this point, let us use the advertising expenditures of the Clinton Company as an example.

Over a period of several years, the management of the Clinton Company has found that spot television commercials were one of the most effective forms of promotion of its products. In 1972 the company's entire advertising budget of \$40,000 had been spent in this manner. In preparing its profit plan for 1973, management considered a variety of actions that might further increase the demand for the company's products, including the price reduction discussed earlier. One alternative was a substantial increase in the company's advertising budget, permitting the use of television stations in some cities in its market region which were not currently being covered. Based on a careful analysis of the results of similar expansions of coverage in 1971 and 1972, executives of Clinton and its advertising agency prepared a list of the most promising potential new markets. This was then converted into a statement of alternative advertising budgets, with a point forecast of the annual sales volume that might be sustainable at each level of expenditure, as shown in the first two columns of Table 7–6.

Table 7–6

CLINTON COMPANY

ANALYSIS OF ALTERNATIVE ADVERTISING BUDGETS

Advertising Budget	Forecast of Total Sales in Units	Change within Interval	
		Quantity	Contribution at $2.75 per Unit
$40,000	100,000		
45,000	105,000	5,000	$13,750
50,000	108,500	3,500	9,625
55,000	110,500	2,000	5,500
60,000	112,000	1,500	4,125

The balance of the analysis displayed in Table 7–6 is straightforward. Successive increases of $5,000 each in the advertising budget are profitable up to a total of $55,000. A further increase to $60,000 would produce only $4,125 of contribution on the additional units sold and would, therefore, decrease the total profits of the company. More generally, this analysis of an explicit demand-creating cost parallels that shown earlier in Table 7–4 where price reductions were used to stimulate demand. For either type of "cost," the critical question is the same: How much will demand be changed as a result of the change in demand-creating costs?

PRICE ADMINISTRATION

The economist's model of price determination assumes an ideal world in which perfect information is always available without cost and in which analysis is effortless. For his major purpose, which is to describe the workings of an entire economic system, the economist views these factors in much the same way that the physicist views friction: as a minor qualification to his broad conclusions.

To the businessman actually engaged in setting a price, however, these factors may be all important. He is an "economic engineer," attempting to apply the abstract principles of the economist to the solution of practical problems. Among the difficulties he faces in this task are a paucity of information, both on demand and on costs in an economic sense, and the sheer volume of pricing decisions which must be made, particularly in a multiproduct company.

There are, in addition, a number of institutional factors which hamper the ability of the businessman to adjust his price continuously to changing demand and cost conditions. For many products, the established price is published in advertising or in catalogs and must therefore be effective over a period of time. In large organizations (and even in some small ones), price making may be delegated to many individuals, such as the field sales force. These individuals must be provided with guidelines; and because of the cost of communication and training, these guidelines cannot be changed too frequently.

The businessman, therefore, usually views his pricing problem in terms of setting a reasonably satisfactory price for a period of time rather than the theoretically optimum price at a given point in time. His overall objective may still be profit maximization, but when the costs of information, analysis, and organizational change are taken into account he may proceed toward this objective somewhat differently than economic theory implies.[5]

Types of Pricing Decisions

To understand how businessmen accommodate to the practical difficulties they face, it will be helpful to consider the various contexts within which pricing decisions may be made.

We may first distinguish between a *policy price* and a *transaction price*. A policy price is a statement of the business' price objective over a relatively long period of time. It may be, for example, a price high enough to cover long-run variable costs, so that if this price could not be obtained on the average over the long run the business would prefer to drop the product. In the short run, however, the business may be prepared to lower this price to meet temporary weaknesses in demand. The

---

[5] Some writers argue, in fact, that it would be more appropriate to view business as seeking to earn a satisfactory profit rather than a maximum profit.

prices actually charged on specific sales are called transaction prices.

For example, it is often argued that the apparent stability of steel prices is really an illusion. What is being looked at are the steel companies' posted prices, which are in fact policy prices. In periods of weak demand, concessions are often offered from these prices, so that transaction prices may show considerably more variation. More familiarly, it is well known that automobile dealers offer concessions below the so-called "sticker prices" of models when they find difficulty in selling them.

We may also distinguish between the pricing of standardized products, usually produced for the seller's inventory, and the pricing of products manufactured to the buyer's order. Policy prices are more feasible in the former case, since in the latter case a new price must of necessity be computed for each order. Even so, some policy guidelines are desirable to assist those who must prepare individual price quotations.

Use of Policy Prices

As noted earlier, a policy price is often set at the level a business believes it must average on the product in question over the long run if the product is to be worthwhile. Stated simply, policy price is determined by a "buildup" or listing of the various accounting cost components (labor, material, and a share of all overhead expenses) to arrive at "total product cost"; an additional amount is then added for profit. The logic of such a pricing system is simple: (1) the price must obviously cover the direct costs such as labor and material; (2) overhead is nothing more mysterious than a common cost which is incurred for the benefit of all products and which must in the long run be recovered in the selling price if the business is to make a profit; and (3) the product must be sold at a profit or it is not worth producing.

The critical problem in this approach is to determine the volume over which to spread the fixed overhead expenses. The more sophisticated companies usually try to estimate a "normal volume," representing an average they expect to be able to achieve over a period of ups and downs in demand. In addition, the portion of fixed overhead expense attributable to "idle capacity," that is, capacity not needed to produce the normal volume, may be excluded from the unit cost calculations. Under these circumstances, the unit cost figure may be a good approximation to long-run variable cost, since in the long run the fixed facilities can be adjusted to the anticipated volume level.

Return on Investment Pricing. In its most sophisticated form, the calculation of "total product cost" may also include an estimate of the "cost" of the capital investment required to produce and sell the product. Conceptually, this approach is an attempt to arrive at a more rational estimate of the appropriate amount of profit to be included in the policy price. "Profit" in this sense is really the compensation earned by the investors who have supplied capital to the firm. These investors have incurred an opportunity cost by investing their money in the firm rather than devoting it to an alternative use, although specifying a rate of return which measures this opportunity cost may be difficult especially for the investment by common stockholders which represents risk capital with a claim only on the residual profits of the company. Nevertheless, attempting to calculate the opportunity cost of the capital investment attributable to a specific product may be worthwhile, particularly in multiproduct companies where capital requirements differ among various products, thus decreasing the usefulness of the less complex calculation of profit as a percentage of sales.

As with the more explicit items of "total product cost," the opportunity cost of invested capital can also be divided into two components: product-related investment which results in a product-creating cost, and capacity-related investment as another type of capacity-creating cost. In conventional financial terms, the product-related investment is usually called working capital and, like other product-creating costs, tends to vary in proportion to the quantity produced and sold. For example, if the product is sold on credit, the investment in accounts receivable will vary directly with the quantity sold, and the cost of providing this capital may reasonably be attributed to the product. Similarly, the required investment in inventories is related to the volume of production, although not always in direct proportion.

The capital invested in production facilities, on the other hand, is part of the cost of creating a productive capability. The magnitude of this cost, therefore, is determined by decisions about how much capacity to have, rather than by the volume of production that actually flows through the facility. The resulting fixed cost of facilities investment may then be allocated to specific products using the same "normal volume" estimate that was used in spreading other capacity-creating costs.

Transaction Prices. Regardless of the care and sophistication used in preparing long-run policy prices, the prices for specific transactions must be set in the short run. Given a policy price as a benchmark, we can raise the following question: "Is the policy price too high or too low for current demand and cost conditions?" An answer requires only local knowledge of the demand and cost curves in the neighborhood of the policy price, rather than the global knowledge assumed in the traditional economic model. The businessman need consider only whether he believes that he can raise his total profit by raising or lowering his price.

Product Line Pricing

The sort of cost analysis used in setting a price policy can be particularly useful in pricing a range of products to be offered within a given product line. Two kinds of situations commonly occur.

If the company has an established product line, pricing a new product to add to the line may pose special problems. Production costs often provide an easily quantified measurement of the relationship of the new product to the existing products in the line. If the goal is to price the new product so that it "fits into the line" in a consistent manner, cost-price ratios for the existing products may be a valuable pricing guide. Such a pricing decision can, and probably should, be made quite independently of the broader question of the appropriate price level for the entire line. Because of the interrelationship of the various items in the line, the demand curves for the individual products will probably be strongly influenced by the prices on other items in the line that are either substitutable or complementary; the products are subject to "cross-elasticity" of demand. The relevant demand curve for a group of related products is the curve for the entire product line.

Another type of product-line problem arises when traditional price classes exist for the quality range of items offered. Familiar examples are women's fashion wear, automobiles, gasoline, and candy bars. Product costs are very important in such situations because the manufacturer can rarely charge an unconventional price—a 7-cent candy bar is unheard of. Rather, the pricing decision is made by deciding to produce a product which will sell in one of the established price classes, and the big problems are in deciding how good a product to offer at that price. Theoretically, this problem is not any different from an ordinary pricing problem in which the product characteristics are fixed and the price is variable. The optimal price is still the one that equates marginal revenue and marginal cost, but in this case marginal revenue is more nearly constant, and it is marginal cost per unit that changes radically, increasing at higher volume estimates to reflect the costs of increasing the quality of the product in order to sell more units.

PROBLEMS

Problem 7–1. A reexamination of the costs of the Clinton Company (used as the illustration in this chapter) discloses that while total variable costs per unit are estimated to be $2.25, this figure constitutes $1.75 per unit of product-creating costs and $0.50 per unit of sales commissions. The salesmen receive a commission of 10% of the selling price and, therefore, the $0.50 holds true only at a price of $5 per unit. Does the additional fact alter the conclusion reached in Table 7–5 that the most profitable price for Clinton is $4.60? Why? If you think this new information is relevant, recompute marginal revenue as in Table 7–4 and total profit as in Table 7–5. Which price will yield the largest profit for the company?

Problem 7–2. The Akron Manufacturing Company produced tires and batteries for national distribution through automotive parts distributors. No sales were made direct to gasoline stations or repair shops. The company maintained two representatives in each of five territories plus a national sales manager to handle national accounts.

For some time the market penetration of the company's products had slipped and the management was actively exploring methods to improve the company's market share. On the basis of the study of 1960 results shown in Table 7–7, it was determined to set up two territories as test areas to study the results that might be achieved by adding to the sales force, but trying two different ways of using the added manpower as described below. The sales department estimated that the average costs per additional representative would be $16,000 per man per year, including travel, meetings, compensation, etc.

A test of one year was devised in which each of the two test territories would be assigned two additional representatives. Each territory would be divided into two districts; one a test area and the other a control area. The additional representatives were to be assigned only to the test areas.

In the A territory, the added manpower would handle distributor accounts as they had been handled in the past. The gain was to come from increased frequency of sales calls and closer attention to complaints.

In the B territory, the added men were only to handle gasoline station or repair shop calls. They were to take no orders, but simply to point out the quality, advertising, public acceptance, and superiority of the Akron Company products, and to refer the active prospects to the Akron Company distributors with a request that they "specify Akron."

The results of the test conducted in 1961 are tabulated in Table 7–8.

Table 7-7

THE AKRON COMPANY
YEAR 1960

	Tires					Batteries				
	Total	Fixed Amount	Fixed Percent	Variable Amount	Variable Percent	Total	Fixed Amount	Fixed Percent	Variable Amount	Variable Percent
Sales revenue*	$6,753					$14,936				
Cost of sales†	5,205	$1,035	20	$4,170	80	13,184	$2,160	16	$11,024	84
Gross profit	$1,548					$1,752				
Distribution expense:										
Selling expense	$84	76	90	8	10	$140	126	90	14	10
Promotion expense	20		...	20	100	120	60	50	60	50
Advertising expense	55	52	95	3	5	200	190	95	10	5
Warehousing expense	73	69	95	4	5	185	176	95	9	5
Total	$232					$645				
Gross profit after distribution	$1,316					$1,107				
Less: Administrative expense	30	28	95	2	5	62	59	95	3	5
Other charges‡	310	310	100		...	430	430	100		...
Net income before tax	$976			$4,207		$615			$11,120	
Percent profit on sales	14.5%			62.3%		4.1%			74.5%	
Total fixed and variable costs		$1,570					$3,201			
Percent of sales revenue		23.2%					21.4%			
Contribution to overhead and profit		Tires: 37.7%					Batteries: 25.5%			

* Net of cash discounts, defectives, freight out, and price allowances.
† Includes product engineering and product division costs.
‡ Includes central office costs, such as legal, executive, interest, etc.

Table 7-8

THE AKRON COMPANY

| | Territory "A" | | | | Territory "B" | | | |
| | Tires | | Batteries | | Tires | | Batteries | |
	Test	Control	Test	Control	Test	Control	Test	Control
Sales—1960	$350,000	$350,000	$ 900,000	$910,000	$375,000	$400,000	$ 875,000	$ 940,000
Sales—1961:								
First quarter	$ 85,000	$ 80,000	$ 225,000	$220,000	$110,000	$ 90,000	$ 245,000	$ 250,000
Second quarter	110,000	100,000	255,000	240,000	120,000	100,000	280,000	250,000
Third quarter	110,000	90,000	255,000	230,000	125,000	110,000	280,000	255,000
Fourth quarter	125,000	100,000	285,000	280,000	130,000	115,000	285,000	265,000
Total—1961	$430,000	$370,000	$1,020,000	$970,000	$485,000	$415,000	$1,090,000	$1,020,000
Sales increase 1961 versus 1960	80,000	20,000	120,000	60,000	110,000	15,000	215,000	80,000
Sales increase 1961 versus 1960—%	22.8%	5.7%	13.6%	6.6%	29.4%	3.7%	24.6%	8.5%

Assignment

The vice president of marketing has asked you to comment on the results of the test. He is interested in the results as the guide to a course of action to be taken for next year.

1. How much better have the test areas done relative to the control areas?

2. Have the tests affected Akron's profitability and by how much?

3. How much additional business must Akron write to cover the cost of an added salesman?

4. What additional action should be taken as a result of these tests?

SYLVANIA ELECTRIC PRODUCTS INC. (B)

The price and policy section of Sylvania's lighting division was the responsibility of Mr. Paul Colton. Mr. Colton considered all problems relating to the division's selling prices and terms, including questions of introducing new lamps into the line.

Proposals to introduce new lamps were generally originated by the sales department, which wanted a new model for competitive reasons, or by the engineering department, which may have developed the lamp. Mr. Colton analyzed all such proposals to attempt to decide whether the lamp could be made and sold profitably.

In September, 1954, Mr. Colton was considering the information he had received on a new type of fluorescent lamp which had been developed by the engineering department. This type, which would bear the code designation 90 T-17 Deluxe Cool White, was basically similar to the 90 T-17 Standard Cool White model, which was carried at a list price of $2.55. The new type would give a better quality of illumination, however.

Mr. Colton had summarized the information he had gathered on a type cost analysis sheet (see Exhibit 1). He had received, as part of the engineering department's report, the information given in Exhibit 1 concerning theoretical material costs for the new model. The engineering department was unable to supply efficiency figures to be applied to these theoreticals since the lamp was not yet in production. Mr. Colton consequently asked Mr. O'Connor, the division's manager of manufacturing costs, to obtain for him the efficiency data on the 90 T-17 Standard Cool White lamp. He realized that actual efficiencies on new types were typically lower than that on types already in production, at least until the "bugs" were ironed out of the new processes, which

366

might take six months to a year. Since the major difference in the new type was in the interior fluorescent coating, the greatest reduction in efficiency would probably occur in bulbs, powder, and solvent. Nevertheless, for lack of any more precise information, Mr. Colton used the efficiencies for the Standard Cool White lamps in calculating the labor costs of the new lamp.

Mr. Colton repeated this process for the direct labor component of manufacturing costs. The theoretical costs were based on estimates by time-study men with the industrial engineering department. The efficiencies reflected recent experience on the Standard Cool White lamp, although Mr. Colton knew that the same consideration applied to those figures, particularly for the coating and baking centers, as applied to the efficiencies on materials.

Standard burden cost of the new type was then determined by multiplying the current burden loading rate for each department by the appropriate standard direct labor cost. Totaling the three elements, Mr. Colton obtained the figure for total manufacturing cost.

Mr. Colton also had to make an allowance in his calculations for trade discount, distribution costs, administrative and central expenses, and profit. He believed that the results for August, 1954, as reflected in the division's profit and loss statement, could be taken as typical (see Exhibit 2).

When Mr. Colton began to work on the cost estimates, he asked Mr. Elbery, the sales manager, to estimate the sales volume of the new type. Mr. Elbery was very reluctant to make such an estimate, pointing out that it was almost impossible to predict the sale of an item that had not yet been introduced.

Mr. Elbery said, however, that he felt that the sales volume would be quite responsive to changes in price, since the lamp would be in direct competition with other similar types, such as the Standard Cool White lamp, as well as with other types of illumination. As an "educated guess," Mr. Elbery advanced the following estimates of annual sales volume at varying prices:

List Price	Anticipated Annual Volume
$3.50	60,000
3.00	90,000
2.75	120,000
2.50	150,000
2.25	200,000
2.00	250,000

The Danvers plant currently had the capacity to produce the maximum indicated volume of lamps without any appreciable increase in investment.

Questions

1. Should Mr. Colton approve the addition of the 90 T-17 Deluxe Cool White lamp to the line of lamps offered for sale?

2. If so, at what price should the lamps be listed?

Exhibit 1

SYLVANIA ELECTRIC PRODUCTS INC. (B)

LAMP DIVISION

TYPE COST ANALYSIS

Copies:					TYPE F90r17/cwk List Price	
Item Class	Theo. Cost/M	% Eff.	Std. Cost/M	Item Class		Std. Cost/M
PRIME COST				MANUFACTURING OVERHEAD		
Materials:						
Bulbs	127.50	88	144.89			
Bases	19.25	91	21.15			
Basing Material	2.13	86	2.48			
Glass Tubing	4.38	76	5.76			
Lead Wires	3.47	87	3.99			
Coils	20.25	89	22.69			
Powder	55.32	81	68.30			
Miscellaneous	3.72	84	4.43			
Packing	68.24	99½	68.58			
Solvents	7.48	—	7.48			
	311.74		349.75	Sub Total		
Transportation			18.50	Departmental Burden:		
			—	Coating	305%	27.39
				Baking	348	24.43
				Flare	250	5.88
				Automount	187	24.07
Sub Total			368.25	Base Prep.	146	3.62
				Finishing	285	274.60
Direct Labor:				Sub Total		359.99
Coating	4.22	47	8.98			
Baking	4.42	63	7.02	Prorates:		
Flare	1.76	75	2.35			
Automount	10.94	85	12.87			
Base Preparation	1.98	80	2.48			
Finishing	79.01	82	96.35			
			—	Sub Total		
				TOTAL MFG. OVERHEAD		359.99
Sub Total	102.33		130.05	TOTAL MFG. COST		858.29
TOTAL PRIME COST			498.30	% to List.		

Prepared by_____ Date_____

GROSS PROFIT		OPERATING CHARGES AND NET PROFIT	
Amount %		Amount %	
List Price		Gross Profit	
Discount		Operating Charges:	
Gross Selling Price		Divisional:	
Deductions:			
Allowances			
Freight			
Cash Discount			
Sub Total	_____	Sub Total	_____
Net Selling Price		Div. Operating Profit	
Cost of Sales:		Central:	
Mfg.			
Sub Total	_____	Sub Total	_____
GROSS PROFIT		NET PROFIT	

Exhibit 2

SYLVANIA ELECTRIC PRODUCTS INC. (B)

LIGHTING DIVISION INCOME STATEMENT, AUGUST, 1954

	Fluorescent	All Other Products*	Eliminations†	Total Division
Gross sales—list value	$2,755,382	$6,942,467	$(224,519)	$9,473,330
Trade discount	1,363,134	3,144,952		4,508,086
Gross sales booked	$1,392,248	$3,797,515	$(224,519)	$4,965,244
Sales deductions:				
Sales returns and allowances	$ 35,076	$ 107,849		$ 142,925
Cash discount	23,830	67,596		91,426
Freight	56,629	163,673		220,302
Total deductions	$ 115,535	$ 339,118		$ 454,653
Net sales	$1,276,713	$3,458,397	$(224,519)	$4,510,591
Cost of goods sold	865,190	2,377,624	(224,519)	3,018,295
Gross profit	$ 411,523	$1,080,773		$1,492,296
Distribution expense:				
Selling	$ 144,597	$ 386,588		$ 531,185
Warehousing	39,714	84,685		124,399
Corporate advertising	15,238	41,262		56,500
Divisional advertising	31,016	83,984		115,000
Total distribution expense	$ 230,565	$ 596,519		$ 827,084
Administrative expense	17,134	46,397		63,531
Total divisional expense	$ 247,699	$ 642,916		$ 890,615
Division operating profit	$ 163,824	$ 437,857		$ 601,681
Central corporate charges‡	43,805	143,959		187,764
Net operating profit	$ 120,019	$ 293,898		$ 413,917

    * On the actual statement, separate columns were presented for each of the other eight product lines.
    †These amounts represent the "transfer value" of goods "sold" from one Sylvania department to another.
    ‡ These charges did not appear in the lighting division's general ledger. They were prorated to divisions for statement purposes only.

GENERAL MOTORS CORPORATION[1]

In an article in the NACA *Bulletin,* January 1, 1927, Mr. Albert Bradley described the pricing policy of General Motors Corporation. At that time Mr. Bradley was general assistant treasurer; subsequently, he became vice president, executive vice president and chairman of the board. There is reason to believe that current policy is substantially the same as that described in the 1927 statement. The following description consists principally of excerpts from Mr. Bradley's article.

General Policy

Return on investment is the basis of the General Motors policy in regard to the pricing of product. The fundamental consideration is the average return over a protracted period of time, not the specific rate of return over any particular year or short period of time. This long-time rate of return on investment represents the official viewpoint as to the highest average rate of return which can be expected consistent with a healthy growth of the business, and may be referred to as the economic return attainable. The adjudged necessary rate of return on capital will vary as between separate lines of industry, as a result of differences in their economic situation; and within each industry there will be important differences in return on capital resulting primarily from the relatively greater efficiency of certain producers.

The fundamental policy in regard to pricing of product and expansion of the business also necessitates an official viewpoint as to the normal average rate of plant operation. This relationship between assumed normal average rate of operation and practical annual capacity is known as *standard volume.*

The fundamental price policy is completely expressed in the conception of *standard volume* and *economic return* attainable. For example, if it is the accepted policy that *standard volume* represents 80% of practi-

---

[1] This case was prepared from published material.

cal annual capacity, and that an average of 20% per annum must be earned on the operating capital, it becomes possible to determine the *standard price* of a product; that is, that price, which with plants operating at 80% of capacity, will produce an annual return of 20% on the investment.

Standard Volume

Costs of production and distribution per unit of product vary with fluctuation in volume because of the fixed or nonvariable nature of some of the expense items. Productive materials and productive labor may be considered costs which are 100% variable, since within reasonable limits the aggregate varies directly with volume, and the cost per unit of product therefore remains uniform.

Among the items which are classified as manufacturing expense or burden, there exist varying degrees of fluctuation with volume, owing to their greater or lesser degree of variability. Among the absolutely fixed items are such expenses as depreciation, taxes, etc., which may be referred to as 100% fixed, since within the limits of plant capacity the aggregate will not change, but the amount per unit of product will vary in inverse ratio to the output.

There is another group of items which may be classified as 100% variable, such as inspection, material handling, etc., the amount of which per unit of product is unaffected by volume. Between the classes of 100% fixed and 100% variable there is a large group of expense items which are partially variable, such as light, heat, power, salaries, etc.

In General Motors Corporation, standard burden rates are developed for each "burden center" so that there will be included in costs a reasonable average allowance for manufacturing expense. In order to establish this rate, it is first necessary to obtain an expression of the estimated normal average rate of plant operation.

Rate of plant operation is affected by such factors as general business conditions; the extent of seasonal fluctuation in sales likely within years of large volume; policy with respect to seasonal accumulation of finished and/or semifinished product for the purpose of leveling the production curve; the necessity or desirability of maintaining excess plant capacity for emergency use; and many other factors. Each of these factors should be carefully considered by a manufacturer in the determination of size of a new plant to be constructed, and before making additions to existing plants, in order that there may be a logical relationship between assumed normal average rate of plant operation and practical annual capacity. The percentage accepted by General Motors Corporation as its policy in regard to the relationship between assumed normal rate of plant operation and practical annual capacity is referred to as standard volume.

Having determined the degree of the variability of manufacturing expense, the established total expense at the standard volume rate of operations can be estimated. A *standard burden rate* is then at standard volume. In periods of low volume, the unabsorbed manufacturing expense is charged directly against profits as unabsorbed burden, while in periods of high volume, the overabsorbed manufacturing expense is credited to profits, as overabsorbed burden.

Return on Investment

Factory costs and commercial expenses for the most part represent outlays by the manufacturer during the accounting period. An exception is depreciation of capital assets which have a greater length of life than the accounting period. To allow for this element of cost, there is included an allowance for depreciation in the burden rates used in compiling costs. Before an enterprise can be considered successful and worthy of continuation or expansion, however, there is still another element of cost which must be reckoned with. This is the cost of capital, including an allowance for profit.

Thus the calculation of standard prices of products necessitates the establishment of standards of capital requirement as well as expense factors representative of the normal average operating condition. The standard for capital employed in fixed assets is expressed as a percentage of factory cost, and the standards for working capital are expressed in part as a percentage of sales and in part as a percentage of factory cost.

The calculation of the standard allowance for fixed investment is illustrated by the following example:

Investment in plant and other fixed assets	$15,000,000
Practical annual capacity	50,000 units
Standard volume, percent of practical annual capacity	80%
Standard volume equivalent (50,000 x 80%)	40,000 units
Factory cost per unit at standard volume	$1,000
Annual factory cost of production at standard volume (40,000 x $1,000)	$40,000,000
Standard factor for fixed investment (ratio of investment to annual factory cost of production; $15,000,000 ÷ $40,000,000)	0.375

The amount tied up in working capital items should be directly proportionate to the volume of business. For example, raw materials on hand should be in direct proportion to the manufacturing requirements—so many days' supply of this material, so many days' supply of that material, and so on—depending upon the condition and location of sources of supply, transportation conditions, etc. Work in process should be in direct proportion to the requirements of finished production, since it is dependent upon the length of time required for the material to pass from the raw to the finished state and the amount of labor and other charges to be absorbed in the process. Finished product should be in direct proportion to sales requirements. Accounts receivable should be in direct proportion to sales, being dependent upon terms of payment and efficiency of collections.

The Standard Price

These elements are combined to construct the standard price as shown in Exhibit 1. Note that the economic return attainable (20% in the illustration) and the standard volume (80% in the illustration) are long-run figures and are rarely changed;[2] the other elements of the price are based on current estimates.

Differences among Products

Responsibility for investment must be considered in calculating the standard price of each product as well as in calculating the overall price for all products, since products with identical accounted costs may be responsible for investments which vary greatly. In the illustration given in Exhibit 1, a uniform standard selling price of $1,250 was determined. Let us now suppose that this organization makes and sells two products, A and B, with equal manufacturing costs of $1,000 per unit, equal working capital requirements, and that 20,000 units of each product are produced. However, an analysis of fixed investment indicates that $10 million is applicable to product A, while only $5 million of fixed investment is applicable to product B. Each product must earn 20% on its investment in order to satisfy the standard condition.

Exhibit 2 illustrates the determination of the standard price for product A and product B.

From this analysis of investment, it becomes apparent that product A, which has the heavier fixed investment, should sell for $1,278, while product B should sell for only $1,222, in order to produce a return of

---

[2] A Brookings Institution Survey reports that the principal pricing goal of General Motors Corporation is 20% on investment after taxes (see Lanzillotti, "Pricing Objectives in Large Companies," *American Economic Review* [December, 1958]).

20% on the investment. Were both products sold for the composite average standard price of $1,250, then product A would not be bearing its share of the investment burden, while product B would be correspondingly overpriced.

Differences in working capital requirements as between different products may also be important due to differences in manufacturing methods, sales terms, merchandising policies, etc. The inventory turnover rate of one line of products sold by a division of General Motors Corporation may be six times a year while inventory applicable to another line of products is turned over 30 times a year. In the latter case, the inventory investment required per dollar cost of sales is only one fifth of that required in the case of the product with the slower turnover.

Just as there are differences in capital requirements as between different classes of product, so may the standard requirements for the same class of product require modification from time to time due to permanent changes in manufacturing processes, in location of sources of supply, more efficient scheduling and handling of materials, etc.

The importance of this improvement to the buyer of General Motors products may be appreciated from the following example: The total inventory investment for the 12 months ended September 30, 1926 would have averaged $182,490,000 if the turnover rate of 1923 (the best performance prior to 1925) had not been bettered, or an excess of $74,367,000 over the actual average investment. In other words, General Motors would have been compelled to charge $14,873,000 more for its product during this 12-month period than was actually charged if prices had been established to yield, say, 20% on the operating capital required.

Conclusion

The analysis as to (1) the degree of variability of manufacturing and commercial expenses with increases or decreases in volume of output, and (2) the establishment of "standards" for the various investment items, makes it possible to develop "standard prices" for each product. The analysis also makes it easier to forecast, with much greater accuracy than otherwise would be possible, the capital requirements, profits, and return on capital at the different rates of operation which may result from seasonal conditions or from changes in the general business situation. Moreover, whenever it is necessary to calculate in advance the final effect on net profits of proposed increases or decreases in price, with their resulting changes in volume of output, consideration of the real economics of the situation is facilitated by the availability of reliable basic data.

It should be emphasized that the basic pricing policy stated in terms of the economic return attainable is a policy and does not absolutely dictate the specific price. At times the actual price may be above, and at other times below, the standard price. The standard price calculation affords a means not only of interpreting actual or proposed prices in relation to the established policy, but at the same time affords a practical demonstration as to whether the policy itself is sound. If the prevailing price of product is found to be at variance with the standard price other than to the extent due to temporary causes, it follows that prices should be adjusted; or else, in the event of conditions being such that prices cannot be brought into line with the standard price, the conclusion is necessarily drawn that the terms of the expressed policy must be modified.[3]

Questions

1. An article in the *Wall Street Journal*, December 10, 1957, gave estimates of cost figures in "an imaginary car-making division in the Ford-Chevrolet-Plymouth field." Most of the data given below are derived from that article. Using these data, compute the standard price. Working capital ratios are not given; assume that they are the same as those in Exhibit 1.

Investment in plant and other fixed assets............	$600,000,000
Required return on investment....................	30% before income taxes
Practical annual capacity........................	1,250,000
Standard volume................................	assume 80%

Factory cost per unit:

Outside purchases of parts.....................	$ 500*
Parts manufactured inside......................	600*
Assembly labor..............................	75
Burden......................................	125
Total...................................	$1,300

* Each of these items includes $50 of labor costs.

"Commercial cost," corresponding to the 7% in Exhibit 1, is added as a dollar amount, and includes the following:

Inbound and outbound freight......................	$ 85
Tooling and engineering...........................	50
Sales and advertising..............................	50
Administrative and miscellaneous...................	50
Warranty (repairs within guarantee)................	15
Total.......................................	$250

---

[3] This paragraph is taken from an article by Donaldson Brown, then vice president, finance, General Motors Corporation, in *Management and Administration* (March, 1924).

Therefore, the 7% Commercial Allowance in Exhibit 1 should be eliminated, and in its place, $250 should be added to the price as computed from the formula.

2. What would happen to profits and return on investment before taxes in a year in which volume was only 60% of capacity? What would happen in a year in which volume was 100% of capacity? Assume that nonvariable costs included in the $1,550 unit cost above are $350 million; that is, that variable costs are $1,550 − $350 = $1,200. In both situations, assume that cars were sold at the standard price established in Question 1, since the standard price is not changed to reflect annual changes in volume.

3. Is this policy good for General Motors? Is it good for America?

Exhibit 1

GENERAL MOTORS CORPORATION

ILLUSTRATION OF METHOD OF DETERMINATION OF STANDARD PRICE

	In Relation to—	Turnover per Year	Ratio to Sales, Annual Basis	Ratio to Factory Cost, Annual Basis
Cash	Sales	20 times	0.050	...
Drafts and accounts receivable	Sales	10 times	0.100	...
Raw material and work in process	Factory cost	6 times	...	$0.16\frac{2}{3}$
Finished product	Factory cost	12 times	...	$0.08\frac{1}{3}$
Gross working capital			0.150	0.250
Fixed investment			...	0.375
Total investment			0.150	0.625
Economic return attainable—20%			...	...
Multiplying the investment ratio by this, the necessary net profit margin is arrived at			0.030	0.125
Standard allowance for commercial expenses, 7%			0.070	...
Gross margin over factory cost			0.100(*a*)	0.125(*b*)

Selling price, as a ratio to factory cost $= \dfrac{1 + b}{1 - a} = \dfrac{1 + 0.125}{1 - 0.100} = 1.25$

If standard cost $= \$1,000$, then standard price $= \$1,000 \times 1.25 = \$1,250$.

Exhibit 2

GENERAL MOTORS CORPORATION

VARIANCES IN STANDARD PRICE DUE TO VARIANCES IN RATE OF CAPITAL TURNOVER

	Product A		Product B		Total Product (A Plus B)	
	Ratio to Sales, Annual Basis	Ratio to Factory Cost, Annual Basis	Ratio to Sales, Annual Basis	Ratio to Factory Cost, Annual Basis	Ratio to Sales, Annual Basis	Ratio to Factory Cost, Annual Basis
Gross working capital	0.150	0.250	0.150	0.250	0.150	0.250
Fixed investment	—	0.500	...	0.250	...	0.375
Total investment	0.150	0.750	0.150	0.500	0.150	0.625
Economic return attainable—20%	—	...	...	...	...	...
Multiplying the investment ratio by this, the necessary net profit margin is arrived at	0.030	0.150	0.030	0.100	0.030	0.125
Standard allowance for commercial expenses, 7%	0.070		0.070		0.070	
Gross margin over factory cost	0.100(a)	0.150(b)	0.100(a)	0.100(b)	0.100(a)	0.125(b)
Selling price, as a ratio to factory cost $(1 + b/1 - a)$	$\dfrac{1. + 0.150}{1. - 0.100} = 1.278$		$\dfrac{1. + 0.100}{1. - 0.100} = 1.222$		$\dfrac{1. + 0.125}{1. - 0.100} = 1.250$	
If standard cost equals $1,000, then standard price equals	$1,278		$1,222		$1,250	

BENTON TEXTILES, INC.[1]

After experimenting for a period of about two years, Benton Textiles, Inc., had perfected the machinery and process for applying a special finish to certain types of textiles.

The company was a finisher of textile materials; that is, it took cloth manufactured by others and printed, dyed, or otherwise converted it to a desired finished product. It did not purchase, and therefore did not own, the cloth but simply took cloth furnished to it by textile manufacturers or distributors and applied the desired finishing processes at an agreed-upon rate per linear yard. The rate of course varied with the nature of the material and processes involved, the size of the order, and the competitive situation. The backbone of the business, with respect to sustained operations, was in the finishing of relatively staple goods, but the real profitability of operations depended upon the continual development of novelty goods which had a relatively short style life but for which the consuming public was willing to pay a premium as long as the goods were in style.

The new process mentioned in the first paragraph above produced a new type of novelty goods, and having developed the machinery and process to a satisfactory point, the company was ready to solicit business for the new product. There were several problems, however, in connection with solicitation, the most important of which could be summarized in the two questions: (1) What type of market should the company solicit? (2) What price should the company charge for its process?

The new process was applicable to goods that would be used for women's dresses, especially evening dresses, and it could also be applied to a variety of materials that would be used for upholstery. In the opinion of the management of Benton Textiles, Inc., the acceptance of the product in the upholstery market was more uncertain than in the dress goods market and would involve much higher promotion expense. Ac-

---

[1] Used with permission from Clarence B. Nickerson, *Managerial Cost Accounting and Analysis* (New York, McGraw-Hill Book Co., Inc., 1962).

cordingly, the management decided to concentrate on sales to the manufacturers and distributors of dress materials, though samples would be sent to manufacturers and distributors of upholstery materials and whatever upholstery business might result from this relatively inexpensive type of solicitation would be accepted if a satisfactory price could be obtained.

In the dress goods field the company faced a problem as to the class of trade it should seek. The new process could be applied to one type of cloth which retailed for $5 to $8 per yard and was used for the more expensive dresses, or it could be applied to another type of cloth which retailed for $2.50 to $3.50 per yard. In each case the processed cloth would not only be retailed as yard goods for retail customers who made their own dresses but would also be sold to cutters who manufactured dresses.

In an effort to determine what probable volume and prices could be obtained in each of these two fields, the company processed a variety of samples and one of the executives, Ralph Benton, spent a little over two months in New York calling on manufacturers and distributors of dress materials. In addition to gaining knowledge in these contacts, Benton had accepted several trial orders at relatively low prices in order that the manufacturers and distributors might test reactions to the products in their markets.

Benton's general procedure in calling on a buyer was to show him samples of goods that would all fall within a limited price range, and after getting the buyer to agree that the goods were attractive, Benton would quote a price that was considerably higher than he hoped to get. The buyer would usually state that he could not possibly handle the goods if he had to pay that much for the process to be applied by Benton Textiles, Inc., and would then make an offer of about half the quoted price. At this stage Benton would pick up his samples and start for the door, whereupon the buyer would call him back and tell him that he liked the appearance of the goods but not the price. The two would then get down to bargaining in earnest and in a good portion of the cases were able to arrive at a price that was mutually satisfactory.

On the basis of this procedure, Benton concluded that in the higher-priced type of goods, it would be possible to get from 30 to 70 cents per linear yard for the Benton process, with an average of 40 cents per linear yard.[2] For the cheaper goods it would be possible to get from 26 to 40 cents per linear yard, with the average at about 34 cents.[2] The differ-

---

[2] Note that these prices covered only the process applied by Benton Textiles, Inc. Since Benton would not own the cloth, it would be paid only for the finishing operation.

ences in price within each type of goods would result from differences in the value of the cloth handled,[3] differences in the amount of material added to the cloth by the Benton process, differences in the complexity of the process as between one type of goods and another, the current competitive situation, and bargaining.

With respect to total demand, Benton had been unable to obtain any idea through his contacts as to the volume that could be expected for processing the higher-priced type of material. The current interest of buyers for this type of product seemed to be reasonably good, and some of the fashion magazines were featuring evening dresses made from Benton-processed materials that had reached the market through the trial orders accepted by Benton as mentioned above. On the other hand, the styles and materials featured by the fashion magazines were often two years ahead of general acceptance, and the market for high-priced materials was extremely fickle.

At the current time there were no competitive products that could compare at all favorably with the goods converted under the Benton process, but this situation resulted for the most part from skill in processing and a secret formula developed by Benton Textiles, Inc., rather than from protection through patents. Furthermore, textile manufacturers were busy developing a process whereby material that looked like the Benton-processed material could be made completely on the loom and would therefore not have to be subjected to the additional finishing operation.

Benton Textiles, Inc., had investigated this situation and found that the mills were faced with technical difficulties that would take at least two years to be ironed out. Furthermore, it was likely that the Benton process would always be less expensive than the mill process that was being developed. On the other hand, the mill process was more flexible and could be used in turning out a wider variety of designs than was possible under the Benton process. In fact, the mills had produced some limited trial orders in a range of designs that the Benton process could not touch and the response was so good that even though the mills could not meet orders because of technical difficulties, the interest aroused might, in such a fickle market, kill the interest in Benton-processed goods of all types. As yet there was no indication that this had happened, but it was within the realm of possibility.

---

[3] The higher the price for either type of cloth, the greater was the margin between manufacturing or purchasing cost and selling price. For this reason manufacturers and distributors of dress goods could be induced to pay more for the Benton process on higher-priced goods.

With respect to the lower-priced materials, Benton was convinced that enough business could be obtained without much effort to run the process at 100% single-shift capacity.[4] He believed that once this market had been opened, it could be counted on for two to three years. Thereafter, the demand might die down, to return some years later, or it might never return. Benton also believed that once this lower-priced market had been opened, it would not be possible to sell in the higher-priced market, because the appearance of the two types of goods was so similar that the more exclusive trade would not be interested in material that could be duplicated so easily in lower-priced dresses.

It has already been stated that the lower-priced goods market would not stand as high charges for the Benton process as would the higher-priced goods market, the expected average charge being 34 cents compared to 40 cents per linear yard. Furthermore, because of the nature of the goods, it was necessary to run the machinery more slowly when working on the lower-priced goods. For example, the 100% single-shift operating capacity working exclusively on the higher-priced goods was estimated to be 1,600,000 linear yards per year (Exhibit 1), whereas the company estimated that the 100% single-shift operating capacity working exclusively on the lower-priced goods would be 1,400,-000 linear yards.

The company had two machines for applying the process and did not contemplate the addition of any more machines. The process on both machines was identical, but one machine was designed to handle narrow widths and the other wider widths. It was expected that the total business received would be about evenly divided between narrow widths and wider widths, whether the company sought the higher-priced goods business or the lower-priced business.

Before deciding which of the two markets should be sought, the company worked out estimates of income and expense. The estimates for the higher-priced goods at 100% single-shift capacity (1,600,000 linear yards) and 10% single-shift capacity (160,000 linear yards) are

---

[4] Later in the case it is stated that the company had two machines for applying its process. Operation at 100% single-shift capacity meant operating both machines 40 hours per week for 50 weeks. In figuring the yardage that could be handled, allowance had to be made for setup time involved in changing from one lot of goods to another. For example, in the higher-priced type of goods it was estimated that production would average 500 yards per hour per machine, once the machine had been made ready. The setup time would be approximately two hours, and the company considered that the desirable ratio of setup time to running time would be one to four. Thus a 4,000-yard lot would require two hours for setups and eight hours for running time (500 per hour), and the average production would be 400 yards per hour for the total time spent on the lot.

presented in Exhibit 1. The company also computed the income (margin per hour per machine, over and above compensation for material) that it would receive on a 4,000-yard order (considered to be an economical lot size) at a price of 40 cents per linear yard (Exhibit 2A). Computations were also made of the prices that would have to be asked for quantities above and below a 4,000-yard order to realize the same income per hour as would be realized when working on a 4,000-yard order. The computation for a 3,000-yard order is shown in Exhibit 2B. Such computation took into account only variance in the size of the lot, but the actual price charged would depend also upon the quantity of material to be added to the cloth in the process, the value of the goods being processed, the complications that might be involved in the given lot, the current competitive situation, and bargaining with the buyer.

Question

As Mr. Benton's assistant, you are asked to write a brief report expressing your opinion on the two questions raised in the third paragraph of the case. You should support your comments with whatever quantitative analysis you consider appropriate. If you think there is additional information which should be obtained before the decision is made, indicate concisely the nature of the additional information.

Exhibit 1

BENTON TEXTILES, INC.

ESTIMATED INCOME AND EXPENSE WORKING EXCLUSIVELY ON HIGHER-
PRICED GOODS

	Single-Shift Operations	
	10%	100%
Sales (at $0.40 per linear yard)......................	$64,000	$640,000
Cost of goods sold:		
Materials ($0.18* per linear yard).................	$28,800	$288,000
Labor (number of employees indicated in parentheses):		
First operation...............................(2)	$ 5,000	(3) $ 8,000
Second operation ....(1)	1,800	(2) 3,600
Third operation.............................(1)	1,800	(2) 3,600
Floor boy....................................(1)	1,500	(2) 3,000
Supervision and design.......................(1)	5,000	(1) 10,000
	$15,100	$ 28,200
Manufacturing expense:		
Power and light..............................	$ 800	$ 2,000
Heat...	600	1,000
Taxes:		
Real estate and excise........................	400	600
Social security...............................	600	1,000
Insurance....................................	1,000	1,400
Depreciation.................................	7,200	7,200
Repairs......................................	600	1,000
Sundries.....................................	1,000	1,000
	$12,200	$ 15,200
Total cost of goods sold....................	$56,100	$331,400
Gross profit......................................	$ 7,900	$308,600
Selling and administrative expense:		

	10%	100%		
Salaries:				
Executive....................$5,000	$10,000			
Office...................... 3,000	4,000	$ 8,000		$ 14,000
Telephone.......................................		1,200		1,200
Postage and office..............................		1,600		2,000
Shipping..		(by factory)	(3)	6,000
Commissions and factoring (10%).................		6,400		64,000
Total selling and administration..............		$17,200		$ 87,200
Net profit...		$ 9,300 (loss)		$221,400

* The cost of materials consumed in the process was expected to be 18 cents per yard for both the higher- and lower-priced goods. All other costs were expected to be the same in total for the higher- and lower-priced goods, except for commissions which would be 10% of selling price for either class of goods.

Exhibit 2

BENTON TEXTILES, INC.

A. Computation of income per hour over and above cost of material on 4,000-yard lot of higher-priced material:

4,000 yards at $0.40 per yard	$1,600.00
Material added in the Benton process ($0.18 per yard)	720.00
Income over and above cost of material	$ 880.00
Setup time	2 hours
Running time (4,000 yards ÷ 500 yards per hour)	8
Total time to process 4,000 yards	10 hours
Income per hour over and above cost of material (880 ÷ 10)	$ 88.00

B. Computation of selling price required on 3,000-yard order to realize the same return of $88 per hour as in A above:

Setup time	2 hours
Running time (3,000 yards ÷ 500 yards per hour)	6
Total time to process 3,000 yards	8 hours
Desired return per hour over and above material cost	$ 88.00
Multiplication of hours by desired return	$ 704.00
Conversion to desired return per yard (704 ÷ 3,000 yards)	$ 0.234
Material cost per yard	0.180
Required selling price per yard	$ 0.414

LIQUID CLEANSE

In early October 1961, Mr. Robert Rudd, product controller for Liquid Cleanse, was given his first major assignment by his immediate superior, Mr. Keith Langan. Mr. Rudd had been employed by Home Cleaning Products upon his graduation from a school of business the prior June but had only recently been promoted into his present position. Mr. Langan asked Mr. Rudd to make an analysis of the effectiveness of the Liquid Cleanse supplemental spending (promotional expenditures authorized to supplement the original budget authorization) in the Philadelphia and Atlanta sales districts for the September quarter of 1961.

This analysis was prompted by a memorandum from Mr. Finn, general manager of the Home Cleaning Products division, asking for an evaluation of promotional effectiveness in these two districts. The pertinent section of his memorandum read as follows:

> The Philadelphia district underspent its budget by $9,910 while the Atlanta district overspent its budget by $4,380 and produced actual sales that were 106% of budget (7,140 excess units) while Philadelphia produced only 98% of budget (a deficit of 12,180). Which of the districts performed more effectively and what accounted for the excess units in one case and the deficit units in the other? It would appear that the Atlanta district met its goal while the Philadelphia district failed to do so. Please apprise me of the effectiveness of the promotional funds spent in these two areas and make any recommendations which you feel would be of assistance in controlling promotional spending and in evaluating sales performance in these two areas.

With Mr. Finn's request in mind, Mr. Rudd began his search for information and data which would enable him to appraise the results of the supplemental spending.

Organization and Product Line

Home Cleaning Products, headquartered in Chicago, Illinois, was one of the larger divisions of American Cleansing Corporation. It produced the following detergents: Cleanse and Liquid Cleanse, Yes and Liquid Yes, White-All and Liquid White-All. The granulated detergents were packed in sizes ranging from one-half pound to one pound, while the liquid detergents generally came in 4-, 8-, and 16-ounce sizes. Each of these products was the responsibility of a product manager who made decisions relative to pricing, advertising, and promotional expenditures, and other questions of marketing strategy. Robert Rudd was responsible to both Mr. Steinmark, product manager for Liquid Cleanse and to Mr. Langan, department head—financial analysis. He reported directly to Mr. Langan but acted as a staff advisor, analyst, and "vest pocket controller" for Mr. Steinmark (see Exhibit 1). Each individual brand was regarded as an independent segment of the business and was operated as a separate and autonomous unit within the Home Cleaning Products division.

From this organization, the concept of brand controllership emerged. This concept specified that each product brand would be assigned a vest pocket controller who should function in a dual capacity as an objective critic of product management performance and as an active member of the product management team. Mr. Rudd's job description (product controller) specified the following functions:

1. Assist the product manager in his efforts to improve the performance, and ultimately, the financial position of its product through:
   a) Control of promotional expenditures;
   b) Evaluation of promotional efforts;
   c) Analysis of historical, economic, and competitive data pertinent to the product.
2. Report to financial management on the performance of product management in meeting agreed-upon objectives.
3. Assist the product group in reporting financial data to management in the long-range, annual, and quarterly marketing plans.
4. Keep track of changes in financial and statistical data pertinent to his product, for example, volumes, margins, costs, etc., and coordinate the communication of this data between product management and financial management.

The continental United States was divided into seven sales regions which were further subdivided into sales districts. The Philadelphia district was in the eastern region, while the Atlanta district was in the southern region. Philadelphia was located in a "high liquid-preference area," or one in which liquid detergents and Liquid Cleanse had met with strong consumer acceptance. Atlanta, on the other hand, was in an "area of low liquid-perference" and one in which major competition was relatively strong.

Home Cleaning Products normally used one, or a combination, of several types of promotion plans. First, and most widely used, was the "label pack." Under this plan each package carried a special label which stated the amount of the price reduction included in the package price, that is, "6 cents off," "12 cents off." This promotion plan might be tied in with national or regional advertising to bring the price reduction to the retail consumer's attention. The plan would remain in effect until all of the specially priced pack had passed from the company to the wholesalers. The second type of plan was the "feature payment." Under this plan, the retailer was given a reduction in price for every case which he purchased during the time period when he was pushing the product in local advertising, window displays, store displays, etc. This offer was open to the retailer for a limited time only (a few days to several weeks), as opposed to the label pack which was in effect until sold to the trade. The third promotional device was the "buying allowance" which was nothing more than a discount per case given to the wholesaler or retailer. This plan was thought to be less reliable than the label pack, since Home Cleaning Products could not be certain that the price reduction given the wholesaler would be passed on to the retail consumer.

ANALYSIS OF PHILADELPHIA DISTRICT
Original Marketing Strategy

The Philadelphia district manager had originally requested and received a promotion budget of $76,800, which was expected to generate the sale of 508,000 units (a unit of liquid detergent was defined as 48 ounces) in the September quarter of 1961. However, on July 3, he requested a supplemental budget of $32,280, which he predicted would generate an additional sales volume of 27,000 units. His request for additional funds contained the following predictions and marketing rationale:

> That additional promotional spending of $32,280 be authorized. These funds are expected to generate an incremental volume of 27,000 units in this quarter without adversely affecting the planned normal quarter-ending retail inventories of 1.4 months' supply. Based on the planned contribution margin of $2 per incremental unit, this spending will result in $21,720 increase in profit before tax.

The rationale for this increased promotional spending was as follows:

1. Liquid Cleanse has suffered substantial share losses during recent months in this market. Our audit shows the following bimonthly market shares:

June–July	Aug.–Sept.	Oct.–Nov.	Dec.–Jan.	Feb.–Mar.	Apr.–May
48.8%	48.2%	47.1%	45.9%	43.4%	40.4%

Our strategy in using the supplemental promotion dollars is to reverse this declining trend by increasing the percent of the total quarter's sales covered by promotions from 55% to 68% while maintaining the present allowance per can.

Because the 8-ounce can accounts for the largest percent of the total volume in the area and since the 8-ounce size has been most susceptible to inroads by Liquid Yes, it has been decided that a 59-cent shelf price will be maintained on the 8-ounce can during the majority of the quarter. Research is not available, but it is strongly believed that the quality image will not be adversely affected by a label continually on the shelf. In addition, one 16-ounce promotion is planned to insure that the volume gains made to date are not lost by a continued price advantage on the 8-ounce size.

See Exhibit 2 for detail on the planned total promotion program including the supplemental budget.

2. The group plans not only to reverse the declining share trend and recapture the lost share but also to introduce Liquid Cleanse to nonusers, and to generate new momentum, thus strengthening the product's long-term acceptance in this area.

The request for the supplemental budget of $32,280 was approved on July 6, 1961 by the general manager, and the district sales manager proceeded to implement the outlined marketing promotion plan.

Results of Marketing Strategy

As shown in Exhibit 2, the plan fell short of its unit goal by 12,180 units but resulted in budget savings of $9,910. Thus, Mr. Rudd concluded, the group had achieved 98% of its unit goal on only 91% of budgeted expense.

Liquid Cleanse's share of the market increased from 42.9% in June–July to 45% in Aug.–Sept. as shown in Exhibit 3. These figures came from the Home Cleaning Product's bimonthly audit, which was compiled from store audit sample results taken from various geographical test areas across the United States. The audit measured retail share of the market, not wholesale share. This report showed that the inroads previously being made by Liquid Yes were halted. Mr. Rudd also learned that the Liquid Yes marketing group had spent 23 cents per unit on promotion in the quarter. Intelligence on competitor spending was generally available only with a three- to four-month delay. Thus, no information was available on current promotional spending per unit by competitors, but indications were that it would be 10% to 20% above prior quarter spending. Liquid Cleanse had been spending from 16 cents to 19 cents per unit on promotion in each of the six preceding quarters.

The retail inventory level declined to 0.7 months of supply, and it was apparent to Mr. Rudd that the goal of not exceeding the 1.4 months of supply level had been attained as of September 30. However, the inventory control section of the product group indicated that whole-sale stocks had increased by 31,800 units, as shown in Exhibit 4. These figures were based on actual counts where possible, but in many cases estimates of stock levels were the only means of obtaining a stock count. It was estimated that these figures were accurate within limits of ± 20%.

Conclusion on Philadelphia District

Mr. Rudd thought he now had the data he needed to appraise the effectiveness of promotional spending in the Philadelphia district. At first glance, it appeared to Mr. Rudd that the district had met its objectives based on the following reasoning: (1) actual volume was 98% of planned volume, while actual cost was only 91% of budgeted cost; (2) the promotion plan had increased market share from 40.4% to 45%; (3) shelf pricing had been maintained at the 59-cent level; (4) the allowance per can had not been increased; (5) 85% of the 8-ounce and 16-ounce volume was moved through promotions; (6) retail inventories had been held below the 1.4 months of supply level. However, before he submitted a report to the general manager, he wanted to make a more detailed analysis of the information he had compiled to make certain that his first impression was correct.

ANALYSIS OF ATLANTA DISTRICT

Original Marketing Strategy

Atlanta was in a competitive infringement area, or one in which Home Cleaning Products was being severely challenged by its major national competitor. Thus, competition in this district was much more severe than in the Philadelphia district. Since brand D was the chief competitor in this area, the Liquid Cleanse product manager was partic-ularly interested in its activity in drawing up his own marketing strat-egy.

The original promotion budget of $41,640 was expected to generate the sale of 102,000 units. However, on July 10, the product manager requested a supplemental budget of $39,600, which he predicted would generate the incremental sale of 12,000 units. Relevant excerpts from his request are reproduced below:

> The product group recommends that additional promotional spending of $39,600 for the current quarter be authorized. These extra funds are expected to generate an incremental volume of 12,000 units during the quarter without adversely affecting the planned normal quarter-ending inventories of 1.4 months of supply. Based on the planned contribution margin of $2 per incremental unit, this spending will result in a $15,600 decrease in profit before tax.

The rationale for this increased promotional spending was as follows:

1. To continue the program started in the prior quarter of maintaining comparable retail pricing with major competitors in those territories (each district was subdivided into several territories) where the brand has been consistently underpriced for a considerable period of time.

The monthly price differential report (Exhibit 5) indicated the price differential existing between Liquid Cleanse and its major competitors. In addition to these facts, it was known that the modal price on Liquid Cleanse was 58 cents, while brand D's modal price was 53 cents or under.

Brand D had been averaging an allowance of 15 cents per 8-ounce can and 22 cents per 16-ounce can during the prior quarter. It was proposed that Liquid Cleanse increase its 8-ounce allowance to 13 cents (12-cent label pack plus feature payment offers) per can and its 16-ounce allowance to 21 cents (18-cent label pack plus feature payment offers) per can, thus reducing its shelf price to a parity level. Major competitors had been using 12-cent and 18-cent label packs for the past several months.

2. To reverse the declining share trend performance in this market, to recapture lost share points, and to sample nonusers by achieving pricing parity and stimulating feature activity.

The following marketing shares had been reported:

	June–July	Aug.–Sept.	Oct.–Nov.	Dec.–Jan.	Feb.–Mar.	Apr.–May
Liquid Cleanse	31.2	28.2	25.7	27.2	24.3	26.2
Brand D	14.3	13.6	15.1	17.4	20.4	18.1
Brand F	3.6	5.7	4.8	5.7	8.5	8.2
Brand E	15.6	16.8	21.4	16.7	15.7	15.0

3. To inhibit the growth of brand D in the liquid detergent market by maintaining competitive pricing and gaining feature support. This is particu-

larly important since brand D has increased its share of the market from 10.6% Feb.–Mar. 1960 to 20.4% Feb.–Mar. 1961, while our share during the same period has declined from 33.5 to 24.3%. (The base periods are not shown above.)

To achieve these objectives, the brand's basic dealing strategy was as follows:

1. The use of label pack as the basic promotion to insure shelf price reflection and controllable costs. See Exhibit 2 for detail on the planned total promotion program including the supplemental allocation.

2. Off-label values designed to provide Liquid Cleanse with shelf price parity or, at the most, a 5-cent differential on both the 8-ounce and 16-ounce sizes. It was believed that Liquid Cleanse could contain competition with a slightly lower value offer (no more than 3 to 6 cents) because of its superior name and consumer acceptance. It was planned that label packs of the 8-ounce and 16-ounce sizes should be a quantity that was equivalent to the projected quarter's sales of these two sizes. Both labels will be offered immediately and continue until the allotment is sold.

The request for the supplemental budget of $39,600 was approved on July 12, 1960 by the general manager, and the district sales manager proceeded to implement the strategy outlined above.

Results of Planned Strategy

The planned promotion resulted in an actual volume that exceeded planned volume by 7,140 units, but additional promotional expense of $4,380 was also incurred (Exhibit 2). It appeared that both volume and expense were 5% to 6% above budget.

The market share held by Liquid Cleanse increased from 28.5% in June–July to 31.5% in Aug.–Sept., thus reversing the declining market share trend by the end of the quarter, as shown in Exhibit 3. It also appeared to Mr. Rudd that brand D's market encroachment had been contained since their share dropped from a high of 20.4% in Feb.–Mar. to 17.4% in Aug.–Sept., although their market share did increase since the June–July reporting period. Mr. Rudd learned from marketing research sources that brand D had spent an average of 29 cents per unit on promotion in the prior (June) quarter and that they were expected to have increased this by 20% to 30% in the quarter under consideration. Final data was not available on competitive promotional spending, but it was known that Liquid Cleanse had achieved shelf price parity (within + 3 cents to + 4 cents) in the quarter. Liquid Cleanse had spent an average of 21 cents per unit on promotion during the preceding three quarters.

During the fourth quarter, wholesale stocks increased by 7,800 units in total, while deal (label pack) units increased to 40,800 units, an increase of 15,000 over the preceding quarter (Exhibit 4).

Conclusion on Atlanta District

Mr. Rudd tentatively summarized promotion effectiveness in the Atlanta district as follows: (1) budgeted volume was exceeded by 6% with an attendant increase in cost of only 5%, (2) the promotion plan had increased market share to 31.5%, (3) brand D's market share advance had been contained, (4) shelf pricing was approximately equivalent to that of major competition (within $+3$ cents to $+4$ cents), (5) 94% of the 8-ounce and 16-ounce volume were promoted units, (6) retail inventories appeared to be holding at about 1.4 months of supply level.

Question

As Mr. Rudd, prepare a report for Mr. Finn in response to his memorandum quoted in the third paragraph of the case.

Exhibit 1

LIQUID CLEANSE

PARTIAL ORGANIZATION CHART

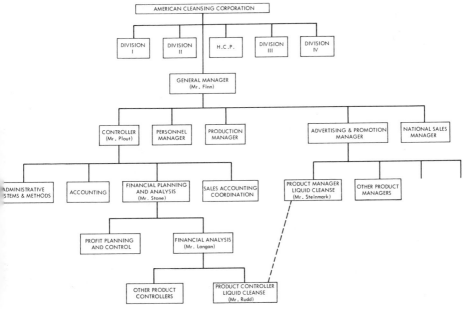

Exhibit 2. LIQUID CLEANSE

REVISED PLAN FOR TOTAL SPENDING AND ACTUAL RESULTS ACHIEVED, SEPTEMBER QUARTER 1961
(Including amount of supplemental authorization)

Type of Plan	Effective Date (All 1961)	Planned Sales Units	Planned Sales Cost	Actual Sales to Wholesale and Retail Trade Units	Actual Sales to Wholesale and Retail Trade Cost*
Philadelphia District					
4¢ label pack/8 oz.	July 12	126,000	$ 30,240	125,640	$30,143
4¢ label pack/8 oz.	August 1	126,000	30,240	122,640	29,430
6¢ label pack/16 oz.	August 4	103,680	33,600	95,220	24,897
Label pack totals		355,680	$ 94,080	343,500	$84,470
Feature payments	July 12–August 1		15,000		14,700
Straight pack/4 oz.		78,500		78,500	
Straight pack/8 oz.					
Straight pack/16 oz.		101,500		101,500	
Total budgeted volume and cost for quarter		535,680	$109,080		
Total actual volume and cost for quarter				523,500	$99,170

Actual cost as percent of planned cost: $99,170/$109,080 = 91%.
Actual units as percent of planned units: 523,500/535,680 = 98%.

Type of Plan	Effective Date (All 1961)	Planned Sales Units	Planned Sales Cost	Actual Sales to Wholesale and Retail Trade Units	Actual Sales to Wholesale and Retail Trade Cost*
Atlanta District					
12¢ label pack/8 oz.	July 10	62,100	$56,160	62,730	$56,590
18¢ label pack/16 oz.	July 25	20,250	14,580	24,360	16,380
18¢ label pack/16 oz.	August 7	11,250	8,100	13,650	10,080
Label pack totals		93,600	$78,840	100,740	$83,050
Feature payments	July 10–August 25		2,400		2,370
Straight pack/4 oz.		13,900		13,900	
Straight pack/8 oz.					
Straight pack/16 oz.		6,500		6,500	
Total budget volume and cost for quarter		114,000	$81,240		
Total actual volume and cost for quarter				121,140	$85,420

Actual cost as percent of planned cost: $85,420/$81,240 = 105.4%
Actual units as percent of planned units: 121,140/114,000 = 106.3%

* Includes amounts of approximately $1,800 in Philadelphia and $600 in Atlanta for the estimated amounts of offers taken by the trade but not yet submitted to the home office for

Exhibit 3

LIQUID CLEANSE

MARKET SHARE REPORT FOR AUGUST–SEPTEMBER 1961
(Abstracted)

Brand	Philadelphia District								Atlanta District							
	Share of Market			Consumption*			Retail Inventories		Share of Market			Consumption*			Retail Inventories	
	Year Ago	Previous Period	Current Period	Units	Percent Change vs. Year Ago	Percent Change vs. Previous Period	Units	Months of Supply	Year Ago	Previous Period	Current Period	Units	Percent Change vs. Year Ago	Percent Change vs. Previous Period	Units	Months of Supply
Total liquid as a % total of market	43.8	45.0	n.a.	780,000	4.1	12.7	378,000	1.0	15.2	14.0	n.a.	210,000	3.1	8.0	249,000	2.3
Liquid Cleanse	48.6	42.9	45.0	351,000	−3.7	18.2	120,000	0.7	28.3	28.5	31.5	66,000	14.6	19.4	51,600	1.5
Liquid Yes	11.0	8.7	7.8	64,800	...	7.1	26,400	0.8	...	0.3	0.2	...	...	−50.0	2,400	12.0
Brand C	...	10.1	10.2	79,800	3.5	14.4	56,400	1.4	5.1	4.8	3.8	8,040	−23.0	−14.4	11,400	2.9
Brand D	...	...	...	...	...	...	...	...	13.6	16.9	17.4	36,900	31.2	11.3	49,800	2.7
Brand E	...	...	...	...	...	...	...	...	16.9	16.5	15.8	33,600	3.3	3.1	27,000	1.6
Liquid White-All	6.8	6.8	6.9	54,000	−6.3	14.1	30,600	1.1	13.2	14.2	13.4	28,500	4.6	2.5	19,800	1.4
Brand F	10.6	11.5	9.4	73,800	−7.4	−7.5	30,600	0.8	4.3	4.0	3.8	8,040	−9.6	2.5	12,840	3.2

* Unit consumption measured only retail sales, i.e., "sales off the shelf" and did not reflect the amount by which trade (wholesale) inventories increased or decreased during a given period. Thus unit consumption was not equivalent to invoiced sales. The % change values were also affected by the constantly changing size of the retail market from one bimonthly period to another. The Philadelphia market was 780,000 units in Aug.–Sept. 1961, 749,300 units in Aug.–Sept. 1960 (780,000 ÷ 104.1), and 692,100 units in June–July 1961 (780,000 ÷ 112.7), a seasonal low. Liquid Cleanse consumption at retail was 364,200 units in Aug.–Sept. 1960 (749,300 × 48.6%), 296,900 units in June–July 1961 (692,100 × 42.9%), and 351,000 units in Aug.–Sept. 1961 (780,000 × 45%). Liquid Cleanse retail consumption in Aug.–Sept. 1961 was down 3.7% from Aug.–Sept. 1960 (364,200 − 351,000 ÷ 351,000). Liquid Cleanse consumption in Aug.–Sept. 1961, however, was 18.2% above the smaller June–July 1961 market (351,000 − 296,900 ÷ 296,900).

Exhibit 4

LIQUID CLEANSE

WHOLESALE STOCK COUNTS
(Quarters ending March, June, and September, 1961)

	March Quarter				June Quarter					September Quarter					Total Change in Stock June–Sept (units)	Gain or Loss in Label Pack (units)
	Total Units	Label Pack Units			Total Units	Label Pack Units			Deal Units, % of Total	Label Pack Units			Total Units	Deal Units, % of Total		
		8 oz	16 oz	Total		8 oz	16 oz	Total		8 oz	16 oz	Total				
Philadelphia district	126,600	2,400	4,800	7,200	134,400		1,200	1,200	1.3%	45,600	78,000	123,600	166,200	74%	31,800	122,400
Atlanta district	34,800			4,800	35,400	13,800	12,000	25,800	73.0	25,800	15,000	40,800	43,200	95	7,800	15,000

Exhibit 5

LIQUID CLEANSE

PRICE DIFFERENTIALS—LIQUID CLEANSE VERSUS MAJOR COMPETITORS

Average Shelf Prices, April–May 1960

————————8-oz.————————			————————16-oz.————————		
Liquid Cleanse	*Brand D*	*Brand F*	*Liquid Cleanse*	*Brand D*	*Brand F*
$0.64	$0.56	$0.55	$1.03	$0.86	$0.86

Percent of 8-oz. Sales at 59 Cents or Below*

	November	*December*	*January*	*February*	*March*	*April*	*May*	*June*
Liquid Cleanse.....	27%	32%	35%	30%	37%	37%	36%	38%
Brand D..........	50	53	53	51	51	51	48	50

Special Weekly Pricing Report Made by Sales Department (Period Covered, May 15–June 26)

	⎯Liquid Cleanse Price⎯		⎯⎯⎯Competitive Differential† (in cents)⎯⎯⎯		
	Normal Shelf	*Lowest Shelf*	*Brand D*	*Brand F*	*Brand E*
8-oz........	$0.69	$0.57	+0 to −9	+3 to −8	+3 to −6
16-oz........	1.13	0.95	+0 to −15	−2 to −18	+0 to −14

* Percent of 16-oz. sales at $0.96 or below is not available.
† + = More than Liquid Cleanse price for the size; − = Less than Liquid Cleanse price for the size.

Chapter 8

COMPETITIVE BIDDING

In the last chapter we discussed pricing decisions. We assumed that there were many people willing to consider purchasing the product and that as the price of the product was increased fewer and fewer people would buy the product. This phenomena resulted in demand curves such as the ones shown in Chapter 7. Many individual decisions of whether or not to buy the product at a given price could be summarized in such a curve, and it could be used to analyze pricing decisions. When the costs were constant for all price levels, the best price resulted where the revenue was maximized or at the price where the product of price and volume from the curve was the greatest.

You should realize that the exact volume to be sold for any given price is not known with certainty. However, if the volume is large enough compared with the amount of the uncertainty, you can use some point forecast of demand to represent volume for each price level. This will allow you to generate a demand curve and perform the analysis as though there were no uncertainty in the volume to be sold.

In this chapter we want to consider a special pricing problem where there is only one buyer interested in purchasing a product and several sellers who are willing to sell it. If you were one of the sellers, you would be faced with a competitive bidding situation. This might occur because the buyer wanted a customized product that you did not carry in inventory and he would ask you for a price quotation. This price would be your bid, and he would compare it to bids from other sellers. We will assume the buyer will accept the lowest bid from all of the sellers who can provide a product of equal quality in the same time period. This problem is quite common for companies selling customized goods or services. Another version of the competitive bidding problem often results when several buyers want to buy a product or service that is limited in quantity. For example, land sales are often conducted under bidding procedures. As one of the potential buyers, you would submit a bid and the seller would sell the product to the highest bidder. We will concentrate our discussion on the first case where the decision maker is the seller. However, the ideas and concepts will apply equally as well to a competitive bid where the decision maker is a buyer.

The competitive bidding problem cannot be analyzed like the problems in the last chapter because no useful demand curve exists. Since there is only one buyer, each potential price or bid will result in this buyer either accepting or rejecting, and thus the volume associated with each price is either one or zero. The bidding problem is further complicated because the uncertainty about whether or not this one buyer will accept or reject any given price cannot be ignored. We cannot use a point forecast for volume as we did in the pricing analysis.

The major goal of this chapter is to develop a model for analyzing the bidding problem. It will be possible to show that the bidder can make an analysis similar to the pricing analysis if he is willing to make a decision based on a criterion of *expected revenue* or *expected profit*.

AN EXAMPLE OF A COMPETITIVE BIDDING PROBLEM

In order to focus our discussion, we will consider the problem faced by Mr. Jacobs, who runs a small general-purpose machine shop. Mr. Jacobs has been asked by Mr. Clark, a local plumbing supplier, to quote a price for machining 30 fittings required by one of Clark's customers. Mr. Clark has told Mr. Jacobs that he has also asked ACE Welding and Supply, another local machine shop, to submit a bid for this job. Mr. Clark has agreed to provide 30 standard fittings to be modified. This job would require about $1\frac{1}{2}$ hours of machining time for each fitting on a general-purpose milling machine. The machine is available and could be set up in about eight hours by the machinist for the run. None of Mr. Jacobs' regular work force is available for this job. However, he knows of a retired machinist who is qualified for the job and wants some part-time work. This man would be paid $4 per hour for all time required for setup and running the parts. Mr. Jacobs believes that there will be some supplies and materials needed in addition to the standard fittings and that he can buy these for about $2 per fitting or $60. He now must decide what bid he will submit to

Mr. Clark who has asked that the bid be quoted in total dollars for the entire job.

It is possible for Mr. Jacobs to quickly determine his minimum bid. The out-of-pocket costs are shown in Table 8–1, with all labor costed at $4 per hour. If Mr. Jacobs bids anything less than $272, he will not cover his out-of-pocket costs. Any bid above $272 will provide some contribution to overhead expenses and profit. Unless Mr. Jacobs is willing to accept a cash loss on this job his minimum bid is clearly $272.

Table 8–1

OUT-OF-POCKET COST FOR THE CLARK JOB

	Cost per Fitting	Cost per Job
Material.....................	$2	= $ 60
Setup labor....................	...	= 32
Machining labor..............	6	= 180
Total cost..............		= $272

We will assume that Mr. Jacobs is not in business to break even on his out-of-pocket expenses but that he would like to make a positive contribution to overhead and profit on each job. How far above his minimum bid should he go? If he wants to consider a bid of $300, he would be faced with the decision problem diagrammed in Figure 8–1.

Figure 8–1

SIMPLE DECISION DIAGRAM
FOR MR. JACOBS' BIDDING PROBLEM

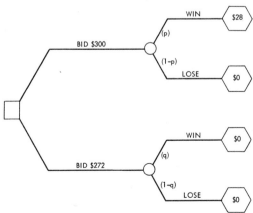

This decision diagram shows only two of the many possible bids available to Mr. Jacobs; we will consider others later. The act fork for each of these two bids is followed by an event with two outcomes, win and lose. The end points of the diagram are valued in dollars of contribution. The probability of winning is represented by the letter p for the $300 bid and the letter q for the $272 bid. The rules of probability then require that the probability of losing for these bids be $(1 - p)$ and $(1 - q)$ respectively.

The result of bidding the minimum bid is zero regardless of whether the bid wins or loses. Thus, Mr. Jacobs should not worry about assessing the probability q because the certainty equivalent must be zero if all the consequences are zero.

The probability of winning with the bid of $300 cannot be ignored if Mr. Jacobs wants to analyze this problem. This probability depends on two factors: The bid submitted by ACE Welding and Mr. Clark's rule for selecting the winner. We will assume Mr. Clark is willing to award the job to the low bidder because he believes both bidders are equally capable of doing the job.[1] Thus, what Mr. Jacobs must really assess if he wants to know the probability of winning with a $300 bid is the probability that ACE Welding will submit a bid above $300. Mr. Jacobs may have some data on ACE Welding's bidding behavior in similar situations that he can use to aid him in making this assessment. More than likely, however, he will only have his judgment to rely on in this situation. He will want to consider many factors; for example, he may want to think about how much work ACE Welding has right now and how badly they may want this job. This assessment is not easy to make and will require some hard thinking.

Finally, after carefully considering all the important factors, Mr. Jacobs has decided that there is a 0.80 probability that ACE Welding will bid more than $300. If he is willing to play the averages and thus let the expected value be his certainty equivalent, he can assign a certainty equivalent of $0.8 \times \$28 = \$22.40$ to the $300 fork on the decision diagram. In addition if he were only considering the bids shown in Figure 8–1, he would select the $300 bid because it has the higher certainty equivalent.

There is no reason for Mr. Jacobs to limit his consideration to only two bids. For any bid he wants to consider he could add a branch as an act fork in Figure 8–1 and follow it with an event having two out-

---

[1] For situations where the award is not given to the low bidder an analysis is still possible, if the rule for determining the winner is stated in advance of bid submission.

comes, win and lose. He would then assess the probability of winning with that bid and calculate that bid's certainty equivalent. The certainty equivalent of this bid can then be compared with other bids to see if it exceeds the certainty equivalent of these other bids. Table 8–2 summarizes such an analysis for several bids considered by Mr. Jacobs.

The contribution for a win is the bid less the out-of-pocket costs. The probability of a win for any bid was assessed by Mr. Jacobs. There is no contribution from a loss, and the probability of losing is one minus the probability of winning. The expected contribution is the product of the probability of winning times the contribution of winning added to the product of the probability of losing times the contri-

Table 8–2

SUMMARY OF MR. JACOBS' BIDDING ANALYSIS

Bid B	Contribution if a Win V(w)	Probability of a Win P(w)	Contribution if a Loss V(l)	Probability of a Loss P(l)	Expected* Contribution E.C.
$272	$ 0	?	$0	?	$ 0
300	28	0.80	0	0.20	22.40
325	53	0.50	0	0.50	26.50
350	78	0.25	0	0.75	19.50
375	103	0.08	0	0.92	8.24
400	128	0	0	1.00	0

* E.C. = $V(w) \times P(w) + V(l) \times P(l)$.

bution from losing. This last step can be ignored in this case because the contribution from losing is zero dollars. In general, this may not be the case, and the losing outcome cannot be ignored. Table 8–2 shows that if Mr. Jacobs were considering only these bids and willing to use expected contribution as his criterion of choice, he should bid $325.

The general nature of the bidding problem can be seen by looking at the first three columns of Table 8–2. As the bid increases, the value of winning increases since the potential contribution goes up for every dollar the bid increases. At the very same time the chance of winning decreases since the probability of winning goes down for every dollar the bid increases. These two characteristics, value of winning and chance of winning, are balanced off when the decision is made on the basis of expected contribution.

THE ASSESSMENT PROBLEM

So far in this chapter we have not treated the competitive bidding problem as unique or basically different from any other decision problem. We have done nothing different from the general decision analysis approach described in Chapter 4. If Mr. Jacobs wanted to consider more bids, he could do so by assessing the probability of winning those bids, calculating the expected contribution for those bids and comparing them to the expected values already analyzed. The most critical step in this process is the assessment of the probability of winning. It is particularly difficult to make this assessment for many separate bids in any consistent manner. This problem can be avoided if a different approach is taken.

FORECASTING THE COMPETITIVE BID

The reason a probability of winning must be assessed for each bid is because we do not know exactly what the competition will bid. In other words, the only real uncertainty is the amount of the competitive bid. We can focus our attention on forecasting this bid and then calculate the best bid using this forecast. The general approach will be to make a probabilistic forecast of the competitive bid. We will then use this forecast to determine the probability of winning for any bid we may want to submit. This probability can then be used in the analytical framework described in the previous section. Remember, we are not trying to make a point forecast of *"the competitive bid,"* we are instead trying to develop a method for making a consistent assessment of the probability of winning for any particular bid.

We will now return to Mr. Jacobs' problem to show how this assessment might be made. Mr. Jacobs knows the only competitor for this job is ACE Welding. He will want to consider all the factors that could influence their bid. For example, their current work load is important. If they are under capacity and have idle workers, they might consider labor costs as fixed and be willing to bid only enough to cover their material costs on this job. If Mr. Jacobs felt this were true, he would want a low range for the bid assessment. However, if ACE has no idle workers, they would want to cover labor costs in their bid and Mr. Jacobs' assessment should be over a higher range of bids.[2]

After much hard thought, Mr. Jacobs has concluded that he believes ACE Welding will not bid any less than $250 or any more than $400 on this job. He believes there is a 50–50 chance the bid will be

---

[2] If Mr. Jacobs had some useful historical data, he might be able to use it in making his assessment. In particular he might have been in competition with ACE on previous occasions and could use the actual bids in these cases to guide his thinking.

Figure 8-2

MR. JACOBS' ASSESSMENT OF ACE WELDING'S BID

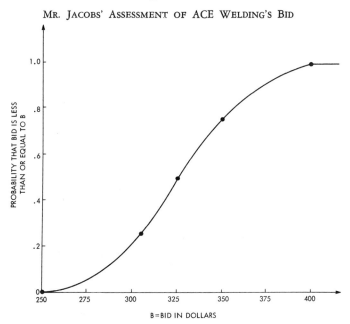

B = BID IN DOLLARS

below or above $325. He also thinks there is only one chance in four that the bid will be above $350 or below $305. His forecast is shown graphically in Figure 8-2.

CALCULATING THE BEST BID

Now it is possible using this forecast to determine the probability of winning with any bid if the rule for determining the winner is known. We believe that Mr. Clark will award the contract to the low bidder. What would happen if Mr. Jacobs were to bid $310? Figure 8-2 shows that he believes there is a 0.32 chance that ACE Welding will bid $310 or less and be the winner. Therefore, he knows that a $310 bid has a 0.68 chance of winning for him. Check Figure 8-2 to see if you agree.

The process of calculating the expected contribution for other bids now can proceed rapidly because Mr. Jacobs does not have to make an assessment of the probability of winning for each bid. This probability can be read directly from the cumulative distribution of the competitive bid in Figure 8-2. From the data in Table 8-2, it looks like the best bid for Mr. Jacobs is between $300 and $350. Table 8-3 shows the calculation of the expected contribution for four more bids in this

Table 8–3

SUMMARY OF BIDDING ANALYSIS USING CUMULATIVE FORECAST

Bid B	Value of Win V(w)	Probability of Win P(w)	Value of Loss V(l)	Probability of Loss P(l)	Expected Contribution E.C.
300	28	0.80	0	0.20	$22.40
310	38	0.68	0	0.32	25.84
320	48	0.57	0	0.43	27.36
330	58	0.45	0	0.55	26.10
340	68	0.34	0	0.66	23.12
350	78	0.25	0	0.75	19.50

range. Of these bids the best one is $320. If Mr. Jacobs wanted more precision, he could try several bids in the range between $310 and $330.

COMPARISON TO THE PRICING DECISION

We began this chapter by saying that the competitive bidding problem was a special case of the pricing problem. We also said that the typical demand curve was not useful in analyzing this special problem. However, it is now possible to develop a special graph for the bidding problem that is analogous to the demand curve. This is the graph depicting the probability of winning versus bid. Using the data in Figure 8–2, you can determine the probability of winning for any bid. These probabilities are plotted in Figure 8–3.

The procedure described in Chapter 7 for determining the best price can be used to determine the best bid if Figure 8–3 is used like the earlier demand curve. One of the weaknesses of the method for establishing a price in practice is the difficulty in obtaining the demand schedule. This is also true in the competitive bidding problem. This assessment requires judgment and the willingness to commit this judgment in a quantitative form. However, for the bidding problem we have presented an alternative to assessing this curve directly that may prove more workable. Namely, we have proposed that the decision maker first make a probabilistic forecast of the bid to be submitted by his competition. This forecast can then be used to calculate the probability of winning versus bid curve.

One word of caution in using the pricing analogy to solve bidding problems. Finding the point on the demand curve that has the highest value for the product of bid times probability of winning is equivalent to finding the price that maximizes total revenue on the price demand

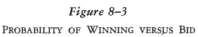

Figure 8–3

PROBABILITY OF WINNING VERSUS BID

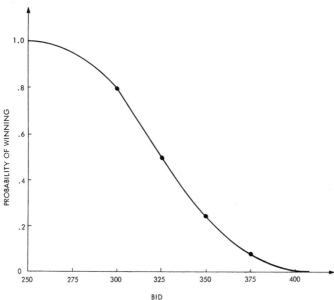

curve. This point may not be the bid that gives the highest expected contribution just as the price that gives the largest total revenue may not yield the highest total contribution in the pricing problem. Special care should be used in bidding problems where there is some cost associated with losing the bid or where different bids have different costs associated with them. In these cases, it may be best to draw the entire decision diagram for the bidding problem to assure that all relevant costs have been considered.

SPECIAL PROBLEMS

So far, we have discussed a simple bidding problem. There are three common situations that are more complex and require special attention.

More Than One Competitor

The first of these situations is when you have more than one competitor in the bidding. This makes the assessment problem more difficult. The important forecast is the *lowest* competitive bid to be submitted.

In general, it is possible to say that the forecasted cumulative probability distribution of the lowest competitive bid will be to the left of the forecast for any one individual competitor. This means that the probability of winning with a given bid is smaller against a group of competitors than it would be if that bid were submitted against any one of the competitors in a two-bidder situation.[3] The forecast of lowest competitive bid cannot be made by thinking about each competitor individually but must be made by thinking about the competition collectively. Techniques for doing this kind of forecast have not been presented in this book. All we will say here is that in bidding situations with more than one competitor some care should be devoted to making the probabilistic forecast of competitive behavior.

Bid Preparation Costs

Another special problem results when there is some significant cost associated with submitting the bid. This is quite often the case in large consulting jobs when a proposal is required before the contract is awarded. This cost can be added to all outcomes, both winning and losing, for all bids. Because this is true sometimes the argument is made to ignore the cost altogether. This would be justifiable if the option of *not submitting* a bid is ignored. However, as long as the option not to bid is open, the bid preparation costs should be included. Suppose Mr. Jacobs had a $30 cost associated with submitting the Clark bid. Assume he must pay this in order to prepare the bid whether he wins or loses. Referring to Table 8–3, all the values for winning and losing would be reduced by $30. Also all expected contributions would be reduced by $30. You can see that this would result in the best bid of $320 having an expected loss of $2.64. This is still the best bid if Mr. Jacobs is going to submit a bid, but he can avoid this cost by not submitting any bid at all.

Often businesses which do a large amount of bidding consider the cost of preparing bids as an overhead cost or a cost of being in business and ignore it on any particular bidding problem. This can result in submitting bids that will not recover their incremental costs. The relevant preparation cost may not be the actual labor or materials consumed in the bid proposal, but the opportunity cost of not having the labor and materials to prepare for a more attractive competition. The alternative

---

[3] In a strict sense we should say that the probability of winning with a given bid cannot increase and it may decrease as the number of bidders increases, if no competitor change their bid.

of not entering the competition is an important one and should not be ignored.

Special Cost Associated with Losing

The final special problem that we want to discuss results when there is some cost associated with losing a bid that is not incurred if that bid wins. This situation might occur if the costs of preparing a bid were reimbursed if you won but were not paid by the buyer if the contract were lost. Consider the example above where Mr. Jacobs had a $30 preparation cost but Mr. Clark would pay for any preparation costs of the winner. Table 8–4 shows the calculation of expected contribution for several bids under these conditions.

Table 8–4

SUMMARY OF BIDDING ANALYSIS FOR $30 PENALTY FOR LOSING

Bid B	Value of Win $V(w)$	Probability of Win $P(w)$	Value of Loss $V(l)$	Probability of Loss $P(l)$	Expected Contribution E.C.
290	18	0.89	−30	0.11	$12.72
300	28	0.80	−30	0.20	16.40
310	38	0.68	−30	0.32	16.24
320	48	0.57	−30	0.43	14.46
330	58	0.45	−30	0.55	9.60

By comparing Table 8–4 with Table 8–3 you can see that the best bid has shifted from $320 to $300 and that the expected contribution for the best bid is lower in this new situation. When there is some unique cost associated with losing, the best bid will be lowered, and the attractiveness of the entire opportunity will decrease when compared with a situation with no such cost. However, it is clear that this condition is more attractive than the case where the cost is associated with both a win and a loss. A useful generalization that can be made from this example is to be careful to include all the consequences associated with losing the bid as well as those associated with winning.

SUMMARY

We would state that the competitive bidding problem can be solved using the general decision analysis framework outlined below.

1. Determine the possible bids you can make. This may mean calculating the minimum bid.

2. Determine the economic consequences of winning and losing with each bid.
3. Assess the probability of winning with each possible bid.
4. Calculate the certainty equivalent for each bid, and if you are willing to play the averages, this will be the expected contribution for each bid.
5. Select the bid with the highest certainty equivalent.

We have also stated that the assessment of the probability of winning for any bid is difficult. This assessment may be easier if a probabilistic forecast is made of the lowest competitive bid. Once this forecast is made, the probability of winning with any particular bid can be read directly from the forecast.

Finally, we have shown that the graph of the probability of winning plotted against the bid is equivalent to the demand curve used in connection with the pricing decision analysis discussed in Chapter 7.

MATS ELECTRONICS, INC.

Mats Electronics, Inc. is a small electronics firm, located in Eastern Massachusetts, that produces a variety of special-purpose analog-to-digital converters, which are used primarily for process control. Its business has grown to a sales level of $5,000,000 per year since its founding in 1959.

The analog-to-digital converters produced by the company are devices for converting readings of instruments measuring such things as temperature, pressure, rate of flow, humidity, etc., into a set of signals for transmission to a central computing facility. The computing facility then analyzes the reading, computes a correction if it is needed, and transmits back this correction so that the process can be adjusted.

Most of the converters produced by Mats make use of linear amplifier circuits of fairly common designs. The specifications of the amplifiers are, in fact, quite flexible; and it is common practice for the Mats purchasing agent, John Greene, to shop around for good buys on batches of them. Whenever he finds a potentially good buy, he obtains a set of specifications of the circuit from the seller and passes it on to his engineering department. The engineering department examines both the electronic characteristics and the physical structure of the circuits to determine whether they can be used without undue modification of the converters in which they will be installed.

Quite frequently, Mr. Greene has been able to purchase batches of amplifiers which have been classified as rejects by the Components Division of Syltheon Manufacturing Company, located nearby. These batches generally contain a high percentage of circuits that are usable by Mats Electronics. In addition to its industrial sales, Syltheon's Components Division acts as the source of silicon diodes, transistors, integrated circuits and circuitry mounted on cards, including amplifiers, for the Product Divisions of Syltheon, including the Consumer Products Division, the Communication Division, and the Military and Aerospace

Division. Each division produces a wide variety of products in large volume. Because of the volume, the assembly of most products is highly automated, thus requiring high accuracy in the location of contact and connection points of the circuits. Hence the Components Division must make tests at regular intervals of both the electronic and physical characteristics of the parts. Should it turn out on inspection that some characteristic of the part tested lies outside the fairly stringent tolerance required for use in one of the Product Divisions of Syltheon, all of the parts produced since the last inspection are put to one side and subsequently sold outside the company. A study made at Syltheon has shown it is not economically feasible for them to sort the batch in the Products Division.

Syltheon always sells these rejects in the same way. A list is kept of purchasing agents who will buy parts with certain characteristics, and these purchasing agents are called and informed when a batch of potential interest is available. Each purchasing agent makes a sealed bid if he is interested, and Syltheon sells to the highest bidder.

Mr. Greene has recently been informed of the availability of a batch of 100 circuits identified by Syltheon as RB1073CQ. Over the past two years, Mr. Greene has bid on fifteen 100-unit batches of these circuits. In every case there had been only one other competitive bidder, a company called Sonarscan which makes a depth-sounding gear for yachtsmen and deep-sea fishermen.

The Syltheon salesman, Robert Williamson, always supplies an estimate of the yield of good parts in each batch. It is in his interest to supply the best estimate that he can since, in the long run, his ability to sell depends on the credibility placed by his customers on his statements. The table below shows his estimate of the yield and what the winning bid turned out to be in the 15 situations in the past when Mats made a bid. The bids which were won by Mats are marked with an asterisk.

Estimate of Yield (%)	Winning Bid ($)	Estimate of Yield (%)	Winning Bid ($)
80	2,425	80	2,375
90	2,750*	90	2,750*
70	2,075	80	2,400
80	2,350	70	2,075
80	2,425	70	2,125
90	2,775*	90	2,725*
70	2,100	80	2,375*
70	2,150		

For the current batch Williamson estimates the yield to be 90%. In each of the past situations where Williamson had estimated a 90% yield, it turned out that Mats had won the bid, so the actual yields were known. They were 87, 95, 96, and 92%. It was Mr. Greene's opinion that with an estimate of 90% the actual yield of the present batch would not be below 80%, and the batch could be almost a perfect one.

With the information from Syltheon on the characteristics of item RB1073CQ, the engineering department has informed Mr. Greene that Mats can use the item now. They have just received a contract to supply 25 pressure sensing and control devices each of which would require four of these circuits.

For Mats to manufacture the same circuit by regular methods, the cost would be $750 for setup plus a cost of $25 per unit produced. Syltheon's price for tested and guaranteed RB1073CQ's in quantities of 200 or less is $55 each. Mats does not carry circuits in inventory.

With these data in front of him, Mr. Greene is about to make his analysis and place a bid. As he looks over the data on the past bids, he remarks to an assistant, "It looks to me as if the Sonarscan people are bidding about $30 per good unit. From what I know of their use of this circuit, their yield of good items should be about the same as ours."

WHITE EAGLE OIL COMPANY (B)

On June 11, 1957, Mr. Carl Young, assistant to the vice-president —contract drilling of White Eagle Oil Company, received a letter (Exhibit 1) from Shell Oil Company soliciting a bid on drilling an exploratory (wildcat) oil well identified as Scharbauer No. 1. Background information describing the operations of the contract drilling department of White Eagle (referred to as H & P) and the methods of preparing contract footage bids was presented in the White Eagle Oil Company (A) case.

When Mr. Young informed Mr. Daniel, the vice-president, of the request for a bid, Mr. Daniel immediately pointed out that the West Texas location of the proposed well was only about 150 miles from where H & P had its deep rig No. 39 stacked. Rig No. 39 had been inactive for six months as a result of reduced drilling programs by many operators in the West Texas–New Mexico area. Mr. Daniel said, "This may be our chance to get that rig back into operation, Carl. Prepare a bid on the job as carefully as you can so that we will have a fair chance of getting the contract. Knowing Shell, I expect they have requested bids from perhaps eight or ten other drillers, so the competition will be rough, especially from the real small outfits. We need the job, though, so we'll have to do the best bidding job we know how."

Rig No. 39 had been purchased by H & P in 1949 and had been well maintained. The gross cost of the rig on the books of the company (before depreciation) was $300,000, including the cost of several major replacements and additions since the date of purchase. The rig was equipped with $4\frac{1}{2}$-inch drill pipe that originally cost $75,000. In June, 1957, the estimated cost of a new rig similar to No. 39, with drill pipe, was $600,000.

Mr. Young's first action in preparing the bid was to telephone Mr. James Pryor, the H & P field engineer in the West Texas area. Mr. Young told Mr. Pryor of the request for a bid and asked him to go out and inspect the site. Mr. Young described all significant features of the offer and requested Mr. Pryor to submit his estimate of the number of days that would be required to drill the well and the number of bits and reamers required. Mr. Pryor was also to investigate the availability of fuel for the rig, and secure a subcontractor's estimate on the cost of drilling the necessary number of water wells.

Next, Mr. Young telephoned Hughes Tool Company and requested a drilling report on all deep wells completed in the area surrounding the Scharbauer site. Hughes Tool Company was a large manufacturer and distributor of oil field equipment, and as a service to its customers operated a clearing house of information on completed oil wells. Drillers and operators filed information of their experience with each well as it was completed. Hughes Tool then made copies of this data available to participating companies at a cost of one dollar per well reported. After checking the area of the Scharbauer site, Hughes submitted reports on two wells (summarized in Exhibit 2), neither of which was really close enough to be indicative of the type of formations and drilling experience that could be expected in drilling the Scharbauer well. Nevertheless, this was the only information available because no other wells had been drilled closer to the proposed site.

Examining the data from Hughes, Mr. Young noticed two significant facts. Both the jobs had been done by Rowan Drilling Company, a reputable independent driller comparable in size to H & P, on a daywork basis. Typically a daywork contract was used in the industry when the uncertainties as to required drilling time were so great that the contractor did not have a reliable basis for making his bid. In such situations it was frequently cheaper for the operator to run the risk of a troublesome job rather than force the drilling contractor to accept the risk and submit a footage bid high enough to protect himself against the possible loss. Mr. Young also noticed that both jobs had started using heavy lubricating muds at a greater depth than that proposed by Shell for the Scharbauer job. The Shell proposal called for native mud, i.e., water, to 3,000 feet and the use of a heavier lubricating mud below that depth. Although he could not be sure, Mr. Young suspected that part of the reason the Terrell A No. 2 well had taken 11 days longer than the Amerada well might be due to the earlier use of mud on the former well.

Inspecting his maps of the area Mr. Young noticed that Amerada Petroleum Company had drilled several wells in their AMROW oil field located approximately eight to nine miles southeast of the Schar-

414　　　　MANAGERIAL ECONOMICS: TEXT AND CASES

bauer site. Realizing that the experience in this field was even less useful than that provided by the Hughes reports, Mr. Young called a friend of his who worked for Amerada. The friend reported that Amerada's experience on 13,000 foot wells in the AMROW field had been that drilling required 65 to 70 days per well.

At Mr. Young's request the accounting department supplied the following information concerning estimated rig operating costs and other cost factors for rig No. 39:

	Cost per Day
Labor and supervision	$371.00
Supplies	39.00
Maintenance	170.00
Home and field office overhead	125.00
Rig depreciation	145.00
Drill pipe depreciation	80.19

Based on his experience, Mr. Young estimated that the cost of having the rig erected on location by a subcontractor would be approximately $3,200. He estimated transportation costs of moving the rig 140 miles to the new location at about $8,000, plus $800 for rig-up and $600 for tear-down transportation charges. The cost of a subcontractor to install the casing pipe was estimated at $1,200, and miscellaneous trucking and other costs would probably amount to $600.

On the afternoon of June 14, Jim Pryor called Mr. Young to report his findings. He said he had inspected the site and discussed drilling problems in the area with other engineers. He said he thought that barring any unforeseen difficulties, H & P could drill to 13,000 feet in about 70 days.[1] He reported that butane was the cheapest suitable fuel available and, although he did not have a firm offer, estimated it could be obtained at about 8 cents per gallon. Rig No. 39 normally required 1,300 gallons of fuel daily. Water wells would cost about $300 apiece, and Mr. Pryor recommended two such wells be drilled. His estimate of bit requirements, with prices supplied by Mr. Young, was as follows:

Size	Number Required	Estimated Price	Total Cost
17½	1	$ 200	$ 200
12¼	13	320	4,160
8¾	84	200	16,800
8¾ (expensive)	4	1,135	4,540
Reamers	10	150	1,500
Total			$27,200

Mr. Pryor also informed Mr. Young that in checking around he had run into several other contractors inspecting the Scharbauer area, and he

---

[1] In addition, two days would be required to set up the rig and two days to tear it down.

knew that at least three of these competitors had stacked rigs located within 50 to 100 miles of the site. This fact put H & P at a competitive disadvantage in terms of transportation costs, which Mr. Young would want to consider in setting his final offer.

In summarizing all the cost data he had collected, Mr. Young was painfully aware of the fact that rig No. 39 had been stacked for six months, and if H & P lost the Scharbauer job would probably not have a chance at another job within economical transportation distance for at least 60 days. He knew that several of the cost factors provided for on the bid form (Exhibit 3) did not represent actual additional out-of-pocket costs, and that any cash contribution from getting the job would be better than allowing the rig to remain idle. On the other hand, he knew that H & P was trying to develop some price stability and a recognition of the value of cost-based bidding in the drilling industry, and to violate that principle in bidding on this job might be considered irresponsible. Finally, he realized the crucial importance of the estimate of drilling days required, and wondered how much of a safety factor, if any, should be allowed for the uncertainties of that estimate.

Questions

1. Complete the bid form provided as Exhibit 3. What price per foot should Mr. Young recommend to Mr. Daniel to submit for the Scharbauer job? What should he recommend as the various daywork bids?

2. Compute the estimated break-even footage bid at which H & P would just be able to cover its incremental costs on the Scharbauer job.

Exhibit 1

WHITE EAGLE OIL COMPANY (B)

SHELL OIL COMPANY

P. O. Box 1810
Midland, Texas

Helmerich and Payne   June 10, 1957
Box 787
Odessa, Texas

Gentlemen:

Shell Oil Company is requesting bids for the drilling of Shell Scharbauer et al 1, located Block 2, League 312, GCSL Survey, Gaines County, Texas ____. The proposed well is projected to an approximate testing depth of _13,000'_, but not to exceed a total depth of _14,000'_, for completion in the _Devonian_. Bid prices should be on footage bases to testing depth. It is proposed to use native mud surface to 3000'; salt gel-starch mud W.L. 15cc or less 3000' to 5450'; Bentonite-Driscose mud 5450' to T.D.W.L. 10 cc or less.

You have in your possession (or there is attached hereto) a sample of our Agreement Form Mid-45 (Revised 1-55). The contract for drilling the proposed well will be identical with this, with the exception of the following modifications:

No standby time without crews.

No cable tool work anticipated.

Paragraph THIRD (C) will read "To keep the hole straight within the limit of not more than five degrees from the vertical at any point in the hole and at all times to have available for use a surveying device acceptable to SHELL. A deviation survey shall be run at least every 250 feet, or oftener if requested by SHELL.

This well will be drilled to permit the contemplated casing program shown below at the approximate depths:

Setting Depth	W.O.C. Time	Size Casing
300'	24 hours	13-3/8"
5450'	36 hours	9-5/8"
13000'	48 hours	7"

The contractor will be required to furnish derrick, a complete and adequate rotary rig, pressure operated blowout preventer equipment, adequate and efficient flow line connections, choke manifold, xmaiixdxiiixmmstkxmmsixinxaiixmmmxxxxxxxxxxxx suitable and adequate power tongs to run 9-5/8" casing, _____, run tubing, complete well, competent and sufficient labor and supervision, drill bits, _fuel_ _____, fuel line, water and sufficient storage for water, vibrating shale shaker, and steel mud pits having adequate facilities for cleaning pit bottoms, settling, mud mixing, and transferring good mud from one pit to another when cleaning, as are essential to the economical handling and maintenance of all drilling muds supplied. Coring, perforating, testing, rat-holing and surveying will be done on day-work basis.

Scharbauer et al 1 _____   -2-   June 10, 1957

Shell will prepare roads and location; furnish casing, casing shoes and collars, tubing, well head connections, mud, mud treating materials, cement and cementing services, testing devices and other devices incidental to the testing and surveying of the hole.   Shell will construct collar _____ .

Additional detailed information in regard to availability of water or fuel, or proposed procedure for drilling and completing the well, etc., may be obtained from Shell's Production Division Office in the Wilco Building, Midland, Texas, if desired.

If you wish to bid on the proposed drilling of this well, please insert your bid price in the space provided below and mail one copy of this letter in the attached envelope to reach this office not later than 10:00 a.m. on   6-19-57   . If you do not have equipment suitable for this work available by   6-19-57   , we will appreciate acknowledgement of our bid and your advice as to the date on which you might be able to undertake the drilling of this well.

It is understood that Shell reserves the right to accept the bid which it considers to be the most advantageous regardless of whether it is the lowest, or to reject all bids. In the event you elect not to bid, please inform us of this decision promptly in writing.

Please fill in the attached form as to the type of equipment you anticipate using in the drilling of this well.

Yours very truly,
/s/ Frank R. Lovering
Frank R. Lovering
Division Production Manager

RDK:
cc - Production Manager - Midland
     Purchasing-Stores - Midland

WORK ITEMS:
1. Drilling price per foot

2. Daywork price with drill pipe

	0'	9000'	
9000'	10000'	
10000'	11000'	
12000'	13000'	
13000'	14000'	

3. Daywork price without drill pipe

	0'	9000'	
9000'	10000'	
10000'	11000'	
11000'	12000'	
12000'	13000'	
13000'	14000'	

4. Standby rate with crews

5. Date equipment will be available

SIGNED: _____
                    CONTRACTOR

Exhibit 2

WHITE EAGLE OIL COMPANY (B)

DATA REGARDING COMPLETED WELLS NEAR THE PROPOSED SHELL
SCHARBAUER NO. 1

OBTAINED FROM HUGHES TOOL COMPANY

Name of Well	Amerada	Terrell A No. 2
Distance from Scharbauer No. 1 site.........	4 miles east	5 miles northeast
Drilled by................................	Rowan Drilling	Rowan
Date drilling began.......................	3/15/55	8/17/55
Date drilling ended......................	5/21/55	11/3/55
Number of drilling days...................	67	78
Total depth of well.......................	12,715 ft.	12,680 ft.
Type of contract.........................	Daywork	Daywork
Hole deviation...........................	2° at TD	4° at 12,514 ft.
Use of heavy mud started at................	10,600 ft.	6,905 ft
Number of bits used:		
17-inch....................................	1	1
12¼-inch...................................	13	1
11-inch....................................	..	9
7⅞-inch—regular...........................	84	87
7⅞-inch—expensive.........................	4	7
Time spent fishing (attempting to recover the end of the drill string that had twisted off in the hole, impeding further drilling until removed).......................	Less than one day at 7,500 ft.	Less than one day at 6,800 ft.

Source: Summarized from reports received from Hughes Tool Company.

Exhibit 3

WHITE EAGLE OIL COMPANY (B)

HELMERICH & PAYNE, INC. CONTRACT FOOTAGE BID

```
                                                    Date_____
                                                    Depth_____
OPERATOR_____  WELL_____
ADDRESS_____  ATTENTION OF_____
STATE_____COUNTY_____  LOCATION_____
BID WITH RIG_____LOCATION_____
RIG UP_____TEAR DOWN_____DRLG._____OTHER_____TOTAL DAYS____
REMARKS_____
```

	Total	Av Per Day	Av Per Ft
DIRECT OUT-OF-POCKET COSTS		____Days	____Ft
RIG OPERATING COSTS			
Labor & Supervision			
Supplies			
Maintenance			
Sub-Total			

```
VARIABLE COSTS
Bits                                               Footage Bid   _____
Transportation
Location_____Dk_____                                 5%    _____
Fuel & Lines
Water & Lines                                          10%    _____
Fishing etc._____Da____
Other_____                                       15%    _____


Sub-Total
```

```
FIXED OUT-OF-POCKET COSTS
Home Office Overhead
Field Office Overhead
Interest & Insurance

Sub-Total

TOT DIR OUT-OF-POCKET COSTS

RECOVERY-OF-EQUIP COSTS
Rig Depreciation
D P Depr._____Da___

TOT RECOVERY-OF-EQUIP COSTS

GRAND TOTAL COSTS

PROFIT

EARNINGS
```

Casing	Depth	No. Bits	Size	Price	Total		Transportation
							Move, Skid:
							____Miles _____
							Rig Up _____
							Tear Down _____
		Rms.___					Incidental _____
		Total					Total _____

ADAMIAN METALLURGICAL
CORPORATION

In October, 1958, Mr. Peter Adamian, president of Adamian Metallurgical Corporation, was engaged in a re-examination of the methods used in setting prices for the services sold by his company. Adamian Metallurgical Corporation (AMC) was a commercial heat-treating company located in Birmingham, Alabama. The company offered a variety of heat-treating services, such as carburizing, hardening, tempering, and brazing, to local metalworking companies and machine shops.

Mr. Adamian had founded AMC in 1946 after being released from the Army. He had taken a degree in metallurgy in 1934 and had worked for several years for a commercial heat-treating company before the war. Between 1946 and 1954, AMC had experienced a steady growth in sales volume and profits; after 1954, sales volume had been relatively stable. A balance sheet as of July 31, 1958, and income and surplus statements for the fiscal year then ended are presented in Exhibits 1, 2 and 3. Condensed income statements for the years 1949–1957 are shown in Exhibit 4.

History of Commercial Heat-treating

Heat-treating is a process whereby the physical properties of a metal may be changed by subjecting it to heat. Typically, heat-treating is done for one of two purposes: (1) hardening the surface of the metal to improve its wearing qualities, or (2) annealing the metal to improve its further workability by removing molecular stresses and strains created by prior metal-forming operations. Another heat-treating operation called brazing is a process whereby two pieces of metal are joined together by applying a compound (analogous to glue) to the two pieces and heating them until the compound "flows" to join the two surfaces. AMC was engaged primarily in the hardening and brazing processes.

Prior to World War II, steel was hardened principally by inducing carbon into the surface. This "carburizing" process was one of the earliest heat-treating methods and was a relatively simple process: the parts to be hardened were covered with a carburizing compound, put in a furnace for several hours, and removed when enough of the carbon had been driven by the heat into the steel to harden it. With the development of specialty steels during the war, and the improvement in cutting tools and other technological advances, a wider variety of heat-treating methods was necessary. In 1958, AMC had six different furnaces and offered a fairly complete range of hardening and brazing capabilities:

1. The box furnace was a firebrick box-shaped gas furnace used for carburizing.
2. The hardening furnace and the tempering furnace were continuous-operation gas furnaces. Trays of metal parts were pushed into one end of the hardening furnace and, after maximum hardness was attained, pushed out the other end and quenched. The parts were then pushed through the tempering furnace where, at somewhat lower temperatures, the brittleness of the metal caused by the hardening operation was modified. The final result was a hardened part with good tensile strength. These two furnaces were always used together, and were regarded as a single process. One hour of furnace time in this process was defined as one hour in each furnace.
3. The salt-pot furnace was another hardening process in which the furnace was in continuous operation. Parts to be hardened were immersed in a hot brine solution until the desired toughening result was achieved.
4. The Hayes furnace was a small, versatile, continuous electrical furnace that would do both hardening and brazing operations.
5. The brazing furnace was an electrical, continuous furnace used exclusively for brazing operations.
6. The induction furnace was another hardening furnace using a relatively new specialized process on the batch method. This furnace had been acquired in 1956, and was rapidly gaining acceptance. Operations of this furnace were not profitable during 1957, but Mr. Adamian felt that after a "shakedown period" the induction furnace would be a profitable addition to his line.

Each of these furnaces were relatively independent of the other furnaces in their operation; that is, a part processed in one furnace would not normally go through another furnace. The main exception to this procedure was that occasionally a part would be carburized in the box furnace prior to hardening in another furnace.

AMC was one of four commercial heat-treaters operating in Birmingham. One of these companies was several times the size of AMC; the other two were slightly smaller than AMC.

An indirect source of competition was manufacturers of metal products who did heat-treating of their own products in their own plants. Commonly this was done whenever the volume of work was large enough to support installation of a furnace, thus limiting commercial heat-treaters to essentially small-volume customers. Large manufacturers occasionally used a commercial heat-treater when the manufacturer's volume was too great for his own furnace capacity, or when a specialized type of process was required which the manufacturer's equipment could not handle.

In 1958, AMC's volume of $165,041 was the result of 10,414 invoices representing individual customer orders. The average size of an order was thus $15.85. Mr. Adamian pointed out that the minimum price for any order was $2.50, and he estimated that 80% of the total orders were for small dollar amounts between $2.50 and $6. The remaining orders included some big jobs running up to $300, thus raising the average order size to $15.85.

Typically, Mr. Adamian said, a customer would bring in parts to be processed and expect to pick up the completed work within three days. The Hayes and induction furnaces were usually operated on a two-shift basis, and the other furnaces were operated 24 hours a day. The plant worked a five-day week. On a rush basis, jobs could be handled in one day and many jobs were completed in two days. Actual processing time for a job varied as a result of the technical specifications to be met; a typical small order being processed through the hardening and tempering furnace might require one furnace-hour. Small orders processed in one of the continuous furnaces did not require the full capacity of a furnace at any time. When technical specifications permitted, several small orders might be in one furnace at the same time.

Because many of his customers were job-order machine shops and small metalworking companies, Mr. Adamian explained that it was practically impossible for AMC to schedule its work load even one day in advance. AMC had several hundred customers, each with a small volume of heat-treating requirements, and the customers could not predict when they would need work done. Mr. Adamian stressed the importance of customer service in maintaining his business. On an initial order a customer might ask for a bid before placing his order with AMC. If the price on that order was acceptable, and the quality and service delivered were good, Mr. Adamian said the customer might become a steady source of business with no future questions about price on later orders.

One of the problems in preparing bids for new customers or pricing the jobs for established customers was that when Mr. Adamian was out of the shop, the pricing might be done by either the plant superintendent or the shop foreman. Since these two men, as well as Mr. Adamian, each had slightly different methods of estimating costs, the price that one man might quote for a job frequently varied from the price quoted for an identical job by one of the other officials. Mr. Adamian pointed out that this occasionally resulted in a request from a customer for clarification on exactly what the price was for a given type of work.

With these operating and customer characteristics in the heat-treating industry, Mr. Adamian said it was very difficult to find an equitable basis for pricing the jobs of steady customers and for preparing bids for prospective orders. One of the primary causes of difficulty was that before World War II, the price for the carburizing process had been fairly well stabilized at 8 cents per pound by all the heat-treating companies in Birmingham. After the war, prices had risen with inflation to about 15 cents per pound, and this was the price that customers had come to expect as the standard price for heat-treating (hardening) service. The reason the 15-cent price was unfortunate, Mr. Adamian said, was that customers expected that this price would cover the heat-treating service they required, regardless of its technical complexity. With the growing variety of processes and increasingly rigid specifications as a result of greater technology, this price was too low to support profitable operations. Nevertheless, Mr. Adamian said, there was great customer resistance to prices quoted above 15 cents per pound for hardening as done in the hardening and tempering, Hayes, or salt pot furnaces. Customers had no such preconceived ideas about a proper price for the brazing and induction furnaces, so Mr. Adamian was able to charge a price which he considered adequate to yield a profit.

One of the solutions to the pricing problem considered by Mr. Adamian was to quote prices on a "per part" basis. Mr. Adamian had found that his customers tended to think about their production costs as being "so much per part," and were receptive to having their heat-treating service quoted on that basis. Mr. Adamian saw an advantage in quoting prices this way in that he was able to quote a per part price that was higher on a "per pound" basis than the 15 cents considered as normal. However, he still had the problem of trying to determine what the per part price should be.

During fiscal year 1958, AMC suffered its first loss in nine years. Mr. Adamian attributed this loss to the recession during that period. "We were able to maintain our volume pretty well, but only by shaving prices to a point apparently below break even," he said. Recognizing the growing seriousness of his pricing problem in April, 1958, Mr. Adamian called in Mr. Richard Showalter, a local management consultant, for assistance.

The Consultant's Analysis

In trying to devise a system for cost-based bidding and pricing, Mr. Showalter reasoned that essentially the service that AMC was selling was furnace time. Mr. Adamian said it was easy to make reliable predictions of furnace time for any job because the time required was determined by the technical specifications of the job. Accordingly, Mr. Showalter decided to distribute all costs to the furnaces in order to arrive at a total cost per furnace which could then be used to determine break-even prices for each type of furnace. The results of this analysis are shown in Exhibit 5.

Mr. Showalter decided to use income and expense data for the calendar year 1957, since he wanted to use the most recent information and final figures for fiscal year 1958 would not be available for several months. His first step was to obtain sales revenue for each furnace. This data was readily available because all sales invoices were classified according to the furnace in which the work had been done. For those few jobs (less than 10% of the total) which had gone through more than one furnace, revenue was allocated between furnaces on a proportional basis reflecting historical "cents-per-pound" prices for each furnace.

In distributing costs by furnace, Mr. Showalter knew that many expense items could not be identified with a specific furnace and would have to be allocated on some reasonable basis. He decided to divide non-assignable costs into three categories: shop overhead, selling expenses, and administrative expenses. In Exhibit 6 the components of each category in Exhibit 5 are related back to the listing of operating expenses shown in Exhibit 2.

Also shown in Exhibit 6 is Mr. Showalter's evaluation of each expense item in terms of its variability with changes in the rate of production. He found that the most variable expense was supplies used in the furnaces (salt, brazing paste, carburizing compound, etc.) which varied almost directly with the volume of work processed. Expenses for repairs and for gas were not directly variable because all the furnaces were usually run every day, although the harder use involved when the furnaces were running full probably did increase gas consumption and necessitate earlier repair work than did running the furnaces partly filled or empty. Similarly, shop direct labor was not completely variable since the same number of attendants were required whether the furnace was completely or partially filled. Further, since customer requirements for processing could not be accurately predicted even one day in advance, AMC usually had the full work force (about 14 men) report each day and the men worked more or less hard depending upon how much work was available. Commenting on this problem, Mr. Adamian had said, "We don't lay men off as much as we should."

Mr. Showalter found that some expenses, such as consulting fees, entertainment, advertising, etc., were neither fixed nor variable by the nature of the operations. He classified these expenses as controllable by management decision.

In preparing his cost distribution, Mr. Showalter did not allocate any cost to the sandblasting operation. This operation was a method used to improve the surface appearance of parts that had been treated in the hardening and tempering furnaces or the salt-pot furnace. Since the cost of this operation was small, it was usually not included specifically as a factor when bids were prepared. Therefore the loss shown in Exhibit 4 was due to an underallocation of revenue to this operation, and to adjust for it the loss was split between the two furnaces using sandblasting. Similarly, the box furnace was, in Mr. Adamian's words, "a necessary evil," for which a detailed cost analysis was not necessary. Since the assignable costs and revenue for this furnace were small, Mr. Showalter ignored it in his allocation of selling expenses and administrative expenses.

In order to determine "break-even" revenue rates, Mr. Showalter needed some estimate of the number of hours that each furnace would be utilized during the year. No actual data on the utilization rate was available. As a practical matter, during the five-day workweek the furnaces were never allowed to cool completely, although the Hayes and induction furnaces were cut back to a standby temperature between midnight and 8 A.M. Most of the rest of the time, all the furnaces were "active" to a greater or lesser extent. Depending on how compatible the different jobs were, a furnace might run completely full, or might contain only one job being processed to unusual specifications.

Mr. Showalter asked Mr. Adamian to estimate the average number of *equivalent* hours each day that each furnace would be completely full. Thus, two hours during which the furnace was only 50% full were counted as one equivalent revenue hour. Mr. Adamian's estimates of average equivalent revenue hours per day are shown on Exhibit 5.

The Beauregard Tool Works Job

Mr. Adamian had still not resolved his pricing policy by October, 1958, when he was contacted by Mr. A. L. Hickory, president of Beauregard Tool Works. Mr. Hickory's company operated four automatic screw machines on a job-order basis in a barn behind Mr. Hickory's home. Mr. Hickory explained that he was dissatisfied with the heat-treating service he had been receiving from one of AMC's competitors, and would like Mr. Adamian to bid on a job that Beauregard was working on. The job involved 1,000 small parts, weighing in total 40 pounds. Mr. Adamian's usual practice was to quote a price immediately, but in this case, realizing that the job might develop a lot of repeat business, he asked Mr. Hickory to give him a day or so to work up a good price on this job that could be used as a pattern for future prices on similar jobs for Beauregard.

Considering the Beauregard job after Mr. Hickory left, Mr. Adamian knew that the "standard" bid should be $6, based on 40 pounds at 15 cents. He knew it would take about an hour to run the job through the hardening and tempering furnaces, indicating a cost of $7.55, to which some allowance for profit should be added. However, this job would probably only require 60% of the furnace capacity while going through, so that if the remaining capacity could be sold, a lower price might be justifiable. Finally, Mr. Adamian recognized this job as a good opportunity to quote a price of 1 cent per part, thus getting $10 of revenue if the bid were accepted.

Questions

1. What price should Mr. Adamian bid on the Beauregard job?
2. For the purpose of making bids and setting prices in the future, should Mr. Adamian figure his costs on a per pound, per part, or per furnace-hour basis, or on some other basis, if at all?

Exhibit 1

ADAMIAN METALLURGICAL CORPORATION

BALANCE SHEET, JULY 31, 1958

ASSETS

Current assets:

Cash			$ 164.34	
Accounts receivable			28,687.04	
Notes receivable			6,752.85	
Work-in-process inventory			340.00	
Supplies inventory			2,055.69	$37,999.92
Investments				9,576.00

Fixed assets:	*Cost*	*Reserve*	*Net Value*	
Equipment	$50,504.27	$25,510.03	$24,994.24	
Office equipment	1,262.29	548.79	713.50	
Trucks	8,836.46	1,627.14	7,209.32	
Total fixed assets	$60,603.02	$27,685.96		32,917.06
Prepaid expenses				1,760.44
Other assets—treasury stock (34 shares)				3,400.00
Total assets				$85,653.42

LIABILITIES AND NET WORTH

Current liabilities:

Accounts payable	$ 3,139.20	
Notes payable	8,381.90	
Accrued expenses	4,404.92	$15,926.02

Long-term liabilities:

Notes payable		8,681.87
Total liabilities		$24,607.89

Net worth:

Capital stock (250 shares issued)	$25,000.00	
Surplus (Exhibit 3)	36,045.53	
Total net worth		61,045.53
Total liabilities and net worth		$85,653.42

Exhibit 2

ADAMIAN METALLURGICAL CORPORATION

INCOME AND EXPENSE STATEMENT FOR THE FISCAL YEAR ENDED JULY 31, 1958

		Amounts		*Per Cent of Sales*	
Income:					
General sales			$165,041.52		89.00
Service sales			20,407.02		11.00
Total sales			$185,448.54		100.00
Deduct: Sales discount	$ 1,067.78			0.58	
Breakage of customer parts	1,803.01		2,870.79	0.97	1.55
			$182,577.75		98.45
Deduct: Service purchases			11,405.39		6.15
Gross income			$171,172.36		92.30
Operating expense:					
Plant expense:					
Shop labor		$66,845.58		36.05	
Supplies		10,006.21		5.40	
Gas		6,140.30		3.31	
Power and light		10,521.02		5.67	
Water		389.75		0.21	
Rent		6,099.96		3.29	
Laundry		684.07		0.37	
Truck expense		5,609.35	$106,296.24	3.02	57.32
Administrative expense:					
Executive salary		$11,500.00		6.20	
Office salaries		8,819.94		4.76	
Office supplies		1,760.42		0.95	
Telephone and telegraph		1,791.60		0.97	
Consulting fees		785.00		0.42	
Audit and tax service		187.50		0.10	
Travel and entertainment		6,508.51		3.51	
Sales salary		7,833.27		4.22	
Sales expense		1,747.06	40,933.30	0.94	22.07
General expense:					
Property taxes		$ 1,155.59		0.62	
Payroll taxes		1,769.38		0.95	
Insurance		4,340.66		2.34	
Repairs		7,097.17		3.83	
Depreciation		6,954.72		3.75	
Interest expense		525.52		0.28	
Advertising		5,044.72		2.72	
Bank charges		11.20		0.01	
Miscellaneous		1,991.98	28,890.94	1.08	15.58
Total operating expense			$176,120.48		94.97
Net operating loss			$ (4,948.12)		(2.67)
Other income: Subleasing part of building		$ 2,606.37		1.41	
Other expense: Accounts receivable charged off		361.33	2,245.04	0.19	1.22
Net loss			$ (2,703.08)		(1.45)

Exhibit 3

ADAMIAN METALLURGICAL CORPORATION

STATEMENT OF EARNED SURPLUS AS OF JULY 31, 1958

Balance August 1, 1957		$43,151.06
Deductions:		
Key-man insurance	$1,852.00	
Health and accident insurance	390.45	
Cash dividend	2,160.00	4,402.45
		$38,748.61
Deduct: Net loss for year (Exhibit 2)		2,703.08
Balance July 31, 1958 (to Exhibit 1)		$36,045.53

Exhibit 4

ADAMIAN METALLURGICAL CORPORATION

CONDENSED INCOME STATEMENTS, 1949–1957

		Expenses			Net Operating In-
Fiscal Year	Sales	Operating	Administrative	General	come before Taxes
1957	$180,441	$103,569	$37,874	$29,475	$ 9,523
1956	165,628	94,543	30,688	30,854	9,543
1955	130,078	79,867	25,291	23,748	1,172
1954	173,063	91,846	34,999	29,825	16,393*
1953	156,082	89,112	27,147	22,671	17,152
1952	n.a.				
1951	99,908	56,839	10,744	15,359	16,966
1950	47,546	31,195	5,983	10,212	156
1949	54,787	38,738	6,580	11,450	(1,981)

* Dividends of $1,250 were paid in February, 1954.
n.a. Not available.

Exhibit 5

ADAMIAN METALLURGICAL CORPORATION

COMPUTATION OF BREAK-EVEN PRICES BY TYPE OF FURNACE, CALENDAR YEAR 1957

	Total	Hardening and Tempering	Brazing	Hayes	Induction	Salt Pots	Box	Sand-blasting
Sales	$173,027	$33,272	$53,135	$22,783	$14,453	$40,913	$8,040	$431
Assignable shop expenses:								
Labor	$51,745	$9,973	$7,990	$9,553	$10,602	$10,936	$2,691	...
Supplies	7,545	335	2,065	865	600	2,857	288	$525
Gas	5,945	960	960	480	...	2,400	1,145	...
Power and light	9,576	2,124	4,266	2,124	1,062	...	...	...
Repairs	6,324	170	3,255	1,766	781	158	194	...
Depreciation	4,460	525	650	1,230	1,198	744	...	113
Payroll tax, etc.	2,500	500	400	450	500	500	150	...
Total assignable	$88,095	$14,587	$19,586	$16,478	$14,743	$17,595	$4,468	$638
Profit after assigned expenses	$84,932	$18,685	$33,549	$6,305	$(290)	$23,318	$3,572	$(207)
Shop overhead—distributed on basis of direct labor cost	$20,988	$4,045	$3,241	$3,875	$4,300	$4,436	$1,091	...
Sandblasting loss—split between hardening and tempering and salt pots		104				103		$(207)
Selling expense—distributed on basis of sales for all furnaces except box furnace	35,978	7,275	11,617	4,981	3,160	8,945		
Administrative expense—distributed equally except none to box	31,913	6,383	6,383	6,383	6,382	6,382		
Total expenses	$88,879	$17,807	$21,241	$15,239	$13,842	$19,866	$1,091	$(207)
Net profit or (loss) before taxes	$(3,947)	$878	$12,308	$(8,934)	$(14,132)	$3,452	$2,481	-0-
Revenue required to break even (sales plus loss or minus profit)		$32,394	$40,827	$31,717	$28,585	$37,461		
Estimated equivalent revenue hours per day		16½	15	9½	8	16½		
per year (260 days)		4,290	3,900	2,470	2,080	4,290		
Break-even revenue rate per hour (required ÷ hours) rounded		$7.55	$10.45	$12.85	$13.75	$8.75		
Available capacity: Shifts per day		3	3	2	2	3		
Hours per day								
Hours per year		6,240	6,240	4,160	4,160	6,240		
Break-even revenue rate per hour of available capacity		$5.19	$6.54	$7.62	$6.87	$6.00		

Exhibit 6

ADAMIAN METALLURGICAL CORPORATION

RELATIONSHIP BETWEEN INCOME STATEMENT AND CONSULTANT'S
COST ANALYSIS

Cost Category Used in Exhibit 5	*Operating Expenses Listed in Exhibit 2*	*Cost Variability Rating*
Assignable:	Shop labor (direct laborers)	Partly variable
	Supplies (approximately 75% of total supplies)	Variable
	Gas	Partly variable
	Power and light	Partly variable
	Repairs (approximately 60% of total repairs)	Partly variable
	Depreciation on furnaces	Fixed
Shop overhead:	Shop labor (supervision)	Fixed
	Supplies (remainder not directly assignable)	Fixed
	Water	Fixed
	Laundry	Fixed
	Insurance on building contents	Fixed
	Repairs (remainder not directly assignable)	Fixed
	Miscellaneous	Fixed
	Breakage of customer parts	Unpredictable
Selling expense:	Shop labor (truck driver)	Fixed
	Truck operating expenses	Partly variable
	Travel and entertainment	Controllable
	Sales salary	Fixed
	Sales expense	Fixed
	Insurance on car and truck	Fixed
	Depreciation on car and truck	Fixed
	Advertising	Controllable
Administrative expense:	Rent	Fixed
	Executive salary	Fixed
	Office salaries	Fixed
	Office supplies	Fixed
	Telephone and telegraph	Fixed
	Consulting fees	Controllable
	Audit and tax service	Fixed
	Taxes—property	Fixed
	Insurance—business interruption	Fixed
	Depreciation on office equipment	Fixed
	Interest expense	Fixed
	Bank charges	Fixed
	Key-man insurance (charged directly to surplus)	Fixed

Note: Payroll taxes, which were directly variable with wages and salaries paid, were assigned to each of the four categories on the basis of a percentage of wages and salaries expense.

J. L. JESSUP & SONS

Early in April 1963, the Western States Power Company (WESTCO) announced plans to sell at public sealed bidding a new $5 million series of its first-mortgage bonds. WESTCO would accept bids for the bonds, which were to mature on May 1, 1988, at its offices in Denver, Colorado, until 11.00 A.M. MDT on Tuesday, May 7, 1963. Bidders were required to stipulate a coupon rate on the bonds in a multiple of one eighth of 1% of par value; the price offered to Western States for the bonds was required to be between 99% and 102% of par value. Western States proposed to award the bonds to the bidder whose combination of coupon rate and bid price represented the lowest annual cost of money to it. It reserved the right, however, to reject all bids if none of them were considered acceptable. The sale was subject to receipt of necessary approvals and clearances from federal and state regulatory agencies. The bonds had been rated Aa, the second highest quality rating, by Moody's Investors Service.[1]

The announcement by Western States was not unexpected at the LaSalle Street headquarters of J. L. Jessup & Sons in Chicago. Jessup & Sons, as a leading securities firm, engaged in a variety of financial activities. As a member of the principal securities and commodity exchanges, it offered brokerage services to institutional and individual investors; it also dealt in the over-the-counter securities markets. The buying department, directed by Mr. Francis E. Jessup, a partner in the firm and grandson of the founder, provided financial services to corporations raising funds through new issues of securities. Mr. Jessup was aware that the recently announced plant expansion program of Western States would require funds in excess of those being generated by the company internally. He also knew that the company had a relatively low debt to equity ratio for the electric utility business, and so he

---

[1] For a brief description of the bond market, investment banking, and public sealed bidding, see the appendix at the end of this case.

had anticipated that the company would decide to finance the deficiency in its funds through a new debt issue. Jessup had already decided that should his anticipations prove correct, Jessup & Sons would submit a bid on the new bond issue of Western States.

Most new securities issues are brought to market by what is called the "syndicate method," under which a number of investment banking firms join in a temporary partnership or "syndicate" for the purpose of buying the issue from the corporation and carrying them in inventory until they are finally placed with investors. Because of the relatively small size of the Western States issue, however, Jessup decided not to attempt to form a syndicate to bid on the issue, but rather to bid individually on behalf of Jessup & Sons only.

On April 24, Western States conducted an information meeting for prospective bidders at its offices. At this time, copies of the various documents related to the new bond issue were distributed to the prospective bidders and discussed with them. The treasurer of Western States presided at this meeting and answered questions raised by the bidders regarding the financial plans and prospects of the company. Five other investment banking firms were represented at this meeting in addition to Jessup & Sons. In the subsequent week, however, Mr. Jessup learned that four of these firms had decided against bidding on the Western States issue, leaving Jessup & Sons with only a single competitor, the Continental Securities Corporation.

On Monday evening, May 6, 1963, Mr. Jessup was reviewing the information he had obtained on Western States Power Company, the new bond issue, and the previous record at competitive bidding of Continental Securities Corporation. Prior to 10:45 A.M. MDT the next morning (11:45 A.M. CDT), Mr. Jessup had to decide on the terms of the Jessup & Sons bid. He would then phone these terms to an employee in his department who would be at the Western States office for the purpose of submitting the final bid of Jessup & Sons.

Determination of Price

The first step in Mr. Jessup's analysis was to determine the price at which Jessup & Sons would reoffer the Western States bonds to investors if it should win the bidding. To assist him in reaching this decision, Mr. Jessup had asked Mr. Edward Bowman, a young financial analyst in his department, to prepare a "spread sheet" listing comparative data on the WESTCO bond issue and on outstanding bond issues with similar characteristics, such as quality rating, interest coverage, maturity, and call provisions. Since the outstanding bond issues were traded on the over-the-counter market, it was possible to get price quotations for them which, Mr. Jessup felt, would give him some feel for the price at which the Western States bonds could be sold to the public. Mr. Jessup felt that considerable judgment was required in evaluating this comparative information. No two bond issues were ever exactly alike, even if they came from the same issuer; differences in maturity, coupon rate, and so forth, could have an effect on the price which the public was willing to pay for the bonds of a particular issuer. Investors might also tend to favor securities of one issuer over those of another for qualitative reasons which were not reflected in conventional financial statistics. Even if corrections were made for these factors of noncomparability, it was necessary to consider the fact that the price quotations from the over-the-counter market represented trades of relatively small quantities of bonds, generally less than $100,000 in par value. It was reasonable to expect that lower prices would have been necessary in order to sell as much as $5 million of bonds.

It would, of course, be possible for Jessup & Sons to buy the entire WESTCO bond issue for its own portfolio and to hold it indefinitely, earning interest on it. This would, however, have been against the firm's normal policy of disposing of any new issue within two weeks of acquisition. The partners believed that it was more profitable to turn the firm's limited funds over relatively rapidly in its main line of business, buying and selling securities, rather than permitting them to be tied up for extended periods of time in a small number of issues; the firm deviated from this policy only when there was a prospect of substantial capital gains, which could not be said of a public utility bond issue. For this reason, Mr. Jessup was concerned with setting a price which, in his opinion, would succeed in clearing the entire Western States issue out of inventory within one to two weeks. Any of the bonds remaining in inventory at the end of two weeks would probably have to be sold at whatever price could be obtained for them.

In addition to the comparative data prepared by Mr. Bowman, Mr. Jessup had available to him reports of telephone calls placed by the firm's retail salesmen to a number of large institutional investors— pension funds, trust funds, and insurance companies. Under the regulations of the Securities & Exchange Commission, it is illegal for an investment banker to accept firm orders for new securities before the SEC has given its final clearance to the issue, a clearance which is granted only after the bids have been opened. For this reason, the salesmen were permitted to obtain only "indications of interest" in the issue from their customers, which could not be construed as firm orders. Further detracting from this source of information was the inevitable tendency of potential customers to try to talk down the price of the new issue in order to make it a more attractive buying opportunity when the final price was set. Thus, this information contributed to Mr. Jessup's "feel" for the market but was by no means definitive.

After reviewing all of the information bearing on price that he had accumulated, Mr. Jessup decided that if Jessup & Sons won the bidding on the next day, the WESTCO bonds would be reoffered to the public with a $4\frac{5}{8}\%$ coupon at a price of 101.25% of par value, for a yield of slightly less than 4.54% to the investor. If a single large institutional investor offered to buy the entire issue from Jessup & Sons immediately after the bidding, Mr. Jessup felt that he would be willing to lower this price to 100.75, since such an offer would immediately eliminate virtually all of the costs and risks which Jessup & Sons might otherwise expect to incur in carrying the issue and in selling it publicly. The exception would be $25,000 in legal fees that would still have to be paid. From the reports received from the sales department, however, it did not seem to Mr. Jessup that there was any possibility that a large institutional investor would be interested in acquiring the entire issue at anywhere near this price.

Considerations Affecting Spread

Having decided on a public offering price, Mr. Jessup's next concern was to arrive at a "spread" which would be subtracted from the public offering price to determine the bid which would be submitted to WESTCO. The spread would clearly have to be large enough to cover anticipated costs if it was to be worthwhile submitting a bid at all. Jessup & Sons would also expect compensation for its risks in carrying the bonds until sold. Beyond that, however, the primary determinant of the spread was probably the intensity of the competition for the issue. Even were there no other bidders, of course, Jessup & Sons would have to be reasonable on its spread, since WESTCO had reserved the right to reject all bids in the event none of them were considered acceptable. Beyond that, the fact that Continental Securities Corporation was also expected to submit a bid exerted a further tempering influence on the size of Jessup's contemplated spread.

Mr. Jessup knew Bob Gordon, his counterpart in Continental

Securities, and was aware of the fact that he had a reputation in the business for a "sharp pencil" when it came to figuring prices and bids. Mr. Jessup checked his files and discovered records of 23 previous occasions when both Jessup and Continental had submitted bids on the same issue. The information from his files on these 23 issues is given in Exhibit 1.

Exhibit 1

J. L. JESSUP & SONS
BIDDING HISTORY OF CONTINENTAL SECURITIES CORPORATION

Issue Number*	Par Value (Millions)	Moody Quality Rating†	Number of Bidders‡	Jessup's Proposed Offering Price§	Continental's Bid§
1	27.5	Aa	4	99.036	98.320
2	16.0	Baa	5	103.356	102.502
3	100.0	Aa	3	99.886	99.305
4	12.5	Baa	3	97.542	96.407
5	20.0	Baa	2	99.028	97.526
6	9.0	Baa	4	101.716	100.834
7	2.0	Aa	5	99.018	97.297
8	17.5	A	3	98.017	97.624
9	20.0	Aa	3	94.340	93.260
10	7.5	A	7	99.524	99.206
11	27.5	Aaa	2	100.526	99.526
12	3.5	Baa	3	103.224	101.813
13	17.0	A	3	99.704	99.120
14	13.5	Aaa	2	100.766	100.089
15	45.0	Ba	4	97.986	96.634
16	22.0	Aa	4	99.172	98.586
17	8.5	A	3	101.276	99.864
18	3.0	Aa	5	99.628	98.610
19	35.0	Baa	4	101.014	99.921
20	25.0	Baa	3	97.248	96.228
21	2.5	Baa	4	99.700	97.626
22	12.5	Aa	3	102.712	101.391
23	5.0	Aaa	7	98.878	98.049

Notes:
  * For identification only; not relevant to characteristics of issue.
  † See appendix to this chapter for description.
  ‡ Including Jessup and Continental.
  § As a percentage of par value. To permit comparability, Jessup's price and Continental's bid have been adjusted to a common coupon rate for each issue. The prices and bids given in this exhibit, taken in conjunction with the common coupon rate, result in the same yield to investors or cost of money to the issuer, respectively, as the actual prices and bids taken in conjunction with the actual coupon rates.

APPENDIX

A *bond* is a contract between a corporation and an investor, under which the investor pays a certain sum of money to the corporation in exchange for the corporation's commitment to pay definite sums of money to the bondholder at specified times in the future. While each bond is a separate contract, it is customary for corporations to enter into a large number of such contracts at the same time; the complete collection of such contracts is called a *bond issue*. As a rule, the individual bond contracts in an issue are supplemented by a trust agreement, called the *bond indenture,* running between the corporation and a trustee or trustees. The individual bondholders are the beneficiaries of this agreement which spells out in somewhat greater detail the rights of the bondholders under their individual contracts.

Major provisions covered in the bond and/or indenture are as follows:

1. *Conditions of Payment.* The corporation's promise to make future payments to the bondholders usually involves two parts. First, at a future time known as the *maturity* of the bond, the corporation promises to make a lump-sum payment to the bondholder which will serve to extinguish the contract and the corporation's liability under it. The amount of this lump-sum payment is called the *par value* or principal amount of the bond and serves as a basis for the reckoning of other payments which will or may be made under the contract. It is not required, however, that the amount paid to the corporation by the bondholder be equal to the par value, although some states prohibit the issuance of bonds at less than par value. When bonds are issued at less than par value, the difference between par value and the amount received by the corporation is called a *discount;* the corresponding difference if the issue price is greater than par value is called a *premium.* It is common for bonds to be issued in denominations of $1,000 par value.

Second, during the life of the bond (the period from issue to maturity), the corporation promises to pay interest to the bondholder at stated intervals, generally semiannually. The interest is calculated at an interest or *coupon rate* which is to be applied to the par value to determine the amount of the payment. For example, 5% interest on a bond of $1,000 par value would require the corporation to pay $50 interest annually, or $25 semiannually. On many bonds, the corporation's obligation to pay interest is evidenced by coupons attached to the bond which may be detached and presented to the corporation or its agent for payment on the specified date; hence the term "coupon rate."

The bond contract may also include a *sinking fund* requirement, which compels the corporation to repay some of the bonds in an issue prior to maturity or to provide for repayment by setting aside a fund of money. The contract may also permit the corporation, at its option, to *call* or repay any or all of the bonds prior to maturity. If these provisions are included, the bond contract will generally state the prices and other conditions which are to govern these repayments.

2. *Security.* Many bonds, particularly those of railroads and public utilities, are backed by a mortgage on specified property of the issuing corporation. In the event of default on any of the corporation's obligations under the bond contracts or the indenture, the trustee may foreclose on the mortgage for the benefit of the bondholders. If the bonds are secured by a mortgage, the indenture will usually set forth its provisions, including a description of the property subject to the mortgage. Unsecured bonds are commonly called *debentures.*

3. *Protective Covenants.* Since purchasers of bonds are looking for a high

degree of certainty that payments will be made to them as scheduled, the indenture frequently includes covenants by the corporation to avoid certain specified actions which, it is believed, might endanger its ability to make these payments. For example, the corporation may be restricted in its right to sell assets or to pay dividends on its common stock. These limitations will be set forth in the indenture.

An investor attempting to determine which of two bonds to purchase is thus presented with a wide variety of different features, to say nothing of the inherent differences in the characteristics of the two issuing corporations. Somehow he must be able to cut through this mass of detail in order to determine which of the two bonds is the better for his purposes.

Regarding the payments to be made by the corporation, it is customary to reduce the entire sequence of payments to a single number, called the *yield*. The yield is the annual return on investment, expressed as a percentage, which the investor would earn by purchasing the bonds at the offering price and holding them until maturity. Published bond value tables are available which make it a relatively easy matter to determine the yield on any bond given its current price, its maturity date, and its coupon rate.

As a means of summarizing the factors bearing on the certainty with which payments called for under the bond contract will be made, several investment advisory services prepare and publish *bond ratings*. The best known of these are issued by Moody's Investors Service, Standard & Poor's, and Fitch's. The essential features of these three rating systems are quite similar, and we will use the Moody's rating system merely for illustrative purposes. Further details on each of the systems may be found by consulting publications of the issuing service.

Moody's analysts classify bond issues into nine categories on the basis of a judgmental estimate of the quality of each bond issue, arrived at by consideration of the issuer's financial position and history and other factors. The highest quality rating is Aaa, which is assigned only to bond issues where, in the opinion of Moody's analysts, there is virtual certainty that payments will be made as scheduled. The next highest quality rating is Aa, and the ratings range down to C. Bonds of the lowest ratings are considered to be highly speculative, with relatively low probability that the contractual payments will be made as scheduled. In many states, banks and trust funds are not permitted to invest in bonds of the lower grades, usually those below Baa.

When a business enterprise wishes to obtain new funds through sale of stocks or bonds, it is customary for it to employ an *investment banking firm* to assist it in determining terms of the new issue, setting the price, and performing the merchandising functions of carrying the securities in inventory from time of issue until sale and of finding buyers. Since the fees charged by investment banking firms are usually small relative to the price of the issue being distributed, even relatively small price fluctuations in an issue during the period of distribution can more than wipe out the entire profit expected by the investment banker in entering into the deal. In an issue of substantial size, these market risks might be more than is tolerable for a single investment banking firm. In addition, a substantial amount of capital may be necessary to carry the issue in inventory until final placement with investors, and no single investment banking firm may have adequate resources foɪ this purpose. For these reasons, it has become customary in the investment banking industry for firms to form temporary partnerships, known as *syndicates* or *buying groups,* for the purpose of purchasing or distributing a particular issue. These syndicates are strictly ad hoc; a firm might be a co-member of one syndicate with another investment banking firm at the same time that it is competing against that firm for another issue. One of the firms in a syndicate, generally the one which took the initiative in organizing the syndicate, is designated as the manager, and has the primary decision-making role within the group.

Whether a single investment banking firm or a syndicate handles the distribution of a new issue, the price to be paid to the company for the issue may be determined in one of two ways: by *negotiation* between the issuer and a single purchase syndicate the issuer has invited to deal with him; or by the solicitation of *sealed bids* from any syndicate which cares to submit such a bid.

The method of negotiation is almost universally used in the sale of new securities issues by industrial companies. Railroad and public utility companies, on the other hand, are required by the regulatory authorities in many states to offer new security issues at public sealed bidding. If the issue is to be offered competitively, the company will publish an invitation for bids in the financial press. This invitation will specify the terms of the prospective issue in some detail and will also give the time and place for the submission of bids. Investment banking firms which specialize in managing issues may respond to this invitation by organizing syndicates to bid on the issue.

A prospective bidder on a competitively offered issue, whether individual or syndicate, will generally start by determining a *public offering price* which he intends to quote to prospective investors should he succeed in winning the bid. The next step will be to determine his spread, or the margin he wishes to retain on the issue to cover his expenses and profits. Finally, by subtracting his spread from his proposed public offering price, the bidder will arrive at the bid he will make to the issuer.

When bonds are offered at competitive bidding, the bidding groups will specify the coupon rate on the bonds as well as the price to the company. Since it is possible that two different bidding groups will specify different coupon rates, the issuer must stipulate some way of standardizing bids for purposes of awarding the bonds. The method commonly followed is to award the bonds to the bidder whose combination of coupon rate and bid represent the lowest annual cost of money to the company. Cost of money is defined as the annual rate of interest paid by the company calculated on the amount it receives from the investment bankers. It is calculated in a manner similar to the investor's yield, although, of course, it is somewhat higher than the yield because of the investment banker's spread. The same bond value tables used in determining yield can also be used to determine cost of money to the issuer.

PART III

Decisions to Create Capacity

Chapter 9

DISCOUNTED CASH FLOW ANALYSIS

In Parts I and II of this book we have discussed product-creating costs and demand-creating costs. Now we want to address the problems associated with decisions to incur capacity-creating costs. Decisions to expand or replace capacity differ from the ones presented in earlier chapters mainly in the time over which their impact will be felt. A decision to build a new plant or to install automated equipment will have consequences that can only be measured by looking years into the future. These decisions cannot be reversed without some cost; even automobiles, for which there is an active resale market, lose a substantial portion of their market value immediately upon purchase. Therefore, the purchaser must anticipate some reasonable period of time in which to earn benefits in order to justify the initial cost. The wisdom of the decision is thus dependent upon events which may not occur until well into the future and which cannot be predicted with any high degree of assurance. All decisions must be analyzed by looking into the future; however, in previous problems this look has not exceeded a year or two. Now we want to consider problems that can only be understood by looking 5 to 10 years into the future.

Two major problems result when the time horizon for decisions is expanded. The first is a measurement problem and revolves around the question: What is a dollar worth sometime in the future? Anyone familiar with savings accounts is aware that leaving a dollar in such an account for one year will result in the dollar plus interest being available one year from now. This simple example shows that having a dollar today is worth more than having a dollar one year from now. The analytical technique we want to discuss in this chapter is aimed at helping the decision maker take into account the time value of money.

The second major problem introduced when the time horizon is ex-

443

panded is a computational one. As the time encompassed by the problem increases, there is a large increase in the amount of uncertainty. The further into the future you look, the more events will be present to influence your decision. It will also be true that the range of possible outcomes for an event will tend to be broader as you look into the future. We have presented a framework for analyzing problems with uncertainty in Chapter 4. This will still be used, but because of the increased amount of uncertainty, the computation needed to analyze a problem with a long time horizon is prohibitive. Therefore, in Chapter 10 we will introduce Monte Carlo Simulation as an analytical technique that will allow us to deal with this computational problem.

Finally Chapter 11 will discuss how the financial structure of a company can influence the decisions to create capacity.

FRAMEWORK FOR ANALYSIS

The framework needed to analyze problems with capacity-creating decisions is no different from the one presented in Chapter 4. The framework can be summarized as follows: (1) determine the possible acts and events and their sequence of occurrence; (2) assign a measure of value to each possible sequence of acts and events; (3) assign a probability to the likelihood of each possible sequence of acts and events occurring; (4) determine a certainty equivalent for each initial act taking into account the information generated in steps (2) and (3). A technique for assigning value to the various act-event sequences is the major topic in this section. In the next chapter, we will discuss techniques associated with handling the probabilities in these problems. For the rest of this chapter, we will assume that the outcome of all events are known with certainty in order to concentrate on the valuation problem.

Cash Flow Patterns

In general, it is possible to measure the economic results of any set of decisions and outcomes in terms of a cash flow pattern over time. In some cases it may not be possible to reduce the costs or benefits of a decision to a cash equivalent, and these benefits or costs should not be ignored. When such intangible consequences are present in a problem, the best procedure is first to consider only those consequences that can be converted to cash flows and perform some analysis that results in a tentative decision. This tentative decision can then be modified based on the intangible consequences according to the decision maker's judgment. The judgmental part of this process is critical, and there is little we have to offer in the way of techniques to improve it. However, it should be easier to apply this judgment if some initial analysis has been performed on the problem. It is with this in mind that we proceed to explain some techniques for handling those consequences that can be converted into cash flows.

A useful method for displaying cash flows is a cash flow diagram. Consider a bond that can be purchased for $1,000. It has a yearly interest of 4% and can be redeemed in 10 years. The cash flow diagram for such a bond is shown in Figure 9–1.

Figure 9–1

CASH FLOW PATTERN FOR A 4% BOND

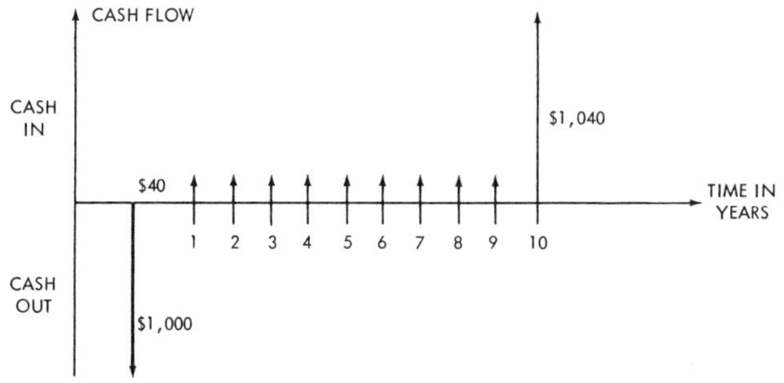

In this diagram the vertical axis represents cash flow; an inflow of cash is shown as a positive amount and an outflow as a negative amount. The horizontal axis is time. It is standard practice to show initial payment being made at the end of year 0, which is the start of year 1. In this example all interest is received at the end of the year. Such a diagram allows you to place in time all the relevant cash flows associated with an investment alternative. A cash flow table can also be used to summarize an investment, where there is one column for each time period and cash outflows are shown as negative amounts. There are many problems associated with determining the relevant cash flows for capacity-creating problems. However, before discussing these it will be useful to discuss how the cash flows would be used once they are determined.

COMPARING ALTERNATIVE CASH FLOW PATTERNS

Once the cash flow patterns of all the alternatives have been identified, the decision maker must decide which alternative he prefers. This is easy if one alternative has higher cash inflows and lower cash outflows in every year. Such an alternative, however, is very unusual. Usually, one alternative has higher cash outflows in some years but higher cash inflows in other years. In this case it would be nice to have a single figure of merit for each alternative that took into account not only the amount but also the timing of the cash flow. In many ways this figure of merit would be like the certainty equivalent in that it would summarize all the important information into one number thus allowing the decision maker to compare alternatives by comparing this single number.

In order to calculate such a figure of merit, we must make one assumption. That assumption is that there always exists some alternative use for the cash that would yield some return to the decision maker. It is not difficult to envision other investment opportunities that could be selected if the cash were not used for the set of alternatives at hand. A common opportunity would be to put the cash into interest-bearing securities. In practice it is difficult to know the rate of return that this other opportunity will yield for the investor. We will discuss various ways of determining this rate in Chapter 11; however, for the moment we will assume that this rate can be determined. The rate that the alternative will yield will be called the *investment opportunity rate.*

We will assume that any cash not required for other investments can be deposited in a savings account earning 10% per year tax-free, figured from date of deposit to date of withdrawal. This savings account is an alternative opportunity to any other act under consideration, and therefore the 10% interest paid on the savings account is the investment opportunity rate.

Suppose you have $10,000 in the special savings account. One year from now, if there are no other deposits or withdrawals, the balance will have grown to $11,000—original balance plus 10% interest on that balance. Two years from now, once again if there are no deposits or withdrawals, the balance will have grown to $12,100—the $11,000 balance in one year plus 10% interest on that balance.[1]

In general terms the amount of cash in the savings account at the end of one year if no deposits or withdrawals are made will be equal to

---

[1] This process assumes that interest is *compounded annually,* that is, the interest itself is added to the balance and commences to earn interest at annual intervals. Interest at 10% per year compounded semiannually is equivalent to 5% interest added to the balance at semiannual intervals.

the starting amount of cash plus that amount multiplied by the interest rate. If we let A_1 be the symbol for the ending amount of cash, P be the symbol for the beginning amount of cash, and i the symbol for interest rate, this relationship can be written as

$$A_1 = P(1 + i) .$$

If the account is ignored for two years, the accumulated cash will be called A_2. But A_2 is equal to A_1 times $(1 + i)$. This means that

$$A_2 = P(1 + i)^2 .$$

In general terms if no deposits or withdrawals are made for N years, the accumulated amount of cash will be

$$A_N = P(1 + i)^N .$$

This relationship is called the compound interest formula. Using this formula it is always possible to calculate what a dollar today will be worth sometime in the future if the investment opportunity rate is known. However, it is often more useful to know what a dollar in the future is worth today. Therefore, we will introduce the idea of *discounting future cash flows into their present values.*

Discounted Cash Flow

Suppose you wished to be able to withdraw $10,000 from the savings account exactly three years from now. How much would you have to have on deposit today? This question is the same as: What balance today would accumulate to $10,000 in three years? Using the compound interest formula, you can calculate that at 10% interest, $1 today will accumulate to $1.10 in one year, $1.21 in two years, and $1.331 in three years. Therefore, in order to have a balance of $10,000 in three years, you must have on deposit today $10,000 ÷ 1.331 = $7,513. For you, with your special savings account, having $10,000 three years in the future is equivalent to having $7,513 today. This is true because the $7,513 could be placed in the savings account and would accumulate to $10,000 at the end of three years. Another way to say this is that the $10,000 three years in the future has a present value $7,513. If this is not clear, take the $7,513 and add 10%. Then add 10% of this total, and then 10% of this final amount. The result should be $9,999.80. The process of reducing future cash flows to their present value is known as *discounting,* and the result is called the discounted cash flow or DCF.

The general expression for discounting can be obtained from the compound interest formula. Dividing both sides by $(1 + i)^N$ will result in the following expression:

$$P = A_N\left[\frac{1}{(1 + i)^N}\right].$$

The term $1/(1 + i)^N$ is called the discount factor and can be found in standard discount tables (see Appendix B). For any investment opportunity rate and any number of years, there is a unique discount factor. With this factor any future amount of cash, A_N, can be converted to its present value, P, by a simple multiplication.

As a test of your understanding of discounting, calculate the present value of $400 six years in the future if your investment opportunity rate is 8%. You should get $252.[2]

Now we can argue that the decision maker should not care whether he receives discounted dollars now or the original amount of dollars in the future, because we have assumed that it is always possible to invest the discounted amount of dollars at the investment opportunity rate and obtain the same original amount of dollars in the future. If this argument is acceptable to the decision maker, we can replace all future cash flows with their discounted values. All of the discounted dollars for each alternative can be added together to obtain a figure of merit for that alternative. This figure of merit is the discounted cash flow for the alternative. The decision maker would then want to select the alternative with the largest DCF. This method of analysis will result in the selection of the alternative that will provide the largest amount of cash to the decision maker at the end of the project life *if all cash generated by the project can be invested at the investment opportunity rate.* It is very important to remember the assumption about the availability of the investment opportunity rate when using DCF to rank or select alternatives.

An Example of DCF Calculation

It will be useful to consider an example of these calculations. Suppose you have to choose between the two investments summarized in Table 9–1.

Investment A requires an initial payment or cash outflow of $1,000 and then returns $400 to you at the end of each of the next five years.

---

[2] The discount factor for an investment opportunity rate of 8% and six years is 0.630. Thus, the present value of $400 six years in the future is $(400 \times 0.630) = \$252$.

Table 9–1

CASH FLOW TABLE FOR TWO INVESTMENTS
($) = CASH OUTFLOW

	0	1	2	3	4	5	Total Cash Flow
			Year				
Investment A.........	$(1,000)	$400	$400	$400	$400	$400	$1,000
Investment B.........	(1,000)	900	500	200	100	100	800

Investment B also requires an initial payment of $1,000 which returns the pattern of cash shown in Table 9–1. Which investment or, more correctly, which pattern of cash flow should you choose if you can take only one?

If your investment opportunity rate is 10%, it is possible to reduce each investment to its net present value. Table 9–2 summarizes such a calculation for each alternative. The discount factors were obtained from Appendix B in the 10% column of Table B–1, entitled "Present Value of $1."

This calculation shows that the DCF of investment A is $516 which is slightly larger than the DCF of investment B. Thus, if your investment opportunity rate were 10% and these were the only investments being considered, you should prefer investment A to investment B.

The fact that the DCF is positive means that the discounted value of the cash inflows exceeds the discounted value of the cash outflows for investment A. Thus, you should conclude that it is more attractive to put the $1,000 in investment A rather than put the $1,000 in your 10% savings account. In order to demonstrate this last point, assume you have $10,000 in your savings account and you can either add $1,000 now or put the $1,000 in investment A. You will also take all

Table 9–2

CALCULATION OF DISCOUNTED CASH FLOW FOR TWO INVESTMENTS

Year	Investment A			Investment B		
	Cash Flow ×	Discount Factor @ 10% =	Discounted Value	Cash Flow ×	Discount Factor @ 10% =	Discounted Value
0..................	(1,000)	1.000	$(1,000.00)	(1,000)	1.000	$(1,000.00)
1..................	400	0.909	363.60	900	0.909	818.10
2..................	400	0.826	330.40	500	0.826	413.00
3..................	400	0.751	300.40	200	0.751	150.20
4..................	400	0.683	273.20	100	0.683	68.30
5..................	400	0.621	248.40	100	0.621	62.10
		DCF =	$ 516.00		DCF =	$ 511.70

the cash inflow from investment A that you receive and put it into your savings account. Table 9–3 shows the two possible results on your savings account.

This comparison leads to the conclusion that a project with a positive DCF is more valuable than investing in the other opportunities represented by the investment opportunity rate.

Table 9–3

SAVINGS ACCOUNT BALANCE WITH INVESTMENT A OR $1,000 DEPOSIT

	Investment A				$1,000 Deposit			
Year	Beginning Balance	Interest Payment	Cash Deposit	Ending Balance	Beginning Balance	Interest Payment	Cash Deposit	Ending Balance
0........	10,000.00	...	...	10,000.00	10,000.00	...	1,000	11,000.00
1........	10,000.00	1,000.00	400	11,400.00	11,000.00	1,100.00	...	12,100.00
2........	11,400.00	1,140.00	400	12,940.00	12,100.00	1,210.00	...	13,310.00
3........	12,940.00	1,294.00	400	14,634.00	13,310.00	1,331.00	...	14,641.00
4........	14,634.00	1,463.40	400	16,497.40	14,641.00	1,464.10	...	16,105.10
5........	16,497.40	1,649.74	400	18,547.14	16,105.10	1,610.51	...	17,715.61

In this example so far we have assumed that the investment opportunity rate was 10%. What would you expect if the investment opportunity rate were 20%? This would mean that current cash flows would be more valuable and investment B would be more attractive than before. As an exercise you should calculate the DCF of both projects with an investment opportunity rate of 20%. What decision would you make in this situation? What will happen to investment A if your investment opportunity rate is 30%?

DETERMINING THE CASH FLOW PATTERN

We are able to rank cash flow patterns using their DCF. Now we want to discuss how the cash flow pattern can be developed for a decision to expand or replace capacity. As we mentioned above, there are many problems associated with obtaining the relevant cash flows for a decision involving capacity-creating costs. Quite often these decisions problems are called capital expenditure problems, and we will often use that terminology in this chapter.

Classification of Cash Flows

As an illustration of the analysis of capital expenditures, we will use the following example: The Beach Company is considering the introduction of a new product, which it anticipates being able to sell at a price of $5 per unit at the rate of 20,000 units a year. There are under consideration two alternative means of producing the product. One method involves the acquisition of a piece of special-purpose equipment for $110,000 installed. With this equipment, the variable costs per unit of product will be $2 and there will also be an increase in out-of-pocket overhead costs of $10,000 per year due primarily to additional supervision. The other method involves the acquisition of less specialized equipment at a cost of $80,000. The variable costs per unit using this method, however, will be $3; and the additional out-of-pocket overhead will be $12,000 per year.

This example illustrates three main categories of cash flows which may often be identified in capital expenditure analyses. They are:

1. *Cash flows which vary on a per-unit basis.* This category is comprised principally of prices and variable costs. Segregating these items into a separate category facilitates investigations of the sensitivity of cash flows to volume changes. We may wish to determine, for example, the volume of cash flow above which the special-purpose machine would be more advantageous than the general-purpose machine. Or we may wish to determine the volume below which introducing the new product would be unprofitable no matter how manufactured.

2. *Cash flows which vary on a per-year basis.* This category is comprised principally of overhead items which are fixed relative to the volume of production but do depend upon which alternative is selected and hence are relevant to the decision. The costs in our example associated with additional supervision fall into this category.

3. *"Lump-sum" cash flows.* The principal item in this category is the investment required for each alternative, which varies neither "per unit" nor "per year." Lump-sum expenditures for major overhaul required at some future date might be another illustration.

To use a more familiar example, we might consider the expenses associated with owning and operating an automobile. The costs of gasoline, oil, tires, and repairs vary, at least approximately, on a per-unit basis, that is, proportionately to mileage. Registration and insurance expenses, however, vary on a per-year basis, while the initial cost of the automobile represents a lump-sum investment.

Special Problems in the Measurement of Cash Flows

There are a few problems in the measurement of cash flows which often seem to create difficulty. The problem areas are accounting amortizations; income taxes; and working capital.

Accounting Amortizations versus Cash Flows. When a business enterprise makes a capital expenditure, it is the common practice of accountants to "capitalize" this expenditure, that is, record its cost as an asset on the enterprise's financial statements. The cost is then "amortized" over the periods during which the benefits of the expenditure are expected to occur, by charging a portion of the cost as an expense of each such period.[3]

If the Beach Company bought the special-purpose machine, its accountants would first record as an asset the $110,000 initial cost. If it were estimated that the machine would be of service for four years, the accountants would then write off a portion of this $110,000 cost as "depreciation expense" in each of the four years. If the straight-line method of calculating depreciation were used, the annual depreciation expense would be one fourth of $110,000, or $27,500.

Depreciation and similar accounting amortizations of capital expenditures, while recorded as expenses on an income statement, are *not* cash outflows. The cash outflow took place when the capital expenditure was made, and the amortization represents only the accountants' subsequent attempt to allocate this expenditure to the benefiting time periods. For this reason, it would be incorrect to include as costs in a given analysis *both* the initial outlay *and* the subsequent amortization of it. Since in our analysis we will wish to calculate the discounted cash flow, the appropriate figure to use will be the actual cash outlay. (As we shall see in the following paragraphs, however, accounting amortizations do have income tax effects which result in relevant cash flows.)

Income Taxes. In earlier decision problems we placed little emphasis on the effects of income taxes. This lack of emphasis was justifiable in problems not involving capital expenditures since income taxes occur essentially simultaneously with the costs or revenue effects and are generally proportional to profits. Thus an alternative which maximizes profits before taxes will usually also maximize profits after taxes in the same period of time.

When capital expenditures are being considered, by contrast, it is not true that after-tax cash flow is proportional to before-tax cash flow. The time pattern of cash flow will not be the same as the time pattern of taxable earnings, so that when the opportunity cost of money "tied

---

[3] When the periods during which benefits may be expected are difficult to specify, as in the cases of advertising and research and development, the accountant might, in order to be conservative in his evaluation of the company's assets, expense the capital expenditure immediately instead of first capitalizing it and then amortizing it.

up" in the project is taken into account, income taxes will affect the relative desirability of the alternatives under consideration.

To be specific, let us return to the Beach Company example, assuming that the Beach Company pays federal and state income taxes equal to 55% of taxable income. Assuming that Beach decides to buy the special-purpose machine referred to earlier, it will have an immediate cash outlay of $110,000. It will not, however, be permitted to write off this entire outlay immediately for tax purposes but instead will be required to capitalize it and take the tax deductions in the form of depreciation charges over the estimated useful life of the machine. If this life is estimated at four years, for example, and if straight-line depreciation is used, the tax deduction will be $27,500. This deduction will result in a credit against taxes of 55% of $27,500, or $15,125 per year. Since taxes represent a cash outlay, the credit of $15,125 per year is a cash savings. The tax credit is not received when the outlay is made, however, so its value is not as great as it would be if an immediate write-off of the expenditure were permitted.

While the federal tax laws do not in most cases permit an immediate write-off of capital expenditures, they do permit the use of two depreciation methods other than the straight-line method, both of which result in writing off a more substantial proportion of the cost of an asset in its earlier years. These two methods are called the *double-declining-balance* method and the *sum-of-the-years'-digits* method.

Under the double-declining-balance method, the depreciation rate used is double the straight-line rate. For an asset with a four-year life, for example, the double-declining-balance rate is 50% per year rather than 25%. This rate, however, is applied to the undepreciated balance of the asset rather than to its original cost, as illustrated in the Table 9–4, for the special-purpose machine. The cash savings due to taxes is the tax rate times the depreciation. The pure double-declining-balance

Table 9–4

SPECIAL-PURPOSE MACHINE TAX SAVINGS USING
DOUBLE-DECLINING-BALANCE DEPRECIATION

Year	Beginning Balance	Depreciation Write-off	Ending Balance	Cash Savings Due to Reduced Taxes
1	$110,000	$55,000	$55,000	$30,250.0
2	55,000	27,500	27,500	15,125.0
3	27,500	13,750	13,750	7,562.5
4	13,750	13,750	0	7,562.5

method would never succeed in writing off the entire cost of the asset, but the tax laws permit the owner to shift to a straight-line write-off of the remaining undepreciated balance at any time. In Table 9–4, this shift has been made after the third year.

The annual depreciation charge under the sum-of-the-years'-digits method is calculated in the following way: First the "sum-of-the-years'-digits" is calculated by adding together the digits representing each year in the estimated useful life of the asset. For example, for the special-purpose machine being considered by the Beach Company, this sum is $1 + 2 + 3 + 4 = 10$. The annual depreciation rate in each year is then determined by using this sum as the denominator in a fraction of which the numerator is one of the years' digits, taken in reverse order. The depreciation rate for the special-purpose machine in its first year, for example, would be $4/10$. This rate is applied to the original cost of the asset. The entire procedure is illustrated in Table 9–5, for the special-purpose machine.

Table 9–5

SPECIAL-PURPOSE MACHINE TAX SAVINGS USING
SUM-OF-THE-YEARS'-DIGITS METHOD OF DEPRECIATION

Year	Depreciation Rate	Depreciation Write-off	Cash Savings Due to Reduced Taxes
1	4/10	$44,000	$24,200
2	3/10	33,000	18,150
3	2/10	22,000	12,100
4	1/10	11,000	6,050

Since either of these alternative depreciation methods provides higher tax credits than straight-line depreciation in the early years, they are used by many companies for tax reporting.

Working Capital. Many capital-expenditure proposals will entail an investment in working capital. This will be particularly true in the case of expansion proposals. In the Beach Company example, since the proposals under consideration contemplate the introduction of a new product, it is probable that additional inventories of raw materials, work in process, and finished goods will be required. In addition, if Beach Company extends credit to its customers, additional accounts receivable will have to be carried.

Even nonexpansion proposals may result in an increase in working capital. Suppose, for example, that the general-purpose machine being considered by the Beach Company requires a periodic setup whereas the special-purpose machine does not. Because of setup cost, it will probably be desirable to manufacture the product in larger lots if the general-purpose machine is purchased, and as a consequence the holding of larger inventories will be necessitated.

If a project requires an increase in working capital, the additional working capital requirement should be considered as a cash outflow at the inception of the project. At the termination of the project, the release of working capital should ordinarily be treated as a cash inflow.

Project Life

In our description of the Beach Company example, one important fact was omitted: the period of time over which the two machines would render service. We will refer to such a period as the *life* of the project in question.

One reason we did not introduce the project life into the earlier discussion is that, strictly speaking, the project life is not a "fact" but is, rather, subject to management discretion. Given a profit orientation, a company will prefer keeping a project in service to retiring it so long as the profits from keeping it in service exceed those from retiring it. When the life of the project is determined, as suggested here, by profit considerations, we will refer to it as the *economic* life.

In our subsequent discussions of the Beach Company example, we will assume that the special-purpose machine has an estimated economic life of four years and the general-purpose machine has an economic life of seven years. These estimates mean that, considering all of the factors discussed in this section, it is the best judgment of the Beach Company management that it will be four years before it is economical to retire the special-purpose machine and seven years in the case of the general-purpose machine.

For future reference, the basic data of the Beach Company example are summarized in Table 9–6.

Table 9–6

SUMMARY OF DATA FOR BEACH COMPANY EXAMPLE

	No Machine	Special-Purpose Machine	General-Purpose Machine
Initial investment	$0	$110,000	$ 80,000
Annual sales	$0	$100,000	$100,000
Variable cost of sales	0	40,000	60,000
Variable gross profit	$0	$ 60,000	$ 40,000
Additional out-of-pocket overhead	0	10,000	12,000
Annual contribution before taxes	$0	$ 50,000	$ 28,000
Taxes at 55%	0	27,500	15,400
Annual contribution after taxes	$0	$ 22,500	$ 12,600
Expected life	n.a.	4 years	7 years

We can use the discounting technique to measure the value of each of the three alternatives available to the Beach Company. We will assume that the investment opportunity rate for the company is 10% after taxes and that the company uses the double-declining-balance method to calculate its depreciation. Figure 9–2 shows the cash flow patterns for each of the Beach company's alternatives. Cash outflows are shown in parentheses. One column is shown for each year including year zero which is now. The initial machine investments are assumed to occur in year zero. The total cash column shows that the general-

Figure 9–2

CASH FLOW PATTERNS IN THOUSANDS OF DOLLARS

		YEAR								
		0	1	2	3	4	5	6	7	TOTAL
GENERAL PURPOSE	INVESTMENT	(80.0)	–	–	–	–	–	–	–	(80.0)
	A.T. OPERATIONS DEPRECIATION	0	12.6	12.6	12.6	12.6	12.6	12.6	12.6	88.2
	TAX SAVINGS*	0	12.6	9.0	6.4	4.6	3.8	3.8	3.8	44.0
	TOTAL	(80.0)	25.2	21.6	19.0	17.2	16.4	16.4	16.4	52.2
SPECIAL PURPOSE	INVESTMENT	(110.0)	–	–	–	–	–	–	–	(110.0)
	A.T. OPERATIONS DEPRECIATION	0	22.5	22.5	22.5	22.5	–	–	–	90.0
	TAX SAVINGS*	0	30.3	15.1	7.6	7.5	–	–	–	60.5
	TOTAL	(110.0)	52.8	37.6	30.1	30.0	–	–	–	40.5
DO NOTHING	TOTAL	0	0	0	0	0	0	0	0	0

* 55% of depreciation charge. Includes some rounding error.

purpose machine will provide +$52,200 after-tax cash flow over the project life, while the special-purpose machine provides only +$40,500 during its life. This total cash flow is a single figure of merit that could be used to compare the alternatives; however, it ignores the timing of the cash flows. Figure 9–2 shows that all of the cash flow from the special-purpose machine is in the first four years, while the general-purpose machine does not provide some of its benefits until year 7. Therefore, a better comparison could be made if all cash flows were converted to their discounted values.

Discount factors for each year at 10% can be obtained from Appendix B at the end of this text. These factors along with the cash flow patterns are shown in Table 9–7. The discounted cash flow is obtained by multiplying the discount factor by the corresponding yearly cash flow and summing the product for all years.

The general-purpose machine has a net present value of $14,500. It is important to remember what this means. If the Beach Company had the imaginary tax-free 10% savings account, they could invest $14,500 in it today and in seven years they would have a balance of $28,275.[4] If instead they borrowed $80,000 from the account today to purchase the general-purpose machine and then deposited all the cash income from the general-purpose machine into the account, at the end of seven years they would have exactly this same balance.[5] Therefore, they should be indifferent between having $14,500 today or buying the general-purpose machine.

Table 9-7

DCF CALCULATION AT 10% INVESTMENT OPPORTUNITY RATE
($000)

Year	Discount Factor @ 10%	General Purpose Cash Flow	General Purpose Discounted Value	Special Purpose Cash Flow	Special Purpose Discounted Value
0	1.000	−80.0	−80.0	−110.0	−110.0
1	0.909	25.2	22.9	52.8	48.0
2	0.826	21.6	17.8	37.6	31.1
3	0.751	19.0	14.3	30.1	22.6
4	0.683	17.2	11.7	30.0	20.5
5	0.621	16.4	10.2	...	...
6	0.564	16.4	9.2	...	...
7	0.513	16.4	8.4	...	...
Discounted cash flow			14.5		12.2

A similar calculation can be made for the special-purpose machine. Table 9-7 shows the net present value to be $12,200. This amount placed in the savings account will have the same balance as the cash flow from the special-purpose machine in the savings account at the end of year 4.

OTHER CRITERIA

Unfortunately, the Beach Company cannot make a decision on these DCF figures as shown in Table 9-7. The DCF for one alternative is based on a project life of seven years, and the DCF for the other alternative is for a four-year project life. It is necessary to determine what happens in the fifth, sixth, and seventh years under the special-

[4] The final balance is obtained by using the compound interest formula. The balance is: $A = (1 + 0.10)^7(14,500) = (1.95)(14,500) = 28,275$.

[5] As an exercise you may want to calculate this balance. Assume that all cash flows are borrowed from or paid to the 10% savings account.

purpose machine alternative before a meaningful comparison can be made. One possible assumption is that the company would discontinue the production of the product, and thus the resulting cash flow in each of the three years would be zero dollars. If this is true the two DCF calculated in Table 9–7 can be compared without further adjustment. The general-purpose machine has the higher DCF and would be preferred to the special-purpose machine. In addition, since the DCF is greater than zero, the general-purpose machine is better than doing nothing.

This decision is based on a rather odd assumption, specifically that the company would not continue production of the product after year 4 if its management decides to use the special-purpose machine. Since management knows that the special-purpose machine has a positive DCF for the first four years, a more realistic assumption would be that it would replace the machine at the end of year 4 with a similar device and continue operations for four more years. This assumption still does not solve the problem of unequal lives for the two alternatives because now one alternative has a life of seven years and the other has a life of eight.

One way of achieving a valid comparison between the two machines would be to consider as the alternatives two sequences of machines:

a) A sequence of seven special-purpose machines,
b) A sequence of four general-purpose machines.

Since each of these alternatives would have a "life" of 28 years, they could be compared on a DCF basis. However, a more convenient way of accomplishing the same result is to calculate and compare the *equivalent annual cash flow* for each alternative.

Equivalent Annual Cash Flow

The equivalent annual cash flow for a project is the amount of cash needed in *each* year of the project life to obtain the same DCF as the actual cash flows from the project. The special-purpose machine has a DCF of $12,200, and this resulted from a four-year project life. The equivalent annual cash flow for this project is some amount, call it X for the time being. The DCF of X cash inflow received in each of the next four years must be equal to $12,200. Table 9–8 shows how this DCF could be calculated and shows how the amount X can be obtained.

Table 9–8

CALCULATION OF EQUIVALENT ANNUAL CASH FLOW
FOR SPECIAL-PURPOSE MACHINE ALTERNATIVE

Year	Discount Factor at 10%	Cash Flow	Discounted Value of Cash Flow
1	0.909	$X	(0.909)X
2	0.826	$X	(0.826)X
3	0.751	$X	(0.751)X
4	0.683	$X	(0.683)X
	3.169		

$$\text{Discounted cash flows} = (3.169)X$$
$$\text{DCF of annual flow} = \text{DCF of actual project}$$
$$3.169X = 12,200$$
$$X = 12,200 \div 3.169$$
$$X = 12,200(0.315)$$
$$X = 3,843$$

The equivalent annual cash flow for the special-purpose machine is $3,849. The advantage of this number is that it does not change when the special-purpose alternative is increased to an eight-year life of two machines having identical cash flows in each four-year segment. In fact, no matter how many identical four-year projects are chained together, this equivalent annual cash flow will remain unchanged. Because of this feature the decision maker can choose the project with the highest equivalent annual cash flow and be confident that he is making the same choice he would make if he converted all alternatives to an equal project life and choose the alternative with the highest discounted cash flow.

Before Beach Company management can make a decision, it must calculate the equivalent annual cash flow for the general-purpose machine. This could be done in a manner similar to that shown in Table 9–8, namely, obtain the discount factors for the first seven years from Table B–1 in Appendix B, sum them, and divide that sum into the net present value of the general-purpose alternative. However, some of this work has already been done and is summarized in Table B–2 of Appendix B. The sum of the individual discount factors is shown in this table entitled "The Present Value of $1 Received Annually for N Years." So it is not necessary to add all the separate factors. The reciprocal of this sum is called the *capital recovery factor*. The capital recovery factor for a seven-year project life at 10% is 1 ÷ 4.868 or 0.205. The DCF of the general-purpose machine from Table 9–7 is

$14,500. Therefore, the equivalent annual cash flow for this alternative is ($14,500) × (0.205) = $2,973. It would be a useful exercise to see whether you can calculate this number using the process shown in Table 9–8.

The special-purpose machine has an equivalent annual cash flow of $3,843, and the general-purpose machine has an equivalent annual cash flow of $2,973. Thus, if the Beach Company plans to replace each machine at the end of its life with an identical piece of equipment, the best alternative is the special-purpose machine.

Rate of Return

So far we have discussed DCF and equivalent annual cash flow as figures of merit for ranking alternatives. A third criterion that takes into account both the amount and timing of cash flows is the *rate of return*. The rate of return of an alternative can be found by determining the discount rate which makes the discounted value of the cash inflows resulting from the alternative equal to the discounted value of the cash outflows. In other words, it is the discount rate which makes the DCF equal to zero. This discount rate is the rate of return, since the equality of the two cash streams signifies that the cash inflows are just sufficient to recover the cash outflows plus a rate of return on the unrecovered balance equal to that discount rate.

In general, except for simple cash flow patterns, calculation of the rate of return on investment involves a trial-and-error process. First a discount rate is selected arbitrarily and the DCF of the alternative is determined at that discount rate. If a positive DCF is obtained, a higher discount rate is selected on the next trial. This will reduce the discounted value of the cash inflows. If a negative DCF results, a lower discount rate is used. This process is continued until a DCF of zero is obtained.

It is obvious from Table 9–7 that the rate of return on both the special-purpose and general-purpose machines is greater than the 10% investment opportunity rate because both have positive DCF. Table 9–9 shows the DCF of each alternative at different discount rates. From this information, we can determine that the rate of return on the special-purpose machine is about 15.7% per year and the rate on the general-purpose machine is about 15.9% per year. Often it is useful to plot a graph with the DCF on the vertical axis and the discount rates on the horizontal axis for each alternative. After calculating several DCFs, a rough graph can be drawn. This graph crosses the horizontal axis at the rate of return because that is where the DCF is equal to zero.

Since the same logic underlies both the DCF index and the rate of return index, in theory the two criteria can be used interchangeably to rank alternatives. There are, however, some practical differences.

One advantage of rate of return is that businessmen often find it easier to think in terms of rate of return than in terms of discounted dollars. This is perhaps because the notion of rate of return is a common one in connection with financial assets, such as stocks, bonds, and savings accounts.

Table 9–9

DISCOUNTED CASH FLOW FOR VARIOUS DISCOUNT RATES

Discount Rate	*DCF Special Purpose*	*DCF General Purpose*
10%	$12,200	$14,500
12	7,600	9,200
14	3,300	4,200
15	1,300	2,000
16	− 700	− 200
18	−4,500	−4,300

Many people also like rate of return because it tends to obviate the need to set a precise investment opportunity rate. If the rate of return of a project has been calculated, it can be decided intuitively whether this rate is satisfactory. Of course, this does not avoid the problem entirely, since difficult borderline decisions will still remain in which the rate of return is close to what the decision maker thinks is satisfactory.

One disadvantage of rate of return is a clerical one: It is difficult to calculate. Whenever the pattern of cash flows is irregular, it is necessary to solve for the rate of return by successive approximations.

A more serious problem in the use of rates of return as decision indicators is that as they are usually calculated in practice, they are not strictly comparable from one alternative to another. For example, a 20% return on a one-year alternative is not necessarily better than a 15% return on a two-year alternative. It all depends upon what opportunities are available in the second year for investing the funds returned by the one-year alternative.

Suppose, for example, the investment opportunity rate for funds in the second year is 8%. Then the 20% investment offers the opportunity of a return in two years equal to $(1.20) \times (1.08) = 1.296$

times the original outlay; while the 15% investment offers the opportunity of a return in two years equal to $(1.15)^2 = 1.32$ times the original outlay.

In fact, the rates of return calculated for the Beach Company are misleading because of this reason. The special-purpose machine cash flow ends in year 4. If we state that the rate of return for this machine is 15.7% and compare it to the general-purpose machine's rate of return of 15.9% for a seven-year project, we imply that funds from the special-purpose machine can earn at a rate of 15.7% in years 5, 6, and 7. This may be correct if we assume that another special-purpose machine can be purchased in year 4, and it will also return 15.7%. If this is not the case, then some other assumption must be made before a rate of return can be calculated.

It is possible to correct the rate of return calculation to compensate for this problem by making an explicit assumption about reinvestment opportunities (as we have done in the last paragraph). This correction increases the amount of clerical effort required, however, and it also requires the specification of an investment opportunity rate, thereby negating one of the previously mentioned advantages of rate of return.

SUMMARY

We have described the following procedure for selecting between alternatives for capital expenditures. First, define clearly all the possible alternatives and determine the cash flow pattern resulting from each over their entire project lives. Next, use some figure of merit to rank the alternatives that gives weight to the amount *and* timing of the cash flow. We have described three such figures of merit: discounted cash flow, equivalent annual cash flow, and rate of return. Care should be exercised when using such figures of merit to assure that the cash flows of the alternatives have been measured over the same time period or that explicit assumptions have been made about what will happen in those years when some alternatives are not generating cash.

PROBLEMS

Problem 9–1. Calculate the discounted cash flow and equivalent annual cash flow at 0%, 4%, 10%, and 16% investment opportunity rates for the following cash flow pattern:

Year	0	1	2	3	4	5	6	7
Cash flow	(500)	200	100	100	100	100	100	200

What is the rate of return for this project?

Problem 9–2. The Harcourt Company is considering the purchase of new equipment to perform operations currently being performed on different, less efficient equipment. The purchase price of the new equipment is $8,000, delivered and installed.

The company estimates that the equipment will produce annual labor and direct cost savings of $2,500 per year. The equipment life is five years, at which time it is estimated there will be zero salvage value. The present equipment is in good working order and can be used for seven years.

The company can borrow money at 10%, although it does not plan to negotiate a loan for this new equipment if it is purchased. The company has a policy requiring a return of 30% on new investments.

Assignment

1. If there are no income taxes, should the Harcourt Company purchase this machine?

For the rest of this problem assume that taxes are 50% and that losses or gains from sale of equipment must be treated as ordinary expenses of income. Also the company policy is to require a 15% return after taxes on new investments.

2. The present equipment has a book value of $4,200 and will be depreciated using the straight-line method over the remaining seven years of its life. The present equipment has no salvage value now. The new equipment will be depreciated using the straight-line method over its five-year life. Should Harcourt buy the new equipment? Why or why not?

3. Suppose the present equipment can be sold today for $1,000. Should Harcourt buy the new equipment? Why or why not?

FEDERAL AVIATION AGENCY (A)[1]

In the early 1960s the Federal Aviation Agency (FAA) decided to standardize on 50 kc/s (kilocycles per second) channel spacing for their radio communications systems operating in the VHF (very high frequency) range for nonmilitary air traffic control because of an anticipated shortage of frequencies.

At that time, the FAA operated many VHF tube-type radio receivers having 50 kc/s channel spacing; however, some of the older sets were of the 100 kc/s and 200 kc/s type. All UHF (ultra-high frequency) receivers used for military air traffic control were of the 100 kc/s type. Narrow channel spacing would permit a larger number of assigned frequencies within a given section of the radio spectrum. Accordingly in 1963 a contract was let for 3,210 tube-type VHF receivers at a cost of $319.70 per receiver.

During 1964, the Agency's Systems Research and Development Service (SRDS) completed development of specifications for 50 kc/s solid-state VHF and UHF receivers that would meet Agency requirements. The Agency's Installation and Materiel Service (IMS) proposed in early 1965 that all tube-type VHF receivers should be replaced by the solid-state type. Supporting this proposal was a brief cost-benefit analysis prepared by the Agency's Systems Maintenance Service (SMS) which indicated that the capital cost of the proposed procurement would be amortized in three to four years.

The Review Process

The IMS proposal was included as a single-line item in the list of total Agency projects being considered for inclusion in the Agency's

---

[1] The case is intended for class discussion only, and certain names and facts may have been changed which, while avoiding the disclosure of confidential information, do not materially lessen the value of the case for educational purposes. This case is not intended to represent either effective or ineffective handling of an administrative situation, nor does it purport to be a statement of policy by the agency involved.

464

five-year plan (FY 1966–70) by the Agency Review Board (ARB). The ARB consisted of the deputy administrator and the four associate administrators, with the director of the Office of Budget acting as secretary. The ARB discussed the IMS proposal in April 1965, and directed the Office of Budget's Requirements Analysis Staff (RAS) to validate the data prepared by SMS.

The RAS had been created within the Office of Budget to provide an independent analysis of major proposed projects. The ARB felt that in order to be able to more properly evaluate the various proposals which came to its attention, it was necessary to have an independent staff group to assess the justifications accompanying these proposals. Most items proposed for inclusion in the five-year plan did not go to RAS for evaluation. Many expenditure proposals fell into categories for which acceptability criteria had already been established and were thus included in the plan.

In the meantime, the Agency's Air Traffic Service (ATS) had prepared a staff study to evaluate an IMS proposal to procure 5,100 50 kc/s UHF solid-state receivers to replace the existing 100 kc/s UHF tube-type receivers. In April 1965, the RAS obtained this ATS study and began to prepare their own evaluation of both the UHF and VHF solid-state receiver procurement proposals separately for presentation to the Agency Review Board. The remainder of this case is concerned only with the VHF solid-state receiver proposal.

Mission of the Federal Aviation Agency

The Federal Airway System was established to increase the safety of aircraft traveling through the airspace over the United States. In 1965 it was the most extensive network of air navigation aids in the world, ranging from small location markers to complex radar systems. Most operated 24 hours a day; a large percentage of them were unattended but monitored and checked on a regular basis by technicians to assure proper operation.

In 1965 there were two FAA approved methods of flying: (1) visual flight rules (VFR) and (2) instrument flight rules (IFR). Many smaller aircraft were not equipped with the instrumentation necessary for flying by IFR; in 1965, there was no law that required an aircraft to have even a two-way radio, although almost all new planes were so equipped. As the number of aircraft and the sophistication of their navigation and communications equipment increased, there was an increasing utilization of FAA facilities and services. In 1965, there were

35.6 million aircraft operations (landing or takeoff) recorded. By 1972 it was estimated that this activity would increase by 69%.

An aircraft flying IFR would be in VHF radio contact with two main types of FAA facilities: (1) airport towers and (2) air traffic control centers with their attendant RCAG (Remote Communications Air/Ground). In addition, Flight Service Stations (FSS) would provide weather and other general information.

A pilot wishing to take off from, say, the Washington National Airport, first received his taxiing instructions from Ground Control over one VHF frequency. When ready for takeoff, he switched to Clearance Delivery on a second frequency to check his flight plan. Tower Control then took over on a third frequency and gave him final takeoff authorization. As soon as he was airborne, he switched to a fourth frequency to communicate with Departure Control. Once takeoff procedures were completed, the Washington Center (Leesburg, Va.) took over on yet another frequency. As he traveled from Washington to, say, Boston, the pilot would be able to communicate with the Washington, New York, and Boston centers directly via RCAG or individually through Flight Service Stations located along his route.

Each VHF frequency used in this process involved a separate FAA receiver on the ground because most of the tube-type receivers in use, as well as all the proposed solid-state receivers, were of the fixed-tuned type.

The Replacement Proposal

The number and distribution of the tube-type receivers, as of December 31, 1964, was as follows:

Type of Facility	—Number of VHF Receivers (Tube Type)—		
	Primary	Backup	Total
RCAG and centers	1,165	1,165	2,330
FSS	955	...	955
Towers	3,220	510	3,730
Total	5,340	1,675	7,015

There were approximately 380 RCAG and centers, 350 FSS, and 300 towers in the FAA system.

Reliability. One of the questions to be resolved if the tube-type receivers were replaced was whether or not solid-state receivers would require the installation of "backup" receivers to be available (in case of failure of the primary receiver) on a one-to-one basis, because of their much higher reliability. In preparing its specifications, the Systems Research and Development Service estimated the following "availability for use" of the equipment: (*a*) solid-state with no backup, 99.93%; (*b*) solid-state with backup, 100.00% (virtually); (*c*) tube type with backup, 99.85%. However, availability was also affected by control equipment and line[1] and power failures. Adjusted availability estimates including these factors were as follows: (*a*) 99.43%, (*b*) 99.49%, (*c*) 99.35%.

Estimated Cost. As part of the SRDS specifications, contract cost data was estimated based on (*a*) replacing all 7,015 tube-type receivers and (*b*) replacing only the 5,340 primary receivers. A contract to purchase 7,015 solid-state receivers was expected to result in an estimated unit cost of $340 per receiver; the cost would be increased to $385 per receiver if only 5,340 were ordered. In both cases the installation cost was estimated at $75 per receiver. If a policy of piece-meal replacement were adopted, the smaller contracts involved would result in a unit cost of approximately $480. Delivery was estimated at 12 months following the letting of the contract, with delivery at the rate of 325 receivers per month.

Although SRDS specifications for solid-state receivers had been prepared by early 1965, no actual receivers had been purchased. Thus, the unit costs quoted above were estimates. Although transistors and other solid-state devices had been in use for almost 20 years for digital applications, the development of transistorized equipment for the analog applications involved in commercial radio receivers had proceeded much more slowly.

Operating Savings. The proposal from the Installation and Materiel Service pointed out that the use of solid-state semiconductor devices, diodes and transistors, would result in an annual savings in power costs, maintenance, and tube replacement costs. Solid-state receivers were also more compact and thus would occupy less space in the facilities than the tube-type receivers. In addition, the longer life expectancy and greatly reduced size of the semiconducting components would significantly reduce the quantity of spares stocked and the storage space required for a given quantity. Additional information about each of these potential savings is given below.

    1. *Maintenance Labor.* Of the total of 7,015 tube-type receivers in use, 620 were multichannel receivers, involving different maintenance and

---

[1] For example, the microwave or leased telephone company cables connecting an RCAG with its center.

utility costs from those for the 6,395 fixed-tuned receivers. The budgeted annual maintenance time for tube-type receivers was 39.6 man-hours per fixed-tuned receiver, and 55.4 man-hours per multichannel receiver. The estimated annual maintenance time per solid-state receiver was 19.9 man-hours. This estimated time for the solid-state receivers represented a 50% reduction from the fixed-tuned tube-type receivers; however, some FAA engineers felt that the potential reduction would possibly be closer to 75%. Maintenance time, which included travel, was costed at $9,602 per man-year of 2,080 man-hours. Additional information about the maintenance activities provided by SMS is given in Exhibit 1.

2. *Replacement Parts.* Annual cost of replacement parts per receiver was calculated at $17.95 for the fixed-tuned tube-type, $73 for the multichannel tube-type, and was estimated at $1.95 for the solid-state type.

3. *Power Costs.* The fixed-tuned tube-type receiver was rated at 100 watts, the multichannel tube-type at 265 watts, and the solid-state type at 40 watts. All receivers, whether primary or backup, tube-type or solid-state, were operated continuously. The cost of electric power was 1 cent per kilowatt-hour.

4. *Space Utilization.* Receivers were mounted in standard racks 83 inches high; each rack cost $100. The tube-type receivers occupied 8.75 inches of vertical rack space, while the solid-state receivers would require only 3.5 inches.

The Replacement Cycle. The oldest tube-type receivers still in use in 1965 were approximately 15 years old, while the average age was from six to eight years. The useful life of the tube-type receivers was estimated at from 15 to 20 years. The life of the solid-state receivers would be at least 20 years.

As noted earlier, at the time of the IMS proposal, the Agency had already contracted for delivery of 3,210 tube-type receivers: 605 receivers had been delivered by early 1965, and an additional 1,083 were regarded as top priority and were being shipped directly to the regions to replace older receivers. Cancellation of this contract would be considered if the solid-state receiver procurement were approved; however, IMS indicated that little, if any, rebate could be expected.

The maximum "salvage value" for the tube-type receivers already in service was estimated at an average of 5% of their original average purchase price of approximately $350 per receiver. It was anticipated, however, that these receivers would probably be turned over to the Agency for International Development or to the Department of Health, Education, and Welfare, with no net return to the government.

A future alternative would be to employ solid-state multichannel combination transmitter/receiver units which would require even less maintenance than separate transmitters and solid-state receivers, would use common components, and would save considerably on space requirements. With these devices, known as "transceivers," one compact "package" unit could suffice. However, availability was not expected prior to 1973. (Present multichannel devices did not permit sufficiently rapid switching from one frequency to another; with solid-state, this would become virtually instantaneous.) If these transceivers were installed, the solid-state receivers requested by IMS would have only limited use, primarily as backup.

Questions

1. Calculate the estimated annual operating savings that would result from replacing tube-type receivers with solid-state receivers.
2. What action would you recommend regarding replacement in 1965?

Exhibit 1

FEDERAL AVIATION AGENCY (A)

NOTES ON THE FAA'S SYSTEM MAINTENANCE SERVICE

The SMS in FY 1965 spent $135 million, of which 70% was for personnel ($94 million), 10% for material ($13 million), and 20% for other ($28 million).

Of the $94 million for "personnel" expenses, 47% was direct labor, 16% was indirect, and 39% was for administrative and leave.

SMS divided the country into 550 sectors, each containing approximately from five to 30 "facilities," or functional groups of equipment requiring servicing. A typical sector may spend $160,000 per year on "personnel" expenses, employing 16 maintenance personnel of whom 14 might be electronic technicians.

Work load for a sector was determined by adding together the "point-counts" or man-hours per year estimated to maintain each individual component within the sector. For example, each receiver was "worth" approximately 50 man-hours per year; a transmitter was worth 100 man-hours per year; and a VOR installation (Visual Omni-Range radio beacon) was worth 1,500 man-hours per year. Each point-count figure included actual repair time, plus allowances for travel, training, leave, relief, etc.

The Corpus Christi, Texas, sector for example, embraced some 25 separate facilities, of which eight involved receivers. For one typical month in early 1965, the actual breakdown of total maintenance time was as follows:

	Electronic		Plants and Structures			
	Routine	*Corrective*	*Routine*	*Corrective*	*Other*	*Total*
Man-hours	1,467	421	112	67	473	2,540

The eight facilities involving receivers consisted of two towers, one FSS, two RCAG, one RCO (Remote Communication Outlet—an unmanned satellite

470 MANAGERIAL ECONOMICS: TEXT AND CASES

FSS), and two **RTR** (Remote Transmitter/Receiver, usually located close to a tower).

Maintenance men typically had to travel anywhere from a few minutes to several hours to reach a remote receiver. Repair time can also vary from a few minutes to several hours.

Maintenance personnel were required to follow mandatory maintenance schedules for VHF receivers, as follows:

Weekly —Check aural quality of all receivers by listening to voice transmissions.

Monthly—Measure and record sensitivity, signal-to-noise ratio, squelch differential and threshold, AVC (Automatic Volume Control) level control and threshold, maximum power output.

Annual —Check selectivity of bandwidth, symmetry and channel frequency.

For an average RCAG, total corrective maintenance time might be divided as follows:

```
Receivers.........................36%
Antennas.......................... 2%
Amplifiers........................ 2%
Controls..........................11%
Transmitters......................49%
```

Other Notes

1. In case of a single receiver failure, the pilot might be instructed to switch to another frequency, if one is available. Emergency procedures also existed for the use of radar transponder code signals, use of VOR, special pattern flying to be picked up on radar, etc., in case of voice communication failure.

2. Spare parts:
   a) Procurement of spare parts was handled centrally in Oklahoma City. When new equipment was to be installed, estimated spares for one year were normally obtained. Thereafter, standard methods were used for determining minimum inventory levels of spares.
   b) Delivery time for spare tubes or transistors was approximately two months (average).
   c) Tubes may be expected to fail at the rate of four or five per tube-type receiver per year, while solid-state receivers were estimated at one failure per 10,000 hours.

MONITOR TEXTILE COMPANY (A)

In January, 1961, Mr. Norman Dixon, superintendent of the Monitor Textile Company, was considering replacement of one of the two industrial forklift trucks operating in its plant at Hickory, North Carolina. The two trucks in the plant were gasoline operated and were three and four years old, respectively. The maintenance expenses of the older truck had been rising steadily, and currently they amounted to about $20 per month in addition to normal servicing, gasoline, and oil. This truck was not dependable and was frequently out of service while awaiting repairs. These trucks were both 1,000-pound capacity Columbia trucks and could be used interchangeably.

Exhibit 1 shows the routes traveled by the two fork trucks. One truck was used on the highway truck dock for loading and unloading packages of mohair wool and cloth from highway trucks. This "dock" truck was used only during the day shift because that was the only time when the company's two highway trucks were in operation. On the truck loading dock it was necessary to use a ramp so that the fork truck could be driven into the highway trucks.

The "inside" truck was used to move goods from machines to storage, from dyeing to finishing, and occasionally to take goods to the repair room, as well as to carry drums of chemicals. When used to take a pallet of goods from the machine that stacked pallets, it was promptly returned to this machine to pick up the next loaded pallet. If the truck was delayed during this operation, the machine had to be shut down. For the most part, the inside truck operated on an intermittent schedule, not following any fixed pattern. During the day shift, there was one driver with the inside truck at all times. During the other two shifts, the inside truck was in use about half the time, that is, a total of about eight hours on the second and third shifts.

The Monitor company processed mohair wool into fabrics for upholstery material. In January, 1961, the company was working nearly at capacity and operating on a three-shift basis, six days a week. A large part of the company's capacity was devoted to the manufacture of a special mohair fabric used in arctic clothing for the Army.

Mr. Dixon was undecided whether the company should buy electric or gasoline operated fork trucks. The Stevens Industrial Truck Company, distributors of Columbia fork trucks, was servicing the two Columbia trucks in the Monitor plant. If a new fork truck were bought, it would be bought through the Stevens company. This company offered a service agreement to users of its trucks which provided for a monthly visit by an experienced serviceman who would lubricate and adjust both gas and electric trucks. The rate was $15 per month for the first gas truck and $10 for each additional truck. A flat fee of $10 per month was charged for each electric truck. The difference between the charge for a gas and electric truck represented the cost of an oil filter cartridge that had to be replaced on gas trucks. If additional repairs for either type of truck were required, the cost of parts and the serviceman's time at the rate of $6 per hour for each hour in excess of the average servicing time were charged to the users of the truck.

The power supply for an electric truck of the type being considered by Mr. Dixon was an 18-cell, lead acid, 6.68 kilowatt-hour capacity battery. The cost of this battery was about $1,000. Mr. Suiter, the sales representative for the Stevens company, stated that this battery would provide sufficient power for the truck to travel continuously for eight hours over a level surface and have sufficient power for the operation of the lifting mechanism. This power supply would be adequate for the operation of the inside truck for the day shift. A second battery would be required if the truck were to be used much in excess of one eight-hour shift. On this basis, Mr. Dixon anticipated that two batteries, each charged once a day, would provide sufficient power for the operation of the inside truck on all shifts.

It was difficult to estimate how much of a power drain the ramp would cause for an electric truck. Although Mr. Suiter was confident that the regular charge was adequate for the inside truck, which operated without going up or down any inclines, he was uncertain whether this normal charge would be adequate for ramp operation. The use of the ramp would result in a very heavy drain on the battery. A power failure on the ramp would be very inconvenient, for time would be lost in getting the battery charged to put the truck back into operation.

The life expectancy of a battery was largely dependent on the number of times it was charged and discharged. A battery which was charged once a day could be expected to last approximately five years. When the capacity of a battery became less than 80% of its initial capacity, it was discarded, and Mr. Suiter stated that the Monitor company could count on at least $50 salvage value.

If an electric truck were to be used inside, it would be necessary to change the battery in the truck twice a day. To facilitate this operation, a heavy metal stand with rollers on its top at the same level as the battery roll-out compartment would have to be constructed. This would require $170 worth of materials.

The installation of battery charging equipment was another cost incurred with the electric trucks. The cost of a charger capable of charging one battery at a time was $550. Mr. Suiter recommended the purchase of independent chargers so that in the rare event of a breakdown of a charger, all batteries would not be disabled. A charger was expected to last as long as an electric truck. The installation of a charger necessitated bringing a 550-volt power line from another section of the plant, requiring materials costing $50. The cost of the electricity required to charge the battery for eight hours of operation was about 10 cents. Mr. Dixon understood that this charge would require about three hours.

The two gasoline operated trucks had been using a total of about five gallons of gasoline per day, at a cost of $0.248 per gallon. Mr. Suiter stated that this rate of gasoline consumption was normal for these trucks. They were equipped with two-gallon gasoline tanks as standard equipment, which the manufacturer considered adequate for eight hours of operation.

The initial cost of a gas truck was $3,600. The cost of an electric truck without a battery was $4,700. It was expected that an electric truck would operate efficiently for at least ten years when operated on a one-shift basis, that is, eight hours a day. The life of a gas truck was expected to be six to eight years on the same basis, assuming a major ($200) engine overhaul sometime after the third year. If operated 16 hours a day, as was the case with the inside truck, the expected life of either an electric or a gas truck would be cut in half, and the overhaul of the gas engine would probably be required at the end of two years.

The company paid an income tax of 52% and used the sum-of-digits method of depreciation. Mr. Dixon said he would plan to depreciate either gas or electric trucks on a five-year basis, the same rate at which the present trucks were being depreciated, and would estimate scrap value as 10% of the original cost of the equipment.

Mr. Suiter explained the longer life of the electric trucks by stating that there were a great many more moving parts in a gas truck than in an electric truck. The gas trucks could be "pushed" to get a job done faster at the expense of increasing wear on the moving parts. Because of the power limitations of the electric trucks, excessive wear was largely eliminated.

Mr. Suiter estimated that for about $1,000 the service department of his company could overhaul the older gas truck. Because of the condition of this truck, however, the Stevens service manager recommended a "factory overhaul" that would include installation of a new engine and replacement of practically all moving parts in the truck. This would cost roughly 75% of the cost of a new gas truck. About a week would be required for either type of overhaul, and the Stevens company would lend the Monitor company a truck for that period. Mr. Hunt, the sales manager, had offered the Monitor company a trade-in allowance of $750 for the four-year-old gas truck and $1,000 for the newer truck. The book value of the trucks, which had cost $3,300 each new, was approximately $525 and $725, respectively, at the end of 1960.

Mr. Hunt stated that the Monitor company could expect shipment of a gas truck late in February, or an electric truck in March. The Monitor company enjoyed a strong working capital position, and funds were available for any expenditure for fork trucks that Mr. Dixon might recommend. Based on recent experience, the company expected that funds committed to new investments should earn at least a 10% rate of return after taxes.

Question

What action do you recommend?

Exhibit 1

MONITOR TEXTILE COMPANY (A)

ROUTE TRAVELED BY FORKLIFT TRUCKS

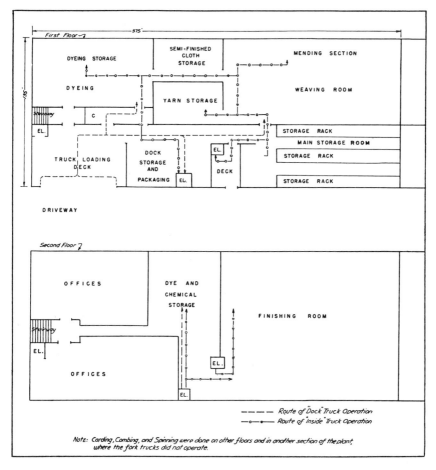

Note: Carding, Combing, and Spinning were done on other floors and in another section of the plant, where the fork trucks did not operate.

NUTHATCH NATIONAL FOREST (B)[1]

Paul P. Barstow walked into the office of Lionel Ursus, supervisor of Nuthatch National Forest, just as Ursus had made his decision on the problems confronting him regarding a sale of timber and a proposed recreation area. (See Nuthatch National Forest [A].)

Lionel Ursus rose to greet his visitor. "How are things in Washington, Paul?"

"Fine, thanks, Leo," replied Paul. "What's new here in Nuthatch?"

"Not much," answered Leo. "I've just decided to. . . ." (Here he explained to Paul his decisions regarding the method of sale, the question of whether or not road A should be paved, and the proposed recreation area.)

Paul sat down opposite Leo, and placed a few sheets of paper in front of him.

"I've got some information here that we've been working on as part of the Service's PPBS [Planning, Programming, and Budgeting System] submissions that may possibly have some bearing on your decision on this sale. Why don't you take a look and see what you think? This first document (Exhibit 1) deals with the decision as to the timing of the main harvest; we could delay it to permit prelogging and commercial thinning. The second (Exhibit 2) relates to the decision about how intensively to reforest the land after the main harvest has been made.

After Leo had finished reading, he said, "I can see I'm going to have to do some more figuring, Paul. Seems to me we might do better by building all roads ourselves this year to take advantage of the additional gains of prelogging and commercial thinning. Of course, that would

---

[1] The case is intended for class discussion only, and certain names and facts may have been changed which, while avoiding the disclosure of confidential information, do not materially lessen the value of the case for educational purposes. This case is not intended to represent either effective or ineffective handling of an administrative situation, nor does it purport to be a statement of policy by the agency involved.

mean postponing the main harvest sale for at least five years, and possibly 15."

"On the other hand," said Paul, "you will have your roads in right away, and you would be able to build your recreational facilities simultaneously. I'd guess you'd be open for the public by June, 1967."

"Well, how about the management intensification figures, Paul? Isn't this a separate decision altogether? Apart from the fact that it looks like an exercise in applying the techniques of discounting cash flows we learned at State U. last year, what bearing does it have on my most immediate problem?"

Questions

1. Using the estimate given in Exhibit 1, calculate the effect of both prelogging and commercial thinning on the proposed timber sale described in the (A) case.

2. Using the data in Exhibit 2, evaluate the desirability of adopting the "management intensification" program.

Exhibit 1
NUTHATCH NATIONAL FOREST (B)
EFFECT OF PRELOGGING AND COMMERCIAL THINNING ON THE ULTIMATE RETURNS FROM A TIMBER SALE

1.   Assume *main harvest* for virgin stands of mixed conifers (60% ponderosa pine, 40% true fir) would average 25,000 board feet per acre harvested, with no prelogging.

2. *Prelogging*

If road systems were built by the Forest Service five years in advance of main harvest, in years 1 through 5 the forester would be able to do "prelogging," without affecting the 25,000 board feet per acre at main harvest in year 6.

Prelogging involves permitting small timber processors to remove from the projected sale area smaller diameter trees which larger operators would reject at the time of main harvest. This would yield some 10,000 board feet per acre with an average stumpage price of $30/Mbf for ponderosa pine and $4/Mbf for true fir. (These prices are calculated assuming that (a) hauling costs for these small timber operators are independent of the type of road used and (b) no components of road building or maintenance costs are included, since this would be the responsibility of the Forest Service.) It would take the so-called "gypo-loggers" in the Nuthatch area a full five seasons to complete their prelogging of the area. During this time, it would not be possible to conduct the main harvest. The gypo-loggers would be able to work without disturbing the recreational use of the forest.

Sales administration costs for this type of sale would amount to $15 per acre, and would be incurred primarily during the year in which the road system was being built.

3. *Commercial Thinning*

Another alternative would be to build the road system immediately and wait 15 years before main harvest. This would permit the Forest Service not only to allow prelogging during the first five years but also to do *"commercial thinning"* simultaneously.

Ten thousand board feet per acre would be available from dead and salvage material, plus a light cut of some of the better quality older trees. This 10 Mbf per acre would be in addition to the quantities obtained as a result of prelogging. However, commercial thinning would mean waiting at least 10 years after it was over to allow the stands to grow back ready for main harvest. At the time of main harvest it would be anticipated that the yield would drop from 25 Mbf/acre to 20 Mbf/acre because of commercial thinning.

Estimated average stumpage prices for the timber removed by commercial thinning would be $37/Mbf for ponderosa pine and $5/Mbf for true fir. Sales and administration expense associated with the commercial thinning sale would be $14 per acre, incurred during the first year of the sale. Again, recreational use of the forest would be possible while commercial thinning was being performed.

During both prelogging and commercial thinning operations, the Forest Service would be responsible for road maintenance. These costs would be $300 per mile per year for paved roads, $600 per mile per year for unpaved roads while used for logging operations, and $200 per mile per year for unpaved roads when not used for logging.

Exhibit 2

NUTHATCH NATIONAL FOREST (B)

PROPOSED MANAGEMENT INTENSIFICATION SCHEDULE FOR
AREAS OF MIXED CONIFER, YIELDING APPROXIMATELY
25 MBF/ACRE AT MAIN HARVEST WITHOUT SUCH TREATMENT

Without this plan, an area, such as the 2,000 acres in the proposed Nuthatch timber sale area, would be left to regenerate naturally after logging, apart from the minimal care laid down by the "K-V Act," for which purpose $2/Mbf of main harvest timber is used (Nuthatch National Forest [A]). The costs given below are therefore incremental costs over and above this minimal treatment following main harvest. Year 0 in the table is the year of the first main harvest of a virgin old-growth stand.

Management Intensification Schedule

| | | | | Stumpage Price |
| | | | *Yield in* | ⌒—(*Mbf*)—⌒ |
Year	*Operation*	*Cost/Acre*	*Mbf/Acre*	*P.P.*	*True Fir*
0........	Slash disposal, site preparation, and planting	$ 6	—	—	—
5........	Precommercial thinning	9	—	—	—
20........	Pruning	12	—	—	—
30........	1st commercial thinning	15 (Admin.)	5	$25	$4
40........	2d commercial thinning	15 (Admin.)	6	30	5
50........	3d commercial thinning	15 (Admin.)	9	30	5
70........	Main harvest	10 (Admin.)	31	40	8

Notes: 1. Stumpage prices will vary from those calculated in (A) case because:
    a) This is a new stand. Hence, even after 70 years, the average diameter of the trees will be less than when the stand was still a virgin, old-growth area. This will mean a lower stumpage price due to less useable timber.
    b) Road construction and maintenance costs do not appear in the stumpage prices quoted in the table, since this will be the responsibility of the Forest Service throughout the period.
    Thus, these stumpage prices should be taken as given.
    2. However, for management intensification of the type outlined here, it must be assumed that road A was paved at the time of the original main harvest in year 0, or before.
    3. The stumpage prices are given in terms of 1966 dollars, as are all figures quoted. However, they are also based on 1966 timber values, and thus assume that 1966 price levels for timber will continue.
    4. In the old-growth stands, the ratio of ponderosa pine to true fir was 60/40. With management intensification, it is estimated that this ratio will change to 80/20.

Schedule without Management Intensification

| | | | *Yield in* | ⌒—*Stumpage Price*—⌒ |
| | | | *Mbf per* | *Per Mbf* | *Per Acre* |
Year	*Operation*	*Cost/Acre*	*Acre*	*P.P.*	*True Fir*
0........	Normal K-V work	...	...	...	...
75........	Commercial thinning	$15 (Admin.)	10	$30	$5
90........	Main harvest	10 (Admin.)	20	37	6

THE ATLANTIC MONTHLY
COMPANY (B)

In February 1964, Donald B. Snyder, publisher of *The Atlantic Monthly* magazine, was reviewing his plans for circulation promotion during the months ahead. Tentative results of the January 1964, direct-mail campaign for new trial subscriptions indicated a substantial improvement over previous years, and Mr. Snyder was trying to determine how, if at all, these new data should influence his future actions. Background data about *The Atlantic Monthly*, its editorial policies and publishing performance for 1959 to 1963, are presented in the (A) case of this series.

The Subscription Cycle

Approximately four fifths of the *Atlantic*'s paid circulation was sent by mail to subscribers who had contracted to receive a series of several monthly issues. The group of *Atlantic* subscribers was constantly changing, and this cycle is illustrated in Exhibits 1 and 2 Stencil List Reports that were prepared for Mr. Snyder each month. Exhibit 1 is a comparison of calendar years 1961 and 1962; Exhibit 2 compares 1962 and 1963. The explanations below are in terms of the 1961 figures, but the same cycle was at work in the subsequent years.

During 1961, the *Atlantic*'s paid circulation delivered by mail averaged 224,136 copies per issue. The stencil list of subscribers had 184,884 names at the beginning of the year and 187,731 names at the end of the year. In addition to stencil list subscribers, there were two other categories of mail-delivered circulation: (1) classroom copies used in high schools and colleges and (2) subscriptions sold by a contract agent. For Mr. Snyder's purpose of reviewing the operations of the circulation department, these two categories of circulation were excluded from the stencil list because neither category was expected to

generate a significant number of renewals. Classroom copies were promoted directly to teachers, but the students changed every year, and
renewals (in terms of names on the stencil list) could not be computed
meaningfully.

The contract agent promoted subscriptions to the *Atlantic* as one of
a group of magazines on which direct-mail customers were offered a
substantial discount for entering several simultaneous subscriptions.
The renewal rate on these subscriptions had historically been so low
that the *Atlantic* made no serious effort to get these subscribers to
renew.

The stencil list subscribers were divided into two categories for
record-keeping and analytical purposes: (1) the long-term list of subscriptions entered at regular rates (including gift subscriptions that
were offered at a $1 a year discount) and (2) the list of trial subscrib-
ers. Changes in the long-term list during 1961 occurred as follows: Of
the 132,000 names on the list at the start of the year, 5,000 canceled
their subscriptions (and received a pro rata refund) before expiration.
Of the remaining 127,000 names, 10,000 subscriptions were not scheduled to expire during 1961; the original terms of these subscriptions
exceeded one year. Thus, the long-term list on January 1, 1961 contained 117,000 names that were scheduled to expire during the year. Of
these, 71,000 renewed their subscriptions (actually, 62.13% of those
expiring[1]); the other 46,000 did not renew and were dropped (after a
"grace" period of a month or two) from the subscriber list.

Total deductions from the stencil list in 1961 amounted to 51,000
names, and 43,000 of these were replaced from two main sources: (1)
25,000 new long-term subscriptions that were sold during the year, the
bulk of these by "catalog agents" engaged in personal selling either
door-to-door or by telephone; and (2) 18,000 trial subscribers who
had originally responded to the *Atlantic*'s direct-mail promotion were
"converted" to long-term subscribers by renewing their subscriptions at
regular rates at the end of the initial trial period.

Exhibit 3 recapitulates the sale of subscriptions in 1961 and 1963.
Of the 89,000 renewal subscriptions sold in 1961, 18,000 were "first
renewals" of the trial subscribers that had been converted to regular

---

[1] Figures quoted in this and the following three paragraphs are approximations.
The actual record keeping by The Atlantic Monthly Company was done in terms of
groups of expires, and the cutoff dates used in cumulating the data for preparing Exhibits 1 and 2 did not coincide exactly with the cutoff dates used in preparing Exhibits
3 and 4.

status, and the other 71,000 were second or subsequent renewals of long-term stencil list subscribers.

The percentage of conversions reported in Exhibit 1 was based on the expiration of trial subscriptions that had originally been sold by the *Atlantic*'s direct-mail promotion; the trials sold by the catalog agent were not included in the stencil list accounting. At the beginning of 1961, the *Atlantic* was mailing copies to 53,000 stencil list trial subscribers, all of whose subscriptions were scheduled to expire during the year. In the early months of 1961 (as shown in Exhibit 4), 26,000 new short-term trial subscriptions were sold. Of these 79,000 trials that expired during 1961, 18,000 (25.81%) renewed their subscriptions at the regular rates. In addition, 65,000 new trials were sold during 1961 that were scheduled to expire in 1962.

Reviewing the figures on Exhibits 1 and 2, Mr. Snyder said:

> The drop in both renewal percentages in 1962 was very serious, but our 1963 results show that the trend has been more than reversed in our favor. The main value of the renewal percentage figures is as an indication of the continuing editorial appeal of the *Atlantic*. By good promotion, we may be able to sell someone a trial subscription, but after he's read it for several months, his decision to renew or not depends solely on how well he's liked what he's read. Some part of the 1962 decline may have been due to the price increase, but I doubt if it had much effect on our long-term subscribers because we gave them a special offer to renew in advance at the old prices. Really, the 1962 figures are so hard to evaluate that I've quit trying to make any sense out of them.

Subscription Promotion Costs

The costs of selling new subscriptions for the *Atlantic* amounted to over $400,000 a year. An analysis of subscription promotion costs for the calendar years 1961 and 1963 is presented in Exhibit 3. The cost and revenue data here presented do not agree with similar data presented in the (A) case for three reasons. First, the (A) case data were for fiscal years ending April 30, rather than calendar years. Second, in 1963, the *Atlantic* spent approximately $35,000 to screen its rented mailing lists before using them in its solicitation of trial subscriptions. Mr. Snyder called this process "unduplicating" the lists, and explained: "We eliminated the names of our regular subscribers from these lists so that they wouldn't be tempted to enter a new subscription at half price rather than renewing at the regular price. This cost is not included in these figures (Exhibit 3) because I can't figure out whether to allocate it to the cost of new subscriptions or to renewals." Finally, and perhaps the most important reason for the difference in promotion results reported in these two cases, the (A) case data were taken from the accounting records and reflect the *Atlantic*'s policies for recognizing subscription revenue and expense; the data in Exhibit 3 represent revenues actually collected (or billed) and expenses actually paid (or incurred) during the year.

The subscription promotion expenses given in Exhibit 3 include all expenses that were directly identifiable with specific subscription promotion campaigns. In addition, the *Atlantic* incurred overhead expenses for salaries, billing, and so forth, of $108,215 in 1961 and $129,490 in 1963.

Reviewing the data in Exhibit 3, Mr. Snyder made the following comments:

There are tremendous differences in the profitability of various sources of subscriptions. Looking at the 1961 figures, for example, we netted $3.31 per 12 copies on classroom business, $3.61 from catalog agents, only 47 cents from our contract agent, and we lost 10 cents on the new trials that we sold by direct mail. These figures don't tell the whole story, though, because the real profit lies in renewal subscriptions. We don't get any renewals to speak of from contract agent business, and the renewals on classroom and catalog agents yield about the same net revenue as new subscriptions from those sources. But the renewals that we get on the trials that we sell are quite a different story. Even though only 20 to 30% of these trials renew, the net revenue per subyear was $5.65 in 1961 and $6.12 last year. And, of course, once we've converted a trial into a regular subscriber, we know that 60 to 70% of them will continue to renew year after year.

The only way, therefore, to compare our contract agent business with direct-mail trials is to take a long-run look at things. We may actually be better off to take an out-of-the-pocket loss on a trial in order to get a series of profitable renewals than we are to take a nominal cash profit on each subscription sold by the contract agent. In fact, the challenge of circulation management is to continually adjust the mix of circulation sources used in such a way that we're using the most profitable combination at any one point in time.

Our circulation picture improved considerably in 1963 as compared to 1961. The average net revenue on new subs rose from $1.31 to $1.99. This improvement can be traced to three factors: (1) the higher subscription price resulted in more revenue per 12 copies; (2) we increased the use of the contract agent and cut back on the sale of trials by direct mail; and (3) we reduced the number of new subscriptions sold during the year, making up part of this drop by increasing our newsstand sale and part of it by reducing our bonus of paid circulation over the guarantee.

We have found, over the years, that the best time to mount a direct-mail campaign is in the fall, when people are faced with the prospect of the long winter nights ahead, and in January. We do our biggest "cold" mailing right after Labor Day, offering a one-year subscription at half price. On the cold mailing in January, we offer eight issues at a cut rate so that those trials also expire in the fall when it's easier to get the first, crucial renewal. Our fall mailing is always more profitable because we get about the same percentage response but collect 50% more revenue from the 12-month trial.

This tabulation (Exhibit 4) summarizes the results of our January mailing for the last several years. Back in 1961, the losses on this source of business became so substantial that we decided to cut back our mailings. The primary advantage of mailing only a million and a quarter pieces, rather than two million, is that we can select only the better mailing lists, the lists that historically have been reasonably successful for us. Cutting back in this way raised our percentage response from 1.27% to 1.64% and cut the cost of getting a sub by nearly a third.

It's hard to compare 1963 to 1962 because the price of our eight-month offer was 34 cents higher. In spite of the price increase, the response to our mailing rose again. Now, we have tentative results of the mailing we made last month, and it's clear that we've scored another major gain. For the first time in several years we show a profit on our January trials, and this is most welcome. This success, of course, raises some questions of its own. In 1962 and 1963, we increased our use of the contract agent by increasing the percentage that we paid for its promoting the *Atlantic*. The agency offers an eight-month, half-price subscription and charges us a commission based on the revenue it collects. In 1961, with a $2.50 offer, we were netting only 32 cents, really 47 cents on a subscription-year basis, or about 13% of the price paid by the subscriber. We sweetened the agent's commission at the time we raised our subscription prices, so that in 1963, we only netted 34 cents on a $2.84 subscription. Actually, the agency would like to sell a lot more subscriptions for us on the terms of the current arrangement, but we've been limiting the amount of business we'll take from them. In fact, it might be more profitable for us to stop using the agency at all.

Another thing we did beginning in 1963 was to increase our newsstand distribution substantially. We did this to counteract the effect of the increase in cover price, and I'm sure our newsstand sale would have declined in 1963 if we hadn't done it. But overdistribution is costly too, and I think this policy needs to be reconsidered in the light of the January mailing results.

Really, these are just the same questions that I have to deal with all the time. Broadly speaking, the problem is one of circulation management, and I'm just glad that I have a fine editorial package and a strong market demand facing me as I tackle the problem this year.

Questions

1. On the assumption that Mr. Snyder has the following alternatives to consider for the fall of 1964, which source of paid circulation would be more profitable for The Atlantic Monthly Company?

   a) Continue the policy of newsstand overdistribution. Assume that of the extra 20,000 copies distributed each month only 6,000 copies will be sold.

   b) Eliminate overdistribution and increase the September "cold" mailing to yield an extra 6,000 trial subscriptions. Assume that these subscriptions would yield $4.50 of revenue, would renew the first time at 20%, and then would continue to renew at 65%. In order to secure these new trials, however, the number of mailing lists used would have to be increased, and the total promotion costs for the fall mailing would be higher by $30,000.

2. What policy do you recommend to Mr. Snyder for dealing with his continuing problem of securing the optimal circulation mix?

3. Do you think it would be profitable for the *Atlantic* to raise its total circulation if that action was coupled with an increase in the circulation guarantee? Assuming that the circulation guarantee was raised from 262,500 to 275,000, the advertising page-rate was raised by 5%, and new paid circulation of 13,000 was provided, find the best combination of the following courses of action:

a) Continue the present policy of newsstand overdistribution.

b) Increase the use of the contract agency.

c) Sell 6,000 new trial subs on the terms described in 1(*b*) above.

d) Sell 13,000 new trials as described, except that the increase in the fall promotion budget would be $72,000.

Exhibit 1

THE ATLANTIC MONTHLY COMPANY (B)

STENCIL LIST REPORT, 1961–62

12 Months of the ATLANTIC through (December 31)	1961	1962	PLUS OR MINUS
STENCIL LIST – "As the Year Began"			
Long-Term List (Regulars & Gifts)	131,527	123,218	
Trial Subscribers	53,357	64,513	
Total Stencils	184,884	187,731	
WHAT HAPPENED TO THE "LONG TERM LIST" DURING THE 12 MONTHS ENDING (December 31)			
Long-Terms & Gifts Renewed @	62.13%	59.67%	
Trials "Converted to Longs" @	25.81%	20.36%	
Long-Terms & Gifts "Not Renewing" were	(45,865)	(40,417)	
Long-Terms & Gifts Canceled were	(5,036)	(5,684)	
Total "Longs" Lost	(50,901)	(46,101)	
New "Long-Terms & Gifts" Sold were	24,871	24,244	
Trials "Converted to Longs" were	17,721	21,847	
Total "Longs" Added	42,592	46,091	
Net Gain or Loss in the "Long-Term List" during the 12 months ending (December 31)	(8,309)	(10)	
STENCIL LIST – "As the Year Ended"			
Long-Term List (Regulars & Gifts)	123,218	123,208	
Trial Subscribers	64,513	53,688	
Total Stencils (as of December 31)	187,731	176,896	
NET NEWSSALE (12 Months Ending December 31)			
Total Copies Shipped to Curtis	1,010,074	975,492	
Total Copies Sold	650,733	593,571	
% of Sale	64.4%	60.85%	
Total Copies Returned	359,341	381,921	
AVERAGE A B C DELIVERY (12 Months Ending December 31)			
Mail Delivery – Monthly Average	224,136	219,918	
Net Newssale – Monthly Average	54,228	48,696	
A B C Average – 12 Months	278,364	268,614	

Exhibit 2

THE ATLANTIC MONTHLY COMPANY (B)

STENCIL LIST REPORT, 1962–63

12 Months of the ATLANTIC through (December 31)	1962	1963	PLUS OR MINUS
STENCIL LIST – "As the Year Began"			
Long-Term List (Regulars & Gifts)	123,218	123,208	
Trial Subscribers	64,513	53,688	
Total Stencils	187,731	176,896	
WHAT HAPPENED TO THE "LONG-TERM LIST" DURING THE 12 MONTHS ENDING (Dec. 31)			
Long-Terms & Gifts Renewed @	59.67%	64.44%	
Trials "Converted to Longs" @	20.36%	25.60%	
Long-Terms & Gifts "Not Renewing" were	(40,417)	(39,193)	
Long-Terms & Gifts Cancelled were	(5,684)	(5,954)	
Total "Longs" Lost	(46,101)	(45,147)	
New "Long-Terms & Gifts" Sold were	24,244	26,211	
Trials "Converted to Longs" were	21,847	18,058	
Total "Longs" Added	46,091	44,269	
Net Gain or Loss in the "Long-Term List" during the 12 months ending (Dec. 31)	(10)	(878)	
STENCIL LIST – "As the Year Ended"			
Long-Term List (Regulars & Gifts)	123,208	122,330	
Trial Subscribers	53,688	49,236	
Total Stencils (as of Dec. 31)	176,896	171,566	
NET NEWSSALE (12 Months Ending Dec. 31)			
Total Copies Shipped to Curtis	975,492	1,300,727	+325,235
Total Copies Sold	593,571	578,341	-(15,230)
% of Sale	60.85%	44.46%	-(16.39%)
Total Copies Returned	381,921	722,386	+340,465
AVERAGE A B C DELIVERY (12 Months Ending Dec. 31)			
Mail Delivery – Monthly Average	219,918	217,935	-(1983)
Net Newssale – Monthly Average	48,696	48,195	-(501)
A B C Average – 12 Months	268,614	266,130	-(2484)

Exhibit 3. THE ATLANTIC MONTHLY COMPANY (B)

COMPARATIVE COSTS OF SUBSCRIPTION PROMOTION, CALENDAR YEARS 1961 AND 1963

	Total	Direct-Mail & N/S Inserts	Classroom	Sources of Subscriptions Catalog Agents	Contract Agents	Misc.
12 Months Ended December 31, 1961:						
Renewal subscriptions—number of orders	88,516	65,430	...	23,086	...	...
Number of subscription years sold	105,937	76,711	...	29,226	...	...
Total revenue	$599,793	$497,214	...	$102,579	...	...
Revenue/subscription year	5.66	6.48	...	3.51	...	...
Promotion costs	64,527	63,484	...	1,043	...	...
Cost/subscription year	0.61	0.83	...	0.04	...	...
Net revenue	535,266	433,730	...	101,536	...	...
Net/subscription year	5.05	5.65	...	3.47	...	...
New subscriptions—number of orders	180,918	82,161	57,825	17,952	18,416	4,564
Number of subscription years sold	126,331	68,988	22,448	17,980	12,277	4,638
Total revenue	$456,286	$269,567	$86,257	$65,724	$6,656	$28,082
Revenue/subscription year	3.61	3.91	3.84	3.66	0.54	6.05
Promotion costs	290,212	276,624	11,952	807	829	...
Cost/subscription year	2.30	4.01	0.53	0.04	0.07	...
Net revenue	166,074	(7,057)	74,305	64,917	5,827	28,082
Net/subscription year	1.31	(0.10)	3.31	3.61	0.47	6.05
12 Months Ended December 31, 1963:						
Renewal subscriptions—number of orders	89,559	67,110	...	22,449	...	...
Number of subscription years sold	105,218	76,823	...	28,395	...	...
Total revenue	$662,232	$543,244	...	$118,988	...	...
Revenue/subscription year	6.29	7.07	...	4.19	...	...
Promotion costs	74,069	73,254	...	815	...	...
Cost/subscription year	0.70	0.95	...	0.03	...	...
Net revenue	588,163	469,990	...	118,173	...	...
Net/subscription year	5.59	6.12	...	4.16	...	...
New subscriptions—number of orders	170,876	61,609	55,626	20,371	27,997	5,273
Number of subscription years sold	117,091	49,957	22,664	20,402	18,665	5,403
Total revenue	$457,039	$224,170	$97,906	$88,780	$9,478	$36,705
Revenue/subscription year	3.90	4.49	4.32	4.35	0.51	6.79
Promotion costs	224,008	205,867	16,400	733	1,008	...
Cost/subscription year	1.91	4.12	0.72	0.04	0.05	...
Net revenue	233,031	18,303	81,506	88,047	8,470	36,705
Net/subscription year	1.99	0.37	3.60	4.32	0.45	6.79

Exhibit 4

THE ATLANTIC MONTHLY COMPANY
COMPARATIVE COSTS AND RESULTS OF "COLD" MAILINGS
JANUARY 1961 THROUGH 1964

	Estimated 1964	1963	1962	1961
Number of direct-mail pieces mailed.........	1,295,000	1,121,323	1,278,614	2,055,121
Trial subscription offered: rate for 8 months...............................	$2.84	$2.84	$2.50	$2.50
Number of orders received..................	32,800	24,115	21,011	26,053
Percentage response.......................	2.53%	2.15%	1.64%	1.27%
Number of subscription years sold...........	21,866	16,077	14,007	17,369
Cost of direct-mail promotion..............	$78,000	$71,853	$68,190	$117,525
Per order received......................	2.38	2.98	3.25	4.51
Per subscription year sold...............	3.57	4.47	4.87	6.77
Subscription revenue per subscription year....	$4.26	$4.26	$3.75	$3.75
Net revenue or (loss) per subscription year....	$0.69	$(0.21)	$(1.12)	$(3.02)

CONSOLIDATED MINING AND MANUFACTURING CORPORATION[1]

In the middle of 1949 the Consolidated Mining and Manufacturing Corporation was considering the storage of a reserve supply of the mineral impervium[1] in order to avoid a repetition of the severe losses which the company had incurred in 1948 after a stoppage of the supply of this mineral had forced the company to shut down the larger part of its manufacturing activities. The Consolidated Mining and Manufacturing Corporation comprised two divisions. Division A extracted ore containing the mineral impervium from a single mine in Mexico and separated the mineral from the ore at a mill located near the mine. Consolidated's production constituted about a half of the total North American production of impervium, the rest being divided among a number of smaller firms. A part of the impervium produced by Division A was sold by Consolidated to a number of outside concerns, but the larger part—about two-thirds of the total—was transferred to Consolidated's Division B. This division manufactured a wide variety of products for both industrial and domestic use. Some of these products contained impervium as an essential constituent, while others used none of the mineral.

In 1947 and 1948 Consolidated had had serious labor difficulties at its mine, culminating in a four-month strike.[2] These difficulties had had no repercussions among the labor force in the manufacturing plant of Division B, which was located in the United States about 800 miles from the mine in Mexico, but the loss of the company's impervium supply had ultimately forced the manufacturing plant to cease production of all products containing the mineral. The losses incurred by Division B as a result of this partial shutdown were so severe, and the labor situa-

---

[1] Fictitious name.

[2] Other impervium producers were not affected by this strike.

tion at the mine continued so unstable, that the president of the company, Mr. Adams, decided to study the possibility of storing a reserve supply of impervium large enough to permit continuous operation of the manufacturing plant in spite of any strike that might occur at the mine in the future.

Mr. Adams realized, however, that the creation and maintenance of such a reserve would involve a considerable investment, and feared that serious operating costs might be involved in addition. He decided, therefore, to have a systematic study made of both the costs involved in the storage scheme and the losses which might be incurred in the absence of such a scheme. The task of collecting and analyzing the necessary data he assigned to Mr. Fox, a young assistant whom he had just hired for this very purpose of making analyses of special problems outside of the ordinary routine of the business. Wishing to profit by as fresh a look as possible at the problem, Mr. Adams outlined the problem to his assistant very briefly. The only specific instructions and information which he gave Mr. Fox were the following:

1. The losses actually occurred as a result of the stoppage in 1948 were not to be considered a reliable basis for estimating losses in case of a future stoppage, since the sellers' market which had prevailed in 1947–1948 had made it possible to shift productive facilities from one product to another in a way which would not be possible under normal conditions. During a strike, Mr. Adams opined, a number of Consolidated's normal customers could be expected to defer shipment on their orders until the end of the strike, so that only about one-half of the normal sales volume for the strike period would be irretrievably lost. Moreover, in view of Consolidated's predominant position in the market, virtually all of the company's customers who had had their requirements temporarily filled by another supplier would return to Consolidated after the strike.

2. It was not a part of Mr. Fox's assignment to predict the exact frequency or duration of future strikes, since this was a decision for which Mr. Adams believed that he himself would have to take the responsibility. The labor situation was in such a state that he had not even reached a tentative decision as yet, although he was convinced that no strike was likely to last more than six months and told Mr. Fox that he need not consider the possibility of a longer strike.

3. Mr. Adams had already definitely decided that if storage facilities were built at all, they should be built in the United States. (Impervium entered the United States duty-free.) The most suitable location was on a 20-acre piece of property which had already been offered for sale to the company in whole or in part at a price of $500 an acre. This property was located a few miles from the plant of Division B and was on the railroad which connected the mine with the plant.

4. In considering the advisability of new capital expenditures, the company had usually been guided by a rule of thumb according to which the least acceptable return was 10% after taxes. (You may assume a tax rate of 50%.)

Mr. Adams told his assistant that he was free to request figures and other information from any department of the company. The first line of inquiry which Mr. Fox decided to pursue was determination of the magnitude of the losses which would be incurred by Division B in case of another stoppage of impervium supplies. For figures on the total amount of sales which would be lost in such a case, Mr. Fox applied to the sales department for information. This department had recently made an extensive study of the probable future annual sales of each of the company's products. The study consisted essentially of the projection on the basis of prewar sales of a "normal trend" for each of the company's products; sales were expected to fluctuate cyclically about this "normal trend." In computing this trend all values had been converted to 1949 prices by use of an "internal" price index, and the projection was on the same basis. A trend was computed separately for each of the company's products, and the total sales trend was simply the sum of the trends for the individual products. This "normal trend" of total sales by Division B showed a value of $70,000,000 for 1950, the first year in which the president expected a more or less normal market. The trend line had a slope of 3.27% per annum. To determine the effect of a stoppage of impervium supplies on the division's sales under normal conditions, Mr. Fox also obtained from the sales department a subtotal trend consisting simply of the total of the trends for all the products containing no impervium. This trend showed a value of $30,-000,000 for 1950, and had a slope of 2.98% per annum. The chart supplied by the sales department is shown in Exhibit 1.

In order to determine the net income which would be lost if the annual rate of sales fell from $70 to $30 million as a result of an impervium stoppage, Mr. Fox first turned to Mr. Walsh, the company's chief cost accountant. Mr. Walsh stated that the problem was very easy to solve, and that he could supply not only the cost figures corresponding to the total predicted sales of $70 million but also a breakdown of these costs into those chargeable to the products containing impervium and those with none of the mineral. This was possible, he said, because standards of hours and materials per unit of product had been carefully set up before the war, and actual performance had been found to be very close to these standards over a long period of time, the only notable exceptions being due to abnormal wartime conditions which had already virtually disappeared. At Mr. Fox's request, Mr. Walsh prepared such a prediction and breakdown on the basis of the volume of sales forecast for 1950, using the current prices for labor and materials. In accordance with the standard policy of the company, established by top management, the cost of the impervium transferred from Division A to Division B was taken at the price F.O.B. mine at which the company sold to outsiders, plus freight from the mine to the plant of Division B. Indirect expenses were allocated to products in the same ratio as their sale value bore to the total sales of the division. Mr. Walsh's figures are shown in Exhibit 2.

Despite Mr. Walsh's confidence in the accuracy of his figures, Mr. Fox was hesitant to accept them, especially as an indication of what the costs would be if only those products were produced which contained no impervium, since he knew that allocation of costs to specific products was generally considered to be difficult and at best somewhat imprecise. As a check on Mr. Walsh's figures, he decided to get the historical costs of operation at a time when total sales amounted to approximately the same sum as the sales department predicted for impervium-free products alone in 1950. Looking at the chart supplied by the sales department, he observed that the year with total sales closest to $30,000,000 was 1920, and he asked the accounting department to supply him with the operating statement for that year. As a double check he asked the accounting department itself to check through all the operating statements and send him the one with total sales closest to $30,000,000. In response to these requests, the accounting department sent him the operating statements for 1920 and 1928, shown in Exhibit 3.

Mr. Fox was considerably puzzled by the inconsistencies among the statements of costs which he had thus obtained, and after studying them for some went in person to the accounting department to see if he could obtain any additional information on the probable behavior of costs if sales should be reduced to about $30 million. Here he was referred to the section in charge of the annual budget, which he was told was the only possible source of information in addition to that which he had already been given. In the budget section he learned that preparation of the budget for 1950 was only beginning, but he was given the following data on the Division B cost budget for 1949:

Direct labor and materials: Expected to vary directly with sales, since the company sold at a uniform markup, and since the company had always followed a policy of immediately releasing workers for whom no work was available.

Factory burden: $1,200,000 fixed expense per month plus $1.057 per dollar of direct labor.

Selling expense: $250,000 fixed expense per month plus $0.05 per dollar of sales.

Administrative and general expense: $135,000 per month plus $0.0125 per dollar of sales.

Further inquiry around the company's offices failed to produce any additional information on the variation of costs with volume, and Mr. Fox turned to the problem of the calculation of the cost of storing a reserve supply of impervium. His first step was to inquire into the existing storage facilities of Division B, and he was told that the very limited space at the manufacturing plant held about ten days' supply at the current rate of consumption. Supplies arrived almost continuously, and since about five days were required in transit from the mine to the plant, this meant that about five days' supply was in transit at any time.

For figures on the cost of the stored impervium, Mr. Fox first got in touch directly with Mr. Spear, the general manager of Division A. Mr. Spear stated that provided that he was not obliged to increase his current rate of production by more than 4,000 tons a month, the "out-of-pocket" cost of the additional production would be $17.35 per ton at the mine. The only other information which Mr. Fox could find on the current cost of producing the mineral was in the company's operating statement for the first six months of 1949, which had just been prepared for internal use. This statement showed a profit for Division A of $319,000 before taxes on a total production of 61,500 tons, all of which had been either sold to outsiders or transferred to Division B at a price of $37.50 per ton F.O.B. mine.

For figures on the cost of building and operating a storage warehouse, Mr. Adams had told his assistant to employ the firm of consulting engineers which the company had used for a number of years on all of its construction projects and whose estimates had always proved very reliable. This firm supplied estimates of costs and of useful lives for warehouses of three different capacities as specified by Mr. Fox; these estimates are shown in Exhibit 4.

Questions

1. Should Consolidated Mining and Manufacturing Corporation build a warehouse to store impervium?

2. Assuming that a strike of three-month duration will occur randomly one year out of four, how big a warehouse should be built?

3. Recognizing Mr. Adams' uncertainty about the frequency and duration of future strikes, how would you recommend he proceed to reach a decision on this problem?

Exhibit 1

CONSOLIDATED MINING AND MANUFACTURING CORPORATION

SALES RECORDS AND PROJECTIONS

(All values in 1949 dollars)

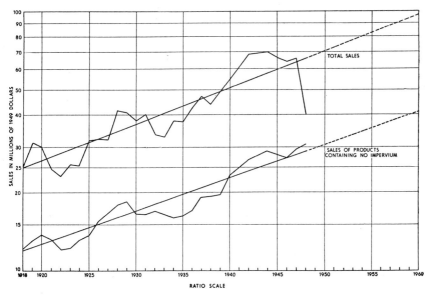

Exhibit 2

CONSOLIDATED MINING AND MANUFACTURING CORPORATION

DIVISION B, PROJECTED COSTS OF OPERATION, 1950

(Based on sales department's forecast of sales)

(All amounts in thousands)

	Products Containing Impervium Amount	%	Products Containing No Impervium Amount	%	Total Amount	%
Sales	$40,000	100.0	$30,000	100.0	$70,000	100.0
Manufacturing costs:						
Direct labor	$ 6,150	15.4	$ 4,350	14.5	$10,500	15.0
Direct materials	7,350*	18.4	3,650	12.2	11,000	15.7
Factory burden	15,100	37.7	10,400	34.7	25,500	36.5
Division B expenses:						
Salesmen, sales office, and promotion costs	3,700	9.2	2,800	9.3	6,500	9.3
Administrative and general	1,450	3.6	1,050	3.5	2,500	3.6
Real and property taxes	550	1.4	450	1.5	1,000	1.4
General Corporation expenses allocated to Division B	2,550	6.4	1,950	6.5	4,500	6.4
Total cost and expense	$36,850	92.1	$24,650	82.2	$61,500	87.9
Estimated profit before taxes	$ 3,150	7.9	$ 5,350	17.8	$ 8,500	12.1

* Including $3 million for 80,000 tons of impervium transferred from Division A at $37.50 per ton. The freight charges on these shipments of $973,600 is a part of the remaining $4,350,000 of direct materials.

Exhibit 3

CONSOLIDATED MINING AND MANUFACTURING CORPORATION

DIVISION B, OPERATING STATEMENTS, 1920 AND 1928

(Not adjusted to 1949 dollars)

	1920 Amount	%	1928 Amount	%
Sales	$13,598	100.0	$30,239	100.0
Manufacturing costs:				
Direct labor	$ 1,619	11.9	$ 3,998	13.2
Direct materials	1,895*	13.9	4,169†	13.8
Factory burden	3,932	28.9	8,144	26.9
Division B expenses:				
Salesmen, sales office, and promotion	1,827	13.4	4,018	13.3
Administrative and general	748	5.5	1,087	3.6
Real and property taxes	54	0.4	73	0.2
General Corporation expense allocation	1,122	8.3	2,281	7.6
Total cost and expenses	$11,197	82.3	$23,770	78.6
Profit before taxes	$ 2,401	17.7	$ 6,469	21.4

* Including $931,500 (before freight) for impervium transferred from Division A.
† Including $2,398,500 (before freight) for impervium transferred from Division A.

Exhibit 4

CONSOLIDATED MINING AND MANUFACTURING CORPORATION

COSTS OF WAREHOUSING IMPERVIUM

CAPITAL INVESTMENT

	Life* (Years)	Cost of Facilities for Storing		
		10,000 Tons	20,000 Tons	40,000 Tons
Land...	....	$ 1,000	$ 2,000	$ 4,000
Land improvements:				
Railways, grading sewers, etc.....................	25	8,500	10,000	12,500
Water supply, electrical connections...............	20	10,000	10,000	10,000
Driveways.......	15	3,500	4,500	7,000
Buildings.......................................	40	123,500	217,000	394,000
Equipment......................................	10	9,500	9,500	9,500
		$156,000	$253,000	$437,000

EXPENSES

Operating costs...................................		$ 1,500	$ 1,750	$ 2,000
Real and property taxes...........................		13,000	24,000	45,500
Insurance..		1,000	2,000	3,500

MEMORANDUM APPENDED TO THE ENGINEERS' REPORT

"Up to the present no method of shipment and storage has been found practical for impervium other than in cloth bags. Unless these bags are replaced every five years, there is serious danger that they will rot and that the mineral they contain will be lost or spoiled. It would be difficult to transfer the stored mineral from old bags into new ones, and would probably be cheaper to renew the stored mineral on a rotation basis. We estimate that the cost of removing mineral from the warehouse and trucking it to the factory, plus the cost of unloading fresh supplies from the freight cars and placing it in the warehouse, will amount to $3.667 per ton exchanged, this figure being in addition to the cost of operating the warehouse given in our estimate above."

* This estimate of the physical life of the facilities would also be used for income tax determination (straight-line depreciation).

Chapter 10

SIMULATION: ANALYSIS OF COMPLEX DECISIONS

In the introduction to the last chapter, we mentioned that there were two major problems in analyzing decisions to incur capacity-creating costs. First, it was necessary to determine a method for assigning a time value to money. Second, some method was needed to help make all the calculations required when a large number of events were present in the decision diagram. In this chapter we would like to describe a technique for solving the second problem. This technique is Monte Carlo simulation.

THE BEACH PROBLEM WITH UNCERTAINTY

In Chapter 9 we discussed a problem facing the Beach Company, namely, whether to introduce a new product, and if it were introduced, whether to use general-purpose machinery or special-purpose machinery to manufacture it. This problem will continue to be our example; however, now we will want to be more realistic and admit that some of our estimates are not certain. Table 10–1 is a list of the point forecasts made by the product manager.

Table 10–1

POINT FORECAST OF PRODUCT MANAGER FOR BEACH
COMPANY NEW PRODUCT INTRODUCTION

Forecast	Special Purpose	General Purpose
1. Purchase price	$110,000	$80,000
2. Sales price	$5/unit	$5/unit
3. Lump-sum overhead cost	$10,000/year	$12,000/year
4. Variable overhead cost	$0.25/unit	$0.50/unit
5. Variable labor cost	$1/unit	$1.25/unit
6. Variable material cost	$0.75/unit	$1.25/unit
7. Initial size of market	20,000 units	20,000 units
8. Market growth	1.2%/year	1.2%/year

498

The machinery purchase price should be known with certainty. We will assume that the price can be controlled by the Beach Company, so this item is also known with certainty. There may be some variation in overhead costs, but for the moment we will assume they too are known for certain. If this assumption is not true, it will become clear in a moment how we could handle these items differently.

The labor and material costs are key forecasts in this problem. The special-purpose machine has a definite advantage if these forecasts are correct. The project manager has been very careful in his estimate, but the manufacturing process is new and the actual labor and material costs will not be known until some experience has been gained in the use of this equipment. The historic experience of the company on this type of forecast has not been too bad; the labor estimates have usually been within 5% of the actual costs, and the material estimates have been within 10%. In fact, after several trials and some frustration, the product manager was able to gather some historical data and make the assessment of forecast error shown in Figure 10–1.

The last two items in Table 10–1 are also not known for certain. The initial market size for the Beach Company product and the market growth will depend on many factors, such as, price, competitive prod-

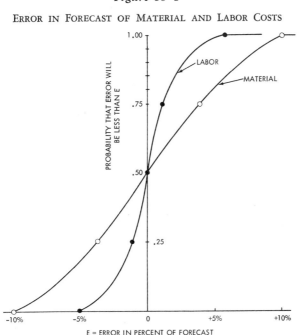

Figure 10–1

ERROR IN FORECAST OF MATERIAL AND LABOR COSTS

Figure 10–2

S = Initial Sales in Units

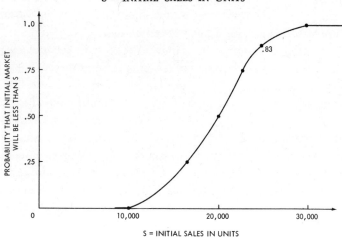

S = INITIAL SALES IN UNITS

ucts, and general economic conditions. The product manager has considered these factors and is willing to assess the probability distributions shown in Figure 10–2 and Figure 10–3 as his best judgment of what these items could be.

Figure 10–4 is a decision diagram for the problem facing the Beach Company. Each of the event forks represents a major uncer-

Figure 10–3

M = Market Growth in Percent per Year

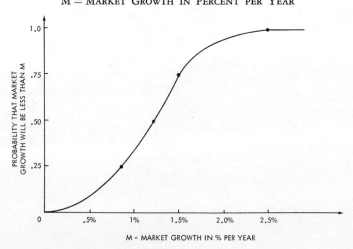

M = MARKET GROWTH IN % PER YEAR

Figure 10–4

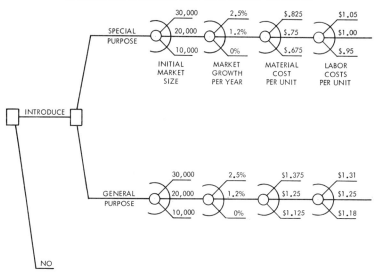

A DECISION DIAGRAM FOR THE BEACH PROBLEM

tainty. Not all possible outcomes are shown on these event forks because the resulting confusion would make the diagram useless. The product manager's point estimate is shown near the middle of the event fork, and the extreme outcomes are shown on the edges. It is possible to calculate the expected value and risk profile for each act by approximating each probability distribution for each event with five representative outcomes. Each event fork would have five branches, and each act could result in 625^1 end points. Each of these 625 end points would have some value for labor costs, material costs, initial market share, and market growth which could be used along with the other estimates in Table 10–1 to generate a cash flow pattern for each alternative. Using one of the measures of value developed earlier in Chapter 9, such as equivalent annual cash flow, this cash flow pattern could be converted into one number. This process of generating a cash flow pattern and converting it to the equivalent annual cash flow could be done for each end point. These values could then be arranged into a risk profile for each alternative, and the mean of the risk profile could be calculated.

This is a rather large computational effort. If more events—like

---

[1] The number of end points is the product of the number of branches for each event fork. Therefore end points $= 5 \cdot 5 \cdot 5 \cdot 5 = 625$.

overhead costs—were introduced, the number of calculations goes up drastically. Suppose that you believe overhead costs are critical enough to require a probabilistic forecast. If this distribution is represented by five typical outcomes along with the other four events, the number of end points for each alternative becomes 3,125.

We propose that the way to handle this computational nightmare is to sample the end points. In much the same way that public opinion surveys can predict public attitudes from the interviews of a small sample of people, we can approximate the risk profile for each act by calculating only a few end points. The key to success is the method of selecting the end points to be calculated.

Random Sampling of End Points

Rather than sample end points directly we will use a method that selects a value from each event fork. It may be useful to think of an interviewer standing at the end of the branch labeled special-purpose machine in Figure 10–4. His job is to calculate enough end points so that he can approximate the risk profile associated with the act special-purpose machine. He has a road map of the territory before him represented by the event forks of the decision diagram. What we must do is to tell him how to proceed along this road map to an end point. Once at an end point, he can calculate the equivalent annual cash flow and return to the starting point. This process we will call making a trial sample. He will continue this process until he had performed enough trials to allow him to make an accurate approximation of the risk profile.

How should the interviewer proceed down the diagram on each trial? His goal should be to calculate the value of a "typical" end point. Suppose he comes to an event fork with only two branches and a probability of 0.50 on each branch. We can tell him to flip a fair coin, and if it comes up heads go along one branch and tails go along the other. During his many trials we would expect him to go along each branch on about 50% of the trials following the coin flipping rule. This is an accurate reflection of the likelihood of encountering each branch when the actual event occurs and, therefore, using this rule should result in "typical" end points. If the probabilities on the two branches were 0.33 and 0.67, we would want to use a different rule. We could tell the interviewer to roll a fair die and if this roll resulted in 1 or 2 he should go down the branch with the 0.33 probability, otherwise go down the branch with the 0.67 probability. In many trials he would expect about one third of his sample end points to be after the one branch on the diagram and two thirds to be after the other branch on the diagram.

The process of selecting outcomes from the event forks for a trial calculation can be generalized for events with many outcomes. To do this we need what is known as a *random number generator* to replace the fair coin and fair die in the examples above. A random number generator must do the following:

1. Provide an equal probability of generating any number in its range on each given trial.
2. Be independent from trial to trial. In other words, the number generated on this trial has the same probability of occurring on the next trial as all the other numbers.

A fair coin is a random number generator for two numbers. A die is a random number generator for six numbers. Lists of random numbers have been generated to avoid having to think up combinations of coin tosses and dice rolls to build random number generators. Appendix A is such a list. If you want a random number between 0 and 99, you merely read a two-digit number from somewhere in this table. As an example if you took the 55th and 56th column and the 7th row, the random number would be 50. You can now proceed from this point in the table to read a list of two-digit random numbers by moving in some systematic manner. Suppose you read down the columns, the next five numbers are 80, 12, 22, 27, 30. You can start anywhere and move in any systematic manner from that point, as long as you do not cycle back on the same sequence, and be assured that this list of numbers you generate will be random.

Now that we have a process for creating a random number generator, we can replace the coins and dice in the instructions we give the interviewer.

Now if he came to an event fork with two branches and probabilities of 0.68 and 0.32, we could tell him the following rule:

1. Draw a two-digit random number from the random number table.
2. If the number is between 01 and 32 inclusive, go along the branch with the 0.32 probability.
3. If the number is between 33 and 100 (100 is represented by 00), go along the branch with the 0.68 probability.

If the random number generator is working correctly, there is a $1/100$ chance of drawing any number between 00 and 99. If the inter-

viewer follows this rule, we would expect him to get a number between
01 and 32 about 32% of the time in his many trials, and we have
achieved a good sampling procedure.

Most event forks have more than two outcomes, in fact all of the
events in our sample problem have many outcomes. Since it is easy to
generate two-digit random numbers, we will follow a procedure of
using 100 typical outcomes to represent an event with many outcomes.
We can divide the vertical axis of the cumulative probability graph into
100 equal divisions and read over to the cumulative graph and down to
the horizontal axis to get the 100 typical values for these outcomes.
Now when the interviewer is making a trial and comes to this event
fork we can give him the following sampling rule:

1. Draw a two-digit random number.
2. Count the list of typical outcomes for the event starting with the
   smallest until your count equals the random number.
3. The outcome where you stopped is the value for this trial.

The probability of any random number between 01 and (00) is
1/100. This rule should select in many trials each outcome about 1%
of the time, and this accurately reflects the 1/100 chance for each of
the 100 typical outcomes actually occurring.

A Typical End Point

We will now follow this procedure for a typical trial through the
Beach Company decision diagram in Figure 10–4. The forecasts shown
in Figure 10–2, 10–3, and 10–4 will be used as the basis for selecting
outcomes leading to this typical end point. First, a random number
was selected to determine the outcome for initial market size; this
number was an 82. We could have divided the market size probability
distribution (shown in Figure 10–3) into its 100 representative values
and counted up to the 82nd value. Instead, the same value can be obtained by going directly to the cumulative graph for initial market
share shown in Figure 10–4 and reading the 0.825 fractile. This value
of 25,000 units is the same one that would be obtained by following
the counting procedure. The next random number generated was an
01, and this was used to select a value of 0% per year for market
growth. The next random number was 86, and this caused a selection
of +6% error in the material cost estimate. This means that the
point estimates for material costs shown in Table 10–1 would be increased by 6% on this trial. The final random number was 88, and

Table 10–2

	Special Purpose	General Purpose
Initial market...........................	25,000 units	25,000 units
Market growth............................	0% per year	0% per year
Labor cost (+2% error).......................	$1.02 per unit	$1.275 per unit
Material cost (+6% error)...................	0.795 per unit	$1.325 per unit

this resulted in the selection of $+2\%$ error in the labor cost estimate. Table 10–2 summarizes the outcome for all events leading to the typical end point that resulted from this sampling procedure.

Table 10–3 shows the cash flow pattern that would result from this typical end point for both general-purpose and special-purpose machines. Table 10–4 shows how the equivalent annual cash flow at a 10% investment opportunity rate can be calculated for each alternative. For this end point, you can see that the special-purpose machine has the higher equivalent annual cash flow: $9,865 per year compared with $6,419 per year for the general-purpose machine.

This is one typical end point, and it is necessary to calculate more typical end points before we can approximate the risk profile for each act. The question of how many typical end points should be calculated in the sample is a difficult one to answer. It is clear that the larger the

Table 10–3

CASH FLOW PATTERNS FOR TYPICAL END POINT
(in thousands of dollars)

	0	1	2	3	4	5	6	7
Special purpose:								
Sales............................		125.0	125.0	125.0	125.0	...	...	...
Labor............................		25.5	25.5	25.5	25.5	...	...	...
Material.........................		19.9	19.9	19.9	19.9	...	...	...
Overhead.........................		16.3	16.3	16.3	16.3	...	...	...
Depreciation*....................		55.0	27.5	13.8	13.8	...	...	...
Profit after tax†		3.8	16.1	22.3	22.3			
Cash flow....................	−110	58.8	43.6	36.1	36.1			
General purpose:								
Sales............................		125.0	125.0	125.0	125.0	125.0	125.0	125.0
Labor............................		31.9	31.9	31.9	31.9	31.9	31.9	31.9
Material.........................		33.1	33.1	33.1	33.1	33.1	33.1	33.1
Overhead.........................		24.5	24.5	24.5	24.5	24.5	24.5	24.5
Depreciation‡...................		20.0	17.1	14.3	11.4	8.6	5.7	2.9
Profit after tax†		7.0	8.3	9.5	10.8	12.1	13.4	14.7
Cash flow....................	−80	27.0	25.4	23.8	22.2	20.7	19.1	17.6

* Double-declining-balance depreciation used.
† 55% tax rate.
‡ Sum-of-the-years' depreciation used.

Table 10–4

EQUIVALENT ANNUAL CASH FLOW
AT 10% INVESTMENT OPPORTUNITY RATE
($000)

Year	Discount Factor @ 10%	Special-Purpose Cash Flow	General-Purpose Cash Flow
0	1.000	−110.0	−80.0
1	0.909	58.8	27.0
2	0.826	43.6	25.4
3	0.751	36.1	23.8
4	0.683	36.1	22.2
5	0.621	...	20.7
6	0.564	...	19.1
7	0.513	...	17.6
Discounted cash flow		31.27	31.25
Capital recovery factor @ 10%		0.3155	0.2054
Equivalent annual cash flow		$9865	$6419

sample size the better the approximations will be. The major constraint on the sample size is an economic one, and when the cost of making a single calculation is large, it is important to determine the sample size carefully. Techniques for calculating the sample size accurately are beyond the scope of this book. However, in most cases where the sampling and calculation are being done in a computer model, the cost of a single trial is small and, therefore, less care is needed in determining the sample size. A rule of thumb in this situation is to take anywhere from 50 to 1,000 trials in the sample. One thing to keep in mind when deciding on a sample size is the number of calculations needed to determine the risk profiles directly. Using five representative values for each event in our example, this would be 625 for each alternative. With this fact in mind and knowing that a computer model was to be used, we have used a sample size of 50 trials to approximate the risk profiles for the Beach Company problem.

Figure 10–5 shows the risk profiles resulting from a Monte Carlo simulation using 50 trials and the forecasts given in Figures 10–2, 10–3, and 10–4.

The means of these risk profiles are $3,933 dollars per year for the general-purpose machines and $5,113 per year for the special-purpose machines. If the Beach Company is willing to play the averages, they can use the mean of the risk profile as their certainty equivalent for each alternative, and they would want to use the special-pur-

Figure 10–5

RISK PROFILES FOR TWO ALTERNATIVES

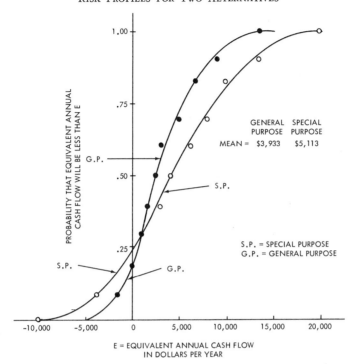

E = EQUIVALENT ANNUAL CASH FLOW
IN DOLLARS PER YEAR

pose machine. They would also choose to introduce the new product because it has a positive equivalent annual cash flow calculated at the 10% investment opportunity rate.

Because this is a major commitment of resources, the company may be unwilling to play the averages. If this is the case, then the company can use the risk profiles shown in Figure 10–5 to determine the certainty equivalent for each alternative. We will mention some of the characteristics of the risk profiles that might help them decide on their best alternative.

The general-purpose machine risk profile has a range of equivalent annual cash flows running from −$5,500 per year to $13,600 per year. The special-purpose risk profile shows that equivalent annual cash flow for this alternative can be as low as −$10,500 per year and as high as $20,000 per year. This indicates that the alternative with the higher mean also has the widest range of possible outcomes and the most negative outcomes. The company may be willing to give up this alternative with its higher expected value in order to avoid any chance of getting these more negative outcomes.

Both alternatives show about a 25% chance of having a negative equivalent annual cash flow. This means that there is a 25% chance that they will not be able to make a 10% profit after tax return. This may be too large a chance of not making enough return and, therefore, the company may want to reject both alternatives.

Another interesting figure to get from Figure 10–5 is the point at which the two alternatives have the same equivalent annual cash flow. This occurs where the risk profile intersect or somewhere near the 0.26 fractile. This means that there is a 26.5% chance that the special-purpose machine will have an equivalent annual cash flow that is less than the flow for the general-purpose machine. The company may have decided for policy reasons that this product must be introduced and that they really only want to decide which process to use in manufacturing. Then it is meaningful to ask which machine is best under most future situations. The answer to this question is that in only 26.5% of the cases is the general-purpose machine better.

An even better method for obtaining this information would be to calculate the difference between each alternative's equivalent annual cash flow on every trial of the simulation. The results of these calculations can then be used to approximate a probability distribution for the differential yearly cash flow between the two alternatives. Such a probability distribution is shown in Figure 10–6. From this you can still determine the probability of the one alternative being better than the other. This probability is shown at the zero differential cash flow on the cumulative curve, and from Figure 10–6 you can see it is about 26%. However, in addition, this distribution gives information about how much better or worse the one alternative is than the other. For example, there is a zero probability that there is any outcome where the special-purpose machine could have an equivalent annual cash flow that is $5,000 per year less than the general-purpose machine. On the other end, this distribution shows that there is no outcome that would cause the special-purpose machine to exceed the general-purpose machine by more than a $6,300 per year equivalent annual cash flow.

You should remember that the probability distribution for differential cash flows is useful only for deciding the best of two alternative production processes. Although one alternative has a larger equivalent

Figure 10–6

DIFFERENTIAL EQUIVALENT ANNUAL CASH FLOW
SPECIAL PURPOSE MINUS GENERAL PURPOSE

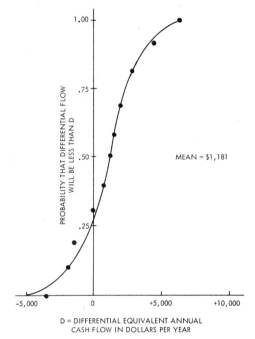

D = DIFFERENTIAL EQUIVALENT ANNUAL
CASH FLOW IN DOLLARS PER YEAR

annual cash flow than the other, this cash flow may not be large enough to justify going ahead with the project.

If the Beach Company does not wish to play the averages, we cannot say for sure which alternative is best. However, the information needed by the company to make the comparison is contained in the risk profiles of Figure 10–5.

SUMMARY

Monte Carlo simulation is a technique that is useful in analyzing a decision problem with a large number of events. You should be careful to remember that this technique is only a portion of the decision analysis process. It is still necessary to: (1) structure the problem using some method like decision diagramming; (2) assess probability distributions for all events either completely judgmentally or with the aid of some historical data; and (3) determine what criterion will be used to measure value. In most capital investment decisions this last step will require using some method that takes into account the time value of money.

Once these three steps have been taken, it is necessary to consider how best to calculate the risk profile for each act fork. It may be possible to take an approximation of the probability distribution for each event by using five typical outcomes and then calculate the risk profile directly. However, if there are more than two or three events, this becomes costly in computational effort. If there are four or more events, Monte Carlo simulation can be used to solve this computational problem. Using a sample of 50 to 1,000 typical end points, the risk profiles for each act can be approximated. To obtain a typical end point, an outcome is drawn from each event fork using a random number generator and the probability distribution already assessed for this event. The information from this sample trial is then used to calculate the criterion of value chosen by the decision maker. Once all typical end points have been calculated, the risk profile and its mean for each act are approximated. This information can then be used by the decision maker to determine his certainty equivalent.

There are several problems with using Monte Carlo simulation that should be mentioned. First, it is important to make sure that all the probability distributions are assessed to meet the needs of the real decision problems and not to meet the convenience of the simulation model. In many real world problems, the probability distribution for one event will depend on the outcome of some other event. As an example, consider some market where one of your competitors is very large and is the price leader in that market. His price is an event in your decision problem, and it is possible for you to assess a probability distribution for that price. The size of the total market is also an event in your decision problem and you can also assess a probability distribution for this event. However, you would be foolish to make these two assessments unrelated, for clearly his price will have a direct influence on the market size. In fact, you should assess one probability distribution for the market size for each of the possible outcomes to the price event. This is true whether simulation or some other method is used to obtain the risk profiles. However, in many cases the builders of simulation models have ignored these interrelationships. This can be disastrous because it will eliminate many of the interesting outcomes in the sampling process and thus give a distorted basis for making the approximations of the risk profile.

A second major problem with simulations is the cost of building the model. The amount of computation needed in simulation, although less than required to obtain the answer by other methods, is large enough that any practical use requires a computer. The building of computer simulation programs can be aided by special simulation languages and subroutines, but it still requires a substantial investment of time. If the model is to be effective some of this time must be spent by the decision maker. Therefore, some thought should be given to this cost before simulation is proposed.

A final problem worth mentioning is a psychological one. Because Monte Carlo simulation requires such an elaborate computational scheme, it is possible to begin to believe that this alone adds some special credibility to the results. This belief should be avoided, and you should remember that the final result is no better than the initial inputs to the model. You must still define alternatives and make assessments for the events in the problem. No amount of computational massaging can make bad assessments or sloppy problem definition into good decision making.

WEATHERBURN AIRCRAFT ENGINE COMPANY

In June, 1957, the Weatherburn Aircraft Engine Company received an order for ten spare ring gears from Sierra Airlines. The ring gear was the largest and most expensive of the gears in the system which drives the propeller.

The Weatherburn company carried in stock part No. 21573, the gear blanks from which the ring gears would be made. This gear blank was a standard size, used in many airplanes. The number of teeth, however, was nonstandard. When Sierra Airlines had bought the airplanes in which these gears were used, its management had decided that flying requirements peculiar to this airline necessitated a gear ratio slightly higher than standard, and Weatherburn had designed a special gear train accordingly. No other airlines used this ratio, and Sierra was on the point of converting its fleet of aircraft to jet operations. Upon inquiry, the production manager of Weatherburn company learned that the lot of ten ring gears would almost certainly last until Sierra's current aircraft had been entirely replaced.

The gear blanks cost Weatherburn about $50 each to make. The first step in the machining process was hobbing. Setup for this operation was very expensive, costing about $500, but the direct cost of hobbing an extra gear was negligible so long as the machine's capacity of 25 gears at one time was not exceeded. After hobbing, each gear was individually subjected to a series of drilling, grinding, and finishing operations, the total cost of which was $90 per gear. In addition, there was a setup cost of $250 associated with these operations. The machined gears were then heat-treated at a cost of about $10 per gear, after which they were subjected to a hardness test the cost of which was negligible.

After hobbing and before the remaining operations, the gears were

512

subjected to a 100% inspection. In the past, an average of 4% of all the hobbed gears failed to pass this inspection and had to be scrapped. The heat-treating operation was much more difficult to control. The test for hardness had rigid specifications, and the Weatherburn company had had considerable difficulty in meeting standards on this type of gear in the past; only 80% of the gears had proved acceptable.

Question

Decide on a scheduling policy to meet the order from Sierra Airlines. Using a table of random numbers, simulate about 20 production runs according to the policy you have decided on. Assuming that any shortage on the first run can be made up *exactly* on the second run (i.e., no overage or underage on the second run), use the data you have simulated to calculate the *expected cost* of your policy. (*Note:* If you prepare this case in a group, it is suggested that each group member use a different policy in order to provide a comparison of expected costs for different policies.)

TOMLINSON STEEL CORPORATION

Tomlinson Steel Corporation operated two docks at a port on the east coast of the United States at which it unloaded iron ore coming by ship from Venezuela. The ships were all of about the same size and type, and it took just about one 24-hour day to unload one. Labor was readily available, and the company was not forced to pay for a crew's time when there was no ship to unload and could go on a three-shift seven-day-per-week basis when the number of arrivals required (360 days per year).

This arrangement had worked out very well for several years. The ships radioed their arrival enough in advance so that a crew was always ready. Not infrequently an arriving ship found both of the docks occupied and had to wait before being unloaded, but the delay very rarely amounted to more than a few hours.

In January 1955, however, management became concerned about the fact that the approaching completion of its new steel mill would increase ore requirements and therefore ship arrivals. A study was undertaken to determine if another dock should be built. This study had the following results:

1. In 1954 one ship arrived about every 15 hours.
2. The steel mill superintendent indicated the new steel mill would require an additional 25% of iron ore; he therefore expected one ship to arrive every 12 hours.
3. As a result of reviewing his past records on ship arrivals, the dock master indicated that under the new setup:
   a) Chances were 1 in 2 that the time between ships would be the 12 hours specified by the mill superintendent or less.
   b) Chances were 1 in 4 that the time between ships would be 8 hours or less.
   c) It was theoretically possible for more than one ship to arrive at once, but very unlikely.
   d) Chances were 3 in 4 that the time between ship arrivals would be 16 hours or less.
   e) Virtually no ships would ever arrive more than 24 hours apart.

With one-fourth again as many ships arriving as was the case in 1954, management was afraid that some ships would be delayed for long periods of time. Every delay of one hour cost the company an additional $100 in charter rate.

Questions

1. Using a table of random numbers, simulate the arrival of 30 ships.

2. Given the above arrival pattern, determine the waiting time and cost with two docks. With three docks. What cost saving per year can be anticipated from building the third dock?

HURLEY HOME PRODUCTS
COMPANY

The Hurley Home Products Company was a major manufacturer of brooms, brushes, mops, and other home cleaning devices. During 1967 its sales had amounted to $125 million, primarily through hardware dealers and grocery chains. To achieve this sales level, the company had spent about $15 million on advertising and sales promotion during 1967.

In January 1968, the executive committee of the company was meeting to determine the advertising and sales promotion budget for 1968. Of particular concern to the committee was a decision as to what to spend on a line of carpet sweepers which had encountered considerable competitive pressure during 1967.

Mr. George Gershberg, the company sales manager, thought that a continuation of present advertising and promotional policies on the carpet sweepers would result in a further decrease in sales. He therefore suggested an increase in advertising and promotion from $50,000 to $100,000 without any change in price.

He said he thought that unless something was done, sales during 1968 would amount to about 100,000 units. He was even unsure of this quantity, estimating that there was even some very small chance that sales might be as low as 75,000 units. He added that the odds were as high as 1 in 2 that the sales would be below his 100,000 unit estimate, and 1 in 4 they might even be below 90,000 units.

When Mr. John Glass, the company controller, asked about how high the carpet sweeper sales might go in 1968 if no changes were made in the advertising and promotional policies, Mr. Gershberg responded that there was almost no chance of their exceeding 120,000 units, and only 1 in 4 chance of exceeding 105,000 units.

Mr. Gershberg said he believed that the proposed $50,000 increase in advertising and promotion was almost certain to increase sales by 10% over these estimates and perhaps by as much as 40% as an upper limit. The increase was as likely to be above 25% as below it, as likely to be between 20% and 30% as outside that range, and as likely to be above 30% as below 20%.

Mr. Glass said that he wondered how competition would react to this advertising and promotion increase. Mr. Gershberg replied that he really was not sure, but that the increases he had just projected assumed that competition would not change their current policies at all. He added that he thought the odds were 3 in 4 that competition would not respond in 1968. Even if they did, he thought there would still be some increases in sales, but probably only 50% of those he estimated, assuming no competitive response.

The sales price of the carpet sweeper to Hurley's distributors was $10 per unit. The variable cost per unit was $7 for production levels below 120,000 units per year, $7.50 for production levels between 120,000 and 180,000 units per year (due to overtime costs). A production level above 150,000 units was not felt feasible by the company's production manager, Mr. Joseph Selman. The fixed production costs associated with the product line would increase by about $8,000 to $10,000 per year at a production level above 120,000 units.

Question

What should the Hurley management do about their carpet sweeper line?

APEX DRILLING COMPANY

In November 1961, Mr. Thomas Grayson, president and sole owner of the Apex Drilling Company, was about to reach a final decision concerning a lease that Apex held on a plot of land in an oil-bearing region in central Kansas. The lease gave the lessee (Apex) the right to drill for oil at any time up to March 31, 1962; it would terminate automatically if drilling had not begun by that date. If drilling was begun before the termination date, it could be continued until either oil was struck or the driller decided to give up; if oil was struck, the lessee was obliged to pay the lessor (the owner of the land) royalties equal to one sixth of the gross revenues received from all oil lifted.

The Apex Drilling Company had been founded in 1954 by Mr. Grayson, until then operations vice president of the Prometheus Petroleum Company, in an effort to "make money for myself instead of for others." Until 1959 the company's business had consisted entirely of drilling exploratory wells for the major oil producers, but in that year Grayson had decided to try exploratory drilling on Apex's own account. Leases had been negotiated for drilling rights on five widely scattered plots of land in central Kansas, and wells had been drilled in 1959 on four of the five plots, but all these holes had been dry and the diversion of Apex's four drilling rigs from paid work for the majors to these private ventures had reduced Apex's working capital nearly to zero and forced Grayson to postpone action concerning the last lease until funds were again available.

During 1960 and the first 10 months of 1961 Apex had been able to secure drilling contracts that kept its four drilling rigs occupied over 90% of the time and had built the company's working capital back up to about $50,000 so that the company was financially able to drill the last of the five sites. The company could not actually do the drilling with its own equipment, however, since in order to obtain the drilling contracts that had kept the equipment so profitably occupied in 1960

518

and 1961 it had been obliged to accept other contracts that tied the rigs up completely until well past the middle of 1962, and accordingly, Mr. Grayson had had his treasurer, Mr. Vance Russell, obtain bids for the drilling from other contract drillers who had rigs in the vicinity of the plot on which Apex held the drilling lease.

The lowest bid received was $9 per foot (after appropriate tax adjustments) from Klimm Drillers, Inc. This offer was applicable, however, only if it was accepted within two weeks since the reason Klimm was able to bid so low was that they currently had a rig in the immediate vicinity of the Apex plot.

Mr. Grayson then consulted with his geologist, Mr. Alden Heffern, as to the depth at which oil was likely to be found in the area. Mr. Heffern indicated that if any oil was there, it was almost certainly between 3,000 and 6,000 feet below the surface. He added that it was as likely between 3,000 and 5,000 feet as it was between 5,000 and 6,000 feet, as likely between 3,000 and 4,500 feet as 4,500 to 5,000 feet, and as likely between 5,000 and 5,300 feet as 5,300 to 6,000 feet. Mr. Heffern also pointed out that the odds were about 8 in 10 of not finding oil even at the 6,000-foot depth. Beyond 6,000 feet the geological formations were so unpromising that it seemed to make no sense to Mr. Heffern to continue drilling.

The value of a successful well depended largely on the rate at which the oil could be removed from the ground (the "production" rate). However, the production rate would not affect Apex directly since Mr. Grayson had already decided that if he did drill and strike oil, he would sell out to a major producer immediately. Apex had a $100,000 bank loan which would fall due late in 1962; and although this loan could probably be extended if necessary, Mr. Grayson thought it was clearly wiser to pay off the loan if he could and put Apex into a really strong position for further ventures than to try to squeeze out a little more profit by lifting the oil himself. The going price at which the majors were buying successful new wells depended, however, on the prospective production rate.

Mr. Grayson thought that he should be able to sell a successful well in the area for somewhere between $300,000 and $450,000 after adjustments for taxes. He further believed that the price was as likely to be above $360,000 as below it, three times as likely to be above $340,000 as below it, and as likely to be between $340,000 and $400,000 as outside this range. Mr. Heffern did not think the price of the well would depend on its depth.

Mr. Grayson questioned Mr. Heffern on the possibility of seismic testing to determine if any oil was present. Mr. Heffern said he could perform a test which would provide almost perfect evidence as to the presence or absence of oil in the area but indicate almost nothing about the depth at which it was located and the anticipated production rate. This test would cost Apex only $3,000 after taxes, and it could be made in a week.

The idea of a seismic sounding at first seemed very attractive to Mr. Grayson as a way of reducing what seemed to him the extremely great risks involved in any decision he could make. If he did not have the test made but drilled a dry hole, he stood to lose as much as $36,000 and be left once again almost without working capital. The only alternative to drilling was to accept a standing offer from Prometheus Oil to buy the Apex lease at any time that would leave Prometheus time to start drilling before the lease expired. The price offered by Prometheus would net Apex only $6,000 after taxes, however, and Grayson felt that if he accepted this offer and Prometheus then struck oil, he would feel that he had lost the difference between $6,000 and whatever the successful well would be sold for.

After a little more reflection, however, Grayson began to think that having the sounding made was in a sense even riskier than not having it made. The result of the sounding would certainly become generally known at once, and he was afraid that if the sounding revealed that the Apex plot was dry, Prometheus would withdraw its offer to buy the lease. A telephone call to Prometheus confirmed his suspicions: Prometheus would not drill on any site if it knew that there was no chance of striking oil and, hence, would pay nothing for a lease on such a site. The Prometheus representative went on to say, however, that Prometheus would be glad to pay a much higher price for the lease than it had originally offered if a seismic sounding revealed that the site *did* contain some oil. Mr. Jackson asked Mr. Russell about the effect of taxes on this higher price and was told that even after taxes were deducted Apex would retain $27,000 of the amount paid by Prometheus.

Question

What should Mr. Grayson do?

Chapter 11

FINANCIAL STRUCTURE AND THE COST OF CAPITAL

The two preceding chapters have relied heavily on the following ideas:

1. The funds which a firm invests have, like the other resources the firm consumes in its activities, a cost, which we have called the investment opportunity rate. This is also called the *cost of capital.*
2. The cost of capital can be expressed in units of "dollars per year per dollar invested" or, equivalently, as a *percent per annum.*
3. The cost of capital can be used either as an integral part of the analysis of an investment project (as, for example, when we calculate the present value of the project using the cost of capital as the discount rate) or as a standard of comparison (if we choose to calculate the yield or internal rate of return of the project).

What we have not done so far is to discuss *how* the cost of capital is itself determined. That is the task of the present chapter.

It is natural to suppose that a firm's cost of capital depends on where and how the firm obtains these funds. Thus the first topic we will take up in this chapter is a consideration of the major sources of funds available to the firm and their respective "costs." We will then present a relatively simple method of calculating cost of capital—a method which, however, opens up a veritable Pandora's Box of theoretical disputes. After hacking away at the theoretical underbrush for a while, we will conclude the chapter with a discussion of a relatively theory-free approach to the financial management of the firm. Understandably, given the disputes of the theoreticians, most practicing financial managers appear to follow an approach similar to that we describe in the final section.

THE FINANCIAL STRUCTURE OF THE FIRM

We assume that most of our readers have already had a course in elementary accounting or in elementary economics in which they have been introduced to the idea of a *balance sheet*. We will need to draw on this acquaintanceship in the rest of this chapter. First, therefore, we will give a brief review of the essential concepts.

For reference, a pair of sample balance sheets of the Jarvis Manufacturing Company for two successive year-ends is given in Table 11–1.

Table 11–1

JARVIS MANUFACTURING COMPANY
COMPARATIVE BALANCE SHEETS
AS OF DECEMBER 31, 1972 AND 1971
(Thousands of dollars)

ASSETS	December 31, 1972	December 31, 1971	Change
Current assets	$3,421	$3,143	$ 278
Less: Current liabilities	1,578	1,518	60
Net circulating assets	$1,843	$1,625	$ 218
Fixed assets, at cost	$5,936	$5,813	$ 123
Less: Accumulated depreciation	3,910	3,547	363
Net fixed assets	$2,026	$2,266	$(240)
Total net assets	$3,869	$3,891	$ (22)
CAPITAL			
Long-term debt	$ 743	$ 815	$ (72)
6½% preferred stock	$1,025	$1,025	$ ...
Common stock	$1,500	$1,500	$ ...
Accumulated retained earnings	601	551	50
Total residual capital	$2,101	$2,051	$ 50
Total capital	$3,869	$3,891	$ (22)

The format and some of the terms used in this exhibit may be a little different from what you are used to seeing, but we hope that these differences will be made clear in the following discussion.

The Meaning of Financial Structure

Looking at Table 11–1, concentrate first on the column of figures headed "December 31, 1972." The totals of the two parts of this column (Assets and Capital) are equal, amounting to $3,869,000. This equality, or balance, between the two parts of the balance sheet as of a given date is, of course, what gives it its name.

There are several ways of interpreting the equality of the two parts of the balance sheet. For our purposes, the most instructive interpretation is as follows. The top, or *assets,* part shows how the firm has *invested* its funds as of the statement date. The bottom, or *capital,* part shows how it has *obtained* those funds. The equality, then, merely reflects the fact that all of the firm's funds must have both come from somewhere and gone somewhere.

We shall use the term *asset structure* to refer to the complex of facts represented by the top side of the balance sheet and the term *capital structure* to refer to the complex represented by the bottom side. When referring to both parts taken together, we will use the term *financial structure.*

Asset Structure

Let us now look at the asset structure of the Jarvis Manufacturing Company in more detail. Note first that there are two main subdivisions: *net circulating assets* and *net fixed assets.* The distinction between these two subdivisions is conceptually very similar to the distinction made in Chapter 1 between variable product costs and fixed product costs respectively. In the present case, circulating assets are those which tend to be adjusted relatively promptly, indeed almost automatically, to variations in the level of sales. Fixed assets are those which are adjusted to the level of sales only in the "long run," although of course in the short run the existence of a given stock of fixed assets implies a capacity constraint and hence a limitation on feasible sales levels.

Net Circulating Assets. As indicated in Table 11–1, net circulating assets is the difference between two quantities: current assets and current liabilities. Current assets include principally cash, accounts receivable from customers who have bought on credit, and inventories of raw materials, work in process, and goods available for sale. Current liabilities include principally accounts payable to suppliers and other vendors, wages due to employees for work already performed but not yet paid for, and short-term bank financing obtained to meet seasonal peaks in fund requirements.

The "circulating assets" idea is illustrated in Figure 11–1. In the firm's normal operating cycle, it acquires or produces inventory, either paying cash for the factors of production or buying them on credit. Sale of goods (if for credit) results in an account receivable from the customer. Collection of the receivable replenishes the Cash account, which is, of course, also used to pay accounts and wages payable as they come due. This completes the major circulation. Since there is generally a time lag between the point at which cash must be laid out to acquire inventory or pay off liabilities and the point at which receivables are collected, the Cash account will be depleted in a period of rising sales. If the sales rise is expected to be temporary (as in the case of a seasonal peak), the firm may meet these temporary cash requirements through short-term bank financing.

Figure 11–1 also shows, through dashed-line relationships, that the circulating assets system is not completely independent of the other

Figure 11–1

ILLUSTRATION OF THE CIRCULATING ASSETS CONCEPT

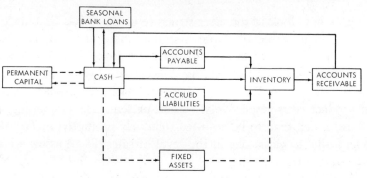

parts of the firm's financial structure. First, cash must be used when fixed assets are purchased, thereby reducing circulating assets and increasing fixed assets. Second, as we have seen earlier in this book, depreciation of fixed assets is usually treated as part of product cost and hence inventory; depreciation therefore reduces fixed assets and increases circulating assets. Finally, the difference between current assets and current liabilities—what we have called net circulating assets —represents a relatively permanent requirement for funds and thus one of the uses to which the pool of permanent funds provided by the capital structure must be put.

Net Fixed Assets. Fixed assets include land, buildings, and equipment. As shown in Table 11–1, fixed assets are usually carried at original purchase price with a separate deduction made for depreciation charges accumulated since time of purchase. The relationships between fixed assets and circulating assets were just discussed.

Capital Structure

There seems to be almost no limit to the ingenuity of finance specialists in devising new kinds of arrangements whereby corporations can obtain funds from investors. We do not have the space to spend on many of these variations. The main issues, however, can be illustrated by using the categories shown on the bottom (or Capital) part of the Jarvis Manufacturing Company balance sheet.

Long-Term Debt. In obtaining funds from investors through the long-term debt route, the firm enters into a contractual agreement to (1) pay the investors a specified amount of interest so long as the debt remains outstanding, and (2) repay them the principal amount (the amount borrowed) according to a specified schedule. The interest requirement is usually expressed as a percent per annum on the amount outstanding. The significant feature of debt, for our purposes, is that the payments called for are firm legal obligations; failure to make them as scheduled can subject the borrower to sanctions up to and including bankruptcy. Interest paid on debt is a deductible expense under the federal tax laws.

Preferred Stock. Like debt, preferred stock calls for specified annual payments to the investors; these payments are called dividends rather than interest, however, and are not tax deductible. In addition to these differences in terminology and tax treatment, there are several other important differences between debt and preferred stock. First, preferred dividends are not an absolute legal obligation in the sense that debt interest is. Dividends on preferred stock must be paid, however, before the common stock may receive dividends (this is one sense in which the stock is "preferred"); in addition, in the event of non-payment of dividends, the preferred stockholders may have certain additional rights, such as the power to elect a majority of the board of directors. Second, preferred stock does not usually have to be repaid. Frequently, however, the corporation has the option of "calling" or repaying the stock for its own convenience.

Common Stock. Investors holding common stock have no legal right to receive *any* dividends but they do (in most cases) have the right to elect the board of directors which has the legal right to decide what dividends (if any) will be paid, to appoint officers, and to exercise general control over the affairs of the corporation. While the common stockholders have no legal right to dividends, all of the earnings of the corporation after payment of interest and preferred dividends is supposed to be used for their benefit. Thus the common stockholders can profit from the growth of the company financed out of retention of earnings. And, of course, there is no fixed upper limit on the dividends they can receive, provided (in most cases) that these dividends are covered by earnings.

Retained Earnings. When the firm earns a profit by selling its products for more than their cost, the differential (if not paid out in dividends) increases the funds available to the firm. As noted in the preceding paragraph, these funds can be considered as "belonging" to the common stockholders.

Some Accounting Issues

There are several accounting conventions used in the preparation of balance sheets which, if not understood, can make them misleading representations of financial structure.

Valuation. The normal practice of accountants is to base the monetary values appearing on the balance sheet only on arm's-length exchange transactions between the firm and outside parties. Fixed assets, for example, are carried at original acquisition cost (less accumulated depreciation calculated on that original cost). These accounting values may not correspond to current market values—indeed, it would be an extreme coincidence if they did correspond.

Rented or Leased Assets. With some exceptions, only owned assets are carried on the balance sheet. A firm may have the use of fixed assets through rental or lease agreements with their owners, but neither the assets themselves nor the obligation to make rental or lease payments appear on the balance sheet. (The payments themselves are reflected as expenses as they accrue.)

Intangible Assets. Expenditures for purposes such as research, development, and advertising may benefit future accounting periods. Accountants generally prefer not to reflect "intangible assets" such as these on the balance sheet; instead they are charged off as expenses as they accrue.

Changes in Financial Structure

So far we have been talking about the financial structure of the Jarvis Manufacturing Company at a given date, December 31, 1972. Decisions made by the firm along with events during a period of time may result in changes in financial structure. A retrospective view of such changes can be obtained by comparing balance sheets as of two different dates.

Table 11–1, for example, also gives the Jarvis balance sheet as of December 31, 1971, thus providing us with the data needed to analyze changes in financial structure during the calendar year 1972. Analysis of these changes can be sharpened by calculating the numerical differences between the two balance sheets; these differences are also shown in Table 11–1. The difference information is also presented in a somewhat rearranged format in Table 11–2. This new format is called a *statement of sources and uses of funds* for the calendar year 1972.

From Table 11–2, we can see that Jarvis Manufacturing Company

Table 11–2

JARVIS MANUFACTURING COMPANY
STATEMENT OF SOURCES AND USES OF FUNDS
FOR THE CALENDAR YEAR 1972
(Thousands of dollars)

Sources of funds:		
Increase in accumulated retained earnings........................		$ 50
Increase in accumulated depreciation.............................		363
Funds provided by operations....................................		$413
Uses of funds:		
Increase in fixed assets..	$123	
Decrease in long-term debt.......................................	72	
Subtotal..		195
Increase in net circulating assets................................		$218

obtained funds in 1972 from two main sources. First, earnings in the amount of $50,000 were retained for use in the business. Second, funds in the amount of $363,000 were, in effect, released from net fixed assets as a result of depreciation charges (compare Figure 11–1, where fixed assets are converted into circulating assets through the depreciation charge).

The funds obtained as indicated above were used as follows: $218,-000 was invested to increase net circulating assets; $123,000 was used to purchase additional fixed assets; and $72,000 was used to repay a portion of the company's long-term debt.

COST OF CAPITAL

Over a short period of time, as Table 11–2 illustrates, a firm may finance its capital budget in a variety of ways. First, it may increase its overall capital structure by selling debt, preferred stock, or common stock, or by retaining earnings. Second, it may draw down its net circulating assets. Finally, it may use funds obtained from the sale of fixed assets or generated by their depreciation.

Only the first source, of course, represents an increase in the total capital funds of the business; the other two sources merely involve a reallocation of existing capital, either from circulating to fixed assets or within the fixed-asset portfolio. Unless the firm's assets are substantially in excess of what it requires to support its sales volume, the two latter sources, therefore, are only temporary expedients. Assets will sooner or later have to be restored to their normal relationship to sales, requiring that new permanent capital be raised.

In determining the cost of capital to be used in evaluating new investments in fixed assets, therefore, it will usually be appropriate to consider the source of the funds to be new capital raised by increasing one or more of the components of the capital structure. In the remainder of this section, we will first consider the measurement of the cost of each component taken separately. Then we will discuss a composite measure of cost, taking all components into account, called the *weighted-average cost of capital.* This will then lead into a discussion of issues raised by the weighted-average concept, which will conclude the section.

Cost of Components of Capital Structure

Two principles which we have emphasized in earlier chapters apply as well to the measurement of cost of capital.

First, relevant costs are *future* costs. When referring to cost of capital, this means the cost of capital yet to be raised, not capital already on the company's books. (Of course, the firm may face the problem of allocating funds already raised, in which case the relevant cost is an *opportunity cost,* but as we said earlier, we are not looking in this section at the issue of reallocation.)

Second, the costs we are concerned with are *after-tax* costs. This is for consistency with our treatment of the returns on capital investments; there we also adjusted the cash flows for the effects of income taxes. In the case of cash flows from investments, we saw that adjustment for tax effects was necessary because different kinds of flows were treated differently for tax purposes. The same is true, as we will see, of the costs of different capital components.

Long-Term Debt. At first glance, the measurement of the cost of new long-term debt appears relatively straightforward. There is a conceptual complication but we will postpone consideration of that until the last part of this section (page 533).

Suppose that the financial advisors to the Jarvis Manufacturing Company report that in their judgment the company could currently sell long-term debt at a net interest cost, after allowing for selling costs of 7.35% per year; this is the *before-tax* cost of new long-term debt. In arriving at this estimate, the financial advisors will consider not only the state of the financial markets and the credit worthiness of the Jarvis Manufacturing Company but also the characteristics of the debt issue itself: its maturity and call provisions in particular.[1]

Since interest on debt is deductible for tax purposes, we must adjust the 7.35% to an after-tax figure. Assuming that Jarvis's tax rate is 48%, this adjustment would proceed as follows:

Cost of debt per year, before taxes	7.35%
Tax deduction at 48%	3.53
Cost of debt per year, after taxes	3.82%

(We have carried this result to two places after the decimal point solely for illustrative purposes. As we shall see particularly later in this chapter, there is enough fuzziness in the cost of capital concept so that Jarvis can probably know what its overall cost is only to within a percent or two.)

Preferred Stock. The cost of preferred stock is even simpler to determine than that of debt, since there is no tax adjustment. If Jarvis's financial advisors report that in their judgment the company could sell preferred stock at a dividend rate of 8.50% per year on the net proceeds after selling costs, that figure of 8.50% can be taken as the cost of preferred stock financing.

Often a company can reduce the apparent cost of preferred stock financing by agreeing to make the preferred stock *convertible* into common stock at the option of the preferred stockholder. If this is done, a schedule of conversion prices is included in the agreement. The preferred stockholders are willing to agree to the lower dividend rate because the conversion privilege permits them to benefit from increases in the value of the common stock if the company prospers. This benefit is, in effect, at the expense of the existing common stockholders, however, who would otherwise be the exclusive beneficiaries of this growth in the value of the common stock. This is why we say that the effect

---

[1] For a brief discussion of these characteristics, see the appendix to the J. L. Jessup & Sons case, beginning on page 436 of this book.

of the conversion privilege is to reduce the *apparent* cost of the preferred stock. Under what circumstances convertibility is to the *net* advantage of the common stockholders is a question beyond the scope of this book.

Common Stock. Measuring the cost of a new common stock issue presents us with the most difficult conceptual problem we have encountered so far in this section. As we have already mentioned, the directors of a company are under no firm, fixed obligation to pay the common stockholders *anything.* In recent years, as a matter of fact, a number of quite successful companies have had a policy *against* the payment of common dividends, arguing that they could use the funds more effectively in the business than their stockholders could for other purposes. This policy has not seemed to have hurt these companies' standing in the securities markets. Does the absence of dividends mean that the "cost" of common stock financing for these companies is zero, in the sense that funds so obtained could be invested to yield *no* return on investment? Common sense (and presumably the common stockholder) would answer No!

What, then, *is* the cost of common stock financing? A number of ways have been proposed to answer this question. These ways differ in operational detail but they come down to this common principle: The management of a corporation should invest the common stockholders' funds in such a way as to meet the stockholders' reasonable expectations. This principle can be justified on ethical or legal grounds, but in most cases it is not necessary to appeal to such an abstract level; a management which fails to meet the reasonable expectations of its common stockholders *may* be voted out of office and *almost certainly* will find it increasingly difficult to raise funds in the future through common stock financing. Thus, the principle of meeting the reasonable expectations of the common stockholders has strong pragmatic justification.

But what *are* these reasonable expectations? A corporation may have thousands or even millions of stockholders, each one of them may have different expectations, and these expectations (even if we asked these stockholders about them) might not be very well articulated. In order to be able to deal with this problem operationally, we need to make some sort of assumption about the expectations of the "typical stockholder." Given the diversity of possibilities, it is not surprising that the literature contains a wide range of suggestions concerning the behavior of this "typical stockholder." Perhaps the most satisfactory of these[2] assumes that the typical stockholder expects two things: (1) a current dividend on his holdings and (2) growth in the market value of his holdings. Each of these two factors can be expressed as a percentage of the current market price of the common stock, and their sum can be considered then as the "return" expected by the "typical stockholder."

For example, suppose that the Jarvis Manufacturing Company is currently paying a dividend on its common stock of $2 per share per year and the stock is selling for $40 share. The "dividend yield" on its common stock is, therefore, $2/$40 = 5% per share per year. Suppose further that the typical stockholder expects that this relationship between dividends and market price will continue indefinitely into the future; that is, as dividends are increased, the stock price will increase in proportion.

Now suppose further that the typical stockholder expects that dividends (and therefore stock price) will increase on the average by 6% per year into the indefinite future. He will then expect a *total* return on his stockholding of 11% per year, as follows:

Dividend return	5% per year
Growth in stock price	6% per year
Total return	11% per year

Exactly what the typical stockholder expects is, of course, a matter of mindreading, but in many cases it is probably reasonable to assume that he expects something like what has happened in the past, so that a study of historical growth will provide a good estimate of stockholder expectations.

One final point: In the paragraph before last we assumed that the typical stockholder assumed that *both* dividends and stock price were growing at a certain rate or, in other words, that the relationship between dividends and stock price is relatively constant. Studies indicate that the relationship between dividends and earnings per share is *also* relatively constant for most companies, since their directors follow a policy of paying out as dividends a relatively fixed percentage of

---

[2] Originally suggested by Myron Gordon and Eli Shapiro, "Capital Equipment Analysis: The Required Rate of Return," *Management Science*, October 1956. One advantage of this approach over some others is its relative insensitivity to detailed assumptions about the typical stockholder. If, for instance, we assume he is relatively uninterested in current dividends, it is because he is more interested in growth. Whatever the relative weights he assigns to dividends and growth, therefore, he will *not* be satisfied if the company *neither* pays satisfactory dividends *nor* has a reasonable growth rate.

earnings. It follows, then, for these companies, that *earnings* per share must grow at the expected rate, so that we can speak of the expected growth of earnings rather than of stock price. Therefore, we can say that the "cost" of common stock financing (as measured by the "return" expected by the "typical stockholder") is the sum of (1) the *dividend yield,* or the ratio of the current dividend to the current stock price, expressed as a percentage; plus (2) the *earnings growth rate,* expressed as a percentage of current earnings.

One of the problems at the end of this chapter asks you to show that the "cost" of common stock financing as defined in the preceding paragraph is the minimum rate of return on capital investments that should be demanded by a company using only common stock financing.

Retained Earnings. Unlike the three sources of capital funds already discussed, the use of retained earnings does not require the firm to go to the capital markets; this source arises automatically as a result of profitable operations. In the past, this had led some authorities to argue that retained earnings are "free" funds, on the grounds that no commitment, either explicit or implicit, has been made to anyone that a return will be earned on these funds.

Nowadays it is generally accepted that retained earnings should be treated as analogous to new common stock financing. The argument is based on the fact that the funds provided by retained earnings could legally be paid out as dividends. From this point of view, the payment of dividends is equivalent to "negative" common stock financing, since it *reduces* the residual interest of the common stockholder. Therefore, the retention of earnings, or the nonpayment of dividends, must be equivalent to common stock financing.

More sophisticated versions of this argument seek to account for the fact that dividends received by stockholders are taxable to them at ordinary rates whereas capital gains (resulting in part from reinvestment of retained earnings) are taxable at lower rates. We will not deal with that sophistication in this book. Instead, we will assume that the cost of retained earnings is *identical* with the cost of new common stock financing.

Composite Cost of Capital

Before going on to discuss a measure of the overall or composite cost of capital, let us summarize the measures we have arrived at for the components of the capital structure of the Jarvis Manufacturing Company. These figures are (on an after-tax basis):

Long-term debt	3.82%
Preferred stock	8.50
Common stock	11.00
Retained earnings	11.00

Since we have agreed to treat common stock and retained earnings as having the same cost, in the subsequent discussion we will lump them both together under the heading residual capital.

Weighted Cost of Capital. The Jarvis Manufacturing Company's net new capital investments can be considered as being financed out of a *pool* of funds, some of the funds coming from the sale of long-term debt, some from the sale of preferred stock, and the balance from residual capital. The cost of the "typical dollar" in this pool of funds will, therefore, depend upon the relative proportions of these three sources.

Suppose, then that the Jarvis Manufacturing Company has *decided* that it will obtain its capital from the three sources in the following proportions:

Long-term debt	25%
Preferred stock	25
Residual capital	50
	100%

The cost of the "typical dollar" in the capital pool is then a weighted average of the component-by-component costs, using the proportions given above as the weights. This gives the calculation below:

	Cost per Dollar per Year	Fraction of Total Dollars	Weighted Cost
Long-term debt	0.0382	0.25	0.00955
Preferred stock	0.0850	0.25	0.02125
Residual capital	0.1100	0.50	0.05500
		1.00	0.08580

Therefore, the composite cost of new capital financing for the Jarvis Manufacturing Company is 8.58% per year.

Deciding on the Proportions. In making our calculation of Jarvis's composite cost of capital, we assumed that the Jarvis management had already decided on the proportions it would use in raising new capital. This assumption waved away several difficult questions which perhaps already occurred to you as you were reading the preceding discussion, such as the following:

1. In any given short period of time, Jarvis Manufacturing Company may obtain funds from only one of its main sources rather than from all three.

Does that mean, then, that its cost of capital would be only 3.82% in a period in which it only sold debt or as high as 11% in a period in which it relied only on retained earnings?

2. Since debt appears to be the cheapest source of funds, why should Jarvis Manufacturing Company ever use *any* other source?

3. How *should* Jarvis Manufacturing Company decide on the proportions in its capital structure anyway?

We will spend the rest of this chapter discussing issues raised by these questions. Before getting into detail, however, it might be useful to consider an analogy in which the facts are more concrete. Suppose that one of Jarvis's products is a widget with a total weight of one pound. Two raw materials are used in making the widget: three quarters of a pound of material A at a cost of 10 cents per pound, and one quarter of a pound of material B at a cost of $1 per pound. The total raw material cost of a widget, then, is given by the following calculation:

Raw Material	Cost per Pound	Pounds per Unit of Product	Weighted Cost
A	$0.10	0.75	$0.075
B	1.00	0.25	0.250
		1.00	$0.325

Now let us raise three questions about the materials cost of the widget which parallel (in reverse order) those raised above about the cost of capital:

1. How *should* Jarvis Manufacturing Company decide on the proportions of materials A and B used in producing a widget? Answer: By considering the desired specifications of the outgoing product and determining what proportions are required to meet these specifications.

2. Since material A is cheaper than material B, why should Jarvis Manufacturing Company ever use material B? Answer: It may well be impossible to produce a satisfactory widget using material A alone; material B, in other words, may have some properties (e.g., hardness) which are essential to the proper functioning of the final product.

3. In any given short period of time, Jarvis Manufacturing Company may purchase new supplies of only one of its raw materials rather than both of them. Does this mean, then, that the product cost of a widget is 10 cents in a period in which only material A is purchased but $1 in a period in which only material B is purchased? Answer: No; we must distinguish between the *purchase* of a raw material and its *use*. The company continues to use the two raw materials in fixed proportions regardless of how it purchases them, making up the differences through fluctuations in inventory.

You can perhaps sense the relevance of the first two answers given above to the corresponding questions about capital structure. The third point is a little more subtle; it relies on the notion that a firm has a *debt capacity,* a limitation on its ability to borrow, which must be replenished from time to time exactly as a physical inventory must. We will now proceed to develop these points in greater detail.

THE DETERMINATION OF CAPITAL STRUCTURE

By drawing an analogy between decisions on capital structure composition and those on the proportions of raw materials in a product, we of course meant to suggest that the components of capital structure must be distinguished on characteristics other than cost, just as materials A and B can be distinguished on characteristics such as hardness, texture, durability, and so forth. It is relatively easy to see the relevance of these other characteristics in something as tangible as a raw material, but in something as abstract as funds many people have been inclined to think that "a dollar is a dollar is a dollar."

Now it is true in a sense that "a dollar is a dollar" whatever its source, but we must remember that in order to *get* the dollar, the firm has had to enter into an agreement with investors and the nature of that agreement does depend on the source. In order to get debt financing, in particular, the firm must incur a fixed obligation to pay interest when due and to repay the face amount at maturity; this obligation continues regardless of the firm's success or failure in investing the funds. No such obligation arises when the funds are obtained through common stock financing or retention of earnings.

In short, although debt financing may generally be *cheaper* than the use of residual capital, it is also *riskier.* Both factors—cost and risk—must be considered in deciding how much debt to use. Cheaper is not necessarily better!

(Preferred stock involves a risk factor which is intermediate between debt and residual capital. In the remainder of this chapter, we will simplify the discussion by ignoring the possibility of using preferred stock.)

Leverage

A useful way to analyze the cost-versus-risk tradeoff in capital structure decisions is through the concept of *leverage.* If you have studied physics, you know that a physical lever serves as a "power multiplier," transforming a force applied at one point into a larger force at another point. Introducing debt into a firm's capital structure similarly multiplies or "levers up" *both* the risk to the common stockholders and (usually) their expected return.

To examine this phenomenon, let us define a firm's *leverage ratio* as follows:

$$\text{Leverage ratio} = \frac{\text{Long-term debt}}{\text{Residual capital}}$$

assuming for purposes of this discussion that the firm has no preferred stock in its capital structure. Both the numerator and the denominator in the right-hand expression should be evaluated at market values. The

Figure 11–2

EFFECT OF LEVERAGE ON COMMON STOCK EARNINGS

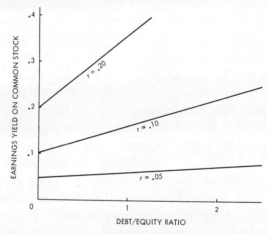

leverage ratio can vary between zero (if the firm has no long-term debt) and infinity (in the unlikely event it has no residual capital).

Suppose that the Jarvis Manufacturing Company has an expected rate of return on total capital employed of 10% per year after taxes and that it can borrow on long-term debt at 4% per year after taxes. Each dollar obtained through debt, therefore, is expected to produce 6 cents in earnings on the common stock.

In Figure 11–2, the line labeled "$r = 10\%$" is a graph of the relationship between the leverage ratio (horizontal axis) and the expected rate of return on common stock, or residual capital (vertical axis), for this case. If there is no leverage, the expected rate of return on common stock is, of course, equal to the expected rate of return on total capital employed. As leverage increases, so does the return on common stock.

The lines in Figure 11–2 marked "$r = 5\%$" and "$r = 20\%$" show how the picture changes if we make different assumptions about the expected rate of return on capital employed (r). The higher r is, the more dramatic the effect of leverage. Of course, if r falls below the interest rate of 4%, then the leverage goes into reverse and reduces earnings.

Figure 11–3

EFFECT OF LEVERAGE ON COMMON STOCK RISK

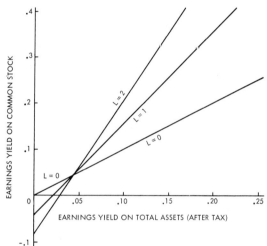

Figure 11–2 gives an idea of how leverage can multiply returns to the common stockholders. Figure 11–3 shows more clearly how it multiplies risk. Remember that the expected rate of return on total capital employed is not a fixed, determinate number but is subject to some uncertainty. In Figure 11–3, therefore, this is treated as a variable represented by the horizontal axis. The figure also includes graphs showing the interrelationship between return on total capital and return on common stock for three leverage ratios.

Note that all three leverage ratios produce the same return on common stock if the return on total capital is equal to the interest rate of 4%; this is true for *any* leverage ratio and not just those shown in the figure. The higher the leverage ratio, the more rapidly the return on common stock changes as the return on total capital changes. If return on total capital falls, a high leverage rate will cause the return on common stock to fall more rapidly and to a lower level than will a low leverage rate. This illustrates the risk factor in the use of leverage.

In Figures 11–2 and 11–3, we have implicitly assumed that Jarvis Manufacturing Company can borrow unlimited sums at an after-tax interest rate of 4% per year. This would not be true in practice. First, increasing leverage increases the risk of nonpayment to the debtholders as well as the risk to the common stockholders; in general, lenders will expect to be compensated for this increased risk by receiving a higher interest rate. Second, eventually the company's leverage may become so high that even higher interest cannot compensate the lenders for the risk of default; higher interest rates, after all, themselves increase that risk. When lenders are unwilling to lend regardless of the interest rate, the company can obviously no longer increase its leverage and has reached its absolute debt capacity.

Theory of Optimal Capital Structure

Increasing leverage has both a good effect (increasing stockholders' expected return) and a bad effect (increasing risk). It seems logical to assume that there is some leverage ratio where the increase in the good is outweighed by the increase in the bad. This point would then represent *the optimal capital structure.*

There has been considerable theoretical discussion of optimal capital structures in the literature over the past decade-and-a-half but not much consensus on operational principles.

The first difficulty which must be resolved is to decide exactly what objective is to be "optimized" in arriving at an optimal capital structure. Most finance theorists now agree that the appropriate objective to be maximized is the market value of the firm's total capital. Assuming that the market value of the debt is relatively insensitive to the leverage ratio (which seems usually to be valid), this translates into the prescription to maximize the market value of the common stock.

If this objective is accepted, the second difficulty arises: determining how changes in leverage affect the market value of total capital. Since nearly everyone would agree that many factors besides leverage affect the market value, sorting out all these factors is a difficult theoretical and empirical problem. Much of the debate in the literature has been concerned with the development and criticism of different theoretical frameworks. One of the early articles, for example, suggested that there was *no* optimal capital structure on the grounds that theoretically the total market value was independent of leverage, but it was quickly agreed that the assumptions upon which this conclusion was based were valid only in a highly idealized world.

What this boils down to is that there is not as yet a satisfactory theoretical approach to the determination of optimal capital structure. In the final section of this chapter, we will present a brief sketch of an adaptive (rather than an optimizing) approach to this problem.

FINANCIAL POLICY AS AN ADAPTIVE PROCESS

Leverage is one way of increasing both risk and expected return to a firm's common stockholders, but there is another way: investing in high-risk, high-return assets. Drilling wildcat oil wells or investing in foreign countries with unstable political situations are two examples. (International oil companies do both!)

In other words, the risk-versus-return tradeoff can be affected by manipulating any part of the firm's entire financial structure, not just its capital structure. If management concludes that it is to the advantage of the stockholders to increase their expected return even at the expense of increased risk, it must still decide whether this is to be accomplished by varying the capital structure, varying the asset structure, or both.

The point we made in the preceding section about the risk-versus-return tradeoff still applies: There is no generally accepted theoretical solution to the problem of finding the optimal combination of risk and return. It does not matter whether this combination is to be arrived at by manipulating the leverage ratio or whether the entire financial structure, assets as well as capital, is subject to change.

Somehow or other, most financial managers are able to arrive at a reasonable resolution of the risk-versus-return tradeoff, even if their decisions do not receive the blessings of finance theorists. How do they do this? Our suggestion is that they do so through an "adaptive" rather than an "optimizing" process. The contrasts between these two approaches will be discussed next.

Optimizing and Adaptive Processes

The main difference between an optimizing and an adaptive approach is that the former seeks, as its name implies, the *best* solution to a decision problem while the latter seeks only a *satisfactory* solution.

For this reason, the adaptive approach has sometimes been called *"satisficing."* The adaptive approach also incorporates procedures whereby a satisfactory solution, once found, can be improved upon, so in a sense the adaptive process may be said to "tend" toward the optimal solution, although it is not guaranteed to get there.

Finding an "optimal" solution to a decision problem requires that there be a *single* measure of merit by which all alternatives can be compared. Only in rare cases is it possible to optimize two or more measures of merit simultaneously. The Benthamite injunction to seek "the greatest happiness for the greatest number" is, for instance, a logical absurdity, because the condition that provides the greatest happiness for me may make you very unhappy indeed! It would be similarly absurd (although some people have proposed it) to seek to "maximize return while minimizing risk," because as a rule higher returns are possible only by accepting higher risks.

If there are a number of partial measures of merit in a decision problem, therefore, that problem is susceptible to an optimizing approach only if these several partial measures can be combined into a single measure which reflects the terms on which the decision maker would be willing to trade off each partial measure against the others. Much of this book has been concerned with developing such composite measures for particular kinds of problems: cost, contribution, and net present value are examples. When we said in the preceding section that there was no satisfactory theoretical solution to the problem of determining optimal capital structure, we meant of course that there was no generally accepted, operationally defined "tradeoff curve" by means of which we could compare different combinations of risk and return.

Since the adaptive approach seeks only a "satisfactory" solution, it can avoid the problem of defining a single measure of merit. An alternative will be considered as "satisfactory" overall only if it is simultaneously "satisfactory" according to each measure of merit considered by the decision maker. In contrast to the optimizing approach, which seeks to *prescribe* the best alternative, the adaptive approach seeks only to *proscribe* unsatisfactory alternatives; and since this can be done with one criterion or measure of merit at a time, it is a much easier task.

It is unlikely, however, that there will be *exactly* one satisfactory solution to a given decision problem after the decision maker has applied all the criteria he can think of. There are two other possibilities: (1) more than one satisfactory solution and (2) no satisfactory solution.

In the first case (multiple solutions), depending upon the amount of time the decision maker thinks it worthwhile to spend on the problem, he may either select one solution more or less arbitrarily or he may look for other measures of merit which he can use to distinguish between the remaining alternatives. In the second case (no solution), again depending upon the amount of time he wants to spend, the decision maker may either search for additional alternatives or he may relax one or more of his requirements so that one of the existing alternatives becomes "satisfactory." This "cut-and-fill" procedure is one reason for calling the approach "adaptive"; by it, the decision maker seeks to adapt his multiple criteria and the set of alternatives he is considering to each other.

A second sense in which the approach is adaptive is this: If there is more than one apparently satisfactory alternative, the decision maker may decide to implement one and *then modify it on the basis of experience.* Experience may lead to modification in several ways. It may reveal new facts which suggest that the selected alternative is less satisfactory (or another alternative is more satisfactory) than was at first recognized. Or it may suggest additional criteria which should have been considered but were not. Action is, in this way, adapted to experience. This possibility is open, of course, only if the decision is in some way reversible, but reversibility is often the case. If a firm increases its leverage ratio, for example, and this proves unsatisfactory, it can reverse the decision over a period of time by retaining earnings, repaying debt, or both.

An Adaptive Approach to Financial Policy

With the concept of an adaptive process in mind, let us see how it might be applied to the determination of financial policy. The approach we will outline is only one possibility, but it seems a reasonable one and is similar to that which empirical research suggests is followed by many companies.

We will develop the approach in the following way. First, we will suggest that financial policy can be reflected in terms of *target values* for these variables: dividend payout ratio, leverage ratio, and asset structure. In the short run, financial decisions are directed at keeping the actual values of these variables close to their target values. Second, we will discuss how the target values are modified over time in accordance with the "satisficing" principle.

Dividend Payout Ratio. This is defined as the fraction of current earnings which is paid out in dividends to the common stockholders. Applied to the current absolute level of earnings, it determines not only the dividend but also the amount of retained earnings available for reinvestment in the business. This ratio may also influence the type of stockholder who is attracted to owning shares in the company; a high payout ratio, for example, will tend to attract those who are more interested in current income than in growth.

Leverage Ratio. This variable has already been defined. As we have mentioned, the leverage ratio affects both risk and return to the common stockholder. Because of this, it may also influence the type of person attracted to owning shares in the company.

Asset Structure. In managing their capital budgets, many companies break the total budget down into categories. Assets within a category are supposed to be relatively homogeneous in character and, therefore, more directly comparable with each other than they are with assets in other categories. Two common types of breakdown are by *function* and by *line of business.* The distinction made in this book between expansion investments and replacement investments is an example of a functional breakdown. The breakdown by line of business is exemplified by the categories used by many oil companies: exploration, production, transportation, refining, and marketing.

When a system of categories is used, the amount of funds going into each category may be controlled to the target values either directly by dollar limitations or indirectly by techniques such as using different hurdle rates. An oil company, for example, may require a 20% after-tax return on its exploration activities but only 10% on refining investments. Since both risks and returns generally differ from category to category, the target values for asset structure will influence the overall pattern of risk and return on the company's investment portfolio.

Satisficing Criteria. What determines whether a given set of target values is satisfactory or not? The minimum requirement is that the set be *viable.* That is, the set must be chosen in such a way that it is possible for the firm to raise the capital to finance the assets in which it intends to invest. Moreover, the set should promise to remain viable into the future.

Viability implies, among other things, that the risk-return characteristic of the firm's capital structure is satisfactory to *some* group of investors, but it need not be so to the present investors. A company which has been relatively stable and has attracted stockholders who value this stability may decide to increase its rate of return by investing in higher risk businesses. This decision may be unsatisfactory, in a sense, to the present stockholders, but as long as there are other investors who find the decision satisfactory and are willing to buy the shares of the present stockholders, the latter are not harmed by the decision.

As the previous paragraph suggests, there may be a number of financial policies which are viable. The external environments of financial markets and investment opportunities do not dictate a unique financial policy. This leaves the management of the firm free to bring in other criteria. At this stage, the personal values of the managers may well play an important part. Some management groups may be oriented toward risk-taking and high expected returns, for example, while others may be more conservative. Even these predilections may change over time, however, and so the character of the company's financial policy may adapt also.

PROBLEMS

Problem 11–1. Assume the following conditions in the markets for Jarvis Manufacturing Company securities and recalculate its weighted average cost of capital:

a) Net interest cost on long-term debt of 8.20% before taxes.
b) Current market price of common stock of $50 per share.
c) Current dividend rate on common stock of $2 per share.
d) Expected growth rate in dividend of 6% per year.
e) Capital structure target ratios as follows:

Long-term debt	30%
Residual capital	70
	100%

Problem 11–2. You are on the staff of the treasurer of The Lowe Corporation. He has asked you to verify the assertion made on page 532 that the expected rate of return to a common stockholder will be the sum of the current dividend yield plus the expected annual rate of growth in dividends, provided that this growth rate is expected to continue indefinitely into the future.

Let:

P = Current market price of common;
D = Current dividend/share, assumed payable one year from today;
g = Annual rate of growth in dividend, expressed as a fraction;
r = Annual rate of return to stockholder, expressed as a fraction.

The problem is to show that

$$r = \frac{D}{P} + g.$$

Verify or complete the following steps in the argument:

a) The value of r solves the equation

$$P = \frac{D}{1+r} + \frac{D(1+g)}{(1+r)^2} + \frac{D(1+g)^2}{(1+r)^3} + \cdots,$$

where the terms on the right-hand side continue indefinitely.

b) The expression above can be simplified to

$$P = \frac{D + P(1+g)}{1+r}.$$

[*Hint:* Suppose you factor out $(1+g)/(1+r)$ from all terms from the second one on the right-hand side of the equation above. Show that what is left is equal to P.]

c) Solve the simplified equation in (*b*) for r.

F. F. FIERCE & COMPANY

In early 1958, Mr. A. B. Bergamot, vice-president in charge of manu-facturing at F. F. Fierce & Company, was considering what action he should take on a proposal that the company should change its capital budgeting procedures. For a number of years the company had been evaluating capital expenditure projects on the basis of annual return on average investment. Although Mr. Bergamot was aware that several members of the management committee had from time to time ques-tioned the company's policies and procedures in this area of financial management, the company's treasurer had always successfully defended the status quo. Recently, however, Mr. Bergamot had received a memo-randum from one of his plant managers, Mr. C. D. Ambrosia, expressing strong disagreement with F. F. Fierce's policies in the area of capital budgeting. Mr. Ambrosia particularly took exception to the fact that the treasurer considered working capital changes related to capital ex-penditures irrelevant to the basic investment decision. In addition, he questioned in more general terms the company's related financial poli-cies regarding growth, debt, and dividends. Mr. Ambrosia requested, therefore, that Mr. Bergamot review these matters once again.

F. F. Fierce & Company manufactured a broad line of perfumes and cosmetics including: make-up, powder, rouge, lip rouge, lipstick, eye shadow, mascara, eyebrow pencil, cold cream, vanishing cream, foun-dation cream, hand lotion, as well as several kinds of perfumes. The company manufactured and sold over 600 individual items. Plants and distribution facilities were strategically located at several centers in the United States as well as in 13 foreign countries. As shown in Exhibit 1, the company had sales of $263 million, earnings of $12.6 million, and total assets of $153 million in 1958.

Industry statistics showed that more than a dozen domestic manu-facturers sold $1.4 billion of cosmetics in 1958. Experience indicated an average annual increase in industry sales of 10%. Although the industry was extremely competitive (out of 1,200 products introduced

during the five-year period preceding 1958 only 200 remained commercially significant), F. F. Fierce & Company had shown unusually
consistent growth in sales and earnings.

The board of directors had defined a basic corporate objective towards which they wanted the company to direct its efforts: "Attainment
of maximum long-term growth in earnings per share." The board believed that complete dissemination of this carefully considered objective
throughout the company would increase the effectiveness of the entire
organization. The objective was derived from each of the stockholder's
desire for maximum return on his investment in F. F. Fierce & Company common stock. Company officials stated that this return was realized both in the form of cash dividends and through appreciation in the
market value of the firm's common stock. Since the company could not
directly control the price of its stock, its objective was related to factors
it could directly influence and which were consistent with the stockholders' goals. The most important of these factors were thought to be
growth of both earnings per share and dividends, which in turn would
influence the market price of the stock. This statement of purpose was
considered to be a stable, long-range objective which would not require
modification to reflect short-term fluctuations in business activity or
profitability.

With this basic objective in mind, and after giving due consideration
to the company's market opportunities, management had long approved
several key financial policies that, as Mr. Bergamot realized, had an important effect on the firm's operations and rate of growth. It had been
decided, for example, that the company should incur no long-term debt.
Along the same line, management attempted to maintain a current ratio
of about five to one. Also, since the key officers owned about two-thirds
of the company's outstanding common stock, it was decided to pay out
an average of only 25% to 30% of earnings as dividends. These major
stockholders received large incomes from the company and were in a
high marginal tax bracket; desiring to avoid even higher personal taxes,
they did not wish to receive large cash dividends from the company as
well.[1] It was thought that the money thus saved could be reinvested
within the company to the benefit of all the stockholders.

Apart from these key debt and dividend policies, Mr. Bergamot

---

[1] At stockholders' meetings management had been asked by a number of the 3,500
outside stockholders why larger dividends were not declared by the board of directors.
These dissenters were advised to sell their stock if they were not satisfied with the company's dividend policy. It was pointed out to them that these policies were in the best
interests of all the stockholders.

noted several other important management decisions. The treasurer had long supported a policy that the company limit capital expenditures to its annual provision for depreciation (see Exhibits 2 and 3). Mr. Bergamot agreed with this limitation and in addition had introduced a very similar requirement that placed a ceiling of 4 million on the amount that the company should spend in any one year on projects affecting manufacturing operations. Both of these policies had received strong support since it was believed that the organization could not effectively handle a greater volume of projects. Mr. Bergamot thought that the company's manufacturing operations became relatively less efficient when expenditures pertaining to manufacturing operations exceeded $4 million. It was found that the company's engineers could not effectively design and administer projects beyond this level. Also, where projects interrupted or otherwise hampered actual production activities, it was often extremely difficult to bring the workers back to a satisfactory level of production. Finally, experience had shown that whenever these policies were violated, management would be overburdened to the near exclusion of many of its other responsibilities.

The actual procedures followed by the company in evaluating investment proposals were considered by company officials to be complex, but nevertheless useful. Projects were first divided into classifications as follows:

Project Class	Nature of Project
A	Obsolete equipment
B	Cost reduction
C	New product
D	Added capacity
E	General

Each of these project classes was handled differently. In the case of Class A projects, involving additional outlays (such as major repairs) on already obsolete equipment, there was no quantitative analysis made at all. In almost all situations these kinds of projects could be justified only where there was thought to be a safety hazard or where unacceptable quality could damage the firm's over-all image. Class B projects were subjected to a complete return on investment analysis. The nature of this analysis is shown in Exhibit 4. These projects were ranked and selected according to return on investment. Class C projects, involving new products, were generally made only if they could be expected to pay back in one to one and one-half years. Class D projects, involving additional capacity, were evaluated on the basis of their effect on production flexibility and expected profit margins. Thus, if the company's production schedules indicated that certain products could not be supplied in sufficient quantity to satisfy forecast sales, the production department had to decide whether to schedule overtime production or to request additional capacity. In general they would do the latter only when the gross profit margin exceeded 65% and when the number of additional required shifts was considered large enough to endanger their production scheduling flexibility. Class E projects were evaluated subjectively by management on the basis of their expected over-all contribution to the company.

All projects involving investments of over $5,000 were submitted to a committee of the board of directors for approval. This committee, consisting of five inside and two outside directors, generally spent one afternoon a week reviewing capital expenditure proposals.

As described above, Class B projects were subjected to rigorous quantitative analysis and were generally ranked and selected according to the return on investment indicated. The company had a target rate of 36% after taxes. Company officials observed that this rate was based on the fact that there were always Class B projects available that would return at least this much. Accepting returns below this cutoff point, in their opinion, would actually be doing the stockholders a disservice. They thought stockholders' interests could best be served by keeping the target rate at a relatively high level. In addition to the return on investment criterion the board also required that the payback period on Class B projects be about three years.

While he was thinking through the implications of Mr. Ambrosia's memorandum, Mr. Bergamot decided to review two capital expenditure requests that had been submitted for his approval. Both of these situations were Class B projects. Typically, the manufacturing staff would submit these requests to Mr. Bergamot who in turn would present them to the board if they amounted to over $5,000.

1. The first of these projects involved the installation of a new processing line, costing $40,000, which was expected to eliminate about $50,000 of inventory. At the present time the company's Eastside plant was producing six different products on its process line Number Four. This meant that whenever one of these six products was run the quantity produced had to be sufficient to last until the line could again be used for this same product, resulting in what was referred to as cycle inventory. By buying the equipment that would be required for a second similar production line, as proposed, it was expected that this cycle inventory could be reduced by $50,000 because the frequency of production runs

could be increased. The plant manager submitting this proposal argued the decrease in inventory investment was *more* than sufficient to justify the required expenditure for a second production line, even though the new line would not show any cost savings as such.

2. The second project involved both a stream of cost savings and a reduction in the inventory investment. This project required an initial outlay of $2,500 and would result in an inventory reduction of $500 per year for three years, or a total of $1,500. The project was also expected to produce cost savings of $100 the first year, $200 the second year, and so on until the savings had reached a level of $1,000 in year ten, the end of its expected economic life. In other words, the project would result in average annual savings of $550 for ten years. It was expected that at the end of ten years the proposed machine would have no salvage value. All told, the company had over 70 machines similar to the one being considered in this proposal. Mr. Bergamot realized that this "test case" could be extremely important to the firm's future.

Mr. Ambrosia, who had submitted this second capital expenditure request, advanced the following analysis, using two methods of calculating the return on investment, in support of his request:

Cash Outlay for Proposal	Method I	Method II
1. Gross cash outlay	$2,500	$2,500
2. Less: Reduction in inventory		1,500
3. Net cash outlay	$2,500	$1,000

Average Return on Average Investment	Method I	Method II
4. Gross annual savings	$ 550	$ 550
5. Depreciation (item 3 divided by useful life)	250	100
6. Gross return	$ 300	$ 450
7. Estimated income tax (at 50%)	150	225
8. Average annual return	$ 150	$ 225
9. Average investment (one-half item 3)	1,250	500
10. Return on investment	12%	45%

While recognizing that "Method I," the management approved method of investment analysis, indicated the project did not meet the required target rate of 36%, the sponsor of the project pointed out that "Method II" did show a return well above the required rate. He requested, therefore, that the proposal be approved.

Mr. Bergamot believed that the treasurer's method of excluding inventory changes from the analysis was the key point upon which the decision in both projects must finally rest. The management committee in its recent discussions of capital budgeting had reached agreement that the company's policies in this area of financial management were quite satisfactory. Mr. Bergamot recalled that at the time there had existed strong sentiment against the introduction of highly complex techniques that management believed were no more useful for decision making than the company's present procedures.

Questions

1. What action should be taken on the two capital expenditure proposals that Mr. Bergamot is considering?
2. Should F. F. Fierce & Company revise its procedures for evaluating new capital expenditures? How should working capital be brought into the analysis, if at all?

Exhibit 1

F. F. FIERCE & COMPANY

STATISTICAL INFORMATION

(Dollar figures in millions)

BALANCE SHEETS

	1954	1955	1956	1957	1958
Cash	$ 15.1	$ 11.4	$ 7.9	$ 8.6	$ 5.3
Marketable securities	2.0	5.5	2.6	7.6	14.0
Accounts receivable	15.1	19.3	19.1	20.0	22.0
Inventories	31.5	34.6	38.6	42.0	41.9
Deferred charges	3.3	3.7	4.4	2.8	3.1
Total current assets	$ 67.0	$ 74.5	$ 72.6	$ 81.0	$ 86.3
Property, plant, and equipment	$ 72.0	$ 75.3	$ 90.9	$ 95.3	$ 101.7
Less: Depreciation, obsolescence, and amortization	32.5	34.8	37.3	40.4	45.8
Net property, plant, and equipment	$ 39.5	$ 40.5	$ 53.6	$ 54.9	$ 55.9
Investment in foreign subsidiaries	5.5	5.6	6.8	6.7	8.7
Other investments	2.1	2.1	2.4	1.9	1.8
Total assets	$114.1	$122.7	$135.4	$144.5	$152.7
Current liabilities	$ 12.7	$ 16.9	$ 18.8	$ 17.5	$ 15.7
Common stock	39.9	39.5	40.6	41.3	41.7
Earned surplus	61.5	66.3	76.0	85.7	95.3
Total liabilities and net worth	$114.1	$122.7	$135.4	$144.5	$152.7

INCOME ACCOUNTS

	1954	1955	1956	1957	1958
Net sales	$202.7	$224.9	$246.5	$260.7	$263.2
Cost of goods sold	126.8	140.4	152.1	157.8	156.0
Selling, general, and administrative expense	49.9	56.6	64.6	71.6	74.8
Depreciation	5.5	6.0	7.0	8.3	9.1
Operating profit	$ 20.5	$ 21.9	$ 22.8	$ 23.0	$ 23.3
Other income or expense (net)	(0.6)	0.2	2.2	1.8	1.8
Income taxes	10.4	10.8	12.1	11.6	12.5
Net income	$ 9.5	$ 11.3	$ 12.9	$ 13.2	$ 12.6

OTHER STATISTICAL INFORMATION

	1954	1955	1956	1957	1958
Current asset turnover	3.0x	3.0x	3.4x	3.2x	3.0x
Accounts receivable turnover	13.4	11.7	12.9	13.0	12.0
Inventory turnover	6.4	6.5	6.4	6.2	6.3
Asset turnover	1.8	1.8	1.8	1.8	1.7
Net worth turnover	2.0	2.1	2.1	2.1	1.9
Gross margin	37.4%	37.5%	38.2%	39.5%	40.8%
Return on sales (after taxes)	4.7	5.0	5.2	5.1	4.8
Return on assets (after taxes)	8.5	9.0	9.4	9.2	8.2
Return on net worth (after taxes)	9.4	10.5	10.9	10.7	9.1

Exhibit 2

F. F. FIERCE & COMPANY

FUNDS FLOW ANALYSIS, 1954–1958
(Dollar figures in millions)

Sources of funds:

Cash	$ 9.8
Deferred charges	0.2
Depreciation	30.2
Current liabilities	3.0
Common stock	1.8
Net income	51.6
	$96.6

Uses of funds:

Marketable securities	$12.0
Accounts receivable	6.9
Inventories	10.4
Capital expenditures	46.6
Investment in foreign subsidiaries and other	2.9
Dividends	17.8
	$96.6

Exhibit 3

F. F. FIERCE & COMPANY

SCHEDULE OF CAPITAL EXPENDITURES, 1952–1958
(Dollar figures in thousands)

Year	Total Capital Expenditures	Capital Expenditures Affecting Manufacturing Operations	Excess (Deficiency) of Additions over Provision for Depreciation
1952	$ 4,260	$2,950	$ (970)
1953	4,875	3,625	(331)
1954	7,612	4,510	2,146
1955	9,456	3,860	3,481
1956	18,179*	4,100	11,149
1957	9,115	3,940	823
1958	9,492	4,025	399

* Company built two new plants at an approximate cost of $9 million. These plants were designed and built for the company by an outside organization.

Exhibit 4

F. F. FIERCE & COMPANY

NEW PROJECT ANALYSIS SHEET

Proposition: *Automatic Filling and Packing Machine*   Life: *Ten Years*

Cash outlay for proposal:

Total cost for which appropriation is requested:

 1. Capitalizable cost of project.............................$14,000

 2. Dismantling of old equipment and cost to be expensed........ 3,000

 3. Total cost... $17,000

Cash provided by income tax benefit:

 4. Book value of present equipment..........................$ 3,000

 5. Dismantling and other costs to be expensed................. ...

 6. Total...$ ...

 7. Less: Salvage value....................................... ...

 8. Net charge to expense...................................$ 3,000

 9. Income tax reduction resulting from expense at 52%..........$ 1,560

Cash from sale of old equipment: ...

 10. Cash returned..   1,560

 11. Net cash outlay.. $15,440

Annual operating savings:

 12. Estimated savings before depreciation.......................$ 7,572

 13. Depreciation (item 1 divided by useful life)................. 1,400

 14. Estimated income, less depreciation from new project........$ 6,172

 15. Estimated income tax at 52%............................ 3,209

 16. Net annual savings after taxes............................ $ 2,963

Years required to recover cash outlay:

 17. Through net savings after taxes (item 16)...................$ 2,963

 18. Through provision for depreciation (item 13)................ 1,400

 19. Total annual cash recovery..............................$ 4,363

 20. Years required (item 11 divided by item 19)................   3.5

Annual return on average investment:

Average annual return

 21. Gross annual savings (item 12)............................$ 7,572

 22. Amortization of net investment (item 11 divided
    by useful life)... 1,544

 23. Gross return...$ 6,028

 24. Estimated income tax at 52%............................ 3,209

 25. Average annual return..................................$ 2,819

Average investment (one-half item 11).........................$ 7,720

 26. Rate of return (item 25 divided by average investment).......   37%

Other financial considerations:

 1. Project will result in an inventory reduction of approximately $7,000.

 2. The machine is the first step towards complete mechanization of this operation and will provide experience for its application in other parts of the company.

MONITOR TEXTILE COMPANY (B)

In January, 1961, the Monitor Textile Company was considering replacement of one of its industrial forklift trucks. Operating data about gasoline and electric trucks, and price quotations from the Stevens Industrial Truck Company for the new trucks, were given in the Monitor Textile Company (A) case (page 471).

The Stevens company also offered to lease a truck to Monitor under four different leasing plans. Regardless of the plan chosen, Stevens would maintain the equipment and guarantee to keep it in serviceable condition at all times. In the event of a major breakdown, Stevens would provide a replacement truck, at its expense, within four hours. The cost of the lease plans, summarized below, varied depending on the minimum term of the contract signed by the lessee:

Plan	Term of Contract	Gas Truck	Electric Truck
1	No minimum term	$25 per day or $75 per week	$30 per day or $100 per week
2	Four months minimum, 30-day cancellation thereafter	$207 per month	$267 per month
3	Three years minimum, 30-day cancellation thereafter	$145 per month	$179 per month
4	Five years minimum, 30-day cancellation thereafter	$132 per month	$159 per month

Questions

1. Why are the monthly payments less on longer-term leases?
2. Which lease is most advantageous for Monitor?
3. Should Monitor buy a truck or lease one?

McCARTHY'S BOWL INN

In August, 1955, Mr. Justin McCarthy was trying to decide whether or not he should make an additional investment in his new bowling alley venture, McCarthy's Bowl Inn. Mr. McCarthy was a partner in a law firm located in Boston, Massachusetts. Having some personal funds available for investment, Mr. McCarthy had decided to open a new business and to operate it in his spare time. After some investigation, he decided that an amusement business, which could take advantage of the increased amount of leisure time being enjoyed by the population, would find a ready market. He finally selected ten-pin bowling as a suitable amusement. Ten-pin bowling was more popular in the Midwest and western parts of the United States, but Mr. McCarthy felt that it was likely to spread into New England, and that a ten-pin bowling alley in the right location in the Boston area would be successful.

During 1954, Mr. McCarthy had spent a considerable amount of his leisure time searching for a suitable location for his first bowling alley. He ultimately selected and purchased two sites, one located on Route 9, west of Boston, and the other on Route 1 near the junction of Route 128. In each case, the lot that he purchased was in a rapidly developing commercial area and had some frontage on the busy highway. The Route 9 location cost $30,000; the Route 1 location cost $25,000.

Mr. McCarthy decided to exploit the Route 9 location first because he thought it offered a better potential for immediate success. In July, 1955, Mr. McCarthy completed a complicated financial transaction with Mr. Anderson, a real estate developer and general construction contractor. Mr. Anderson purchased the Route 9 location from Mr. McCarthy for $30,000 and agreed to erect on the site a building suitable for a 16-lane bowling alley. Mr. McCarthy obtained a 15-year lease on the building at a monthly rental of $1,400, with an option to renew for an additional ten years at a reduced rental. Mr. Anderson was responsible for paying all taxes, insurance, and maintaining the building. The lease provided that the building was to be air-conditioned, with the initial equipment and the maintenance of it to be the responsibility of Mr. Anderson. Mr. McCarthy knew that bowling was a seasonal sport, being more popular in the winter, but he hoped that providing an air-conditioned facility would reduce the seasonality of his business.

Mr. McCarthy had had no previous experience in the bowling alley business, but he had attempted to estimate what his operating expenses would be. He planned to hire a full-time manager because he would be able to devote only general supervision to the operation of the business. He estimated the manager's salary at about $6,000 per year. He also knew that he would need to hire two additional persons: a cashier-clerk at $4,000 per year and a janitor and utility man for about $3,600 a year. He estimated his heating and electricity bill at approximately $4,000 a year, to cover the costs of lights, operation of the air-conditioning equipment, and heating of the building during the winter. Supplies and maintenance were difficult costs to estimate, particularly the latter because when the alleys were new they would require a minimum amount of maintenance, but as they aged, maintenance costs would no doubt rise. He estimated an average annual expenditure of $8,000 for these expenses. Payroll taxes and workmen's compensation insurance would amount to approximately 5% of his labor costs. Income taxes would be about 40% of net profits.

In late July, 1955, Mr. McCarthy contracted with a firm in Chicago, Illinois, for the installation of 16 bowling alleys. The cost of these alleys and accessory equipment was just under $4,000 each, a total of $60,000. The Chicago firm told Mr. McCarthy he could expect a life from the hardwood alleys of about 15 years. Mr. McCarthy made a down payment of $30,000, and the supplier permitted him to pay off the balance over five years with equal payments (interest and principal) of $625 each month.

Mr. McCarthy planned to permit an outside operator to establish and run the concessions in his first Bowl Inn. These concessions, which would rent bowling shoes and lockers as well as offering a full line of refreshments, were expected to provide Mr. McCarthy with a net income of $10,000 per year.

Thus, by August, 1955, Mr. McCarthy's plans for the Route 9 Bowl

Inn were complete except for the decision as to the method to be used to reset pins. Mr. McCarthy was trying to decide whether to use pinboys or whether he should buy or lease pinsetting machines.

Pinboys

Mr. McCarthy knew that the initial cost would be low if the decision were made to use pinboys. He was afraid, however, that there was a chance that the presence of pinboys might have an adverse effect on the type of customers he hoped to attract. He expected that a large part of his business would come from children, families, and mixed bowling leagues. He had noticed that pinboys working at other alleys sometimes behaved in a manner which might not make the best impression on this type of customer. In any case, he knew that careful supervision would be necessary.

The only additional investment required if pinboys were employed would be about $25 per alley for pinsetting guides. The going rate in the area for setting pins was 12 cents a string; payroll taxes and other fringe benefits would add about 8%. Five boys were usually needed to operate four alleys; a total of 20 would be required for the proposed 16 alleys. These employees would have to be drawn from the 16- to 18-year age group since the minimum legal age was 16 and boys over 18 could normally find higher paying jobs.

Pinsetting Machines

Two makes of pinsetting machines were available: "Speedy" pinsetters, made by the Griswold Machine Corporation of Everett, Massachusetts; and "Reliable" pinsetters, made by Old Reliable Machine Tool Corporation of Akron, Ohio. Both machines could be either bought or leased.

Both machines had a list price of $3,600 per machine, and 16 machines would be required. Freight and installation charges on the Reliable machines were paid by the manufacturer, but the customer paid for these charges on the Speedy machines. Griswold Corporation charged $125 per machine for installation and estimated that the freight cost to Mr. McCarthy would be $10 per alley. The parts of Reliable machines were guaranteed for one year; Speedy's warranty covered only 90 days. If the machines were purchased for cash upon completion of installation, both manufacturers offered a 20% discount off the list price; the net cash price was $2,880.

Financing could be arranged by both companies. Reliable agreed to finance 75% of the net cash price over 48 months, and Speedy would finance 80% over 36 months. Both firms charged interest of 6% per year on the total original amount of the loan, based on net cash price. Thus, if 16 machines were purchased from Speedy, the total cash price would be $46,080. If the purchase was financed, Mr. McCarthy would make a down payment of $9,216, and in each of the three following years he would pay $12,288 on the principal (one-third of 46,080 − $9,216) plus $2,212 in interest (6% of $36,864). The installment payments of $1,208.33 would be paid each month for 36 months.

Speedy and Reliable machines could be leased under the following conditions: The rent on the Speedy machine was $720 a year for four years, and would probably be $420 thereafter. An initial lease of four years would be required, followed by four-year leases at the option of the lessee. The uncertainty of the rental fee after the initial lease period was due to the fact that very few machines had been in operation for four years, and fees for subsequent lease periods would be subject to negotiation. Freight and installation costs on the Speedy machine would be paid by the lessee; insurance on the machine would be paid by the manufacturer.

The rental fee on Reliable machines was 10 cents a string, with a minimum fee of $40 a month on an initial lease for four years. Subsequent four-year leases could probably be negotiated at 5 cents a string and $40 a month minimum. The manufacturer of the Reliable machines paid the freight, installation, and insurance costs. The manufacturers of both Speedy and Reliable pinsetters employed servicemen to do major repair work on the machines; most alleys, however, did their own minor repair work and maintenance. If the machines were purchased, Mr. McCarthy expected that, after the initial warranty period, maintenance services purchased from the manufacturer might cost an average of $50 per year per machine. These services would be provided at no cost by the manufacturer if the machines were leased.

The lease arrangements for the Speedy machines gave the lessee an option to buy the machine at three different points during the four-year lease. When the machine was six months old, it could be purchased with 80% of the total past rental payments applied to the original list price. At 24 months, 60% of the past rents could be applied to the purchase price; at 48 months, 40% of the past rents could be applied.

There was also included in the Speedy lease an option to substitute a seven-year lease at $540 a year. This option could be exercised only after 16 months of the original lease, and would thereby extend the total lease period to eight years, four months. If this option were elected, the purchase option would no longer apply unless the $15 a month difference were paid for all the months in which the reduced rent had been paid. If the machines were purchased, they could be depreciated for tax purposes over an eight-year life, and Mr. McCarthy planned to use the double-declining balance method. Lease payments were deductible for tax purposes in the year in which paid.

Volume of Business

One of the important considerations, in Mr. McCarthy's opinion, in deciding between pinboys and pinsetting machines, concerned the expected volume of business that the new Bowl Inn might achieve. In his initial planning, Mr. McCarthy had tried to estimate the volume of business under the assumption that he would use pinboys. He planned that the alleys would be open daily from 2 P.M. to 11 P.M., although he knew that the evening hours were much more popular for bowling. Initially he had expected to charge 25 cents a string before 5 P.M., and 35 cents from 5 P.M. until 11 P.M. Mr. McCarthy thought that with an alley in constant use, a pinboy would set an average of six strings an hour. He expected to obtain 100% utilization during the hours of 7 to 10 P.M.; about 60% utilization during the hours of 5 to 7 P.M., and 10 to 11 P.M.; and perhaps a 40% utilization during the afternoon hours. The Bowl Inn would be open every day of the year.

The capacity of pinsetting machines was about eight strings per hour, and was one of the primary advantages of the machines over the pinboys. If he acquired the machines, Mr. McCarthy was uncertain as to how he should exploit this advantage. He knew that most bowlers, and in particular, league bowlers, like the greater speed of bowling with the machines and might be expected to pay a premium for this advantage. Thus, he felt that if he offered machines, he might be able to charge a price of a nickel a string more than if he used pinboys, without suffering a decline in his expected volume. On the other hand, if he kept his prices at 25 and 35 cents, which were the going rates in the area for manually set pins, Mr. McCarthy felt that he might achieve a greater volume with the machines, particularly in the evening hours, because of the greater capacity of the alleys. He was dubious that afternoon bowlers would pay any premium for the use of machines.

Some Additional Factors

There were some additional factors which Mr. McCarthy had to consider. Each machine would require electrical power extensions costing about $150 per alley. If he bought the machines, his annual property insurance costs would rise $14 per alley. He would have to hire a maintenance man for around $75 a week whether he bought or rented the machines.

Electrical power costs were expected to be relatively insignificant. Each machine had six fractional horsepower motors: a one-third and one-sixth horsepower motor ran continuously; the other four, which amounted to one horsepower (about 1,000 watts), ran 11 seconds during each cycle; about 12 cycles were required, on the average, to process a string. The electrical power would cost $0.01 per kilowatt-hour.

Mr. McCarthy examined both makes of machines in operation and came to the conclusion that there was little difference in their reliability or speed. The Speedy machine was perhaps slightly less noisy, but on the whole each did the job satisfactorily. In addition, there seemed to be no reason why one machine would last longer than another, although just how long they would last was difficult to determine. They would surely last for five years, and probably for ten. All machines could be easily modified as a part of normal maintenance activities, the manufacturers said, to keep abreast of design improvements. If this were done, the machines would almost certainly last for ten years. There had been almost no major improvements over the past three years, and none of the companies appeared to be working on any radical improvements for the near future.

Mr. McCarthy was quite optimistic about the potential success of his Route 9 Bowl Inn. He felt that his judgment in launching the venture had been substantiated because he had recently been approached by Mr. Carl Peterson, the operator of a nearby amusement park, who had offered to buy him out (that is, take over the lease and make the remaining payments on the alleys which were being installed) for $40,000. Mr. McCarthy felt that this prospective $10,000 immediate profit was partly in compensation for his efforts in locating the site and getting the business underway, but also reflected the potential high profitability of the enterprise. Mr. McCarthy declined to sell because he did not need the money and was hoping to use the Route 9 Bowl Inn as the first of a chain of such ventures.

Mr. McCarthy still had approximately $15,000 available for investment in his bowling alley venture. He thought that about $5,000 would be needed for working capital and a "safety margin" at the Route 9 location, and the remaining $10,000 could be used to make the down payment on the pinsetting machines if he decided to purchase them. As an alternative, however, he was also toying with the idea of proceeding immediately with the exploitation of his Route 1 site. Assuming that the land could be sold and leased back as he had done on Route 9, the $25,000 proceeds plus his available $10,000 would be sufficient to make the down payment on the alleys and provide working capital at Route 1.

Mr. McCarthy was less confident of the immediate profitability of the Route 1 location because he knew that his operating expenses would be about the same as on Route 9, while his best estimate of the volume was that it would range between 15% and 30% lower to begin with. On the other hand, he was convinced of the ultimate profitability of the Route 1 location, and felt that establishing it as soon as possible might discourage any potential competitors from building in that area.

Question

What course of action would you recommend to Mr. McCarthy?

APPENDIXES

Appendix A

RANDOM NUMBER TABLES

By Stanley I. Buchin

0- 4	5- 9	10-14	15-19	20-24	25-29	30-34	35-39	40-44
25251	28614	92995	38300	48205	75604	19773	93563	21276
81383	29079	42026	62640	42210	82713	16390	84991	17792
14774	30927	70095	91419	54924	31062	85270	00988	00639
79798	04590	40428	87688	31201	53375	39438	18397	17585
65703	83735	42154	23591	24304	64579	37662	37973	19946
99623	47137	41573	87348	18854	13423	17630	78190	65828
66003	24820	23815	68087	63113	28037	24490	01392	78341
33907	29356	42873	34222	81620	50647	93592	05723	54156
10712	45891	65366	10243	73165	02161	85551	18144	69973
86568	64681	86377	05320	16667	84134	14319	59776	16213
73949	68521	85029	47418	43536	96597	56681	26072	15226
25568	13194	73338	76640	61940	75093	24170	24545	91419
13481	51552	74411	13564	96612	81285	23380	13216	93162
38502	30461	98393	54063	94200	78627	17179	50790	19053
03747	97466	44290	43904	26957	04458	27891	91573	36273
44459	17662	43693	20699	68811	13004	58726	21749	70890
51215	25690	31057	03702	80555	74301	14024	14972	26623
41409	22557	00515	24363	27972	79639	95010	15449	99743
66409	80855	18519	38778	65993	46951	80982	63335	44383
71863	19016	22691	40708	57535	09904	22669	16872	21499
40138	49611	67490	89514	60745	83126	83124	14822	49887
10181	10754	66112	55244	29670	18677	24680	55701	29585
72929	92342	28763	27932	15510	65958	30830	25980	26985
96583	38832	19105	27287	22846	98278	83039	29959	87762
01999	34240	73877	51468	46183	76030	40535	83223	58113
55865	28455	58341	35721	82471	42262	35622	95517	21428
09687	27139	17606	23523	58398	25108	18279	55212	67214
01444	95503	53239	15266	81368	06172	35790	45621	82690
33238	50189	84547	96115	77908	26702	59039	26063	97936
53640	27805	13124	52783	85010	35007	00313	24669	31627
93468	72989	21011	69164	12312	51395	83990	41379	16653
30781	50812	45341	76882	53225	20623	37927	41952	41443
52136	58349	83019	04044	30069	06963	09012	84615	50870
22029	23472	31091	06365	96225	71521	58576	00979	78684
57676	48551	34366	31381	40105	18964	50297	35854	24595
27327	41090	18095	04715	95862	25947	79356	11541	86114
59509	38667	89635	58732	69966	22279	28263	00136	84305
41234	54504	18038	49111	18751	63721	82493	52540	97085
14050	51016	66075	68379	77741	13177	10463	37400	16660
26942	29325	82049	97295	07470	31311	22723	72762	00993
89454	22421	60508	47686	17228	82511	99442	16193	64319
96313	53876	11799	54840	09277	31025	20158	48507	27126
27452	64377	25621	98618	98975	99506	99471	94490	64911
45493	18649	95671	33537	41376	77489	92552	20051	18406
32938	20787	90418	93281	26391	30352	93163	23666	89961
13830	55791	96704	78099	22547	32390	24125	64513	38879
19550	27831	22103	88922	89961	17495	35144	70915	09189
69284	24151	45633	56436	58992	08171	18092	28230	99767
10309	09864	59620	24302	58098	64433	25860	44193	49916
77528	03315	53210	44785	51964	39792	33219	03324	58829

RANDOM DIGITS

45-49	50-54	55-59	60-64	65-69	7C-74	75-79	80-84	85-89	90-94	95-99
16657	57028	61183	15990	89998	18766	89C44	C3225	80093	75820	27294
72901	32634	63978	90159	96225	28060	88767	17918	95037	25567	02207
88160	16419	91506	25676	29181	37218	09256	58428	22622	77106	41577
71C06	50069	18698	30490	C7873	28184	60385	26160	82418	49680	63625
40064	60867	14906	26913	20541	05315	71307	39355	66412	44279	61178
84471	45446	36726	73485	10371	60391	92463	21809	29528	11954	17514
97851	15484	50655	51001	12254	83438	23257	83597	47626	57673	48470
28785	78518	8C967	41280	43259	19107	18526	71237	31186	70266	82050
96985	81614	12080	57933	25306	99362	23776	10539	73538	01737	79652
28216	40885	22433	04487	49311	20266	67161	06999	37544	48701	85376
80994	C4288	27852	01172	79269	89355	84850	98123	87228	33471	71135
06286	77C84	30217	61160	29435	95093	61000	34452	50925	26556	38863
64315	71714	13593	36133	11962	84431	23216	34778	30793	78540	80537
50420	31C39	7C306	28911	65CC2	29809	62758	25773	58738	37071	29208
48840	97649	30243	19789	70833	31388	36969	70389	89610	35231	60256
16026	58145	91064	23073	05294	30892	24135	28928	32059	80579	63868
42496	02935	86112	14546	43338	96432	45490	60411	84122	92106	57679
83704	28819	19578	25982	40471	26486	56822	02555	03934	93819	20725
89497	19719	60174	52501	35584	91794	29299	80716	07032	46318	04050
70363	15116	57430	94965	52921	18200	01834	71490	36721	01199	94064
52351	27266	3C288	84909	05786	C6115	97972	26014	60766	30467	04838
97707	66541	44170	59363	89714	13580	29181	07084	14183	14559	52922
59157	12074	93670	88157	79122	74537	28335	99176	95397	73008	03764
25865	964C0	0C971	62427	45548	17557	88626	11600	62388	84863	78758
55503	72143	64402	30337	71326	41357	30491	17515	10318	11051	66661
31054	86687	27063	13265	60309	28898	99537	92496	52353	88766	85895
37447	31896	34005	48032	13221	15961	69992	31659	84309	89849	42454
85546	31207	72689	24196	23C42	94215	95768	19891	19573	31634	31145
08405	31145	28726	98836	89839	42727	03170	03401	85086	04196	21543
98810	46073	42508	02536	01569	79807	89008	77925	59689	50022	25075
20722	50161	78247	68143	97848	04873	38154	56321	66038	20411	52414
33165	48514	23673	43264	64025	25848	47785	71584	30505	51319	07514
67975	81086	91536	03685	60425	84743	95704	73677	05008	98027	36307
87582	79477	81842	37899	65C39	23313	78812	82590	94127	83592	47619
87029	38673	C4136	67941	27897	17078	75679	55728	46468	39398	80319
37103	C2953	21645	20794	26533	52786	95417	97430	19038	99499	49940
28895	07330	19151	42703	25408	30265	83992	00491	09158	83581	85143
09652	46286	77277	47090	11330	13095	69817	56405	03290	12097	70365
25503	51055	16521	32845	48378	25737	56872	27098	19665	98396	37679
82172	08384	41826	61929	26214	68845	63578	24003	96099	98422	18851
26606	49695	76214	29613	87404	26831	05418	60615	94800	23259	72786
64045	26563	07258	19774	17255	56631	53417	72966	88109	42570	19561
63345	58013	40115	11787	47541	65592	96756	21279	19009	72037	28256
78547	43484	78271	78265	27292	14728	49523	51013	22514	28857	48776
64628	024C8	32795	61526	73996	21313	17268	18576	49259	38665	98815
45870	56383	56534	93901	54601	73579	18268	47397	03810	53000	39068
16898	36186	65032	64515	63946	65185	77740	20783	27073	06460	01760
99888	94635	62035	44782	03589	87419	16500	43297	28781	20867	90459
32832	25995	66956	36705	27892	15343	37678	05487	31672	27077	69333
78418	72120	20171	71947	40838	64455	19183	59288	52009	40606	37699

	1	2	3	4	5	6	7
1	1.29	2.46	C.11	0.14	0.79	0.62	1.32
2	0.C4	0.90	0.82	0.46	C.63	0.09	0.48
3	3.38	0.80	1.14	C.11	0.24	C.07	C.C8
4	C.47	0.18	C.C4	2.96	0.39	2.86	4.41
5	1.24	1.23	1.12	0.20	0.12	0.66	1.35
6	C.30	0.51	C.46	1.38	4.84	C.14	C.42
7	1.C0	1.13	2.26	0.03	1.31	C.02	C.42
8	C.27	0.63	C.24	0.18	C.72	4.75	0.24
9	C.33	2.82	0.63	C.06	0.81	5.09	C.24
10	0.04	0.4C	0.74	1.29	0.45	C.17	1.11
11	0.74	1.55	C.62	0.32	1.75	0.68	0.46
12	1.36	C.74	1.21	0.14	1.31	0.70	0.14
13	1.4C	1.01	0.27	1.49	1.20	0.C1	1.43
14	2.39	0.03	1.C7	1.95	0.23	1.18	1.C0
15	0.05	C.13	C.43	1.1C	0.87	2.04	0.21
16	0.04	1.44	0.09	1.38	2.93	1.47	C.14
17	C.14	1.88	0.66	2.43	0.61	0.06	0.22
18	C.04	1.19	C.23	0.30	0.C2	C.10	6.21
19	C.14	0.38	1.49	0.43	0.56	1.03	C.32
20	C.15	0.34	0.C0	4.36	1.64	2.99	3.66
21	1.C6	C.3C	1.81	2.52	0.10	0.48	C.60
22	2.C7	C.29	0.46	4.C0	0.11	2.07	C.54
23	1.C4	0.44	C.45	0.11	C.C8	0.42	3.19
24	0.81	0.61	C.96	1.C6	0.16	C.11	0.14
25	0.C9	1.14	2.77	0.11	0.26	1.82	0.19
26	1.50	1.86	C.54	0.52	0.72	0.93	C.29
27	0.02	5.70	1.68	2.78	2.16	C.76	3.60
28	1.41	0.31	0.52	0.18	1.92	0.95	0.54
29	C.38	1.32	1.11	C.33	1.C5	0.21	0.66
30	2.C9	0.27	C.35	0.67	0.€4	0.16	C.52
31	0.22	0.21	4.23	1.96	2.C3	0.42	0.93
32	1.77	C.0C	0.46	0.84	0.22	2.00	1.91
33	0.70	1.87	2.08	1.07	0.20	0.53	C.55
34	0.13	4.11	C.C7	2.14	0.63	5.64	2.05
35	C.32	C.28	C.16	0.66	C.C1	1.97	0.81
36	C.33	0.45	1.64	0.29	1.69	C.19	1.08
37	C.30	0.78	C.87	0.87	C.C6	0.18	1.74
38	0.84	0.6C	0.5C	0.13	0.10	0.17	1.80
39	2.47	C.33	1.85	0.02	0.56	0.09	0.08
40	C.66	3.14	C.01	0.36	0.42	0.72	C.36
41	0.29	1.4C	2.14	0.55	0.71	0.05	0.06
42	1.50	3.4C	1.77	1.55	1.66	0.03	C.15
43	0.76	0.35	1.31	1.78	3.30	0.09	C.21
44	1.19	0.79	C.34	0.27	3.60	C.70	1.15
45	C.03	3.0C	0.88	3.62	0.C3	0.54	0.04
46	C.13	0.C7	0.29	0.3C	1.C1	0.44	1.52
47	C.04	0.74	1.29	0.07	5.C8	0.15	C.03
48	0.19	0.45	1.05	2.36	0.48	0.49	2.84
49	C.22	0.09	0.65	0.24	0.57	0.89	C.00
50	1.40	0.45	0.64	0.83	0.27	1.45	0.93

EXPONENTIAL
RANDOM
NUMBER
$\lambda = 1$

8	9	10	11	12	13	14	15	16	17	18	19	20
2.69	0.21	0.13	0.12	0.09	1.08	2.06	0.96	0.28	0.44	0.32	1.24	0.30
0.64	1.15	0.46	0.97	1.76	0.14	0.90	3.22	0.10	0.50	0.18	3.38	0.85
0.35	1.65	2.44	0.76	1.61	1.80	0.11	1.21	2.28	2.43	2.60	0.65	1.96
1.14	1.00	2.22	0.74	3.91	0.28	1.34	0.33	0.52	0.45	0.54	0.44	0.17
0.64	2.61	0.88	2.78	4.05	2.36	1.31	1.89	0.53	0.44	0.40	0.77	0.11
0.11	1.68	1.87	0.40	1.88	0.20	0.45	0.07	0.67	0.75	0.73	0.94	0.23
0.49	1.13	0.85	0.04	0.27	1.92	0.66	2.65	0.12	0.13	2.26	0.86	3.62
0.75	1.93	1.27	0.19	0.75	2.55	0.53	0.39	2.52	1.01	2.00	1.32	0.37
0.73	1.60	0.60	0.29	0.18	0.00	0.72	3.29	0.11	0.10	0.89	2.85	0.16
1.19	0.64	0.83	0.06	5.36	0.86	2.52	1.02	0.12	0.37	0.43	0.91	0.22
0.11	0.76	0.49	0.38	0.07	0.66	3.42	0.23	0.37	1.08	0.13	0.41	3.75
0.33	1.38	1.37	1.23	0.18	0.49	0.25	1.90	0.75	0.42	0.59	2.43	0.71
0.82	1.72	0.67	0.33	2.49	0.34	1.51	0.11	0.29	0.24	0.59	2.45	0.55
0.04	1.56	1.26	0.86	0.58	2.33	0.98	0.61	1.42	0.21	0.25	0.31	1.63
0.42	0.06	1.49	0.42	0.16	2.06	1.51	0.32	0.96	0.85	2.12	0.49	0.71
3.08	1.17	0.51	0.02	0.33	0.59	0.41	0.58	1.48	0.04	0.05	0.74	1.40
0.28	0.59	0.48	0.09	0.52	1.00	1.78	0.30	0.86	2.84	1.23	0.21	0.24
1.11	0.23	0.33	1.87	0.12	1.22	0.80	1.66	0.15	0.74	0.36	0.16	2.38
4.41	4.19	0.13	1.29	0.28	1.11	0.82	0.01	0.26	1.56	1.43	0.51	0.03
0.43	0.18	0.16	0.45	1.23	0.08	1.20	4.88	0.72	2.47	1.52	0.63	2.87
0.65	3.01	0.49	0.22	1.51	1.71	0.02	0.51	0.64	0.72	0.11	0.58	0.63
0.68	0.66	2.55	0.12	1.80	0.63	0.17	0.00	0.00	1.43	0.04	0.36	1.52
1.32	0.29	2.52	1.16	1.63	1.14	0.08	1.08	0.47	0.54	1.79	1.05	0.91
0.20	1.27	0.34	3.77	1.26	1.68	0.79	1.31	3.74	1.59	1.48	1.24	0.35
2.52	0.88	2.05	0.79	3.08	0.02	0.15	1.34	0.73	1.47	0.18	2.75	0.25
1.36	0.48	0.20	0.31	0.49	0.14	2.14	2.03	0.95	3.88	1.14	0.17	0.33
0.82	0.20	0.57	0.75	1.19	0.33	0.21	1.60	1.88	1.00	3.91	1.14	0.26
0.34	0.39	1.97	1.09	0.76	0.63	0.22	0.56	0.54	0.91	0.03	1.18	2.02
0.14	1.67	1.23	0.04	0.75	0.23	2.67	0.44	0.82	1.54	0.26	0.54	0.23
2.52	0.51	0.75	1.06	1.20	0.43	0.26	0.28	0.93	0.80	0.21	1.45	0.09
1.49	0.45	0.23	0.19	2.37	0.44	0.23	0.11	1.62	1.12	0.08	2.65	0.09
0.87	0.58	1.29	0.02	0.98	0.00	0.09	0.04	1.40	0.56	0.46	0.08	0.04
1.26	0.44	0.67	4.53	0.07	1.04	2.98	1.72	0.14	0.61	0.15	0.47	1.32
0.36	0.06	1.64	0.57	0.85	0.01	0.05	0.13	2.74	0.91	0.44	0.46	0.15
0.41	0.62	1.03	3.64	3.46	1.21	4.19	0.17	1.76	2.21	0.03	0.70	0.25
0.36	0.01	0.90	1.82	1.34	0.86	0.24	0.62	0.26	1.18	0.54	0.84	0.03
0.89	2.37	0.51	0.37	0.44	2.06	0.40	0.19	0.61	1.93	0.73	0.84	0.54
1.89	0.87	2.43	2.69	1.00	1.95	0.08	4.02	0.05	2.20	4.11	0.53	0.26
1.48	0.75	1.06	0.11	2.17	0.27	0.16	0.11	1.17	0.13	1.66	0.25	3.60
0.32	0.39	0.24	1.50	0.70	0.07	0.20	0.64	0.92	1.72	2.12	0.34	1.68
0.06	1.14	0.18	2.73	3.62	0.14	3.12	1.05	2.11	0.07	2.05	0.81	0.22
1.09	0.83	0.12	0.61	1.78	1.71	0.21	5.69	0.92	1.11	3.13	1.03	0.02
5.48	0.39	1.17	1.85	1.84	0.17	0.25	1.05	0.23	0.78	0.22	2.30	2.26
0.21	1.19	0.33	0.14	0.31	0.97	1.62	1.08	0.14	0.17	0.54	1.62	0.71
0.33	0.86	0.23	0.25	1.27	1.32	0.05	1.22	0.72	0.30	0.29	0.90	0.43
0.34	0.47	0.04	0.40	2.82	0.27	1.02	0.10	0.48	0.19	1.17	1.22	1.26
0.37	0.28	0.07	2.08	1.50	0.23	0.36	0.01	0.01	0.43	1.42	0.89	0.32
0.02	1.60	0.67	0.44	0.26	1.14	0.75	1.01	1.08	0.22	0.30	0.79	0.85
0.43	0.47	0.95	0.46	0.33	0.43	2.01	0.37	2.47	0.16	1.90	0.19	0.41
1.83	0.15	0.60	0.16	1.05	0.57	1.01	0.02	0.18	0.29	2.12	0.89	0.63

Appendix B

TABLES FOR THE ANALYSIS OF CAPITAL EXPENDITURES

By Jerome Bracken and Charles J. Christenson

Table B-1

PRESENT VALUE OF $1

Years Hence	1%	2%	4%	6%	8%	10%	12%	14%	15%	16%	18%	20%	22%	24%	25%	26%	28%	30%	35%	40%	45%	50%
1	0.990	0.980	0.962	0.943	0.926	0.909	0.893	0.877	0.870	0.862	0.847	0.833	0.820	0.806	0.800	0.794	0.781	0.769	0.741	0.714	0.690	0.667
2	0.980	0.961	0.925	0.890	0.857	0.826	0.797	0.769	0.756	0.743	0.718	0.694	0.672	0.650	0.640	0.630	0.610	0.592	0.549	0.510	0.476	0.444
3	0.971	0.942	0.889	0.840	0.794	0.751	0.712	0.675	0.658	0.641	0.609	0.579	0.551	0.524	0.512	0.500	0.477	0.455	0.406	0.364	0.328	0.296
4	0.961	0.924	0.855	0.792	0.735	0.683	0.636	0.592	0.572	0.552	0.516	0.482	0.451	0.423	0.410	0.397	0.373	0.350	0.301	0.260	0.226	0.198
5	0.951	0.906	0.822	0.747	0.681	0.621	0.567	0.519	0.497	0.476	0.437	0.402	0.370	0.341	0.328	0.315	0.291	0.269	0.223	0.186	0.156	0.132
6	0.942	0.888	0.790	0.705	0.630	0.564	0.507	0.456	0.432	0.410	0.370	0.335	0.303	0.275	0.262	0.250	0.227	0.207	0.165	0.133	0.108	0.088
7	0.933	0.871	0.760	0.665	0.583	0.513	0.452	0.400	0.376	0.354	0.314	0.279	0.249	0.222	0.210	0.198	0.178	0.159	0.122	0.095	0.074	0.059
8	0.923	0.853	0.731	0.627	0.540	0.467	0.404	0.351	0.327	0.305	0.266	0.233	0.204	0.179	0.168	0.157	0.139	0.123	0.091	0.068	0.051	0.039
9	0.914	0.837	0.703	0.592	0.500	0.424	0.361	0.308	0.284	0.263	0.225	0.194	0.167	0.144	0.134	0.125	0.108	0.094	0.067	0.048	0.035	0.026
10	0.905	0.820	0.676	0.558	0.463	0.386	0.322	0.270	0.247	0.227	0.191	0.162	0.137	0.116	0.107	0.099	0.085	0.073	0.050	0.035	0.024	0.017
11	0.896	0.804	0.650	0.527	0.429	0.350	0.287	0.237	0.215	0.195	0.162	0.135	0.112	0.094	0.086	0.079	0.066	0.056	0.037	0.025	0.017	0.012
12	0.887	0.788	0.625	0.497	0.397	0.319	0.257	0.208	0.187	0.168	0.137	0.112	0.092	0.076	0.069	0.062	0.052	0.043	0.027	0.018	0.012	0.008
13	0.879	0.773	0.601	0.469	0.368	0.290	0.229	0.182	0.163	0.145	0.116	0.093	0.075	0.061	0.055	0.050	0.040	0.033	0.020	0.013	0.008	0.005
14	0.870	0.758	0.577	0.442	0.340	0.263	0.205	0.160	0.141	0.125	0.099	0.078	0.062	0.049	0.044	0.039	0.032	0.025	0.015	0.009	0.006	0.003
15	0.861	0.743	0.555	0.417	0.315	0.239	0.183	0.140	0.123	0.108	0.084	0.065	0.051	0.040	0.035	0.031	0.025	0.020	0.011	0.006	0.004	0.002
16	0.853	0.728	0.534	0.394	0.292	0.218	0.163	0.123	0.107	0.093	0.071	0.054	0.042	0.032	0.028	0.025	0.019	0.015	0.008	0.005	0.003	0.002
17	0.844	0.714	0.513	0.371	0.270	0.198	0.146	0.108	0.093	0.080	0.060	0.045	0.034	0.026	0.023	0.020	0.015	0.012	0.006	0.003	0.002	0.001
18	0.836	0.700	0.494	0.350	0.250	0.180	0.130	0.095	0.081	0.069	0.051	0.038	0.028	0.021	0.018	0.016	0.012	0.009	0.005	0.002	0.001	0.001
19	0.828	0.686	0.475	0.331	0.232	0.164	0.116	0.083	0.070	0.060	0.043	0.031	0.023	0.017	0.014	0.012	0.009	0.007	0.003	0.002	0.001	
20	0.820	0.673	0.456	0.312	0.215	0.149	0.104	0.073	0.061	0.051	0.037	0.026	0.019	0.014	0.012	0.010	0.007	0.005	0.002	0.001	0.001	
21	0.811	0.660	0.439	0.294	0.199	0.135	0.093	0.064	0.053	0.044	0.031	0.022	0.015	0.011	0.009	0.008	0.006	0.004	0.002	0.001		
22	0.803	0.647	0.422	0.278	0.184	0.123	0.083	0.056	0.046	0.038	0.026	0.018	0.013	0.009	0.007	0.006	0.004	0.003	0.001	0.001		
23	0.795	0.634	0.406	0.262	0.170	0.112	0.074	0.049	0.040	0.033	0.022	0.015	0.010	0.007	0.006	0.005	0.003	0.002	0.001			
24	0.788	0.622	0.390	0.247	0.158	0.102	0.066	0.043	0.035	0.028	0.019	0.013	0.008	0.006	0.005	0.004	0.003	0.002	0.001			
25	0.780	0.610	0.375	0.233	0.146	0.092	0.059	0.038	0.030	0.024	0.016	0.010	0.007	0.005	0.004	0.003	0.002	0.001				
26	0.772	0.598	0.361	0.220	0.135	0.084	0.053	0.033	0.026	0.021	0.014	0.009	0.006	0.004	0.003	0.002	0.002	0.001				
27	0.764	0.586	0.347	0.207	0.125	0.076	0.047	0.029	0.023	0.018	0.011	0.007	0.005	0.003	0.002	0.002	0.001	0.001				
28	0.757	0.574	0.333	0.196	0.116	0.069	0.042	0.026	0.020	0.016	0.010	0.006	0.004	0.002	0.002	0.002	0.001	0.001				
29	0.749	0.563	0.321	0.185	0.107	0.063	0.037	0.022	0.017	0.014	0.008	0.005	0.003	0.002	0.002	0.001	0.001					
30	0.742	0.552	0.308	0.174	0.099	0.057	0.033	0.020	0.015	0.012	0.007	0.004	0.003	0.002	0.001	0.001	0.001					
40	0.672	0.453	0.208	0.097	0.046	0.022	0.011	0.005	0.004	0.003	0.001	0.001										
50	0.608	0.372	0.141	0.054	0.021	0.009	0.003	0.001	0.001	0.001												

Table B-2

Present Value of $1 Received Annually for N Years

Years (N)	50%	45%	40%	35%	30%	28%	26%	25%	24%	22%	20%	18%	16%	15%	14%	12%	10%	8%	6%	4%	2%	1%
1	0.667	0.690	0.714	0.741	0.769	0.781	0.794	0.800	0.806	0.820	0.833	0.847	0.862	0.870	0.877	0.893	0.909	0.926	0.943	0.962	0.980	0.990
2	1.111	1.165	1.224	1.289	1.361	1.392	1.424	1.440	1.457	1.492	1.528	1.566	1.605	1.626	1.647	1.690	1.736	1.783	1.833	1.886	1.942	1.970
3	1.407	1.493	1.589	1.696	1.816	1.868	1.923	1.952	1.981	2.042	2.106	2.174	2.246	2.283	2.322	2.402	2.487	2.577	2.673	2.775	2.884	2.941
4	1.605	1.720	1.849	1.997	2.166	2.241	2.320	2.362	2.404	2.494	2.589	2.690	2.798	2.855	2.914	3.037	3.170	3.312	3.465	3.630	3.808	3.902
5	1.737	1.876	2.035	2.220	2.436	2.532	2.635	2.689	2.745	2.864	2.991	3.127	3.274	3.352	3.433	3.605	3.791	3.993	4.212	4.452	4.713	4.853
6	1.824	1.983	2.168	2.385	2.643	2.759	2.885	2.951	3.020	3.167	3.326	3.498	3.685	3.784	3.889	4.111	4.355	4.623	4.917	5.242	5.601	5.795
7	1.883	2.057	2.263	2.508	2.802	2.937	3.083	3.161	3.242	3.416	3.605	3.812	4.039	4.160	4.288	4.564	4.868	5.206	5.582	6.002	6.472	6.728
8	1.922	2.108	2.331	2.598	2.925	3.076	3.241	3.329	3.421	3.619	3.837	4.078	4.344	4.487	4.639	4.968	5.335	5.747	6.210	6.733	7.325	7.652
9	1.948	2.144	2.379	2.665	3.019	3.184	3.366	3.463	3.566	3.786	4.031	4.303	4.607	4.772	4.946	5.328	5.759	6.247	6.802	7.435	8.162	8.566
10	1.965	2.168	2.414	2.715	3.092	3.269	3.465	3.571	3.682	3.923	4.192	4.494	4.833	5.019	5.216	5.650	6.145	6.710	7.360	8.111	8.983	9.471
11	1.977	2.185	2.438	2.752	3.147	3.335	3.544	3.656	3.776	4.035	4.327	4.656	5.029	5.234	5.453	5.937	6.495	7.139	7.887	8.760	9.787	10.368
12	1.985	2.196	2.456	2.779	3.190	3.387	3.606	3.725	3.851	4.127	4.439	4.793	5.197	5.421	5.660	6.194	6.814	7.536	8.384	9.385	10.575	11.255
13	1.990	2.204	2.468	2.799	3.223	3.427	3.656	3.780	3.912	4.203	4.533	4.910	5.342	5.583	5.842	6.424	7.103	7.904	8.853	9.986	11.343	12.134
14	1.993	2.210	2.477	2.814	3.249	3.459	3.695	3.824	3.962	4.265	4.611	5.008	5.468	5.724	6.002	6.628	7.367	8.244	9.295	10.563	12.106	13.004
15	1.995	2.214	2.484	2.825	3.268	3.483	3.726	3.859	4.001	4.315	4.675	5.092	5.575	5.847	6.142	6.811	7.606	8.559	9.712	11.118	12.849	13.865
16	1.997	2.216	2.489	2.834	3.283	3.503	3.751	3.887	4.033	4.357	4.730	5.162	5.669	5.954	6.265	6.974	7.824	8.851	10.106	11.652	13.578	14.718
17	1.998	2.218	2.492	2.840	3.295	3.518	3.771	3.910	4.059	4.391	4.775	5.222	5.749	6.047	6.373	7.120	8.022	9.122	10.477	12.166	14.292	15.562
18	1.999	2.219	2.494	2.844	3.304	3.529	3.786	3.928	4.080	4.419	4.812	5.273	5.818	6.128	6.467	7.250	8.201	9.372	10.828	12.659	14.992	16.398
19	1.999	2.220	2.496	2.848	3.311	3.539	3.799	3.942	4.097	4.442	4.844	5.316	5.877	6.198	6.550	7.366	8.365	9.604	11.158	13.134	15.678	17.226
20	1.999	2.221	2.497	2.850	3.316	3.546	3.808	3.954	4.110	4.460	4.870	5.353	5.929	6.259	6.623	7.469	8.514	9.818	11.470	13.590	16.351	18.046
21	2.000	2.221	2.498	2.852	3.320	3.551	3.816	3.963	4.121	4.476	4.891	5.384	5.973	6.312	6.687	7.562	8.649	10.017	11.764	14.029	17.011	18.857
22	2.000	2.222	2.498	2.853	3.323	3.556	3.822	3.970	4.130	4.488	4.909	5.410	6.011	6.359	6.743	7.645	8.772	10.201	12.042	14.451	17.658	19.660
23	2.000	2.222	2.499	2.854	3.325	3.559	3.827	3.976	4.137	4.499	4.925	5.432	6.044	6.399	6.792	7.718	8.883	10.371	12.303	14.857	18.292	20.456
24	2.000	2.222	2.499	2.855	3.327	3.562	3.831	3.981	4.143	4.507	4.937	5.451	6.073	6.434	6.835	7.784	8.985	10.529	12.550	15.247	18.914	21.243
25	2.000	2.222	2.499	2.856	3.329	3.564	3.834	3.985	4.147	4.514	4.948	5.467	6.097	6.464	6.873	7.843	9.077	10.675	12.783	15.622	19.523	22.023
26	2.000	2.222	2.500	2.856	3.330	3.566	3.837	3.988	4.151	4.520	4.956	5.480	6.118	6.491	6.906	7.896	9.161	10.810	13.003	15.983	20.121	22.795
27	2.000	2.222	2.500	2.856	3.331	3.567	3.839	3.990	4.154	4.524	4.964	5.492	6.136	6.514	6.935	7.943	9.237	10.935	13.211	16.330	20.707	23.560
28	2.000	2.222	2.500	2.857	3.331	3.568	3.840	3.992	4.157	4.528	4.970	5.502	6.152	6.534	6.961	7.984	9.307	11.051	13.406	16.663	21.281	24.316
29	2.000	2.222	2.500	2.857	3.332	3.569	3.841	3.994	4.159	4.531	4.975	5.510	6.166	6.551	6.983	8.022	9.370	11.158	13.591	16.984	21.844	25.066
30	2.000	2.222	2.500	2.857	3.332	3.569	3.842	3.995	4.160	4.534	4.979	5.517	6.177	6.566	7.003	8.055	9.427	11.258	13.765	17.292	22.396	25.808
40	2.000	2.222	2.500	2.857	3.333	3.571	3.846	3.999	4.166	4.544	4.997	5.548	6.234	6.642	7.105	8.244	9.779	11.925	15.046	19.793	27.355	32.835
50	2.000	2.222	2.500	2.857	3.333	3.571	3.846	4.000	4.167	4.545	4.999	5.554	6.246	6.661	7.133	8.304	9.915	12.234	15.762	21.482	31.424	39.196

Table B–3

Present Value of Sum-of-Years'-Digit Depreciation

Years of Useful Life	2%	4%	6%	8%	10%	12%	14%	15%	16%	18%	20%	22%	24%	26%	28%	30%	35%	40%	45%	50%
3	0.968	0.937	0.908	0.881	0.855	0.831	0.808	0.796	0.786	0.764	0.745	0.726	0.707	0.690	0.674	0.658	0.621	0.588	0.558	0.531
4	0.961	0.925	0.891	0.860	0.830	0.802	0.776	0.763	0.751	0.728	0.706	0.685	0.665	0.646	0.628	0.611	0.572	0.538	0.507	0.479
5	0.955	0.914	0.875	0.839	0.806	0.775	0.746	0.732	0.719	0.694	0.670	0.647	0.626	0.606	0.588	0.570	0.530	0.494	0.463	0.435
6	0.949	0.902	0.859	0.820	0.783	0.749	0.718	0.703	0.689	0.662	0.637	0.613	0.591	0.570	0.551	0.533	0.492	0.456	0.425	0.398
7	0.943	0.891	0.844	0.801	0.761	0.725	0.692	0.676	0.661	0.633	0.606	0.582	0.559	0.538	0.518	0.500	0.458	0.423	0.392	0.366
8	0.937	0.880	0.829	0.782	0.740	0.702	0.667	0.650	0.635	0.605	0.578	0.553	0.530	0.508	0.488	0.470	0.429	0.394	0.364	0.338
9	0.931	0.869	0.814	0.765	0.720	0.680	0.643	0.626	0.610	0.580	0.552	0.527	0.503	0.482	0.462	0.443	0.402	0.368	0.338	0.313
10	0.925	0.859	0.800	0.748	0.701	0.659	0.621	0.604	0.587	0.556	0.528	0.502	0.479	0.457	0.437	0.419	0.378	0.345	0.316	0.292
11	0.919	0.848	0.786	0.731	0.682	0.639	0.600	0.582	0.565	0.534	0.506	0.480	0.456	0.434	0.415	0.397	0.357	0.324	0.297	0.273
12	0.913	0.838	0.773	0.715	0.665	0.620	0.580	0.562	0.545	0.513	0.485	0.459	0.435	0.414	0.394	0.376	0.338	0.306	0.279	0.257
13	0.907	0.828	0.760	0.700	0.648	0.602	0.562	0.543	0.526	0.494	0.465	0.439	0.416	0.395	0.376	0.358	0.320	0.289	0.264	0.242
14	0.902	0.818	0.747	0.685	0.632	0.585	0.544	0.525	0.508	0.476	0.447	0.421	0.398	0.377	0.358	0.341	0.304	0.274	0.250	0.229
15	0.896	0.809	0.734	0.671	0.616	0.569	0.527	0.508	0.491	0.459	0.430	0.405	0.382	0.361	0.343	0.326	0.290	0.261	0.237	0.217
16	0.890	0.799	0.722	0.657	0.601	0.553	0.511	0.492	0.475	0.443	0.414	0.389	0.367	0.346	0.328	0.312	0.277	0.248	0.225	0.206
17	0.885	0.790	0.710	0.644	0.587	0.538	0.496	0.477	0.460	0.428	0.400	0.375	0.352	0.332	0.315	0.298	0.264	0.237	0.215	0.196
18	0.880	0.781	0.699	0.631	0.573	0.524	0.482	0.463	0.445	0.413	0.386	0.361	0.339	0.320	0.302	0.286	0.253	0.227	0.205	0.187
19	0.874	0.772	0.688	0.618	0.560	0.510	0.468	0.449	0.432	0.400	0.372	0.348	0.327	0.308	0.291	0.275	0.243	0.217	0.196	0.179
20	0.869	0.763	0.677	0.606	0.547	0.497	0.455	0.436	0.419	0.387	0.360	0.336	0.315	0.296	0.280	0.265	0.233	0.208	0.188	0.171
21	0.863	0.754	0.666	0.594	0.535	0.485	0.442	0.424	0.406	0.376	0.349	0.325	0.304	0.286	0.270	0.255	0.224	0.200	0.181	0.164
22	0.858	0.746	0.656	0.583	0.523	0.473	0.431	0.412	0.395	0.364	0.338	0.315	0.294	0.276	0.260	0.246	0.216	0.193	0.174	0.158
23	0.853	0.738	0.646	0.572	0.511	0.461	0.419	0.401	0.384	0.354	0.327	0.305	0.285	0.267	0.252	0.238	0.208	0.186	0.167	0.152
24	0.848	0.729	0.636	0.561	0.500	0.450	0.409	0.390	0.373	0.344	0.318	0.295	0.276	0.258	0.243	0.230	0.201	0.179	0.161	0.147
25	0.842	0.721	0.626	0.551	0.490	0.440	0.398	0.380	0.364	0.334	0.308	0.286	0.267	0.250	0.236	0.222	0.195	0.173	0.156	0.142
30	0.818	0.683	0.582	0.504	0.442	0.393	0.353	0.336	0.320	0.292	0.269	0.249	0.232	0.216	0.203	0.191	0.167	0.148	0.133	0.120
35	0.794	0.648	0.542	0.463	0.402	0.355	0.317	0.300	0.286	0.260	0.238	0.220	0.204	0.190	0.178	0.168	0.146	0.129	0.116	0.105
40	0.771	0.616	0.507	0.428	0.368	0.323	0.286	0.271	0.257	0.233	0.213	0.196	0.182	0.170	0.159	0.149	0.129	0.114	0.102	0.093
45	0.749	0.586	0.476	0.397	0.339	0.296	0.261	0.247	0.234	0.212	0.193	0.178	0.164	0.153	0.143	0.134	0.116	0.103	0.092	0.083
50	0.728	0.559	0.448	0.370	0.314	0.272	0.240	0.227	0.214	0.194	0.176	0.162	0.150	0.139	0.130	0.122	0.106	0.093	0.083	

Source: Jerome Bracken and Charles J. Christenson, *Tables for Use in Analyzing Business Decisions* (Homewood, Ill.: Richard D. Irwin, Inc, 1965).

INDEX OF CASES

Adamian Metallurgical Corporation 420
Almond Apparatus Company 143
Apex Drilling Company 518
Astra Company, The 202
Atlantic Monthly Company (A), The 88
Atlantic Monthly Company (B), The 480
Benton Textiles, Inc. 379
Bill French, Accountant 196
Bob Mogielnicki 139
Condon Leather Company 102
Conerly Chemical Company 255
Consolidated Mining and Manufacturing Corporation 490
Davison Press, Inc., The 319
F. F. Fierce & Company 545
Federal Aviation Agency (A) 464
Forest Service (A) 330
General Motors Corporation 371
Hurley Home Products Company 516
J. L. Jessup & Sons 432
Liquid Cleanse 386
Lockbourne Company, The 160
McCarthy's Bowl Inn 554
Mats Electronics, Inc. 409
Monitor Textile Company (A) 471
Monitor Textile Company (B) 553
Newporter Fashions (A) 315
Newporter Fashions (B) 317
Nuthatch National Forest (A) 221
Nuthatch National Forest (B) 476
Post Office Department (B) 206
Post Office Department (D) 146
Prendergarth Shipping Company 7
Sherman Motor Company 156
Stardust Grinder Company 217

Sylvania Electric Products Inc. (A) 48
Sylvania Electric Products Inc. (B) 366
Technotronics Corporation 264
Tomlinson Steel Corporation 514
Waco Wildcat Company 266
Walsh Company, The 327
Warren Agency, Inc. 257
Weatherburn Aircraft Engine Company 512
Weston Manufacturing Company 259
White Eagle Oil Company (A) 67
White Eagle Oil Company (B) 412

SUBJECT INDEX

A

Accountant's concept of cost, 19
  economist's concept distinguished, 19, 116–18
Accountant's role, 20
Accounting amortization as cash flow measurement problem area, 451–52
Accounting conventions, 256
Accounting costs as cost minimization problem, 113–16
Accounting records as information source, 24, 34–35, 45, 108, 113
Acquisition cost, 19–20, 23
Acts
  best worst case, 233
  certainty equivalent for, 237–39
    expected value as, 239–41
  defined, 229
  most likely outcome, 232–34
  payoff table, 231–32
  probabilities, 234–37
  ranking scheme, 233–34
  risk profile, 286–88
  selection of, 229–30
    decision guides in, 232–34
  sequential choices of, 245–47
Actual costs, 24–26
Administrative expenses; see General and administrative expenses
Advertising
  expenditures, 23, 171
  influence of, 342
A/F ratio, 310–11
Allocated plant costs, 115–16
Allocation of resources; see Resource allocation
Analysis; see also specific topics
  break-even point, 165–69
  complex decisions, 498–511
  decision-making, 227–54
  discounted cash flow, 443–63

Analysis—Cont.
  historical data, 35
  make-or-buy, 119–22
  overhead variances, 41–42
  pricing decisions, 340–65
  prime cost variances, 38–41
  profit changes, 35–38
  volume variances, 42–44
Asset structure, 523–24, 542
Average, 280
Average direct cost per unit of production, 21, 354

B

Backward induction, 247
Balance sheet, 522; see also Financial structure
Bentham, Jeremy, 4
Best price, 341, 397
Best worst case, 233
Bidding; see Competitive bidding
Blending problem, 123–24
Break-even chart, 166–67
Break-even point
  analysis, 165–69
  cost-price relationships, 189–90
  cost-volume relationships, 178–82
  defined, 166
  price-volume relationships, 171–73
Break-even price, 168–69
Break-even volume, 168
Budgets, 23
  overhead, 30, 32–35
Business problems, classification of, 109–10
  advantages of, 110

C

Capacity
  consumption of, 23
  decisions to create, 6, 441 ff.
  defined, 5
  forms of, 22

Capacity-creating costs, 22–23, 27
Capital, cost of; *see* Cost of capital
Capital expenditure analysis tables, 569 ff.
Capital expenditure problem, 109
Capital expenditures, 451–52; *see also* Cash flows
Capital recovery factor, 459–60
Capital structure, 525–26
   cost of components of, 528–32
   cost-versus-risk tradeoff, 535
   determination of, 535–39
   leverage concept, 535–38
   optimal, theory of, 538–39
   risk-versus-return tradeoff, 539
Cash flow analysis; *see* Discounted cash flow analysis
Cash flow diagram, 445
Cash flow patterns, 444–45
   comparing alternatives, 445–50
   determination of, 450–57
   typical end point, 505
Cash flows
   accounting amortizations, 451–52
   after-taxes, 452
   before-taxes, 452
   classification of, 450–51
   depreciation methods, 453–54
   income tax problems, 452–54
   lump-sum, 451
   per-unit basis variations, 451
   per-year basis variations, 451
   project life, 455–57
   special problems in measurement of, 451–55
   working capital problems, 454–55
Certainty equivalent for an act, 237–39
   expected value as, 239–41
Circulating assets, 523–24
Classification of cash flows, 450–51
Classification of costs, 20–24; *see also* Cost *and specific type of cost*
   conventional, 28–29
Classification of resource allocation problem, 109–10
Coefficient of elasticity, 345–46
Coin tossing illustration, 299
Common stock, 525–26
   cost, 530–32
   dividend yield, 532
   dividends, 525–26
   earnings growth rate, 532
   preferred stock convertible into, 529–30
Competition
   monopolistic, 342–43
   perfect, 342–43
Competitive bidding, 397–408
   assessment problem, 401–2

Competitive bidding—*Cont.*
   bid preparation costs, 406–7
   calculation of best bid, 403–4
   decision diagram, 399–400
   example of problem involving, 398–401
   forecasting in, 402–3
   more than one competitor, 405–6
   one buyer, several sellers, 398–405
   out-of-pocket expenses, 399
   pricing decision comparison, 404–5
   problems giving rise to, 397–98
   simple problem, 398–405
   solution framework, 407–8
   special cost associated with losing, 407
   special problems, 405–7
Consumer tastes in relation to demand, 341–42
Contribution, concept of, 163–65
Contribution per unit defined, 164
Cost; *see also specific type*
   accountant's concept, 19
   acquisition, 19–20
   actual, 24–26
   analysis of, 23, 35–45
   capacity-creating, 22–23
   classification, 20–24
   conventional classification, 28–29
   data source, 24; *see also* Accounting records
   defined, 19
   demand-creating, 22–23
   different uses of term, 19
   economist's concept, 19
   estimating, 24–35
   future, 19
   historical, 19
   objectives, 22–24, 27
   opportunity, 19–20
   overhead, 20–21
   overhead budgets, 30, 32–35
   price determination factors, 353–55
   prime, 20–21
   product-creating, 22, 24–45
   product identification, 20–21
   standard prime, 29–32
   types, 19–47
   variable, 21
Cost of capital, 527–35
   after-tax costs, 528
   before-tax costs, 529
   common stock, 530–32
   composite, 532–35
   defined, 521
   expression of, 521
   long-term debt, 528–29
   preferred stock, 529–30
   relevant costs, 528
   retained earnings, 532

Cost of capital—*Cont.*
  use of, 521
  weighted-average concept, 528, 533
Cost control, 33–34
Cost of goods sold, 25
Cost minimization, 110
  accounting costs, 113–16
  alternatives available for, 110–13
    comparison of, 118–23
    evaluation of, 113
  formulating problem of, 110–13
  judgment, importance of, 122–23
  least cost alternative, 113
  make-or-buy analysis, 119–22
  opportunity costs, 116–18
Cost-price manipulation, 186
Cost-price relationships, 163, 184–92
  break-even point, 189–90
  cost-price squeeze, 184, 186–90
  inflation, 187
  new product feature exploitation, 184–86
  profit margins, maintenance of, 190–92
Cost-price squeeze, 184, 186–90
Cost-versus-risk tradeoff, 535
Cost-volume relationships, 176–83
  break-even point, 178–82
  design costs versus product demand, 180–81
  fixed costs versus variable costs, 177–79
  project break-even point, 178–79
Criterion problem, 3–5
Cross-elasticity of demand, 361
Cumulative graph, 278
Cumulative probability distribution, 272, 275–77
  approximating, 278
  smooth curve, 304–5, 308
Current assets, 523
Current liabilities, 523

D

Debt capacity, 535
Decision analysis, 227–54; *see also specific topics*
  acts, 229
  backward induction, 247
  diagramming, 245–51
  events, 229
  payoff table, 231–32
  sequential choices of acts, 245–47
  uncertainty, 228–29
  value of information, 242–44
Decision diagramming, 245–51
  act forks, 245
  bidding problem, 399–400
  complex problem, 248–51
  event forks, 245

Decision diagramming—*Cont.*
  probability distribution, 283–85
  sequential choices of acts, 245–47
Decision-making, 34
Decision problems; *see* Decision analysis
Degeneracy, 126 n, 128–29
Demand
  consumer tastes, 341–42
  controllable factors, 341, 343
  cross-elasticity of, 361
  decisions to create, 5–6, 269 ff.
  defined, 5
  economic conditions, 342
  elasticity of, 344–46
  environmental factors, 341–43
  factors affecting, 341–43
  forecasting of, 292–314; *see also* Forecasting
  measurement of, 350
  revenue, effect on, 347–50
  shifts in, 347
  unitary, 345–46
Demand-creating costs, 22–23, 170–71, 355–57
Demand curve, 345, 397
  shifts in, 347
Demand function, 163
Demand schedules, 163, 343–47
Department foreman costs, 115–16
Depreciation, 452
  double-declining-balance method, 452
  straight-line method, 453
  sum-of-the-years'-digits method, 453–54
  table, 572
Depreciation expenses, 115–16
Design costs, 180–81
Dice rolling illustration, 299–302
Direct costs, 21, 23
  factory overhead, 22
  labor, 20, 29, 117–18
  material, 20, 28
  overhead, 21
Discounted cash flow (DCF), 447–48
  example of calculation of, 448–50
Discounted cash flow analysis, 443–63; *see also* Cash flows
  cash flow patterns; *see* Cash flow patterns
  discounted cash flow concept; *see* Discounted cash flow (DCF)
  equivalent annual cash flow, 458–60
  framework for, 444–45
  method of calculation, 456–57
  rate of return, 460–62
Discounting defined, 447
Distinguishable event in probability distribution using historical data, 305–9, 311–12

Dividend payout ratio, 542
Dividends, 525

E

Eastern Europe, managed allocation of resources in, 2
Economics
  defined, 1–2
  managerial economics distinguished, 1–2
Economist's concept of cost, 19
  accountant's concept distinguished, 19, 116–18
Efficiency variance, 41
Elasticity index, 345–46
Elasticity of demand, 344–46
End points
  random sampling of, 502–4
  typical, 504–9
  uncertainty in new product introduction, 499–502
Environmental factors affecting demand, 341–43
Equivalent annual cash flow, 458–60, 506
Equivalent gamble, 295–96
Error curve, 310
Events
  cumulative probability distribution for, 275–77
  defined, 229, 272
  mass probability distribution for, 272–75
  outcomes, 230
  payoff table, 231–32
  probabilities to outcomes of, 234–37
  selection of, 230–31
Expected profit, 398
Expected revenue, 398
Expected value
  of an act, 239–41
  of perfect information (EVPI), 244, 252
Exponential random number $\lambda = 1$, 566–67

F

Factory overhead costs, 20, 29; *see also* Overhead costs
Factory payroll, 26–27
Financial policy
  adaptive process, 539, 541–43
  optimizing process, 538–41
Financial structure, 522–27; *see also specific topics*
  accounting issues, 526
  asset structure, 523–24
  capital structure, 523–26
  changes in, 526–27
  meaning of, 522–23

Fixed assets, 22, 523–24
Fixed costs, 21, 23, 29, 177–79
  price as function of, 187–88
Fixed facilities, opportunity costs of, 354–55
Forecasting, 23, 227–28; *see also* Probability distribution
  competitive bid, 402–3
  defined, 271–72
  demand, 292–413
  models, 309–11
  point, 272
  probabilistic, 272, 292
Fractiles, 281–82, 292
Fringe benefits, 27
Future cost, 19

G

General and administrative expenses, 20, 25, 170
General Motors Corporation, 2–3
Graphic method of linear programming, 133–34

H

Heat, light and power costs, 115–16
Hidden persuaders, 342
Historical cost, 19, 29
Historical data; *see also* Accounting records
  analysis of, 35
  cumulative relative frequencies of, 303, 308, 310–11
    stairsteps graph, 303–4
  probability distribution, use in
    distinguishable event, 305–9, 311–12
    indistinguishable event, 298–305

I

Idle capacity, 359
Income taxes as cash flow measurement problem area, 452–54
Incremental cost, 354
Incremental revenue, 353
Indirect labor costs, 115–16
Indistinguishable event
  defined, 299
  probability distribution using historical data, 298–305
Inflation, 187
Information
  perfect, 242
    expected value of, 244, 252
  source of; *see* Accounting records
  value of, 242–44
Input, 20, 31
Intangible assets, 526
Inventory adjustment, 44
Inventory valuation, 34

Investment opportunity rate, 446, 448–49, 461
Investment pricing, return on, 360
"Invisible hand" doctrine, 2
Iterative procedure, 125, 135

K–L

Keynes, Lord, 6

Leased assets, 526
Leverage concept, 535–38
Leverage ratio defined, 536, 542
Linear programming, 123–37
  activities, 123–24, 135
  assignment method, 125
  blending problem, 123–24
  characteristics of, 124
  constraints, 123–24, 135
  general method, 132–34
  graphic solution, 133–34
  iterative procedure, 125, 135
  marginal cost and/or marginal revenue, 124, 135
  product mix problem, 123
  program, 123
  rates of substitution, 124, 132
  resource allocation problem, 123
  shipping problem, 124
  simplex method, 132
  transportation method, 124–32
Long-term debt, 525
  cost of, 528–29

M

Make-or-buy analysis, 119–22
Make-or-buy problem, 109
Managerial decisions, economics of, 1–6
Managerial economics
  defined, 1–2
  economics distinguished, 1–2
Manufacturing costs, 26–29, 113–16
Marginal analysis, 351–53
Marginal cost and/or marginal revenue, 124, 135, 353
Marginal revenue, 348–50
Market system
  effectiveness of, 2
  functioning of, 2
Mass probability distribution, 272–75
  approximating, 279
Mathematical programming, 123–37; *see also* Linear programming
Maximin criterion, 233 n
Mean, 280
Median, 281–82, 292–94
Minimax criterion, 233 n
Mode, 280–82

Money as resource, 108–9, 120
Monopolistic competition, 342–43
Monopoly, 342–43
Monte Carlo simulation technique, 498–511
Most likely outcome, 232–34

N

Net circulating assets, 523–24
Net fixed assets, 523–24
New product feature exploitation, 184–86
New product introduction
  cash flow analysis, 443–63
  uncertainty, elements of, 498–511
Nonlinear programming, 124
Northwest corner rule, 126

O

Objectives of costs, 22–24, 27
Opportunity cost, 19–20, 23, 243
  capital structure components, 528
  cost minimization problem, 116–18
  defined, 108
  fixed facilities, 354–55
  invested capital, 360
Out-of-pocket expenses, 399
Outcomes, 230
  collectively exhaustive, 231, 235
  cumulative graph for, 278
  defined, 272–73
  mutually exclusive, 231
  probabilities to, 234–37
Output, 20
Overhead budgets, 30, 32–35
Overhead costs, 20–21, 29, 115–16
  contribution to, 163–65
  expense budgets for, 30, 32–35
  variable budget for, 32–33
Overhead variances, analysis of, 41–42

P

Payoff table, 231–32, 241–44
Payroll taxes, 115–16
Perfect competition, 342–43
Perfect information, 242
  expected value of, 244, 252
Period costs, 21, 23
"Playing the averages," 241
Point forecast, 272, 312, 397
  demand schedule as, 343
  new product introduction, 498
Policy price
  defined, 358
  use of, 359–61
Preferred stock, 525
  callability, 525
  convertible into common stock, 529–30

Preferred stock—*Cont.*
  cost of, 529–30
  dividends, 525
Present value tables, 448–49, 459–60
  $1, 570
  $1 received annually for N years, 571
  sum-of-years'-digit depreciation, 572
Price administration, 357–62
Price changes, price-volume relationships
    affected by, 173–76
Price-cost relationship; *see* Cost-price rela-
    tionships
Price determination, 350–55
  average direct cost versus incremental
      cost, 354
  change of production technique, 355
  marginal analysis, 351–53
  opportunity costs of fixed facilities, 354–
      55
  profit maximization, 351–53
  relevant costs for, 353–55
Price leadership, 186
Price policies, 341
Price-profit relationship, 163
Price-quantity relationship, 163
Price-sensitivity of market, 344
Price-volume relationships, 169–76
  break-even point, 171–73
  demand-creating costs, 170–71
  price change, effect of, 173–76
Pricing decision analysis, 340–65; *see also*
    specific topics
  competitive bidding problem compari-
      son, 404–5
  complexity of problem, 340
  demand, 341–50
  other demand-creating costs, 355–57
  price administration, 357–62
  price determination, 350–55
  types of decisions, 358–59
Pricing problem, 109–10
Prime cost, 20–22
Prime cost variances, analysis of, 38–41
Probabilistic forecast, 272, 292
Probability, 234–37
  bidding problem, 402
  defined, 234
  measuring uncertainty, 271–91
  rules for assigning, 235
Probability distribution, 272–77; *see also*
    specific topics
  approximating, 277–79
  average of, 280
  cumulative distribution, 272, 275–77
  decision diagram, 283–85
  equivalent gamble, 295–96
  final outcomes, 286–88
  fractiles, 281–82, 292

Probability distribution—*Cont.*
  historical data, use of
    distinguishable event, 305–9, 311–12
    indistinguishable event, 298–305
  lack of data for, 293–98
  mass distribution, 272–75
  mean of, 280
  measures of, 279–82
  median, 281–82, 292–93
  mode, 280–82
  obtaining one from another, 282–86
  risk profile, 286–88
  wheel illustration, 294–97
Product
  decisions to create, 5, 17 ff.
  defined, 5
Product costs; *see* Cost *and specific type of
    cost*
Product-creating costs, 22, 24–45; *see also*
    Cost *and specific type of cost*
  function of, 23
Product demand, 180–81
Product divisions, 2–3
Product identification costs, 20–21
Product line pricing, 361–62
Product mix problem, 123
Production technique changes, 355
Profit, contribution to, 163–65
Profit changes, analysis of, 35–38
Profit margins, maintenance of, 190–92
Profit maximization
  marginal condition for, 353
  pricing for, 351–53
Profit plan, 36, 173–76
Profitgraph, 166–67
Programming of interdependent activities,
    123–37; *see also* Linear programming
Project break-even point, 178–79
Project life, 455–57

                      R

Random digits, 564–65
Random number generator, 503
Random number tables, 563
Random sampling end points, 502–4
Rate of return, 460–62
Rate variance, 41
Rates of substitution, 124, 132
Rented assets, 526
Repairs and maintenance costs, 115–16
Resource allocation, 1–3
  automatic, 2
  criterion problem, 3–5
  managed, 2
  measurement problem, 109
  problem classification, 109–10
  problem of, 108–38; *see also* Cost min-
      imization

Resource allocation—*Cont.*
 programming of interdependent activities, 123–37; *see also* Linear programming
 types of decisions, 5–6
Resources
 allocation of; *see* Resource allocation
 money as, 108–9, 120
 types, 108–9
 value of, 108
Retained earnings, 526
 cost of, 532
Revenue
 demand as affecting, 347–50
 incremental, 353
 marginal, 348–50
Risk profile, 286–88, 507
Risk-versus-return tradeoff, 539
Rules of thumb, 341

S

Sales commissions, 23
Satisficing, 540
Satisficing criteria, 542–43
Seasonal trends, 309
Selling expenses, 20, 25, 170
Service-creating costs, 22
Shipping problem, 124
Shop supplies costs, 115–16
Short-run cost minimization, 108–38; *see also* Cost minimization *and* Resource allocation
Simplex method of linear programming, 132
Simulation, 498–511
 problems with using, 510–11
"Skimming the cream" off the market, 186
Smith, Adam, 2
Smooth curve, 304–5, 308, 310
Special-purpose machine; *see* Cash flows *and* Discounted cash flow analysis
Spending variance, 43–44
Spoilage allowance, 31
Stairsteps graph, 303–4
Standard cost system, 38–44
Standard prices, 31
Standard prime costs, 29–32
Statement of sources and uses of funds, 527
Sticker prices, 359

T

Total product cost, 360
Tradeoff of fixed and variable costs, 179
Transaction price
 defined, 358–59
 use of, 360–61
Transportation method
 alternative combination, 127, 135
 assignment method variant, 125
 computational methods used in solution, 136–37
 degeneracy, 126n, 128–29
 excluded routes, 127, 135
 final program, 129–31, 135
 improving the program, 128, 135
 included routes, 127, 135
 initial program, 125–26, 135
 interpretation of row and column differences, 131–32
 northwest corner rule, 126
 pricing of alternative combinations, 126–28, 135
 relative locational advantages, 131
 solution of problem, 125–31, 135
 statement of example, 125

U

Uncertainty
 decisions under, 228–29
 measurement of, 271–91
 new product introduction, 498–511
Unit costs, 26
Unitary demand, 345–56

V

Valuation, 526
Value of information, 242–44
Variable budget, 32–33
Variable costs, 21–23, 29, 177–79
Viability, 542–43
Volume variances, analysis of, 42–44

W

Waste allowance, 31
Weighted-average cost of capital, 528, 533
Working capital as cash flow measurement problem area, 454–55

This book has been set in 12 and 10 point Garamond # 3, leaded 1-point. Part titles, chapter numbers and titles, and case titles are in 18 point Garamond Bold. Part numbers are in 24 point Garamond Bold. The size of the type page is 27 × 45 picas.